Advance praise for *The Collected Letters of Alan Watts*

"Alan Watts has touched so many lives, then and now and forever into the future. The Chinese name I have chosen for him is 'Ai-Lan,' with two symbols — 愛蘭 — depicting 'the *love* of *orchid*': the man who loves the beauty and the quality of being a highly cultivated human being. These letters offer us further insights into the Man with Many Qualities we can admire and emulate. I am forever grateful to him as my mentor, colleague, and friend."

— **Chungliang Al Huang**, founder and president of the Living Tao Foundation and director of the International Lan Ting Institute

"Alan Watts's influence in the USA, which began to really flourish in the mid-1950s, was remarkable. Alan was so clear and such a good writer, and so well grounded in the teachings and worldview he extolled, that he was taken by some as 'easy' and glib. Without artifice, a truly human life and heart, he was both deep and accessible, and made no effort to impress. Consequently, he was impressive, and he lived his life fully and to the end. The East Asian Zen world had always shown itself as both playful and severe. Alan skipped the severity and thus sometimes disappointed those who had a secret hope for difficulty. This is so difficult! I knew Alan over twenty-five years, and he was always a grand and instructive friend to me. Yet it took some years after his death before I could see and appreciate the whole. This collection of letters will entrance and challenge you, and be with you for decades."

— **Gary Snyder**, Pulitzer Prize–winning poet

"Though I knew Alan Watts from his first days at the American Academy of Asian Studies in 1951 until his death in 1973, I did not appreciate the extent of his interests or the range of his friendships and influence until I read the letters collected by his daughters Anne and Joan for this book. At Esalen in recent years we have noted his growing influence among our program participants young and old. The humor, playfulness, and generosity of spirit with which he framed his teaching is especially winning today, besieged as we are by rancor and divisiveness not only in politics but in philosophy and religious studies as well. We miss the light touch, the wit, the imaginative embrace of paradox and nuance, the sheer fun he brought to difficult issues.

"Alan was a prime catalyst for the transmission of Buddhist, Taoist, and other Asian philosophies to America and Europe during the 1950s and '60s through articles, books, radio, and television; and you can find him now around the world through YouTube and other media that did not exist back then. But this collection of letters adds to all that, revealing more about him than we'd known before, his faults as well as his many virtues, his weaknesses as well as his strengths, and turns of his wisdom not to be found in his books. He called himself a philosophical entertainer, but he was much more than that. You can learn a lot about Chinese and Japanese aesthetics from him, about secrets of language, about the satoris of everyday life. What a life he lived!

"Yeats said of Oscar Wilde that he left half of what he had to say in conversation instead of his written works. I can testify that Alan, too, left much of his genius unwritten. If Wilde was the greatest conversationalist of his day, Alan arguably was the greatest of his. Fortunately, though, he has left us his recordings and these letters."

— **Michael Murphy,** cofounder of Esalen Institute

"Alan Watts once told me, 'In fifty years, nobody will remember me.' To the contrary, his books, essays, and recorded lectures have gained in stature in recent decades, and the claim that he simply popularized Eastern wisdom has been eclipsed by a recognition of his scholarly insights. I never knew Alan to utter a boring sentence or write a dull word. This collection of his letters bears testimony to my impressions. His keen observations, his witty rejoinders, and his depth of knowledge are reflected in this incredible collection. Brava to his daughters for their diligence, and bravo to their father for taking the time to write his circle of friends and acquaintances!"

— **Stanley Krippner, PhD,** coauthor of *Personal Mythology* and
Extraordinary Dreams

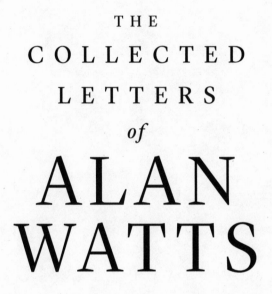

THE

COLLECTED

LETTERS

of

ALAN

WATTS

THE
COLLECTED
LETTERS
of
ALAN
WATTS

Edited and with commentary by

JOAN WATTS & ANNE WATTS

New World Library
Novato, California

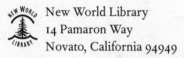 New World Library
14 Pamaron Way
Novato, California 94949

Text design by Tona Pearce Myers

Library of Congress Cataloging-in-Publication data is available.

First printing, December 2017
ISBN 978-1-60868-415-1
Ebook ISBN 978-1-60868-416-8
Printed in Canada on 100% postconsumer-waste recycled paper

 New World Library is proud to be a Gold Certified Environmentally Responsible Publisher. Publisher certification awarded by Green Press Initiative. www.greenpressinitiative.org

10   9   8   7   6   5   4   3   2   1

Dedicated to Alan's children, grandchildren, great-grandchildren,
and all future descendants, and to Alan's many followers,
past, present, and future, so that they will see the man as he was,
an extraordinary teacher subject to human frailties.

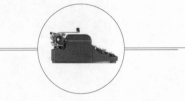

In Memoriam

Richard Buchan Watts
February 4, 1955–July 30, 2017

As this book went to press, we learned of Richard's death.
He is the first of Alan's progeny to pass on.
May he rest in peace.

CONTENTS

FOREWORD

Alan Watts. It is amazing to us what mentioning this name at a social gathering will often evoke. Overwhelmingly, the reaction is "You've got to be kidding! He's your father? His books changed my life!" Other reactions have included such statements as "May I kiss your feet?" "Can I touch you?" or "You seem too normal to be his daughter!" Alan Watts, philosopher and interpreter of Eastern philosophy and religions and Christian doctrine, had for years answered the big questions — "Why are we here?" and "What is the meaning of our existence?" His explanations resonated with people of all walks of life and beliefs. It has been over forty years since his death, and yet his writings and lectures are more popular than ever worldwide. Glance through YouTube to view him lecturing or Google his name, and you will find many sites with information about him. Wikipedia has a long synopsis of his philosophical beliefs, personal life, accomplishments, and bibliography, as do many other sites. His books are published in more than twenty-seven countries and in many languages including Chinese, Korean, and Japanese. There are at least five Facebook pages dedicated to discussions about his life and writings. Amazingly, there are murals that bear his portrait on public buildings in at least three countries.

We are the first- and second-born children of Alan's seven. I (Joan) was born in 1938, the year Alan married his first wife, Eleanor Everett, and the year he immigrated to America to avoid the oncoming event of World War II in Europe. Anne was born in 1942, the year he entered seminary to become an Anglican priest in Evanston, Illinois. By his second wife, Dorothy DeWitt, he fathered five more children: Marcia (Tia), Mark, Richard, Lila, and Diane. One could say that we've had the longest relationship with him except for his father, Laurence, who died at age ninety-three, a year after Alan.

We often wonder how, in the magnificent plan of this universe, we came to be the children of a world-famous thinker, writer, philosopher, and authority on Christian and Asian religions. After all, we could have been the children of a parent involved in any sort of occupation. But the universe thought we should be daughters of Alan Wilson Watts, a precocious child born to an English couple of modest means in a suburb of London — Chislehurst, Kent. Alan, our father, born in 1915 during World War I, was the only surviving child of Laurence (Laurie) and Emily Watts. Our grandmother, Emily Mary, who was thirty-nine when Alan was born, apparently had six pregnancies. Three produced infants who lived, two of them only briefly. (I suspect that she was RH negative, as I myself was later diagnosed with this hereditary condition.) Alan survived with the help of his Aunt Gertrude (Gertie or E.G.B.) Buchan, a nurse who brought him formula and baked potatoes during bombing raids. Emily, who prior to her marriage had been diagnosed with breast cancer and had had a double mastectomy, was unable to nurse infant Alan. We've been told by members of the medical profession that it was highly unlikely that she actually had cancer that young: she lived to the age of eighty-five.

Alan was absolutely cherished by his parents, who doted on him, encouraging his intellect and interests at every turn. Alan was equally devoted to his parents, and, as the reader will see, stayed in constant contact with them throughout his life with letters, addressed to "Dear Mummy and Daddy." Although he grew up in a modest home, his mother was very creative. She taught gymnasium and needlework to the daughters of missionary families, who often presented her with items from the Orient. Embroidered silks, china, figurines, and other art objects graced the walls, cupboards, and mantelpiece of their home. These objects stirred Alan's imagination, as did the many books his father read to him, especially *Just So Stories*, *The Jungle Book*, and *Kim*, all by Rudyard Kipling. His father worked for the Michelin Tyre Company and eventually for the government, in the capacity of director for The Lord Mayor's Hospital Sunday Fund, a nonprofit organization for the benefit of London hospitals.

We both had the opportunity to live in his birthplace with his parents, Joan for one year and Anne for five. We loved Rowan Tree Cottage, as the home was named, and the exquisite garden our grandparents had created. They had the equivalent of an acre and a half, artfully designed, with flower beds, grassy paths accented by beautifully trimmed shrubs named for Queen Mary and Queen Elizabeth, rose trees, fruit trees of all kinds, a vegetable patch, and a henhouse. It was just the way we would imagine the garden in *Alice in Wonderland* to look, with nooks and crannies, rabbit holes, and trees where one might hide.

This is the environment in which Alan grew up. Eventually his parents realized they should send him to a school where he might get a better education than at the local school he had been attending. So at seven, he was sent off to Saint Hugh's School, a boarding school near Chislehurst and then eventually, at age thirteen, to King's School, Canterbury, in 1928. He discusses his experience of boys' boarding-school life at length in his autobiography, *In My Own Way*, in which he writes about his education as considerably more than "book learning."

When Alan was fourteen, the family of a schoolmate at St. Hugh's took him to Paris and introduced him to the European lifestyle, which he found to be more stimulating than the rigid environment of King's School and Britain itself. Alan began to picture himself as an adult. During his years at King's School, he discovered Zen Buddhism. Eventually he became involved with the Buddhist Lodge in London after he had submitted a pamphlet entitled *Zen*, and was invited to speak to the members, who were shocked to learn that Alan Watts was a mere lad of fifteen. This was also his introduction to his mentor, Christmas Humphreys, and others involved in Buddhism. Alan's father went with him to lodge meetings and eventually became the institution's treasurer.

As his parents didn't have the means to send him to university, he set about to learn more on his own, voraciously reading the works of D. T. Suzuki, Friedrich Nietzsche, Lao-tzu, H. P. Blavatsky, Lafcadio Hearn, Bernard Shaw, Robert Graves, and C. G. Jung, to mention a few. All this literature was considered "oddball" and had been screened out of his general school curriculum. At this point, he was seventeen. He was also being influenced by many of the people he met in philosophical circles. It was during this time that he met Suzuki, the philosopher Dimitrije Mitrinović, and Jiddu Krishnamurti. He was quite active with the World Congress of Faiths, held in London in 1936.

By the time Alan reached twenty, his first book, *The Spirit of Zen*, was published. He (and others) had discovered that he had a gift for wordcraft, the ability to describe the meaning of what he was writing in a way that is easy for anyone to grasp, almost as if he were painting a picture with words. Through all this, he learned that he wanted to experience life on his own terms, not necessarily according to the societal or ideological mores of the time.

After Alan's death, among his manuscripts, journals, and articles, we found many copies of correspondence he'd had over his life. An avid and eloquent writer of books and journals, he also wrote wonderful letters. Early in his career they tended to be quite long and very descriptive. As he got older they became shorter, perhaps because his many books so plainly stated his thinking. We felt that it was time to share this other form of his writing with his many followers. Herein we've attempted to give you his more interesting correspondence with a variety of individuals. Alan made carbon copies of most of his letters, but we are certain there are other letters out there that we don't know about. There is a broad range of subject matter, ranging from very personal issues to church and religion, counseling, politics, lifestyle, psychedelics, and general commentary. Unfortunately, shortly after his death, there was a loss of some stored literary papers and manuscripts, which were damaged beyond recognition by floodwaters at a storage company.

In the process of editing Alan's letters, we've attempted to keep them as pure as possible. He tended to use a mix of British and American spellings, and words or phrases that were of British origin. While we felt there was a certain charm to his usage of these, in some cases we did fix spelling, punctuation errors, and inconsistencies. Where letters were repetitive, we deleted repetition as shown with [...]. Anne and I have added commentary before and after certain letters. For clarity, our commentary is in italics introduced with our initials: *JW* for mine and *AW* for Anne's.

— Joan Watts

PREFACE

These collected letters give the most complete and vibrant perspective into Alan's very full, rich life ever published. They enable us to follow the development of his mind, philosophies, and personality. We get to witness his brilliance, his kindness, and his foibles. I remember as a child having the thought, "The greater the person, the greater their faults." It seems to be a part of our human condition to put people on pedestals and expect them to be perfect. Of course, no one lives up to these expectations, not Gandhi, not Martin Luther King Jr., not even saints! The sad thing about putting someone on a pedestal is that there is only one way to go — off. Once their "imperfections" are discovered, they are often discounted as completely no good. This is a great shame. In Alan's case, given the huge numbers of individuals worldwide and over the years whose lives have been positively affected by his work, it is my hope that the readers will keep that which is illuminating and valuable to them and leave the rest.

Alan tried valiantly not to be put on a pedestal, calling himself an entertainer, a trickster/coyote, and other such names. My hope is that the readers of this book will be nourished by his brilliance and have compassion for his human failings, as he so clearly had for others'. I once had a conversation with Ram Dass (Richard Alpert), who knew him well, in which he said of Alan, "He knew IT, and he wasn't IT." That made sense to me.

This is a treasure trove of writings through which my sister and I have had a deep, emotional, and bonding journey.

— Anne Watts

PART I

Early Letters

1928-37

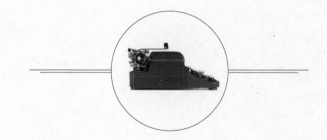

JW: Incredibly, Alan's parents, Laurie and Emily Mary, saved most of the letters that he wrote them during his lifetime. The earliest date is from Saint Hugh's in Bickley, Kent, when he was just thirteen. From there, he was sent to King's School, Canterbury, where he entered in the fall of 1928 and remained until 1932. As was, we believe, traditional among boarding schools, one was required to write a weekly letter home to one's parents. (We both attended Farringtons Girls School in Chislehurst when we lived in England, and writing home weekly was required.) We have included a few of the more interesting letters he wrote during this time. Unfortunately, there are none for 1930–31.

The first section of Alan's letters are from this period — the time when he was sent off to boarding schools until his early twenties, at which time he became acquainted with D. T. Suzuki, Sokei-an Sasaki, Ruth Fuller Everett, and her young daughter, Eleanor, our mother. These introductions would determine the future course of his life.

Letters home always seemed to follow a basic format: thanking Mummy and Daddy for their letters and for sending things he'd asked for; a synopsis of the academic and sports activities for the week and what was coming up in the week ahead; asking for things he needed or for money; and, as closure, asking how they were, how the rabbits were, and similar things. Alan was very fond of rabbits, and they figured in much of his storytelling and artwork, even as an adult. He apparently had a special rabbit named Oberon ("Ob"). He always asked after Oberon and was very concerned when a new home had to be found for him.

ST. HUGH'S SCHOOL, KENT | JUNE 21, 1928
Dear Daddy,
When this letter reaches you it will be your birthday, and I am sending it to you to wish you many happy returns. [...]

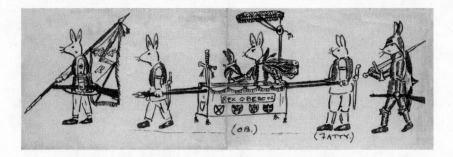

I don't think it's fair that you shouldn't have a birthday procession:

I have no chance to get you anything for your birthday yet, but I will get something as soon as possible.

With much love and best wishes from,

Alan

GRANGE HOUSE | KING'S SCHOOL, CANTERBURY | OCTOBER 7, 1928

Dear Mummy & Daddy,

Thank you so much for your last letter, I have not written before because I find that Sunday evening is the proper time.

I have been assigned to the Gryphon's Tutor set.

Auntie and Miss Bentinck came down this afternoon, and I showed them round the cathedral and the other interesting places in the town and school.

I have played no rugger yet, but have only been for runs, my feet are tired and blistered, and I find physical drill etc. rather difficult.

I shall soon be wanting more money, it fairly flashes away.

The archbishop was in the cathedral at morning service today, and the Bishop of Dover preached. I don't know what the sermon was about for I didn't hear a word!

I have written to Alf — have you seen him lately?

I hear that you have no more embroidery to show! Rather a catastrophe, if you have done really well over the exhibition, you have got plenty of money behind you to go on with. How are the rabbits? Are the mills taking wool? How is "Ob"? Just the same I expect, give him my love.

All is well here, I hope all is well at home. Well, I must stop now.

Your loving son, Alan

JW: In the letter above, Alan is referring to his mother's embroidery. She was an incredibly talented needleworker and was commissioned by Queen Mary to embroider a jewel box, beautifully done in silk with a flower garden on all sides. She was also commissioned to do altarpieces for various churches. When I lived with her in Chisle-hurst, she taught me featherstitching, cross-stitch, smocking, French knots, and hem-stitching. Even though her hands were crippled with arthritis, she managed to produce beautiful pieces. I have a few lovely pieces she did — needle cases with delphiniums and daisies, English robins, red squirrels, and a charming sampler piece on linen with rabbits, flowers, birds, trees, fruit, and caterpillars.

One of his more remarkable letters (below) involved the enthronement of a new Archbishop of Canterbury on December 5, 1928. Alan was selected to be one of His Eminence's two trainbearers for the event, which was reported on the front page of the London Daily Express *with the headline "New Primate Enthroned in St. Augustine's Chair in the Presence of Nearly 5,000 People."*

GRANGE HOUSE | KING'S SCHOOL, CANTERBURY | DECEMBER 2, 1928
Dear Mummy & Daddy,
Thank you for your last letter. I have got crowds of news for you this week. I shall see the enthronement of the Archbishop all right, another boy and myself have GOT TO CARRY HIS TRAIN!!! We have got to dress up in all sorts of complicated affairs, we have got to wear ruffs! — and red cassocks! I have been to several rehearsals for the service and it is going to be a very pompous affair. The Premier and the Lord Chancellor are going to be there and the Lord Mayor of London. We have got to go to the Arch B's Palace and wait in the Hall till he comes, and then pick up his train and follow him!

On Thursday I played for the "Colts B XV" in a match against the Junior School. We won easily because most of their good men had left and were playing for us.

On Thursday evening a Mr. Edmonds gave us a lantern lecture called the "Road to Endor." It was all about some prisoners who tried to escape from Asia Minor in the Great War. It was exciting.

Do rats come out in wintertime? I want to do some trapping in the hols [holidays].

How is everything at home? Rabbits, studio, "Ob," etc.?

Well I must stop now, from your loving son, Alan

THE GRANGE | KING'S SCHOOL, CANTERBURY | MAY 12, 1929
Dear Mummy & Daddy,
My chief news this week is about Ascension Day. Well, first of all, I must thank you for your letters and for sending me the map; it arrived in time. After Cathe-dral we were given our lunch, we changed and set out. I went with a boy called

Forrester. As soon as we were outside Canterbury we came into glorious country, big hills of pastureland and plots on either side of the road. We saw some lambs, comic creatures, they looked at us like this:

Puzzle:— which end is which?

    The first town we came to was Chartham, but the road led past it. Then we passed through a few little villages and we turned onto the road to Charing at Chillam. Through more pastureland and some lovely primrose woods then when the Ashford road met us we got off and went to an old farm tearoom and had a 2d [pence] glass of ginger beer, the best I have ever tasted. I think it must have been homemade. Then we went on through more country till we came to the top of Charing Hill, near the house we once proposed to buy. Here we branched off and had our lunch in some woods. After that we got to Charing by some winding lanes and fair shot along the big main road. Halfway down a gradual slope I stopped outside a tea shop. Forrester, who was behind me, not looking where he was going, crashed into me. He was flung off but received no hurt. Our bikes only got minor scratches. Well we went into the tea shop, had another drink, and then walked up Charing Hill. Then we returned to Canterbury. Having plenty of time we went on to Herne Bay — the most dreary seaside place I have ever seen. I can't think how anyone ever goes there. I shan't go again in a hurry. We had tea there and then come home. I had a supper of fish and chips, went to bed — and slept.

    Well how are you? Have you found a decent home for "Ob" yet? I can't see why he would be so much trouble at Shaftesbury House. Well how is the School?

    By the way, I am getting all the numbers of *L'Illustration* this term. I have got two already. They are fine.

    From your loving son, Alan

THE GRANGE | KING'S SCHOOL, CANTERBURY | MAY 26, 1929
Dear Mummy & Daddy,
I suppose Daddy has told you all about the Field Day. Today, I went up to the scene of battle and found five dummy cartridges in a clip. I went to that pond we passed but there were no water hens there.

I went to the baths on Saturday afternoon, it was fairly warm.

I have written to thank Mrs. Macfarlane for the toffies.

How did you enjoy the drive in Lady Wadia's car?

Can you possibly move that bench from upstairs into the room you have thought of giving me? Please don't put a bulky chest of drawers in there. Put in the small ones out of the spare room if there must be some in there. I would rather there weren't any.

Have you been up to St. Hugh's?

Have you found anything for me to read? Preferably small editions of RLS [Robert Louis Stevenson], Dickens is too ponderous for private reading.

Do you know when Ivan is trying for a "School"? How is Fausset getting on?

Well, I am afraid I must stop now, from your loving son, Alan

PS. Love to "Ob." What have you done with him?

THE GRANGE | KING'S SCHOOL, CANTERBURY | JUNE 9, 1929
Dear Mummy & Daddy,

Thank you so much for your letter. After thinking it over I have wondered whether I might go in for the Senior Scholarship just to get experience in the papers and to know what standard I must aim at in order to get one. I should like to know what you think as soon as possible, in any case before the 22nd.

Will infection spread in letters? If I want to write to Ivan or Ronald would mumps or anything go in the letter? Please answer this soon.

It is rather a pity I can't go home for half term. Still a good many people are staying behind and I shall go to Canter[bury] for one day.

I suppose there is no chance of your coming down at half term? I suppose you are too busy.

How are things getting on? Have you been up to St. Hugh's? I have written to Auntie.

Is my design for a programme cover good enough to exhibit?

How is Oberon in his new home?

Well, I'm afraid I must stop now, from your loving son, Alan

JW: According to Alan's autobiography, In My Own Way, *it appears that he went to France in the summer of 1929 via the Isle of Jersey, with Francis Croshaw and his son Ivan, one of Alan's good school friends. This is where he got his first taste of a more cosmopolitan way of life: elegant hotels with restaurants serving sumptuous gourmet foods, fine wines and fancy cigars in cafés, horse races and bullfights. He returned from this adventure to King's School, feeling that he had become an adult, and found the curriculum at King's boring and irrelevant. It was shortly after this that he discovered*

Lafcadio Hearn's Glimpses of Unfamiliar Japan *in a bookshop. He became fascinated with Oriental culture and with Chinese and Japanese art, which led him further into the exploration of mysticism and Oriental philosophy.*

In this next section of letters written from school, we start, interestingly, with a letter written to Sokei-an Sasaki. Little did he know at the time that this Zen priest would eventually become his stepfather-in-law.

Sokei-an Sasaki was of the Rinzai Zen lineage and was sent by his Zen master to teach Zen in America. Sokei-an's father was a Shinto priest; his mother was a concubine taken by his father because his wife was unable to bear children. Sokei-an was sent to art schools, where he learned woodcarving as a young man prior to studying Zen. When he arrived in America, he traveled extensively through the Pacific Northwest and San Francisco. He was briefly an art student at the San Francisco Art Institute. Eventually, after several trips back to Japan, at age forty-eight he was ordained a Zen master and went to New York City in 1928. There he started teaching Zen to a handful of followers. In May 1931, Sokei-an and others signed the incorporation papers for the Buddhist Society of America, which eventually became the First Zen Institute of America. He met our grandmother, Ruth Fuller Everett, in 1933, and they became friends. She became a formal student of his in 1938. He was interned during World War II but was released in 1944 because of ill health. Ruth and Sokei-an were married shortly after that, but the marriage was brief: he died in 1945.

I'm not sure how Alan initially came to communicate with Sokei-an Sasaki. Perhaps the Buddhist Lodge in London had published Sasaki's writing. His communication in 1932 with Alan, then aged seventeen, showed respect for his interest in Zen. In answer to Alan's letter below, he cautioned that "it is very hard to judge the ultimate attainment of Zen without observing the daily life and establishing a close contact between teacher and disciple in order to make certain whether attainment is one of mere conception or that of really standing in its center." He ended his response saying, "I am quite sure you are on the way of Zen and I hope some day in the future we will meet each other." They met in person in 1938, when Alan and his young wife, Eleanor Everett, arrived in America under the wing of Eleanor's mother, Ruth.

BROMLEY, KENT | FEBRUARY 18, 1932

Dear Mr. Sokei-an Sasaki,

Many thanks for your most interesting letter of the 1st.

From what you say there and from what I have read elsewhere the essence of Zen is to regard Existence universally or impersonally, or so I understand. Instead of thinking "I walk," you think, "There is a walking," until you begin to see yourself as a part of the Universe not separate from other parts while the "I" is as the whole. I have tried this and the result is that there comes a feeling calm, of indifference to circumstance.

In the Sutra of Wei-Lang (Hui-neng) 6th Patriarch, I read that one should get rid of the pairs of opposites — good and evil, joy and pain, life and death. Surely it is by the personal attitude to Existence that these opposites arise; by thinking "I do," instead of "There is a doing." By regarding oneself objectively in this manner one becomes detached and an idea of "oneness" prevails. Is this what you mean when you say, "The master regulates his cognizance of the body of relativity (i.e., the pairs of opposites?). Ceasing to follow its movement (ceasing to think 'I like' or 'I do' or 'I hate'?), he realizes serenity"? Surely this is seeing Existence from the standpoint of Tathata, which is the very basis of Existence and yet is undisturbed by it? It is really rather hard to explain! But I somehow feel that as soon as I start looking at things impersonally, the "I" which thinks about opposites vanishes, while a sort of calm, "universal" feeling takes its place. Am I on the right track?

Yours sincerely, A. W. Watts

JW: Around the years of 1930–31, Alan's friend Francis Croshaw began lending him books from his vast library. One book in particular caught Alan's interest: The Creed of Buddha *by Edmond Holmes. Inserted in the book was a pamphlet written by Christmas Humphreys regarding the work of the Buddhist Lodge in London. This prompted Alan to write the lodge forthwith, become a member, and subscribe to the lodge's journal,* The Middle Way. *He apparently submitted a pamphlet he wrote entitled* Zen, *and was asked to lecture to members of the lodge, who upon meeting him, were shocked that he was a mere lad! Christmas Humphreys ("Toby"), a prominent London barrister, and his wife Aileen ("Puck"), ran the lodge out of their London flat and took in the young scholar as if he were their son.*

The Humphreys were Theosophists, followers of H. P. Blavatsky, and members of the Cambridge branch of the Theosophical Society. Together they founded an independent "Buddhist Lodge" of the Society. They introduced young Alan, still in his teens, to an incredible assemblage of scholars and artists from around the world involved in the lodge's activities. This is where Alan met D. T. Suzuki.

Alan began writing articles for The Middle Way, *and by 1932 he was editing the publication.*

In the following letters I note his appreciation for the donation for a typewriter. Alan was an amazing typist. He made very few mistakes, and I was fascinated watching him rapidly type using only three digits of each hand — thumb, index, and middle finger (as I was taught in typing class to use all fingers and thumbs!).

Referring to "lunch with the Ashton-Gwatkin" — this was Canon Trelawney

Ashton-Gwatkin, rector of Bishopsbourne and his son, Frank Ashton-Gwatkin, who had been attached to the British Embassy in Japan. Alan would frequently lunch with them. "John P." refers to Frank's pseudonym "John Paris," under which he wrote realistic novels about Japanese life.

The reference to Wesak is apparently an event put on by the lodge celebrating the traditional festival honoring the Buddha on the full moon in May.

Alan did not finish his final term at King's School, Cambridge. Although, at the age of seventeen, he was a senior prefect and member of the sixth form (roughly equivalent to a high-school senior in the United States), and in his words "I had had enough of this juvenile atmosphere." After all, he was adult enough to be a contributing writer and editor for the journal of the Buddhist Lodge and had published a booklet on Zen, and he had no use for going on to university. He had created his own study plan, which launched him into an environment that he obviously enjoyed immensely.

We have no letters for the period of 1933 until October of 1936, when we find a letter to C. G. Jung. Imagine, a twenty-one-year-old Alan taking on sixty-one-year-old Jung! Another, from December 1936, is addressed to Sokei-an Sasaki but regrettably is missing its last page.

THE GRANGE | KING'S SCHOOL, CANTERBURY | MARCH 13, 1932
Dear Mummy and Daddy,
Many thanks for your interesting letters. I'm so glad you've been to see Mr. Humphreys; he's a fascinating man isn't he? As a matter of fact — my pamphlet won't be quite the same as his; Knight writes: "...your MS is already in print and should reach me any day now...The pattern of the cover...is a yellow and looks quite nice."

A Religion for Modern Youth is an excellent pamphlet, but I've never read Carus's book; it's very good I believe, but of course the best book on the subject is *What Is Buddhism?*, published by the Lodge.

Thanks awfully for the contribution for the typewriter...we can see about it in the holidays. Rather a pity that March's machine is old-fashioned; the worst of it is that a brand-new one costs about 10g [guineas]! Secondhand ones can be had for about 4d [pence] and even cheaper.

About the Hardings' dance...well you know I can't dance and haven't the vaguest idea what the latest dances are like...and it's quite useless to go unless I have a partner to go with...and who is there????? I think the only thing to do is to accept and, if I can't get a partner or anything else, to arrange for a convenient headache on the night. What do you think? RSVP I haven't answered yet!

I went to lunch with the Ashton-Gwatkin today; their son was there and we talked a bit about Japan.

Well this is Sunday and we are so bored with Cathedral — going and continual psalm-singing that we hardly know what to do. In fact two people have come
and *asked* me for Buddhistic literature and one of them is so keen that he has written to the Lodge for further information which I have not time to give. *Modern
Youth* is very inspiring! And I haven't even been trying to spread propaganda!
An article I wrote last holidays has appeared in the current issue of *Buddhism in
England*...it's one of my best.

So sorry to hear about your cold; I have a bit of one too, but we shall recover
in time.

By the way...please don't be worried about my giving up too much time
to Buddhism etc....this letter may sound as if I am, but sometimes I feel so lazy
that it needs a jolly hard application of Buddhism to make me work...and then it
comes quite easily. I get lazy because school is boring! It's only relieved by work,
Buddhism, a few friends and games (such as there are). The rest is just blank! A
little world all of its own, shut away from real life like a monastery — the only
connection being the Postal Service! I wonder if it is good for one to be shut up
after 17? The atmosphere of repression throws the River of Life into the wrong
channels.

Well, well — "Aim at extreme disinterestedness and maintain the utmost
possible calm!"

From your loving son, Alan

THE GRANGE | KING'S SCHOOL, CANTERBURY | SUNDAY, MAY 8, 1932
Dear Mummy and Daddy,
Probably you got that very disreputable postcard I sent you from Etham or
some godforsaken spot. As a matter of fact I found it in my raincoat pocket and
thought some use had better be made of it! Well, we had a most enjoyable day
and I'm sure it's done us a lot of good. The weather kept fairly good and we only
had about three mild showers; for the rest of the time there was plenty of sun.

That dressing gown has turned out marvelously; please give Mrs. White-
house my congratulations! And thanks for forwarding all the various letters —
there will no doubt be more forthcoming! The Roerich Museum sent me quite a
decent-sized book about themselves — gratis, and it contains some rather interesting information and photographs.

My eyes seem to be going a bit straighter and I'm gradually getting used to
being without glasses.

I went out to lunch with the Ashton-Gwatkin again today and found "John
P." there. He wants a copy of my pamphlet to send to some Japanese gent so I

suppose I must get hold of one. I really ought to have had about twenty specimen copies!! Mr. Humphreys hopes to be able to sell quite a number at Wesak.

The supply of news having run out I must stop…

From your loving son, Alan

THE GRANGE | KING'S SCHOOL, CANTERBURY | OCTOBER 9, 1932
Dear Mummy and Daddy,
Thanks awfully for sending along all the various oddments; the shorts and stockings are the right size.

We had a most successful afternoon with the dean on Tuesday; he is rather a jolly fellow. He sleeps almost out in the open on the top of one of his towers — summer and winter. His bed is a rough camp-bed and his bedroom a sort of glorified kennel! These, I understand were habits picked up in China. He showed us all his photos of his journey, some of which were remarkably good. He penetrated as far as the great Kumbum monastery in Tibet, and had to undergo all sorts of adventure with bandits and whatnot. I'm afraid I didn't get a chance of mentioning your church work!

Then I have been out to Mrs. Gatherer again. She was unable to go up to town last week but is going this one.

I have had a talk with the Chief about that religious conference and am getting him to take some active measures. We are going to have a discussion circle (how American) to deal with the matter.

It is quite definite now that we are going to do the "Meistersingers" in the Choral Soc. here and it ought to be great fun. The rest of the stuff is by Elgar — "St. George" and "As Torrents in Summer." They were thinking of doing Stanford's "Last Post," which perhaps you remember being done at St. Hugh's.

C'est tout pour le moment…

From your loving son, Alan

SOUTH EATON PLACE, LONDON | OCTOBER 17, 1936
Prof. C. G. Jung | St. Katharine's Precinct, London
Dear Sir,
I was rather surprised to hear you say in your lecture at Caxton Hall last night that you had never found any mandalas with six divisions. Of course, the Buddhist "Wheel of Life" is almost always divided into six, but perhaps you have some reason for not regarding this as a mandala in the strict sense of the word.

I am enclosing herewith a reproduction of a Tibetan Wheel of Life, which you may like to add to your collection if you have not already got it. Apart from the six divisions, another feature, which distinguishes it from the usual mandala is its centre. Almost all the examples you showed, except some produced by pathological cases, had at the centre some kind of "holy of holies" — a temple, an egg, or a golden ball. The Buddhist Wheel, however, has a cock, a snake, and a hog, the symbols of lust (raga), ill-will (dosa), and stupidity (moha).

I have never come across any instance of its being used for magical purposes. Probably it is only used as a formal representation of the six worlds of samsara — a picture rather than a symbol. The unusual centre, however, seems to mark it as an essentially "world-denying" picture. That is to say, enlightenment or individuation does not consist in going to the centre of the circle, but in escaping from it altogether.

For this reason it might be called the "reverse side" of the usual mandala. It represents the philosophy of "neti, neti" as distinct from "Tat tvam asi," although the two are really opposite ways of doing the same thing. Or, as is said in "The Secret of the Golden Flower," "between the All and the Void is only a difference of name."

It is interesting to note that in the many Tibetan wheels of this kind, the figure of the Buddha appears in each of the six divisions to show that the phenomenal world is actually a manifestation of the Buddha nature. In this particular wheel, the Buddha only appears in four sections.

If you do not already know the work, a large number of these wheels will be found in L. A. Waddell's *Buddhism of Tibet: Or Lamaism, with Its Mystic Cults, Symbolism and Mythology, and Its Relation to Indian Buddhism* (Heffer, Cambridge, 1934, new ed.). Other works are: *Waddell's Buddhist Pictorial Wheel of Life*, Calcutta, 1892; Caroline Foley in the *Journal of the Royal Asiatic Society*, 1894, p. 388, and Vallee Poussin in the same journal, 1897, p. 463.

Unfortunately I cannot at the moment give you the history of the enclosed example, beyond the fact that it is taken from a rather curious work by Basil Crump called *Evolution as Outlined in the Archaic Eastern Records* (Luzac, London, 1930).

I think I am right in saying that this wheel is quite different from the Tibetan "khylihor," which is always used for magical purposes. (See David-Neel, *Mystiques et Magiciens du Tibet*, Librairie Plon, Paris, 1929).

Yours very truly, Alan W. Watts

The six divisions, starting from the top and going clockwise, are as follows:

Heaven World
Titan World

Tantalised Spirits
Hot and Cold Hells
Animal World
World of Men

There are twelve figures within the rim (outer) representing:

Avidya, ignorance
Samskara, propensities and impulses
Vijnana, consciousness
Nama-rupa, personality
Chadayatana, six gates of sense
Sparsa, contact with world through sense
Vedana, feeling
Trishna, craving for separate existence
Bhava, becoming, or the course of life
Jati, birth of an heir, maturity or giving rebirth to another ego
Jarmarana, decay and death
There is a twelfth, but the reproduction is so indistinct in places that I cannot detect it.

The demon clutching the wheel is Trishna, clinging to samsara. Note his eight limbs, four of them coiled with snakes.

Bromley, Kent | December 30, 1936
Dear Sir [Sokei-an Sasaki],
You sent me a letter some time ago on the subject of Zen which puzzled me very much. But now I think I understand what it means, for I am sure I have come to a close intellectual understanding of Zen. You wrote:

We train ourselves to concentrate upon something according to the power which is beyond our everyday consciousness, and yet which is within us. So we yield entirely to our true or real nature which is connected with all nature. To practice this, one must give up one's own intention — shut off as it were one's own brain action — to drive one's mind in an egotistic sense.

Just let go as you would with a stream, not rowing your own boat with your own strength or purpose. Go with the stream of nature. Do not try to go against the stream. Of course this is practice for the beginner, but using it you will find entrance to Buddhism.

I then read this passage from Suzuki:

> The Zen ideal is to be "the wind that bloweth where it listeth, and the sound of which we hear but cannot tell whence it cometh or whither it goeth."
>
> Lieh-tze [Lao-tzu], the Chinese philosopher, describes this frame of mind graphically as follows: "I allowed my mind without restraint to think of whatever it pleased and my mouth to talk about whatever it pleased: I then forgot whether the 'this and not this' was mine or another's…in and out I was thoroughly transformed; and then it was that the eye became like the ear, and the ear like the nose, and the nose like the mouth: and there was nothing that was not identified. The mind was concentrated and the form dissolved, and the bones and flesh all thoawed [*sic*] away I did not know where my form was supported, where my feet were treading; I just moved along with the wind, east and west, like a leaf detached from the stem, I was not conscious whether I was riding on the wind or the wind riding on me."

You will excuse me for quoting like this — I quite realize that it is not in accordance with the principles of Zen, which declared that such passages are "gems belonging to others," but I am forced to use the words of others as I have only just found the right finger pointing to the right moon. You can imagine how utterly perplexed I am by this sort of thing:

"One day Goso entered the hall and seated himself on the chair. He looked one way over one shoulder, and then the other. Finally he held out his staff high in his hand and said, 'Only one foot long!' Without further [next page(s) missing]

PART II

Coming to America

1938–41

JW: The years 1936 and 1937 were an expansion of Alan's self-imposed university. He pursued his work with the Buddhist Lodge as a protégé of Christmas Humphrey's, editing and writing for The Middle Way, *and eventually becoming the lodge secretary. During this time, Alan became somewhat of a man about town, enjoying the social activities of theater, symphony, and opera; visits to art exhibits at museums; and dating young women. He relished hanging about in bookstores, finding more books on Eastern philosophies and art. He wrote* The Spirit of Zen *(1936), and in an attempt to bring together Buddhism, Vedanta, Taoism, Jungian psychology, and Christian mysticism, he wrote* The Legacy of Asia and Western Man *(1937), which he later characterized as "a somewhat immature book."*

In the summer of 1937, he again attended the World Congress of Faiths, this time held in Oxford, and found conversations with many illustrious scholars informative and stimulating. He met Jiddu Krishnamurti, from Benares, India, adopted son of Annie Besant. She was a leader of the Theosophical Society who promoted Krishnamurti as the vehicle of the coming World Teacher. Krishnamurti disavowed such a notion, along with allegiance to any particular religion, but became a speaker and philosophical writer that Alan greatly admired all his life.

Another notable was Dimitrije Mitrinović, originally from Bosnia-Herzegovina and living in London as a self-styled guru, whom some of Alan's friends considered a black magician. Connected to some of the notable mystics of the era, Mitrinović was quite active in philosophy, psychology, and European politics, and inducted Alan into his "secret society." Alan worked for one of Mitrinović's publications, The Eleventh Hour, *doing copyediting, book reviews, and layout.*

Around this time Alan also met Frederic Spiegelberg, a noted scholar of Asian philosophies who had escaped the Third Reich and eventually moved to San Francisco, where he established the American Academy of Asian Studies. Years later, Spiegelberg would hire Alan as dean of the academy.

It was in 1937 that our grandmother, Ruth Fuller Everett (later Sasaki), a Chicago socialite with an avid interest in Buddhism, arrived in London. She had brought her young daughter, Eleanor (our mother), there to study piano with George Woodhouse. Ruth had studied Zen Buddhism in Kyoto, where D. T. Suzuki had introduced her to Nanshinken Roshi of Nanzen-ji Temple, of the Rinzai sect. She totally immersed herself in the study, practicing zazen and receiving koans. Eleanor, then fifteen, had lived in Kyoto with her for a time. In London, they sought out the Buddhist Society and became involved in activities there, with Ruth discoursing on what it was like to live in a Buddhist temple and participate in the day-to-day rigors of a disciple of a Zen master in Japan. Of Eleanor, Alan states in his autobiography, "I fell hopelessly in love with this young attractive American woman who loved to dance the hula."

When Ruth left to return to her duties in America, she left Eleanor in Alan's care (something that profoundly surprised me, knowing our grandmother). As Alan often told me with a pat on my rear end, I was conceived on the Commons in Chislehurst. Counting on my young fingers, I found I was born seven months after their wedding in April 1938.

Eleanor's father, Edward Warren Everett, twenty years older than Ruth, was a highly successful criminal attorney in Chicago, known for his fierce courtroom tirades and apparently being equally fierce at home. Warren, as he was known, was crippled, because he had suffered from polio as a child. By the time Alan met him in 1937, he was quite ill with arteriosclerosis and was eventually placed in a sanitarium in upstate New York, where he died in 1940.

Just prior to the holidays in 1937, Alan and Eleanor were engaged to be married and sailed to New York City aboard the HMS Bremerton to properly introduce Alan to the Everett family and friends. They took the train from New York City to Chicago. Alan was amazed at the cities and countryside, and upon arriving, at "Swan House," the Elizabethan-style mansion Ruth had had built in Hinsdale, Illinois, he was taken with the grandeur of the Everett lifestyle and with the generosity of his future mother-in-law. He also apparently shared Warren's love for fine brandy and cigars and formed something of a bond with the irascible family patriarch.

The couple returned to England after the holidays to prepare for what Alan and Eleanor alike thought was a strange wedding for two Buddhists — to be wed in an Anglican church. The wedding took place on April 2, 1938, at the parish church in Earl's Court, London, with Buddhist Ruth Everett making it a grand event, while Alan's parents were somewhat bewildered by the whole scene.

With rumblings of a war beginning in Europe, Alan and Eleanor lived only briefly in an apartment in London, and as Eleanor neared term with her pregnancy, they again boarded the Bremerton and left England for a new life in America. Alan's arrival in the United States to live was a nearly mystical experience for him. It was

exhilarating to come from the small island of Great Britain to the vast lands and open
skies of the American landscape. Although Alan had no idea what he was going to do
to provide for his wife and child when he arrived, he had no need to worry, with mother-
in-law Ruth and her connections at hand.

    The following series of letters are mostly to "Dear Mummy & Daddy." He wrote
his parents often, portraying his life in America, his associations, and eventually his
writing and being published. It is obvious that Alan loved to write, as his imagery of
life in America, his rather painterly descriptions of the landscape, his thoughts about
class and world politics, and the war in Europe are quite effusive. These letters cover
the period from his arrival in New York City in September 1938 through his decision to
enter seminary in Evanston, Illinois, in the summer of 1941.

New York | September 21, 1938

Dear Mummy & Daddy,

Well here we are at last and I expect you will have got my cablegram about our
safe arrival. We were 12 hours late getting into port as there was a bad fog outside
New York and we had to wait about in the entrance to the harbour.

    Although there was rather a stiff wind at times we had a very steady cross-
ing. The *QM* [*Queen Mary*] is a fine ship from the engineering point of view, but
accommodation and service [are] poor. However, we both survived it all right
and got plenty of good sea air. As table companions we had a delightful American couple and were able to pass the time very agreeably with them. I think the
only other thing of interest that happened on the voyage was that I won a prize
in a competition for guessing the names of passengers from clues on the principle of a crossword puzzle. The prize being a cigarette case, which will do as a
Christmas present for someone. We arrived to find Mrs. Everett in great form,
looking extremely well and feeling it too. She seems absolutely overjoyed to have
us, and has been busy looking round for things for me to do, with the result that
prospects look good. She is very friendly with the chief of one of the biggest
publishing concerns in New York — Doubleday Doran — and she seems quite
eager to help me. This afternoon we go to meet a prominent literary agent, but I
don't suppose much will be done for a week or so as we are going on a trip into
New England to see the countryside and visit Mr. Everett.

    Last night Mrs. E. took us for a jaunt about 30 miles up the Hudson River,
and although it was pouring with rain we had a fine time. All that part of the
country is incredibly beautiful, for the banks of the river are astonishingly steep
[—] wooded, rocky slopes almost 700 feet high and the roads run along the tops
of them. The views are simply gorgeous and the roads so well built that you can

cruise along so evenly that you seem to be gliding uninterruptedly through the air. On the way home we called in for supper at a wayside tavern. Beer was not on sale owing to local elections! However, we had a lobster each. But the amusing thing was the tavern itself, constructed almost entirely of wood and its walls covered from ceiling to floor with a vast collection of old arms, pewter, paintings, warming pans, clocks, spinning wheels, flags, and whatnot. Then we returned to the city after dark, and a more thrilling sight than New York lit up at night can hardly be imagined. It's an entirely new kind of sensation.

In this hotel we have rooms 16 floors up looking out straight over the river. We are going to make it our headquarters, but we shall be traveling about a good bit and I think it would be as well to address letters for the time being to c/o American Express, 605 Fifth Avenue, New York City. This weekend we shall be away, and shortly afterwards we shall be going by road to Chicago to visit the family there. I have written to Uncle Willie and shall try to arrange a meeting with him.

According to Mrs. E. the local Zen master, Sokei-an Sasaki, is a trump, and we are going to work a good bit with him. He has been translating all kinds of Chinese and Japanese texts with Mrs. E. He is really a dear; came down to the dock to meet us and is anxious to do anything he can for Buddhism in England.

I can't think of any more news at present as we've only been settled in a day and a half. I shall be sending you some photographs soon. Mrs. E. has let me have the use of her Leica camera, which is a beauty and can do almost anything.

In the meantime rain continues to pour — just streams of solid water, but it will be over in a day or two and is usual at this time. Eleanor is feeling fine and she and Mrs. E. send all love to you.

I'm afraid you must be missing me terribly, but you are hardly ever out of my mind even though there is so much to do here. But I'm certain I've got a grand opportunity to get some good work done this winter, and you can be sure I shall spend my time well.

So here's so long until the next letter, and all my love to you,

Alan

NEW YORK, NEW YORK | OCTOBER 4, 1938
Dear Mummy & Daddy,
Well, here we are again, and I'm trying to get this written in time to catch the *Queen Mary* on its way back. I hope it won't be late, but we've been away from New York the last two days visiting Mr. Everett at his sanatorium up in Hartford, Connecticut, which is about 100 miles from here. He is much worse than when

I last saw him, but there is no doubt that he is now in good hands. We went all the way there and back by car, and you've no idea how gorgeous the country is now that the leaves are turning. Connecticut is very like England in some ways, except for the architecture. Almost all the houses are of white wood with red or green shutters to the windows, and the whole countryside is covered with trees of every colour from dark green, pale yellow, orange, and deepest red to a fiery gold which just takes your breath away. And from time to time you pass enormous hills of these colours with lakes and rivers at their feet. The only thing that spoils it is the trail of wreckage left by the hurricane, which you may have read about in the papers. It came just after we arrived, and although we had little trouble in New York, to the north there were storms and floods, which have made a mess of dirt and broken trees and houses all over the place. Today we passed through an area where tobacco is grown, and hundreds of the huge sheds in which it is stored have been completely wrecked, and their roofs blown clean across the road. Even so we haven't seen the worst of it.

However, you mayn't have heard much about this owing to ructions in Europe. You must have had a terrible time with that war scare, and although opinion over here seems rather strong against Chamberlain, I can't help feeling he did a marvellous piece of work. I doubt if England could have afforded to take a strong line with the rearmament business uncompleted, and C. had to play for time but can't very well say so in public.

Last Saturday we spent the day with Eleanor's friends the Stursbergs at their country house in Norwalk, Connecticut (you'll need a map to follow all this!), and on Sunday we went up the Hudson River to Nyak [Nyack] again to visit an old friend of Mrs. Everett's, Dr. P. A. Bernard. He is in charge of a huge estate right on the top of a hill, and is a most remarkable man having an encyclopaedic knowledge of some of the more out-of-the-way branches of Eastern philosophy and mysticism. He is also interested in circuses and keeps an astonishing collection of wild animals: 3 elephants, tigers, monkeys, a baboon, white peacocks, a golden cockerel, ravens, and heaven knows what else. His place is run as a sort of club where lectures are given and I have his permission to use his library, which Mrs. E. tells me is an absolutely unique collection of books, most of which concern the East.

Eleanor has now got herself a new doctor (name of Kozmak), who was recommended to us by the Chicago obstetrician de Lee who is supposed to be just the last word at the job. This man seems an excellent fellow, and he was simply astonished at Eleanor's condition. Told her that people like her ought to bear the world's children and give some of the other "poor females" a rest! After a most thorough examination he pronounced everything so okay that he doubted if the birth would give the slightest trouble as E. is absolutely built for it. So much so that we may expect it earlier than we had thought for the appropriate muscles and whatnot are so arranged with E. that the infant is calculated almost to drop out.

I have seen quite a lot more of our local Zen master, Sasaki, who is really a fine fellow with the most amazing store of wisdom. I feel I simply can't miss the opportunity and am going to have him teach me Zen in the orthodox way. Mrs. E. has worked with him all summer, and the change in her from when she left England is almost miraculous. Herewith is a snap of them both doing their Chinese translations. The other snaps are just a few odds and ends of my first attempts with a Leica, but I will send you better ones soon.

I have made several friends at Columbia University, including one of the professors of philosophy who has given me the entrée to the university library so that I need not want for books. I have also seen a good bit of Spiegelberg, who is now lecturing there, and he seems to be finding his feet all right. Of America he says that nature is hostile but man friendly! This week I am getting in touch with Dutton's (Murray's counterpart here), and am already making friends of the New York Watkins' [bookstore].

Had a letter from Uncle Willie, but little news of his family as he is away from home in Dakota. There is just a chance he may have to come to New York on business, and if so we shall meet as we have arranged to stay permanently at this hotel. In a few days we shall be going into new apartments on the top floor (16th) overlooking the river. E. & I will have three rooms and Mrs. E., two. So from now on please address letters here. These American flats are lovely; each room has its own bathroom and our flat will have a kitchen as well so that altogether we shall have a living room, a bedroom, a nursery (pro tem my study), 2 bathrooms, and kitchen, and all for a lot less than one pays for the same in London. Service is included in it, and very good it is here. Mrs. E. is being [an] angel but no words will convince her of it as she is more than relieved that she did not have to come to England what with Mr. Everett's illness and the political situation in Europe.

Well that's all the important news for the present. There will be more when we get settled in properly, for at present we're still rather living in trunks. Please pay my respects to Puck & Toby and also to Douglas and say that I will write shortly. I have a lot of news for Toby, but some of it must mature before I write him. So here's all my love to you both, and am longing to get a letter from you. Perhaps one is waiting at the American Express so I will call in there tomorrow as it is now late and we've only just got back from Hartford.

Your loving son, Alan

NEW YORK CITY | OCTOBER 18, 1938

Dear Mummy & Daddy,

I'm afraid this must be rather a hurried note, but I've realized there is just time for it to catch the *Queen Mary*. I was so glad to get your last letter but terribly sorry to hear about the burglar. I do hope the stuff was insured, but you can never replace a gold watch like that. I think it's an absolute shame that they should take things like that from people who can't afford to have much in the way of gold and jewels in any case. Hope the police get him; they ought to take some trouble after the help you gave with the Hollands.

I don't know that there's anything special in the way of news to give you. We have been taking things quietly in the last week or so. I'm getting along fast with my work for Murray's and Eleanor is getting along fine. Her doctor very much regrets that he can't possibly find anything wrong with her! And I'm glad to find that he belongs to the good old-fashioned school, which doesn't believe in all these new-fangled drugs and things which are used here for giving "painless" but highly complicated and dangerous births. E. was most anxious to avoid anything of that kind.

I have started Zen work good and proper with Mr. Sasaki and find it most beneficial. I have learnt more about Buddhism in the past weeks than I have learnt for years, and I never realised there was so much to be known. Dr. Spiegelberg and I are arranging to give lectures together next month. He is being a great help to me and is talking about my books and things all over the place. Incidentally, the American edition of *The Legacy of Asia* has just come from the Chicago University Press, and they have made a fine job of it. Now we await some press reviews.

Well, I will write at more length in a day or two, as this one has to go off quick. Eleanor and Mrs. E. send their love to you, and as for me, well, I'm always thinking of you and how I wish there wasn't 4,000 miles of water between us!

Your loving son, Alan

NEW YORK CITY | NOVEMBER 17, 1938

Dear Mummy & Daddy,

Well, I suppose you got quite a surprise, and we were almost caught napping too. The doctor had told us to expect the baby somewhat earlier than usual, but the creature made such a rush to get into the world that we only got Eleanor to the hospital just in time. The baby weighs six pounds four ounces; the doctor says it's rather small but there's nothing wrong with it. It's impossible to tell what it's going to look like just at present, the only distinctive feature being the hands, which are unusually large, with long fingers and beautiful nails. Eyes are hazel, and the eyelashes rather dark, so it may be a brunette. Everyone at the hospital is astonished at Eleanor. She had no pain at all until after six in the evening, when it started coming every fifteen minutes; I took her to the hospital between 7:30 and 8 and by this time they were coming every three minutes. At 9:15 they phoned us to come along as it had already started to come, and by 9:30 it was all over. Just after 10 [AM] I went in to see Eleanor, found her bright and cheerful and feeling like getting up to cook breakfast, and now we expect her to be out of hospital by the 31st. The doctor says that next time she will have to go round with a wash-basket in case of emergencies!

I go round to see her twice a day now, and it's amazing what a difference it has made to her appearance. She looks five times as beautiful and has suddenly acquired an exquisite skin, and has no longer any inclination to bite her nails. She's nursing the baby herself. We had been told that American hospital nurses are none too kind to mothers, but this was either a myth or else Eleanor has struck it lucky, for she has just the ordinary hospital day and night nurses and they are as delightful as can be. The doctor's name is Kozmak, in spite of which he appears to be an Irishman about 65, rather gruff but with a delicious twinkle in the eye. As soon as the baby has grown into some sort of recognizable shape I will send you a photograph; at present she's much like other babies and rather dirty as Kozmak won't allow them to be washed for four days except for their faces. He says washing too soon creates skin irritations. At present its only activity is to suck everything in sight, and to gaze round at things as if there was something on its mind. It squawks, but not very noisily, and is given to blowing bubbles.

I'm not quite sure what I'm going to do with a girl, but I seem to get on all right with the Spiegelberg's baby girl so I suppose I shall learn. Jimey doesn't understand things at all; he's not allowed at the hospital, and whenever I come back I smell of Eleanor, which is most mystifying.

This has all been such an event that I can hardly think of the rest of the news. I got a pleasant surprise the other day. I told you I had written an article for *Asia* — 3,000 words for which I should usually be paid at most 6 guineas, more generally 4½. But one morning a cheque arrived for $60.00, which is about 12 guineas, by far the most profitable 3,000 words I've ever written.

You must have had a miserable time with your teeth, and I do hope they have made some new ones which fit you well. Has it changed your face much, and if so what about sending us a photograph?

We did very little in the week before Eleanor went to the hospital as she couldn't go about much and I was busy with my work for Murray's, which will soon be finished, leaving me time to get ahead with my novel.

Lots and lots of love to you both from us all, and I do hope you like being grandparents! Baby has to be just plain Joan Watts, as Eleanor doesn't like her mother's name Ruth, and if we called it Emily or Eleanor as well it would have such unfortunate initials.

All the best from your loving son, Alan

JW: In Alan's letter about my birth I was surprised at his discomfort in acknowledging that I was a girl! He refers to me as "it" throughout most of his letter. I guess he'd had little or no experience with babies or children, although he mentions Frederic Spiegelberg's infant daughter, who was born about the same time as I was. He sounded almost disappointed that I wasn't a boy, although his fascination with me as I grew is obvious in subsequent letters. Jimey was my mother's Pomeranian dog, which lived a very long life. I believe he was about twenty years old when he died.

The issue of my name was also interesting. I've always disliked being just plain "Joan Watts," a sum total of nine letters in my name. (Anne was just plain Ann Watts; she would add the "E" later in life.) When I was young and read the Raggedy Ann *books, I always wanted to be Marcella; it was more substantial and romantic. But the part about an appropriate middle name actually shocked me. The initials "JEW" being not acceptable, was apparently a dilemma at that time in New York among certain factions of society. The large influx of European Jews, due to the Hitler regime, was bewildering to the rather stuffy, proper upper classes of the city, which found them boisterous and pushy. In some ways, our Grandmother Everett could be somewhat of a snob, and I'm sure our father absorbed some of her ideas at the time. On the other side of the coin, though, she was always very respectful of her "colored" help, paying them quite well, and she always said that Jews made the best lawyers, doctors, and dentists. Obviously, Alan grew beyond racial definitions during his lifetime.*

NEW YORK CITY | DECEMBER 6, 1938
Dear Mummy & Daddy,
I'm afraid it's rather a long time since you heard from me last but I've been terribly busy finishing off Ingrams' book for Murray's and getting to work again on my novel. But first of all you will want to hear about your granddaughter. I think she is going to be a most beautiful child. She has got splendid eyes and an excellently shaped head, and my, is she strong! At three weeks she can roll herself over, lift her head, and shout fit to raise the roof. Has a grip like a vice and is learning to kick! I'm really very pleased with her. Photographs aren't ready

yet, but I hope to be able to send you something soon. Eleanor is getting along all right too.

I have had several letters from Ivan [Croshaw] who is now in Canada and expects to be coming here soon. Apparently he is looking for a job in the new aircraft factories, but I don't think he has had any luck yet. Nevertheless he appears to be in high spirits.

Yesterday I had lunch with the president and lecture secretary of the Analytical Psychology Club (Jung Society), and they want me to give them a lecture quite shortly. Evidently the APC here is rather a bigger concern than the one in London, especially if they can pay their lecturers $50.00, which is what I am offered. The president is a Dr. Baker (woman), who is not a psychologist but a research worker in a most fascinating branch — tissue culture, which apparently means keeping dead things alive. She is the assistant of Dr. Alexis Carrel, who works with Col. Lindbergh on strange scientific experiments. They have chicken liver, which they have kept going for years and some kind of ovary which is still fertile after twenty years in a bottle! A very delightful and intelligent woman.

I had a most exacting intellectual exercise the other night when Sasaki made me a present of a set of Japanese chessmen and taught me the game. It is far more difficult than our chess. The board has 81 squares instead of 64, and though the pieces have more restricted moves they can change their character when they get into the enemy's territory. And, horror of horrors, when you take one of your opponent's men you can use it against him, putting it down on the board wherever you like! Add to this the fact that the men are not to be recognized by shape; they are just flat bits of wood inscribed with Chinese characters, and you have to remember them by these.

I was simply delighted to hear about the amenability of RHM and the Finance Committee. It was about time, too, and I hope the raises were reasonably large. Talking of hospitals, we struck it very lucky with Eleanor at the Woman's Hospital here. I've never come across a more pleasant crowd of nurses, and the atmosphere of the place was astonishingly friendly. We have discovered that our doctor was not an Irishman but a Jew, though you wouldn't think it. He made a fine job of things and has a special way of fastening up the navel so that it looks perfectly normal only a day or two after birth and the baby doesn't have to wear any sort of bandage.

As to [a] Christmas present, I think a book would be the best thing to send and we have both been wanting to read a new publication of Murray's called *Laughing Diplomat* by Daniele Varè. The best way for you to get this would be to ring up Murray's warehouse, which you will find in [the] telephone book under

John Murray, say you are ordering it for me, and ask them to deliver it to the office. You could pay the messenger and you should get a discount of 33 percent on retail price, which is about 16/s [shillings]. If there is any difficulty about it, produce enclosed.

We have had some lovely presents for the baby, among them some of the finest knitting I have ever seen done by an old woman in Chicago — a coat and bonnet done on some great grandmother's needles, which must be about the thickness of a pin. They are of the softest wool, beautifully edged with silk, but as yet the baby is a little small for them, though she now weighs 6 lb., 13 oz.

Well, I've got an awful lot of work waiting, so I'm afraid I must stop now. So here's lots of love from us all and a bubble from Joan.

From your loving son, Alan

New York City | December 14, 1938

Dear Mummy & Daddy,

Well this is to wish you both a very happy Christmas, and I think it should arrive just about in time. And here are the first photographs of Joan. They were taken over a week ago, but it takes time to use up these Leica films, to get them developed and enlarged, so I'm afraid I couldn't get them to you sooner.

I am sending you by parcel post a book (for Daddy), and something for Ma to put in a handbag. Eleanor has one and it looks very smart. It's rather a small thing, but I felt I ought to send you something direct from America. But it isn't all because your other present must come from England. Please will you take the enclosed to Harrods whenever convenient and get any kind of plant you want for the garden.

Well now as to news. I have finished the Ingrams book for Murray's and am getting to work quietly on my novel, which I'm going to try and get published over here first. I expect to be through with it by early January. We have to stay here at least until the cold weather is over because of baby, and we took a 6 months' lease on the flat (you can't do it for less in this hotel).

We had a perfectly gorgeous time last night. A friend from Chicago came and took us out for dinner and dance at the famous Rainbow Room, which is right on the top of Radio City, the second highest building in New York. The view from there by night is quite one of the most astonishing things I've ever seen, the chief feature being the line of lights on Fifth Avenue, stretching right away to the horizon as the crow flies. And below you in every direction is just a display of inverted astronomy. The Rainbow Room itself is rather a credit to its situation; there's none of the vulgar, rowdy crowd, for the music is beautiful and the company select, being too inexpensive for the flashy set, the right price for the more "old-fashioned" society, and too dear for a mob. We were very much entertained by a rather respectable-looking middle-aged couple, both of them rather tall and slender, who, we were told, come twice a week just to dance and have a glass of champagne. The man was quite the most exquisite dancer I have ever seen, and when it came to Spanish tangos everyone else just deserted the floor and watched them. Mrs. E. had never been there before and was so smitten with it that she wants to arrange a small party there on Eleanor's birthday.

When we go out at night we get our Irish maid, Teresa, to look after the baby. She is nothing short of a stroke of luck, and her only drawback is that she chatters a bit much, but being Irish what would you expect! And how she enjoys the job, so much so that it's all I can do to make her take an extra tip for it.

Mr. Everett's mental condition has decidedly improved in the last month so far as his disposition is concerned. But he's getting much weaker in body and mental strength. Yet whereas he was once so bad tempered that everyone fought shy of him, his room is now quite a gathering place and he is always wanting people to come in and talk to him. It's made everything so much easier for everyone, particularly for Mrs. E. He is tickled to death at being a grandfather.

On Sunday we had a most amusing Japanese family to lunch. He is one of the chief men of the big Mitsui Corporation over here, Mitsui being the owners of almost every big business concern in Japan. He has two small daughters, one 15 and the other 6. The eldest one seems rather underdeveloped, but that is because, being the eldest, she had to have a Japanese education and speaks little English. Yet she is a great beauty and the family got me to take some photographs of her. But as for the younger one — what a caution! She's perpetually on the go and has more brains for a child of her age than I thought possible. There's nothing at all of the demure Japanese woman in her, being a thoroughly emancipated Western woman, and I think they will find her a problem when she grows up. I can tell you I had a full afternoon entertaining those two. I had managed to pick up a miniature edition of that Chinese Rings conjuring trick — you know, Major Branson's old game of joining together apparently solid steel rings. Were they mystified, but then I let them into the secret and set them fooling their parents.

Joan is caroling away now as it's just feeding time. This afternoon I was literally "left with the baby" as the two womenfolk went out for a day's shopping. I had to feed the brat and change its nappies. Here we have an ingenious business called a diaper service, invented by two young bachelors who have made a fortune out of it. You have no trouble washing nappies. The service supplies you with 100 per week and as you use them you put them into a special disinfected drum and they collect them and take them away all for $7.00 a month. Progress!

Joan's godparents are to be the Matthiases and Mrs. Forman. We got your parcel and were just delighted with the woolly jacket and my old robe with the fine lace. Did I really wear that? The Matthiases were Eleanor's guardians in case of the death of her own parents and they have another daughter called Joan as well.

It's rather difficult to write coherently at the moment as I'm trying to listen to Wagner's *Rienzi* overture on the radio at the same time. There is a broadcasting station here that puts out almost nothing but first-rate music, mostly from records. There is almost no advertising on it as it appears to be run for charity. We also have two stations, which give only Italian programmes, and do we get some fine tenors! The only trouble with the Italians is that they talk too much. Otherwise, the programmes are mainly jazz and advertising, with occasional plays and a man who comes on in the morning to sing the most terrible hymns to the accompaniment of a cinema organ.

Well, it's right on bedtime and I'm going to have a hard day's work tomorrow, so I had better bring this to an end with lots of love from us all for Christmas.

Your loving son, Alan

New York City | January 3, 1939
Dear Mummy & Daddy,
First of all I want to thank you very much indeed for giving us a subscription to *Punch* for Christmas. This will be a lovely thing to have, and it was a most thoughtful and original idea, so we shall look forward to receiving copies as they come. I hope you received our parcel and the photographs okay. We have had several cards from England — a most amusing one from Puck and Toby, done by Puck herself, one from the Blyths, from Douglas and Christine, from Graham Howe, Ronald MacFarlane, Mrs. Burke, Auntie G., and others.

We had a very jolly Christmas here; it was not nearly so hectic as last year's, so were spared the inevitable indigestion that comes from too much American party food. And on Eleanor's birthday we had one of the chief men from Doubleday Doran, the publishers, to dinner. He is going to help me with the publication of my book, and we got on rather well together, finding we had several common interests; he is also a keen photographer. On my birthday we are going to celebrate with another visit to the Rainbow Room, which I told you about, and Eleanor has already given me a lovely set of chessmen as a present. She is so fascinated with it herself that she broods over the board playing single-handed games when I am busy, and I never thought chess would "get her" like that!

I have got the chance of a small, peculiar, and rather lucrative job for, of all people, a world association of hairdressers! They are having a special book made to contain the biographies of 30 of their chief members, and they want someone to write them up in decent English at $5.00 a time — each biography to occupy about a page of the book. There is also a chance that I may be able to get the actual work of writing them into the book, which is to be exhibited at the New York World's Fair, but that is very much in the air at present. The idea came through Mrs. E.'s hairdresser, who is the president of the association.

We haven't been out much lately as I have been so busy with writing and Eleanor with the baby, who is steadily putting on strength and shows the first signs of being able to crawl. We have found a new way to stop her howling. Mr. Sasaki gave her a *mokugyo* for Christmas — a small Buddhist temple gong, being a hollow ball of wood shaped like a cuttlefish. When you knock it, it makes a melodious noise, which the baby finds rather fascinating. Everybody is giving us advice about what to do with her, all of which we ignore and go on our own sweet way because all the advice is quite contradictory! The only problem is that she hates being weighed and will never keep still on the scale unless she is tied up tight in a blanket.

By the way, I have given orders for the piano, wireless, gas stove, and refrigerator to be removed from our flat pro tem [in London], as there is no point paying rent on them while we are away and they may as well be overhauled in any case. So if you go there and find them absent please don't think we have had a burglary.

I expect we shall be getting about more in the New Year as the weather gets better, though at present it's nothing to grumble about. Today is quite warm and the only big fall of snow was at the end of November. I may be going up to Toronto shortly to lecture to a rather large branch of the Theosophical Society there, which wants to start a Buddhist group. If so I hope to meet Ivan if he does not come here before then, but I have had no news from him lately.

Now I really don't think there's much more news for you — oh, except that just this minute, a gorgeous parcel of towels, flannels, etc., for Joan has just arrived from the Minneapolis family.

I just wish you could be here looking out of my window with me. It's just the most lovely sight, and every evening we get the finest sunsets I've ever seen. Ships are almost always passing and often huge convoys of barges come up early in the morning, some of them from as far away as Chicago and Canada. And my, isn't the air good! I'm getting fat by degrees, and the suit I had made for my wedding no longer fits. The waistcoat, the coat, and the trousers are just about bursting their buttons.

Well, here's all my love to you both, and good wishes for a happy New Year. We got your telegrams, and were very glad to have them.

Your loving son, Alan

New York City | April 29, 1939

Dear Mummy and Daddy,

Ivan has suddenly decided to return to England so I am taking the opportunity of dashing off a short note to send by him and also let you have the enclosed just to go on with. Hope to let you have something better and of us all soon.

This new address is a place some German people have let us have while they are out of town for the summer. It is really delightful, a huge saving on the Park Crescent, furnishing modern but very tolerable and with a lovely view over Central Park showing us quite a third of the city's length.

News in brief: the other morning we were surprised by the arrival of a barrage of press photographers wanting pictures of yours truly. Why remains rather a mystery, but apparently some literary paper is giving me a write-up. Busy pressing Wisdom of the East; result, Dutton's sent large repeat order to London and have advertised in *Asia*, the latter, incidentally, being about to take another of my effort. No news of novel yet, but am starting another book on psychology of acceptance, relaxation, etc., from the viewpoint of East & mod. psychology. Probable title *The Anatomy of Happiness* [published under the title *The Meaning of Happiness*, 1940] after Burton's *Anatomy of Melancholy*. Was a paragraph about me in NY *Herald Tribune* the other day. This is equivalent of London *Daily Telegraph*, just to say that I was now in New York, famous English writer, blah, etc. As you say, thank God I got out of the New Britain affair. Those cuttings [reviews] were terrible; I knew them both well, but the offender was [a] wild Irishman. Am having a bout with the dentist, having at last found a man who is reliable and no fancy stuff. The tooth which others would have said would have to come out he is saving by draining it. Have been engaged in long correspondence with Cranmer-Byng; we are improving the format of the books. This year I make over £15 out of the series, which is about 30 percent on original investment. Not bad!

Well, Ivan is in a hurry to get off so I must stop. Am sending a load of odds and ends.

Tons of love to you both, Alan

New York City | May 29, 1939

Dear Mummy & Daddy,

I'm sorry Ivan delayed in posting your letter. I have been waiting to hear from you before writing again. Consequently you haven't heard from me for some time as I was always expecting to hear from you by the next delivery!

No, apparently Eleanor didn't read over her letter. Our apartment is not quite so mixed up as it would seem. There are 1½ bathrooms, i.e., one with a shower only, and the beds in the study are divans. There is also a proper bedroom with the most amazing double bed ever conceived; it defies description, and is most comfortable. There is a grand piano (hence the request for music) and we are both teaching ourselves. I now play a Bach minuet, a Chopin mazurka (the one in *Sylphides* which comes on the first side of the turn-over record in your collection — side 3, I think) and the *Tannhäuser March*.

I wish you could see the New York World's Fair. We have been twice and are going again on Friday. It's quite the loveliest thing of its kind either of us have seen, especially at night when everything is floodlit and they have a fountain symphony. This is produced by a lake of 1,000 fountains which can be operated from a central panel together with appropriate music, coloured lights, fireworks, etc., all very skillfully put together. The architecture is astonishing, "pièce de résistance" being the USSR building. We went with Mrs. E. to see a troupe of Japanese dancing girls doing traditional acts, which was [a] real treat. I have taken a lot of photographs of these things, some of which I will send. Various odds and ends are enclosed, especially the guardsman and his dog, which will amuse you. I should explain that he is eating what they call here a "hot dog," i.e., a long bread roll with a frankfurter sausage inside.

Dagg has given me [the] job of being American agent for the *Modern Mystic* pro tem, which adds considerably more grist to the mill, with promise of directorship in [a] new company they hope to form in less than a year. I told you he had been over here conducting an advertising lecture tour on a grand scale. He has been quite successful in the east of America, and had crowded houses. They are putting me on to the job of lecturing in Boston soon on any relevant subject I like. Manager of these lectures will be a delightful old man called Max Gysi, who knows lots of my friends in London — the Watkinses, for instance, for whom he has boundless admiration. All this business ought to get me an extra $1,000 p.a. at least directly, and more indirectly as it increases "my public." The tough job is now to make the *Modern Mystic* into a really good magazine as I don't like to sell things in which I don't believe through and through, but there is every possibility of doing this. However, "softly, softly, catchee monkey"; it must be a diplomatic business.

The New York summer has begun in earnest. Am sitting at an open window in shirtsleeves with an electric fan buzzing and an iced drink at my elbow. But I am still hot! As yet we cannot fry eggs on the pavement, but this is no doubt to come, which is one of the occasions when I thank God I'm an author and that my office is at home. Everyone is going about the streets today in light hats, no coats, and gabardine trousers, and, as in London, the underground is the one cool spot. The summer has its blessings, however. Strawberries are now under a shilling per large basket, and all kinds of strange fruits are arriving — watermelons, cantaloupes, huge cherries, succulent avocado pears. I have never known such a country for eating.

Most restaurants leave English visitors (unaccustomed to Simpson's) gasping. But my training at Simpson's has stood me in good stead.

On Sunday we had one of the theological professors from Columbia Univ. to tea — Dr. Hume, a dear old parsonic fellow who went into ecstasies over Joan. He is a most learned scholar of comparative religion and brought some old works on Buddhism, among them a bibliography published in the sixties, which contains many items in English not listed in the Lodge biblio. I am making notes of them to send to Toby.

Joan's first front teeth are showing and she shows signs of crawling in the proper way — instead of progressing about the floor by rolling. She really enjoys getting herself as dirty as possible and is trying to eat everything in sight, even the door-handle of the car.

I have had letters recently from Graham Howe and John Grey Murray. Howe is wanting me to find a publisher for his books here and Murray is getting married! — which explains the mysterious and beautiful house at Richmond, so obviously furnished for a lady.

Correspondence with Cranmer-Byng continues regularly, and shortly you will see the next Wisdom of the East volume somewhat transformed in appearance to the pleasure of all concerned.

I'm afraid I owe apologies to Mr. Forsdyke, but the postal authorities are really to blame. The first announcement I saw of the Atlantic airmail was when I opened my morning paper at 9 AM. It was to the effect that the service had suddenly decided to start and that all letters must be received by 9 AM that same morning! The only other announcement was at midnight on the radio the night before. But as soon as the service runs direct to England I will see what can be done. Apparently they sprung it as a surprise so as not to be overwhelmed with letters.

Where we are living now is not so very far from Mrs. E., who is still at 150 Riverside. New York is laid out in rectangular blocks, so things are easy to find. 150 Riverside is at 87th Street, i.e., 10 blocks north of us and 5 blocks west, as there are 5 main avenues between here and Riverside. North-south roads are avenues, and east-west are streets, with the exception of Broadway, Riverside Drive, and Central Park West. All these are really avenues, but are not called so. We are on the corner of 77th Street and Central Park West, looking south and east over the park. We calculate about 8 blocks to the mile, but I think it should be more like 12. Manhattan Island, the main part of New York City, is really quite small, and when the *Queen Mary* arrives and departs it can be heard all over the city.

When you are next at Courtfield Gardens I wonder if you could do something for me. Among my papers there is a book called *Mythos und Schiksal*, having a black cover with white lettering. With it is a portion of a MS (carbon copy), which is a translation of parts of the book. Would you mind collecting these together and sending them to Mr. Philip Metman of Carlton Hill [London]. I feel terribly guilty about not having sent these to him before.

Re: addressing letters to America. An American citizen, being a republican, is "Mr." A British subject, being a monarchist, is "Esq." But the form "Esq." is sometimes used here; I have seen letters addressed to Mr. E. in this way from American people, and I was once addressed thus by a firm who had no reason to think I was British.

Well, much work awaits me, and I think I have given you most of the main news. We have a busy week ahead, every day filled with something, and now I have got to prepare a lecture on meditation for tonight!

Lots and lots of love to you both. I will send you more photographs when Joan is a little less grumpy about her teeth.

Your loving son, Alan

NEW YORK CITY | JUNE 14, 1939

Dear Mummy & Daddy,

First of all, thanks for all your letters. We will arrange to meet Miss Everington and see that she doesn't get lost, stolen, or strayed. With regard to the second of these, we guarantee nothing definite! I hope she is expecting us.

You must be having a time of it at the Fund this year without extra help, but I do hope the hard work will get Douglas his raise at the end of the year. It's about time that his good qualities had some substantial recognition.

At present I am piled up with work, and in the past few months I have met so many people that my head begins to reel. This is called "building up a following," and before long I think I shall have collected together so many people interested in Oriental philosophy in New York that I shall be able to give at least one lecture a week. Just now it's one a fortnight, and to the last of them came Mr. Koizumi from London, who was most useful in the subsequent discussion.

We may be going out of New York for a month later in the summer to take a farm cottage somewhere in Connecticut, either by the sea or among the lakes and hills. It will be lovely for Joan, who is now taking a very active interest in life.

She crawls all over my study while I am working. I put her down beside Eleanor on the far side of the room and the next thing I know is that something is tickling my feet. She is now about to explore the bathroom, and I suppose I shall soon have to rescue her from trying to eat a radiator pipe. More photographs soon, as she seems to change every day.

We have had Lady Bateman over here. I don't know if you remember her, but she came to the Lodge once — a perfectly delightful person with a rather weak memory, which seems to be getting much better. She dined us in glory on the roof of the Hotel Pierre. Was on her way back from a tour in India and Japan.

I'm glad you liked the article in *Asia*. There will be another shortly, which I will send you in due course. The lecture was, in a sense, intended to leave people on the horns of a dilemma. In another sense there is no dilemma because I let the cat out of the bag for everyone to see. The only trouble with this cat is that although he is walking right out in the open, he is black and the night is dark. To put it in another way, accordance with Tao is difficult because it is too simple for the human mind to grasp. When it is said that everything is the Tao, that is a plain statement of fact, and there is really no more to be said. If this is so, there can be neither getting into accord with it nor getting out of accord with it. This is what is meant in Buddhism when it is said that there can be no attainment of Nirvana because there is no one to attain it. I do not think the analogy of a musician learning a symphony is quite relevant here, because from the standpoint of Tao it does not matter whether the musician hears his own part as in harmony with the rest or not. In fact, his not hearing it so is just as much Tao as his hearing it so. Does it matter from the musician's standpoint? Yes and no. It matters in that he feels himself out of harmony with life, which makes him unhappy. But this feeling is also Tao. Of course, in another way the analogy is relevant because, as you say, trying to accord with the accordance and lack of accordance is necessary if only to demonstrate its own futility. In a way it comes back to the saying, "Which of you by taking thought can add one cubit to his stature?" We cannot bring ourselves nearer to the Tao, or increase our spiritual stature until we reach heaven, for Tao and heaven are here and now. People think that to find Enlightenment they have to do something about it, i.e., to make themselves different or worthy of it. But this is false pride, because Enlightenment is not a reward which one can get. It is something we have in spite of ourselves. We long for the heights of spirituality, but "Tao is like water in that it seeks the lowly level which men abhor." In other words, it is so simple that it is complicated, because we think something so great ought to be complicated.

I discovered an interesting thing the other day, which you might like to try out. Playing cards was said to have been invented to conceal mystical philosophy and yet preserve it where no one would think of looking for it unless "in the know." I puzzled about this for some time and then got a hint. The four suits run as follows, representing the 4 elements and the 4 faculties of man: Diamonds are fire and intuition; spades are earth and sensation; hearts are water and feeling; clubs are air and intelligence (the aggressiveness of thinking). Arrange the suits to form a cross, diamonds opposite spades, clubs opposite hearts. Start with the 2 in each suit on the extremity of the arms of the cross and work inwards to the centre, counting ace high. Put the joker in the middle at the end. It is a symbol which can be read in crowds of ways, and pay particular attention to the court cards, especially king and queen, noting the symbols which they hold in their hands. As you put the cards down to form the arms of the cross (from the 2 of each suit inwards), you will be able to read a special meaning at each stage. I wish you'd try it when you've a spare moment and let me know what you get from it, and you might get Toby on the job as well. As I've tried to figure it out, it's a completely Zen answer.

I have got a lovely new suit for the summer, just the kind I always wanted, but in England they're difficult to get away with. It's gabardine in what they call "natural colour" cloth, i.e., very light greyish brown (fawn is it?), worn with straw sailor hat, brown and white shoes, and gay Paisley tie. In England it would be uproarious, but here in the summer men go in for colour. Bright yellow socks are quite usual!

The heat here is becoming quite bearable, especially living at some height from the ground. The other day I got a special kind of kimono called a *yukata*, which the Japanese wear in hot weather. Mr. Sasaki gave me a fan, and so I am comfortable! The only person who suffers is Jimey with his thick coat, but we don't like to shave him because it would be a terrible blow to his pride. He spends his time on the cold bathroom floor.

Well, I don't think there's any more special news for the time being, so here's lots of love to you both from,

Alan, Eleanor, Joan & Jimey (paw print)

NEW YORK CITY | NOVEMBER 26, 1939
Dear Mummy & Daddy,
I'm sending this letter in duplicate and at an interval of several days so as to be sure that you get it. Since writing last I have received your letters 1 and 2, and also a letter from Daddy. We also received Joan's lovely birthday present, with which we were just delighted. She is now walking all over the apartment and weighs 22 lb.

As to Christmas presents. I think we shall be sending off something in the way of a book in the next few days, but I don't quite know about your sending things here. We have loved having *Punch*, but what with the state of shipping and what with income tax at 7/6 we simply hate to ask you for anything, unless you would like to chance sending some small thing for Joan.

I am getting busier and busier, gradually collecting a little money. A few people have been supporting my lectures quite generously and it looks as if it might be the beginning of something decent. I now have four groups a week, one of which is composed of some of the most intelligent and thoroughly well-educated old ladies I have ever had the pleasure of meeting. They are a group of friends from a place in New Jersey, and, my, there are no flies on them! Another group is made up mainly of Jungian analysts, and they are a little deadly; they think they know it all, and it's like talking to a wet blanket. Then I have another composed of, among others, two rather prim schoolteachers and two business men, very much American, one in advertising and the other in whisky! This is rather riotous and jolly. The other night someone brought along a tame publisher in the shape of the religious editor of Harper, and we are now talking business in the shape of a book. I think I told you I was writing one to be called *The Anatomy of Happiness*, being the practical contributions to said problem of Oriental and Western psychology. Well, he seems to like the idea and we shall see what we shall see.

I now have a list of some 50 people more or less actively interested in my work and I have started sending out a bimonthly (fortnightly) mimeographed letter to them on various aspects of Oriental thought. The latest is enclosed. You can imagine that to keep abreast of things I have to do quite a bit of reading, while Eleanor helps me with secretarial work and with hashing over the various problems and the best ways and means of impressing them on those concerned. Another game is the publishing of essays on various subjects for private circulation among the groups. We get people to subscribe and then have them mimeographed, and I am just bringing out some notes on meditation of which I will send you a copy when it appears. It will be followed early next year by one on Zen stories.

I have been meeting all kinds of interesting people. The other day I had lunch with a Robert Ballou, who has edited a remarkable book called *The Bible of the World*. It looks like being a bestseller. 10,000 copies were ordered before publication and you will soon be getting it in England. It contains great chunks of all the important scriptures of the world, including the entire Tao Te Ching (Ch'u's translation), many Zen texts, and Lord knows what else besides. He made a beautiful job of it, and even went so far as to include a version of the Cowherding Pictures.

Then we met Mrs. Cary Baynes, translator of some of Jung's books into English, and also the peculiar Mrs. Fröbe-Kapteyn, who runs that Ascona Congress where all the European orientalists and psychologists get together every year on the Swiss end of Lake Maggiore. She is somewhat of an intellectual snob, but otherwise interesting.

Mrs. E. continues to flourish and to set herself up in grander and grander style, but I'm afraid Mr. E. is just about finished. It will be just as well for he is in a terrible condition and has little more mind than a helpless animal. He's so weak that he can hardly move.

You do certainly send some interesting letters these days. Don't you find all this business a terrible nervous strain? I wish you could get over here for a holiday and be out of it all for a while, but I reckon the ocean will have to be safer and my pocket longer first. But the day will come, and (in peace-time), you can cross the Atlantic with almost no exertion at all. But I've got to keep my nose to the grindstone for quite a while yet; it's very hard going, but it is going and I enjoy every moment of it. The important thing is that it means constantly keeping oneself up to scratch because this country always wants the best out of you.

I really wish you could meet Joan; she is such a personality. The other day we bought her some slippers like white rabbits with a squeak in them, and was she puzzled! She walked a step and then sat down to find out what it was all about: very disconcerting! She is particularly attached to matches, books, pieces of paper, cigarette butts and ashes and we have the greatest trouble keeping her out of the ashtrays. She also has a teddy bear made like a glove so that you can make it come to life; it's a most convincing illusion, and Eleanor, I think, likes it even more than Joan does. Our colored maid is so good with her; takes her out for a walk every afternoon, accompanied by Jimey, when she meets all the other babies in the district and makes friends. The maid (Nettie) is Joan's great love, and we have to see that she doesn't spoil her sometimes. Now I wake up most mornings to find this small creature round my neck, writhing and kicking around all over the bed with the most delicious gurgles. But she will hit me over the head with anything that comes to hand — not because it's my head — but just because she loves hitting things. Much of the day is spent pounding things around with wooden blocks and a back-scratcher.

Well, I must bring this to a close. I guess it will reach you around Christmas, and please let it be a very happy one. We shall be thinking of you all right.

From your loving son, Alan

ALAN W. WATTS, NEW YORK CITY
Newsletter #2
These letters are now being sent out twice every month to various people who are interested in the study and practice of the philosophy of the ancient East from

our modern, Occidental point of view. As I said in the first letter, there are a number of us already meeting regularly at my apartment to discuss these matters on the basis of informal lectures, and those who would like to join us will always be welcome if they will let me know in advance when they would like to come. Further details of our meetings are at the end of this letter.

A question, which we often discuss, is the relationship of modern, civilized man to nature. For, seemingly, those of us who are city dwellers are in rather a different position from the great philosophers of the Orient who never had to live in our "artificial" world of steel, concrete, automobiles, telephones, and canned food. Our life and circumstances are almost purely man-made (or so we think), and there are many people who believe that we can never achieve any great degree of spirituality until we return to a closer contact with nature. For the laws of the spirit are the laws of nature, and it is thought that while our lives are ordered on a purely human basis, while every advance of our science is directed to the conquest of nature and while we try to solve all our problems by the exercise of unaided human reason, in such conditions we shall always be lonely, unhappy orphans (or prodigals), shut off from the true source of life. But this idea is both true and false, false because the idea that we are independent of nature is a tremendous conceit, and true because we are, relatively speaking, divorced from nature by that very attitude. Strictly speaking, New York City is no more artificial than a bird's nest, for man is just as much an aspect of nature as a bird and the difference between man and bird is chiefly that man is somewhat more complicated. A secondary difference is that man is self-conscious; he believes himself to have an ego, a separate, self-contained, self-directing entity which has to figure things out for itself, whereas the bird just lets nature or instinct take care of its problems. But nature is powerful and when man disagrees with it he feels his loneliness and impotence; this is the great unhappiness. The Buddhists call it *sakayaditthi*, or the "heresy of separateness," which is another name for being "taken in" or fooled by the sense of selfhood.

While we are thus fooled we are caught in the conceit that we are very peculiar people, having a secret pride in our loneliness and isolation and an open pride in the wonderful achievements of our unaided reason and intellect. But are we so lonely? Might it not be that our self-conscious ego and its power of reason is a device, a trick (*maya*), employed by nature to achieve certain results? Nature arranges for us to feel that we are separate selves in order to manifest aspects of natural power for which the animal is not equipped. Thus, it is most important that we should have this feeling, *provided we are not fooled by it*. Two things are therefore involved. On the one hand, if we are to be true to nature, we have to behave whole-heartedly *as if* we were separate selves; on the other hand we have to recognize that self-consciousness and rationality are devices making it appear that we live our lives, whereas in fact nature lives them under this disguise. Selfhood means that nature is playing at being lots of different, separate, and self-ruling beings.

In truth, however, there is no absolute division between the self and nature. Nature plays at being a self, but without this play, without this universe of countless separate objects, there would be nothing to be called nature; there would only be a void. Selves and nature are essential to each other, and in truth neither one is master, for when the self acts, nature acts, and when nature acts, the self acts. The initiative appears to come sometimes from one, sometimes from the other, but this is appearance. If you ask, "Which of the two comes first? Which is master?" the answer is a very old conundrum, "Which came the first, egg or hen?"

When this absolute and unavoidable interdependence is known and felt in the very depths of one's being, then you have what Oriental philosophy calls the realization of unity with Tao or Brahman, which it describes as understanding that the self and the not-self are two appearances of one fact which cannot be known apart from its appearances.

This and other aspects of Oriental philosophy are the subjects of informal lectures and discussions at my apartment to which all are welcome provided they let me know beforehand when they would like to come. There is no fixed charge for admission to those lectures as they are supported by purely voluntary contributions. We are now meeting every Monday at 8:30 PM, every Thursday at 3:15 PM, while on Monday, November 13th, we shall start another regular meeting at 3:15 PM, and another on Wednesday, November 15th, at 8:30 PM. In the meantime I shall gladly welcome and answer any comments on these letters if those who write would be so kind to enclose a stamped return envelope.

Alan W. Watts

November 10th, 1939

ALAN WATTS, NEW YORK CITY

Newsletter #4

Once upon a time there was a lunatic who used to pass the time by sitting in a corner and beating himself on the head with a brick. When asked the reason for this interesting behavior he replied, "Well, it feels so pleasant when I stop." Very often the lunatic is nothing more than a caricature of people supposed to be sane; we call him a lunatic only because he expresses fundamental traits of human nature in the most obvious and concrete manner, whereas sane people carry on the same processes in more veiled and mysterious ways. And the performance of beating oneself on the head with a brick is an exact caricature of man's chief spiritual problem, for we have to realize that our apparent lack of what Oriental sages call Enlightenment (*bodhi*) or spiritual freedom (*kaivalya*) is due to our not having ceased to knock ourselves on the head with a brick. Naturally, the realization of Enlightenment is accompanied by an enormous sense of relief — not because we have acquired something new, but because we have got rid of something old. Enlightenment, wisdom, or a sense of harmony with life and the universe is present within us all the time; it becomes apparent when we cease to use the brick just as the moon becomes visible when the clouds are blown away. But we appreciate the light of the moon more keenly when it emerges from the clouds; if it had been shining openly all the time we should never have experienced the sudden ecstasy of light breaking in upon darkness. And for this sudden ecstasy we have to be thankful for the darkness as much as for the light.

At the same time, our lack of Enlightenment or freedom is only apparent, for in a special sense "the light shineth in darkness; and the darkness comprehended it not." In this sense the darkness is also a manifestation of the light but does not understand it. Therefore as soon as we understand that our very lack of realization is itself an aspect of Enlightenment, our ignorance turns into wisdom. Thus a Buddhist text says, "If the accumulation of false imaginations is cleared away, Enlightenment will appear. But the strange thing is that when people gain Enlightenment they realize that without false imaginations there could be no Enlightenment." In Vedanta philosophy and Buddhism alike Enlightenment is the nature of the universe; all possible forms and aspects of life are manifestations of Brahman or "Buddha nature" because there is only one ultimate Reality. Thus maya, which in one sense is darkness or illusion, in another sense is the creative power of Brahman. Now Enlightenment is the condition of union with that power, and we realize its freedom in understanding that not even in ignorance or darkness can we be deprived of that union.

There is a Buddhist story of a disciple who asked his teacher, "How can I find liberation?"

The teacher replied, "Who is putting you in bondage?" "Nobody." "If so, why should you seek liberation?" And for this reason it is often said that Enlightenment cannot be found by *doing* something about it, for it is always a question of being rather than doing. Hence the saying, "Seek and you will find not; become and you will be." Become what? Become what you are. Thus the Orient has always sought wisdom in meditation rather than action, but from this it should not be supposed that meditation is a passive way as distinct from an active way. Both activity and passivity are forms of doing; the latter is indirectly doing by not doing. Therefore the West has found it difficult to understand what is really meant by meditation. Meditation is not only sitting still like a Buddha-figure, nor is it thinking *about* something, for the Upanishads say that the stars, the trees, the rivers, and the mountains are meditating — unconsciously. Conscious meditation is a knack, and as an exercise it is a way of learning that Enlightenment comes to pass in us as much when we are doing nothing to produce it as when we are in the midst of activity. Thus the "sitting-still" meditation of the Orient is so much valued as a way of enlightenment because in it we are able to realize that our spiritual freedom consists not in our manner of doing and thinking, but in the fact of our being.

Enlightenment and realization is the main theme of our informal lectures and discussions at my apartment during the first few months of this year, and future letters will keep those who cannot come acquainted with the course of our work. We shall be studying first the Hindu and Chinese views of Enlightenment and the technique of its realization on the basis of readings from original sources and also from that famous allegory of the "Oxherding Pictures." We shall then go on to consider the expression of Enlightenment in Chinese art and in the mental and physical culture of the Far East as a whole. Finally we shall compare our findings with Western equivalents of the way to Enlightenment — in particular with Christian mysticism and analytical psychology. This letter is a cordial invitation to those of you who do not already come to join us. Groups are now meeting on Mondays at 8:30, on Wednesdays at 8:30, and on Thursdays at 8:30. The last of these is generally speaking reserved for those who have already some knowledge of these matters and who do not feel the need of any introduction to basic principles. The group which meets on Thursdays at 3:15 has not yet been started again, but will begin as soon as arrangements can be made, and those who would like to come on Thursday afternoons would assist me by letting me know as soon as possible. And may I say again that comments on these letters will always be welcome and will always be answered.

January 1940
Alan W. Watts

JW: Reading the newsletter above made me aware of the wonderful ability Alan acquired as a young man (he was only twenty-five) in explaining metaphysical concepts — ideas that may escape many of us because they are too complex to articulate. A theme throughout many of Alan's books and lectures is that life is full of opposites; otherwise we wouldn't be aware of the concept of difference. He states it beautifully in the example of the moon hiding behind clouds, or pain versus lack of pain, etc. Enlightenment is the "aha!" moment of the realization of not being able to know one without the other.

NEW YORK CITY | JANUARY 3, 1940

Dear Mummy & Daddy,

I do hope you received my last letter safely and also the things we sent for Christmas. I have yours of the 5th December (#3), but I wrote you quite a long one just before then, and as I sent it in duplicate you ought to have received it by now.

Well, the important news is that Harper has accepted my new book, *The Anatomy of Happiness*, and it will be published probably in March or April. Their religious editor, Eugene Exman, signed me up for it before it was even finished, and I took it along to him yesterday. That is one reason why I have not written more often. They wanted it by the first of the year so I had to set to work very hard to finish it. Now he wants me to write a book on the religions of the world for children, with illustrations, so that will be the next job. Harper is just like Murrays — the same old-fashioned, courteous kind of people; I had lunch with their president, Mr. [Cass] Canfield, the other day and found him interesting but a little shy and rather hard to open up. Maybe he was trying to open me up! But we had a very pleasant chat. I have been extremely lucky to get Harper because their standing is quite as good as Murrays and they're an even bigger concern — and rather more alive.

The book is subtitled "The Quest for Freedom of the Spirit in Modern Psychology and the Wisdom of the East" and is rather longer than *The Legacy of Asia*. It is written for a wider public and brings in some new ideas; I gained a lot from reading Meister Eckhart, a great Christian mystic of the 13th century, and so have been able to use Christian terminology rather more freely. Now that it's finished I shall be able to take a rest for a week or so before starting anything else; I shall need it! But the next book will be real fun because it will involve a lot of drawing and painting — an art which I've been practicing lately and it makes a wonderful change from writing.

I have done almost everything for this new book from the writing to the designing, including the drawing of a number of diagrams to illustrate various points. I will arrange for a copy to be sent to you as soon as possible.

We have had a lovely Christmas. I am wondering if our Christmas cards reached England. We sent one to the Forsdykes, the Blyths, and to E.G.B. care of you; so please let me know. Thank you both ever so much for another subscription to *Punch*; I didn't want you to spend so much on us, but we love having it. But, my, doesn't it change with war circumstances! The jokes, the stories, the advertisements — everything. Mrs. E. had a fit of the wildest generosity and presented us with a combination radio and phonograph (I mean gramophone, excuse my American!). It's rather like Toby's, having an automatic record changer, so we have been reveling in music. I think I told you once that there is a marvelous radio station here which plays almost nothing but first-rate music with a minimum of talking and advertising. Late at night we can get English stations on the shortwave.

On the 6th we are giving a party for my birthday and on Eleanor's 21st I took her out for a spree. She was just delighted to receive your cablegram and asks me to thank you very much indeed.

I have just had a very pleasant letter from Jung saying all sorts of kind things about *The Legacy of Asia* and giving me permission to use his privately circulated notes on the more "occult" aspects of his work. He also sent me a copy [of] his introduction to Suzuki's *Introduction to Zen*.

The inimitable Dr. Bing is here and is probably going to settle in the US permanently. We had him round on Christmas Eve and spent a most loquacious evening. My, that man is a scholar. He *speaks* Latin, and Ciceronian Latin at that, which is no small achievement!

Joan is getting along fine and can now climb up onto a low armchair. She says, "Oh my!" when surprised — something she has picked up from Nettie, who constantly uses that expression! Now she spends most of the day trotting around the apartment and getting in Jimey's way. We have a lot of fun with her because she loves being swung around and tickled. Eleanor dances to music and Joan tries to imitate; the effect is priceless. I think I have at last found time to take some more pictures of her, and will let you have some in due course. I think she is a very good-looking baby.

Well, we must be going out now so this must stop. But I will write more often; that is a New Year's resolution which will NOT be broken. Eleanor asks me to send all her love to you both. Please have a very happy New Year and write again soon. Lots and lots of love to you both,

From your loving son, Alan

PS. This copy comes by ship; the other by airmail. Please let me know which reached you first and by how long.

NEW YORK CITY | FEBRUARY 9, 1940
Dear Mummy & Daddy,

We have just received your letter #6, and I hope you will by now have received the letters which both Eleanor and I have written since November 26th. From you we have also had the subscription to *Punch*, the mountain book, and the handkerchiefs, etc., for Joan — all of which are just splendid. The mountain photographs are simply beautiful, in addition to which they contain many useful photographic hints for yours truly. I think Eleanor has already told you how much we liked the things for Joan; it was certainly good to see some of your handiwork again, especially that squirrel.

Eleanor told you in her letter that Mr. Everett died January 18th. We went out to Chicago for a weekend for his funeral and spent two nights at Eleanor's old home in Hinsdale. Fortunately the end came very quickly and he had no pain; it was just a quick bout of pneumonia. Chicago was 2 below freezing when we arrived, having been as much as 13 below. In winter it can be the most incredibly dirty place, being surrounded and permeated by factories and railroads. Joan, having just recovered from an abscessed ear, remained at home with Nettie and Jimey, and it was good to get back to them. After Chicago, New York seems absolutely spotless.

Arrangements are going ahead rapidly for the publication of my book, the title of which has been changed to *The Meaning of Happiness* and Harper seems to expect quite a good sale for it. I have just finished reading the proofs, and yesterday they sent me a dummy to show what the binding and general format (which I designed) will look like. And am I pleased with it! They have given me a two-color title page, terra-cotta red and black; the cover is also terra-cotta with gold lettering with a device of crossed *dorje* (Tibetan thunderbolts) in cream beneath — it's a symbol of the power of wholeness. It will run to about 250 pages, having some 8 chapters, so you see it's a good bit longer than *The Legacy of Asia*, and is also written for a much wider public. It should be published about the beginning of April, but I will try to get a copy to you as soon as possible. It seems so odd to see one's work all in American spelling, and you've no idea how different it is from English. For instance, there's no such word as "practise," both the noun and the verb being "practice." "Technique" becomes "technic," which I would not allow because "techniques" are utterly different things from "technics"! And then there are such odd anomalies as "behaviour" changing to "behavior," while "glamour" remains with the "U."

Here are the latest photographs of Joan, and also one of the family at home. How do you like our screen? We put her in a kimono that was sent us from Japan, and if her hair was black I think she would look just like a Japanese baby. Everyone remarks on this, and I tell Eleanor that the reason is surely that she ate so much rice while carrying her. We were always going to the Japanese restaurant. The other day we took her for a haircut and shampoo, so she looks a bit shorn at the moment.

Next week I have to go and lecture to a lot of schoolchildren, aged about 11 or 12, at the Dalton Schools here. Two teachers at this school come to my classes, which continue to go ahead although quite a number of people are away in Florida at present. When they come back we shall have a full house!

Did I tell you in my last letter that Murray's have asked me to find books for them over here? This will give me the entrée to several places as their official representative, and I ought to get to know the publishing world quite well. John Grey Murray put it that I was asked to be their "American Eye."

Have you any news of what has happened to Watkins' bookshop? A lady here tells me she is unable to get in touch with them. Apparently Nigel is in the censorship, as in the last war, and I am wondering if the business is being carried on.

Just before going to Chicago I gave another talk on the radio, and an influential friend who listened in says I have a voice worth $1,000,000! She wants to introduce me to people in radio, so I am getting some records made. [...]

So here's our love to both of you — and please don't suppose that you will be leaving this world before we meet again. You have yet to see the USA, which, I assure you, is well worth living to see! One day soon we hope to have a little house in the hills of Connecticut or on the banks of the Hudson, where there will naturally be a spare room for you. Incidentally, New York and environs is now packed with English people.

But while on the subject, I entirely approve of your leaving the cottage to [Emily Buchan Watts's niece] Joy, though if she should marry and her husband not approve of it other arrangements would have to be made, and if anyone has to sell it I would rather you did than she. And do you think it would be advisable to let me have a copy of your will? I have taken note of the other matters mentioned in your letter.

Well, once again, here's all our love to you, and please drink success to my book sometime!

Your loving son, Alan

NEW YORK CITY | MARCH 19, 1940
Mummy & Daddy,
I meant to write you more than a week ago, but bronchial flu of some kind got hold of me and I was in bed for a week. But what with Eleanor's nursing and Dr. Taylor's homoeopathy I soon got on my feet again.

So you will see I haven't been doing much lately and there isn't an enormous amount of news. But things are beginning to get busy again. On Easter Saturday we are giving a party for all our moderately young friends (of whom we have acquired quite a number lately). Previously we seemed to know no one but the greybeards! Then on Easter Sunday I am going up to the Riverside Church to talk to two of their Sunday school classes. Did I ever tell you about this church? One of the women who come to my lectures works there and Harper's Mr. Exman (who took my book) is also connected with it. So now I go there from time to time to talk to the children so that I can get some experience for writing my next book. It is a very famous church built by the Rockefellers for Dr. Harry Emerson Fosdick. You've probably heard of him; Hodder & Stoughton publish his books in England, and he's quite a remarkable man — so much so that in this Sunday school they learn all about the other religions of the world before they even start on Christianity. The kids act ancient Egyptian and Mayan rites and the teachers never damn other religions with faint praise. It's really a very impressive effort.

I am trying to make arrangements now for the publication of my book in England. Proofs have been sent to Murray's as John Grey Murray has shown some interest to see it. If, however, they don't want it I have asked them to send the proofs to you, and I wish you would consult with Toby about sending them somewhere else. The best second choice in my own opinion would be Routledge, and next John Lane. We are arranging to secure English copyright in my own name. It will be out here about April 4th, but I expect to have some copies in a few days' time, and Harper will send one direct to you.

Joan is becoming dangerously intelligent these days. Almost nothing in the place is beyond her reach, but luckily she understands a good deal of what is said to her. So far her own vocabulary only extends to "Bye-bye," "Dada," "Oh my," and "See!," the latter with a finger pointed at the object in question. She can climb all over the furniture. The other day I was changing into my outdoor shoes and taking off my slippers. She came and picked up the slippers, put them away in the closet, and shut the door. So she may turn out quite useful! There are some more photographs of her with this letter, and one of Eleanor which I took recently. Another picture of me you will find on the dust jacket of my book when it reaches you; don't be too surprised at it. I chose it to look a bit Svengalian and impressive!

I'm still carrying on with my private lecture work with rather interesting results. The people have divided themselves into two distinct classes, those who really want to learn something of practical value and those who come merely for information. The former are about 10 in number and all are people we find very easy to get on with. The joy is that they really mean business, and I think they will form a nucleus for some very interesting work. For the others I am shortly going to start out a series of lectures on the symbolism of magic! — from the standpoint of modern psychology. Looked at from that angle it's a reasonably profitable subject. Jung has done some interesting work on it, which I have been able to see since he gave me permission to use his private seminar notes, copies of which several people have here.

Ashton-Gwatkin is here now and I have been in touch with him. He had to go straight to Washington when he landed, but he wrote me a note and said he would come and see us when back in New York. He is here with Prof. Rist from France to consult with the State Department about American neutrality rights.

I enclose a picture from today's paper which gives you a remarkable view of the north of this island, showing you how they build roads here. The bridge in the background is the famous George Washington over the Hudson River, joining Manhattan and New Jersey. It leads almost straight into open country, and the high rocks on the far side of the river are the Palisades, from which you get some of the loveliest views in the world — especially higher up the river. I'm also enclosing a copy of a previous letter, which I hope you received safely.

We are trying to get rid of the lease on the flat [in London] and I have asked Toby to find me a competent solicitor to negotiate, giving him full details. Well, I guess this is about all for the time being, so here's lots of love to you both and we look forward to another letter from you soon.

From your loving son, Alan

NEW YORK CITY | APRIL 10, 1940
Dear Mummy & Daddy,
I have your letter #11 and was so glad to hear that you received the pictures safely. Another lot should have arrived by the time you get this letter. Also the book is on the way to wish Mummy many happy returns on the 15th; it is being sent direct from Harper, and looks much fatter than I thought it would — quite a tome! I have heard nothing definite from Murray's about it yet, but I hope they will take it.

Isn't it odd that Daddy and I should have had more or less the same trouble! But I must say I feel very much better after it. Did I tell you that the doctor thought he ought to check up and see if there was any TB, and that both X-rays and laboratory tests found everything absolutely clear. So my usual thinness is just the nature of the beast!

Eleanor and I celebrated our anniversary on the 2nd with an evening out dancing, and came home to a bottle of champagne. I thought of you then, and wished you could have shared it with us! The first copies of my book arrived that day, very appropriately, as it's dedicated to Eleanor.

I seem to have been going around a lot with church people lately, started by my contacts with the Riverside Church. The other evening we had dinner with

James Riggs, a minister whose job is to travel all over the country inspecting Presbyterian and other churches and trying to put some life into them. He told us some absolutely extraordinary tales of the queer forms of religion practiced in the back of beyond, among the southern mountains [the Appalachians] — inhabited by people we call hillbillies or "poor whites." They are mostly of old Scotch, Irish and English extraction, and in some places their language hasn't changed since the 17th century because they are completely isolated from "civilization." Religion is their only interest outside work, and thus they put all their emotional life into it; the results are amazing, such as the "holy-roller" revivals that may go on for a whole day or more.

I have just had a delightful letter from Suzuki, who, for some reason or other, has started a fairly regular correspondence with me. He is doing some very interesting work now and wishes I would go to Japan before he dies. But there's little chance of that now, as he must be over 70. He sent me some fascinating material on Shin Buddhism, which prompted me to write an article for Toby; ask him to let you know if it reaches him safely. I have a copy of it if it doesn't.

The book will be out officially here on the 18th, and my friends at the Gateway Bookshop are sending out 500 letters to their customers about it. So I am hoping to ride in on the tide! Harper advertises rather more extensively than Murrays, and in the meantime I'm getting all my friends talking it around.

Well I hope Hitler's latest is his big mistake. The wider you spread the butter, the thinner it gets. Napoleon found that, too.

There is no more important news at present, as I am sort of waiting for various developments with my tongue out. But I will write again soon. By the way, I am filing your last letter with details about the silver, etc.

Well, here's heaps of love to you from us both, and as it's time for lunch (which is always ready exactly when Nettie says so and not a second later!), I must stop.

From your loving son, Alan

NEW YORK CITY | APRIL 30, 1940
John Murray | London, England
Dear Murray,

Thank you so much for your letter of April 11th. I am, of course, delighted to hear that you want to publish my book, and I have asked Harper to send you a set of sheets. They tell me that sheets are not available actually in sheet form; they are already sewn for binding, but they thought this would not present any difficulty as they themselves always photograph from the bound volume.

I appreciate the difficulties about spelling; I decided to regulate my behavior (*sic*) in this matter on the principle that in Rome one should do as Rome does. I suppose, however, that if you felt it necessary to alter certain pages in any way they could be set separately in 11-on-13 Garamond Linotype. But perhaps the English reader would put up with American spelling if he sees that the preface is dated "New York City, 1940"!

On a separate sheet I am enclosing some remarks on the comments from the reader's report, which I return herewith. I enclose also the circular and an advertisement to show the kind of advertising copy they are using.

One or two questions of layout are involved. I wish, if possible, you would use the same title page layout; this is in Weiss Roman caps and Caslon Roman and Italics. The triangular piece in italics should have been set a little higher, together with the publisher's device. Now I don't think you have a device of your own, so perhaps you could use the phoenix I drew for the Wisdom of the East series.

You will see that the Wisdom of the East series is mentioned on the dust jacket, in the biographical note, but I think it should also be mentioned on the page facing the title page, where my other books are listed. With regard to the dust jacket, I note that many English publishers are economizing and perhaps you will not be able to use a two-color process on glossy paper. But as long as you avoid the apparently prevalent fashion of Trafton Script on greenish-blue I shan't mind.

The royalties of £9.12.2 arrived safely as $33.53, for which many thanks.

I wonder if you could give me an approximate idea as to publication date, because there are several people in England who would like to know and who will get busy advertising the book by word of mouth. When the time gets nearer I will send various suggestions about review copies, etc.

With all good wishes,

Yours ever, Alan Watts

The following are notes to John Murray in regard to publishing *The Meaning of Happiness*.

p. 37: Relaxation. Yes, but here the word is in quotes, showing that it is used in the more popular sense of something to while away the time without menial strain. You might substitute *playthings* if you think it necessary.

p. 126: Bad man. Again *bad* is in quotes, for the term is used very loosely to denote one who is evil in the generally accepted sense — i.e., he bears the taint of original sin. "Lord have mercy on us, miserable sinners." As the Americans say, "This means you."

p. 147: Pearls before swine. I suppose the comment means that I am not following the example of the Buddhist scriptures and that I am at least trying to put the thing in language that all can understand and bear to read. But I don't say that I advocate the Oriental attitude of putting the pearls in a place where the swine can't reach them. Being a white man I try to make it all plain; that is the white man's nature; it may be his misfortune, but being a white man myself I have to behave as one. An author would have a short life if his books were as long and as involved as the sutras. So the reader should note the difference of technique and make due allowances for the necessities of modern life!

p. 61: Clew is American for clue [*sic*].

Ch. 8: Gratitude. I'm a little puzzled by this comment. The gratitude in question can't really be defined because it can only be known fully as a result of spiritual experience. Then it is expressed in different ways, according to the nature of the individual. Does the comment mean that I have not sufficiently described the ways of expression or that I have not said enough about gratitude itself? I don't see how any more can be said about g. itself, because it's just one of those things we feel or don't feel — like joy, sorrow, fear, etc.

The moral code. I left this alone because it has been discussed plentifully elsewhere. I feel rather that the individual must figure out his own moral code. Anyway, codes are for those who want to be told what to do. I feel morality is art, not science, and cannot be codified.

NEW YORK CITY | MAY 6, 1940

Dear Mummy & Daddy,

I have just received your letter #14 saying that the book had arrived safely. Actually, I think the letter should have been #13 as the last one we had was 12, mailed on April 1st.

Well I'm so glad you like the latest effort. Murray's have accepted it for publication in England, so you will be having plenty of copies over there before long. They are going to photograph it from the American edition and print it that way as it saves composition costs. So the spelling will have to stay as is. It seems to be going reasonably well here, in spite of the fact that Harper is pushing it very lazily; I'm going down this afternoon to give them a pep talk. So far I have seen no reviews of it but I've had quite a number [of] comments. One that pleased me was from Dr. Strong, one of the leading psychologists at the New York Medical Center and a pupil of Jung; he says he agrees with everything in it, and thinks it will prick the consciences of some of Jung's misguided pupils — of whom there are too many in this city. They, he says, will hate it, but that would please Jung a lot!

Anyhow, it's resulting in something of a spurt for my lectures, and on Wednesday evenings I have a very full house. We had 15 in the other night, and our place was jammed. This includes a young Englishman who is a teacher of dancing, and I'm going to him for lessons. He teaches me Rumba, Waltz, etc., and Eleanor teaches him the Hawaiian Hula, so we live by taking in each other's washing.

Sunday before last I had another bout at the Riverside Church — this time talking to both parents and children, and next week I am to talk to the teachers of an adult school. Last Monday we went out to Connecticut to see over rather an unusual school in Greenwich run by one of the most delightful women I have ever had the pleasure of meeting. She was about 60 odd — a Miss Langley — one of those practical, humorous people with a deep knowledge of human nature and that delightfully brief, laconic way of talking which relies on few words and conveys everything by the twinkle in the eye. She kept us in fits all through lunch. She has a wonderful little school there for both boys and girls, and they really are a fine crowd of kids.

You certainly seem to be doing things around the estate these days. The front path needed looking after and it sounds as if you had made a good job. Isn't it queer the way the Minneapolis people write? We have had several letters from them, but I guess the New York papers give us better news. You are very sensible to start a good vegetable garden going again, but I suppose the position is very well put in a joke I saw in *Punch*. "My dear," says one lady, "just as I've got used to margarine they go and double the butter ration."

I'm glad you liked the pictures of Eleanor. My photograph on the book was specially chosen for a certain atmosphere of learned mystery, not so much for good looks! Mrs. E. is reading the book and is finding it very interesting. I think it's the first time she has really read any of my work.

Joan is getting along wonderfully. She has breakfast with us now, and can manage her own drinking. This morning we took her out shopping and she walks all over the place so that we hardly need the pram anymore. She is about 2 ft. 8 in. high. She is beginning to understand quite a lot, knows exactly what to do when Eleanor tells her to kiss Daddy good-night. She walks in, goes up to me, and says, "Night, night!" Now she waves at people on the street and says, "Bye-bye" as we pass, turning round and almost falling over her mother's feet.

[Letter continued.] May 20th

Oh dear, this delay is awful! But I've been kept hard at it this last week or so. The book is getting around, there was an extra lecture last week and a lot of preparation to do [blacked-out section]. (No, not the censor; just a piece of news

I have already given you!) I am hard at work with the dancing, which gives me splendid exercise and I seem to be getting along very well.

Toby has sent me the proofs of his new book to see if I can do anything with it over here. It's rather difficult because he has made it very Theosophical in tone and his style has become a little too oratorical. However, we shall do our best.

Well I certainly hope you are bearing up under the strain of new developments in the war. I get horribly worried about you sometimes. I have faith that something good will come out of this in the end like the phoenix out of the fire. But in the meantime it's almost impossible to know how to plan for the future. Things here are as good as can be expected, but under such strains you never know when people are going to go crazy! Sometimes I get the queerest feeling that things going on in the world around one, are in some odd way reflections of things happening in the depths of one's own mind. It is almost as if the world gets calm as you keep calm yourself, and vice versa. Yet it would be absurd to imagine that one could actually control the course of events in that way because this would imply the belief that oneself alone is real and all else a figment of thought. But it convinces me more and more that there is a universe inside one, which contains Hitler and all forms of human madness as well as love and beauty. I suppose too many of us have been accustomed to think of life in too protected a way. After all, when you read history it seems as if what we understand as security is quite a recent invention. There never has been any such thing. But modern civilization (while it lasts) so protects us from the sight of death and destruction that it makes it difficult for us to believe that such things actually exist. Whereas, in former times they were well in evidence every day.

Please will Daddy write again soon (when he has time). Yes, I always get those letters, and I think they only *seem* to have missed my attention because I write to two people at once, which gets your grammar a little mixed incidentally!

Mrs. E. asks me to send her love to you both. She seems very well and perky these days. The other day we all took Joan to the zoo, where she had a simply wonderful time, and my how that child can walk! There is so much energy in a tiny body, and we have difficulty trying to get her to take things easily.

Well, I must hurry to get this off to you by airmail, so here's lots of love to you both from all of us and do let us hear from you soon.

From your loving son, Alan

NEW YORK CITY | JUNE 11, 1940
Dear Mummy & Daddy,
I have just gotten your letter #14 of May 14th, but actually I think it should have been numbered 15. I think there are two of mine on the way which you had not

received by then, and to make sure that you get this one I'm sending two copies, one by air, the other by ship.

Things are moving horribly fast these days and you must find the conditions of life in England very much changed, although some of the letters I get (particularly from John Murray) talk as if the war were a mild fracas in some remote part of the world.

This summer we are going to combine business with pleasure by going up to Rockport near Boston for July and August. It is a great summer spot for Bostonians and I am going to try to raise a clientele there, while Eleanor is going to do some work with our friend the teacher of dancing. He is an expert on eurhythmics and we are working together on all kinds of things. Incidentally, he has introduced us to an amusing group of people who do old American country dances. Once a fortnight we go to their place (a large loft) and have the most glorious fun with the "Grapevine Twist," "Turkey Wing," "Birdie-in-the-Cage," and so on. It is really the healthiest kind of fun and very good exercise. We wear our oldest clothes and get absolutely soaked with perspiration. There are usually about 50 or 60 people there, all young, and the dances are led by a "caller" who, with a delightful mixture of shouting, singing, and hollering, tells you just what to do. It looks complicated, but actually is quite simple if you use your head.

I don't know yet what our address in Rockport will be, but I will cable it to you as soon as we know. I shall try to get something through to Daddy for his birthday, but don't expect it to arrive on time! Did you get the cable I sent for April 15th?

Rockport, by the way, is an old fishing village on a very rocky part of the coast. It stands on an island joined to the mainland by a single bridge, and I think we shall take a cottage on a hill with a view of the ocean on one side and all the surrounding country on the other. Possibly I shall spend 10 days at a summer camp run by an athletic coach with a flair for mysticism. Sounds the rarest mixture, but such is America! There has been a tentative invitation to me to take charge of certain activities. It is called the "Camp Farthest Out," being on an island ten miles from Portsmouth, New Hampshire, about 30 miles from Rockport.

Joan grows and grows. She is going to be quite a tall creature from the look of things, for she is much larger than other kids of her age and can walk a lot further and a lot faster. We have given up using the pram for her. When we get away I shall take some more pictures for you.

I am finishing up my lecture work for the season now. Last Sunday we gave a party for many of the people who have been coming and had a glorious time. On such occasions we have to enlarge our living room by moving all the furniture back against the walls and bringing in all available chairs. We find that an inexpensive and delightful way of feeding the multitudes is to buy a mass of radishes, celery, carrots, olives, and endives and then serve them raw in a bowl with ice. The radishes here are vast, and only 3¢ a bunch.

I have had another letter from Suzuki recently. He has sent me some of his recent works and tells me a number of very interesting things about Zen and a new way he has of presenting it for the West. This involves getting away from the notion that Zen is pantheism and has anything to do with the Yoga idea of identifying the "Seer" with the "seen" — i.e., the individual with the universe. The idea is approximately that such an identification is beside the point because there is no need for it. It is "taking coals to Newcastle."

Mrs. E. has finally sold her house in Hinsdale, which was very lucky because few people are buying this kind of property now. Fortunately the buyers are old friends of Eleanor's (a young couple just married).

Yours of May 24th has just this minute arrived. I can't think why you haven't heard from me since April 10th. I'm sorry to hear about the Whitelys, but the old man must have been getting on in years. I wonder where the Andersons have gone. John was in the HAC for a long time before the war started, so I imagine he's quite a "high-up" by now. If the new man is part Italian what becomes of him now??

I am doing a fair amount of studying now in preparation for work next autumn. The supply has to keep up with the demand! And people really want to do some work, so [I] am presented with the fascinating but difficult task of contriving methods of applying Oriental philosophy that really suit the Western mentality. Fortunately I have reasonably competent people to help me.

This is all the important news for the present. Other things develop, but "chicken not crowing before egg laid."

With lots of love to you all,

Your loving son, Alan

NEW YORK CITY | JUNE 24, 1940

Dear Mummy & Daddy,

Daddy's letter of May 21st has just arrived and I have also had one from Mummy, written just after the Dunkerque business. That seems an age ago, and things now move so fast and so monstrously that I'm afraid my letters to you must seem rather like the circumference trying to talk to the center. In some ways the whole thing seems so enormous that it's difficult to have personal feelings about it; it seems more like an earthquake or a flood than a war — a point of view that may seem strange when you are right in the middle of things. I can only guess what your real feelings about it are; my own are at present very definite though not easy to express.

Perhaps I can give you a hint of them by saying that to me the most cheering thing in your letters is the way you are both working hard on the land. In other words, you seem to be following the advice of Matthew 6:28–34, and to my mind we have had nothing but increasing wars and revolutions for the last 150 years because that advice has been neglected. There has been too much faith in man's ingenuity and too little in nature's, so now we are learning where purely human ingenuity leads. I think we are sort of driven to take this advice by the frightful pressure of events, because when we want to rest our minds from them we naturally turn to things which go on as if nothing had happened — trees, vegetables, stars, birds, and clouds — and see that for all their lack of cleverness they are not one part so crazy as man. They have a secret we have to relearn, and I believe the deep, underlying cause of present events is that life is forcing us to discover it. In other words, this is not an ordinary war; it is a birth and death paroxysm in one, and as for Germany's role — "it needs be that the offence must come, but woe to him by whom that offence cometh."

I was so glad to hear that the Fund struck it lucky this year because I was afraid that it would be going through very hard times, and its money must be needed more badly than ever. I was glad, too, to hear that the Lodge is meeting again, and I hope this is still being kept up because there is an awful lot for you people with a long vision to do.

We have changed our plans for the summer. Rockport is really too far away, so we shall be going into Connecticut near our friends the Stursbergs. Address after July 15th will be The Longshore Club, Westport, Conn., for a month and then there is just a chance we may go to Dorset, Vermont, for a few weeks. If you lose this address letters will always be forwarded from New York.

I am being offered a job (part time), in a school for teachers to start in the autumn, but I have no concrete details yet of just what they want me to do. It's called the School of Related Arts and Sciences, and I have already been to talk to a number of their seminars.

It was good to hear from you at such length about *The Meaning of Happiness*, as I had indeed been wondering whether your work would leave you any time to study it! Apparently I worked so hard on it that it's difficult to gather the momentum to start really serious writing again, but at last I am getting moving. It takes about three months or so for one's thoughts to become modified to the extent of being compelled by them to write again, realizing that you can still give your ideas a more complete expression than you have done before.

Whenever I cease to outgrow my work will be a bad day for me. When I finished that book I thought it reasonably free from inadequacies, but now each week shows me another hole in it. There are all sorts of things left unsaid and I say to myself, "There are more things in heaven and earth than are dreamed of in your philosophy."

Things here are quiet just now as almost everyone is going out of town for the summer, though the weather has been none too hot as yet. There is, of course, a political furor over the forthcoming presidential election, and it's impossible to tell what the results of it will be. It will be very evenly contested, and as far as I can see the only hopeful rival to Roosevelt would be Wendell Willkie, who, if the Republican Party nominates him, should be an extremely capable president. The others are old fogies. [...]

Well, I think this is all our news (except that Joan grows daily louder), for the time being. I must return to work. Am instructing Murrays to pay you my royalties and Wisdom of the East dues for the time being. There should be something due for the W of E about now, as I have had nothing yet. If it crosses my letter I will send it back. May as well keep the pounds where they belong and you will have a use for them. All our love to you both and do let us hear from you again soon.

From your loving son, Alan

PS. We have gotten rid of the lease on the flat. Am closing my London bank a/c, so please pocket small proceeds enclosed.

New York City, New York | September 22, 1940

Dear Mummy & Daddy,

I got your letter of August 22, but don't expect to hear from you too often. I guess you will need all odd bits of spare time for sleep, but just drop a line from time to time to let us know you're all right. [...]

I hope you received the pictures of Joan safely. I shall be sending you another lot shortly, but ever since we came back from the country I've been so busy that I haven't been able to get to work on them. For the last two weeks I've been at it almost day and night, writing, editing, and arranging my lectures. There is another book on the stocks, and I have just written an article in which I quoted from one of your letters. Harper is loading me with things to do and we seem to be getting really on our own feet. But you never know what will happen these days.

If the US comes into the war I doubt if it will be until the early part of next year — when the elections are safely over. Test votes show a high percentage of people in favor of full financial and economic aid to Britain, but

98 percent against actually going to war. The facts seem to be that effective help, while much desired, is difficult to supply, the US having only a one-ocean navy, a purely potential army, and a very small but extremely efficient air force. A two-ocean navy will not be ready until 1943–44, unless there is a tremendous speedup. At the same time there is a very definite movement for a tie-up with Canada, and the exchange of destroyers for bases is looked upon as an absolute scoop for the US. The real fly in the ointment is Japan, the fear being that as soon as the US becomes involved in the Atlantic the whole Orient, including Australia and New Zealand, will be at Japan's mercy. We have news, however, that Japan's economic condition is really serious.

I have just heard from Miss Skinner, who was connected with the Sufis in England; she is over here now, and I expect to meet her again soon. My lectures look as if they are going to be popular this fall; we start with almost four times as many people as we had at the beginning last fall — I mean autumn, American is so infectious and in Rome one does as Rome does.

Our friend Bing is still around, and always asks to be remembered very kindly to you, also to Puck and Toby.

Joan is a monkey as well as a full-time job for Eleanor. Every day less and less of the house is beyond her reach, and more and more of her head is filled with ideas. However, she's a beautiful child and often so mirth-provoking in her naughtiness that we just have to hide our faces. Like yours truly, she is given to laughter in her sleep.

I sometimes turn on the BBC late at night when we can pick it up quite clearly on the shortwave. The trouble is that German and Italian stations use the same wavelengths but someone manages to cut them out. It is so curious to get London just as loudly as Radio City only a few blocks away. And then the German stations always shut off when the RAF goes over, but London keeps up just the same whatever is happening.

Joan is at the moment disappearing under the bed on some dark errand; I suppose I must investigate. No, the desired object is out of reach!

Eleanor is in wonderful form these days and helps me no end. Her mother has been so much happier since Mr. E. went off, and lately has given me a great deal of encouragement in my work. She keeps pretty busy. I'm glad you like her *Cat's Yawn*. Sokei-an is Mr. Sasaki, our tame Zen master. The cat's yawn is a symbol of something without purpose and indicates the Zen ideal of living like the universe, freely and without any fixed aim — the wind that bloweth where it listeth. Not a bad idea. Human beings have interfered with everything so much that they are now in a wonderful mess. Better to have left it alone, as God made it!

At present there is still not much real news from here. It's just work, and that means so many words per hour. I have finished editing the minister's book, but more awaits me. I will write again soon when more things develop, but in the meantime don't bother to write any long letters. Sleep, rest, relax, and eat all you can, and please take care of yourselves.

From your loving son, Alan

[Continuation of the letter above.] September 23

Yours of the 10th arrived this morning. We called up the British Consul and find that we can only send 5 lb. of sugar at a time, but we will send off a supply at once and follow it up later. This can be sent direct to you, marked "Gift." They had no information about any special address to which larger consignments could be sent. Now I am not quite sure whether we can get the kind of sugar you want; Eleanor doesn't think they have it here, but we shall try a very big grocer and at any rate get you the nearest thing possible. The brown sugar here is finer ground (or whatever they do to it) than Demerara (spelling?) and not so sweet. But as this might not suit you I will either get the nearest possible or send both brown and white or whatever the grocers advise.

You said that the Iveses had been sending you seeds. I wonder if we could let you have some. There is a brand of lettuce here which you might be able to grow; it comes up very large and is almost solid heart, about the size of those wooden balls they use for bowls, you know, the old gentlemen's game. One lettuce will make about four salads for 2 people. It's very compact inside. There is also a white cabbage which grows in much the same way but is about as big as a football. You can cut it into shreds (raw) and mix it with dressing to make what is called coleslaw, which is an excellent dish. You might also try eggplant. This is a large, egg-shaped aboveground vegetable — purple. Sliced and fried in breadcrumbs it is wonderful. I suggest these things because I know you get rather tired of the same old vegetables; and when veg. and fruit is all you can grow you may as well make it as varied as possible. I think your gardening encyclopedias would tell you whether they would grow in England, and if so, let me know.

We hear the Germans find the shooting too accurate now to indulge in many daylight raids. I don't wonder you get tired of stargazing when they sometimes bring down 185 in a day. I only hope they don't land on the premises. But the Nazis are exceedingly stupid in some ways, because if they go on sinking refugee ships they can expect to find the US in the war before long. That's the one thing that makes people here really angry. Americans are slow to anger, but when they get going *** [*sic*]!!!

I wish you had a better shelter than that coal cupboard. Is there any way it could be strengthened with extra beams and corrugated iron? One idea would be to put the bookcase against the opposite side of the wall. Books in double rows are astonishingly solid. — A.

NEW YORK CITY, NEW YORK | OCTOBER 6, 1940
Dear Mummy & Daddy,
I have both your letters, Sept. 15th and 22nd, and some days ago I sent off 5 lb. of sugar. More will follow and I do hope it will be of use. We can't get Demerara here; it just doesn't exist, but this is Jack Frost light brown and is the nearest thing to it. Let me know as soon as the first package arrives whether it is satisfactory. I shan't wait to hear before sending another. I have asked Toby whether he wants anything, and I am also going to send you some tea.

The season's work has now begun — four groups a week and 38 regular attendants and more coming after the 1st of November. We had our first meeting last Thursday, consisting almost entirely of people from the Riverside Church, which gives me a strong contingent. The work is growing so fast that I can't keep it in our apartment (except for special work) much longer. Soon I shall have to take a small hall or a large studio once a week and open it to the general public. At present all people come by invitation only and are not encouraged to come for individual lectures. They are expected to take the whole course, and consequently we have no drifters. Apparently troubled times are creating increased interest in these subjects, for at the same time last year we opened the season with only 10 people. However, I must take things fairly easy as the doctor says I have to live carefully; he had some X-rays taken a while ago and they show a patch of arrested TB at the top of one lung, but as long as I don't burn the candle at both ends and in the middle it won't start again.

I think I shall be able to send some more pictures of Joan with the copy of this letter. As you will see, she found herself a boyfriend! He is the small nephew of a friend. In this letter I enclose some small prints taken down at Westport. Her vocabulary now includes quite a lot of things: "Sit down," "See you later," "All right," "Coming" being recent additions. She can understand much more than she says. She will fetch her chair when asked, will put away her toys and actually shut the drawer, will put away our shoes in the closet and bring out any pair you ask for. When naughty she is told to go to her room, which she does, shuts the door, and comes out again when she feels better. We have several books of animals and she can call most of them by name. One morning she got into the living room before we were up and started tidying. She took the cups and glasses of the night before out into the kitchen. After meals she clears away, brings me the silver from the kitchen, and helps put it away. How long such tidiness will last is another matter. Most of it is picked up by watching the maid.

Does Daddy have to be out in the open in those raids? Or has he one of those conical steel boxes to pop into? I imagine Toby is a warden or something because he just wrote me about inspecting damage after raids in a tin hat. Apparently he must have some position of importance because he drives a car around. *Punch* is full of jokes about people wandering around stargazing and Toby says he finds people in the middle of the street always doing just exactly what they are advised not to do. In any trouble there are two kinds of people: those who go below ground and those who rush for the best possible point of observation, such as the top of a roof. The same thing happened here when we had that fatuous scare about an invasion from Mars, but I guess you know that story.

I am just going out for a drive with one of our "parishioners" as Eleanor calls them, for our job is much like running a church — minus the bazaars, weddings, and funerals. Today is Sunday and the weather is gorgeous and I suppose we shall run up the Hudson River or somewhere.

Yes, I know Theos Bernard who wrote the book on Tibet. He is an old friend of Eleanor's family, but although he pretends to know a lot about Tibet his knowledge is terribly sketchy. Runs a bogus Yoga school in a swank hotel. His father is a famous character, known as "Oom the Omnipotent" and has a huge colony at Nyack up the Hudson where he teaches Hatha Yoga, keeps a zoo, a baseball stadium, runs a bank, and administers most of the surrounding property.

Well, having returned home from the drive we begin again. We went exploring the west bank of the Hudson, driving along precipitous roads and looking down at the river through trees, which are taking on their autumn colors — blotches of brilliant red and gold among the green.

Sorry, I don't think I'd better send you tea; I hear the duty is very high. I will try and find out what things are not so dutiable.

I hear a strange noise: "Woo-ooo-ooo-oo-o Ooo-oo-oo-o!" Joan has a set of crayons and is drawing in an exercise book; each "ooo" represents a sweep of the crayon, and the result reminds me of Picasso and the New York Museum of Modern Art. Title: Study of a Fugue in Hyper-space. However, I prefer "Woooo."

This, I think, is all the news for the moment. Don't we both mark off the days to the end of this business! The only trouble is you don't know how many days have to be marked, but latest news seems to justify taking off a week or two. All the best to you both, lots of love from us all.

From your loving son, Alan

[Continuation from above.]

Yours of the 30th arrived this morning (Oct. 8) — only eight days! We were very much intrigued by it, and you have us guessing. I will turn on Priestley one night soon. The trouble is we are working three nights out of the week and it will soon be more. I am terribly sorry about the Mordaunts; if you see them, please offer condolences, as well as congratulations on escaping themselves. That Widmore Rd. property is a nuisance to you; how much do you need to get rid of the mortgage?

How I wish you could both get a holiday. Aren't there parts of Devon, Cornwall, or South Berks which are fairly quiet? The Berkshire hills are the loneliest parts of England I know, and as I remember the industrial towns are all in the northern part of the county, along the river.

E.G.B. [Gertrude Buchan] is very plucky taking on that DN work without car or bicycle, and I bet she had plenty to do. I will write Uncle Willie about it, and I know they will be delighted to have news of you all.

Please let me know of any other things you need besides sugar. — A.

NEW YORK CITY, NEW YORK | NOVEMBER 12, 1940
Dear Mummy & Daddy,
You made a perfect guess in sending Joan those Beatrix Potter books; she loves them and hasn't got either, although Eleanor bought some of the others for her a while ago. They arrived safely this morning, as well as the *Wisdom of the East* account. I have letters from you dated Oct. 7th and 21st, and Mummy's of the latter date has a great hole in it! What an adventure Derrick had, and what a stroke of luck; I suppose bad weather caught them.

Weekend before last we were down at Atlantic City in New Jersey spending Mrs. E.'s birthday with her, and since then have had one hectic time with record attendances at my lectures, presidential elections, etc., etc. All Eleanor's relatives are coming to live in New York and we are becoming a large family. One of her cousins has married a perfectly delightful wife (who, incidentally, has transformed him into quite a person) and they have come to live just round the corner. Then you remember Bobbie — she may be coming here soon, and marriage has done a lot for her!

Today is very wintry, although bad weather has only just started, and we hear the severe cold is coming eastwards. I wonder if it will reach you and, I sincerely hope, hold up air raids and make things most uncomfortable in Europe. The Italians seem to be having rough going all around, and I expect you're glad the earthquake messed up the Rumanian oil fields.

A perfectly extraordinary national revival is sweeping this country which is a sight for sore eyes. I think Wendell Willkie, the "unsuccessful" presidential candidate, is responsible for it. People who have never been interested in political matters before are offering their services to him, and he got more votes than any Republican candidate has ever had even though Roosevelt just beat him. The man has a peculiar quality which I think can best be described as an infinite capacity for believing in other people. I think in a way he will be more effective as a private citizen than as president, and he has made people so aware of their liberties and responsibilities that it will now be exceedingly difficult for anyone to interfere and take them away. There are certain dangerously fascist elements here, though not of foreign origin. I don't ever remember having read or heard of a politician so fair, honest, and self-effacing as this Willkie; the result is that, with complete Taoism, he can't help being extraordinarily conspicuous.

Joan is getting much too big for our apartment, and we plan to move to the country next year. Somehow I shall have to find a studio in town for my lectures, though we shall then be in a position to shift a good deal of the work to the country. It's now tied up with a lot of relaxation exercises, etc., to soothe the highly strung and reduce the number of psychic ruins.

How Joan chatters! She now calls herself Doey, or Doughy, which is an attempt at Joany, but I suppose now her own version will stick to her as a nickname. She has a wonderful capacity for sympathy; if anyone knocks themselves she comes up and strokes the hurt place with a worried frown, saying, "Oh, moushey, moushey!" which is meant to be mousey, but she can't get a pure "s." She is in league with Jimey to give him all the food he wants and shouldn't have. But she also knows what her Daddy wants and when, and brings him shoes, cigarettes, and other odds and ends without being asked. But work in the morning is becoming rather difficult as she rampages up and down, and I have to do all heavy concentration while she is resting in the afternoon or at night — so sometimes I have to catch up on lost sleep in the morning. In the late afternoons I play with her, play hide-and-seek, draw pictures of things round the house so that she can go and identify them, cut out paper figures for her (which she adores), teach her to scribble with pencils, to dance, sing, do gymnastics, and talk. It's a wild riot. Sometimes when she is late going to sleep she roars with laughter at appropriate points in my lectures and carries on rival lectures to her teddy bears in utterly unintelligible jargon. This child is a PERSON, and how!

She is usually present when people come to tea, very often to have a business interview with me, and she sits very quietly beside me in the big arm-chairs and hoots with mirth when we laugh. Then she passes the cigarettes and tries so hard to be grown-up and useful — but usually gets side-tracked in a fight with Jimey over a biscuit.

At the moment I have the awful consciousness of millions of things to be done and not knowing which to begin with. Life is very full and never boring, even though trying at times; yet nothing to what you have to put up with. Eleanor is like having acquired a second brain because she understands what I don't, and we still stay awake talking to each other about everything under the sun. She is a wonderful stimulator. It's like having married a bottle of encouragement.

Well, I have to be going out now. I hope you will get the sugar I have sent you. Everyone asks me about your news and how you are getting along, and you get a full share of the admiration which Americans are feeling, with a considerable mixture of awe. Tons of love to you both, and I will get another letter to you well before Christmas and will find out something useful to send you (having consulted the Consul about duties!).

Your loving son, Alan

NEW YORK CITY, NEW YORK | FEBRUARY 10, 1941
Dear Mummy & Daddy,
Your letter of January 23rd has arrived, and we were delighted to have the recipes. If your Christmas packages have not arrived when this letter reaches you, please let us know at once and we will claim the insurance and send them again.

We have definitely decided to move into the country next summer, and we are going to look for a house somewhere on the east bank of the Hudson River, which is simply beautiful. Little Joan is much too big for a town apartment and it's not fair to her to keep her away from fields, birds, and trees any longer. I shall have to have a studio of some kind in the city as an office and lecture room. Joan is getting along wonderfully. Every morning she has to speak to her grandma on the telephone, and it's beginning to become more or less intelligible, though somewhat pidgin. We have given her a set of crayons and she is doing a lot of drawing — strange monsters which are just beginning to be human faces. It has passed the stage of mere scribble. Anything circular is a moon to her, but she now knows most animals by name — horse, lion, monkey, kitten, chicken, bird, camel, fish, whale, goat, sheep, etc. Giraffe and elephant are too much of a mouthful, but she makes an attempt.

I suppose it was you who sent her that perfectly lovely book of nursery rhymes. That really is a joy. I am now real busy with my book on religion for children, and I hope soon to send you photographs of some of the colored illustrations I have done. There will be seven of them in all — Man first uttering the name of God, Ra fighting Apep, Krishna and Arjuna, Buddha under the tree, Lao-tzu, Job, something Mohammedan which I haven't yet decided, and Jesus. I have now done four of them. No, that makes eight! The difficulty is that they are so expensive to print, but I think the book would sell well enough to justify it. I am doing them in a highly detailed, rather fantastic style. The whole approach of the book to religion is through the wonder and beauty of nature, and therefore I have taken Job for the Jewish example because of the great 38th chapter, which I think is the most gorgeous thing in the Old Testament. Then there will be a lot of black-and-white drawings of symbols, diagrams, gods, etc.

I have been wondering for some time whether I could do anything for the HSF [Hospital Sunday Fund] here. It would be a popular charity just now, as people are working hard for war relief. But it seems a little late to start for this year. However, I might approach the Riverside Church, where I have contacts, and one or two others. Suppose you send me a letter of authority to represent the Fund, last annual report, and any details you have of the war work of the hospitals. Then I will see what I can do. I would tell them to remit money direct to London as it would be very complicated to handle it here, and much more satisfactory to pass it direct to the Bank of England earmarked for the Fund's account.

You might try adding the *New York Herald Tribune* and the *New York Times* to the Lord Mayor's letter to the press. Both are very sympathetic to war re-lief, and are generally regarded as interventionist papers. But you should stress these two points: the hospitals' contribution to the actual defense of London; and how their work is protecting the whole world, including America, from the pandemic diseases started by war. To your list also add the *Baltimore Sun* and the *Washington Post*. I could give you the names of many others if you think it worthwhile, but they have to be carefully chosen for their policy. Address these last two, "Baltimore, MD" and "Washington, DC" If it would help I could draft a letter suitable for the American press which you could get LM [Lord Mayor] to sign. I think this is a good idea, because the *New Yorker* devoted many pages this week to an account of war work in St. Thomas's and I'm sure lots of people would like to help it.

Eleanor takes Joan out for walks every morning now so that I can get some peace for work. She goes to the zoo and to the little park by the river near where there are other children to play with. Unfortunately most children are so protected by their snobbish nurses that a child out with its *mother* is not quite nice to know! But when Nettie takes her along, that's different. Still, it's so difficult to find com-panionable children in the city anyhow, and we have got to get her into the coun-try to find some friends. We thought of trying to find a nursery school, but they all have such cranky ideas about children that it's not worth exposing your brat to so many "child psychologists" with lots of university degrees and no common sense!!

(u :i 9 ..l ohg) That is Joan's work. She has just come in and is very interested in the typewriter. She is now wandering around with her overcoat on back-to-front, having no idea how to get into it any other way.

I'm afraid I must get on with my work. There is no special news as I have settled down to a more or less regular routine of writing and lecturing, which is beginning to net me about $2,000 a year. It should grow a bit soon, but I can't take on much more lecturing. Already 3 nights a week is enough and the room won't hold any more.

Well, here's all our love to you both, and please let me know as soon as possible about the Fund.

Your loving son, Alan

PS. Yes, your airmail letters are *always* stamped with the right amount. I hope mine are, too!!

NEW YORK CITY, NEW YORK | MARCH 21, 1941

Dear Mummy & Daddy,

I have been frantically busy of late, and I'm afraid this letter is behind-hand. But for the last few weeks I have given all available time to working up my latest series of lectures into a book, which will probably be called *The Psychology of Christian Faith*. However, I have received all your letters, including the one for Joan, and have enjoyed them very much. That little girl is beginning to talk fast and to take an intelligent interest in life. Eleanor took her out to Chicago for a weekend to see her great-grandmother, who didn't know she was coming. All the previous notice she had was that her birthday present would be at the front door at 9:30 in the morning. So when Eleanor and her mother arrived, they put Joan on the doormat with a bunch of violets, rang the bell, and hid. Great-grandmother opened the door and little Joan walked right in, said "Hullo," and took everything as a matter of course. "Whose little girl are you?" asked g-g-m. At this point, Eleanor couldn't stop laughing, so they showed themselves. A wonderful time was had by all.

Now the main thing I want to tell you about is that [I] am planning a peculiar but important affair, which may not after all surprise you. At present it's somewhat in the air, but everyone here thinks it a magnificent idea. My work is taking a very logical course and has brought me more and more in contact with church people, who have turned out to be most responsive — much more so than anyone else. I have been wondering for a long time how to extend that work and make it really effective, and it seems to me that the obvious way is to cooperate 100 percent with those forces in the churches which are feeling out along these lines. For this purpose it would be of enormous value to be a minister, and I have found that everything I want to say can be said in Christian language. In working up this last series of lectures I have delved fairly deeply into Christian theology and found that, given a certain point of view, the whole scheme is admirable good sense, provided you emphasize its psychological symbolism and do not tie yourself slavishly to a merely historical or metaphysical interpretation.

As I went to the King's School and worked all the time under C of E [Church of England] auspices the obvious course would be to join up with what is here called the Protestant Episcopal Church, which is the exact counterpart of the C of E. I have sounded out the possibilities, which look inviting, and am shortly going to discuss the proposal with a number of ministers from here. But I shall probably need certain information from England. Most important is the copy of my School Leaving Certificate, which you have in your drawer of papers. If you can do so without any danger or inconvenience, would you have a photostat copy of this made (or, get a local photographer simply to photograph it, actual size) and send it to me as soon as possible, the original by airmail and the copy by ship. Don't send it in its cardboard roll; just fold it flat. Would you also let me know exactly when and by whom I was baptized, and if you have it, send the certificate of baptism. I know it was at the Christ Church, Sidcup (or was it St. John's?) and the man's name was Chancellor (or was it?) and it was sometime in 1915. Perhaps it would be as well to make two copies of the School Cert. and keep one yourself in case others go astray, but I don't want you to spend too much money, and will reimburse you for expenses. There may be other helpful papers in your files: I forget what you have, but at one time I had a reference from Birley which isn't here and which you may have. But, quite emphatically, for no reason at all do I want you to risk running around London after photostat people except in foul weather when there couldn't be a raid. Maybe you are used to going around under fire, but please, not on my account! A local photographer would do as well. [Handwritten note on side of paragraph: "Have called you about this."]

So much for that. Please don't talk to Toby about this just yet; I will write him in due course when things are more definite. But I feel strongly that in these times when our institutions are threatened there is no purpose in dividing our efforts into thousands of little sects and groups. I feel I am kind of cut out for this work by inheritance and education, and that I would be wasting my talents elsewhere. I believe it was at one time your own idea for me. Don't worry if for any reason you can't send the papers, because I will push ahead on my own resources; but it would be helpful and save time to have them.

I was so glad that some of the Christmas parcels arrived, but I'm afraid the extra sugar and canned meat that I sent you went astray. Mrs. E. got your letter about prospects for the HSF here; if I get a chance I am going to put in a word among certain ministers and get them interested.

There isn't much other news beyond this for the time being. Spring is just beginning here, but early March brought some bad weather coupled with a bus strike that upset everything.

Why is it that children always pick up one's BAD habits without even knowing they are bad?? Original sin?! Sometimes Joan's are very original.

Lots of love to you both from us all, and let's hear from you soon. I think your garden sounds lovely; I wish we had one.

Alan

PS. Have also cabled King's School for verification of my confirmation. Had to send it to Canterbury, because I don't know what town in Cornwall it has moved to. Do you? I think I took First Communion at Chis. Parish Ch. Would they be able to verify confirmation if I can't get in touch with King's School? — A.

NEW YORK CITY, NEW YORK | APRIL 15, 1941
Dear Mummy & Daddy,
I have just a pile of letters from you as well as the copies of the School Certificate, which arrived promptly, and thank you very much for getting it over so soon. I have letters from Daddy dated March 14 & 20, and from Mummy March 15, 22, 24, and April 2 (airmail) which arrived April 14. By this time you will have had mine of March 21, which explains why I want the School Cert. I also received the certificate of my confirmation from Canterbury a day or two ago, so things are moving.

Well, I've been a busy person what with writing and interviewing parsons. The latter has been most productive as I seem to have made a good friend of the leader of the movement to reconcile analytical psychology with the church and use it in what they call "personal counseling." He is the rector of one of the big New York hospitals, and we had an hour talk the other day about matters of mutual interest, and he is coming to dinner quite soon. He tells me that he has had quite a bit of success and recognition with the ecclesiastical powers-that-be, and he is having theological students trained in hospitals by doctors — quite a thorough course. The corresponding movement in England is the Guild of Pastoral Psychology, of which Jung is the patron and Graham Howe and other friends of mine are in it.

We discovered a relative of Eleanor's in the Church living quite near us and he has been a lot of help. There is some difficulty about my not having a university degree, so I may have to go to Harvard and take theological and some courses for an ordinary degree concurrently. I have some good introductions there through Harper. But all that remains to be seen. Harvard has much the same standards as Oxford and is less red-taped than other places; they let you specialize, which suits me!

Little Joan is getting on wonderfully, and I shall soon have some more pictures of her which I took at Easter. She talks a blue streak — syntax poor but vocabulary wonderful! We gave her a doll's pram for Easter — but it won't go straight on the street and Joan arrives in the hedges in no time. Then she goes round to the front and pulls it round and out, walking backwards. I also painted up some eggs (hard-boiled) for her as rabbits and Mickey mice and stuck ears on them. Then I sometimes draw faces on her ordinary breakfast eggs, which causes great glee.

Mrs. E. has bought a house here — a gorgeous place with five floors and almost 20 rooms!! She is going to bring her mother from Chicago and give her an apartment there. Also she is going to give the Buddhist society quarters in it as they have an enormous room which will make a wonderful temple. She will have her own suite, complete with wisteria-covered terrace. She will move in about mid-August.

We are thinking of Mummy's birthday today and wish you a belated many happy returns. We want to send you some more edibles — BUT, we have heard here that you have to deduct what you receive from abroad from your rationed allowance, and we have also heard complaints that receiving food can be rather a nuisance. I don't know if this is some Nazi propaganda, but I would like to know about this.

Daddy's letter of March 26 has just this minute arrived, and we are enclosing with the airmail copy of this letter a cheque for 16/[shillings] to cover your costs.

Our arrangements for the summer are rather in chaos owing to new developments. However, our friend from California is going to be in town with his car and we shall take plenty of weekends in the country. He gave us the most gorgeous potted rosebush for Easter — those little puffy roses; the thing's enormous.

We met Mrs. Croshaw's friend Reginald Pole again today, just by chance in [a] bookshop. He is lecturing here on Krishnamurti, and I expect we shall see him again soon. We are very curious to know what you think about my plans; there has to be a little subtlety on matters theological, but I think I "know my onions" as they say. However, my friends say, "If *you* have a church I'll come to it." Working as I have done, I have almost reached saturation point in the people I can reach and it mustn't stop there, while I have found church-people ripe for a new vision and open to it if you change the language. The Episcopal

Church offers great freedom, and in New York they have every kind of church from something next to Rome to a theosophical church. Both extremes have their points! The Anglo-Catholics can put on a service which hits you in the pit of the stomach with the sheer beauty of unaccompanied Gregorian chants and 13th century rites, but their moral theology is, in plain American, lousy. Not an inappropriate adjective in view of "hair shirts." But somehow all those grand symbols of Christianity have to be freed from the associations they have gathered in their transit through musty minds and soured souls — and that is the work to be done.

The other day Joan drew a face all by herself but then went and spoiled it. Next time she does one I will snatch it away and send it to you.

Our love to you both and do let's hear from you soon. We do so enjoy your letters, and you certainly keep us well posted.

Your loving son, Alan

New York City, New York | May 24, 1941
Dear Mummy & Daddy,
Mummy's letter of May 13th came this morning, and there are one or two others which I haven't answered yet because the last few weeks have been HECTIC! Now I have a moment's breathing space, so here goes.

Last week we were in Chicago, I to see the Bishop of Chicago and arrange about my training, Eleanor to see her grandmother who is getting very weak and old. Bishop Conkling was very agreeable and I think he would like me to study in his diocese. We have a very good introduction to him and so went to him in preference to any other bishop. If I work under him I shall go to the seminary in Evanston, which is a rather beautiful suburb of Chicago on the shores of Lake Michigan. On the other hand I may go to Philadelphia. Both seminaries are ready to accept me without examination, on the basis of an English classical education, of which they think quite highly. I go down to Philadelphia on Monday, and our friend from California, Adolph [Teichert] (what a name, but a good fellow!), will drive us down.

Then we have been busy joining up with a New York church, getting Eleanor confirmed and making friends with the rector, who is a dear with a terrific sense of humor — a man of strange, almost ascetic simplicity, with no nonsense about him. The church is famous for its music. It has two choirs, one mixed, which sits at the back in a loft, the other of six men who take your breath away with those gorgeous Gregorian chants. The church itself is very large and quite beautiful, having some lovely stained glass and vestments and altar front that would appeal to you — all of them made by women belonging to the congregation. It's rather high, but am sick of New York low churches where all the socialites go to see each other's hats rather than worship.

The Harvard plan is off because bishops don't like their men to go to inter-denominational schools. Yes, Harvard is just outside Boston —

Home of the oyster and scrod,

Where Lowells talk only to Cabots,

And Cabots talk only to God.

Evanston has the advantage of being attached to Northwestern University and of having plenty of trees, open space, and grass, which is now essential for Joan.

I am just about at the end of my new book, which I hope will be out in the fall. It turned out to be a rather big job, involving some very hard thinking and research, and is longer than any other I have done. But it has been a very wonderful education for me and has brought me into a new and inexhaustible field of thought and experience.

We are very relieved to hear how well the garden is supporting you, though I had no idea the food problem was quite so difficult. You didn't say in your letter whether food packages were still acceptable or whether they got you into rationing difficulties. We have heard that this is so, but in these days you believe about one-hundredth of what you hear and only half what you see! Quite apart from believing a great many things you don't hear or see. In any case I will send more sugar.

Mrs. E.'s new house is coming on, but it's rather hard to explain its exact location. I think I sent you a large map of New York some time ago. 65th Street is north of 57th, running from Central Park to the East River. [It] is between Park Ave. and Lexington Ave. Her mother [Eleanor's grandmother] and David [Mrs. E.'s brother] won't come from Chicago as she is much too weak to travel. If we go out there, I think they may move to Evanston where we can keep an eye on her.

I have finished my lectures for the season and will probably start theological work in July or September. Meanwhile I have to polish up my book, and we may get a few trips into the country, which is just lovely at this time of year, though rather desolate in the winter.

We have put little Joan into pigtails for the summer. It's wonderful what she can do for herself now — dress, wash, go to the bathroom, open doors, brush her teeth, clear up the living room, feed herself (occasional spills), and even draw a face, of sorts, one of which I enclose. She's rather slow in talking, but uses what vocabulary she has quite fluently, but that's what comes of having parents that talk too much anyhow! You get her to draw a face by first asking for a moon. She makes a circle. Then you ask for eyes, nose, and mouth, result — face. What a noisy babe! But you get used to it, and I am sure it improves one's powers of concentration.

I never knew it was Jean's 21st, or maybe I forgot. I'm afraid I'm horribly absent-minded, but it's almost difficult to stop working. I feel such a brute for delaying letters to you, but New York has very few post offices and you have to go such a way to get an airmail stamp. I think I had better buy a supply of them.

Next week is all parsons to dinner, including Rice who I told you about, who works at St. Luke's Hospital and is also a psychologist. Apparently he is very much respected in the Church and our rector has strongly advised me to take his advice, in the matter of where I should study. I am hoping to get a chance to work under him at the Hospital soon.

I was sorry to hear old Sir Walford Davies died. His radio talks were so fine and I have always liked his book *The Pursuit of Music*. Do you remember the series he gave on *The Melodies of Christendom*? The other day I picked up a recording which he played of a Russian choir singing the most astonishing creed. We are trying to take it down and, with the help of Adolph and Anne, his girl, who are both very competent musicians, we shall have a usable version of it for future use.

Poor Uncle Harry — what a blow about the RW hall, and I wonder what he will use instead. I had a letter from Mrs. Burke saying that she is bearing up in the midst of London and that, wonderful to relate, their windows are still unbroken.

Your last letter certainly came through in a hurry, only 10 days! We were out at La Guardia airport yesterday and saw the clippers, two of them, on the water. Planes leave and enter that place continually; it's just a queue, like taxis at a railway station, and from there you can get across this whole continent, some 3,000 miles, in 16 hours! It's really rather terrible, but I guess good planes from here cannot be too few. Every now and then a bomber in British colors goes by our window on the way to Floyd Bennett Field, from which they go to Canada. Some pilots from England going to Canada to pick up planes brought newspapers from London to New York in less than 24 hours, which was a record. In a few months they may send you some charming monsters that will run 7,000 miles without stopping. There is only one at present.

Well, I expect to have more news about my plans in a few days and I will let you know at once when things are decided. In the meantime, all our love to you both with a bundle of sugar on the way!

Your loving son, Alan

NEW YORK CITY, NEW YORK | JUNE 12, 1941
Dear Mummy & Daddy,

Daddy's letter with the Wisdom of the East papers has just come to hand. Don't have any compunction about using that money for yourselves if you need it. That's really why I wanted you to have it, but if you prefer to invest it, that's okay by me. I have sent off more sugar to you (5 lb.), which I hope will arrive intact.

Last week Bishop Conkling of Chicago accepted me as a postulant for holy orders, so the first important step has been taken. After a year's work I become a candidate, and then after a year or two a deacon, all depending on how fast I can do the work. You become a full-fledged priest as soon as you get an appointment. I am very much puzzled as to why you should think I am taking a "shortcut" or going about it without deliberateness, or even why the whole approach should be so peculiar. Three years' hard work in a seminary is hardly a shortcut, and there is certainly no lack of deliberation. It may certainly seem peculiar in view of my previous affiliations, but have I not said for a long time that Christianity is the religion of the West and that the whole point of studying Oriental religions is to re-inform it with certain mystical insights and techniques which it has either lost or neglected — a matter on which several priests I know are in full agreement.

Therefore it has become more obvious to me than ever that the Church needs full cooperation rather than criticism from without. This is not only because the Church can be improved, but also because it contains spiritual treasure and means of life from which I, for one, cannot afford to separate myself. It is a definite, authorized field of service, teaching, worship and in which you can work as a servant with others, instead of being on your own with all the temptations and dangers of self-imposed authority and "mastership." My work has turned out to be a priest's work. My entire background and training is in that direction, and I have the choice of trying to do it on my own (and becoming a freak), or going in with the spiritual tradition of the West in a perfectly normal way.

I have explained this position to the "powers that be," making it clear that my work in Oriental philosophy and modern psychology have enabled me to appreciate Christianity as otherwise I might not have been able. Of course, there are points on which I do not agree with some churchmen's interpretation of Christianity. These points of difference are already in the Church, and do not have to be introduced by such a person as myself going into it. My contribution, as I see it, is not to make differences, but to find ways in which existing differences can be healed by the application of new viewpoints, which, even so, are not so very new. One of the most outstanding of modern Christian writers — Nicolas Berdyaev of the Greek Orthodox Church — is a person with whom I find myself in almost entire agreement on every point, and the Archbishop of York has called him the most important and profound writer on such matters in our time. In other words, there are trends already in the Church which I find wholly and honestly supportable, and you probably know that while Berdyaev is a Greek Orthodox there has for time been discussion of uniting the Anglican and Orthodox Churches because of their close sympathy. Then again, I find myself agreeing all the time when I read Barry and Streeter (both Church of England), and even Chesterton's version of Catholicism (though it is not always the Church's) is not at all unpalatable.

Over here we have, too, a group of priests called the Order of the Holy Cross who have put out some of the most stimulating teaching on Christian mysticism that I have ever seen. (Incidentally, they run some of the best boys' schools in the country.) So when I see such trends at work I feel bound to work along with them. The Church here has also had the good sense to employ such men as my friend Rice, who is priest-psychologist, to be guide, philosopher and friend to all the seminaries and religious orders in this diocese, and to think very highly of his work. I find myself in agreement with him also, so there is no question of my making an entrance on false pretenses among people with whom I do not honestly sympathize and agree.

Furthermore, I am sick of simply extending "my" work, for insofar as it is purely and merely mine its extension is a wearisome and unprofitable burden. But insofar as my work can be absorbed into that of a really God-inspired Church, it ceases to be mine and becomes both outwardly and inwardly an eternal work of which I am simply a helper. Therefore I have no notions of introducing wild innovations or conducting outlandish experiments. Insofar as I have any personal object at all, it is to try to stimulate fresh and deeper understanding of time-honored traditions and teachings. This can be done, is being done, and will, I believe, be thoroughly acceptable to those in the American Church who are not simply moribund. It so turns out that here, generally speaking, the "low" churches are in a sort of rigor mortis with stodginess and complacency, whereas the "high" churches are apt to be full of liveliness, humility, and genuine spirituality. The low churches (as also the "free" churches with the exception of the Quakers) have unfortunately turned religion into a matter of vague political and ethical aspiration rather than union with God. You go to church to hear a good lecture, the minister's personal views on almost anything, instead of to worship and be united with God, and the result is that free-church people are starved for religion but well-informed on politics. As you know, I have lately worked with many free-church people, and they took so readily and eagerly to talks on the mystical and religious aspects of Christianity that I was amazed. Things have come to such a pass in this matter that a common devotion to real religion has, in a particular instance, brought a group of Quakers and High Anglicans (Episcopalians) into sympathetic cooperation! Extremes meet in God, but it seems that the neither hot nor cold are spewed out of the mouth.

The day before yesterday we had Joan baptized. She looked, and behaved, like an angel in a white dress and veil, and although she loathes having her hair washed she didn't object at all to quite a thorough soaking — poured upon her from a silver scallop shell. At the moment she is *not* being an angel! Violent screams and protestations from the bathroom.

I have just had a letter from Toby, who says he is grimly enjoying life though his home seems to have been battered about a bit. I wrote him the other day about my plans, and sent Clare [Cameron] some money for reestablishing the magazine, Sanders' place having been wiped out.

Do remember me to Jessie, and say I hope her crowning glory is more glorious than crowned. Eleanor has just written to Minneapolis, and we expect to hear from them again before long.

I shall have to spend the next two months brushing up my Greek and History, as I plan to start work at a seminary in September, and though I have not yet heard from the dean, I expect this will be the Seabury-Western Seminary in Evanston, Illinois, which is just north of Chicago on the shores of Lake Michigan — a glorious place. The dean is Bishop McElwain, who is perfectly delightful.

Well, I will let you know how things go as they turn up. In the meantime, lots of love to you both from us all.

Your loving son, Alan

NEW YORK CITY, NEW YORK | JULY 1, 1941
Dear Mummy & Daddy,
Yours of the 18th arrived this morning, and we were delighted to hear that you are going to Ruthin this month. I certainly hope you will get some peace there for a while. I forget the date of my last letter as I sent you both copies, but I don't think it would have arrived by the 18th. I told you I had sent off some more sugar. I shall also have some more pictures of Joan for you next week.

We are just cooking in the heat here. Day after day the temperature is over 90, and so humid that you become a mass of stickiness. Joan doesn't seem to notice it, so I suppose it depends on what kind of climate you are brought up in.

I wonder what you think of the new turn of events in the war. Many people here sincerely hope both parties will exterminate each other, but Russia's power is a mystery and I doubt if the first few battles will tell anything. A steamroller takes time to get going, and Russia is bigger than the USA, and much worse to travel over. But we may get Napoleon's troubles over again, because as they burnt Moscow then, they will probably destroy the Ukrainian wheat and oil fields now.

I start getting practice in things priestly tomorrow, as I am to serve at early Communion, complete with red cassock and surplice! Eleanor feels nervous for me, but it's a fairly simple business of carrying books around, ringing bells, and saying a few responses. They are also going to let me serve at the 11 o'clock on Sundays, which is sung Eucharist. With the choir away for the summer all the music is unaccompanied plainsong (male voices), which is perfectly exquisite. All the serving is done by men, as we have no choirboys.

Our home seems to be flooded with ministers these days — high, middle, low, and free. We have some very good friends, husband and wife, he being one of the "big shots" in the Presbyterian Church — quite an elderly man with the interesting job of going all over the country and reviving decrepit churches. They were in to dinner last night, and we had a fascinating time discussing the state of the nation. He has astonishing tales of some of the queer little towns out West where one church has to do for all kinds of people, of the terrible poverty down South where they have to paper their walls with newspaper and the average annual income in some counties is only $50 a year. The South is very backward. Mentally, they are still fighting the Civil War, and still regard colored people as outcastes. Well, some Negroes are a bit difficult, but others are almost paragons of virtue. There could hardly be a more delightful person than Nettie, our maid, and recently I read the story of George Washington Carver, the Negro scientist who discovered more than 100 uses for the peanut, started crowds of new industries, and always insisted that he himself had found out nothing, but that everything had been shown him by God. The strange thing about Negroes is their way of working; they never hurry, never get flustered, and always get things done. They don't fume and bluster in hot weather, and on a day like this are a lesson to everyone.

New Yorkers don't seem to realize that this is really a tropical city. We are on the same latitude as Madrid and Naples, and try to live as if we were in Edinburgh. However, the summer is very quiet, and there's nothing much doing. I am trying to do some serious study, but your fingers stick to the paper and your mind goes like an overboiled cabbage. One consolation is the discovery that I haven't entirely forgotten my Greek, and can read the New Testament fairly easily. But I have to work up all the history I never did at school — Greek, Roman, and Mediaeval, also the history of Western philosophy, which is quite something.

I'm very sorry things are not going well for the Fund this year, but you have a terrible problem. That reminds me: Does St. Jude, Courtfield Gardens still exist? I want a copy of my marriage certificate, as the original was abducted by the government when I came in. Should these be obtained from the church or from Somerset House? I wonder if you would make enquiries and get me a copy if you can. I don't know what the fee is, but will reimburse you.

I hope the telegram for Daddy's birthday arrived on time. I meant to send it much earlier in the day, but got hung up that morning as well as the night before.

In the copy of this letter I enclose another of Joan's drawings, which is a bit better than the previous one.

Lots of love to you both, and a very happy holiday —
Your loving son, Alan

New York City, New York | July 14, 1941
Dear Mummy & Daddy,
They are too heavy for airmail, so I am sending you 5 pictures of Joan by ship, putting them in two lots in case one goes astray. I think they are the best I have done. The one sitting with her mother has curly hair, which was taken on her second birthday. The one out of doors was taken at Easter, and those in the white dress were taken just before her baptism last June. So you see she's growing up.

Your lovely letter of July 3rd came this morning, but we were terribly sorry to hear that your lung had been bothering you again, just when you were going to have a good time in town; I think that was horrid. Do take things as easily as you can.

I have written to Toby about my plans, so the subject is no longer for family consumption only! I don't know yet what his reactions are. I have also announced it to all the people who came to my lectures, and it has had on the whole a very good reception, though some people can't imagine what I can possibly see in the Church and await developments with puzzlement. I am now learning the ropes by doing as much serving as I can at our church, which is most interesting. On Wednesday mornings I serve the 9:30 service, and on Sundays I have just started in at the 11 o'clock as crossbearer. We are close to the altar all the time and see everything. Yes, they wear vestments, not the [Roman Catholic] lace and ruffles, but the really old kind consisting of amice, alb, maniple, stole, and chasuble. They follow the ancient designs and patterns, which is to say, they are symbolic and floral and have no fussy pictures or landscapes on them! But the work is very beautiful. A cope is worn at the beginning of the service, but these are not so good as the other vestments. Not many Episcopalian churches have them as it's considered Popish in some quarters, though the movement for restoring such things is growing. The priest wears them to distract attention from his personal identity to his office, and because he is supposed to symbolize Christ.

The symbolism of the Church is astonishing, but seldom understood, and I find as I learn more about it that every part of it is important and is a dramatic way of presenting a real mystical truth. When you perform symbolic acts with body and mind at the same time, it has far more effect than with the mind alone. Many people complain that church services seems to have no relation to life, being an obscure mumbo jumbo that cannot be of value in ordinary, everyday life. This is always a danger when their meaning is not understood. Unfortunately the clergy do not explain it enough, for fear they might explain it away. But I don't find it works like that. If you know something of what is really signified, it does things to you. Human beings need this drama, for without it religion becomes too much in the mind, where it is apt to be elusive. "Out of sight is out of mind" applies all too well to our modern culture, for men can't practice religion by a mere decision of conscious will. Therefore I discover our church teaching the interesting and profound doctrine that prayer is not man praying to God, but God praying in man. In other words, religion is not something we do off our own bat, but is an activity of God already in us, which becomes apparent when we assent to it. How Buddhistic!

I have recently been doing some painting which has turned out rather well. It's a good activity for the hot season when the temperature is too high for hard mental work. I'm going to send you some photographs of it. I have discovered some new techniques, such as getting the effect of enamel by putting varnish over watercolors on paper, and then fastening the paper to a firm base, such as wood. Very interesting results may be obtained by mixing watercolors and inks, or using black Indian ink as a base for watercolor designs, drawing them on first in Chinese white. For the enamel effect you have to put the colors on heavily. I have a blue which by this process can give a fair imitation of some Limoges and Byzantine work. With the varnishing process you use gold paper. While the paste beneath it is still moist you can work designs on the gold with a stylus; the paste dries and the design hardens.

A Frenchman has published a book in England called *You Can't Ration These* or some such title, which I think you should get. It tells how to make attractive dishes out of all kinds of odds and ends that people never thought of eating — things that may be found about the countryside, and certainly in a place like Chislehurst. Let me know in good time when the jam-making season comes around, and I will send plenty of sugar. I hope you have the consignment I sent last month. Tell me how much will be needed.

I don't know yet what is happening about my book; the publishers have had it more than a month now, and no decision yet. It's rather a tough subject, and I gather they are getting several opinions. There are suggestions that I should write up the same subject in a book about the size of *The Spirit of Zen* for popular consumption.

Well, there is not much actual news, so this had better stop for the time being. I will write again soon.

All our love to you both — Alan

AW: In the following letter to Toby (Christmas Humphreys, president of the Buddhist Lodge in London, which became the Buddhist Society in 1943), Alan responded to a book of Toby's poetry in such an inspired fashion that I found myself feeling a sense of unexpected joyful expansiveness! This started with his comment regarding Toby's poetry as "introducing life, freedom, and even passion into the somewhat arid ground of pure principle."

I was moved by Alan's descriptions of principles being derived from a deeper reality connected with elemental forces, the beauty of freedom, and irregularities that are grounded in order. I will not attempt to say more, but will rather allow his words to say it all.

One other thing struck me: Alan was twenty-six years old at the time of this writing, and fourteen years younger than his mentor, Toby, who was then forty. Alan writes fully as an equal.

NEW YORK CITY, NEW YORK | JULY 21, 1941
Christmas Humphreys | Founder of The Buddhist Society of London and Barrister
My dear Toby,
Your letter and the book of poems arrived today. We are delighted. I have read and reread many of them, for most I had never seen before, and am moved to comment. First, I am very glad you published them, because they reveal a side of you that does not ordinarily come out. And, second, it's a side, which while somehow you don't seem to take it quite seriously, has a certain essential red-blooded reality. It makes your more philosophic work mean more, introducing life, freedom, and even passion into the somewhat arid ground of pure principle.

"No More," "Madrilene," "Etude," "Humanity," and several others are really beautiful examples of that rare quality — molded, restrained, and truly valued *feeling*. They show a very human bondage which is at heart more free than that living from an ultimate reality of principle and law which you seem to suggest in the *Middle Way*. You have always said that principles are alive, but it seems to me that their life is very much derived from a deeper reality. Principles become alive for us when we associate them with elemental, cosmic forces.

Yet such forces thrill us not because they are blind, cold, utterly principled, and law-abiding, but just because we feel, in the bottom of our hearts, that they are not. They suggest immense life, vast freedom, and terrific power.

In Mahayana, all principles are derived from sunyata. Philosophically, we may think of this as the full void, the potency of absolute space, but this misses the most important part of its nature. Sunyata is absolute freedom, and hence absolute life, all-inclusive, and hence all-loving. But what does it do? It fulfills its freedom by limiting it; it is free to be bound. Instead of remaining quiescent on the one hand, or bursting into crazy chaos on the other, it constricts itself in limited law and form.

Zen sometimes speaks of sunyata as standing in the midst of a void with freedom to move in all directions. But this freedom of sunyata is not *realized* unless a movement is made in certain particular directions, not all directions at once, which would be chaos. To be realized, to mean anything at all, this freedom must be sacrificed. Naturally, this involves the life of principle and law. But I think we mistake the real nature of the process if we regard principle as the ultimate, because this makes the universe like a machine whose operations may be taken for granted. The beauty of a principle is not that it is there anyhow, but that it is produced at a price, at a sacrificial cost, to a free, living Reality — a Being or Be-ness, and not simply a cold mode of behavior.

When principles are seen as grounded in a living freedom, they become tolerable. For if the ultimate reality of life were absolute, immutable law, it would be like the Nazi state, which is the vicious circle of going round and round, the stultification of the perfect circle and perfect symmetry. Even in manifestation, the living freedom of that reality is shown by certain delightful irregularities. The solar system is redeemed because the earth goes round the sun in 365¼ days, and not a neat 360; its orbit is elliptical, but near enough to a circle not to be crazy. Chinese art is superb because of the same subtle off-centeredness. Your poetry supplies this same element to the rest of your work, introducing that side of you which is not quite reasonable.

For, from the standpoint of the life of pure principle backed by "cold, indomitable will," our bondage in love, of whatever kind, and its handmaid, sorrow, is unreasonable — an involvement in maya. We seem to be loving a fair courtesan, but I sometimes wonder whether in your poetry you think you are just toying with her, ready to cast her aside for the more serious bedfellow of Law. Is this lady's name Maya after all?

The schoolmen used to say that all human love, altruistic or bestial, is at root the love of God, that our bondage to love, however much in ignorance, is an aspect of God's self-giving and self-limitation. Hence the symbol of the suffering

God-man on the cross of manifestation, and of the God incarnated and limited, freely and voluntarily, in human flesh. But in each one of us, when we suffer through love, and in his own nature, God who is *the* self really experiences this pain, and the self-limitation of reality is not a mechanical law, but the free act of a living self. Therefore we cannot possibly take it for granted. We are able to accept and affirm life, to reconcile the opposites, and so experience enlightenment, because such acceptance is already the basic nature of being. But it is not so just because it had to be, because we just found it lying around as something like the law of gravity. Acceptance and love may be a law, but a law achieved at a price and not to be trifled with.

The idea that our human, and not always very altruistic, loves are mere involvement in maya is often clothed by poets with a beauty which makes it seem an exquisitely perfect and beautiful principle. Yet to give that idea of maya all its beauty and force, they are compelled to borrow that beauty from the maya they would spurn. Lafcadio Hearn in his essay "Within the Circle" makes his point about the illusoriness of life only because he borrows those illusions to make it — "borrows from the heavens a tongue, so to curse them more at leisure."

But compel the poet to be logical, to be fair, strip him of all his borrowed goods, and leave him with the principle itself; he must then be dumb. But to this extent he is right; we are bound, and because of bondage we certainly suffer. More than that, we suffer from ourselves, "none else compels." But is that really so stupid? For ignorantly and usually poorly, we are doing the most divine of all things, and it seems to me best not to stop what we are doing but to realize what we are doing, and shape it accordingly.

Yet, consciously, we do not know what it is to be absolutely free. Therefore the constriction we feel in our bondage cannot be compared to that known by the great self. But only because of that cosmic bondage, freely taken, are we able to live and love, whether for evil or for good. We use that sacrifice to do all that we do and to be all that we are, and any deep understanding of this must make its misuse horrible. To grow in wisdom and experience enlightenment we have to learn the essential union between our ignorant, unconscious self-abandonment and the consciously free self-abandonment of God, sunyata or the great self. We then see that there is a peculiar exhilaration in this accepted bondage over and above the love and suffering it involves. We experience the ultimate paradox of finding freedom in surrendering it. But to do these things we have to employ the Original Sacrifice, because we do not love with our own love or accept with our own acceptance. To imagine so is real dualism and a cause of awful pride, coupled with that loneliness and self-isolation which is the real heresy of separateness. These pitfalls are avoided by gratitude, an affection which can hardly exist very consistently in a worldview ruled by immutable law, to which we can't be grateful because it can't be anything save what it is.

Gratitude seems to imply a dualism, in common with its outward expression — worship. But this is using duality to achieve nonduality. I think we must go about it this way to avoid the more subtle and pernicious dualism of mere one-ness, which is the death of uniformity, Monophysitism, determinism, and spiritual Nazism. "When the many are reduced to the One, to what shall the One be reduced?" Zen has always recognized that oneness is still within duality. But within real nonduality there is room for difference, room for duality, room for Giver and receiver, worshipper and Worshipped. The nondual is free to be dual; thus merely one is not. There is room in God for creatures different from God, but in the pantheistic Absolute there is not. It cannot include difference, and so falls short of complete freedom and the total inclusiveness of nonduality. Here orthodox Zen and orthodox Christianity have common ground, in the light of which it is specially interesting to read Suzuki's Zen *Buddhism & Its Influence on Japanese Culture*, pp. 215–237.

Sorry, I'm wandering rather far and not talking about your book. The pity of "Madrilene" is that over here it's the name of a widely advertised tomato soup. Otherwise, it is so lovely that I wish our poet had been a little bolder and not so content with his hoped-for dream! Such a whetting of the appetite! "The Pilot" is a splendid example of something quite different, slightly troubled by vagueness in the last two verses but one. "The Burden" says a world of truth; at least, I think it does, though it depends how you take the last verse. "Bandol" starts splendidly, but I don't quite like the strange choice of words in later verses because there seems to be beauty of sound at the expense of clear meaning — "The spiral fumes from watching mouths betray the altar of content" in another context might be a little clearer. "No More" is quite heart-rending and never sentimental, which is some job. But all is a treat after the biological sentiments and indifferent technique of so many of our moderns.

Yours truly is working away, brushing up his Greek, and learning the vast intricacies of ritual, clad in a red robe, waving candles, ringing bells, and having a wonderful time. We get this over before turning to more serious business. In September we go to Evanston near Chicago where I shall meet "doctor and saint, and hear great argument, about it and about" — a monkish life, save that I shall have a wife and live out. I had to assist a tame monk at the altar the other day, complete with cowl and habit. He belongs to a remarkable order of mystics that live up in New York State somewhere, and they put out some exceedingly good literature, and did he know how to conduct a service!

If you have any more *unpublished* poems of war, I think the *New York Herald*

Tribune (daily) would like them; they should be short. I will see what I can do about the book; might do something with serial rights — are they tied up in any way, and if so to what extent? That is to say, republication in magazines here.

I haven't had the July mag. yet; I wonder if mine has gone astray.

All the best to you both, and more power to you.

Yours ever, Alan

NEW YORK CITY, NEW YORK | AUGUST 24, 1941
Dear Mummy & Daddy,
Well, we have found our new home in Evanston. Eleanor and I went out there last weekend and discovered a delightful house which will accommodate us all beautifully. It has nine rooms, study, living room, dining, kitchen, and five bedrooms. The two bedrooms on the top floor will be a bed and sitting room for Nettie. The living room is on a mezzanine and has a sunporch attached to it. There is a small garden and two garages, one of which I shall use for a workshop and studio, and in the other we shall put a car. We shall have to have one now as travelling is difficult in the Middle West without it, and we can pick up a secondhand one very reasonably. The house is only two blocks from the lake and a bathing beach, five from the seminary and one-and-a-half from the station. For all that (the station) it's in a beautiful locality with lots of trees and open spaces. We pay the same rent for it as for our three-room apartment in New York! We shall be there after September 11th. It will certainly be grand to live in a house once again, and we are looking forward to going there and starting work at Seabury-Western very eagerly. I will send you some pictures of it when we are settled; the house doesn't look so much from the outside, but it's most pleasant in.

We had a long letter the other day from Auntie Jean. Young Jean has just graduated (see photo) and goes to work in a school at Grand Rapids, Michigan, which isn't really so very far from us, and we may be able to drive over and see her or put her up in Chicago on her way through for holidays. Betty has two more years to go as she is taking a longer course. Uncle Willie is at present away on a long trip, but I think we shall try to see them all soon as we can make the trip to Minneapolis in a day from Chicago.

Mrs. E. will move into her new home about September 15th in NYC, but I shouldn't be surprised if it's a few days later than that. Defense work is beginning to hold up all ordinary commerce, and certain materials are hard to obtain.

I am getting busier and busier with church affairs, and the other day assisted at a wedding, which was quite one of the most delightful ceremonies I ever saw. It was done in one of the small chapels of our church, and comprised the ordinary wedding service and Communion for the bride and groom. The joke was that the bride and most of the congregation were RCs, and it was the first time they had heard it done in English. They were duly impressed, for the RCs make no effort whatever to instruct their people in the contents of the missal, so they really don't know what they are doing. They go to mass and say their rosaries all the time, being encouraged in a state of abysmal ignorance. That's particularly true of New York where all the priests are Irish, with all the particular eccentricities of Irish priests.

Our trip to Chicago will be rather amusing as we have to take baby, dog, canary, and two fish; it will almost be a procession. Nettie goes with us (thank goodness) and will help take care of the livestock. Our first call will be at great-grandmother's house. The poor dear is getting terribly frail, and is almost crippled with lumbago. I'm afraid she can't last much longer. She still manages to walk slowly round the apartment, but will soon be confined to bed.

I had a long letter from Toby the other day. He seems to approve of my going into the church, but wonders how on earth I am going to fuse Christianity, psychology, Zen, and all the rest. That's not so hard once your basic principles are straight, for then everything works out perfectly logically. The more you study them, the more each detail of Christian teaching and practice fits perfectly into the scheme. But without a knowledge of basic principles they are a maze of confusion and improbability — not to say superstition. Yet there is a point of view from which every ancient doctrine and practice of the Church is absolutely relevant and meaningful, without any offence to reason. The only real difference from the higher forms of Buddhism or Taoism is that Christianity is inseparable from belief in a living, conscious God, since the impersonal Principle is less than man, and is setting up as God something which is a creature of the human mind — machinery. I find this a very acceptable point of view, for I have often quarreled with a mechanistic view of life without understanding the full implication of what I was saying, namely, that if ultimate Reality is not a machine the only other thing it can be is a living Being.

Peg Everington has also written to us. She seems very happy and busy with her work. Have you heard anything lately of Douglas and Christine? And what about Ivan? He has to all intents and purposes disappeared.

Joan is coming along splendidly, learning to talk more and more, and saying the funniest things, which are rather hard to convey without the particular tone of voice. She has grasped the principle that "a soft answer turneth away wrath," for if you get angry with her she raises a finger and quietly reprimands you for losing your temper.

I think that's all the news for the time being. I hope you had a good rest and a grand time in Wales and found everything in order on returning home.

Love from us all to you both,

Your loving son, Alan

PS. (Aug. 25) Yours of the 11th came this morning. I see the Minneapolis folk have written you direct. I love your comment on the hourly news broadcast! That's nothing to what it was last May and June (1940). Of course, we have many more radio stations, because they are all privately owned. New York has at least 20, and their broadcasts are pandemonium, idiocy, and advertising. There is, however, one rational station to which we stay permanently tuned when we listen to the radio, which is not often. This station broadcasts almost nothing but recordings of fine music, so that you can have a first-rate concert any time you like, which is even better than the BBC. So it seems that extremes of good and evil go together! But gramophone records have now been reduced to half normal price, so that there's not much need to bother about the radio. We shall miss that station in Chicago, though they may have an equivalent. Fortunately, on the whole, our stations are not as powerful as European ones, being designed to cover strictly limited zones.

I really should adore to have that stole, but there's no hurry about it and I know church work is terribly expensive, so don't want you to be out of pocket. The brocade is, as I remember, the chief item, though you say you have this already. It should have a Greek cross (i.e., all arms of equal length) at the center, which is at the neck. There seems considerable liberty of choice for designs at the ends, but I will figure out something and send you patterns in due course. It should be 2½ yards long, and very slightly widened at the ends. Meanwhile, you may have some suggestions, for I know you have made them before.

The enclosed is a new bookplate I have designed, with a trick of perspective which shows the nearness of what seems to be far away. *Pulsate et aperietur vobis* — knock and it shall be opened unto you. — A.

JW: The letters above span a period of three years. They cover Alan's arrival in New York as a young man with wife and, weeks later, a child, his adaptation to life in the United States, the vastness of the country, and the mix of humanity and the social scene into which he married. He left behind his own family in England, which became war-torn; places in his old neighborhood bombed out, food scarce and money short, friends lost. He saw the politics of his new country in stress over the war in Europe and the economy at home. It must have been quite a feat to absorb all this and to intellectualize it in terms of philosophical and religious beliefs. In his autobiography, published in 1972, he described himself as a pacifist, stating, "The energy and treasure which Germany and Japan alone put into World War II, and which the United States has squandered in Vietnam, could have gone a long way towards ending poverty over the whole earth. Would that have been peace without honor?"

Given those circumstances, I suppose it is no wonder he gravitated towards the more insular environment of the church. I am not a theologian or a scholar of Buddhism. I am, however, amazed at the progression of his thinking through these letters. He was able to go from interpreting Eastern philosophy to New York "society" in his adroit fashion to becoming involved with the higher-ups of Christian faiths. He came to the point of feeling that somehow he could combine the philosophies and make "it" all more understandable, "it" being human existence in relation to God, earth, and the universe, through merging the more palatable tenets of both Christian doctrine and Eastern philosophy. I had always thought that his decision to enter the church was based on a need to avoid the draft. I must have garnered that thought from the adults around me, as I was only a child at the time, though there is no mention of that thought in his letters or autobiography.

With the obvious closeness he felt to his parents, it must have been wrenching to hear of the bombings, food shortages, fear of being outdoors, and other hardships they had to suffer. His wish that there would be a way to shore up the space under the stairs, his parent's bomb shelter, was poignant. When I lived in Chislehurst just several years later, I would walk up to town with my grandparents past the shells of bombed-out buildings, overgrown with grass.

There was also his concern for his father's livelihood with the Lord Mayor's Hospital Sunday Fund: he was worried that the HSF was not being adequately funded and that his father's salary might be diminished. I had the opportunity to attend a children's party fundraiser for the HSF. My grandmother cleverly made me a lovely gown out of a piece of French silk that had been a gift to her; it was printed around the bottom with beautiful garden flowers. She topped it with some dark green velvet, making a bodice with puffed sleeves and peplum. I still have the invitation to the ball and a photo portrait of me in the dress (see photo insert).

Alan's observations of our national politics at the time are quite interesting. I'm sure some of his opinions were influenced not only by his mother-in-law's, but also by his concern about the pending US involvement in the war in Europe and his parents' safety in Great Britain.

In reading his many letters written during his church years, we noted Alan's love of ritual and the trappings involved. He came by this, I believe, from attending the Church of England school (King's) at Canterbury. His early letters reflected some of this. In his search for the "right" church denomination in New York, this background obviously played a big part. As the reader will see in the next group of letters, he took ritual very seriously, down to the hem of his vestments, the choir, processions with incense, the intoning of prayer, and the significance of the sermon. This all seemed to be the "mystical" calling of the Spirit of God, wherein all things were both finite and infinite. From some feeling innate within him, the church became a calling.

We regret that there is no copy of the letter Alan sent to Toby (Christmas Humphreys) about becoming a priest; there is only the mention of it in his letter of July 14, 1941, to his parents, in which he comments about "symbolism" in the church. He does a total switch in his letter to Toby of July 21, 1941, regarding Toby's poems, and delivers quite a treatise on Buddhism.

One of their friends, Adolph Teichert (introduced to our parents by our grandmother Ruth's California friends Blanche and Russell Matthias), figures into all this as a musician and apparent enthusiast of liturgical music. Adolph ("Tolly") was the son of a Sacramento building magnate and in New York was a student of the famous harpsichordist Wanda Landowska. Adolph becomes part of the Evanston scene in the following letters.

As an aside, I have to say that I am blown away by Alan's interest and involvement in my development from infant to child. I blush with embarrassment at his fascination with my growth, noting my behavior in detail. I wonder how many people have such a chronicle of their development, both physical and intellectual. What a gift in a time capsule!

PART III

On Becoming a Priest — The Seminary Years

1941-44

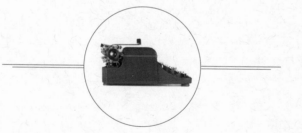

JW: The following group of letters will take the reader to Alan's ordination as a priest in May 1944. He became completely involved in the church as a "postulant" or student, immersing himself in the required religious studies. He was, apparently, an astute scholar, mastering Greek, Latin, doctrine, and other subjects. At the same time he was being invited to take part in services, both Anglican and secular, speaking publicly, either as guest lecturer or "lector" for not only the Anglican Church but others, such as the Theosophical Society and the Russian Orthodox cathedral. He assisted at Christmas Eve mass in New York City, while visiting Eleanor's mother, Ruth, in 1941. He established friendships with celebrants of other faiths, including the Greek Orthodox Church, visiting the various cathedrals in the Chicago area and marveling at the beauty of the architecture and decor, the gilding and frescoes and stained-glass windows. He took in the various rituals involved in the services and, with another student, actually incorporated some of these features into seminary services. Although he was not yet a priest, he had already established himself as an authority on ecclesiastical dogma. Alan felt that the mystery and symbolism in ritual was important in mass, that "in taking away the miraculous and wonderful it leads us to forget the essential mystery of life and religion."

All this while he was still managing to pursue his writing. In his autobiography he states, "During all this study I was trying to get my inner being over the conflict of atmospheres between Buddhism and Christianity." He was troubled by the concepts of sin and forgiveness as much as he decried the idea of a paternalistic universe and the belief that God was a "he." Alan was also troubled by the notion that he was a pantheist. He wrote: "If one asserts that the universe is God, and by 'the universe' means an ordered collection of separate things, then I am certainly no pantheist because I do not hold this conception of the universe."

Alan's daily schedule was fairly grueling. He had to be at the seminary at 6:00 AM, and often stayed late in the evening, and when at home, he had his studying, reading, papers to write, and preparation for exams. This had to be hard on Eleanor. Anne and I agree that she must have held some unhappiness and resentment, especially as the United States entered World War II and rationing and financial worries began. And then there was the second child, born in the summer of 1942 — Anne. There was some disappointment that she was not the infant son for whom they had hoped. I carry the image to this day of my mother leaving our home while in labor, valise in hand, striding resolutely up the hill to the boulevard where the hospital was located. A walk of about three long blocks. Apparently Alan was not reachable.

Alan briefly mentions Sokei-an Sasaki's internment. Much to our grandmother Ruth's dismay, Sokei-an was summarily arrested by the FBI as an "enemy alien" on June 15, 1941, and removed to the internment camp at Ellis Island. Over the years, Alan felt indebted to Ruth and Sokei-an for much that he had learned from them.

In 1943, during Easter vacation at Grandmother Ruth's house in New York, Alan met Aldous Huxley. Alan had read Huxley's Grey Eminence, *where he had come upon reference to Pseudo-Dionysius the Areopagite and had found the Greek text of Dionysius's* Theologia Mystica *(*Mystical Theology*) in a dusty volume in the seminary library. Alan had taken upon himself the daunting project of translating the text into English (mentioned in his letter of June 26, 1942). He and Huxley became good friends, and it was through Huxley that Alan eventually met other British "mystical expatriates" in California, including Gerald Heard, Felix Greene, and Christopher Isherwood. For Alan's ordination, Huxley gave him the gift of a microfilm of a treasured sixteenth-century book,* Regula Perfectionis *(*Rule of Perfection*), from the British Museum.*

Alan's increasing immersion into Christianity, particularly the more Catholic approach, is seen in his letters leading up to and culminating in his ordination as a priest. His long letter to his parents in October 1943 was an apparent move on his part to justify his choice to become a Christian priest. Was he arguing himself into the choice? I, as an atheist (or agnostic), found all this dialogue (with himself, as it were), almost tedious, where I'm sure others will find it profound. My immediate reaction was, "So what? We are here, so why ask how or why? Live in the moment!" The idea of a supreme entity is not comprehensible to me despite my upbringing. Again, in his letters to Clare Cameron (at the Buddhist Society) regarding her notion of becoming a Christian, he shares with her his total absorption in Christian doctrine. I am assuming that since he was so immersed in his studies at the seminary he had little time to continue his interest in Buddhism, either solely or comparatively, as very little is mentioned on the subject during this time.

Alan was obviously quite enthusiastic about his pending ordination and the prospect of being assigned to a specific parsonage. He was ordained a deacon in May 1943 and was told in April 1944 that on his ordination as a priest, he would be the Episcopal chaplain of Northwestern University and reside in the chaplain's house on the campus.

At the time, it was a relief to both Alan and Eleanor not to have to move from Evanston. The ordination mass, held on May 18, 1944, was a High Mass, with all the ritual that Alan imagined. His uncle, Willie Buchan (brother of his mother), expressed dismay that Alan had "bent his energies to restoring superstitions of the Dark Ages."

EVANSTON, ILLINOIS | SEPTEMBER 28, 1941

Dear Mummy & Daddy,

This is just about the first chance I've had in what seems an age to sit down and write. Not only have we had to move in here and redecorate at the same time, but Eleanor's grandmother died as soon as we were out here, and we had to stay up several nights looking after things. But at last we are more or less settled, and work at the seminary is about to begin.

Our house is just lovely. It seems enormous after an apartment, and now that we are spread over it, I can't imagine how we lived in three rooms. As soon as the curtains are up I will take some pictures and send them to you. Of course, it is a sheer delight for Joan and Jimey, who can at last stretch their legs and take some exercise. After New York City this seems a haven of space, Evanston being much like Chislehurst enlarged with the addition of a university and innumerable churches, being almost the religious center of the Middle West.

As soon as we came out here we made some very good friends among the younger clergy, and I am beginning active work in St. Luke's parish where they are letting me help with the children and also give some lectures at evening services. St. Luke's is a huge organization, but all at "sixes and sevens" because the congregations consist of several factions with rather differing ideas.

The seminary looks as if it will prove most interesting. Bishop McElwain improves and improves upon acquaintance, and although the rest of the faculty is rather stuffy it contains one or two fine scholars. There are two beautiful libraries, and the most amazing assortment of students you could imagine, varying from the thin, ugly, and monkish to the vast, muscular, and bullish. A few seem endowed with imagination, and all promise to be pleasant company. We started with what was for me a thorough reeducation in church chanting, taking Gregorian plainsong instead of the Victorian "Cathedral Psalter," cutting out jiggy rhythms and reverting to the pointing of natural speech. It's a vast improvement. Serious work starts on Tuesday, with courses in Old Testament history and criticism, Christian Origins, Christian Doctrine, and reading from the Greek New Testament.

This ecclesiastical life alters one's whole tempo of living, as we begin the day around the indecent hour of six to set out for various churches or chapels for Holy Communion (or, as my more lofty brethren call it, Mass). The seminary chapel is dull, but the most beautiful place in the neighborhood is a tiny box of a chapel owned by Methodists but used by Episcopalians where there is some of the most gorgeous stained glass you could wish to see. The services here are taken by a most agreeable Anglican monk, who has the job of pastor to some 500 students of the university. It is interesting to note how the more Catholic an Episcopalian becomes, the more he dislikes Rome. Whether it is a case of protesting too much I don't know, but I find their company excellent, their religion sincere, and their knowledge of human nature far more profound than among extreme Protestants. They have the hard job of reviving the practice of an ancient faith and rite which Rome has brought into well-deserved disrepute. But even so, so much of it is on the surface, locked in symbols, and you have to stick to essentials in order not to be lost in a labyrinth of minor details.

Just after we came out here we were treated to an astonishing display of northern lights. I have never seen these before, and this was a particularly unusual type. It seemed to come from directly above us — a mass of rays spreading out from a dim center, shifting in shape and color, and forming now and then into huge masses of light like beings with wings. It lasted so long that we got very stiff necks, but it was worth it.

We have other natural novelties: our garden is visited by tiny green hummingbirds and a common creature is a large butterfly which you know as the milkweed — brown with black stripes. But we shan't see them for long as autumn is coming on fast with falling leaves and cold winds. The heat is already on in the house; boilers terrify me, but this is supposed to be a very good one. We do, thank heaven, have one fireplace — a large open one — in my study, and we shall soon have crackling logs on it.

I think one of your letters will probably have gone astray. For some days the New York post office made a mess of forwarding our mail, and it may be returned to you. So don't think we have vanished into the blue.

From so many points of view it is perfectly wonderful to be here. The clergy make so much better friends than so many of the youth of New York, whom one usually had to throw out at 3 AM in a drunken stupor wherein they sought escape from neurotic tangles. However, it taught one something about life, and made the need to take orders quite evident. Luckily our gentlemen of the cloth are quite human, and you don't have to sit on the edge of your chair and be proper. With such people there is a chance to do work that really matters in this world. Also our two immediate bishops, Conkling and McElwain, are both men of real culture and wisdom, not to mention spirituality, which among bishops is rare, seeing that they are so often chosen for their ability to manage. In a few years this should be a very fine diocese.

Joan is now nearly three. How the time seems to fly, for it won't be long before we shall have to send her to school. She runs up and down the stairs here like nobody's business, and is already up to Eleanor's waist. I have some delightful colored pictures of her playing with other children, and as soon as I can get prints of them (at present they are on slides) I will send them along. Here she can pick up acorns, chase squirrels, and see a few birds, and will be able to have just the life a child needs.

Under a separate cover I am sending you a book about Northwestern University with a bird's-eye view of Evanston so that you can see the kind of surroundings we have.

I have a year of hard work ahead of me and am going to give all my attention to getting the work of the seminary done very thoroughly. I don't expect I shall be able to write another book for a while, but St. Luke's will keep me in practice for public speaking. They are hoping that after Christmas I will give the series of lectures on Christian doctrine which I gave to Fosdick's people in New York. This is a mercy, because I was afraid I should get out of practice or be taught some fearful kind of parsonic diction at the seminary.

My library has had a very welcome addition from a whole lot of books Mrs. E. didn't want, and is now a very imposing array of volumes, and useful ones to boot. She has now moved into her new house, and I think we shall visit her at Christmas. She came out here for her mother's funeral, and was very pleased with our new home. How I wish you could see it too. There is a very good spare room, you know.

We have picked up quite a bargain in the way of cars, and shall probably have it next week. I shall have to learn to drive, for in this part of the world you have to cover such distances that it is quite essential.

I'm afraid I must stop this now, but as soon as I settle into seminary routine I will let you know all about it.

All our love to you both, and please forgive this delay in writing — but times have been hectic and so much of a change needs some getting used to.

Your loving son, Alan

PS. Two letters of yours have just arrived, dated the 1st and 15th. Dear me, I am a terrible slow correspondent! The time flies, and sometimes a month seems like a week. Yes, I remember Floy, and what a chatterbox. What has happened to Auntie Kittie? I haven't heard of her for ages. I thought Peg was going to get work on the propaganda department of the BBC, and am wondering if this is the new war work you speak of. She wrote to us a short time ago.

Your ideas for the stole sound good, especially the idea of using the St. Hugh's designs. I think I will leave it entirely to you. I am having a purple stole made here, for this type is most frequently used. Now as to colors. When the stole is being worn with chasuble or cope and full vestments, it does not show, but should match the rest of the set. If, however, it is worn simply with surplice (as in saying morning and evening offices) it need not match the altar frontal exactly. I prefer the olive green. I shall have a set made out of that yellow Chinese silk we used for curtains at Courtfield Gardens. I have consulted liturgical experts about this, and they say it would be absolutely in order to use this silk as "festal white," for Easter, Christmas, and other great feasts. The uniform width should be 4 inches (for a stole), and only very slightly widened at the ends. Actually, stoles without any widening are more correct.

Well, I must get this finished and put it in the mail on my way to the seminary. Our love to you again, and let me know if the second lot of Joan's pictures have arrived by now. — A.

EVANSTON, ILLINOIS | DECEMBER 7, 1941
Dear Mummy & Daddy,
It's a terrible long time since I've written, but do I have some work to do here! I hope you got Eleanor's letter to fill the gap. The first term will be over in two weeks, and in about eight days we get the final term exams, just like being back at school. I find that my powers of memory have developed quite a bit since I last did this kind of thing, and it's all rather amusing. Next term they give a course in comparative religions, from which I am excused, as the fellow who [gives] it says he doesn't want to be tripped up too often! He's a perfectly delightful person — also the professor of theology — and we have wonderful times with him. Instead, I am going to take some special work in Church history, which hasn't yet been decided.

The work this term has really been very profitable. Old Bp. McElwain has managed to get me really quite interested in the Old Testament, as his courses have been extremely good. We have also made some excellent friends among the students, who are just about the most congenial set of people I've ever had to work with. Some of us felt that while the seminary was providing a lot in the way of scholarship, there was precious little in the way of religion, so we discovered a young monk who is giving us weekly lectures on mystical and ascetic theology, which are very profound and most stimulating. He is one of those rare, genuine, and unaffected people who is a real priest, is perfectly at ease in any kind of company, and really knows how to do his job among the sort of people who don't know a chalice from a cocktail glass.

For Christmas we are sending you a number of odds and ends, including more sugar, a set of colored photographs of our house and other pictures, and one or two small things besides. Conditions being what they are please have patience for their arrival, as we never know how long it takes to get things through. Joan has a note of thanks on the way for Milne; it's just a little old for her yet, but at the rate she's going it won't be long before she will love it. Her drawing is coming on splendidly, and her talking as well — and you've no idea how this can be developed with a toy telephone! She mimics Eleanor giving orders to the grocer, and dissolves us into a weak pulp from laughing.

Eleanor is busy with Christmas cards; we have about 200 to send out this year, which is exactly double last year's lot! I think we told you that we shall be spending Christmas in New York, and one advantage of being a potential parson is that you travel half price on the railways, not to mention getting a 10 percent discount on clothes and suchlike. Well, we have to work for it, and what we are doing at present is a mere picnic to what follows. Our present schedule involves getting up at 6 or 6:30 most mornings for early service, and sometimes the nights are very late. However, the fresh air and the worth-while-ness (excuse that horrible word) of the work make it pretty healthy. Following early service, we have sung Mattins [morning songs], and classes run from 9:15 to 12:45, with Evensong at 5. Sometimes there are classes or choir practice in the afternoon, and evenings consist of study, church "affairs," or deep discussions with the students. You know how men are when they get together.

I still try to get some writing done, and am trying hard to evolve a more simple presentation of things, for which preaching at St. Luke's has been good practice. The best method is to work with stories and parables, and I've had quite some success with a tale about a fish ["The Fish That Found the Sea," published in *Holy Cross* magazine, 1944], which I will send you.

I am trying to find time to write to Toby, so when you see him, please tell him that I haven't altogether forgotten him. Unfortunately, I cannot do much for him now in the way of getting books published as I am away from New York. I think the calendar this year frankly stinks, but don't say I said so. The idea isn't bad, but that particular fool seems to me to lack wisdom because he is trying so very hard to be a fool. Too much of a muchness.

Well, I have now to set about reading several books of the Bible, one volume on theology, one vol. on Church history, not to mention some Greek grammar, and finish it all in a week. This is typical, so please excuse my too-infrequent letter writing. Also there is next Wednesday's "sermon" and 2,500 words on some of the "early fathers of the Church" expected of me.

I hope you will both have all possible peace and happiness for Christmas, and I only wish you could be with us here with Joan and make a wonderful family party. There are two Christmas trees growing at the front door, and we shall have colored lights on them at night. Everyone does this, and Christmas nights in these small towns are an enchanting sight.

All our love to you, Alan

The following letter refers to the fact that on December 7, 1941, Japan bombed the US Navy at Pearl Harbor. During the next few days, the United States declared war on Japan, Germany, and Italy.

EVANSTON, ILLINOIS | DECEMBER 12, 1941

Dear Mummy & Daddy,

This must be a very short note in answer to yours of November 5th, which has just arrived. We would love to have *Punch* again for Christmas, but I always feel it may be a bit expensive for you, and in these times you need everything. But we do love having it, and hardly a number goes astray.

Well, things have certainly blazed up in just the way no one expected, and everyone is so vague and running around in circles so fast that it's impossible to know what is happening and still less why. Even in this stolid Middle West all opposition to taking part in the war has vanished, and plenty of people here are roused to fury. It may take a while to do anything very effective.

Apart from the general uproar there is no news, except that I am working hard for exams, and we are still planning our trip to New York for Christmas. I shall be assisting at the midnight celebration at St. Mary's on Christmas Eve and we are very much looking forward to seeing our friends there again.

Well, here's lots of love to you both, a very happy Christmas and New Year, and all possible blessings.

Your loving son, Alan

EVANSTON, ILLINOIS | JANUARY 14, 1942

Dear Mummy & Daddy,

Your letter of the 27th arrived today, which was a bit quicker than the last, asking about *Punch*, which took a month to get over! Well, we had rather a hectic time in New York, with Mrs. E. very upset about the war with Japan and able to talk about almost nothing but air-raid precautions! Please, have you some leaflet which tells the householder exactly what to do in case of such? If so, please send her a copy. So far as I know the book you sent to New York for Joan has not arrived yet; but *The Pie and Patty-Pan* came, which is just a delight. Perhaps

Mrs. E. has received it by now, but forgotten to forward it; Eleanor is writing to her and will find out.

I was kept pretty busy in New York at the church, where Christmas was an enormous success. The midnight service was packed, and didn't finish until 2 in the morning; and though I had to kneel for half an hour on a stone floor, every minute of it was beautiful. Christmas Eve we had a carol service in the afternoon for the children, to which Joan went, and saw the crèche. Then we met a lot of old friends, and were kept on the run the whole time. Evanston seems very quiet and peaceful after that, and it's really rather a relief to be back here. Tell me, how was the Christmas service at Chislehurst P[arish] Church? Was it much as I remember it when I last saw it? I think in the days of Little Jack Horner, who used, if I remember rightly, to celebrate in the oddity of a cope. Is Hardman still rector? We have some of his books in our library, among them a learned and rather excellent work on ascetic theology.

That copy of *Picture Post* came, but I don't understand — that surely wasn't St. Hugh's Chapel, and yet there was your reredos [decorated screen or wall behind the altar] with all the St. Hugh's fixings. I wish the inside of our chapel here was that beautiful, but it's rather a mess, although the exterior is gorgeous and I have sent you some pictures of it.

This Christmas everyone went clerical on me, and I got a very lovely traveling pyx [box for carrying the consecrated Host] from Eleanor and a surplice from Mrs. E.; plus an altar-size copy of the new *American Missal* for my birthday. This is a new prayer book being published by a liturgical society in our church, as the old one had almost 2,000 misprints.

The work here is getting more and more interesting as the time goes on, and not the least valuable part of it is the people you meet. It has opened up an entirely new world to me in which I am just a beginner, and it's rather like being born again. But the old school training which you gave me is suddenly proving almost alarmingly useful, so that I got honours on every course last term, scoring 99.5 percent in one paper on the Old Testament. Greek is gradually coming back to me, but we don't seem to have any need for Latin. Yet although the seminary is called a graduate school its standards seem rather low, and you can get away in everything but theology with little more than a good memory. They are still thinking in pioneer terms, of preparing men to go out and bang Bibles in the back woods among lumberjacks and hillbillies. They don't seem to see that the menace to everything sacred is from the intellectuals, the universities, the clever-clevers, both here and abroad, who have no religion at all. The backwoodsmen may be Fifth Day Adventists or Pentecostal Brethren, but that *is* a religion of some sort. Whereas over here middle-class Presbyterianism or Methodism isn't a religion at all; it's a means of purveying moral platitudes, uplift, and social ideals, with the result that people who want some real religion go either half-crazy or to Rome. We have a big job in providing a third alternative.

This afternoon our musical instructress made a record of my speaking voice, which was the first time I ever heard me, and was I surprised! I don't seem to have suffered much from the Middle-Western accent, if at all, but I talk much deeper than I ever imagined. She is going to make a singing one soon, and I hope I don't get a nasty shock.

And now, preserving the most exciting news to the end (take a deep breath), towards the end of August you will be twice grandparents, as Eleanor will produce another sublime little nuisance. We are praying for a boy this time, for a Laurence Wilson Watts II, as a counterbalance to little "Doey" (of all the awful names to have given herself), which is badly needed. We have all Joan's layette, so the production line is ready for the baby to go right through. One of our tame priests has a girl who is a nurse in the maternity ward of the Evanston Hospital, and she has found us a doctor. It's rather hard to have to have it during the hot summer, but we tried, without success, to arrange it for the spring.

Poor Eleanor gave her ankle a slight sprain the other day and I've been helping her take the adhesive tape off her leg most of the evening. Now we both stick to everything and are completely exhausted; the bathroom is positively clammy, the tape has come off but most of the glue is still on. She has gone to bed, so I must go up now and keep her company and also put some more work in on my reading.

The last few days we've had a cold spell, down to 20 below zero! Everything froze in all directions, and now it's as balmy as spring; what a climate! I bought myself a black sealskin cap and look like something between a lama and a Cossack, but otherwise your ears drop off.

Lots of love to you both, and I hope you receive all our Christmas odds and ends intact.

Your loving son, Alan

EVANSTON, ILLINOIS | MARCH 13, 1942
Dear Mummy & Daddy,
We have just finished the rush of term-end examinations, and breathe freely again! We have the queerest system of terms; the next one begins on the 17th and breaks off in the middle for a ten-day recess at Easter, and then continues until June 3rd. After that everything shuts down until the beginning of October! Which is really a vast waste of time, but here the summer is so hot that almost

everything closes down. Still, I don't understand how that can be managed in wartime.

Your two letters of February 10th have arrived, and we were delighted to have them, and especially to hear that there is news of Leslie, which must have been an absolute godsend to Uncle Douglas. Mrs. E. has received your ARP [air-raid preparedness] booklet, but the needlework book has not arrived. That little animal you sent Joan was adorable; where on earth did you find such a creature?

We are all very pleased to hear that Temple has been made Archbishop of Canterbury. His "Malvern Declaration" is one of the few really sensible pieces of social thinking that has been put out for years. I wonder when he will be enthroned; he will certainly be an improvement after that stuffed shirt with a golden voice!

I had a very interesting time the other day visiting the priest of the local Greek Orthodox Church, who is an extremely charming person. We had a long talk and he showed me over his church, which is principally for the fairly large Greek population of North Chicago. Their churches are quite different from either our own or the Roman; they just glow with gold and those stylized Byzantine paintings on windows and walls, for they use the color gold as a symbol of God and their churches are supposed to represent the transfigured world where all things are seen as contained in God. Their liturgy is again quite different from ours, although nearer to the American and Scotch than the English, but it is exceedingly beautiful. He rejoices in the name of Athenagoras Theodoritos Kokkinakas, and we share a common interest in modern psychology and the psychology of religion — so he has asked me to write for his magazine.

Spring is just beginning to show itself around here. The robins (so-called, they are red-breasted thrushes), have returned from the south and birds are beginning to sing early in the morning. Sometimes I get up just about sunrise and walk over to the early service at the seminary or the little chapel of the university, and the sun coming up over the lake is a sight for the gods. You can just see the lake as you walk along, showing between groups of trees, and as it comes up everything starts moving — squirrels, birds, everything but people, who don't get up until a bit later. Yesterday afternoon there was the weirdest bird-like cawing and chattering out in a tree at the back, only it turned out to be an angry squirrel, scolding away like fury and cracking a nut. I have strung up a coconut to see if tits can be attracted, but perhaps it's a bit early at the moment.

Eleanor has been busy this week — down to the church every day and ironing albs and surplices, knitting for Red Cross and so on. Luckily there won't be much to do in that way for the new baby as we still have all Joan's layette. The other Sunday we went out to Wheaton where the American Theosophical Society have their headquarters, and I gave them a lecture on mysticism which they loved and didn't really understand, because they might not have loved it so much if they had! They have a gorgeous and magnificent estate there and eat the foulest vegetarian food ever perpetrated. Even a substitute for gelatin has been found, to ward off the contaminating "vibrations" of animal bones. It melts on sight.

I can't quite remember which picture of Joan is the one you like so much. I seem to remember sending two recently — one with curly hair and one standing by a drinking fountain. Her hair is pale gold, blonde but not platinum. The colored pictures give you a fairly good idea. Both those pictures were taken last August or September, so she would be just turning three. Yes, *Punch* is coming through regularly, and we always enjoy it. In the copy of this letter I am enclosing a picture from the *New Yorker* (our equivalent of *Punch*), which seems to remind me of something!

Joan is now busy with her toy telephone — calling up the grocers with long orders and calling her various friends, babies down the street, the local clergy, and a legendary Mr. Bomfish, who I invented. She has made friends with a sweet child from Texas living a few doors down, but unfortunately they had to leave, though another family has moved in with a child Joan's age; they are recently from South America.

We are arranging for Jean to come here for a weekend from Grand Rapids sometime in April. More pictures of Joan soon.

I don't think I should run to another page because of airmail. Lots of love and a happy April 15th to Mummy.

Your loving son, Alan

EVANSTON, ILLINOIS | MAY 4, 1942
Dear Mummy & Daddy,
The book on needlework has arrived safely, and we are very glad to have it as it looks very comprehensive and has just the things that Eleanor wants to know. To get acquainted with all these things she is working on the church altar guild, which keeps her busy.

The weekend before last we had Jean over from Grand Rapids to stay with us. She is very grown-up now and is perfectly delightful. A party of seminarians came over on Saturday evening and were much charmed by the lady! We drove out to Hinsdale with her and introduced her to some of Eleanor's friends there, and spent the rest of the time chatting about our respective relatives and everything else under the sun. I don't suppose it will be long before she gets married; there are, I gather, a few suitors on her track and she does her best to pretend that they don't mean much to her — though that doesn't fool anyone! It's really rather cute (sorry, but there's no English word that quite puts it). I took some pictures of her with Joan, which I will send when they are ready. Mummy, we all think that, save for the chin, she looks like a young edition of you. She is getting on very well with her work, and there is a possibility that she may get a teaching job at the University of Minnesota. While in Chicago she introduced us to an old friend, Mrs. Doremus, who knows E.G.B.

My work here is making it almost impossible for me to do anything more with the Wisdom of the East series. The difficulty is that I'm out of touch with publishing activities, which are all centered in New York. I am therefore negotiating to sell out, probably for about £50, which will be paid over to you as no money can be sent out of England. I can't tell yet when this will happen, but you will be kept informed.

This being away from New York is also rather a disadvantage for my writing work, but on the other hand it is perhaps just as well that I practice some more before publishing anything else. The terminology of Christianity is not too easy to handle because in comparison with Zen it is extraordinarily complicated. It has so many more doctrines, symbols, and practices that you have to say three things for what could formerly be said with one. But this is always the difficulty with a religion that dramatizes and symbolizes so much. The meaning of drama and symbol has to be brought out, because I find more and more that in practice the ordinary run of Church teaching just isn't cutting any ice — and I mean ice, for on the whole it leaves the average congregation absolutely cold. Yet they still come to church, and sit like lumps on logs, from force of habit and because few have ever known what it is to be really warm. Both clergy and people feel they ought to be getting something out of it, and because they will not admit frankly that they are not they go around whipping the dead horse like mad. The result is inward frustration, a gnawing, dimly conscious sense of futility, and some bad dispositions. The only people who are really moved are the Bible-banging revivalists on the one hand, and the extreme Anglo-Catholics on the other — and a good deal of that is emotional stuff without lasting effect. Well, somehow I've got to break that ice without breaking anyone's bones; it's a nice tough job — something you can really get your teeth into!

We have just found some perfectly exquisite recordings of a boys' choir singing Gregorian chants. I have heard the temple and King's College and Chapel Royal, but this is absolute perfection. I have never heard anything like it in my life. It is the choir of the RC College of the Sacred Heart in New York, and what puzzles me is how mere kids can sing with such restraint and depth of feeling and perfect maturity. I played them to the seminary organist and he immediately bought a set for himself, and is going to play them to us all this afternoon as we are going to sing the same music for an ordination service on Ascension Day. He is one of the students — a perfect genius with the organ and a grand choirmaster. The official choir mistress is hopeless, but one afternoon with him makes up for all the mess she makes in a year.

A short time ago the Rev. Professor of Greek came with us both on a trip to Chinatown, as he has some Chinese friends at his church. The church secretary is a Chinese girl, and she joined the party, to which was later added her father and mother. The father is quite a big noise in the Chinese community, so we got around that night, ending up at a huge party for China War Relief where all the Chinese and their wives and children were present, all as happy as larks and as pleasant as could be. The Chinese gamble as readily as the English drink tea, and the proceeds that night must have amounted to something. They had policemen there in uniform to guard the money, which covered the tables in piles. Even the little brats had their own table, but the whole atmosphere was as unlike the usual gambling outfit as anything could be. It was just a happy family gathering, with that delicious Oriental happiness — expansive and unself-conscious. After three glasses of wine the Rev. Professor began to recite Greek and Latin poetry. He is a priceless person, as ugly as a mug, cross-eyed, piebald, short, and fat, but as sweet and kindly as anything.

His trouble is a rather shrewish wife from whom I am sure he will welcome a vacation! To get HER would be a task worthy of St. Francis Xavier and Assisi rolled into one. Militant Methodist, from which breed good Lord deliver us.

Talking of "Good Lord deliver us," the organist and I have composed a new setting for the litany, based on a Russian chant, which really brightens up the usual dreariness of that office. We picked up the idea down at the Russian Cathedral, where we had a meeting the other Sunday at which I was speaker. It was followed by Russian Vespers, with the barbaric splendour typical of our Orthodox brethren. I sat next to their bishop at dinner, but I think my talk was a little too revolutionary for the stuffy conservatism which afflicts the Orthodox Church in these parts. However, he is a wonderful old soul just glowing with saintliness.

Mummy's letter has just come, saying, among other things, that Daddy is getting more and more like the Pater. Now, to finish the job off and to keep all three generations in accord, how about growing a nice little "Imperial" or goatee??? It would be highly distinguished — and the small kind don't look too disreputable in process of growing.

I am very glad E.G.B. is looking in this direction again. We shall love to see her and of course would like to have her to stay with us for a while on her way to or from Minneapolis. If she sails to Quebec she could come via Detroit to Chicago. It was news to us that Malcolm had gone into partnership with WPB. Or she could go out via Winnipeg and back our way, sailing from New York.

I have got to run out now, take Joan to school, and mail this letter.

A very happy Christmas to you both and a specially good New Year — including a trip to this side of the water.

Love from us all, Alan

Evanston, Illinois | June 26, 1942
Dear Mummy & Daddy,
Oh my, how the time flies! It is now almost a month since the term ended and I've hardly noticed it, as I seem to be harder at work now than when the term was on. I am tackling a job which I never thought I would be able to do — translating from the Greek one of the more interesting early Fathers of the Church [Dionysius]. All translations of his works are out of print, and I thought I would have a shot at one of them as he is most important for the history of mysticism.

We are having the most disgusting summer weather; for almost a month every day has been cloudy and chilly, whereas less than a hundred miles on either side of us it is blazing. As a result we haven't had anything in the way of swimming; the only day we went down the water was much too cold, although we have a perfectly lovely beach almost at our door. But there are compensations: a bush of red roses in our garden produced such a crop of blooms that it was just weighed down with them, and though we have cut lots for the house it is still going strong.

Mrs. E. is very disconsolate as there is trouble about her Zen master [Sokei-an Sasaki], who apparently is being confined as an enemy alien. It will be an awful blow to her, as her life was completely absorbed in working on translations of Chinese Buddhist texts with him, and now she will be at rather a loose end.

Next Sunday I have to go out and take the morning service at a mission church not far from here, which will be a maiden voyage of this kind. I have no idea what sort of a place it will be, so will have to go in an adaptable frame of mind, as a short sermon is also required! A letter has just come from Toby, who says he recently had lunch with Bishop Conkling's brother-in-law, who is Warden of St. Columba's College in Dublin. I see he hasn't moved into his new house yet, though he writes most enthusiastically of it.

Eleanor is getting along splendidly and the doctor is very pleased with her. We have gotten rid of our maid as finances are rather reduced with taxes, buying war bonds, and trying to help get churches out of debt. But Eleanor is most relieved to have the house to ourselves, and the work involved seems surprisingly small. However, we shall get someone in just before and after she has the baby.

Joan is learning to draw surprisingly well. A short time ago we gave her a set of colored crayons, and she is concentrating on faces, some of which I am sending with the copy of this letter. I'm afraid my pictures of Jean haven't turned out very well; there was a fault in the film I used, but if I can possibly manage to get some sort of decent print from it I will send it along. Another set of pictures taken at the end-of-term celebrations at the seminary is still awaiting development.

Arrangements in regard to the Wisdom of the East series are still unsettled. I have retracted my original notion to withdraw from it as when the war is over something can be done with it here, so I have suggested putting my share of the profits back into the business for a period.

In fairness to Cranmer-Byng, who has done all the work recently, I think this is the only right thing to do. I might have sold out if he had some other partner in mind, but he has not, so I am holding on. If I can possibly make up the income to you, I will do so; to some extent this will depend on the sale of recent writings in this country, or, alternatively, of their publication in England. To date I have completed a short book called *The Way of Acceptance: An Introduction to Creative Mysticism* and in a few weeks my translation of St. Dionysius's *Mystical Theology* [*Theologia Mystica of St. Dionysius*, Holy Cross Press, 1944] will be ready. Here you might help me. In regard to the latter, Watkins are very interested in this type of book and I wonder if you could get either Nigel or the old man on the phone and ask if it would be worthwhile to send a copy of the MS to them. The book will consist of a translation of the text together with a longish introduction by myself. At the same time, could you ask him to send, and bill me for, two books: (1) *The Cloud of Unknowing*, etc., edited by Dom Justin McCann, London, 1924, in a series called The Orchard Books. I already have Underhill's edition of this work, which Watkins publish. (2) *The Divine Names & Mystical Theology of Dionysius*, trans. by C. E. Rolt, London, 1920. I believe both are out of print.

Pictures of Temple's enthronement have finally come out over here, and what an improvement on the last effort! He really looks like an archbish.

Nothing much is doing at present as most people are away, the seminary is more or less closed and all is quiet. However, we have had sundry of the Rev. Professors to dinner and they us, which has all been very pleasant. Now I must get this off to the mail, enclosing pictures — the one of Joan is with the little girl next door and a boy from across the street.

Lots of love from us all — Alan

EVANSTON, ILLINOIS │ JULY 23, 1942

Dear Mummy & Daddy,

I have been meaning to write to you for two weeks, but the heat has been simply terrific and all energy vanishes; paper becomes clammy to touch, and one is fit for nothing but cold water. Now it is somewhat cooler, so I can catch up with arrears of letter writing and work.

I am terribly sorry, I completely forgot Daddy's birthday, which is what comes of getting too absorbed in Greek and things. But I have sent off a volume containing the complete works of Thoreau — a contemporary of Emerson whom I don't think you have ever read and whom I am certain you will enjoy immensely. He is one of the greatest nature writers that ever wrote, and his *Walden* in particular is a most delightful book when you get fed up with the world of men. Modern America has almost nothing like him. Like Emerson, he was a lover of Vedanta and Taoism, and the influence of the latter is quite obvious in his work. It is a book you can begin anywhere and read in short spells.

There has been some vagueness hovering around the Wisdom of the East business; Toby wrote a somewhat nebulous letter from which I gathered that he would buy me out just after Cranmer-Byng had written that he would be an unacceptable editor because [he is] an axe-grinder for Buddhism. However, I sent an authority for you to sell to him just in case C-B had accepted him, and now a second letter from Toby tells me I guessed right! He must have cast spells on C-B, and I am glad he has done so because I didn't want anyone else to have it. He will arrange the terms with you, and I have put the whole matter in his hands, as I trust him to be fair.

Joan is having a wonderful time these days. She just loves the water and insists we take her to the beach every day, and during the hot weather the lake has certainly been wonderful. I am as brown as wrapping paper. Very often we go swimming in charge of all the children in the surrounding houses and Eleanor looks like the mother of all creation! They are a fine lot of kids and splendid companions for Joan. Just now they are all having a grand time in our spare garage where I have made them a playhouse, building a bench and a table out of packing cases, painting pictures on the walls, and making a pair of short stepladders so that they can go in and out by a window. Five of them are out there now — just as busy as can be, sweeping and tidying and playing at being a family, with the older girls the mothers and the little girls the children. It is a great thrill for them as heretofore they have mostly played in the street; apparently the modern parent is too busy with bridge and golf and country clubs to pay much attention to their children, and as a result the poor parents get stuffy and over-adult and can't ever let their hair down. Some of the kids are very interesting; there are two sisters of 10 and 7 who have recently come from Switzerland, the father being a Swiss doctor and the mother an Englishwoman with the strangest mixture of an English and Swiss accent. The younger sister doesn't speak English properly yet and has to be helped out with French; she is a delightful child and is in and out of the house at all hours. It is interesting to see how children of such different ages get along together; there is one other Joan's age, and the rest are between 7 and 10, and though I may be mistaken they all seem older than English children. Next door there is a girl of 12 who looks about 16; they seem to miss the "gawky" stage completely, jumping from childhood to young womanhood overnight, though the boys develop more slowly.

Eleanor expects the new baby in about four weeks, and when it comes I will send you a wire. If it's a boy it will be Laurence Wilson and if a girl, Ann. Female names are a problem, for some strange reason, and of all possibles Eleanor and I can only agree on about two that we like! I wish you could see Joan now; she is a beautiful little thing, with the most astonishing poise. Her back is as straight as a larch, and she has the sweetest little white swimsuit with a skirt which shows her off better than anything; I will get you a picture in this outfit, but the trouble is that you can't convey the quality of movement, where so much of the beauty lies.

I am still working on *Dionysius*, and the more I study it the more I realize its importance, for here is a traditional link between Christianity and Oriental mysticism, and what is more, the Catholic Church accords him all the respect due to an ancient apostolic father. For me this is a very useful discovery for here are approved grounds for a mystical technique which is blessedly free from the sanctimonious sentimentality and emotional stuff generally handed out.

All the babes are now having lunch in their house — what a riot! They suddenly decided on a picnic and rushed home to get sandwiches. Then there will be a clamor to go swimming, and it's becoming quite a puzzle as to when I am going to get some work done, though Eleanor insists that I relax more and itch less to be getting things done!

Well, this is all the news for the time being; let me know if your book doesn't arrive in about six weeks at the most. Parcels take a long time. All our love to you both, to which Joan adds one of her special wet kisses and stranglehold hugs!

With love, Alan

EVANSTON, ILLINOIS | AUGUST 20, 1942
Dear Mummy & Daddy,
Well, as you can imagine, I've been very much on the go since August 2nd as everything happened so early that all our domestic arrangements misfired and

I had to supervise the house and number-one babe (who is a handful). We had a terrific thunderstorm in the small hours of the 2nd and probably this started Eleanor off, just the same way as before. Nothing much happened, however, until five in the afternoon when she walked over to the hospital and had the baby at 6:24, with less than 1½ hours' labor. Immediately afterwards she was bright and cheerful, demanding a meal, and has continued to bounce along ever since. The baby weighed 5 lb. 10 oz. and was 19½ inches long, has a perfectly round head, nice flat ears, and blue eyes, and has rather more of a nose than Joan had. We shall call her Ann, and she will be christened by Bishop Conkling in a few weeks. She was three weeks earlier than expected, and to keep things running at home I finally stole a maid from the seminary who is just a treasure (a colored woman again) and a superb cook. I'm sorry it wasn't a boy, but two girls are really much easier to look after.

Joan is absolutely thrilled. As soon as we brought the baby home she presented her with her best doll, and it was a little while before we could tactfully persuade her that it wasn't quite wise to place odds and ends of toys in the crib at all hours. When Jimey realized what had happened he gave Eleanor a dirty look and walked off under a table. "Another of those nuisances!" Joan used to telephone her mother at the hospital every day (she is quite expert on the phone now), asking if baby sister was there, and whether she could talk to her.

Lady Bateman has given Ann the most exquisite little dress trimmed with Irish lace. It was in a shop in town here, and Eleanor had seen it in the window several times and set longing eyes upon it. It arrived at the hospital quite unsought, which was a surprise, like everything connected with this strange being who is the mother of coincidences. Lady B. is quite something; she has recovered her memory astonishingly since I first met her and is vastly saner, which I can only attribute to the way she has been training herself in formal Western philosophy, learning to concentrate and follow a logical line of thought. I had lunch with her yesterday, and she showed me photographs of her place in Herefordshire, Shobdon Court, which is a truly colossal and amazing establishment — one of those 18th-century palaces with walls and towers and cauliflowers, ironwork gates and vast urns on top of columns, formal gardens and huge cedars. She was born in America, and, to judge from early portraits in Empire dresses, was a raving beauty. She married Lord Bateman of Shobdon, now dead; he was a Hanbury and fabulously wealthy, and she owns book and art collections that would make you gasp. The best of it is now in a warehouse in Paris, and she has ceased to care about it, finding so many possessions an intolerable responsibility. Although staying, pro tem, in a small house in Evanston she is the last word in refinement (which is a little trying), and has us to lunch there almost every week, keeping me busy for the rest of the afternoon in philosophic discourse, at which she is becoming quite adept. Nominally a Roman Catholic she is temperamentally almost anything else, which is quite amusing. Formerly, a convert of that astute English Jesuit, Fr. Martindale of Farm Street.

Think of it, we had a blackout here the other night, just for practice, as they are afraid that since Chicago is the same distance from Norway as New York we might get trouble. Am to be a fire-watcher or something. But to try and find a shelter in our house is almost impossible because it's one solid window, and the only possible places are near the boiler, which isn't exactly ideal. The possible objective around here is Gary, where there are huge steel mills, though that's almost 30 miles away across the lake. But this over-the-top-of-the-world geography gets you all mixed up in your distances, for one is apt to forget that the world is round and that "Mercator's Projection" is a terrific distortion.

We have gotten to know our Swiss neighbors quite well, and oddly enough he is a psychiatrist and we have some friends in common; he knows Jung quite well and several others. They are most charming people and a lot of fun to talk to in a town where real culture is a trifle skin-deep, Northwestern being a monument of what a university should not be. But Chicago Univ. is really good, modeled on Oxford lines by President R. M. Hutchins, who has picked up its standards tremendously, so much so that it will soon be as good, if not better, than Harvard and Yale.

I hope you will get Thoreau safely, and be sure to let me know if it doesn't come by the end of August. Now I must to work, for I have soon got to start my engine ticking over for next term's work. I wish I could get these preliminaries done with and start doing something really constructive. However, I am preparing some future work on quite a large scale, and for this a good deal of quiet consideration and preparation is necessary.

Our love to you all, twice grandparents, and since Eleanor is agitating (mildly) for another, you never know what you will end up as!

As ever, Alan

EVANSTON, ILLINOIS | OCTOBER 4, 1942

Dear Mummy & Daddy,

This letter is terribly late, for the last few weeks have been choked up with getting ready for the term's work, which has just begun. I have been slaving at my Greek and for the first time ever did quite successfully at an examination in the stuff, with which the term's work began. We have a much heavier schedule this year and I have a mountain of reading to do. The new class of men looks fairly promising; one of them in particular appeals to me, having a considerable knowledge of Oriental religions and an interest in mysticism — so at last I have someone to chew the rag with. He comes from Harvard Divinity School and unfortunately will only be with us for a year.

Little Ann was, successfully and quietly, baptized by Bishop Conkling; she didn't make a murmur. The godmothers were two of Eleanor's old friends from Hinsdale, and the godfather was Fr. Flagg, the university chaplain. Bishop Conkling came to our house afterwards and a good time was had by all. She refrained from yelling until the bishop had gone, which was really most tactful. The child is now putting on weight rapidly and has hair like peach fuzz on top of a perfect sphere of a head. I really will let you have some pictures soon, but in the dull and rather chilly weather we are having at present photography is a little difficult. The day of her baptism it was pouring wet.

I have been putting in a lot of time with one of our professors who instructs in Greek and Hebrew and has a special interest in the Eastern Church, which I am studying on and off. We visited together the Ukrainian Church in Chicago the other day, which is quite the most gorgeous thing of its kind I have ever seen. It is built on the lines of the great St. Sophia Church in Constantinople — a blaze of gold mosaic, icons, interlacing patterns edging the arches, with a vast dome towering over all. The altar is set in a huge apse, a half-dome, entirely gold with a figure of the Virgin in the upper center, beneath which is a panorama of the last supper. The altar itself is a vast square of white marble with six giant candlesticks across the center, and from the back of the church makes the most impressive silhouette against the shining apse. He and I are now getting ready to celebrate one of the Eastern liturgies in the seminary chapel, for which we shall use the Anglican formulary for the Church in India, which is one of the most beautiful services in the world. He will be celebrant, and I shall be lector — the person who leads all the responses and is master of ceremonies. We are allowed to have unusual services from time to time for the benefit of the class in liturgics and the history of worship. Furthermore it will be as well to give our own High Church or Catholic party an occasional push towards the East instead of Rome because a union with the East is very possible before long, at least in America, and theirs is a much more sensible religion.

Some of the students have asked me to give them an informal course of lectures on Christian mysticism this year; whether this is a momentary flash of enthusiasm or not remains to be seen, but at least it is a straw in the wind.

Joan's godmother has given her the sweetest little silver brooch specially made for her; it is a figure of Jimey cut out of a flat piece of silver by some jeweler in Philadelphia. To say thank you Eleanor got Joan at the typewriter and managed to dictate, letter by letter, a short note, which came out quite well. This is a marvellous way of learning letters, and I will get her to write one to you one of these days. Just think of it — Joan will be going to school next year!

I am now a full-fledged driver, having passed the state test. Yesterday I drove all the way out to Hinsdale, which is over 30 miles, but gasoline rationing will soon cramp my style until I am ordained or otherwise put in charge of a church — which won't be long at the present speed. The clergy have special gasoline and tyre privileges, and you need them around here because everything is so far apart.

All the trees are turning now, and the woods are a sight for the gods. We have a lot of maples around, and they give you a blaze of red and gold. And talking of such matters, I am so glad you like Thoreau. I have only read his *Walden*, and if, as you go through it, you come across a passage about some mysterious folk who dwell in trees and have a lichen as their emblem, please give me the reference. I read this as a quotation in some other book, and have always wanted to track it down.

As to the Wisdom of the East business, I have put the entire matter in the hands of Sir John Murray, and you will doubtless hear from him in due course. I have given him an authority to sell to C-B if he thinks wise, but have pointed out that the proposed arrangement is utterly unsound. However, he is the publisher and stands the financial burden, so if he wants a mess he can have it! I don't know yet who will publish my *Dionysius*, but Harper has asked to see it.

Well, to work! Love to you both from all four of us, and to make up for this long silence I will write again very soon — with some pictures.

Your loving son, Alan

PS. Jean was with us here a while ago — did I tell you about this? I get rather hazy as to when I last wrote, not having kept a copy.

EVANSTON, ILLINOIS | NOVEMBER 1, 1942

Dear Mummy & Daddy,

Your last two letters have arrived — Daddy's considerably earlier, though seminary work kept me from answering it right away. (They are giving us more of it than usual this year.) Please keep and use all royalties paid to you for whatever you want. That £10 must have been a pleasant surprise, and don't hesitate to use it for current expenses. As to the Wisdom of the East business, I see it has been a first-class mess. I wish you would get in touch with Sir John Murray and find out what he has finally decided to do about it; I think I told you that I put the final settlement of the matter entirely in his hands, he, as publisher, being the one who stands the financial burden. He has authority to let C-B have my share if he thinks fit, so that I won't be responsible if a total incompetent takes my place! C-B apparently gave him the impression that everything was settled, but I wrote to him a second time and was very emphatic that he should have the last word. Toby should take a lesson or two in tact and diplomacy, for he has muffed a good thing. Sir John seemed to think that £25 was a fair settlement, and I took his advice because it is very important that I should have good relations with Murrays.

Mrs. Everett is coming out here at the end of this week, and will stay for three weeks, being here for Joan's birthday. Yesterday afternoon she went to her first party, the birthday of a little boy across the street, and as it was Allhalloween they had a riotous time. On this occasion the children dress up, and after dark run from house to house ringing for sweets; if you don't give them something they howl and hoot and put soap on the windows! We got the customary pumpkin, cut a diabolical face on it, put an electric light inside, and set it in the window. I also constructed a hideous white vampire bat and suspended it from a thread running from an upstairs window to a tree; it was made so that when you pulled the thread the wings flapped, and the kids had a lot of fun out of it. Joan will have a party on the 14th, and I think that Bishop Conkling's two children will be there among others.

I have now passed through the second stage towards ordination, being admitted as a candidate; at first you are a postulant. I had to go before the Standing Committee of the Diocese, and they asked me all about Canterbury and my work with the H[ospital] S[unday] F[und]. One of the men asked after Sir Sydney Nicholson of Chislehurst; is he still alive? I shall take the exams for the diaconate in the spring, but I don't suppose I shall be made a deacon until the winter or the spring of 1944. Ordination to the priesthood is usually six months later.

This term I am concentrating on doctrinal studies, and among other things have been working on the problem of relating the Vedantist theory of nonduality to the Christian doctrine of God. The results promise to be quite interesting, and two members of the seminary faculty are interesting themselves in it. The Indian method of logic seems to offer a way of eliminating the difficult element of dualism which the doctrine of God seems to involve, while at the same time steering clear of pantheism.

Doctrine is an intensely fascinating subject, especially when you read the great Christian philosophers like Thomas Aquinas and such moderns as Temple, Berdyaev, von Hügel, and Gilson. This work has brought before me very clearly and persuasively the inadequacy of certain aspects of the Hindu and Buddhist conceptions, especially the emphasis upon Reality as a law or principle which inevitably makes of Reality a mechanism instead of a living spirit. The idea that God is personal is a rather clumsy way of saying that God is immeasurably alive.

The ultimate reality of a universe which has produced man must, it is argued, be more than man; a mere law or principle is less, so that we should think of God as one who is at least a person — a being who is the maximum of consciousness, life, and intelligence. Once this is admitted, many other doctrines become clear. The Incarnation of God in Christ, for instance, becomes the historical symbol of the marriage of God and the world. God is perfectly united with man, yet in such a way that man is still man and God still God — a seeming dualism which can only be resolved by the Oriental nonduality concept, for which a thing is most perfectly united to God by the very fact of being itself and not God. For if God were unable to create and manifest what is other than himself, he would not be absolutely free; he would exclude otherness and difference, and so be dual. The same idea is expressed in the Holy Communion, which perpetuates the Incarnation, the wedding of God and the world. The bread and wine [are] bread and wine (representing our own body and blood) and yet [they] become the body and blood of Christ without, on the other hand, ceasing to be bread and wine. One has to let oneself be rather primitive and childlike to grasp this symbol, to be in a position to appreciate a mystery. I think all our Protestantism and modern philosophy is too intellectual; in taking away the miraculous and the wonderful it leads us to forget the essential mystery of life and religion.

But Catholic worship seems to me to remind us of the mystery, and to help the mind to center itself in God. Thus the center of the service is not the preacher but the altar, upon which is not a *mere* symbol or sign but an utterly incomprehensible mystery — the union of the infinite God with the very finite world. I find that in churches where this attitude exists you cease to be conscious of all the stuffiness of "Sunday-best clothes" and of human pomposity; you can relax and get rid of physical and spiritual rigidity. The three ministers at the altar and their servers are like participants in a sacred dance (emphasized by their genuflections and other ritual movements) — a dance which absorbs us in the melody rather than ourselves; it reminds one of the great cosmic dance of the stars and all nature which, as Dante says, is moved by love. Once you become accustomed to it this ritual ceases to fidget and distract you, and becomes a new language just like speech, music, or painting. You forget the technical details and speak it naturally, and it becomes the perfect language of worship.

I tell you this because it will give you some idea of the why and wherefore of what we are doing out here, and why we may seem to you to be so terribly "High Church." It is not that we want to traffic in superstition and popery, but to restore to our churches the sense of worship and mystery, and above all of beauty so that the people are cleansed of that involuntary and subconscious impression of God as a pompous cosmic patriarch. Obviously this method has dangers which it does not always avoid. The Mass and the cult of the Virgin can easily degenerate into superstition, unless it can be made understood that the one shows the mystery of the union of God and the world, and the other the reflection of the feminine prototype in God which is neglected in our purely male symbols of the Father and the Son. If these things are taught in merely abstract and philosophical terms, thousands of people will never be able to understand them; and even if they grasp no more than the symbols, it helps to bring an element of grace, beauty, and wonder into a world made crazy by too much logic, mechanism, and intellectualism. The human soul craves mystery, and if it does not get the sacred mysteries of the Church it goes to the diabolical mystagogy of Nazism and State-worship. But we need, what the RC [Roman Catholic] Church doesn't provide, an esoteric understanding over and above the exoteric — and that can only flourish in the greater freedom of Anglicanism and Eastern Orthodoxy. Roman Catholicism is strangled in its terrible legalism.

Children adore this kind of thing (because of a certain amount of natural wisdom), and every Sunday I sit among them and explain and teach them how to participate in the Mass, and a better-behaved crowd of brats I have never seen. Some people think it's too much over their heads, but after all we don't really understand everything ourselves — so why pretend we do? But what, of course, so many of our Anglo-Catholics do not see is that so much symbolism and ritual has to go hand-in-hand with something like Zen — lest the living spirit should be strangled in formalism. Oddly enough, Zen itself, with the exception of Lamaism and Shingon, is the most ritualistic form of Buddhism when it comes to worship. But on the mystical side it wipes out imagery, for without such a radical cleansing of the mind doctrine, dogma, and ritual cannot be used really freely; they enslave, for it is like trying to draw a picture on a sheet of newspaper instead of a clean white page.

Yesterday we had two sergeants in the radio division of the Army Air Corps to dinner. They were introduced to us a while ago by a friend at the seminary, and they have been out here several times. One is going into the priesthood when the war is over — a Harvard graduate who will probably go a long way in the army. They are perfectly delightful company, and their account of what is being done in their branch of the service is really quite encouraging. On the other hand, what they say of the general effect of the war and military life upon men's minds makes one realize what a tremendous problem the aftermath will bring in the way of social service. If our Church is going to be in any way fit to handle it there will have to be some quick changes made, most important of which is disentanglement from our subjection to certain apathetic and wealthy churches like country clubs, no tramps or mere working people allowed. This fear for the Church's respectability is behind the move to join up with the Presbyterians in this country, who are, on the whole, even stuffier. Doctrinally we have much more in common with Methodists, Lutherans, and Orthodox — but only personae non gratae go to these churches! Fortunately the new Archbishop of Canterbury gives a different kind of leadership, and he is making certain circles here very uncomfortable.

Little Ann gets longer and bulgier, and has now added cereal to her diet. I will get some pictures of her to you by Christmas, but I don't take so many pictures now as prices are going up and it's a bit expensive. Taxes, too, have made a sharp rise and we are economizing all round. At the moment the dear baby is making a rare fuss about taking her cereal, and strangled cries come from upstairs! Meanwhile Eleanor lays down the law with a heavy hand. We have masses of squirrels around, and now that the leaves have fallen it's fascinating to watch them run from tree to tree and do a tightrope walk along the telephone cables. They are quite tame, and, believe it or not, there is a coal-black one in the neighborhood. The other afternoon two of them chased each other up and down a tree and over the roof of the house for quite half an hour, providing hilarious entertainment for the family.

I suppose I must finish up now and turn to other pressing business; I have yet to get our Christmas card ready, and start making various presents for people, and on top of that professors want their assignments done. Oh well, it's hard to be bored! Our love to you both, and I will write again very soon.

Your loving son, Alan

EVANSTON, ILLINOIS | DECEMBER 1, 1942

Dear Mummy & Daddy,

We have been rather puzzled as to what to send you for Christmas, but books seem to be the easiest things and less subject to duty than other goods. So there are two on their way to you, coming separately. One is Lin Yutang's *Importance of Living* (its title in the English edition is *The Art of Living*). I don't think you have read this, but if you have let me know, and I will send something else. The other is what appealed to me as a perfectly fascinating book about trees, with lovely colored illustrations. I am very fond of Lin Yutang's book. His metaphysics are sometimes inadequate, but the general attitude is most refreshing, and no book could be more pleasing to one who loves the little pleasures of life. He is a guide to getting an enormous amount out of very little.

Your letter of Nov. 14th has just arrived, and I have written to Richard [Weeks] and am sending him some cigarettes and other things. I don't think he'll be boxed up there for long at the present rate, for it now looks as if the war in

Europe will be over before very long, and Italy will probably crack first. The real trouble is going to be with Japan.

I am terribly sorry to hear about old Macfarlane. I wonder where Ronald is now. I suppose a captain in the Black Watch is quite somebody. But it was good to hear that E.G.B.'s operation was successful, though what a pest for all the strain to bring you down with the shingles. I don't quite know how this sort of thing behaves, but I hope to goodness it has cleared up by now. Do take care of yourself, my dear.

I don't think Joan had had her birthday party when I wrote you last. It was a great success, the high spot being a treasure hunt in which presents attached to different colored threads were hidden all over the house and the threads trailed upstairs and down and all around. Bishop Conkling's two children came; they are 11 and 4, the eldest one a very bright girl but the other somewhat subdued. She loved your book of kittens, all furry beasts being her special loves. I wish she could see your rabbits. We have plenty of wild ones around here, but never see the babies.

We have just had our first fall of snow and of course Joan is thrilled, and has been out all morning with her sled. Little Ann looks almost exactly like Joan used to, save that she has rather less hair. She is coming along perfectly and has signs of lower teeth appearing. After we got rid of all the baby doctors she settled down to behaving beautifully; it is a perpetual marvel to me how much fuss a doctor can create with babies and how little good it does them! Yet they would persuade you that you should take them for inspection every month.

I am working at another church now, preparing a class of children for confirmation. This church is rather closer in to Chicago than St. Luke's, and incidentally a much better place. The architecture isn't so flossy, but the rector and the people are much to be preferred, not being suburban "aristocrats." We are going to have the Christmas Eve Midnight Mass there, and I am to assist the rector as subdeacon, which means that you wear a dalmatic [vestment worn over the alb by deacons], chant the Epistle, and assist the celebrant at the altar.

I have discovered a perfectly lovely book in my library, which has been there for ages, and I had never looked at it. It is Tagore's translation of the *Songs of Kabir*, a Hindu mystic of the 15th century. You should get hold of it, as I think it is the absolute acme of mystical poetry, which is a terribly hard thing to write (especially on bhakti lines) without getting slushy. Perhaps Toby has a copy, but if not it is a must for the Lodge library. I haven't seen the November *Buddhism in England* yet, but I'm glad you liked my little article. I am having rather a difficult time in getting things published at the moment because the man in charge of the religious department at Harper violently disagrees with my point of view, and not being in New York it is difficult to make the right approaches to someone else. But he is now sold on the frightful stuff Aldous Huxley and Gerald Heard are advocating — a completely world-denying mysticism of self-annihilation in the absolute mixed up with the cult of superman — a sure way to spiritual infla-tion, with the usual aftermath of spiritual flatulence! However, I keep at it, and drops of water will eventually wear the rock away.

The seminary is humming along, and another term is nearly over. My Greek seems to have made considerable progress as I am coming out on top of this course, and the instructor is a dry-as-dust scholar from N. Ireland who has nei-ther illusions nor imagination, but a very keen wit — Prof. Arthur Haire Forster, known from his second name as the Rabbit. I think I should get some enlighten-ment out of this term's history course as the prof. has let me have English mystics of the 17th century as a research subject. The history work I did at Canterbury is now becoming useful, as we are covering the period in which I specialized. Sometimes it strikes me as rather silly to be back at school again like this, but soon I shall be able to get back to serious work again. I only wish my Rt. Rev. Superior, Bp. Conkling, weren't quite so prissy and pseudo-English. He seems to have his religion tied up in such *nice* little watertight compartments, but he has only been a bishop for a year, is fairly young, and so has hope!

This morning Eleanor worked out an arrangement for sharing cars with our next-door neighbor, Mrs. Liegl, as gasoline rationing came in today, and we can only get 4 gal. a week. Fuel oil for heating is also rationed, and has been a tre-mendous piece of bungling. There is no shortage of oil, but the govt. wanted to save tankers and their tires. This they have wonderfully "achieved" by making it necessary for tankers to deliver their rations to customers in penny drops once a month, instead of in one load per six months or year. So you can see that where a customer lives some distance from the retailer, the saving on the tanker's tires is terrific! However, it's not easy to think frightfully logically in these times, and I suppose things will straighten themselves out; we learn by mistakes.

We are hoping for a real old-fashioned snowy Christmas, and possibly we may have Eleanor's mother with us as she couldn't get out before. Well, I hope this airmail won't take five weeks, and will come in time to give you all our love for a very happy Christmas and New Year — with a quick end to the war.

Your loving son, Alan

EVANSTON, ILLINOIS | MARCH 24, 1943
Dear Mummy & Daddy,
This letter is very late because I have been sick in bed for the last three weeks with a rather complicated arrangement of ailments. Looked as if it was starting

up with pneumonia, so they gave me sulfadiazine and then it developed into intestinal flu and then into jaundice. I went the color of a rather dark grapefruit and looked like a mandarin, and now I just have to sit and rest.

Well, it gives me time for a lot of reading and thinking!

I have to take exams for the diaconate immediately after Easter, and there are dark hints that I may possibly be ordained early in the summer. One or two remarks dropped by Bp. Conkling and odds and ends of information that come along the grapevine seem to indicate this, and from "a usually reliable source" I hear that the bishop has some idea of my doing teaching work, whether in the seminary or elsewhere I don't quite know. The good man has taken quite an interest in us; he came for dinner one night before I got laid up and last Sunday paid a two-hour call. Like most bishops he is something of a politician, moves in a mysterious way his wonders to perform, and you are never quite sure what he has in mind.

We are not going to St. Luke's in Evanston anymore, for luckily I have been able to get under a man who has a much better church in Chicago itself with a more friendly and sincere congregation. I have been teaching some of his rather difficult children in the church school, and now that they have been safely confirmed I am to be the church master of ceremonies, and polish up the conduct of the services.

This letter should arrive sometime around Mummy's birthday, which I hope will be a very happy one. As soon as I can sit up a bit more I will finish a certain little job I have been working on for you, but I have to sit on a couch for the rest of this week as I only got out of bed on Sunday.

In a few weeks we shall be planting out a vegetable garden as the food situation is becoming rather a problem. It takes Eleanor almost 2 hours to do her marketing in the morning as you have to go from place to place trying to find fresh vegetables, canned vegetables being rationed. Fortunately my diet excludes fats, for no butter, margarine, lard, shortening, or anything like that has been available for a week. But we can't grumble; it has been infinitely worse for others. Our car is very economical on the gas, and four gallons a week is ample. The tires will last quite a while, so we shall be able to get around, and as soon as I am ordained we shall have an increased ration.

Little Ann has sprouted two teeth and is coming along splendidly, continuing to be bubbly and happy all day. Joan is learning some simple spelling and can write a few words like cat and dog. Soon I will get her to send you a letter. Our friend Adolph Teichert from California is staying with us for a few days on his way back from New York. He is going to work as a subcontractor for Henry Kaiser, the great shipbuilder who can turn out a cargo boat in two weeks.

Submarines have rather a job keeping pace with him. Adolph stopped by in Detroit with an uncle who is a crack inventor for General Motors and other concerns, and he is one of those (sometimes I think they are misguided dreamers) who foresee a super-machine era after the war with helicopters instead of cars. Bishop Conkling says he will purchase one for travelling around the diocese, and appropriately descend from the skies with the gifts of the Holy Spirit! The big-time industrialists in Detroit really seem to be taking all this quite seriously, but there are others who only foresee chaos and scarcity.

If I should be ordained early in the summer (around Ascension Day) this means that I shall probably be ordained to the priesthood at the beginning of next year, serving six months odd in the diaconate, all of which would speed matters up considerably more than I had expected. I am hoping very much to be able to get work within easy reach of Evanston as we are anxious to be able to stay in this house. Moving with all my books is rather an expense, but they are such essential tools of trade that I just have to have a vast library. It is now well over 2,000 vols., and I think getting close to 3,000!

I told you I was going to start up my informal lectures again, and though being laid up has interrupted them, I have had two sessions with a very delightful group consisting of a wonderful mixture of musicians and church people.

We are working on the basic principles of mystical psychology, and meet on Friday evenings.

As I have not been doing much there is not much else in the way of news. I have to stay at home another ten days because this jaundice business is supposed to be liable to back up on you, but I feel perfectly well and it's rather a bore.

Love to you both from us all. Let us know how the HSF is going and don't work yourselves to shadows. (I should talk.)

From your loving son — Alan

EVANSTON, ILLINOIS | MAY 25, 1943
Dear Mummy & Daddy,
This must be rather a short letter as I have a pack of letters to write to tell all who are interested that I shall be ordained on June 3rd at St. Luke's, Evanston, at 10 AM. This will be to the diaconate, and the bishop has indicated that I shall be advanced to the priesthood a year hence. I am sending you a telegram today, and I will tell you all about it after the service is over. I couldn't let you know for certain before as the Standing Committee of the Diocese had to approve it, and there might have been a hitch as the time elapsed is rather shorter than is normally permitted. But I think the bishop is very anxious to hurry things as we

seem to get along rather well together. The other day he was very excited about one of my sermons, which he is going to publish, anonymously, in the interests, I suppose, of holy humility! And then I did quite a job with the examinations, getting nothing less than 98, and 100 on several papers; but they were kind of easy. What work I shall do when ordained remains in doubt, but the bishop wants me to help resuscitate a decrepit parish about 60 miles away (going there on weekends) and my present rector wants me as his assistant. So they will have to fight it out, but I should much prefer the latter.

The ordination service should be rather impressive — almost as impressive as it will be long, because there will be some four or five deacons and at least one priest, and if you will consult a prayer book you will see that this is quite something! How I wish you were here to see it, and, by the way, to lend your expert hand to some needlework! They solemnly vest us with stole and dalmatic, the latter being an embroidered tunic, and we have to provide ourselves with amice, alb, and various odds and ends. The stole I have bought is nothing like your work, but the alb is quite lovely.

Well we received those photographs you sent us, and are absolutely thrilled with them. My, what a gorgeous job you have done with the garden, and I think they are the best pictures of you both that I have ever seen. That stream looks delightful; I always wanted a stream there with a rock garden beside it, but there are one or two mysteries I should like explained. Where does the stream flow to, or is it really an elongated pond? And who is the owner of the short trousers peeking out under a tree? And what supplies the pump? Did you have a well dug or is it just tap water?

Since the examinations I have been resting up a bit, taking the time to study local birdlife which is rather interesting. Our next-door neighbor knows quite a lot about birds, and we have all been out with field glasses looking at them. We have a tremendous variety of warblers, which are extremely graceful and colorful little creatures. Once we saw a glory called the scarlet tanager, whose body is a brilliant velvety scarlet and his wings jet-black. Eleanor was sitting in the garden the other day when a cowbird came up to her and fed out of her hand; he looks something like a cuckoo, but isn't. The American cuckoo doesn't cuckoo, but he has the usual bad habits. Then we have a lot of blue jays, who have an interesting call and the most exquisite plumage, while the best song belongs to the cardinal, who is also bright red with a neat little crest. He likes rain, and has been getting it. We have had solid rain for nearly three weeks, and in some places, though not here, there are bad floods.

I have planted scarlet runners, which seem to be rather a novelty around here as hardly anyone has heard of them. The usual equivalent is called the green bean, but doesn't taste so good, and I have kind of an itch to see those tall plants with their bright flowers again. Our radishes are already eatable, and the peas and lettuce are coming along. Carrots, beets, and tomatoes are to follow.

I enclose some pictures. The ones of baby Ann are not so hot, but she would screw up her face every time the camera was aimed at her. As for me, I have somewhat changed the pattern of the foliage to the shape of Grandpa Watts, which is more becoming. I think Eleanor told you in her letter the story of how it all happened, because of the bishop's squeamishness about priests' moustaches. After all this time with hair on my face I should feel naked and clammy without it, so as it has to be all or nothing it shall be all!

Well this must be all for the moment. Oh, by the way, I received the letter sent to me c/o Murray's and your copy, for which many thanks — and again for those lovely pictures.

Your loving son, Alan

EVANSTON, ILLINOIS | JUNE 8, 1943
Dear Mummy & Daddy,
I am so disturbed about the slowness of our letters in arriving, but I think that by now you should have received a very long letter from Eleanor, sent in duplicate by both air, and ordinary mail, and a letter of mine sent by ordinary mail, written at the end of May. I hope also that you received my telegram saying that the ordination would definitely be on, June 3rd.

Unfortunately the day before the ordination both Eleanor and Joan came down with measles (from which they are now about recovered) and so they missed an extremely lovely service. However, ordination to the priesthood is a more important occasion, and that is yet to come — I suppose this time next year. How I wish you could have been here too. It was at St. Luke's here in Evanston at 10 in the morning, and lasted until about 12, and despite the heat and the length I enjoyed every minute of it. Some photographs were taken by friends, and I will send copies to you as soon as they can be obtained. Bishop Conkling was a sight for sore eyes in his cloth-of-gold cope and red-and-gold mitre, with two attendants in red dalmatics. The seminary choir sang the service quite well, in the Gregorian settings, and amidst much anointing, censing, and vesting we were safely deaconised. We were each presented with a copy of the New Testament and a marvelous certificate which tells "all the faithful in Christ Jesus through-out the world" that I am a "deacon in the One, Holy, Catholic and Apostolic Church" — our bishop being in no mind to think of our communion as a mere sect called the Protestant Episcopal Church! Not the least fascinating thing was the experience of being ordained, for Bp. Conkling is one of those individuals with power in his hands, and when they have been laid on your head you don't feel at all the same afterwards. It was utterly unlike being confirmed.

The following Sunday I went to work at the Church of the Atonement, delivering the chalice at mass, and this coming Sunday I am to preach there. Shall also be chaplain to the bishop at the seminary commencement service (which means, by some weird paradox, the end-of-term service) this Thursday. I shall be working at the seminary for another year yet, but strictly as a special student, which means that I don't have to follow the usual routine and can specialize on various lines that interest me. Aside from the work necessary for taking the examinations for the priesthood, I shall be able to put in a lot of study on the art of spiritual direction, which means the whole field of prayer and mystical theology. I am familiarizing myself with the very rich body of literature which the Church has produced on this subject, and I have found much of great profit. It is a study of endless surprise, for I find more and more that the outward appearance of traditional Christianity is very deceptive; it appears crude and sometimes even superstitious, but if one will take the pains to use imaginative appreciation the hardest dogmas turn out to be statements of extraordinary depths. They do not fetter thought but introduce it to a new realm of wonders in which it expands almost indefinitely. The difficulty is that we are too familiar with these ideas, and yet do not really know them at all. And it is so exasperating to watch so many clergy and seminary students swallow them at face value, and develop that spiritual flatulence which keeps so many millions away from the Church. On a lower level, it is like watching someone gulp down a glass of Napoleon brandy at one draught. I have been guilty of such gulping myself, and it ruins everything for you.

A week or so ago Jean and her new husband came to visit us. He lives only a few miles north at Kenosha, Wisc., and so they will be quite close to us this summer. Eleanor and I were rather disappointed; he is a very pleasant but taciturn bull. There's more than six feet of him and quite 200 lb. And while Jean is a charming girl, she's just [a] wee bit of a prig and is doing her best to make hubby the same. Maybe she gets it from her mother, because Uncle Willie doesn't strike me that way. It must be that commendably strenuous but horribly unimaginative Presbyterian religion! They came with only a few hours' notice on a Sunday evening and I was so embarrassed because we couldn't give them any supper, the rationing being such that by the end of the week there's absolutely nothing left in the house.

The last few days I have done the marketing and experienced all the complexities of rationing. But I think I came out quite creditably, and brought back large supplies while parting with very few coupons (or stamps, as they are with us). I have also been doing all the driving, and seem to manage Jenny (our car) quite capably except that to get her in and out of our lopsided garage and to back her into a parking space is rather a job.

The week after next I shall be spending a few days at a clergy conference at Racine, Wisc., and the next week Eleanor and I will go up to Algoma, Wisc., (some 250 miles north) for the ordination of a very good friend, with whom we shall spend a day or two.

I still look at those lovely photographs you sent us and which we have shown to so many people who have enjoyed them with us. Now that the garden is more flowery I will try something like them for you, but I can't promise anything so good.

With all our love to you both, and many happy returns for June 23rd, Alan

The following letter is addressed to Clare Cameron Burke, editor of the Buddhist Society's periodical, The Middle Way.

EVANSTON, ILLINOIS | JULY 8, 1943

My dear Clare Burke,

I was so glad to get your letter of June 10th, and also to hear that my letter had reached Richard safely. I will write to him again on the strength of that, though I am not sure whether I still have his address correctly; will you drop me a line with a note of it as soon as possible? By now you should have received another letter from me.

Yes, I remember the Plane Tree Restaurant, and I am sure the lodge will find itself in very congenial surroundings, right by Kegan Paul, Luzac's, and the British Museum. It will be grand for you to have a proper office, and while I agree with you that a paid secretary is the ideal it will be good for you to have some help. The part I always found exasperating was keeping the accounts, but Eleanor is a perfect genius at that game, so I don't worry about it anymore.

I am much interested in your mention of Gnostic Christianity, being a subject which I have investigated fairly thoroughly; and only the other day I had a long conversation with a priest of the Greek Church who wanted to revive Gnosticism in Christianity. He, however, did not really know what Gnosticism is, and many people are under grave misapprehensions about it. In the true sense of the word Gnosticism is, or rather, should be the gnosis or knowledge of God, in which sense it is only another term for mysticism. The historic Gnosticism of Valentinus, Basilides, Bardesanes, and the Hermetics proves, upon investigation, to be a very disappointing and unattractive business, even in the hands of its partisans, such as G. R. S. Mead. I was always in the hope of finding in it some key to the mysteries of Christianity, but when you get down to the bottom of it you have the sad old story of dualism and contempt of the world. For historic Gnosticism was loath to ground this everyday world in the ultimate reality. This was the work of the Demiurge, a virtually Satanic power who had in some way fallen from the spirituality of the pleroma, for which reason this world is intrinsically evil.

Catholic Christianity opposed Gnosticism on two principal grounds, first, that all things whatsoever, whether earthly or heavenly, material or spiritual, are the work of one God, representing and manifesting his nature and will. Thus matter is not intrinsically evil, but has been perverted for evil purposes by a malefic *spiritual* power. Second, that the purpose of true religion is to transfigure and redeem the material world, for which reason God became man, the eternal Logos became flesh. Gnosticism couldn't possibly accept this, for it thought the union of God and flesh to be an outrage upon the dignity of God. Therefore Gnosticism resisted the great Catholic symbol of the union of God and the world, the doctrine of the Incarnation — that Christ is at once completely God and completely man, for, as Athanasius said, "He became man that man might become God."

Thus the Gnostics, in common with so many Theosophists, pseudo-Buddhists, and the like of modern times, thought there was something necessarily unspiritual, something degrading and even positively evil about the physical world. Fleshly existence was of necessity an obstruction to the life of the spirit. From this follows a whole world of nonsense — fantastic dietetic and sexual fads, extreme asceticism, and, worse still, spiritual pride. For contempt of bodily existence, the idea that one must rise superior to "mere" dust is that dangerous pride which forgets that God loves the dust. It imagines spiritual progress as man's raising himself above the material level by his own power, whereas the only real spiritual progress comes from the acceptance of the descent of God to man. It is therefore not surprising that the historic Gnostics were rather horrible people, who exercise over us the glamour of strange rites and occult symbols. But when you penetrate that romantic facade, you do not find one atom of the profundity of true mystics, who are all very simple people having no truck with Aeons, Demiourgoi, Abraxides, Emanations, and whole hierarchies of cosmic principles which remove the human soul further and further from God. In practice Gnosticism was not a knowledge of God but of the structure of the psychic universe, with all the pride of supposedly secret knowledge.

There is, nevertheless, esoteric Christianity, but it has nothing in common with historic Gnosticism. Its esotericism does not consist in hidden or withheld information, but in (a) mystical intuition and (b) profound understanding of simple statements, such as the articles of the creeds. You find it in Dionysius, Eckhart, Ruysbroeck, Julian of Norwich, Nicholas of Cusa, John of the Cross (but scratch him deeply), Brother Lawrence, de Caussade, and, in our own times, R. H. J. Steuart, Berdyaev, and many another. Mixed company, but highly stimulating. (I should add Baron von Hügel.)

No, Gnosticism is a sad disillusionment, for it is so promising on the outside. It is a spiritual schizophrenia, disintegrating the universe into the pneumatic and the hylic, the true spiritual and the false material. Mother Nature is made a harlot and cast like Hagar into the desert, whereas in the Catholic tradition Mother Nature is exalted to the heights in the symbolic personage of Mary. In her, God and the world are united because she brings forth the God-man, Christ. And when we say that belief in Christ is necessary to salvation, we mean that there is no salvation (union with God) unless you, as man, can accept the gift of union with God as you are, i.e., without ceasing to be man. If you cannot believe in the union of true God and true man, how on earth can you be united with God? Will you try to become something more than man? Will you try to raise yourself by your own belt? Those who try to do this so spiritualize themselves that they become perfectly awful. You can't have a drink with them; you can't talk about anything but religion in their company; they are incapable of relaxing; they have no sort of Zen. (See *Essays in Zen*, vol. 1, p. 331, about Goso. Von Hügel said just the same thing about certain Christians who could think and talk of nothing but religion and the spiritual.)

Well, well, please forgive this diatribe on the subject of Gnosticism, but there would have been no point in exploring it myself if I could not pass on some of the results to others. And I would like to save you any disappointment on that score.

With all good wishes,

Very sincerely, Alan

EVANSTON, ILLINOIS | JULY 15, 1943

Dear Mummy & Daddy,

Your letter of June 29th has just arrived, and I'm afraid this one is a little overdue. I have been on the run since the seminary closed for the summer; first I had to go to the diocesan clergy summer school, then to New York for a couple of days to help Mrs. E. with some business, and then up to Algoma, Wisconsin, for a week to stay with a very good friend who was being ordained to the priesthood. So when I got back there was a mass of business to be attended to.

At last I have some pictures which I am sending to you with these letters (some with the top copy and others with the carbon). The big one was taken just after the ordination and shows all of us standing with the bishop. Another is just me with the bishop, and another shows me being chaplain to him at the seminary graduation ceremonies. I don't think they're specially good pictures; Conkling is rather hard to take because his snow-white hair catches the sun and makes him look much older than he really is.

I had a fascinating time at the summer school, meeting a whole lot of people. It was held at a big retreat house near Milwaukee, and we had as our chief lecturer Fr. Whittemore, the superior of the Holy Cross monks; with a few more like him the Church would be a mighty powerful outfit; I think he is one of the freest souls I have ever known. A man of 52 but looking like 40, and as gay and open as a child but a mind as sound as a bell. There were 85 clergy present out of about 120 in the whole diocese.

Mrs. Conkling called me the other day about a Mrs. Shakespeare whom she wants me to meet. Now I think you wrote to me about her in a letter which miscarried, for Mrs. C. said that Mrs. S. had had a letter from you. The old lady apparently had an accident the other day; she went to light the gas stove (which had been turned on for some time) and there was an explosion which blew her across the kitchen and broke a vertebra. But she is recovering and we will get together as soon as Mrs. C. gets back from her vacation.

The country up round Algoma is perfectly lovely although it was rather cold there, especially after being in New York where the temperature was 105 in the sun. My friend has the loveliest little church there, and I went to help with his ordination service conducted by Bp. Sturtevant of Fond-du-Lac, Wisc. We went up on one of those streamlined diesel trains which makes a 260 mile with several stops in 3 hours. Wisconsin is all rolling hills, heavily wooded, interspersed with the most glorious lakes which are famous for fishing. Had a talk with a Red Indian on the train who was just coming home on leave from an army camp way down in Tennessee.

I am continuing to work at the Church of the Atonement where I am now able to preach every few Sundays, but I can't do full-time work yet as I still have seminary work to do. Besides, there's not an awful lot that a deacon can do. Meantime, Eleanor is getting ready to make me a set of vestments for summer and travelling use. We make this kind out of a crepe silk which doesn't crumple easily, and they are very simply constructed with orphrey material which you can get by the yard from ecclesiastical supply houses. Eleanor doesn't feel up to church embroidery yet, and, besides, it's just about impossible to get any gold thread. However, she has been making some winter clothes for Joan which are simply gorgeous — little suits with jackets embroidered in cross-stitch, one bright red, another forest green.

I heard through Clare Burke the other day that my letter reached Richard Weeks. I'm going to write him again right away, for at the present rate he should be rescued before long! I see the lodge is going to take premises on Gt. Russell St., though I gather that Clare is getting a little restive under all the work she has to do. Toby must be on the make to be branching out like this.

Ann is getting lots of teeth and has begun crawling around the house. We have to keep a sharp eye on her as she loves to bite the connection wires of electric lamps! After saying Da-da-da-da and Ma-ma-ma-ma for a while her conversation has withdrawn into so many incoherent but rather joyful noises.

Twice a week I am giving lessons in drawing to the little girl aged 10 next door and it's rather fun. As a start I'm getting her to play the "sedulous ape" and yesterday she made quite a decent copy of the head of Botticelli's Venus. Her parents got fed up with the way they teach drawing at school — you know those frightful daubs with poster paints these modern educationalists encourage, getting the little dears to "express themselves," as if they didn't express themselves enough anyway.

Love from us all to you both, as always, Alan

The following letter is addressed to a friend of Blanche Matthias and Ruth Sasaki. Blanche Matthias was Joan's godmother.

EVANSTON, ILLINOIS | AUGUST 2, 1943
My dear Mrs. Leggett,
I am so sorry to have delayed so long in answering your kind letter of July 15th, but I have lately had a spell of work which has occupied all my energies. Dr. Baker was here a short while ago and spoke of you, and Mrs. Matthias mentioned your name to me when she last came through Chicago.

I do not think there is any further chance of my coming east this year. I made two short visits to New York in February and June, but had not time to get around much. I am sorry about this, because I certainly should have liked to have a talk with you.

I think Dr. Baker told you of the work I am doing now, and I have not published anything since *The Meaning of Happiness* (aside from a few articles) because I have been thinking along new lines of which, in my previous works, you will find only the germ. It may possibly have struck you that the purely psychological standpoint of *The Meaning of Happiness* left a number of very important problems unanswered — as, for instance, just why the realization of our union with the Tao should result in a life of gratitude and love as distinct from any other kind of life. Obviously an individual who is consciously at one with the ultimate Reality will only be moved to such a life if that Reality has a specific character. Now it was possible for anyone having finished my book to lay it down with the question, "So what?" Yes, we are united with Reality and cannot get away from it, but unless that Reality is in some profound sense absolutely good and beautiful, what is the use of bothering to think about it? In other words, I described a psychological process without any metaphysical foundation. It was like telling people how to eat a certain dinner which had been offered them, and then forgetting to describe the dinner. I am afraid I fell in to this pure psychologism from being too much under Jungian influence (for one reason), for I think Jung's refusal to relate his psychology to any system of metaphysics is its profound weakness. Psychology has to be related to metaphysics in the same way as the conscious has to be related to the unconscious; an isolated psychology is as neurotic as an isolated ego; it is a flower without roots.

The problem then arose as to what system of metaphysics provided the most adequate ground for the spiritual experience I was feeling after. Now as Jung himself has said, Oriental metaphysics are very inadequate. They are not really metaphysics at all; they are really a symbolic psychology, based entirely on subjective experiences. For instance the spiritual experience (satori) of Zen Buddhism results in a particular kind of life — a very *lively* life — and an art (i.e., Chinese painting), which has an astounding sense of the eternal significance of momentary details, such as the turn of a bird's wing or the kiss of the wind on a particular blade of grass. Metaphysically, this life and this art are explained as the result of realization of the Void, in which the enlightened ones are able to live and move with perfect freedom. But in the Void you can move in any direction. Why, then, did Chinese art hit upon that particularly beautiful direction? The only satisfactory answer is that ultimate Reality is a void only to human understanding and perception. It is a veil of invisibility and intangibility hiding a positive life, beauty, and goodness, and such qualities cannot possibly be ascribed to a mere principle or law. As well try to explain the beauty of Chinese art in terms of pure mathematics. I found it impossible to deny that Tao has a character, that Tao is a *personal* life, understanding the word *person* not as the *persona*, the mask, but as a self-sufficient center of infinite life, consciousness, intelligence, and beauty. If Reality is not this, it is a law, a mechanism, and if this be true the universe is dead.

There is only one metaphysical system that really allows for the experience of Reality as a preeminent life, consciousness, and beauty, and that is Christian theism at its highest, as you will find it in St. Thomas Aquinas, St. Bonaventure, and the really profound doctors of Catholic theology. Or, in modern times, in

Maritain, Wust, Berdyaev, Gilson, et al. And as St. Thomas used Aristotle to expose the true depth of Christian revelation, so we can use Buddhism, Taoism, and Vedanta. Many intelligent people today react against Christian theism because they do not know what it is. They have only the crudest notions of the idea of God, imbibed from the Sunday school and the popular preachers. For myself, I can only say that after studying this theology as it really is, and not as the average Sunday school or preacher presents it, all other metaphysical systems seem utterly puerile, narrow, and dead, even though many of them have partial glimpses of this vision.

I tell you this so that you can evaluate my previous work more correctly and understand its hidden direction; also that you can tell it to others of your acquaintance who have been interested in my thinking. I should say, too, that this conclusion is no sudden enthusiasm, seeing that for two or three years I have resisted it in every way, only to find its sanity, rationality, and beauty overwhelming. The pity of it is that, with some few exceptions, the Church is not alive to its own treasure, and one still has to put up with the frightful mediocrity of modern Christianity. But times are changing.

Sincerely yours, Alan Watts

EVANSTON, ILLINOIS | AUGUST 4, 1943
My dear Clare [Cameron Burke],
Well, I have tried again, but I don't seem to be able to reduce the thing to less than five pages! However, see how you like this one; it has, I think, more material of interest to your average reader and is less involved. Like a fool I didn't keep copies of the others, but I don't want you to insert any material that was in my private letter to you. If the thing is still rather lengthy, why not have the part between the two red lines in the margin set in 8-point type?

I have received the July–August number, and found the Wilmshurst article interesting but a trifle screwy, especially on the subject of the creation of the phenomenal world, where he exhibits that peculiar Gnostic prejudice against matter of which I spoke in my last letter. How much more sane and *integrated* is the Catholic version of the subject — "*All* things were made by him, and without him was not anything made that was made." The phenomenal, material world is not the result of the fall; it has been perverted by the fall, but it is as inherently united with God as the psychic or supernatural realms. The whole philosophy of the Incarnation is based on this, for in Christ the eternal Logos became flesh — our concrete physical flesh — and thereby raised concrete and complete humanity into perfect union with God. "He became man," said St. Athanasius, "that man might become God." And do you know that wonderful prayer that is said at the blessing of the water in the Mass? "O God who didst create the dignity of human nature in wonder and honour, and in wonder and honour hast renewed the same; grant by the mystery of this water and this wine that he who was partaker of our humanity may make us partakers of his very Godhead…" .

This philosophy is at the root of the Christian sacraments, which so many people have difficulty in accepting — which is odd, because they are so easy to accept, and purposely so. Nothing is easier than to be baptized and to eat bread and drink wine, but for modern intelligentsia it is most difficult. They feel that submitting to such simple forms and making their union with the life of God depend on such little material details is an insult to their intelligence and spirituality. As if, they argue, the almighty and infinite God would descend to such trivial practices to communicate his life to me; as if he would make such a lofty matter as the spiritual life depend on mere historic facts and ritual actions! But God is not proud, and small material things are not alien to him, as anyone may tell from the marvelous construction of the ephemeral snowflake or a single leaf. Heaven is not reserved for the intelligentsia, and if they cannot "lower" themselves to receive the gift of God in the simple and humble means that he provides (so that *all* may receive it), they cannot have the least understanding or sympathy with the divine love. To spurn this offering as idolatrous, unspiritual, and crude is surely the height of spiritual pride. It is, indeed, a subtle and insidious type of idolatry in itself, being an attempt to *confine* God to the spiritual and suggest that it does not become his dignity to associate himself so intimately with material things. God, however, can very well take care of his own dignity.

The whole point of this kind of thing is missed if one does not have the childlike approach with its all-embracing sense of wonder, a sense which gives life, color, and mystery to the simplest things. It is the approach of God himself to the creation, for the universe is ultimately intelligible only as a tremendous playing. Thus in Proverbs 8:31 the Wisdom of God says, "I was with him forming all things and was delighted every day, playing before him at all times: playing in the world." It is absolutely in keeping with this attitude that the mystery of redemption should be communicated to man in a story, a drama, and a ritual because the universe itself is a drama and a ritual; there is a unique and special way of redemption because every created being is unique and special. Uniqueness is the keynote of creation because every individual thing is an object of the divine love, and is wonderful in its eyes.

Clare, if you decide to go more deeply into Christianity you should think over this side of things very carefully because it is the essence of Christianity, and if you cannot accept it fully there are certain things that will always irk and annoy you. It would be better to remain Buddhist than to accept the compromised pseudo-Christianity of Gnosticism. You must remember, too, that the institutional side of the Church is a necessary part of the divine drama, but, because it is in human hands, is at present diseased, and it is our job to help in its healing. For this reason you would not be happy in the Church if you went into it before you felt almost compelled to do so; you have to be 100 percent convinced. It might help you to clarify your mind by reading something decent on these lines, and I unreservedly recommend Steuart's *World Intangible* (Longmans), Noyes's *Unknown God* (Sheed & Ward), both of which have the mystical and poetic element that you will love, and, for more solid reading, either Gilson's *Spirit of Mediaeval Philosophy* (Sheed) (for a grasp of theology in its sublimest mood) or Evelyn Underhill's *Worship* (for an introduction to the life of the Church). And if all that excites you enough, you might have a talk with Dom Bernard Clements (an Anglican Benedictine) or his successor at All Saints, Margaret Street — monks being generally saner and more profound than secular clergy. Please let me know your reactions.

Yours ever, Alan

This letter is addressed to a friend of Alan's from seminary, whose surname is unknown.

EVANSTON, ILLINOIS | AUGUST 4, 1943
My dear Bill,
I was just delighted to get your letter, and hasten to reply because you should be kept abreast of the news. So first I will clear off the gossip. Carl Moss has apparently joined the Army (or Navy) Air Corps, but he left behind a trail of debts like a small comet. Apparently he left RC Seminary last September, and first went to our Franciscan monks at Little Portion; he was about to apply for postulancy to Bp. De Wolfe of Long Island, when he did a vanishing stunt and came out to us. Bp. Conkling found out about this from his friend Fr. Thomas, who at that time was trying his vocation with the Franciscans. Carl left us after the Standing Committee had found out that he was not a Mundelein student. All the details are too long to tell, but piecing things together, it looks as if he had been a seminarist at the Catholic University of Washington, DC, and had perhaps been taking one or two special courses at Mundelein. My guess is that they found he had some psychological trouble and were going to subject him to special discipline, when he quit. There are a lot of vague and rather fishy aspects to the whole business, which are too long to go into and not very conclusive.

Fr. Buck has left the Atonement to go east, and Fr. Matthews is now priest-in-charge until they can find a new man. I am rooting for a certain person, whose identity you may be able to guess (he is from NY), and the vestry seems interested. But that is strictly sub rosa, as it's none of my business. What we need is a real Catholic in these parts, and that demands a certain attitude to life rather than a certain set of ritual and intellectual formulae — although those go with it. So please don't mention my activities in this matter to anyone!

I was down buying some books at Benziger's the other day and had a long chat with the chief RC chaplain at Great Lakes, who at first took me for a Jesuit! Apparently the only RC priests who wear beards are religious, for at another place where I wanted to buy a crucifix they asked me if it was for a monastery. As to books I have been reading Jacques Maritain with great profit, also Christopher Dawson and Peter Wust, all of them leaders in the Romanist revival, and those boys really have something. That Thomist philosophy and mystical theology [are] to the kind of thing we get in seminary as a Gothic cathedral to a Methodist tabernacle. Also read a lot of von Hügel — his *Letters* and *Mystical Element of Religion*, both of which are full of good stuff. The latter quotes the following brilliant passage from St. Thomas's *De Beatitudine*:

> Already in this life we ought continuously to enjoy God, as a thing most fully our own, in all our works...Great is the blindness and exceeding the folly of many souls that are ever seeking God, and frequently de-siring God: whilst, all the time, they are themselves the tabernacles of the living God...since their soul is the seat of God, in which he con-tinuously reposes. Now who but a fool deliberately seeks a tool which he possesses under lock and key? Or who can use and profit by an in-strument which he is seeking? Or who can draw comfort from food for which he hungers, but which he does not relish at leisure?

Maybe you have heard something like that before?? And it relates, doesn't it, to that problem of *time* which you raise, to that every flying present moment which seems to be pushing you relentlessly along so that you can't even stop to find the presence of God in it.

> "Then dared I hail the moment fleeing —
> Ah, still delay, thou are so fair!"

Isn't the difficulty that you are trying to keep up with it, or else trying to race it? That is just like trying to grasp and possess God — a headache, an impossi-bility, for it is God who must possess us. For as we can neither grasp the moment nor yet escape from it, we can neither grasp nor escape from God. And as we can live nowhere but in the moment so we can live nowhere but in God. It holds and carries us forward just as God holds and carries us. In fact, you don't have to accept the moment; it has already accepted you! — just as God has already united himself with you and is loving you in spite of yourself. To try to get it is to hide from yourself the fact that it is already a gift, quite literally a Christmas present, which we have to use until it becomes conscious and we are perfect in its use.

I see now that without Christ this given union with God is a terrible thing and a judgment, a Hound of Heaven, a consuming fire. It is like being swept along in a stream with your back to its goal, fighting madly against it. But Christ has turned human nature around so that it faces the goal, and the given union becomes a joy instead of a terror. For this reason I think a Jew must have read the 139th Psalm with fear and trembling, but a Christian with ecstatic joy.

Nevertheless, I think you will best realize the presence of God in the present moment (which is a figure of the eternal now of heaven) in the unhurried regularity of monastic life. The monk with a real vocation to his life has a sanity and a depth so obviously lacking in the majority of secular clergy, who, when they happen to be Catholics are so preoccupied with ridiculous wrangles with the laity, or the absurd "club-life" aspect of PE churches, that they forget about religion.

As to your friend Tallisferro (spelling?), please give Mrs. T. our address and phone number and we shall be of service if we can. I can well imagine that he is in for an inner conflict between Catholicism and Rosicrucianism, for they cannot mix. I shall have to bone up on my Rosie Cross, but as I recollect that is one of those Gnostic religions that suffer from the contempt of matter, and *that* cannot be reconciled with the incarnational and sacramental essence of Catholicism. Nor, as you say, can reincarnation for this minimizes the worth of the physical body as a component of the total personality, and denies the ultimate re-creation and transfiguration of its dust. I cannot, however, press him to a solution of that problem, but perhaps you can, oh so very gently, suggest that he might talk with me if he ever has difficulty with it.

The candle in the font is of course as Freudian as the Virgin birth! The mystery of Christ entering the womb of Mary. That blessing of the candles is a strange thing; it intensifies rather than solves the problem of evil, and suggests the thought that evil magnifies the glory of God without any credit to itself. The more evil fights him, the more it reveals his love; but this does not justify evil, because it does not *add* to his love. And if there were no evil, there would be no need for his love to be revealed: it would be perfectly obvious. Thus the fault is only happy in retrospect — as something forgiven and transfigured by the divine love. But it certainly gives one the idea that forgiven sins are not simply wiped out but turned from lead into gold.

I know you are now a busy man, and have not the time, and probably not the inclination, to write rambling letters like this, but do please keep in touch with me, and let me know if you read or think anything interesting, and also how your work goes along. Eleanor and Joan send their love, and we all miss you very much. Give our regards to Hud if you see him.

Very sincerely, Alan

EVANSTON, ILLINOIS | AUGUST 5, 1943
Dear Mummy,

I have your letter of July 15th, and am just delighted that you will be able to work a stole for me. Now I know you have precious little time these days and that you have to go easy on your eyes, so I am sending some designs that I think will be fairly simple. There's no hurry about it, so just take your time.

What I need most are reversible stoles in white and purple — white one side and purple the other. This type of stole has a lot of uses — for baptisms, hearing confessions, and visiting the sick. Other types of stoles are seldom used, at least, that is true of separate stoles which do not match a complete set of vestments including chasuble, veil, burse, and maniple. However, a red stole would be useful, as these are worn at ordinations over surplice by assisting clergy. It is not liturgically proper to wear a stole at the Morning and Evening Offices. But I don't want you to have to spend a lot of money buying that terribly expensive silk, and if you have some red on hand why not go ahead with that? I have one white and purple reversible, and though it is not very good it will do.

The accompanying designs are made for the laid gold crosses you have already made. I have outlined some suggested color schemes, but you have such a good sense of color that I would really prefer you to use your own judgment. On red the flowers (formal roses) could be either yellow or white, but if the latter I think it would be an idea to have the stems and leaves in light blue instead of green. If you do a white one, however, I think I would like something close to the color schemes in the drawings. The design for the small cross at the neck is made so that it can be worked separately, cut out round the green edge, and appliquéd over the join. The eight letters are IC-XC-NI-KA, the Greek abbreviation for IHCOYC XPICTOC NIKA, "Jesus Christ the Victor." This design would of course be worked on a piece of the same material as the stole itself.

As to the shape and size of the stole, you know they are best made in two sections of double material (lined with a cheaper material is best if they are not reversible) having a peculiar curve at the neck, which I have tried to outline in actual size as best as I can. Overall they are some 80" long, 2½" wide at the neck and 5" at the base. When the two sides are joined together and laid flat, it is almost the shape of a boomerang. There should be a gold silk fringe at the base each end, not more than 2½" long. The small cross at the neck could be worked in gold silk or, if you have any of that rarity, gold thread. The bordering or edging would look best, I think, in French knots. Alternatively, you could work it in gold silk and do the edging in gold thread, but here again use your own judgment.

I don't think there is any need for me to send patterns of materials, for not only are they difficult to match but here again I trust your judgment. I only ask that the purple be blue rather than red and that the green, if you get any, is not olive-drab.

The rector, Fr. Buck, has left the church where I work and we are looking for a new man. I am trying to persuade the vestry to call a friend of mine from New York, and they seem interested in the idea. The present locum tenens is an old dear but rather a duffer. I have been doing a lot of studying this summer, and swimming by way of recreation. Today the water was just gorgeous — nice big waves and sunshine. Eleanor carried Joan in and she enjoyed it hugely.

I wonder if you would ask Daddy to do me a favor — if he can possibly manage it, but if it's at all inconvenient please don't hesitate to say so. I want to give Clare Cameron a subscription to *The Middle Way*, but at present it is a frightful complication to send small amounts of money over. So do you think he could send her 10/- [shillings] for me? If it's a hardship just don't do it, and I will figure some other way, and I really mean this because I know your taxes and whatnot are worse than ours. I have been having quite some correspondence with her in regard to an "open letter" I have sent for publication, formally announcing to friends of the lodge just what I am doing and why; and she is so much in sympathy with my point of view that (I have a hunch) it won't be long before she's in the Church herself. For when you really get down to the depths of Christian teaching, it's quite an eye-opener — an astonishing blend of mystical profundity and childlike wonder; it gives you a point of view that transforms everything. It has made me do a lot of rethinking, and when next I publish anything you will see that there have been some changes made!

Eleanor wrote to you a day or two ago, and I think she has given you all the recent news. By the way, if you can think of any improvements on these designs, just send me a pencil sketch of your ideas. I'm not quite happy about the small cross.

All our love to you both, as always, Alan

The recipient of the following is Lillian Baker, a former student of Alan's in New York and assistant to Alexis Carrel at the Rockefeller Institute.

EVANSTON, ILLINOIS | AUGUST 9, 1943

My dear Lillian,

Thanks so much for your letter, which I ought to have answered immediately, but the last few days have been very full and very hot. Here are two letters which arrived after you left, and I hope they are not too overdue. I should have asked you for your forwarding address when you were here.

We are hoping that Chicago will continue to be your destination, and are looking forward to seeing you again around the 25th so that we can have some more talks. I entirely sympathize with you in finding that Christian terminology is depressing; for me that was the biggest difficulty of all, the reason being that it has feeling associations of a very inferior quality. Popular, and especially Protestant, Christian piety has never attained to anything corresponding to the intellectual maturity of theology, and when we are subjected in childhood and youth to piety at its worst it takes a long time to live it down. It seems incredible that so many people actually *like* that kind of thing, but in matters of religion the taste of most civilized people is perfectly dreadful. The peasant, however, has a certain natural good taste; one has only to compare a folk song with any modern ballad (unless it has the saving grace of Negro influence) to see that modern man does not know how to *feel*. Compare also the hymns of peasant production (old Christmas carols are a good example) with such monstrosities of sentimentality as "Rock of Ages" and "What a Friend We Have in Jesus." The former are of the very essence of Christianity; the latter... I don't want to be profane! But they are self-conscious, maudlin things which, if we had a theology of feeling as well as a theology of intellect, would be regarded as heretical.

One is enabled, in some measure, to get rid of these false associations by understanding just what they are, where they come from, and by realizing how wrong and positively dangerous they are. The other side of the process must be to discover what the true meanings are that lie behind the words and terms to which these associations have become attached. At one time it was very difficult for me to *feel* any real relations between the beauty of nature and the Christian God. When I woke up on a fine morning, and the sun was rising through a dewy haze and the air was fresh and invigorating, I would feel almost hostile to this God. I would want to rush off and be a thorough pagan, and have no more to do with this Being who lived in ugly buildings called churches, and who was at one in my feelings with varnished pews, prayer books, bad stained glass, stuffy clothes, and ugly old women.

To overcome this I "soaked" myself in the conceptions of our classical and Catholic theology, which is to the theology of the popular preacher as Chartres

Cathedral to a Methodist tabernacle. And here I found the teaching, familiar in a way to anyone with an Oriental background, that God escapes the forms of feeling as much as the forms of thought, for which reason God can possess those who do not try to possess him in some image or state of thought or feeling, especially, we may add, in 19th-century Gothic feeling! This was the basis of a spiritual experience which I find it intensely hard to describe, not because it was overwhelming and sensational, but because it was subtle though peculiarly pervasive and real. The more I tried to possess God in some form of feeling (a form that would be a counterblast to bad associations), the more I realized the total inadequacy of any such form. The attempt to feel God was just what destroyed the possibility of any true feeling, blocking up the channel of spiritual life. I found, however, that as soon as I gave up the attempt to feel God in any way, as soon as I gave myself wholeheartedly to the living of ordinary life and the experiencing of present experience, instantly there came what I can only describe as a true feeling of God. But this wholeheartedness was something more than either simple acceptance of the moment or just doing and being things thoroughly and wholly. It was faith. Not faith in life or nature, not faith in the moment as such, but faith in the immediate but wholly unknowable presence of God in all things. The attempt to feel God presupposed lack of faith in his reality. But if I accepted that real presence of God as absolutely given despite my not feeling or knowing it, to give myself wholly to the living of the moment was to act upon that faith and *use* it. For I knew that I could afford to live the present moment freely and wholeheartedly just because it was entirely in God. Instead of presupposing, subconsciously, that God was *not*, and then trying to feel him, I presupposed that he was, and instead of trying to feel him in the moment, I let myself freely feel the moment because it was in God. The result was an entirely unmanufactured and wholly given feeling of God which blew the old and horrid associations to the winds.

Really, I am so sorry about the beard, but it is only a joke (on myself and the bishop), and don't feel yourself estranged to me because of a few hairs — even though a Buddhist proverb says, "A hair's breadth, and heaven and earth are set apart." It is a stockade defending my moustache, and a very inconvenient one. But then what is one to do with a wife who thinks that a kiss without a moustache is like a stew without salt? So circumstances have forced the thing upon me, and I can only ask you to bear with it as I do, and see the sunny as well as the funny side of it. Whenever I go into an RC shop they mistake me for a monk!

Love from us all, yours ever, Alan

EVANSTON, ILLINOIS | SEPTEMBER 16, 1943

My dear Clare [Cameron Burke],

Thanks for yours of August 29th. By now you should have received mine of August 4th with the revised letter. I hope this is satisfactory, because if I wait to write something new in view of the correspondence in the September mag., I doubt if you will be able to insert it until January; letters take so long to travel now. But if you would rather do it that way, I will cooperate. However, I will write you commenting on the correspondence when I have seen it.

I am writing to Toby by this mail, telling him, among other things, that at last arrangements have been made for the publication of my translation of the *Theologia Mystica of St. Dionysius*, with an introduction and notes. It is going to be done by our monks of Holy Cross, New York, who have their own press, and I will send you a copy for review.

I certainly sympathize with your efforts to try and give the magazine that breadth which it could never really have as a specifically Buddhist journal. I had the same problem. On the other hand, there is always the difficulty that if you aim at too many people, you will satisfy none. Aims and objects must always be definite. I believe that to be true also of one's own spiritual life. Certainly the genuine mystic attains a standpoint that is in some sense universal and beyond confessional boundaries; but we have bodies as well as souls needing transfiguration and redemption, and a body is a definite thing with a local habitation and a name. A completely amorphous religion having no roots in the earth is rather like a thin wine; it has no body, and is thus not fully satisfying. The function of an institutional religion with its concrete fellowship, its rites and sacraments is to provide that necessary element of earth and body; and perhaps one reason why Buddhism, for instance, has taken no true root in the West is that it exists among us in bodiless form. It has no temples but drawing rooms, and no ritual but conversation and discussion. When these are not present it is impossible to be spiritual bodily, to unite the body as well as the soul with God, and therefore the whole man is not abandoned to the divine life.

You will always find that the highest and best mysticism flourishes within the boundaries of a concrete religion. Only because of this can it afford to be universal, just as a light can only illuminate a large space if it be definitely lodged in a lamp. A light not so grounded is a will-o'-the-wisp. The mystic who can flourish outside a definite religion is a rare soul — Kabir for example, and perhaps the religious founders themselves. But Patanjali, Sankhara, Hui-neng, Jami, St. Francis, St. John of the Cross, St. Teresa, Ruysbroeck, Ramakrishna, etc., have all a definite confessional background which they employ as the necessary instrument of mystical knowledge, just as we have to employ the definite English language to give expression to ideas that are beyond language. But even the solitaries, the founders, have employed some confessional language. The Christianity of Christ has solid roots in Judaism, and were it not for those roots Christianity would have been a terrible religion like Gnosticism. It has always been the Hebrew element that has kept the feet of Xty on the earth, saving it from Gnostic dualism and the contempt of matter.

I think you received, quite a long time ago, my article on "The Fullness of the Void" and I hope you will be able to use it.

I have not read *The Golden Fountain* although I have seen it once or twice. Böhme is interesting and has had a powerful influence on Berdyaev, especially in regard to the idea of Ungrund, the meonic darkness, the primal void, laying as it were beyond and beneath God the Trinity. I don't quite like the idea myself, for though there is a void it is surely not prior to God (in any sense) but the aspect under which God appears to our sense, thought, and feeling. Böhme is a little in danger of dualism because of the apparent moral difficulty of reconciling the God of love with the wrathful aspect of creation, and tries to solve it by finding a tension, a conflict even in God — an eternal transmutation of wrath and darkness by love. Certainly the love of God is what maintains things in being and preserves them from relapsing into nonbeing. But nonbeing simply is not, even though there can be that tendency towards it which we call evil. But to make a kind of entity out of nonbeing is to introduce an illogical and spiritually harmful dualism into one's theology. I have the feeling that Böhme's mysticism is a rather groping affair under a romantic alchemical exterior, but full of inward darknesses. I am more drawn to the equally mystical but triumphantly reasonable and luminous thought of St. Thomas.

With love from us all, Alan

EVANSTON, ILLINOIS | OCTOBER 4, 1943
Dear Mummy & Daddy,
I have your letter of September the 8th, and let me first answer some questions. Mattie is our Negro maid, whom we have had for nearly two years now — a delightful soul and a wonderful cook. The address of the seminary is Seabury-Western Theological Seminary, Evanston, but there is no point in sending anything to me there as I keep all my vestments, books, etc., at home. The sample of purple thread is a grand color, but when I spoke of a blue purple I meant something a little lighter, which would not, I imagine, appear black in artificial light. However, I leave such matters to your own judgment for you have a faultless sense of color. There is no special point in matching a veil and burse to a stole, because the main thing which they should match is the chasuble, and in this part

of the world we never celebrate in surplice and stole. But those white and purple reversible stoles are most useful, and if you are sending one for Christmas it will be exceedingly welcome. I see why the neck shape I sent would cut into extra material, and I think it would be quite all right to shape the neck as per drawing in the margin.

The 3" fringe is also okay, and I like that idea of a Runic or Celtic cross on black, and by a black stole I presume you *don't* mean a tippet, but a regular black stole for use at funerals.

Yes, we use the maniple, though it is largely ornamental and is occasionally used to drive away flies if they happen to come buzzing around the altar! But this, too, has to match the chasuble. Eleanor is making me a set of chasubles with all fittings to match in the five colors. So far the black one is complete and looks perfectly lovely. The set is for traveling and for summer use, made very light, of crepe silk so that it won't crush in a bag, and the orphreys are woven with various designs. They are simple but attractive, and we have some delightful color combinations — dark crimson on white, gold on dark green, a bright Wedgwood blue on Chinese red, and red Roman purple on blue purple.

I don't quite understand about the cross and chalice design, which you mention at the end of your letter. Is this an alternative to the design I sent you, or something extra? It sounds all right, so again I leave it to your judgment. In any matter of doubt Mr. Howes will be able to advise you if he understands that our vestments are the same as those used at such places as All Saints, Margaret Street — i.e., the normal Western Catholic types, excluding the square Roman chasuble, all-lace albs, and lacy surplices with bows at the neck! We also exclude certain freakish Anglican garments such as the ankle-length surplice, the tippet, the Canterbury cap, etc.

Joan is apparently having a wonderful time at school. One of the assistant teachers in the kindergarten is a friend of ours and we hear that Joan is the life of the party. The other day the man who superintends all the artwork of the local schools came round to look at their drawings. Joan had a drawing of a boy with a bow and arrow, and promptly corrected him when he suggested that it was a drawing of something else. Then he went on to the next child's picture, and as the little artist didn't seem quite sure what she had drawn, Joan volunteered a long story about it. And then she proceeded to give him a personally conducted tour of all the other drawings, inventing tales about each to which the kids offered no objection. Finally they came to the picture of a girl who had drawn a house without any windows. "It's a funny house," he said, "with no windows." "Oh no," said Joan, "they're all on the other side." Ann is now walking all over the place, and is still very cheerful and happy, though at the dangerous age when you never know what they will get into next.

I don't think I told you in my last letter that my translation of *Dionysius* is to be published sometime this winter, and I will of course send you a copy. The introduction of the translation will first appear as two articles in the magazine published by our monks of Holy Cross, New York, and then they will print the whole in a small book on their own press. Their magazine is a very fine job, beautifully produced and edited, and it will mean a lot for me to have something in it. It's the only magazine in the Anglican Church devoted to mystical Christianity. They are a wonderful group of men — wise as serpents, gentle as doves, and all of them superb preachers. They have quite a large monastery on top of the rocky cliffs overlooking the Hudson River, some 50 miles north of New York City. They specialize in home mission work and the training of clergy in the spiritual life, though they have one foreign station in Liberia.

I am still working on Sundays at the Church of the Atonement in Chicago, taking the children's service and teaching them, which I enjoy immensely. We are shortly getting a new rector, Father Duncan, a Scotsman from Rhode Island on the East Coast, and everyone who knows him thinks most highly of him. I have found that the best way of teaching kids is to keep drawing illustrative pictures on the blackboard; it holds their attention better than anything!

Under separate cover I am sending you a small piece of manuscript work [embellished text] I have done recently. It's rather difficult to get perfect finish on so small a scale, but I hope you will like it. I have done some big ones that really have some polish, but it would be rather difficult to send one.

Seminary has now started up again, and we are having a fascinating course from Bishop Conkling on pastoral care, parish administration, etc., etc. That man really has something to say, and the more I get to know him, the more I like him. The other courses are a little on the dull side. Among the new students is another delightful person from Texas who is an expert with the organ. I don't know why Texas produces so many interesting people, but so far all the seminarians I have liked most have been Texans. And they all seem to have a mystical strain so conspicuously absent in most of our clergy, who are often just as "parsonic" as anything you find in England, though, on the whole, we do seem to be preserved from "parsons' voice."

I am so sorry that you have had difficulty in getting clothes. As yet we have no real clothing problem, although Eleanor makes most of her own and Joan's things. We are having trouble with meat and butter, and fish is not too plentiful either. Being 1,000 miles from the sea we have no good sea fish, but Lake Michigan produces very good trout and whitefish, which is to my mind the best fish in the world, especially when smoked.

We are expecting a young couple and their baby girl to spend the night with us, coming from New York on their way to California, where they are going to live. The baby was born at the same time as Ann, but is much bigger.

I think this is all the news for the moment. You know, we lead a fairly settled life these days (for a change!) and one day is much like another though we are not a bit bored. I am only hoping that the bishop won't go and stick me in some small-town parish around here; the inhabitants of such places have a provincial psychology, which I don't understand, and their minds go like molasses in winter! That is getting too settled, and I am more attuned to the problems and pace of the city.

Your loving son, Alan

PS. Over the page I have drawn some typical vestment combinations which may interest you. AW

Vestments for Mass —

Alb · Amice · Cincture · Stole
Maniple · Chasuble.

Vestments for :-
Solemn Evensong
Marriages
Funerals, etc. etc.

Surplice · (Stole) · Cope.

Equipment for Chalice :- Veil, burse, (silk)
Corporal, Purificator (linen) – Pall (linen covered)
Lavabo towel for credence table.)

Also occasionally used is the Humeral Veil :-

EVANSTON, ILLINOIS | OCTOBER 21, 1943

My dear Clare,

I was very interested to get your letter of Sept. 25 with the news about yourself, and about Richard whose future as a Dominican may be either a romantic dream, to which sort of thing he was once much given, or a piece of stark sanity. I have recently read a book by a Dominican which contained some of the clearest and sanest thinking I have ever had the pleasure of following.

I read the correspondence in the last number of the magazine, which, as you say, was very illuminating. I never liked Hardy myself. But if only such "rationalists" could see how utterly irrational they are! If this universe is grounded, as they say, in nothing more than a fortuitous mechanism, then obviously they themselves, as parts of this universe, are also so much fortuitous mechanism. From which it follows that their brains and their arguments are of the same nature, and thus are not arguments at all. Their notion that the universe is meaningless and mechanical is also meaningless and mechanical. But then if you tell them this, they up and say that truth is superior to mere logic, by which means they try to have it both ways!

The origins of Christianity, and the relation of those origins to the present Church is an interesting problem. The *trouble* with what we loosely call the Church is at present a prevalent lack of spiritual insight, of fire, of mysticism, of vital and productive union with God. But please, Clare, do not be misled by vague assumptions. In certain circles it is a dogma, an article of infallible truth, that there is an abysmal and fearful discrepancy between the faith (*not* just the practice) of the Catholic Church and the original message of Christ. I have searched anxiously for this discrepancy; I have wanted to find it terribly badly. Still more I have wanted to find out just what the *different* and more esoteric message of Christ was. I have consulted the latest researches of modern critical scholarship to find out. I have also tried to get a line on this discrepancy from the deep insight of the mystics. But the further I investigate, the less discrepancy I find. Of course there is a discrepancy between Christ and the Catholic faith when the latter is understood crudely and naively, and especially when it is not put into practice. But you don't have to understand it in that way, no, not even as a member of the Church. St. Thomas didn't; Nicholas of Cusa didn't; St. Augustine (of Hippo) didn't.

Now you may not like the practice and the atmosphere of the Church as it is today. It is frankly rather vile. I don't like it myself, and often get very depressed by it. But honesty with oneself demands that we should look at the faith of the Church and find out whether that really diverges from the teaching and the actions of Christ. To make it do so you must arbitrarily reject certain parts of the gospels as spurious, and, in the light of modern research it is becoming increasingly hard to do this. For since Strauss, Robertson, Dibelius, Harnack, etc., critical study has gone a long way.

I haven't read Kingsford and Maitland, so do not know the precise points on which they say that the Catholic faith has departed from the original. But I have read much on what I suppose are similar lines, where you will find it said that the Church has made Christ the only son of God, whereas he only claimed to be a son of God and that all men are in fact sons of God equal to Christ. That whereas Christ's spirit may have appeared after his death, the Church has perpetrated the irrational crudity of making his physical body rise up. That the Church has fabricated the wild and incomprehensible doctrine of the Trinity for which there is no basis in the New Testament apart from the (spurious) passage in Matthew 28. And so on. It is a profitable, but tedious, job to take all these issues to the bar of pure evidence and prove conclusively that those who maintain these things are not offering evidence at all, but only theories of what Christ ought to have said and done. But it is less tedious to try to discover the real meaning of the Church's teaching. When this is done the discrepancy vanishes.

Certainly the faith of the Church has been buried in materialism; but one mustn't go too far to the other extreme and blow it away with spiritualism, as did the Gnostics with their contempt of matter and of humanity, and of such human things as history and institutions. God does not reserve himself for the highbrows; he wants all men to be united with his divine essence, and consequently reveals his nature to them by very humble and simple means that any child can appreciate. To declare such means crude and irrational is often a rationalization of mere pride, of feeling affronted at God's eagerness to be loved and lived in by very ordinary souls. Note that only Christianity has ever thought of admitting little children to the mystic vision; every other religion would demand their reincarnation or some long probation in an intermediary plane, where they too can become highbrow and so *deserve* the vision. But no one deserves it. It is a free gift which anyone can enjoy who is capable of enjoying it, and the child is very capable.

But I would be very interested to know just in what respects you believe that the faith of the Church has buried the truth in materialism. It might take you a while to think them out and write them down, but after all you owe it to yourself to face the issue squarely and find out what the truth is. For example, the claim that Christ is the only Son of God does not exclude the Catholic dogma that we also are sons of God. It does exclude the notion that we are actually God in an absolute sense. We are God perhaps in the sense that a square is red, but as the squareness is not the redness, so our we-ness is not our God-ness. At the same time, it does affirm that Christ is God in a different and more intimate sense. And you can accept the rationality and the beauty of that claim if you can really accept the fact that God loves the universe and man so much that he will reveal his nature to us in a way that the simplest minds can grasp. And what more simple than to emerge, to manifest himself on the plane of time and history as a specific character. Mystical minds sometimes react against this because it seems to remove us from intimate union with God. They feel excluded from union because another person was the *only* Son. But the teaching of the benighted Church has cleared up this difficulty. Christ was not so much the Son of God as God the Son. He was God in an absolute sense, and in your heart of hearts you do not want to be that. You do not want to be God to the annihilation of your own individuality, for then there would be no "you" to enjoy being God. For underlying this is the tremendous mystery of nonduality, which is quite other than mere oneness. You are truly one with God to the degree that you are not God, to the degree that you are your own distinct self. For in ceasing to be yourself you would deny God. It is the creative will of God (and God is his will) that you should be you; otherwise you would not exist. To deny that will is to deny God. But to accept it is to accept God, and to be one with God in the profoundest way. For herein you realize that you are an action of God, something God is doing — so much so that all your actions are really actions of God. But this does not make you his irresponsible puppet, for one of God's actions is your very freedom. Our space-time minds find it a little hard to catch on to that.

I think I know just a little of that dweller on the threshold, and can appreciate and sympathize with your difficulties. I haven't gotten rid of him by a long shot in my own life, but I do know that his name is Pride, and that he is utterly outraged in affronted dignity at any move I make to let down my hair and play with God — who intended this universe to be a jolly business with the sun, moon, and stars to play with — while the enemy has perverted it all into a Very Serious Task.

For some weird reason I have turned into a voluminous letter writer, and trust I don't weary you. I wrote Toby quite a screed the other day, to which he will no doubt react with a "you'll-grow-out-of-it-one-day" attitude. But I do hope I don't confuse you; sometimes I wind people up terribly, and for peace of mind refuse further discussion. It happens at the seminary when I start in on mysticism, so I have to pray for the gift of Holy Brevity! As the bishop said the other day, "Well I hope *you* know what you mean."

With love from us all, Alan

EVANSTON, ILLINOIS | OCTOBER 24, 1943

Dear Mummy & Daddy,

It's a little difficult to tell how long it takes letters to reach you now, but at this time of year the load on the mail grows, and I want to be sure that one reaches you shortly before Christmas. They are already urging everyone to mail their Christmas packages for men in the forces, and I am getting some books for you as they are the easiest things to send. If possible, I will also try to send you some pictures of the family, but film is so hard to get these days.

I am afraid that most of my letters to you have been things in which you have had to read too much between the lines, and that they haven't really told you very much about me other than a lot of externals and trivialities. But no end of a lot of things have happened to me during the last five years, and it's only recently that I have really been able to see what they were. Before that, my own version of them was not the real version, for I have done a lot of things for stupid and silly motives which by the sheer grace of God, and nothing else, have been turned to my own advantage. For instance, I had the queerest reasons for going into the priesthood, and the moment I decided to do so everything "clicked" to move me in that direction as if there were a prearranged plan. But while I thought I was arranging the plan, it subsequently became obvious that the plan was arranging me. So I can't claim any credit at all for what has happened, having done anything but to deserve it; for there is a wisdom which employs all the weaknesses and foolishnesses of this world for its own purposes, and people are used by it in spite of themselves. It makes you feel such a fool, but a grateful one!

As I said, I went into my present work with the idea that I knew just "what the score was," with the notion that I had inside information on the true meaning of Christianity which was just what the Church needed to make it over. Through a lot of ups and downs I found out otherwise, and that in truth the Church had just what I needed. And what that will ultimately do for and with me remains to be seen. As we always used to discuss these things together in the past, I feel you should be in on the discussion now.

Over here I have been introduced to a side of the Church which I knew almost nothing about in England, a side for which most English people seem to have little sympathy because it is associated with bitter quarrels and prejudices. In England the Church, or the major sections of it, are so identified with the nation that it is a little difficult to grasp its eternal and supernational character. Because of this identification the greater good is apt to be obscured by a lesser good — the Church by the nation, the work of God by the work of man. But where the emphasis is put upon the eternal character of the Church, certain aspects of its teaching are brought out which are otherwise toned down. Where the Church is too much one with the state the emphasis is on ethics, service, and social work, all of which are right and necessary, but by themselves turn the Church into a kind of super boy-scout organization where the morality of Christ is changed into a kind of superior *bushido* or code of chivalry, which, however lofty, tends to the glory of man rather than the glory of God. But when the Church is more conscious of its eternal mission, the proportions of its teaching are restored. We learn that it exists simply and solely for the glory of God, to bring all men to the vision of God. And when men like St. Thomas Aquinas describe that ideal it takes your breath away. With logic so perfect that it has all the beauty of Gothic architecture in its mere technique, he reveals the astounding richness of the idea of God, the necessity of this idea to all thought and action, and the truth that this God is the only possession worth having.

I used to think that the highest conception of God lay in some kind of pantheism. *The Meaning of Happiness* is full of the notion of God as a vague force which everything is. I felt that God as a person was a limited and inadequate God, a mere caricature of the unthinkable mystery of reality. But I have found that this reality is still more caricatured by an idea which denies to it even the attributes of man — intelligence, consciousness, personality — and makes God look something like an electric current, a thing undoubtedly inferior to man, a thing which could never have produced man. That which produced me must have at least all my qualities; if it does not, where do those qualities come from? If my cause is a mere law or force, I, as a part or consequence of it, am also a mere law and a mechanism, for which reason my ideas are as meaningless as any other purely mechanical process. But because I did not want to admit that God was personal, and, on the other hand, because I did not want to degrade everything to mechanism, I took refuge in vagueness.

Then, too, I said that all things were identical with this God because I felt that our union with God was a given fact and not a product of our own manufacture. I overlooked the truth that in becoming aware of this union one did not become aware of God's own interior knowledge; and if I am really God, you would expect that to happen. Therefore this given-ness of union with God cannot be explained by identity, and if not it must have a more exciting explanation. It is a free gift from another, given out of perfect love and generosity — not something you can take for granted like so much water from a tap. The more I tried to explain away the personal, the free, spontaneous, and living quality in the giver, the more I found I was like a person sawing off the branch of a tree on which he is sitting. In denying the personality of God I was denying my own.

Furthermore, I could never explain satisfactorily why the realization of union with an impersonal God should have certain definite results. A person filled with the power of such a God might become either a saint or a devil, but I maintained in *The Meaning of Happiness* that such realization would produce gratitude and love. But why should it if there is just as much wrath, darkness, and demonism in the nature of God as there is love and light? If God is not preeminently good, what on earth is the use of making any fuss about him at all? And if he is less personal than I am, could he possibly be very interesting? One might read *The Meaning of H* through to the end, and simply comment, "So what?" Or, "If there is nothing better than the acceptance of everything just as it is, why did you bother to say so?" It was much to Eleanor's credit that she pestered me with such comments until I had to be honest, and really think out what I meant.

Now once you have admitted that God is really alive and that he is loving enough to abandon himself and his power to people who don't deserve it, a lot of consequences follow. For instance, it becomes utterly rational and fitting that this God should have emerged on the plane of time and history as man, as a historic character. If God wants all men to be united with him, he will reveal himself in a way that any child can understand, and not just in some esoteric fashion that can only be grasped by highbrows. If everything that exists is an action of God, he must have an alarming humility, since he is not above employing his whole being to produce an ordinary housefly. It becomes highly probable, then, that he would not be above becoming a man. Not just all men, because you couldn't explain that intelligibly to a child, but a particular character. Now if he has done this, the obvious character is Christ. No one else ever claimed to be God outside a lunatic asylum, and Christ certainly claimed to be God, not too obviously perhaps, although he forgave sins, and to the Jewish mind that is most certainly claiming to be God.

The key to the thing is that God gives himself to all, and not just to the highbrows, the mahatmas, and the pandits. In that light the Christian religion becomes intelligible, and I mean the original Christian religion which lives in the old-time Christmas carol rather than the nasty self-conscious evangelical hymn. I mean the sacramental and concrete Christian religion, which sees no inconsistency between God and humble material objects by means of which all can receive him, and not the over-spiritualized and theoretical forms of Christianity where such associations of God with humble things are regarded as crude and superstitious. I mean also the jolly Christian religion where it is recognized that God made the universe for the same reason that men will sometimes dance and sing — because he is vastly happy and wants to share that happiness infinitely, and not, therefore, those forms of Christianity where we have to be stiff and stodgy, can't let our hair down, and which one associates with that awful phrase "a godly, righteous, and sober life" — coined by that old misery Archbishop Cranmer.

Now there are only about three kinds of Christianity quite like this, the Eastern Catholic, the Roman Catholic, and the Anglo-Catholic. But they are all Catholic, and the essence of Catholicism is the Incarnation, the Word made flesh, the transfiguration by God of this physical world. Hence the Mass, hence sacraments, hence a lot of things which proceed from the revelation of the child-likeness of God, for "of such is the kingdom of heaven." To put myself on a plane supposedly superior to this kind of Christianity made me feel like a skeleton at a banquet. Or it was rather as if Joan, for instance, had come into the room with a dandelion for me, and I had been too much absorbed in "higher things" to be interested. For the child bearing the gift of God is, of course, the whole point about Christmas; the whole point about the Incarnation. And the further point came when the gift was refused and the child crucified — by the Jews because they worshipped law, by the Romans because they worshipped the state, and by the Greeks because they were highbrows and thought it all foolishness.

Of course the whole thing is symbolic, but not merely symbolic. Modern biblical scholarship of the most critical kind is failing more and more to poke holes in the story of Christ. The great Olmstead of Chicago University has even gone so far as to say that much of the fourth gospel is the oldest material in the New Testament, and there is more actual evidence for the story of Christ than for a great many other historical events which we believe implicitly, such as the Battle of Thermopylae. Four different biographies of one character is almost unheard of; we haven't even as much near-contemporary material for Virgil or Homer or Alexander the Great. So too, the evidence piles up to show that the practice of the early Church was not, in essentials, so very different from modern Catholicism (esp. in its Eastern form). I've done my damnedest to prove it otherwise, but it just won't work.

Yet while it is childlike, the Catholic Church is not lacking in mysticism; that's how it preserves such a wonderful balance. There is really no formal and final dualism of God on the one hand and the creation on the other, nor is it true to say that the God of Catholicism is made in the image of man. On the contrary, man is the very inadequate image of God; but he is not formally separate from God as one man is separate from another. According to the best theologians, God is indeed other than man but nonetheless the true life of man. Man and all that he thinks and does whether good or evil is an action of God; we are lived by God; but since our freedom of choice is also an act of God we are not his irresponsible puppets, for which reason evil is an abuse of God, and returns to soil your own face like spit flung at the sky. Christian mysticism is therefore the increasing realization that we are already as abandoned to God as corks on the sea, and as united with God as the song with the singer. But because there is always a tension in man's heart, a fear of the consequences, which prevents him from letting go of himself unreservedly and accepting that union with his whole being, God has entered into our life and done the letting-go for us. That is the meaning of the Sacrifice of the Cross, of God as the man Christ abandoning himself to God on behalf of all men. But again we come back to the idea of union with God as a gift, not to be earned, but to be accepted and used. But what makes it exciting is that it's a *real* gift. It isn't something that we had anyway automatically, by force of immutable and impersonal laws to which we can't say, "Thank you." It's a gift of love and not of law.

I have found that other forms of Christianity emphasize one or more aspects of the Catholic whole at the expense of others — the moral at the expense of the mystical, or the mystical at the expense of the sacramental, service at the expense of worship. But I'm convinced that all are necessary. We have souls *and* bodies; for which reason we need the sacramental and the concrete just as much as the purely spiritual . . . However, that's only a little part of the story of how I unintentionally became convinced of [the] truth of Catholic Christianity. And, looking over the reasons, I find they appear quite conventional and ordinary. But it's like looking at the moon. You might be convinced for years that it's just a flat disk, and then suddenly wake up and find that it's a sphere. But I suppose what plays so strong a part in all this is the men you meet, the power of example — Fr. Taber in New York, Fr. Whittemore of Holy Cross, Bishop Conkling out here, are those I think of most; not just good men — there's a little "something else" beyond that which saves goodness from dullness, the salt that hasn't lost its savor. Yet on the other hand the present state of the ministry is, as I've said before, none too happy, because by and large the Episcopal Church is still much of a social club for polite religiousness on Sundays at 11 AM (Mattins). By a strange irony all the worship that the Protestants have left themselves is an abbreviated form of the monastic offices of Lauds and Prime, to which "early service" has become an appendix.

It's a funny thing. The last war queered a lot of people on Christianity, but this one seems to be having the opposite effect. I've just heard that Richard intends to become a Dominican father when he gets out; he was always rather a romanticist, but he's been through enough hell to make him a realist I should say. Clare Burke is heading fast that way, and even Toby isn't quite so cocksure as of old to judge by a few straws in the wind. I know a lot of others.

I wish you could see your two granddaughters. Joan gets more beautiful every day, and Ann can best be described "cute." She's a regular imp, walking all over the house and into every place where she shouldn't be — electric wires, wastebaskets, Jimey's food, etc. And talking of getting beautiful, so is Eleanor, having reduced her volume by some 30 lb. of late. She has also become quite a student, and eats up Latin authors as if they were novels. And we *still* get involved in the longest conversations at late hours. You would think we ought to have talked ourselves out (at the rate we jabber) by now, but it keeps on coming. I married a real companion.

Lately we have been raking and burning leaves, which is such fun because it fills the crisp autumn air with a lovely tang. In the morning the skies are a wonderful pearly tint, and I wake up to see them between the black branches and trunks of trees; it always gives me a thrill somewhere down inside. Then I often get a walk to the seminary for mass at about seven, and the sight of the sun rising over the lake is a dream. The street is quiet and squirrels are romping everywhere.

Perhaps I will be able to get another letter to you for Christmas if this one arrives a while beforehand. But in case not this will bring you love from all four of us for much joy and happiness.

Your loving son, Alan

The following is a letter to an unknown fan, possibly in regard to The Meaning of Happiness.

Evanston, Illinois | December 1, 1943

My dear Mrs. Burch,

Your delightful letter of November 23rd has been forwarded to me, and I hasten to thank you for it as it is always so cheering to know that one's work is appreciated. Let me first answer your two minor questions. *The Spirit of Zen* is published in this country by E. P. Dutton of New York; I think it is still in print, but if not it can still be obtained from the English publisher, John Murray.

As far as I know, Dr. Beatrice Hinkle is still working. She lives in New York City, where there is a large group of Jungian psychoanalysts. She is quite old now, being, as it were, the grandmother of psychoanalysis while Freud is the grandfather. She is more or less a follower of Jung, but I think prefers to regard herself as one of the prophets of the new psychology in her own right.

I think I know just how you feel about the realization of spiritual freedom being hidden right round the next bend in the road, about to turn up at any minute, yet always somewhat elusive. Of course the important thing to understand is that this freedom, this union with God, is a gift, a reality, which exists by its own power quite independently of you seeing or feeling it. You do not possess it, but it possesses you. You therefore come to the knowledge of it not by trying to possess it, but by faith in and wholehearted assent to the fact that it possesses you. To try to possess it puts you further away from it because it is quite unnecessary; it is like adding legs to a snake or putting red paint on roses. It's a gift, and you don't have to feel it to have it because it has you. You *seem* to be trying to find it, but in truth your attempt to find it is its attempt to reveal itself to you.

The solid, objective fact of this gift which is quite independent of our perception of it is a truth which has impressed me more and more ever since I wrote the book. In the last chapter I said something about the overwhelming sense of gratitude which faith in this fact inspired, and that has led me to do a lot more thinking about the nature of the fact itself. For if this gift of union with reality or with God fills me with love and gratitude, it must itself be of a loving character — otherwise it might just as well fill me with indifference or even hate. And if it exists and possesses me quite apart from my attainment of it or my knowledge of it, it must in some mysterious sense be quite other than me. These were two points which I did not discuss in the book because they are metaphysical and not psychological questions, and I was confining myself to psychology.

I find, now, that the book lost something very important by being too psychological, for life is more than psychology (although I know so many psychologists who don't seem to realize this). But by leaving metaphysics out of the picture, I gave no real reason for not assuming that the ultimate reality is (a) a sort of blind, mechanical principle, neither good nor evil — a mere impersonal condition of is-ness; and (b) a principle that is simply and solely the indivisible sum of existing things — i.e., nature. Now I cannot get excited about a mechanical principle or a condition of is-ness. If I am united with such an affair, I see no reason to be grateful, for the fact is no more inspiring than the fact that two and two are four, which has always struck me as a rather arid proposition. Someone who read the book several times got the impression that this was the kind of reality I was writing about, and remarked that the only thing that remained to be said about our union with such a reality was, "So what?" Nor should I have given the impression that this reality was simply nature, for I know I am one with nature; any fool knows that, and it's nothing to rave about. But what was and is really worth raving about is that this gift is not a gift of mechanical necessity (and thus not a real gift at all), but the gift of a giver who, so far from being a machine, is tremendously alive and free. Thus the gift was not union with a mechanism called nature, or is-ness, but union with a life called God. And this gift was independent of my knowing or feeling it because God is independent of me, and other than me as color is other than shape.

Furthermore, if, as the book suggested, God and myself and all things are *necessarily* one, there is no gift and no reason for gratitude. Such a state of affairs excludes and opposes itself to the possibility of difference, and thus is a subtle but dreary form of the old mess of dualism. But if God has no opposite, he does not exclude and oppose the existence of things other than himself. Thus we have the wonderful and divine paradox of a thing being truly united with God, not by being God, but by being its own distinct self! We have also something to be thankful for, because the gift of union with him is a real gift, and consists in union with One about whom it is possible to be really enthusiastic. All this has, of course, been thought up long ago, and the works of the great exponents of Christian theism are full of it. Their metaphysic was the only one that really fitted my psychology and the experience I was trying to describe. The trouble was that I did not know what they had said, and was confusing their idea of God with its degraded descendant — the alternatively doting and crotchety old man with a white beard on a golden throne.

If and when you have the opportunity, you might communicate some of these "subsequent reflections" to your friends who have also read the book.

Sincerely yours, Alan Watts

The following letter refers to The Perfect Way, *by Anna Kingsford and Edward Maitland, originally published in 1882. They are the Kingsford and Maitland mentioned above in the letter of October 21, 1943. The book is also mentioned in a letter from February 19, 1944.*

EVANSTON, ILLINOIS | JANUARY 15, 1944

My dear Clare,

I have three things to thank you for — your Christmas card, your letter and poem of Dec. 18, and *The Perfect Way* which arrived this morning. The Christmas card and the piece about the bell was beautiful — *very* good and sound. I will read the book very shortly and write to you about it; I have already been through the contents summary, and it certainly looks interesting. I have a Christmas–New Year present on the way to you, a very lovely work by the poet Alfred Noyes call *The Unknown God* — and I believe you may find him a kindred spirit.

I am very glad that you have grasped the simplicity of the Kingdom of Heaven. That is the hardest thing to get people to see; they look beyond the horizon to find what lies at their feet. The fish in the water says he is thirsty, and with a lighted candle in his hand man looks for fire. The presence of God is as present as the present moment, and just as unavoidable. People fail to see it because they are looking for it so hard. They just can't believe that it's absolutely given, and that to try to find it or feel it is to imply that it has not been given.

It's as the Capuchin [Friar Minor Benet] Canfield says in his *Regula Perfectionis*, those who would see God and feel him on the surface of the soul "do not see that they have already That which they seek." Why desire him "as though he were absent"? Instead of desiring "One absent," one must "enjoy him as present." For the soul must realize that "her Bridegroom is as truly present as herself, more so indeed, more within her than she is in herself, more her than herself." There is a wonderful passage in a work attributed to St. Thomas to the same effect, where he likens this search for God as though he were not already here and now to a man looking all over the place for a tool which he has already in his toolchest... You see, Clare, I burrow into theological tomes to be able to prove to those who won't believe me that their own authorities give them the lie. What is more, I *like* doing that kind of thing; it is my peculiar vocation, but that doesn't mean that it's everyone's vocation. It's just so much light reading, and though the volumes are large and often dusty they neither bore me nor weigh my spirit. Hell, can't I have any fun?

Your news of the lodge was very interesting. Now I would very much like to hear more from you about Toby's state of mind. From his letters to me one would gather that his self-assurance is as mighty as ever. But the magazine reflects much uncertainty, however valiantly dear old Jackson may try to hold the fort of Buddhist orthodoxy! Really, he should first find out what the Christian idea and experience of God is, before comparing it with the lofty conceptions of Mahayana. The reverse of his method would be to compare St. Thomas or St. John of the Cross with popular Amidism or degraded Lamaism. That wouldn't be at all fair!

I don't want to overwhelm you with the voluminosity of my letters! Guess I find writing too easy. But I am so very interested in what you are doing, in the revolution that is taking place in so many of us that have formerly worked upon certain lines. Yet I know I sometimes *bother* my friends unmercifully, and many of my former students in New York are shaking their heads dubiously at the progress of my craziness, and at the sad story of a "potential spiritual genius" being fast lost in the dust-laden mists of rite and dogma. They don't know the half of it. Not being in the Church, they have only the barest glimmering of its present rottenness. But what if I do choose to go and live in the swamps? It's better than the madhouse.

Enclosed in the book, whether by mistake or intention, was a receipt for the TS [Theosophical Society] in Wheaton, Ill., which I am sending on to them. And herewith is a poem, which if you have not seen it before, I am sure you will love.

Happy New Year and love from us all — Alan

EVANSTON, ILLINOIS | JANUARY 24, 1944

Dear Mummy & Daddy,

The two books — Jeffries and Chiang Yee — have just arrived and I am simply delighted with them, especially with the Jeffries, for he is, I think, the most beautiful nature writer that ever was, and the photographs in the book are very lovely indeed. I have read some of the essays already, and have yet to read the Chiang Yee. He wrote a very fine work on Chinese painting, and the *Silent Traveller* promises to be a treat. There are so many things to thank you for; the birthday telegram, *Punch*, and those perfectly grand books which you sent Joan. Those are the best children's books I have seen for a long time, and I am particularly fond of *Ploof the Duck*. When another suitable occasion arises, I wish you would send her *Mischief the Squirrel*; I know this would appeal to her as we have so many squirrels around here.

We had rather a hectic Christmas, which is why I have been so long in writing to you. Mattie got sick on Christmas Eve and has been so ever since; the heating plant went on the blink and we had a lot of fuss with that; both the children were down with nasty colds immediately after Christmas; the sewer backed up into the basement; I had a double dose of church work — and so on, and so on.

I hope you got all the things we sent to you. There were three books — an autographed copy of Jan Struther's *Mrs. Miniver*, Chesterton's *Colored Lands*, and an amusing little work called *The Screwtape Letters* which should give you a good laugh. Also, I have subscribed to the *Holy Cross* magazine for you, as the first two numbers will contain my articles, and I think you will like the contents in general. As church magazines go, this is rather a high-class job. There is nothing else like it.

I find that there is a way of sending church goods, such as stoles, over here duty free, and when you get the opportunity you might consult Whipple's about it. They have to be sent to a church and not to an individual, and the address of my church is Church of the Atonement, 5749 Kenmore Avenue, Chicago. Our street numbers must seem prodigious to you, but the reason is that they begin high. Each block is counted as 100 numbers, even if there are only one or two houses on it. Thus on our street, there are only two blocks between us and the lake containing some 12 houses. House numbers are to help you find your way around. Thus 5749 tells you that the church is 57 blocks north of Madison Street, which is the centerline of Chicago.

Glad you liked my letter in *The Middle Way*. The situation at the lodge, I should say society, is very curious; I get a lot of letters from Clare, giving me the "inside dope." She has resigned, but is going to edit the magazine for two more months, and writes that Toby has lost much of his former self-assurance and feels the whole business very unsatisfactory. Clare, unfortunately, has gotten all hyped about one of the less profitable varieties of esoteric Christianity — a lot of stuff written down "under inspiration" by Anna Kingsford, and I can't persuade her to read anything decent to show it up for the mess that it is. Nor do I want to tell her just what I think of it in so many blunt words, because this would be uncharitable, and it might be knocking away a valuable stepping-stone to something better.

Eleanor surprised me at Christmas with a lovely set of white vestments made by her on the QT. They are made with the simplest materials but look perfectly stunning — white crepe silk with red orphreys having a design of gold roses with green leaves. She also gave me a gorgeous book on mediaeval art. Got a splendid bunch of books for my birthday — oh, how that library grows and grows!

Fr. Duncan has asked me to draw up some ideas for a new altar and reredos for the church, and I have been busy with that the last few days. I wish I had you at hand, Mummy, as consulting architect! Having only $3,000 to spend on it we can't be too fancy, but I have an idea for a perfectly plain wooden altar with frontals surmounted by a Gothic baldachino (canopy on pillars) in wooden poly-chrome, the whole backed with a deep-red dossal curtain. Above is a stained-glass window. Our job will be to convince the vestry this is a good idea, as the senior warden has some ghastly plan for using the money to surround the whole choir and sanctuary with cheap wainscoting, and make the place look like a fourth-rate Methodist church. In matters ecclesiastical the public taste is unspeakable, and the clergy have an unending battle to get them to accept good things, whether in art, music, liturgy, ceremonial, etc. Our special bête noire out here is showy and unnecessarily ceremonial, which suggests that the worship of God is a good show *put on* for the entertainment of the congregation, together with operatic and fussy music instead of plainsong. What people are trying to get are the mere externals of Catholic worship without the life and the practice.

Whew, did I get a workout last night. Had [to] go down to the church to take care of a young people's group and spent most of the time playing badminton with them! Today I can hardly hold a pencil. None of them were any good at it, so I didn't look too stupid.

There's no further excitement for the present, and as we hope to get Mattie back this week we trust things will run along a bit easier. I must get me to reading many books, as I have soon to deal with the priest's exams. Love from us all, and again many thanks for your lovely gifts —

Your loving son, Alan

Dear Mummy & Daddy,

Your letters of December 5th, 9th, and 30th have arrived and I hope you have received mine of Jan. 24 safely, thanking you for your Christmas and birthday gifts. A very busy season begins for me now, what with study for priest's exams, at least five sermons for Lent, three special sermons for the bishop, and so on and so forth!

We spent a very interesting afternoon yesterday with Canon B. I. Bell and his wife, who is known as the "gadfly of the Episcopal Church" because of his highly stimulating and critical, though constructive, writings about the present state of the Church. He is a good friend of the rector, who arranged the meeting. He made some most amusing but unfavorable comparisons between the Church in England and the Church in America, deploring the lack of sound education in the latter, and told me a lot about various English priests whom I knew by name but had never met. He was particularly enthusiastic about a certain Fr. Gage-Brown of S. Kensington (or Earl's Court).

I am very sorry to hear of all Joy's difficulties, and wonder very much what the underlying trouble is. If someone is not very careful, she will turn into a bitter old maid, and should either marry or get an absorbing interest in life. The poor girl was brought up under somewhat depressing circumstances, and it seems as if much of her sickness may be rooted in psychology. I am so glad that she spends a few days with you occasionally.

So glad you liked *The Colored Lands*. I specially love the section on demonology, the poem about "Stilton," and "Homesick at Home." *Screwtape* is very clever; I think his knowledge of human nature is marvelous. Did *Mrs. Miniver* arrive safely?

No doubt you have seen the storm in a teacup aroused by my letter to *The Middle Way*. Toby has got everything exactly the wrong way round, but I guess it's no good telling him so, because I have found that the real block to the perception of certain truths has to do, not with argumentation, but with the basic attitude to life. I only wish he wouldn't be quite so proprietary about me!

Daddy's remarks about the personality of God were very interesting, and very much in accord with the book of St. Dionysius that I have been working on. But it all depends on what you mean by this curious word *personality*. God certainly appears in personal form so that the human mind may understand something about him, but theology does not maintain that God is a person in the same sense that the historic, human Christ is a person. When St. Thomas says, in his special jargon, that "no term can be applied univocally to God and to creatures" he means that God has no attribute or characteristic in the same sense as any creature, and this is especially true of personality. As applied to God it means simply that he is spirit (not law, form, or matter), that he is alive, conscious, intelligent, and an undivided, integrated whole. It does not mean that he has personal whims and peculiarities, or that he differs from you and me as we differ from each other. In himself God is absolutely mysterious and unthinkable, but he is not impersonal in the sense of being an abstract principle or state of being which we have to find, which passively awaits our discovery. He is a "something" which actively loves and creates, and actively communicates himself to us. God finds us; we do not find God. Hence union with God is not attained but given (to those who will receive and accept it). And that is why we believe that Christ was not a man who attained union with God, but God "descending" to unite himself with man, so that the credit goes to God and not to man. Hence all the thanksgiving.

Reason has, however, a part to play in the knowledge of God, for by themselves intuition and experience are too subjective. Reason has surely been given us as one, among other, means of approaching God, and perfect reason reflects the divine nature in some degree. Christianity envisages a union of the whole man with God, body, mind, feeling, and will. Thus for the body union is given through the physical aspect of the sacraments, for the mind through reason, for the feelings through the aesthetic side of religion and through "affective prayer" (bhakti), and for the will through self-oblation and the intuitive processes of contemplation.

Mattie has now returned to work, we have a nice new heating unit, and life isn't quite so hectic. Joan is, of course, back at school and the other day received a report card that was so vague and impalpable that I had some very specific comments to make. "She expresses herself well before the group... Her attention span is lengthening... Her muscular coordination has developed." This modern education! Quite on the side we have taught her to write all the letters of the alphabet, to spell a few words, to count up to about 20, and to do some adding. For the latter we have a dice game called Parcheesi which she loves, and learns to add without knowing that she is being taught! Winky [Anne] (known also as the Pig) says a few words, eats tremendously, and makes faces. If she eats much more she will be like the sculptor who makes faces and busts.

Sorry to hear that old Preb. Ellison has gone; he will be a loss to the Fund I'm afraid. But I wish people wouldn't try to improve on the traditional way of having funerals!

Lots of love from us all, Alan

EVANSTON, ILLINOIS | FEBRUARY 9, 1944

My dear Mrs. Burch,

Thank you so much for your letter. I am very sorry that I was so confusing, and I blame myself, not your "lack of background." I will answer your questions in order, and try to express the ideas more clearly.

1. You ask why a state of being which is pure oneness, and which excludes all difference and diversity, is a subtle form of dualism. First of all, it is subtle because not immediately obvious. One might think that all dualism, all opposition, was completely resolved in such a state. But it has not been resolved because it has been excluded and rejected, not accepted. This may be understood best in relation to a practical problem. Suppose you have a pain. There are two ways of relating that pain to your spiritual life. According to one, you may declare that the pain is really an aspect of God and thus not really a pain. This would be your logical course if you actually believe that all things are one. Pain, although apparently different from God, is really God, and must be received as God and not as pain. You must therefore treat the pain as an illusion. That's very hard to do and requires a lot of self-convincing. It also splits your experience asunder into the dualism of the one God to be accepted and the illusory forms of that God to be rejected.

According to the other way, you accept that pain as a real pain. In other words, instead of trying to get rid of the tension of pain by fleeing to a state of oneness in which no tensions exist, you receive and accept that tension as it is. This is a much more effective way of dealing with pain; it sometimes has the most surprising results. Why? Because such acceptance is a truly godlike action, whose symbol is, of course, the cross of Christ. For the unity of God is not a uniform oneness that excluded all distinctions; it is a unity of love which accepts and includes distinctions. If it thereby abolished those distinctions and made them unreal, it would not truly be including them.

2. This leads naturally to your second question, about the difference between a God who has no opposite and a God from whom nothing is different or other. The difference between the truly nondual God who has no opposite and the God who is simply a oneness from which nothing is different is this: — that the former is all-inclusive, and the latter all-exclusive. If nothing is different from God, God cannot be said to include anything but himself; and that is not real inclusion. It is the dismissal from reality, from God, of all diversity. Personally, I find such a God highly uninteresting and unlovable. If I am God, if all things are God, what is there to get excited about in being united with God? The only answer to such a proposition is, "So what?" And, furthermore, there is the difficult question, "If

all things are God, what happened to God that, in me, he became subject to the illusion that things were different from himself; whence came this highly diverse creation?" If all things are God, their apparent diversity is some ghastly mistake, and the whole system of creatures is rendered purposeless and vain.

But union with God is really exciting if God is including me in himself, not as himself, but as me. Then there has been a real union, a real inclusion, and there is then some point in the existence of my individual personality. It is not just a bad dream to which God, in me, became subject. Furthermore, opposition is not the same as difference. Shape and color are different, but not opposed. Black is opposed to white, and long to short, but white and short are not opposites. A man or thing united with God is God in the sense that a circle is red. But he is not God in the sense that the circularity is not the redness.

All this is very abstract and philosophical, but has practical implications. It means that we find union with God not by the rejection of our humanity, but by the acceptance of it. It means that the state of union with God includes our normal, everyday experience; it is not an exotic state of consciousness which pushes it out of mind and contests place with it — as many pseudo-mystics believe.

3. As to books in which you will find these things stated from the standpoint of Christian theism, the difficulty is that the relevant passages are very scattered, and many of the works out of print. But the following should be discoverable in any large public library: *World Intangible* by R. H. J. Steuart, SJ (Longmans); *Dionysius the Areopagite* by C. E. Rolt (Macmillan); *Companion to the Summa*, vol. 1, by Walter Farrell, o.p. (Sheed & Ward), esp. Ch. 8; *Nicholas of Cusa* by Henry Bett (Methuen) esp. Part ii; *The Presence of God* by Alan Whittemore, OHC (Holy Cross Press, West Park, NY). The first and the last on this list are very simple and stimulating, though the latter is of a highly "devotional" character which may or may not be to your taste.

4. Eastern methods of meditation. Underhill's books are very sound. By "Eastern methods" I refer to Yoga with its complex physical and psychical exercises. Beg, borrow, or steal her *Mysticism*, and read Part 2 before Part 1. It's a perfectly magnificent book, but one to be read slowly.

I'm afraid I've spread myself at some length without getting down to your last and really important question about how to "grasp" the present fact of union with God. The way differs with every individual, and there is no uniform sure method. It would take ages and pages to describe all the ways and devices. You *might* be helped by something I have found useful. Our given union with God is like our union with the present moment. As you can't live anywhere but in the moment, as you can't get out of the present moment, you can't get out of God.

As the present moment carries you along all the time, so does the power of God. You don't have to do anything to remain in the present moment, for it stays with you; you don't have to exercise yourself to stay with it. Treat this present moment as an image of God, as that eternal now which is the reflection in time of the Timeless One, and you may be able to "get the feel" of what this given union is.

I have a small work coming out very shortly — *The Theologia Mystica of St. Dionysius*, with an introduction, from the Holy Cross Press, West Park, NY. This work is the foundation of the main tradition of Christian mysticism.

Sincerely yours, Alan Watts

EVANSTON, ILLINOIS | FEBRUARY 19, 1944

My dear Clare,

I see I aroused quite a furor in the last number of *The Middle Way*, but as there's no use arguing when (a) the other party is terribly uninformed, and (b) there is little chance of someone being enlightened, I am not going to pester you with replies. Toby's little outburst was just a wee bit contemptible, and had all the facts about my own attitude completely the wrong way round. Really Hardy's attitude is very logical. He knows what he wants and what he thinks. He is an atheist and I respect him for it, because he is not quite so self-deceived as certain other atheists who think they believe in some sort of a God by giving a fancy name to very dead concepts.

It's time for me to let you have some reactions to *The Perfect Way*. I have not yet been able to study the book as thoroughly as I would like. It is very interesting, and its symbolical reasoning most stimulating and often very competent — especially in regard to the Mother of God. In other places its interpretation of symbols seems most questionable. But let us get behind symbols to meanings.

While the method of interpreting the symbols is in many ways novel, the resulting meaning, the underlying philosophy of God and the world, is not. It is Neoplatonism almost pure and simple, very much à la Plotinus, a mystical philosophy which has quite a bit to be said for it. But whatever its label, the great questions are, Is it true? and, Does it Work?

Going right to the heart of things, which is always the relation between man and God, *The Perfect Way* is a champion of the idea that the two are of one substance — i.e., ultimately identical. "For as the Mystic knows, there is but one substance of man and of God" (p. 39). The universe is a "projection of God's substance, that is, of God's self," and were it not for this projection God would remain in potentiality, unknown, unloved, etc. (p. 41). "Of Whose Substance are the generations of Heaven and Earth" (p. 301). Now it is true that doctrines about God are much like shape trying to describe color, that the experience of mystical union is beyond all formulations, and that this identification of human and divine substance seems to be a very convenient way of indicating the content of that experience. Pantheism, which is what this is, is very attractive — if it is not pushed too far and made to reduce all being to a valueless, colorless, undifferentiated wodge of uniform oneness.

For a long time I myself was perfectly content with this way of doctrinalizing a certain spiritual experience. But I soon discovered that, so far from expressing that experience, it was repressing it; it was preventing the content of that experience from becoming creative to its fullest extent. Because I wanted to adore, to worship, and to thank the something that had undoubtedly caused this experience and continued to maintain it, something that was certainly not my own ego. How did I know it was not myself that caused it? Because the whole essence of the thing was this: that I perceived myself to have a union with God in spite of myself. When I tried to grasp it, it fled. But when I realized that it existed independently of what I thought and did, when I realized that I couldn't escape it, that it had me, not that I had it — then it was consciously present.

So I was compelled to adore and to thank. But the personal God of Christianity as I understood him did not seem to be an adequate or satisfactory object of this urge. The idea was repellent, and conflicted with my pantheistic explanation of the experience, which was that in spite of my individuality, ignorance, mental ups and downs, I was somehow necessarily one with God. The union was a necessary fact discovered — not a gift. But then the urge to adore and to thank didn't fit with this, not, at least, until I found out that it really was a gift, until certain supremely convincing *intellectual* arguments showed me that truth of theism. Then I saw that this gift is offered to all, but that it is a gift, and act of supreme love, and not at all a necessary and inevitable thing which may be taken for granted (to use an expressive but illogical phrase).

For the "perfect way," the union, even the identity, of God and man is *necessary*. God *needs* to manifest himself as the creation because otherwise his love would be potential, he would be imperfect, his nature would be unfulfilled. To my mind, that idea destroys the very glory of our union with God — the one thing that makes this union worthwhile, splendid, and meaningful. The glory of this given union with God that is offered to all, which is our raison d'être, is that while it *need* not be, it *is*. In other words, it is a gift of love, a *free* gift, for a necessary gift is not the result of love. Love must be free. You would not respect the love for you of someone to whom you had given an aphrodisiac!

Union with God can only be the result of love, of God's love, if God does not need man and the universe — if God is perfectly self-sufficient without the universe. Christian thought can conceive God as love, as self-sufficient, without the universe because of the doctrine of the Holy Trinity. God the Father is the loving subject, God the Son the beloved object, and God the Holy Spirit the relation of love between the two. Between these three eternal distinctions in God there is a relation of free love which makes God perfect and self-sufficient for all eternity, without the universe. The creation of the universe does not add to his glory or to his love, for infinity plus the finite is still equal to infinity. He makes us, not for his glory, but for ours, as St. Thomas says.

Now I don't want to fuss you with a close philosophical argument. But I think you will grasp the point that any form of pantheism makes the union of God and man necessary, and thereby destroys the glorious fact of love. To say that all things are united in love is not at all the same thing as saying that all things are necessarily one. I can be united with God through his love only if I have no right to such a union, if God can do perfectly well without me, if it is an utterly free gift. It is this love which puts a heart in reality, a meaning in it, a value in it. For if God is subject to any necessity, necessity and not God is the ultimate reality, the first cause. And necessity is the nature of the machine. The root of all being is then made mechanical and lifeless and meaningless — in fact, dead. That is Theosophy, etc., which you abhor so much. In principle, though not in form, *The Perfect Way* comes to the same thing — our union with God is a brute, necessary fact, which law compels. In other words, you are united ultimately not with God but with that blind law of necessity which determines him. If that be true, — so what? What is there to rejoice about? To love? To adore? To contemplate and enjoy in eternity? What is more: How, then, can you explain yourself, with your own love, intelligence, and personality, your basic yearning for eternal love? If all that proceeds from the law of necessity, then eggs [are] rabbits, for an effect is without adequate cause.

Of course I hated to admit it, but the *only* religion which thoroughly and consistently taught that God was perfectly free and alive, and so could really be said to be love, was Catholic Christianity. It permitted me to give thanks for a real gift, and to adore without trying to kiss my own lips. I therefore felt obliged to *do* something in return for the gift, at the least to acknowledge myself in unrepayable debt, which is most humiliating but unavoidable if you are to *realize* this given union. It's the whole principle of realization. And I decided that the central truth was so splendid that it more than amply made up for the present and superficial quirks and unpleasantness of that religion — although many of these became acceptable when the underlying principle had been grasped.

All this, and only one point of the book covered! But it is the crucial point, with which I will leave the matter until I hear further from you. Being about midnight, I must stop.

With love from us all, Alan

EVANSTON, ILLINOIS | MARCH 19, 1944
Dear Mummy & Daddy,

I'm afraid this can't be a very long letter, as this is the ecclesiastical all-out season. I am preparing busily; for the final exams, reading Greek till I dream about it, but that will be cleared up during the second week after Easter. Ordination is set provisionally for Ascension Day May 18th, but it is not yet settled where I am going to work, though I am trying to arrange for something in connection with a university or college. I'll let you know as soon as there is anything definite. Sunday evenings in Lent I am giving talks at the Atonement — also trying to train up a choir of girls of 10–13, who take some handling, the monkeys, in preparation for a special children's service on Easter Day. It will be Solemn Evensong with all the works.

Eleanor went to New York for a few days a while ago to consult with Fr. Taber of St. Mary's about my future, and he was very helpful. Also to see her mother, who is fine, and is coming out here to see us at the end of the month.

My little book on Dionysius should be out any day now. I have had the proofs and all is set to go. I want to have it in time to present to the Examining Chaplains as a thesis for the special subject in which advanced study is required — little me having chosen the field of mystical theology!

I have just recovered from the German measles, which lasted for three days this week, and messed things up beautifully. Now I suppose Eleanor and the babes will get it just when her mother comes out! It is still very chilly here, with flurries of snow, although we have had one or two gorgeous days. But I long for spring, and am always amazed how every year you get a yearning in your bones for the coming season and a weariness of the one that has gone. A little while ago snow was such a thrill, but now I can't wait to see the last of it and the coming of the green. In winter America is all brown, when the snow doesn't cover it. It probably sounds terrible but after a while it grows on you.

Mrs. E. has bought me a perfectly lovely chalice for an ordination present. It is of beaten silver, of the earliest Celtic type, with a red enameled Celtic cross on the base. The lines are extremely simple, and it is perfectly proportioned and weighted — the latter being a very necessary requirement. You should see some of the things you have to lug around and try not to spill! Fr. Taber has just been given one that is so ornate that the decoration cuts and pricks your fingers — all in solid gold. He hopes someone will steal it.

No further news of the Minneapolis folk, although Eleanor wrote them just after Christmas. I have an idea that Jean's husband is in the army by now.

Yesterday I had a letter from Bishop Conkling to say that he was considering a scheme to attach me to a church alongside the University of Chicago so that I should be able to work among the students and faculty. That wouldn't be a bad idea. The church is about the best (spiritually speaking) in the whole diocese and the U of C promises to be one of the finest universities in the country, being run on European-English lines rather than American. American colleges are not, as a rule, much more than glorified secondary schools. Chicago has a high academic standing, and at the moment has a nice little nucleus of students and professors interested in the philosophy of St. Thomas. Unfortunately the church has precious little money, and it will need a hefty grant from the diocese to put me there. But I am also fishing on the QT for a much better job at the University of Wisconsin at Madison — of which more anon.

Now I have to get to work on my talk for tonight, so I must wind up. These talks are given in the "meditative mood" with the speaker sitting at the back of the church — so as not to offend or distract the eye! Not a bad idea, being a trick borrowed from the monks.

Love from all four of us, Alan

PS. More on the "softly-softly-catchee-monkey" method of learning arithmetic — Joan is now quite an adept at dominoes, which I play with her before she goes to bed.

Sorry to hear of HM's [the Lord Mayor of London's] death — thank you for the *Times* obituary. Who, I wonder, will succeed him — I hope someone with whom you can work agreeably. Also received the cutting about Beatrix Potter, who is a great favorite here as well as in England. Saw a recent copy of the *London Church Times* and found it very interesting. They don't seem to like His Grace of Canterbury very much!

EVANSTON, ILLINOIS | APRIL 20, 1944

Dear Mummy & Daddy,

Just a short note to give you the news. I have been appointed Episcopal Chaplain for Northwestern university, which is here in Evanston, to begin July 1st. We shall move into our new home, on the university campus, about June 14th — address, Canterbury House, Sheridan Road, Evanston. At the same time I shall also continue to assist at the Atonement, as I am anxious to continue work with Fr. Duncan, and it will bolster up the old salary somewhat!

The ordination will be on May 18th, at the Atonement, the exams having been successfully dealt with. You can imagine that we are very busy with preparations — as a lot has to be done to put the new house in order. The work has been very incompetently run for a long time, and with the bishop's enthusiastic cooperation, I intend to go in and build it up. The house is quite large, has a garden, and contains its own chapel, dedicated to St. Thomas of Canterbury, which I am going to have a lot of fun redecorating. It is next door to the seminary, and thus a position of some considerable potentialities. I am very pleased indeed about the whole business, as it is really just the kind of work I wanted.

Lots of love from us all, Alan

EVANSTON, ILLINOIS | MAY 8, 1944

Dear Mummy & Daddy,

The two books for Joan, about Squirrel Jane and the Saints, arrived this morning, and they look so delightful. You certainly find the loveliest things to send her, and we have looked at those French ones you gave her for Christmas over and over again. She is so pleased to have them, and demands immediately that they be read to her!

By now you will have received my telegram and a letter telling you about the ordination and the work I am to do. There are so many things to be done in advance; among others I have to train a master of ceremonies and acolytes for all the ceremonies, which are quite complex! And then we have to get Canterbury House set in order, and its basement is a mess of junk and dust which is perfectly frightful. However, the upstairs is nice and clean, and we have had some very welcome help. My friend Adolph Teichert, mentioned in the Preface of *The Theologia Mystica*, has given us $700 for the redecoration of house and chapel. He has been making a small fortune in the contracting business out in California, and much of it is going to the Church. He has given hundreds and hundreds to the Order of the Holy Cross and to St. Mary's, New York.

The chapel, dedicated to St. Thomas of Canterbury, is actually in the house and is really no more than a small oratory for weekday use. For Sunday services we shall probably use the chapel of the seminary, which is next door just across the street. But redecorating it is going to be a lot of fun. As the backdrop behind the altar we shall use our large Aubusson tapestry (predominantly green), which will cover the whole wall; it depicts the finding of Moses in the rushes — the Old Testament "type" of the Baptism of Christ, which is shown in a small medallion in the top center. All the characters are dressed in 16th-century style. The walls will be papered, and for this we have chosen a pattern similar to the all-over wall painting you often see in chancels and sanctuaries — a simple, stylized passionflower in white and blue on grey, without stems or leaves. I am having the altar tabernacle specially made from cedarwood, and the decoration on the door is to be a lovely reproduction of a highly elaborate Celtic cross which is part of the illumination of the *Lindisfarne Gospels*. On either wall within the Communion rails I shall put two icons, one of Jesus and the other of the Virgin and Child. I wish you were here to help us with frontals. Eleanor hasn't time for them at present, as she is my ultra-efficient secretary and treasurer, for whom I am uproariously thankful!

I have already started some of the work in connection with Northwestern, which involves being a sort of unofficial chaplain to the huge navy unit stationed here. I had a sailor in tonight for instruction, and others are to follow, while for some days I have been instructing one of the girls in college. These just arrived on the doorstep, so the grace of God carries on the work even when there's no chaplain in residence! I shall never be able to run proper confirmation classes as people can never manage to get together all at the same time. But this individual work, though harder on the priest, is more worthwhile.

In addition to the work at Canterbury House, I am to remain the assistant at the Atonement under Fr. Duncan, which pleases me mightily as he is perfectly splendid. I shall have charge of the whole outfit during August when he takes his holiday, and this will be some job as it's quite a large church. Another advantage of the place is the charming congregation, which is so friendly and so different from the all-too-frequent snobbish crowd who adorn the Episcopal Church because it's said to be the church of the "best" people.

This week, on Wednesday, we are going up to Fond du Lac in Wisconsin, for a three-day retreat at the convent of the Sisters of the Holy Nativity, when Eleanor will be received as a lay-associate of the order, and I shall be able to get a little meditative peace and quiet before all the fun begins. Later in the year I shall become a priest-associate of the OHC [Order of the Holy Cross], and we support these groups in this way because they deserve every bit of help in the grand work they do for us all. They are *the* training centers for work in meditation and the spiritual life, and without them the Church might well suffer from a fearfully arid formalism.

Last Sunday evening Jean and her husband dropped in for a while, with a pleasantly surprising ordination gift for me — Kahlil Gibran's book *The Prophet*, which I had meant to read for a long time, but never got around to buying. I don't know if you know it, but it is a mystical prose-poem of some power. I think Jean must have unsuspected depths, for the exterior has still its somewhat Presbyterian frigidity. The husband is taciturn, but nice. Uncle Willie has more work than he can manage, but not enough gas (I mean petrol!) to get around.

Mrs. E. is coming here for the ordination, and also Fr. England and his wife from Algoma, Wisconsin, so we shall have quite a house party. Meanwhile letters are coming in from all over. I heard from Aldous Huxley the other day, and he has sent me his microfilm copy of an excessively rare mystical book of the 17th century which I had been trying to find for a long time. I mean to translate this when I have time (from the Latin), as it contains profoundly interesting material. The author was an English Capuchin, and his work is based on Dionysius.

If I am to get to bed this must stop. Your letters come through regularly, for you are the most wonderful correspondents — a virtue which I'm afraid I didn't inherit!

Lots and lots of love from us all, Alan

PART IV

The Priesthood Years

1944–50

JW: The move to the university campus seemed to give Alan and Eleanor new purpose in their relationship. He now had a job (actually two jobs), and Eleanor had a new home to decorate. Their friend Adolph Teichert made a donation of money to help with the sprucing up of the somewhat worn interior. Alan refitted the chapel in a room at the front of the house, where he held occasional mass. The house quickly became a refuge for students and returning servicemen, as Alan became quite popular. He was, after all, an attractive young man (now just twenty-nine) with interesting ideas about reli-gion, and he was a published author as well. He also had a wonderful speaking voice, which he used to good effect when delivering sermons and lectures. He was an excellent conversationalist and easily held court at the soirees at Canterbury House. Eleanor too enjoyed the conviviality of the student-faculty gatherings. She was a good hostess, and the fact that she had two young daughters was incidental (I was six, Anne two). She spent a good deal of time sewing vestments, knitting, and reading. She was also a good pianist and would frequently play at gatherings.

Meanwhile, Alan would spend days in his third-floor office at Canterbury House. There he spent many hours composing sermons, writing, reading, and counseling stu-dents. It was his inner sanctum, where my sister and I rarely went. During this time, he wrote Behold the Spirit *(published in 1947, for which the faculty of the seminary awarded him a master's degree in theology),* The Supreme Identity *(published in 1950), and* Easter *(also published in 1950).*

This letter is addressed to the British-born author Aldous Huxley, author of The Doors of Perception *and* The Perennial Philosophy.

CANTERBURY HOUSE | EVANSTON, ILLINOIS | MAY 22, 1944
Dear Mr. Huxley,
Thank you very much indeed for your letter of May 9th. I appreciate the gift of the microfilm of the Regula tremendously, and would have written to you

before had I not been away, "in retreat." I took the time to read Dom Chapman's *Spiritual Letters*, which you quoted in a previous letter and found them most profitable. He has a faculty for the accurate description of the contemplative processes, which is most unusual, while his tolerance and breadth of vision is most refreshing. It all goes to show the presence of a certain *disciplina arcana* in certain sections of the Church which it is most interesting to track down.

Yours sincerely, Alan Watts

This letter is addressed to a friend of Alan's from seminary. (Compare his letter from August 4, 1943.)

CANTERBURY HOUSE | EVANSTON, ILLINOIS | MAY 22, 1944
My dear Bill,
I was so glad to get your letter with all your news, and now that the ordination and the attendant festivities are over I have time to write you at more length. Of course, everything was wonderful, and the ordination went off amidst a terrific outburst of solemn ceremonial. I also discovered yesterday that it was rather easier to celebrate High Mass than Low Mass, but both provided the fascinating experience of being present and not present. Maybe it will wear off, but I still can't believe that it was *me* doing those things.

So you will soon be an oblate, and round about September 14th I shall be priest-associate if I can manage to keep up the rule, for which I am really very thankful. The use of the Breviary Offices certainly carries you along over the dry places, and somehow I have found time and will to carry them through since the beginning of Lent. Now I think I should feel a bit lost without them.

Before the ordination Eleanor and I went up to the Convent of the Holy Nativity at Fond du Lac for a retreat, in the course of which I read that astonishing book the *Spiritual Letters* of Dom John Chapman, OSB. It gave me a wonderful eye-opener, and some of it seemed particularly relevant to certain parts of your letter. I am thinking of those which speak of contemplation as something carried on almost unconsciously during your ordinary work, and even during sleep! You see, there is a conflict between contemplation and other activities when our contemplation, our consciousness of God, depends too much on a *technique*. A technique is something that you do; and strictly speaking *you* can only do one thing at a time. But contemplation is really something that God does in *you*, and its technique is so confusingly simple that it isn't really a technique at all. God *is* here and now, and a technique for grasping him and holding him is as unnecessary as a bucket to a fish. The secret is to abandon every idea, method, and device which you use for grasping the fact of God's presence — because the important thing is that the fact should grasp you, not you the fact. In attempting the latter, the former is not realized. You might think that such an abandonment of technique and method would deliver you over to nothingness. So it does — but to no ordinary nothingness, but rather to that mysterious void, the divine darkness, from which the power of God emerges. The thing works because God truly and objectively *is* quite apart from one's own thought and imaginations about him.

This abandonment of technique is not, however, quietism. It is faith. Quietism is doing nothing in order to find God, and this studied "doing nothing" is still a device, a technique, for grasping the ungraspable, and presupposes lack of faith in the truth that God is here and now and holds us in spite of ourselves. Therefore it still falls short of handing the mind and will entirely over to God. The point is to give the mind to God himself and not to our own method of conceiving him. He will do the rest. Our consciousness of God is then determined by God himself and not by our thoughts and feelings about him. But I don't think you can tell that to a person who hasn't struggled with a technique for some time!

I am tremendously interested in Tolly. The poor fellow hardly dares open his mouth around seminary for fear of howls of "Heresy!" Of course, they are a narrow-minded bunch who don't know what orthodoxy is because no one has told them. Why, they don't even know St. Thomas, and if they did would probably accuse him of everything from Protestantism to Theosophy. Even such a thorough Romanist as Dom Chapman is perfectly ready to admit that Buddhist, Hindu, and Sufi mystics attain a very high degree of union with God. Lord, how I wish people would read the right books! If they would only go to the really big men, to Maritain, von Hügel, Gilson, Aquinas, John of the Cross, Ruysbroeck, et al. — instead of Hall and other so-called Anglo-Catholic obscurantists — they might learn what the faith is about. Tolly himself has to work on these writers, and until he does so he will not be able to express himself with confidence, knowing that he speaks with the doctors of the Church. Fortunately this Fr. Duncan "knows his onions" in this field. Eleanor has taken him as her director, and his counsel is of the best. His popularity with seminarians grows and grows, and he threatens to present them with copies of *The Cloud of Unknowing*.

Gossip: The new dean of the seminary is to be Dr. Alden Drew Kelley, late of the Church Society for College Work, and of St. Francis House, Madison. Good, I guess, though I hope he won't try to interfere too much in Canterbury House. The Church's College Work has been most on paper — reams and reams of it! Fr. Duncan has raised hell at the Atonement and now has the place just where he wants it. This year we had the Holy Week ceremonies in much fuller style. We actually sang the Praeconium and the Blessing of the Font, together with four of the Prophecies and the full Mass of the Presanctified, together with "creeping to the cross" — i.e., veneration of the crucifix, to which no one objected. Those are the greatest parts of the liturgy.

Love from us all, and do let's hear from you again soon,

As ever, Alan

CANTERBURY HOUSE | EVANSTON, ILLINOIS | MAY 30, 1944

My dear Mrs. Brooks,

I was so glad to hear from you again, and I would have written to you before had I not had so many things to do after the ordination, including moving into a new home, on the campus of Northwestern University, of which I have been appointed Episcopal Chaplain.

I would love to be able to have a talk with you, and if and when I get to New York again I will certainly look you up, though I do not think I shall be there permanently for quite a long time yet. Do you still go to the Church of the Ascension? — though since you speak of the "rector" I imagine it must be somewhere else, as Dr. Aldrich is in the army. Or since you speak of taking part in the rituals, could it be St. Mary the Virgin's? If it were so, I should certainly feel you were in the right place.

I think I know very well what you mean by the feeling that God is not real to you. That is a feeling that the greatest of the saints have to put up with sometimes, in what is called the dark night of the spirit. It means that they are getting very close to God indeed, for, to use a figure of speech, when you are carried in his arms you cannot see his face. The nearer the lamp, the deeper the shadow. Even Christ on the cross asked why God had forsaken him; so you are in very good company with your experience. This feeling is to be found at every stage of the spiritual life in one form or another. It is rather more intense for the saints and the advanced souls, but what enables them to put up with it, even to welcome it, is faith. They trust themselves to the darkness, to the God who cannot be seen, felt, or understood; for they know that you cannot possess God as an experience, a feeling, a state of mind. The only way to possess God is to be possessed by him, and that is true already. Whether you feel it or not, you are utterly possessed by God; you can't escape him any more than you can get out of the present moment — but no one expects you to understand *that*. You can't even see or understand your own self; how much less the Self of your self! So instead of trying to grasp God, the only thing to do is to be happy to *be* grasped, to submit your state of mind to his will and let him run it, come what may. And he always does it!

And, honestly, you don't have to have gotten to the point of God being "real" to do that. No one ever made God real to himself; it works the other way — God makes himself real to you, just as soon as you are willing to let him do it in his own time and way, just as soon as you gladly accept the truth that you are possessed by him whether he reveals himself or not.

However, you are doing the right thing in simply exposing yourself to the sacramental life of the Church. There is a life in those things which communicates itself to us as surely but as unconsciously as the food we eat strengthens our bodies.

With very good wishes from us all,

Sincerely yours, Alan Watts

CANTERBURY HOUSE | EVANSTON, ILLINOIS | MAY 30, 1944

Dear Mummy & Daddy,

We have just received your letter of April 20th and are rather worried about your not having heard from us more than twice this year, as both Eleanor and I have written many more times than that! During the last two months especially we have written at least four times, and Eleanor sent you a long letter at the beginning of Lent. I will try mailing copies again, and send one by air.

Well, the ordination is successfully accomplished, and in a week or two I shall be sending you a set of the photographs which were taken of the actual ceremony by the press. They are really rather interesting. It was a perfectly lovely service. Mrs. E. sent a mass of flowers for the altar, and I have had letters galore from all over the place — including one from Uncle Willie, which was very nice, but expressed his doubts and his sadness that I was bending my energies to restoring the superstitions of the dark ages!

Now that the preliminaries are really over I can get to work, and we are having a splendid but hectic time getting Canterbury House ready. I think it is going to look very lovely. It has a delightful little garden with a lot of trees, but it has been allowed to run wild and at the moment is a jungle. We have the chapel almost complete and it sure is looking good since we have been able to get a cloth-of-gold frontal with bands of deep blue-green velvet, matching the blues in the tapestry which hangs behind. We have not had any services there yet, but have had several down at the Atonement, including the great High Mass of Whitsunday; it's a very strange experience. You feel as if you are there and yet not there, as if someone else had taken you over for the time being, and you come out of it wonderfully refreshed.

From your letter I gather that you are having a tough time of it, and I have been rather puzzled because our papers have had nothing to say about raids on the London area. We certainly pray for your safety, and you were remembered specially at the altar last Sunday. They are, of course, joking, but the English RAF boys over here say our thunderstorms are worse than the blitz. I must say they are scary and they go on all summer, and if they are anything to go by I guess a blitz would reduce me to a jelly! I was talking to a merchant marine officer the other day who was raided off Casablanca while carrying a load of high-octane gasoline. When they got on board he was told that they were giving them parachutes instead of life rafts! He said he was terrified out of his wits until he got angry, and then he felt a lot better. They shot them all down.

I hope you have been receiving *Holy Cross* regularly. I have two more articles coming — one with my parable about the *Fish Who Found the Sea*, and another about the practice of the presence of God. When we are more settled, I may have time for more extensive writing work, including (did I tell you about this?) the translation of an exceedingly rare and exciting work of the 16th century of which Aldous Huxley gave me a microfilm copy from the Brit. Mus. — a book called the *Regula Perfectionis* by an English Capuchin. I have had a considerable correspondence with Huxley, and have hopes of drawing him towards the Church one of these days. A lot could be done with men of his ability, and he really needs some of that "bringing down to earth," which the discipline of the Church and its sacramental life provides.

I hope my *Dionysius* arrived safely. This was really to be Mummy's birthday present, but it came out rather later than I had expected. This will, I think, be in time to wish Daddy a happy June 23rd, for which I am sending a copy of the *Letters of Evelyn Underhill* which have just been published. Mummy, I wanted to dedicate the *Dionysius* to you but the printers were so miserly about paper, and the publishers insisted on keeping costs so close to the bone that I was not allowed the extra page. However, you really shall have the next one, which is mostly written, but awaiting revision. To my own, I suppose hopelessly biased, judgment, it is the best I have done.

When I send the photos of the ordination I shall tell you more about the service as explanation to the pictures. Every one of them has in the foreground the chalice which Mrs. E. gave me. Unfortunately none show Eleanor's vestments and I shall have some additional pictures done with these; they are very simple yet most effective.

We had a perfectly splendid time at the convent before the ordination. It was real peace, and the sisters were perfectly charming — one especially, a dear old thing of 81 who does the most exquisite illumination work. It is a huge building, the sisters' quarters rather bare but clean and beautiful, and the guests' quarters all in the most perfect of Victorian taste. But I'm afraid the art of really fine Church embroidery is dying out; they just can't get the younger ones to do it.

All our love to you, and just as soon as those pictures are ready I will write again.

Your loving son, Alan

This letter seems to be addressed to a friend from New York City.

CANTERBURY HOUSE | EVANSTON, ILLINOIS | JUNE 16, 1944
My dear Arthur,
I am most grateful to you for your long letter of June 11th, and I do not know whether I can really begin to answer all its many questions. The above address is the student center of the Church for Northwestern University, of which I have been appointed chaplain, and both the work and the new home are very congenial to me. Just what I wanted.

Now you ask how what you so charmingly describe as the "fresh wine" of my spirit is getting along within the traditional form of the Anglican Church. I scent a strong opposition in your mind between fresh wine and traditional form. It might be, but it isn't. The traditional form of the Church is much like the traditional form of the English language: once you have mastered it, you can forget it and use it like any other technical means of expression — especially in its more rich and colorful and *Catholic* form, with all its tremendous heritage of mystical knowledge and experience from such great ones as Ruysbroeck, St. Dionysius, St. John of the Cross, and St. Teresa of Avila. Believe it or not, that kind of thing really does flourish in the Anglican Church, though its principal devotees are as yet mostly monks and nuns, who have no truck with the ordinary stuffy Park Avenue Episcopalianism. They are spiritually explosive people who make the respectable ones so uncomfortable!

You see, we have a form so that all the mere externals of worship can be forgotten or at least can cease to bother you. You can't live without form, and you have to invent a new one each time if you don't have one that's fixed. In so doing you can't get beyond externals; more especially you can't get beyond the externalism of trying to do without externals! Supposing you had to invent a new method of notation every time you wanted to write down some music!

I know that Christianity is traditionally permeated with the atmosphere of sin and dualism. The former is a tremendous question which I simply cannot enter into at present for sheer lack of space and time. Sufficient to say that while the nature of sin and evil is to oppose God, it is inherently futile because God, having no opposite, cannot be opposed. Sin is at root the pride, the conceit, of trying to be the equal and opposite of God. But the goodness, truth, and beauty of God belong to the nondual order. Theologians speak about them in dualistic terms because, on their own admission, they are forced to do so by the nature of human thought and language. Yet the goodness of God is not just greater in degree than any human goodness; it is other in kind as color is other than shape, and cannot be described in terms of shape. Even so, it is not well known but it is the very truth that according to St. Thomas Aquinas and the best theologians,

God has no opposite. The fact that he creates things other than himself does not involve dualism. God would be involved in dualism if he could *not* create what is other than himself, for in such case his nature would exclude and *oppose* that capacity. If all things were simply one, we should have dualism since oneness of its nature excludes and opposes many-ness. That is good Mahayana Buddhism and good, orthodox Christian theism. Sin is therefore an attempt to do that which can't be done — a folly like trying to live on nails; it is trying to oppose God.

Prayer in its essence is, of course, the contemplation of God as the living void, or, in the theological language, the "luminous darkness." That is to say, the aim is to reach the point where you abandon all images and concept of God whatsoever, as well as all specific techniques of prayer. You enter into a darkness of the mind in which you have no mental contrivance whatever to rely on, putting complete trust in the *fact* of God's invisible and unimaginable presence. Result — having given up every attempt to possess and grasp God by your own power, you are able to realize that God always possesses and grasps you. By these contrivances of our own we try to *make* union with God. But that union is *given*, and in trying to manufacture it we suggest to ourselves that it is not given, and hence fail to realize it. It is like trying to paint a picture of the sky on a window instead of looking through the glass to the real sky beyond. But as St. Paul says, now we see through a glass darkly, for the light of God beyond the window is so bright that it blinds. It appears as darkness, as a void. Only trust it, plunge out into it in faith, and we find it truly light. You will find all this in *The Cloud of Unknowing* or my own new work *The Theologia Mystica of St. Dionysius*, just published by the Holy Cross Press, West Park, NY.

I say this to show you that the spiritual life of the Church has an inner aspect which simply is not preached far and wide because it would be misunderstood. Most people simply would not be interested in it. Yet because of this I am afraid that many priests have failed to study it, are ignorant of the treasure that is theirs, and so when someone comes along who needs this kind of thing they have nothing to offer. At the same time, religion is not for highbrows only, and the more exoteric practices of the Church have the twofold object of conveying the gift of union with God to children and simple people in ways that they can [comprehend], and of extending that union to our *physical* as well as our spiritual life.

Yes, our devotional literature speaks much of the unworthiness of man. On the other hand, do you know the prayers of the blessing of water at Mass — "Oh God who in creating the dignity of human nature didst marvellously ennoble it, and hast still more marvellously renewed it; grant…that he who vouchsafed to partake of our humanity may make us partakers of his divinity." All the same, there *is* an unworthiness. Does your ego *deserve* either a union with God or even the light of the sun? Can you earn these things to have them by right? If you have union with God by right and by necessity, what is there to get excited about? It would then be just a mechanical affair, a matter of the fulfillment of iron laws, a sort of "sorry-go-round."

I have not for many years been inclined to regard the external world as the projection of our inner consciousness. I can't see any reason why it shouldn't be perfectly objective and concrete, and why all this to-do to explain matter away? Why not accept the earth? That is the essence of the doctrine of the Incarnation — "The Word was made flesh." New thought lands up eventually in Gnosticism, Manichaeism, and all the other flesh-despising, world-hating outfits. But "God so loved the world."

Just at present I've had to drop the mimeograph letters, but I am contributing articles on the spiritual life fairly regularly to the *Holy Cross* magazine, published by our monks — the Order of the Holy Cross. My fish story has gotten quite a reputation, and they will be printing it very shortly.

How grand to hear that you are bringing up a brood. We have another since coming out here — Ann, who is cute and very naughty and very dirty, in fact raising hell right now. She is nearly 2. Listen, this really has gone on long enough and I could ramble on forever. Why do I bore people with so many sheets of paper?

The very best to you and yours from us all, and let's hear from you again one of these days.

Sincerely, Alan Watts

AW: In Alan's autobiography he writes of a certain Jim Corsa, who described himself as a penniless hermit living on Captiva Island off the coast of Florida. He requested a copy of Alan's newly published book The Meaning of Happiness *(then in its second printing) in exchange for a collection of seashells. Clearly Alan was intrigued, acknowledging that shells had once been used as money. He sent the book, and shortly thereafter received "a box of true miracles recently washed up on the same beach from which Anne Morrow Lindbergh received her [inspiration for]* Gift from the Sea.*"*

CANTERBURY HOUSE | EVANSTON, ILLINOIS | JULY 19, 1944

Dear Mr. Corsa,

Thank you for your letter of July 13th. The word *ahimsa* is, as you observe, not at all equivalent to *caritas* or *agape*, since it denotes merely harmlessness. The nearest equivalents to these Christian terms in Pali, the language of Hinayana Buddhism, would be *metta*, although this signifies a weak order of love, at most tenderness or "kind regards." But I don't see how you can say that *caritas* has never been more than a mere ethic in the Western world; this may be true of much of the debased ethical Christianity of modern Protestantism, deprived of all its mystical content. But for St. Bernard, St. Thomas Aquinas, or St. John of the Cross, *caritas* is anything but a mere ethic; it is the nature of God himself mirrored in the human soul, and uniting the soul with God and with all creation. *Caritas* is nonduality, i.e., the all-inclusive which has no opposite, though, indeed, there are those who would *like* to oppose it if they could. But *Deo nihil opponitur* ["Nothing is opposed to God"], as the schoolmen said.

I think the most interesting non-Canonical sayings of Jesus are those discovered at Oxyrhynchus, and included in James's *Apocryphal New Testament*. I do not know the Bernhard Pick collection, but will look it up. After some recent study of Essenism I very much doubt if Jesus was connected with this order; it is surrounded with an aura of romance, but on investigation turns out to have been a very dull and narrow-minded group of body-haters, certainly influenced by that Persian dualism which caused so much trouble in the early Christian era and left its cantankerous imprint on Christianity itself. Jesus is quite untouched by it, and it reaches Christianity not through the gospels but through Manichaeism and Gnosticism. It was, I believe rightly, regarded as heresy, because if Christ is God emerging on the plane of time, space, and matter, there can be no dualistic opposition between God and the world, the Logos and the flesh. Christ as the Logos made flesh is the very archetype of nonduality, of that at-onement [*sic*] of God and the world which is the goal of all true mysticism and religion.

But because of the infiltration of Manichaeism through some of the Eastern monastic orders (esp. in Syria), Christianity has always had to walk the knife-edge path between an asceticism based on loathing of the body, and an asceticism based on so great a reverence for the body that it is offered entirely to God. From the doctrinal standpoint, the latter is the only justifiable type of Christian asceticism, though in practice the former has often crept in.

Apocryphal sayings, gospels, and acts are largely suspect just because a great number of them (e.g., the *Acts of John*) are clearly Gnostic and dualistic in character. This is not true of some of the isolated logia. But since many of these have only been discovered recently, and since the Church is now divided into several conflicting parties, it would be impossible to obtain the consensus of the Universal Church as to their canonicity. The Apocryphal material that has been known for some centuries was excluded by wonderful good sense, not only for its dualistic doctrine, but also for its fantastic character. This material is a great proof of the authenticity of the four gospels, since it shows how the men of those times wrote when they set out to *invent* a story out of their own heads.

I think that the correct answer to the Hindu is that if we are to extend the same type of *ahimsa* to all creatures that we extend to human beings, we should logically land in the absurd predicament of not being able to kill germs with disinfectant or even to eat vegetables, since they too, according to the researches of Bose, are thoroughly sentient and alive. Personally, I don't fancy the kind of diet it would then be necessary to follow! While I admire Hindu spirituality I deplore its lack of humor, which is surely an acute sense of proportion.

Sincerely yours, Alan Watts

CANTERBURY HOUSE | EVANSTON, ILLINOIS | JULY 28, 1944
Dear Mr. Corsa,
Thank you so much for your interesting letter of July 25th. Yes, it is true that I have become a priest in the so-called Episcopal Church, which has perhaps the disadvantage of being so labeled that some people will think they know what I believe even before I open my mouth! However, I don't think their guesses will come out right because those who know what the Church really does teach are extraordinarily few — even, I regret to say, among clergy.

And I think one of the things that people both inside and outside the Church understand least of all is the real meaning of Christian theism, which you and millions of others find unable to accept for the good reason that it is so seldom properly taught and explained by those who should know. There is some doubt in my mind as to how far Hinduism and Mahayana Buddhism can be called theistic; for while an indubitably genuine mystical experience is attained in these systems, its metaphysical explanation is very poor — if it can be called an explanation at all. Like the Christian mystic (St. John of the Cross or Ruysbroeck), the Mahayanist arrives at an experience of the great void (sunyata), out of which seeming nothingness comes terrific spiritual power, liveliness, joie de vivre, and creativity. Obviously mere voidness cannot be the source of this power, but Mahayanist metaphysics seems almost to think that it can.

The problem then is this: What is the true nature of the void which the mystic experiences as that ultimate reality in which we live and move and are, and from which we emerge? There can only be three answers: (1) that it is mere empty chaos; (2) that somehow it enshrines a principle of absolute, immutable law (*Hinayana*); (3) that it contains a *life*, a being, which so transcends our powers of thought and feeling that it can only be grasped by them as a void. Agnosticism, the position that we can't possibly know or think anything about it is, of course, not an answer.

Answer (1) cancels itself out, for to say that reality is chaos is necessarily to make a chaotic statement, since both speaker and statement are part of the reality. The argument undermines itself hopelessly. Answer (2) has rather the same effect; for if reality is mere law (i.e., machine), both speaker and statement are simply mechanical phenomena of no more relevance to the problem than the rhythms of a metronome. For the answer to the question is simply, "Tick-tock," which can mean anything you like. You can't have a "living law," or "life principle" any more than you can have a black white. Answer (3) is that of the best Christian theology — with this addition — that if reality is alive, is a living being, its motive in creating phenomena is to communicate itself, to share its life and interior joy. This it does by what is called revelation. But revelation as embodied in dogma and doctrine is only an *analogical* description of the content of the void; it is like trying to describe color in terms of shape, or light in terms of sound. Consequently the description is not at all accurate unless analogically understood. That God is personal is an analogical statement. It is like trying to show that an invisible sunset is beautiful by playing beautiful music to a blind man. It does not tell him what the sunset is like. But it assures him that it *is* beautiful. So revelation assures us, by symbols, that in some incomprehensible way, reality is alive, is a living being. But whereas human personality is complex — a composition of parts — divine personality is simple, uncompounded, individual in the true sense. Now the only reasonable alternative to this proposition is to cut one's own throat — intellectually, morally, aesthetically, and physically: which is just what answers (1) and (2) achieve! (3) creates all kinds of thorny problems; but it is still possible to *have* problems. It is not suicide.

The best Christian mystics, St. John of the Cross, the Victorines, Tauler, Ruysbroeck, Dame Julian, Catherine of Genoa, de Caussade, et al., are *not* heretical in the eyes of the Church. They interpret dogma analogically — but so does St. Thomas himself, and so do his modern interpreters like Maritain, Gilson, and Garrigou-Lagrange, with the fullest approval of authority. But the general public just doesn't read such books; nor do most ministers. Consequently there is a tremendous gap between what the Church actually teaches and what she teaches and believes popularly. Hence, a tremendous exotericism which is largely due to spiritual and intellectual laziness. The powers that be aren't very disturbed about this, assuming, Oriental fashion, that those who are too lazy to discover the inner meaning don't deserve to have it.

But the Church does condemn mystics when they become pantheists, for the excellent reason that pantheism is a form of dualism. If all things are simply one, the reality excludes and is *opposed* to diversity and differential — a point fully grasped by the Zen Buddhists, who see that reality is free to include what is other than itself! Mere oneness is a term of duality, because it has an opposite, i.e., two-ness or many-ness. But God has no opposite, and such a being cannot be intellectually conceived. The pantheistic mystic makes the mistake of trying to enshrine his experience in a rigid intellectual form. He tries to capture the wind of God in the bag of an intellectual concept which does *not* claim, as does theology, to be merely analogical.

(I am afraid I am writing a tremendous amount without getting to some of the main points of your letter — but it seems I write either long letters or none!)

I am puzzled as to why you find in the teaching of Gautama (i.e., the Pali Tipitaka) a more developed doctrine of *caritas* than in the gospels. I do not see that the Hinayana scriptures are a development at all; they remind me more of something that has decomposed — an endless analysis, lists and lists of bits and pieces of things, as if the beauty of a woman might be explained, or explained away, by dividing her up into her smallest component parts and arranging them in classified groups. Naturally the conclusion is that there is no woman, and especially no beauty. The music of Kreisler is merely the scraping of cats' entrails with horsehair. Man has no soul because he is only an aggregation of blood, bones, and pus; the universe has no God for similar reasons. I grant you that the *Dhammapada* and odd bits here and there show that much of this material was written by bored monks on wet afternoons with nothing better to do — that underneath there is a core of sense. But all that remains to us of what may have been Gautama's own teaching is so slight that it doesn't even begin to compare with Lao-tzu, the Upanishads, the Gita, etc.

Krishnamurti has a great deal "on the ball." He is perfectly marvelous as a spiritual cathartic. But he has only one idea, albeit a very good one. But it isn't a new idea; I have been reading page after page of what amounts to the same thing in Dom John Chapman's *Spiritual Letters* — of the tremendous debunking, the utter loss of God, which one has to go through in order to find God. Krishnamurti tries to push his followers straight into the dark night of the soul, and like so many Orientals, he derives great power from the void of the dark night but doesn't know how or why. He says it's the power of life, whatever that may be. Yet though he won't or can't admit it, he is talking about God. He shies away from the word. One must sympathize, because that word has some very bad associations attached to it.

I think Oriental religion is of value to us in rather the same way that Aristotle and Plato have been of value to Christianity. First, their terrific mysticism is an eye-opener to the *average* Christian who is too close to his own religion to see it properly, and too misinformed about it to enjoy it. Second, Mahayana Buddhism has a philosophic *method* which it doesn't carry out fully, but which Christianity can adopt. Cardinal Nicholas of Cusa almost found it in the 15th century. I refer to the way in which, say, the *Lankavatara Sutra* states the problem of nonduality, employing a logic unknown to the Greeks and the Western tradition of philosophy. Oriental religions are a wonderful bridge between infantile and adult Christianity — for those who have revolted from the former.

Sincerely yours, Alan Watts

CANTERBURY HOUSE | EVANSTON, ILLINOIS | AUGUST 28, 1944
Dear Mummy & Daddy,
Well here's taking time off from my wonderful "summer schedule" which involves running Canterbury House and the Atonement. Eleanor wrote you a week or so ago to fill in the gap, and I think things will be letting up for me in a few days' time when Fr. Duncan returns. Thus far I have had three masses and a sermon every Sunday, and the afternoons and evenings taken up with entertaining servicemen here. Then during the week I have to get up at 5:45 every morning except Monday and Tuesday for a 7 AM mass at the church, spending the morning down there making calls or taking Communion to the sick. Afternoons I come back here and there are always sailors or seminarists in for conferences, chats, and meals. It's a great life, and I like it tremendously. But when I shall be able to do some serious writing again heaven only knows! There are three books I want to write very badly. Add to that Toby wants to print a new edition of my old *Outline of Zen*, and I don't want to have that juvenile effort around anymore unless totally rewritten.

I enclose the latest photograph of yours truly for your amusement. I look rather angry because of the bright light straight in my eyes. In a week or so I shall have some enlargements made. I had it done for the press.

Yes, the above is the family insignia. I traced it through the crest back to a Watts who lived in the north of England back in the 18th century — a priest of the Church of England. The shield is "quarterly a field argent; 1st and 3rd two crosses crosslet jules (red) above a fesse jules; 2nd and 4th ermine, a fesse jules in chief (at the top) with a bezant between two billets or (gold)." A bezant is a round gold coin from Constantinople harking back to the time of the Crusades. A billet is a brick. The snake in the crest is an amphisbaena, i.e., a snake having a head at both ends. The motto means "Firm of purpose." Pure swank, but sort of pretty! If I remember right the original owner was a Rev. William Watts who lived in Northumberland; I believe he was a canon.

I have to rush off to Chicago early this afternoon to see a poor woman who is dying of cancer — I think, maybe, I shall have to give her the last rites. She is only just over 40 and has a girl of 14. Divorced from her husband. It's a terribly sad case, and in the past she has been so temperamental and difficult to handle that she's alienated almost every priest in town. I get stuck with some queer situations at times. And there are problems in life which absolutely no amount of sweet reasonableness will solve, where there is absolutely no advice or consolation that can be given. You feel so utterly powerless in the face of these things and wish to heaven you could work miracles. Sometimes the use of the sacraments bridges the gap and gets through to the person's heart because they speak the language of a deeper level of the soul than the conscious mind. If it were not for them there would be many a time when one could do absolutely nothing for people because mere talk would be just so many noises in the air.

I have now had to do almost all the regular things a priest is called on for — baptize, bury, say Mass, take Communion to the sick. On Saturday comes the first wedding! Looking after a parish sure gets you around to see plenty of things. Oh yes — and also to hear confessions, where you soon learn the essential *monotony* of sins. In practice that turns out to be about the most useful thing that we do; it's operating the human safety valve, or, shall we say cleaning out the dirty basement. To get rid of what is passed on to you, you have to develop a forgettory instead of a memory. It isn't too difficult after the first few.

In September we are going to get to work on the garden, planting things for next year. I saw in the paper the other day that some big shot from England reported that he had seen more houses surrounded with empty tin cans over here than gardens. I think he must have been only around the slums, and tales like that give the strangest impression of this country. Almost every house in this town has a garden, some of them are very lovely but if all you see are the houses along the edges of railways the impression is never very good. We shall have crocuses in the lawn under the trees, lots of daffodils, and then various odds and ends in the beds arranged to flower in succession. We already have irises, peonies, hollyhocks and japonica, and one climbing rose. The garden is fenced all round and contains several trees, one of which now bears a nice crop of apples. The place has been full of butterflies because we are surrounded by all kinds of gardens. The other day I saw a peculiar type of hummingbird hawk moth with gossamer wings and a yellow tuft on its tail. A neighbor has grown tomatoes as large as the bigger cooking apples, and has his patch fenced with the most exquisite show of blue morning glory. This is how we are situated: [the] alleys have hedges all along, and are rather like country lanes in the summer. There is a whole system of them, going all over the town.

All along the front of the house is a verandah or porch, screened to keep out flies, and we spend most of the summer on it, being the coolest place. It's about 200 yards from us to the seminary.

I hope you are having less trouble from the doodlebugs; at the rate things are going in France there soon won't be any place to shoot them from.

Lots of love from us all — Alan

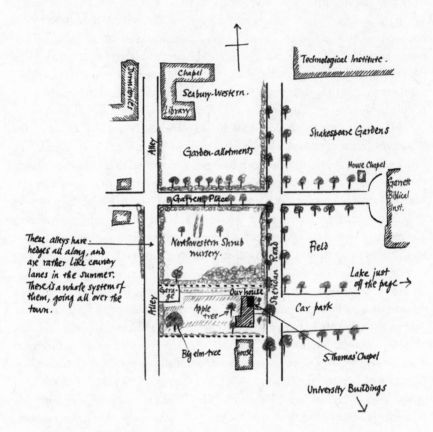

CANTERBURY HOUSE | EVANSTON, ILLINOIS | NOVEMBER 22, 1944

Dear Mummy & Daddy,

It really has been a terrible long time since I wrote to you. I am awfully sorry, but really my life is just too full. It is weeks since I have been able to do any serious reading or writing at all. The two jobs, Canterbury House and the Atonement, are too much and with the New Year I shall have to give up the latter although it may mean less money, but it's absurd to make money only to pay it out in doctor's bills! Students are in here all the time, and most of the work consists in giving instruction. For the sake of thoroughness I do this individually, making each instructee come one hour a week and take notes, and the course covers from seven to eight weeks. I am making such a point of this because almost all our people seem to be terribly badly informed. Think of it, there is not one single decent manual or textbook covering the whole teaching of the Church which you can give to an intelligent person without advice to take much of it with a grain of salt! All the existing manuals enlarge upon relatively unimportant details and neglect fundamentals, devoting pages and pages to Church history, the nature of the Mass, etc., and dismissing the doctrine of God in a few paragraphs. The Holy Cross Press [is] getting me to write a booklet on the doctrine of God for student use, and when this is done maybe I can save myself some time and vocal-chord strain!

This month we have Adolph Teichert from California staying with us, and he is great fun. He is a marvelous pianist and thus a huge asset in entertaining students. He stops by here on his way to New York, where he wants to talk with a number of the more experienced clergy about the possibility of his becoming a priest; and if it turns out that he really has the vocation he may come here to Seabury-Western. He gets on very well with the bishop, who was in here the other night with his wife. We had a grand time, and "his lordship's" chaplain told me he enjoyed himself so hugely that he stayed out to an unprecedentedly late hour. He sure was relaxed, and even allowed himself the unheard-of indulgence of a whisky. I think it's Eleanor's influence; she has a way of reducing the most lordly personages to the ordinary human level. Not that the bishop is a Pooh-Bah, but he is very conscious of his office and authority.

Eleanor and I have had wretched colds; mine went to my chest and I had to go to bed for a couple of days and take things very easy. Now it looks as if Joan has the mumps and I'm scared stiff of getting them, as that was one of the children's diseases that never hit me!

In spite of all, however, I would rather be doing this work than almost anything I can think of. The students keep you young, and some are really delightful to know; the great majority are girls. December is going to be a busy month despite the closing of the university for the holidays. Among other things I have to go to Beloit in Wisconsin to lecture on Buddhism at a college there, and to conduct a short retreat for the lay readers of this diocese at the request of the bishop. And then Christmas! This year it's a Monday; and so there will be non-stop church for two days and one night.

We are sending off packages for you both, and as this letter should arrive around Christmas it comes with all our love and wishes for your happiness. I know I ought to have written about this long ago — but we still love to have *Punch* if that is what you are sending. If you ever want to make a change, we should welcome a subscription to (don't laugh) the *Church Times*. I have seen several copies recently and it is absolutely invaluable for keeping up with English publications. Don't be afraid that without *Punch* we might get too horribly serious; we do get *The New Yorker* (which is the American equivalent of *Punch*) and is uproariously funny if you know the life of the people intimately. Otherwise much of its humor would be obscure.

Joan is delighted with her robin needlebook, and all of us love to have your work in the house. They are so good to *stroke*. Joan has lots of pictures of English robins, but this one is almost the real thing. We took her to the zoo on her birthday, and she had lots of presents, including one from a student which fascinated the whole family — a kaleidoscope. I think we play with it more than she does!

Winky is at the stage where she talks a blue streak without much meaning, although it sounds tremendously intelligent. However, she does make sense occasionally. She is, I think, a little more backward than Joan, though her good spirits are utterly irrepressible. And she is very naughty. Quite the nearest thing you ever saw to perpetual motion.

A very happy Christmas to you both, free, we pray, from flying gas mains and other horrors.

With love from us all — Alan

CANTERBURY HOUSE | EVANSTON, ILLINOIS | DECEMBER 7, 1944
Dear Adolph [Teichert],
It was good to be able to talk to you today, though so much runs through my head that if it were to be said on the phone the charges would be as phenomenal as the duchess's rumblings abdominal. [Quote from a limerick, we believe. Alan loved limericks.]

While the return of 13,000,000 men and women in service is an Event with a capital *E*, the future of the Church does not, of course, depend upon how the present ministry deals with it. Somehow I suspect that the fundamental weakness in Rice's attitude is perhaps that he does not actually and profoundly believe in the Church. It is good while it works psychologically, and the reality of its sacraments consists in their subjective effect upon the recipient. But I wonder how far he conceives the Church as a divine and metaphysical rather than a human and psychological organism? Whatever happens in the immediate future, "truth will out," and if the Church is an integral part of objective truth, nothing can ultimately suppress it.

This is, of course, a colossal question. The two general attitudes towards it underlie two very different kinds of priests now operating in the Church — those who believe that the efficacy of Church and sacraments depends largely upon man, and those who believe that it depends on God. The former class are essentially Protestant, however much they may employ the sacraments and the externals of Catholic worship. They are in the large majority, and they lack any deep faith in the *given-ness* of God and his power. Their thinking is based on the Greek philosophical tradition of God as a somewhat impassive and static being whom human effort *discovers*. On the other hand, the essential Christian tradition is the thought of the living God who gives and reveals himself through prophecy, sacrament, and mystical grace.

Now everyone who wants to think straight about the Church, and especially everyone who seeks or exercises the priesthood, must make up his mind about this question. To clarify it through a particular case: Is the presence of Christ in the Blessed Sacrament a good thing to believe in because it answers a need in the psyches of some or most human beings? Or is it good to believe simply because it is true? The same question may be applied to any other sacrament or article of faith — to the Incarnation, the Resurrection, to the very existence of God. To put it in another way: Is the goal of the Christian religion psychological integration, or is it God?

The modern, cultured Protestant mentality goes for the first answer. It judges by *immediate* results, asking (rightly but too hurriedly), "Does it work?" And if it doesn't work, immediately, this impatient, untrusting mentality is going to *make* it work — it, or some other procedure or creed. But naturally, to try to make God work presupposes the inner conviction that he doesn't. All liberal Protestantism presupposes that. God doesn't really appear in Christ, but in Christ a man becomes godlike. God doesn't really come to us in the Sacrament, but man reaches up to God. The logical result of this kind of thinking is to make religion depend entirely on man, upon our feelings, our efforts, our cleverness — and since these are all most undependable, the return of 13,000,000 disillusioned doughboys will of course knock the Church for a loop.

There are many variants of both these attitudes, some of them unexpected, for it is even possible to conceive of one in the Catholic camp of dependence on God who might believe that while much of Christian dogma is in fact myth, it is nonetheless God's myth planted in the human mind by the Holy Spirit. He would resist violently the notion that the myth originated merely in the needs of the human soul, wish being father to thought.

The point is that the essence of Catholicity and spiritual sanity is faith in the God who exists, gives, acts, and unites himself with us quite independently of our belief or our efforts.

The disappointing, the positively discombooberating [*sic*] thing about current church life is that such faith is at a minimum. This fact goes beyond party lines, and is as true of many so-called Catholics as of Protestants. Its symptom is invariably a great show of religious busy-ness. With the Protestants this takes the form of emotionalism and "social service." With the "Catholics" you find it in very self-conscious piety — the sort of piety where you *make* such a wonderful meditation, with so many acts, considerations, and resolutions, that the silence in which God dwells is dinned right out. Or else you find it in the busy-ness of spiky ceremonialism, discussed ad nauseam as a substitute for the spiritual life. When there is no true faith, we do anything to get away from the silence, from the ordinary things of the moment, because they might after all be a void and a banality, instead of places where God actually *is*.

If you have even a molecule of faith, this busy-ness is the curse of the priest-hood — the interminable flurry of "activities," the ersatz, professionalistic piety which cloaks inner emptiness, the bun-fights, bazaars, whist drives, and all the other busy-nesses which take up so much of the ordinary parish priest's time. We have to draw deep for the waters of the spirit, and in case they might not be there it is easier to pour tap water into the well and have the sensation of "getting something out of it."

Religion depending on oneself is the ultimate headache; it would mean that your spiritual life stopped when you went to sleep, or when you had to concentrate entirely on boiling an egg. And if that were true, could we dare to sleep, or have eggs for breakfast?

As to the rule. It depends where you are, but so long as you are in places where a full sacramental life is possible, I would suggest the following:

1. Communion at least weekly. More often if adequate preparation can be made. Do not withhold from it as if familiarity might breed contempt. You may think you can have too much of a holy thing, but the holy thing cannot have too much of you; it demands and desires all of you all the time.

2. Prayer — morning (longish period) and night (shorter); I think your habit of noon is also to be kept up, though to this or to the morning period add five minutes of meditation. Use as a seed thought some phrase taken from current spiritual reading and treat it koan-fashion. Distractions are not to be fought but offered to God; just *let* your distracted mind be in his hands.

3. Reading — before meditation read some passage from the masters of the spiritual life. For this purpose try to get hold of any of the books of R. H. J. Steuart, SJ, (all published by Longmans; best is *World Intangible*). Also de Causs-ade's *Abandonment* (Benziger); St. Bonaventure's *Life of St. Francis* (in the Everyman *Little Flowers of St. Francis*); Maurice Zundel's *Splendor of the Liturgy* (Sheed & Ward). These are all quite slim volumes! Short chapters.

4. Confession — every month to the day, if possible. And provided it be

thus regular there is no need to rush to the sacrament with every lapse. An act of contrition suffices with intention to include it in the next confession.

5. Recollection — or the practice of the presence of God. The ideal is to have this running constantly through the day. The point is not to try to feel God's presence but to recollect that, like the present moment, you cannot get away from it even if you try. Recollection is coupled with the *enjoyment* of this fact. You don't necessarily enjoy God directly, for you can't feel him; but you enjoy your freedom to live and move in him like the fish in his inescapable sea. Obviously, all periods of prayer or meditation begin with recollection. Also, all meals begin with it — and thanksgiving. You might add drinks, too.

That, I think, is enough. We can omit the daily ten minutes with the scourge, and at this stage you can of course do as you think fit about the Divine Office; it is only of obligation for religious and clergy. If you do want to take it on, it's best to begin at first with Prime and Compline only.

We had a swell time last night with Dean Kelley and wife. He is really making that seminary over, and at last I have hopes for the place. The wife is somewhat like Eleanor several years older.

Golly, but this has turned out to be an epistle, and before I collapse with stenographical delirium tremens I must cease. Be sure to talk matters over with Taber, and let me know his reactions.

Love from us all, as ever, Alan

The following letter seems to be addressed to an otherwise unknown fan.

CANTERBURY HOUSE | EVANSTON, ILLINOIS | JANUARY 8, 1945
Dear Mr. Chandler,

Thank you very much for your kind letter of December 27th. I especially appreciated the paper enclosed with it, which says so many of the things that I am repeatedly saying myself. The Church is in a state of terrible rot for the very reason that the devotional and mystical life is not cultivated, and those who hunger for it are driven from the Church to seek it in all kinds of cults.

So far as my experience goes, I find that right now there are, by and large, only two kinds of Christians who are doing anything serious and solid in this way, and they represent two extremes — the Quakers and the Catholics (both Roman and Anglican). I notice that you quote Douglas Steere, who with Howard Brinton, Erminie Huntress, and others are leading lights in the Quaker revival of spirituality. Steere's recent book *On Beginning from Within* is a great job, though I feel that he lacks an adequate metaphysical background, as my own book *The Meaning of Happiness* lacked it. In both the spirituality is too subjective, too psychological, lacking sufficient sense of dependence on the God who exists and acts quite independently of our faith and our feelings. And in my own book the perception of the nature of this God was still somewhat vague; there was not the definite assertion that God is *alive*, and not simply the impersonal, natural force. It is the liveliness, not the mere abstractness and vastness, of God that places him beyond the reach of thought and imagination. Thus when the Church speaks of God as "personal," the word is intended to mean liveliness and not, as many think, composite form and structure.

But of course most of the doctrines of the Church are misunderstood for the very reason that the spiritual life is not cultivated. They are grasped only on the formal and historical plane, and people seldom go deeper to understand them as symbols of God himself. Understood profoundly (i.e., as historical and theological symbols of God) the full richness of Catholic doctrine is really a remarkable and glorious spiritual treasure. Protestantism is greatly impoverished because it has thrown out the baby with the bathwater, the life-giving symbols with the superstition. To change the metaphor, it has made the mistake of despising the shell which contains the kernel; and we can never have the kernel without the shell which protects it while it grows. Conversely, the more naive forms of Catholicism have never suspected that there is a kernel within the shell. As a result, Protestantism has largely lost spiritual power, and purveys mostly ethical platitudes, while run-of-the-mill Catholicism blindly goes through the motions of thoughts and actions whose inner significance is lost. The great task of the Church is now, through the spiritual and mystical life, to discover the inner meaning of its own doctrinal treasure. But it is awful hard going to get people to see that!

At least, it's particularly hard for the ordinary parish priest. It's not quite so tough for me because I am now a college chaplain here at Northwestern University, and the young have open minds.

Sincerely yours, Alan Watts

This letter is addressed to an otherwise unknown friend.

CANTERBURY HOUSE | EVANSTON, ILLINOIS | FEBRUARY 12, 1945
My dear Charles,
I really must apologize for my long delay in thanking you for the two Kelly books and the Pennington pamphlet. In the first place, I wanted to read them before I wrote to you, and in the second, the approach of Lent has given me quite a bit of extra work.

The *Testament of Devotion* is really a wonderful job, and I think quite the best part of it is the essay on holy obedience. I think the value of the book is "inspirational" rather than "directive," for he makes the call to the complete abandonment of one's being to the divine will extremely powerful. But I wonder: Can you simply set out to surrender your life to God? Of course, one has to try, but the more you try, the more you are humiliated to discover that, by yourself, you can't do any such thing. The human will is subtly twisted and perverted in the first place, so that "when the wrong man uses the right means, the right means work in the wrong way." And we are all "the wrong man"! Our attempts to abandon ourselves to God are subtle, indirect attempts to get God for our own, since the will is chronically self-centered.

Yet the humiliation of discovering that we can't do it is a very necessary part of the purgative way. It teaches us to depend more on God, and to learn that when any "abandoning" is done, it is done not by ourselves but by God in us — and we have to wait on his will and trust him to act in his own time and way.

This is something which the modern mind seems to find it very hard to understand. It has the Greek conception of God as a passive hidden treasure awaiting our discovery, rather than the Hebrew idea of the God who *acts*, who says, "You have not chosen me; I have chosen you." If God is just hidden treasure, then by the right means we ought to be able to dig him out by simple application of the right spiritual technique.

I do not, however, believe that God's choosing of us is purely arbitrary. In one way or another we are all chosen, we are all already abandoned to God by God himself; and the will has to learn through its own humiliation, through the abortiveness of its own efforts, to fall back on union with God as a *totally undeserved gift*. This gift is ours *now*; but it is so hard to accept just because the perverted *will* makes the very act of acceptance an attempt to *get* God for its own, and so escape the final humiliation of confessing complete impotence. Yet still the gift is given quite apart from our acceptance of it, which leaves us with precious little to do except to praise God with everything that we have!

Thank you so much, and do let's hear from you again when you have time to write.

With all good wishes,

Very sincerely yours, Alan Watts

Canterbury House | Evanston, Illinois | April 26, 1945

Dear Mummy & Daddy,

This is a terribly overdue letter, but you know what the Lent and Easter season is for clergy — and Eleanor has been filling in the gaps. But the work has been very fruitful and made quite considerable strides. Not only has it advanced things for us financially, but I think we are really "getting somewhere" with the students.

I have started a choir — a small one of six girls — for the singing of Gregorian plainsong. They made their first appearance at our Easter Midnight Mass, which was a huge success — for Northwestern — where we are really just as much missionaries as if we were in darkest Africa. We borrowed a small but very lovely Methodist chapel across the street for the occasion — built in the most perfect Tudor Gothic style, with really exquisite stained glass. I don't suppose the poor place will ever be the same again — after all the incense and stuff we threw around!

The special service for Holy Saturday is the very ancient blessing of new fire and the Paschal candle — supposed to be the oldest part of our liturgy other than the Lord's Prayer, the Psalms, and other biblical material. It begins in complete darkness, in which the new fire is struck and carried from the west door to the altar, where it is used to light the Paschal candle and all others in the church. The blessing of the candle is sung to a hauntingly beautiful chant, the words having to do with the mystery of finding light in the very depths of darkness; you should read them sometime — one of the A[nglo-]C[atholic] clergy would lend you a copy — it is a thing of the greatest spiritual depth and value. The Mass followed this immediately, and I was amazed at the real devotion and sincerity of the group; so many will ordinarily come to a thing like this just to see the show.

Thank you very much indeed for sending over the legacy, and for settling my account with Mr. Koizumi. The receipt is returned herewith. Thank God you are now free from rockets and bombs. I am afraid that last bout with the V-2s must have been simply horrible. Before long the actual war in Europe will be over, but I am afraid that the Continent itself won't recover for a very long time — maybe a couple of centuries. I hope you both enjoyed yourselves in Tunbridge Wells.

At last I too have a copy of Evelyn Underhill's — and find it *very* good. She was so sane and down-to-earth, and in work such as hers I see the English Church at its absolute best. We can't have too much of her approach.

Today I had to go down to the National Broadcasting Co. to make records of morning and night prayers for the opening and closing of a day's radio program. They are inviting clergy all over the country to do this. The records are made on 1'6" discs of black glass, and take a perfect impression. It's so surprising to hear the sound of your own voice — especially when you discover that you have such an English intonation! I find it quite impossible to read prayers with any sort of American pronunciation; it simply won't go with Elizabethan English. But I am happy to find out that I have *not* acquired a parson's bleat or any other clerical cacophony.

I'm still kept busy with the counseling and instructing side of this work, and find it intensely interesting. Among other things I am now preparing a Jewish girl for baptism, which is a rather unusual proposition. But I run into an awful lot of quite hard psychological problems, neuroses and the like, which are tough going — the more so when you've seen so many professional psychologists fail at them! And book learning is just no good in dealing with them, even though one goes on reading and reading to try and get a little light.

With luck I may get a chance at writing a new book this summer, a book which has been boiling up for a long time. But I've first to get another pamphlet for Holy Cross completed, which they will first run in the July and August issues of their magazine. Hope you liked the article in the April issue. We shall probably be in New York for a few weeks in July or late June. I was there over Passion Sunday, assisting at St. Mary's and visiting with Ruth.

We are getting our garden into shape; the tulips are lovely, and we have had a gorgeous show of apple blossom and lilac. The other day we had a visit from two *real bluebirds* — simply gorgeous creatures, who stayed for a few minutes and passed on. The blue on the backs, wings, and heads is truly vivid. The red cardinals are all around now with their wonderful song, and just loving the April rains.

Hope our birthday gifts for April 15 arrived safely; you will find them very useful, even if there is duty to be paid.

Lots of love from us all — Alan

PS. The consignment of cigarettes has just arrived — and they are very, very welcome! Thank you so much. The shortage is now worse than ever. They reached us in excellent condition — as those tins protect them perfectly. It's funny, but you can get all you want in Canada, but just across the border, nothing doing!

JW: By now, Canterbury House was a bustling center of activity with students coming and going at all hours. The weekly soirees had as many as thirty people and more, discussing the problems of life, politics, and the church, all this mixed with a party atmosphere. Our mother would share the piano bench with Tolly (Adolph) and then Carlton Gamer. They would play songs and sing along and get very silly (from a child's perspective), a favorite being an advertising jingle that Tolly made up about a laxative called "Jumbo Dump." They'd all double over with laughter at the punch line.

Northwestern students John Gouldin and Jacqueline "Jacquie" Baxter became good friends with Alan. They were a lively and creative pair. Jacquie was very pretty and would tease the men by lying down on the floor, challenging them to pick her up — which they could not do. Alan and John would get into all sorts of high jinks, from making rockets of tinfoil and match heads and shooting them off in the backyard, to

driving around town at night shooting out lights in tunnels and on occasion, stealing
gravestones. They actually took me along on some of these escapades.

The morning after such gatherings, Anne and I would creep downstairs, finding
the light in the living room diffused by lingering cigarette smoke. We'd go through
the sofas and easy chairs looking for lost coins, which we always found, and would
set about tidying up, taking drink glasses, and ashtrays into the kitchen. If the maid
wasn't there, we'd wash the dishes with the hope of being paid a quarter.

CANTERBURY HOUSE | EVANSTON, ILLINOIS | APRIL 27, 1945
Dear Charlie [a fan],
I hope you will forgive the long delay in answering your letter of March 16th, but
this Easter has been very busy indeed, and I wanted to be able to do justice to it. I
am most grateful for the Larsen book, which I find very good, and I am returning
it under separate cover this week.

It is true that the idea of surrender to the will of God can seem cold — especially when in the dim background of one's mind there is a somewhat Calvinistic
association with the phrase "the will of God." I think all of us reared in a Protestant background have something of that association. But the good impulses that
arise in your own heart, together with everything that you experience at every
moment, are indeed the very touch of God upon your soul — the movement of
the Spirit experienced as the present moment.

Theology falsely interpreted does indeed make the will of God seem an external thing, though properly understood there is no "inside" or "outside" in
relation to God, as if he could be bounded by spatial limits and excluded by a wall
of flesh. But terminology — theological, metaphysical, philosophical — always
blunders around helplessly in the realm of mystical experience, and this is as true
of a theistic as of a pantheistic theology.

I note how much in your paper you incline to the pantheistic-impersonal
way of expression, a way to which you are drawn (a) because of the very intensity of the experience of union, and (b) because the traditional conceptions of the
divine personality need a thorough cleansing from anthropomorphic elements.
But it seems to me more and more that both the theistic-anthropomorphic and
the pantheistic-impersonal conceptions of God are absurdly inadequate to the
reality. The former makes God seem so external and distant and limited, and
the latter so impotent and vague and neutral. But that impression is precisely
what you do *not* wish to give, because your experience is one of intense life. The
impersonal pantheist, whether Buddhist, Hindu, or Taoist, never actually means
what he says. He feels one with God to the point of identity, and yet because
this does not make him omnipotent, omniscient, etc., he is forced to describe

God as impersonal — i.e., lacking those distinctly personal powers. At the same time, this is felt as an experience of intense life, for which reason he describes the divine nature with such contradictory phrases and "living principle" or "impersonal life."

The trouble is that "personality" is a terrible word. I would not say that man is *the* expression of God's personality, because man is only very incompletely personal. Man is part living spirit and part machine, more of the latter than of the former. The higher the life, the more personal (i.e., spiritual) it is, the more alive, the more conscious, the more integrated, the more individual (i.e., undivided). We think of personality as complex, as human personality is, being a composition of many parts. But the personality of God is simple; it is pure life, pure spirit, the absolutely uncompounded One. The Hindus were right in calling God the Atman, the Self, which is the same as the Hebrew name Yahveh, the "I am."

I am interested in what you say about the reason that so many of us do not live in a "constant condition of uplifted heart." You know, there has always been considerable misunderstanding about the *constant* mental state of the great mystics, as to whether or not they were in continual ecstasy. Saudreau regards ecstasy as a weakness — a reaction of an infirm psyche to the inpouring power of God. In time they grow out of it! But even the intense periods of pure spiritual joy seem to be relatively short, though it would seem that there is always a semi-conscious undertone of joy in union with God that persists and underlies all other experiences as the mirror underlies its images.

With many thanks, and all good wishes,

Very sincerely, Alan Watts

CANTERBURY HOUSE | EVANSTON, ILLINOIS | DECEMBER 17, 1945

Dear Mummy & Daddy,

At last the main work of the term is over, and this really is the first moment I have had for weeks to sit down and write a letter. I think it will reach you in time to wish you a very happy Christmas. This term has been a particularly active and successful one for us, as the whole work has been making great strides. Yesterday we had a perfectly lovely pre-Christmas service for the last Sunday of term. The choir was in great form — sang carols, including Praetorius's "Lo How a Rose E'er Blooming," specially harmonized for girls' voices by our organist. There was a splendid turnout despite the bitter cold and the imminence of final exams. It is below zero today.

Just to show you what I have to do: I have given 109 hours of instruction to 16 students since October, and 8 hours of personal counseling, preached a sermon and given an informal lecture every Sunday, conducted about 60 services. We have more than tripled our attendance since this time last year. I shall shortly be sending you some pictures of self with some of my chief student helpers, recently taken for the university yearbook.

We have received your Christmas gifts, but are keeping them wrapped up for the day. I think ours should reach you in time. I am sorry, but we shall have to dribble those apricots through to you one can at a time; as regulations do not permit more than 2 lb. of one kind of foodstuff per person per month.

I have plans in mind for that candlestick, haven't had a moment to sit down and draw it. It seems the piece of wood will make one large candlestick hold the Paschal candle, and I think I shall be able to make the design during the holidays.

Adolph Teichert is on his way from California and will arrive tonight, his train having been delayed 12 hours by a blizzard. He will be staying with us until the end of the week, and then goes on to New York. After that Ruth comes to stay with us over Christmas. Fr. Duncan has invited me to celebrate the Midnight Mass at the Atonement, and I'm looking forward very much to being there again for that occasion.

A few weeks ago Fr. Whittemore of Holy Cross stopped by to see us on his way through Chicago, and we had a delightful time with him. I am more and more impressed with his astounding insight and spiritual genius. He has shown me some writings of his (private notes), which top anything I have ever read on mystical religion. He and Winky had a wonderful time together playing bell button on her nose.

There is a terrible dearth of things to buy for Christmas gifts, and I imagine it is much worse with you. We have been trying to get gramophone records, but almost everything we want is out of stock. Someone has loaned us Landowska's harpsichord version of the Bach *Chromatic Fantasia and Fugue* and the *Italian Concerto*. That old biddy certainly has technique. I am becoming a terrible purist in music; everything later than the 17th century is wearing thin, with the exception of one or two moderns and Beethoven's piano concerti. But I can listen to Bach by the hour. It's terrible to get so limited in taste, but I can't help feeling that the Romantics were awfully trite. (I'm afraid my literary composition of letters is vile; three "terribles" in one paragraph!) How is BBC music these days? I hope as good as ever. Broadcasts here, except on Sunday afternoons when we get the NY Philharmonic, are utterly atrocious (not to say terrible) — as Aldous Huxley says, "news items, mutually irrelevant bits of information, blasts of corybantic or sentimental music, continually repeated doses of drama that bring no catharsis, but merely create a craving for daily or even hourly emotional enemas." That's one place where we could really do with state ownership to get rid of the advertisers.

Bill McGovern is back on campus from the war. He was an assistant to the general staff. This cold weather ought to bring out his Tibetan lama cap and fur coat again. The whole family came over for tea the other Sunday; he has managed to bring up some wonderfully intelligent children, which considering the school system is something. He is professor of political science here.

I had lunch this week with Prof. Carlson, a particularly charming member of the history department. He hopes to go to England this coming year to do research at the British Museum, and is rather worried about finding a place to stay. Do you by any chance know of any hotel, boarding house, room, or whatnot in Chislehurst where he could be put up? He is quite a young man, much interested in religion, and I hope one of these days to slip him quietly into the Church. If he could meet the right people in London... who knows?

Your loving son, Alan

JW: William Montgomery, or Bill, McGovern mentioned above and in the letter below, was most likely introduced to Alan by our grandmother Ruth. I remember visiting his home as a child and being amused by his appearance. He was noted for looking somewhat disheveled and had a large red nose. Bill was an explorer and had spent time in the Himalayas and Japan, where he studied at Nishi Hongan-ji Temple in Kyoto. He gained a reputation during World War II for delivering confidential daily briefings on enemy preparedness to President Roosevelt and his Joint Chiefs of Staff. Bill also served as a foreign correspondent for The Chicago Sun-Times *and taught Chinese at the University of London (he spoke twelve languages). As a professor at Northwestern University, he taught a very popular political science course, insisting that his students learn to write one Chinese character a week. Northwestern considered him their very own Indiana Jones.*

CANTERBURY HOUSE | EVANSTON, ILLINOIS | FEBRUARY 12, 1946
Dear Mummy & Daddy,
I just hate to think that the delay between my letters gets longer and longer. I wish you could see my appointment book: almost every day is planned for me until the middle of March! I think Eleanor has told you more or less what goes on in the way of work. However, we do get some relaxation. This afternoon we went to the concert of the Chicago Symphony, and heard Rubinstein play the Beethoven Piano Concerto No. 4 and Bizet's 4th Symphony, both of which were

very lovely. After that we bought some records, including a suite by Corelli, of whom we have heard rather a lot lately.

On Saturday we went to a delightful party at Bill McGovern's house, and met some interesting people — for a change. Save for the students, the residents of Evanston are apt to be rather dull — especially the churchy ones. There was a particularly pleasant Count Ostrowski there, a young man from the Polish Consulate, of whom we hope to see more. He is said to be one of the leading authorities on French history, and he certainly was astonishingly learned for his age.

Speaking of diplomats, I have also had a visit from a certain Mr. Groth of the American Foreign Service who has read my books and came by on his way out to Denver to discuss Oriental philosophy. He is rather a find — an oldish man of particularly fine type; one of those long, lean Yankees of the old New England breed. He is coming again on his way back, and then expects to leave for Hamburg.

While on this subject — how about your passports? Would it help if I wrote a note to Frank Ashton-Gwatkin; I am sure he would be glad to help, and we have kept in touch fairly constantly. Let me know at once if the bureaucrats are being too absurd, and I will drop him a line.

I was so pleased to have the *Memorials of Canterbury Cathedral* for Christmas. I have read a lot of it with great enjoyment — mostly late at night before going to sleep, which is when I get much of my reading done. The pile of books waiting to be gone through is rather formidable, and as for those I ought to write — well, that's another story. I haven't been able to do a lick on my own since last summer.

Our choir is reaching quite a remarkable degree of proficiency these days, and we are looking forward to some extremely interesting music at Holy Week and Easter. We have been able to obtain copies of the ancient melody for the singing of the Passion on Palm Sunday, where the various parts — the narrator, the Christ, Pilate, the crowd, etc., are divided up between cantors and the choir. Then we shall be having an Easter Midnight Mass again, and this time in the large seminary chapel with the big organ. Since January we have added a men's section to the choir, singing separately from the women (echo fashion), and their special job is to take care of the "propers" — the ancient forms of introit, gradual, etc. As a result we are attaining some fame as the only Anglican Church for miles around which specializes in mediaeval church music.

We are still having a fight with the university about our house, but the bishop has plans to keep everything under control. Actually we shall *have* to think of a bigger place before long, for at present our living room is hardly large enough to accommodate the Sunday evening groups. We have nearly 30 — sometimes more — every Sunday evening. Adolph Teichert gave me a balopticon for

Christmas — that's a glorified magic lantern which will project ordinary picture postcards upon the screen. It hasn't arrived from the manufacturers yet, but should be here by the end of the month, when I shall start using it for lectures on Christian art and architecture.

Daddy, do you ever get a chance to go by the British Museum? They used to publish lovely colored postcards of illuminated MSS and other treasures of ecclesiastical art. If these are still available, I should like to have anything and everything of this kind, and if you can possibly stop by the museum any time, I can allot from £2 to £3 for suitable pictures for our lectures. They should not exceed 6" x 6".

Please don't buy much in the way of clothes before you come here. The prices you mention are absurd, and you can get them better and cheaper here and wear them on you when you return. Men's shirts are still scarce. I have no trouble with this as I get specially made black ones, and have a large stock on hand. This enables me to take off my coat in hot weather without showing all the false fronts, strings, pulleys, straps, and buckles that some clergy employ in order to be black below the collar.

Uncle Willie and family are thinking of coming by this way rather soon. I had a somewhat tempestuous letter from him around Christmas, harping as usual upon my popery, which is howlingly funny because I am a terrible liberal despite the external labels. I try to be as nice to him as possible, but he will hit me on my argumentative funny bone. He said that if ever it were absolutely necessary to prove by irrefutable logic that black is white, he would employ me to do it!

When will I get around to designing that candlestick? O Lord, when? At least I have bought me a wonderful gadget to draw the design — a ruler which takes the shape of any desired curve. It will have to be about 4'6" high, made in two pieces. Possibly I can get after it tomorrow evening. Is the wood you have dark in color? I think I would like the wood left quite unstained; if necessary soak it a little in linseed oil. I don't quite know what problems are involved with very ancient wood.

The proofs of my pamphlet *The Case for God* have come from the printers, which means that it should be in circulation fairly soon. I need it badly for my work here. I am seeing the editor of the *Holy Cross* magazine very soon, and will enquire about Fr. Moore-Allen's subscription. There are some delays in foreign subscriptions.

Am mailing you a photograph of self with my chief student workers. They are a wonderful bunch of kids.

Well, it's about time we went to bed. Tomorrow is a full work day, and I have to be up at 6:30 for Mass. Please let me know about the passport question.

Joan and Winky are *most* excited to see you, and are getting very questioning about their English grandparents. They send their love, with which ours goes too, as we count the months to your coming.

As always, Alan

This letter is addressed to his seminary friend who received the letter of May 22, 1944.

CANTERBURY HOUSE | EVANSTON, ILLINOIS | MARCH 14, 1946
Dear Bill,
I can't say how glad I was to hear from you again — and from such an address. I sincerely hope that now that you are delivered from the cares of parish life I shall hear from you more often. There will be much praying for the certainty of your vocation, and I wish you a million blessings.

How can you say that the lines on which I (perhaps) started you thinking were "unorthodox"? Provided you keep that adjective in quotes, I won't argue. However, your present superior, Fr. W., and I have had some considerable discussion of these matters and find ourselves in almost total agreement. Indeed, he can put things even a little more extremely than I have put them, and I would draw your attention to a remark in his problem paper "Are All Men Mystics?" on p. 2 (bottom line), continuing on p. 3. He believes those statements tremendously. He bases his whole life upon them. The more you can get to know him the better; he has more real insight than any other priest I know.

As to the invocation of the saints. Our relation to God works in two ways — direct and indirect, through his immediate presence and through one another. Prayer (of the intercessory type) is quite unnecessary to God; but so is our existence. God cares for everyone, so from one point of view it is unnecessary for us to help another person. However, when we help or pray for another person we have the privilege of sharing in God's love for them, and that draws both of us into a fuller realization of union with God. Remember too that your prayers for another are not really yours; they are the action of the Holy Spirit in you. God uses your prayers to help another, just as he uses a doctor's medicine to heal the sick.

Now the saints in that fullness of union with God which is heaven are most actively sharing in his love for the world: that precisely is their prayer for us. God loves us directly, and through them; that is their privilege, which God will certainly not deny them, any more than he denies the doctor the privilege of healing when a miracle from heaven would do instead. When you ask the prayers of the saints it is again the Holy Spirit which moves you to ask. By this means the love which God has for us and for them is made to move consciously through them to us, and through us to them. By such means we all grow in the realization of our corporate union with God, which is the communion of saints. It would be of no point to ask their prayers if oneself existed alone with God.

And about the "entry of another being into the essence of God" — there ain't no such thing as the *time* concept of entry in *eternity*. "I have loved thee with an everlasting love." So long as we have existed we have, from God's standpoint, been in union with him, again from his standpoint, even before we existed. What we call entering into union or attaining union is not entering or attaining at all. It is simply waking up to the fact that we are already in, and love it! The "respond to responsiveness," the joy which God has in our awakening is an *addition* only to the joy of our Lord's divine humanity, which is God's participation in time. You may have to read that rather carefully, but this business of relating time to eternity is rather subtle. Of course, we don't really understand it, and I don't feel inclined to quarrel with God if my awakening to union with him doesn't add a drop to his infinite ocean of joy. For he has focused that whole infinite ocean on me already, and what else *could* I want?

I'm glad you see that in religion you aren't striving after holiness but only giving thanks for the gift of union. The suspicion hits me occasionally that some brethren don't know that. Did you read my review of Huxley's *Perennial Philosophy* in a recent number of *Holy Cross* magazine?

This work here is the hardest and happiest I've had for a long time, and we are making some strides. Am instructing day in and day out, bull sessioning and trying to build up a university church. We have taken over the seminary chapel on Sundays, and have a rather good student choir, specializing in plainsong and early polyphony. Plan to do the Liturgy of the Palms and an Easter Midnight with the *Praeconium*.

Love from us all, and God's blessing on you —
Faithfully in XPO, Alan

CANTERBURY HOUSE | EVANSTON, ILLINOIS | MAY 8, 1946
Dear Mummy & Daddy,
With the work of Easter and its aftermath over, here is at last a chance to sit down and write! All through Lent the work went ahead rapidly, and reached its climax at our Easter Midnight Mass when we filled the seminary chapel with a congregation of 125 — twice what we had last year. It was a beautiful service, and I enclose a program so that you can get some idea of it. We also had large

congregations for Palm Sunday and Good Friday Tenebrae, and the choir sang exquisitely.

Last week I went down to Dallas, Texas, for a priests' conference to give a lecture on Christian marriage, and flew back by plane in the wee small hours of Saturday morning. The sensation is hardly different from travelling in a large motor coach, although your ears occasionally feel the change of pressure and you occasionally hit a bump in the air. The greatest thrill was looking down upon brilliantly lit cities at night. Flying over the clouds is reminiscent of an ocean voyage, for sometimes they look like a vast expanse of water. Dallas is rather a delightful city, and I was most hospitably entertained, while the lecture was received with considerable enthusiasm. They are going to print it as a pamphlet. It was an expansion of an article that has already appeared in the diocesan magazine with mildly sensational results, and is to be reprinted in one of the national Church papers.

I seem to be getting around! I have been invited to give another lecture at a conference near Boston in July on the subject of the priesthood. I have promised Toby a new booklet on Zen, am preparing another on the technique of meditation, and have still my own large "opus" to get ahead with. So I shall be pounding the typewriter quite a bit this summer, starting now as work quietens down somewhat after Easter.

The future of this job here is still unsettled, as nothing has been done yet about our house. The university still wants it back at the end of September, and the diocese still has no money for a new one. If they don't come across with something suitable I shall get me another job. It oughtn't to be difficult as I have already had a tentative offer from the Diocese of Dallas to be their director of religious education.

Texas is a long way from Chicago, but don't worry — when you reach New York we shall transport you to wherever we are. And I shall write Ashton-Gwatkin this week to see if there is anything that can be done to hurry things along. Have you tried any of the American lines, and if so what is the specific difficulty with them? If it is expenses en route we may be able to take care of that.

Uncle Willie [Buchan] and Aunt Jane dropped in here on Sunday for tea. They seemed very well and happy, and anxious to know when you and E.G.B. [Gertie Buchan] are to be expected. Willie is extraordinarily reminiscent of Uncle Harry [Buchan] — except for the chin. Auntie is as Scottish as Scotch can be; I have never heard a burrrr stick like that after so many years in this country. Betty is now in North Carolina with her husband, who plans to be an accountant and is now in his apprenticeship.

Toby has written me from Japan to say that he has obtained the translation rights of six books which Suzuki wrote during the war. He seems to be having the time of his life, and has found Kyoto quite undamaged; all its great temples and art treasures are intact.

Too bad that Paula couldn't make Girton. Why doesn't she try Oxford? One of our girls here has a scholarship to Girton, and will be going over in about a year's time. She is very brilliant and beautiful but not nearly so pleasant as Paula.

Did you get a copy of my *Case for God* in pamphlet form? I am sending another by separate mail in case not. Ruth was out here last week, and plans to get sent to Japan for a month this summer on government business as a "cultural relations" envoy. She would go and return by plane, presumably on Uncle Sam's payroll!

I suppose there is still a paper shortage in England, but I do want to get Murrays to reprint my books. If the *Legacy of Asia* sold 250 copies last year it must be doing pretty well, and I think I shall try to write them this week and see what the chances are.

Our love to you both, as always, Alan

JW: Our English grandparents (Alan's mother and father) came to visit in late 1946. It was an event we remember well. They got to know a number of the students and would ask after them on their return to Great Britain. An interesting note was that after the war, his parents were sending him cigarettes, as they were rationed here! Our Granny Ruth (Sasaki, Eleanor's mother, whom Alan often refers to as "Mrs. E.") would visit over holidays. She would stay in the third-floor bedroom, small and under an attic eave. She always arrived in grand style, with a full set of matched Mark Cross luggage, in tweeds and furs, hat, gloves, and sensible shoes, and when she hugged you she smelled of powder and violets. Ruth, through the help of her lawyer and George Fowler (a student of Sokei-an's who had been a commander in the navy and later became a professor of history at the University of Pittsburgh), was able to get Sokei-an released from internment, and they were married in Arkansas in 1944. Regrettably he lived for only ten months after his release and died in June 1945.

CANTERBURY HOUSE | EVANSTON, ILLINOIS | JANUARY 17, 1947
Dear Jim Corsa,
It was good to hear from you again, and especially to get a letter so full of news and ideas. I'm glad you have seen old Tai Hsu; I never met him myself, but a close friend who saw him when he came to London said he was one of the world's spiritual giants.

Yes, I have read Hu Shih's article, and your letter prompted me to read it again to refresh my memory. I think he has something; it is certainly true that

Hui-neng's writings disparage yoga meditation, and there is no reference to za-zen with koans in the greater part of early Zen literature — even the great Rinzai makes little of it. Although koan meditation certainly existed in China, I have an idea that the real father of the modern koan technique was Hakuin. I can't say for certain.

Koan meditation came into being as the monasteries began to be filled with people who had no vocation to be monks, boys who were just sent there by their parents as 18th-century families in England automatically sent the third son into the priesthood. Christian methods of meditation (Ignatian, Sulpician, Salesian, etc.) came into being for much the same reason: people with no real interest in religion had to be given some sort of a mill to go through to keep them busy.

In other words, all great religions, although their inner essence is esoteric and inevitably the province of the few, have to make some provision for the world at large. This involves a hardening and conventionalizing process which renders all popular religion (whether Christianity or Buddhism) superficial — an imperfection which is simply inevitable, but which we must no more resent or deplore than the fact that children of six cannot be taught the calculus. When certain persons insist that this exoteric religion is the whole truth, and that there is no other way of salvation, we have fanaticism, which is also almost inevitable.

Little real harm is done by this process, so long as a nucleus of persons maintains the interior religion, which is substantially the same in all places and periods. I see no particular point in changing the external religion of the West from the Christian form to the Buddhist form. Indeed, I think it would do a great deal of harm. My concern is that the inner religion should flourish within official Christianity so that the Church will be able to instruct and guide the increasing, but still relatively small, number of persons who are ready to profit by it. Furthermore, where such a nucleus does not exist, there is a general decline of the entire religious and social order. But the constructive influence of such a nucleus is out of all proportion to its numbers. I do not think that interior religion should be given a name or form so as to be externally recognizable, for it will thus be rushed into the position of a sect and involved in argumentation, propaganda, and controversy, the terms and methods of which are radically inapplicable to mystical knowledge.

Thus it will not follow at all that a Christian who wakes up to mystical knowledge in its supreme degree will forsake Christianity for any other external religion, for there is no real inconsistency between the Christian dogmatic system and mystical knowledge, since the two are as incommensurable as shape and color. Moreover, it is supremely easy to understand dogma in a mystical sense without departing from formal orthodoxy. You just have to equate such terms as "supernatural" with "nondual" (which is its strictly accurate meaning) and "heavenly" with "interior," and the whole picture changes almost miraculously.

Oh, do be careful of Sinhalese bikkhus! I edited *Buddhism in England* for some years and had plenty of dealings with these gentlemen. They are dreadfully bigoted and narrow on the whole, for Sinhalese Buddhism is markedly sterile. And I certainly wouldn't involve myself in any close economic relationships with them, unless you are feeling highly adventurous.

I think you would be greatly interested to read Guénon's *Introduction to the Study of the Hindu Doctrines*. You can get it at Orientalia — also his *Crisis of the Modern World*. They are thought-provoking books if wordy and discursive at times, and a few gems may be extricated.

With all good wishes,

Sincerely, Alan Watts

CANTERBURY HOUSE | EVANSTON, ILLINOIS | FEBRUARY 7, 1947

Dear Mummy and Daddy,

Ever since you left things have piled up on me and even now I am snatching the moments to write. I am delighted you got back safely and had no trouble with customs, but it must be depressing to find rations even briefer, and *Punch* is full of jokes about lack of warmth! We are in the midst of a bitterly cold spell, started off by a hailstorm so intense that the ground is now covered with four inches of solid ice.

I have just heard from John Grey Murray that they want to go ahead with the publication of my book [*Behold the Spirit*] and would like to start printing just as soon as I can send them the final corrections. So I have to get busy with that — but it's very welcome news.

Business has picked up during the last two weeks owing to a lecture I gave on marriage at a local church to a very large crowd including many university people. Many of the students have asked after you; you seemed to make a great hit with them. Last Tuesday we had a gathering of some of the professors and made some good new friends. They want to start a group for discussion which will be a nucleus for doing a more active work with the faculty. Priscilla Clark is thinking of applying for a scholarship to Oxford next year.

The other day we sent you two cans of ham, and we have other packages done up ready to mail in penny numbers! Let us know about the big Marshall Field package. We will investigate the question of firms with Danish agents. Under separate cover I am sending you the first batch of the stamps.

The tray, when unpacked, was found in perfect condition. I had never realized what a beautiful thing it is, and you can be sure it will add a most opulent atmosphere to our entertaining facilities.

I hope everything went all right at the office while you were away. Probably you were snowed under with work on returning, and I shan't expect to hear from you about Watkins, etc., until you have had time to settle down; so don't hurry yourself. You might tell Watkins about the new book and say that I will have details of it sent to them in due course.

There is no other particularly important news, except that your grandchildren are always talking about you and about England and how far away is it (?).

In haste, and with lots of love from us all, as ever, Alan

CANTERBURY HOUSE | EVANSTON, ILLINOIS | FEBRUARY 24, 1947
Dr. F. S. C. Northrop | Silliman College, Yale University | New Haven, CT
My dear Dr. Northrop,
This letter is to thank you for the tremendous intellectual stimulus of your book *The Meeting of East and West*. As one who has studied Oriental religions for many years I was very deeply impressed with your treatment of Taoism, Buddhism, and Vedanta for the reason that you have presented their true unity and have grasped what they are talking about in a manner all too uncommon among many of our Western scholars.

I am hoping very much that your book will go into further editions, and that if this gives you the opportunity to make certain revisions you might consider two suggestions.

1. In your discussion of the method of realizing the "undifferentiated aesthetic continuum" you have given principal emphasis to the negative, apophatic approach of Indian Yoga, which involves a considerable degree of isolation from the world. It might be valuable to give more space to the other approach found preeminently in Ch'an or Zen Buddhism. Here the continuum is realized, not by emptying it of contents, but by *accepting* all contents as the undifferentiated surface of a mirror accepts all images. (Cf. Giles's *Chuang-tzu*, pp. 97–98.) I attach to this letter a quotation from the *Tan-ching* of Hui-neng which admirably indicates the process.

2. An extremely important aspect of your argument in regard to St. Thomas does not seem to me to have nearly enough explanation, because you do not take enough space to point out just where and why his Aristotelian theology is inadequate. In view of the great Neo-Thomist revival it would seem a little lacking in caution to dismiss St. Thomas quite so briefly, and it gives some readers the impression that you may be the victim of an unexamined assumption. It has

become so usual for the modern philosopher to hurry through the scholastics with some few remarks to the effect that "all that has now been superseded," that one wonders if they know why it has been superseded! I am doubtless airing my own ignorance, but I would like to know in what way, for example, the "five proofs" of St. Thomas have been invalidated by Galilei's study of projectiles. Perhaps you could recommend some bibliography. What troubles me, as one relatively uninitiated in certain aspects of Western philosophy (which has always seemed so much of an epistemological squirrel cage), is that minds of the caliber of Maritain and Gilson seem so unaffected by the alleged collapse of the Thomistic-Aristotelian system. Incidentally, have you seen E. L. Mascall's recent book on this matter, *He Who Is* (Longmans, 1945)? I have not found a better exposition of modern Thomism.

I have often wondered whether not only modern science, when coordinated, but also Oriental philosophy may not play the part in future Christian theology which Aristotle played in the Middle Ages, something like it happened before, with the introduction of what amounts to pure Vedanta through pseudo-Dionysius and Erigena into Catholic mysticism. But I hope your book will do something to minimize the absurd prejudices that exist on this subject among ecclesiastics.

With many thanks,

Sincerely yours, Alan Watts, Episcopal Chaplain, Northwestern University

CANTERBURY HOUSE | EVANSTON, ILLINOIS | APRIL 7, 1947
Mr. Kurt Wolff | Pantheon Books, Inc. | New York, New York
Dear Mr. Wolff,
Very many thanks for your letter of April 4th and for sending me Mr. Binsse's report, most of his suggestions being very much to the point. I enclose herewith a memorandum for Mr. Binsse which seeks clarification on one point in particular, and I would be obliged if you would pass it on to him.

Should you decide to publish the book, I enclose also a number of corrections and additions on the basis of Mr. Binsse's suggestions. I think they are clearly enough indicated for one of your office staff to insert them in the MS, and I believe they will do a great deal to eliminate offense that might have been given to Catholics of Mr. Binsse's type.

I realize only too well the difficulty of fitting this book into any of the existing theological and denominational pigeonholes. That was why I sent it to a publisher who does not seem to be afraid of rather unusual books! As to advance statements from religious notables, and other means of getting publicity, I have these suggestions:

Neither Maritain nor Niebuhr would be particularly sympathetic. The former expressed a view of mysticism in his *Degrees of Knowledge* which made it a very remote pinnacle, and Niebuhr doesn't like the subject at all. I can't remember his name, but Henry Luce has a "theological adviser" who would be well worth contacting, and if you haven't heard of him I will find out who he is. Certain prominent Anglicans might also be sympathetic, to wit Canon Bernard Iddings Bell, who contributes to *The Atlantic* and is a good friend of mine; also Canon T. O. Wedel of the College of Preachers in Washington, Bishop Pardue of Pittsburgh, and, perhaps, Bishop Conkling of Chicago. I had a most sympathetic review of a former book from John Haynes Holmes; he might fall for this one. I would also try Dr. F. S. C. Northrop of Silliman College, Yale, author of *The Meeting of East and West*. I have been in correspondence with him. Harvard psychology professor Gordon W. Allport might be interested; he knows of me and has read former works with apparent approval. You might consider, too, Paul Tillich of Union Theological, and two outstanding Quakers, Rufus Jones and Elton Trueblood. Maybe some others will come to my mind, and let's not forget Robert M. Hutchins!

The question of the title [for *Behold the Spirit*] is difficult. I don't like "The Games the Angels Play" for the excellent reason that this is a book about incarnational and not purely spiritual mysticism (which would be eminently suited to angels!). I'm not entirely satisfied with the present title, but I wanted something that would indicate fairly clearly what the book is about. What do you think of these: "Now Is Eternity"; "Spirit Descending"; "Out of the Broken Shell"? I will give this a good deal more thought.

With many thanks,

Sincerely yours, Alan Watts

Memo: To Mr. H. L. Binsse

1. Your comments are on the whole very much to the point and most helpful, and I wonder if I may have your permission to express my thanks in the preface.

2. Comment to p. 28, on the obscurantism of "contemporary" Roman Catholicism. The word *contemporary* was to go hand in hand with the 19th-century Gothic revival. But I see this was misunderstood and have changed the passage to avoid confusion. True, there are very many *present-day* movements in the Church which are anything but obscurantist. But I was thinking of the regime of Leo XIII, etc.

3. Stained glass. Oh, but look what the Victorians did with it; I feel that it was an unconscious rather than a conscious artistic sense which preserved the Middle Ages from such abominations. But I have added a note about miniatures.

4. The muttered Mass. Here I am in doubt, and would like your opinion in greater detail. I am under the impression that Low Mass was not at all unknown at this time, but that, on the contrary, had been developed by the chantry system and the celebration of other private masses to a wholly excessive decree. Furthermore, even at High Mass the canon was, and still is, said almost inaudibly save for those in the immediate vicinity of the altar, and in those days they did not have vast quantities of small missals for the laity. In England many popular superstitions arose among the disaffected about what the priest was doing at the altar, and for this very reason the reformers demanded that the Lord's Supper be held in full view of the congregation on a table in the middle of the church. Until a generation or so ago, one could still find in remote country places the notion that the priest had a crab on the corporal, and that all his funny motions were to keep it from crawling off!

5. Civilized and peasant Catholicism. A verbal misunderstanding, I think. I have now made a plain distinction between "civilized" (i.e., urbanized) and "cultured."

6. I admit frankly that I have been unfair to the liturgical reformers, and have remedied this extensively. Sometimes these folk are a little on the "precious" side, but I certainly would not want to include the Benedictines of Maria Laach in that class. You have prevented a bad mistake here, for which many thanks. It had slipped my mind, for since writing those sentences I have been reading "Orate Fratres." — AWW

CANTERBURY HOUSE | EVANSTON, ILLINOIS | APRIL 21, 1947
The Rev. Dom Gregory Dix, OSB
My dear Father,
I was among the audience at your first lecture at Seabury-Western last Wednesday, and found it of particular interest in that it tackled the historical roots of a subject which has long been of concern to me — the obstruction to a full realization of the Incarnation offered by the anti-materialism of Greek theology. In particular, it has always been a source of astonishment to me that we have seldom had what to my mind is quite essential for the proper development of Catholicism — an incarnational mysticism. Christian mysticism has constantly leaned to a contempt for the physical aspect of life, and has never seemed quite in harmony with the sacramental aspect of religion; it has sought to rise above the flesh to God, forgetting that God has come down into the flesh.

If the alternative to this is either the "prophetism" of Heiler, or a strictly (or maybe, excessively) analogical knowledge of God (i.e., kataphatic), would we not be excluding from Catholicism one of the most highly creative types of spiritual experience?

Your lecture seemed to imply an almost irreconcilable conflict between points of view that might be tabulated thus:

GREEK	SYRIAC
Impersonal God	Personal God
Spiritualism	Materialism
Immortality	Resurrection
World denial	World affirmation
Eros	Agape (in Nygren's sense)
Mysticism	Sacramentalism
Apophasis	Kataphasis

I am wondering to what extent this conflict is real and necessary, and whether there is not a value in the Greek view which, if it is not allowed to run wild, is the necessary complement of the Syriac.

You said, for example, that it was only in the Syriac culture that we find a genuine conception of the living God. A cursory examination of Vedanta, for instance, gives the impression that its God, like that of Greek philosophy, is impersonal. But after studying this subject for a long time I am convinced that the contrary is the case, and that what we have in Vedanta is in fact an extension to the realm of thought and emotion of the Hebrew prohibition against idols. God is so infinitely alive that *no* form can contain him, whether the form (eidos) be of wood, stone, imagination, or intellect. (This is especially true of the Vedanta of Sankhara and, even more, of the little-known school of Kashmiri Tantra; also of certain types of Mahayana Buddhism.)

The idea that no form can embrace God may produce, and in some Greek and Indian circles, *did* produce, the notion that the life of form and matter is *incompatible* with the divine state. Here is the source of the trouble. It is here that the extreme askesis and even acosmism of the predominant forms of classical Christian mysticism have their origin.

Such a notion, however, does not necessarily follow — as in fact many of the Oriental, and especially Chinese, philosophers and mystics have seen. God conceived thus is no more incompatible with form and matter than a mirror is incompatible with its images. Just because the mirror has no form and no color, it can reflect the whole variety of forms and colors. Thus by analogy: just because God is beyond form (a "No-thing") he can create and embrace the multi-form universe. But this is quite a different thing from saying that God is *merely* impersonal; it is saying that because he is infinitely alive, no finite form can comprehend him — whether wooden image or determinate proposition.

But as the indeterminate God creates a determinate and ordered universe, so the indeterminate mystical experience of God may be trusted to produce a determinate moral life. This would be a morality genuinely inspired by the indwelling Holy Spirit, and not the mere imitation of legal principles, or even of the character of our Lord codified into a new law — which is a real reversion to Judaism.

Judaic legalism has its parallel in a determinate conception of God, which is conceptual idolatry, a God to be imitated by man. But doesn't the Christian dispensation of grace involve an indeterminate God, who, despite outward darkness, formlessness, and invisibility, is nonetheless so real and living that whoever trusts himself unreservedly to this apparent No-thing will be filled with creative power and sanctity? Surely this is what we are to understand from our Lord's utter surrender of himself to the darkness of death, and from the "*Eli, Eli, lama sabachthani*" followed by "Father, into thy hands..." For out of this entry into "nothing" comes the Resurrection.

In sum, then, it would seem that the Indian-Greek view of God takes the Hebrew antipathy to idols to its full conclusion, but draws the wrong inference that God and the world are incompatible. On the other hand, the Hebrew mind gets the point that the world is God's compatible creation, but draws the wrong inference of an essentially determinate God — a personalized law. The Christian and Catholic synthesis is that by the gift of the Holy Spirit man is brought into immediate contact with the indeterminate "unmoved mover" who, in man's life, freely determines by free grace, the physical and formative expression of holiness. The essentially formless Word takes form in the flesh.

It doesn't seem to me that Catholic (much less Protestant) spirituality has at all fully developed this view. The reaction of both Reformation and Counter-Reformation to acosmic mysticism was a "Christocentric mysticism" amounting mostly to the legal imitation of a vividly imagined Christ. (Dom John Chapman called it "reversal of tradition.") But, "If I go not away, the Paraclete cannot come unto you."

One other point: I don't know so much about Persian religion, but how, in view of its alleged dualism (to which Isaiah 45:7 is surely a violent reaction) can you class it with the Syriac group?

This has turned out to be a terribly long epistle, but if you should ever want to develop your theme in print, it occurred to me that these would be points to be considered. And please don't bother with a reply unless you think it worth discussing further.

Faithfully in Christo, Fr. Alan Watts

CANTERBURY HOUSE | EVANSTON, ILLINOIS | JUNE 21, 1947

Dear Mummy and Daddy,

Mummy's letter to Eleanor arrived yesterday. I hope you're not killing that broody hen! A substitute *is* on the way, but what with all the flu and the rush at the end of the academic year it took us a while to get it off. The photographs have come in good condition, and we're delighted to have them.

I have been up in Wisconsin all week conducting a retreat for 85 women! They seem to have had a wonderful time, and you can imagine what it was like to be one man among such a multitude — all of them under rule of silence! Of course I enjoyed myself immensely as this is the type of work I find most congenial, because it is possible under such circumstances to get below the surface. It was held at Kemper Hall School, a girls' school run by the Sisters of St. Mary, and was for the associates of the community. The sister in charge of the retreat said that of all the many retreats which she had run, this was the only one that had left her really relaxed and rested. There are some very remarkable women in the community, and they certainly run some excellent schools.

The book is going ahead rapidly. Almost all the proofs are corrected now and it seems to read better in print than it did in typescript. Murray's are also going to reprint *The Spirit of Zen*, and as certain corrections must be made to it I am putting Ruth to work to help me decide what should be done. She is out here with us for a fortnight, and plans to take Joan back with her for a month's holiday at Walker's [Everett, cousin] farm in Connecticut.

Our own plans for the future are still uncertain. We do not know yet whether this house will be available for another year. If not, we certainly do not plan to stay on this job. Eleanor couldn't stand two moves in short succession, and this climate gave her a terrible time this May — a cough that kept her awake night after night. Even now it's still cold, and we wonder if we are ever going to get any summer. I bought her a sunlamp which is doing some good. Much will depend on the book as to what I do next.

Can you give us some more definite information as to Auntie Gertie's plans and itinerary? It is possible that we may go away for the first three weeks in September, as Dorothy will then be available to stay with the children. Eleanor and I are thinking of driving out to Colorado and staying with friends who have a ranch there. I shall be in New York sometime around the first week in August, to collect Joan and to see my publisher.

This summer Eleanor and I want to get to work on a new book on Taoism. Such a thing as an actual book on the subject apparently does not exist! As an addition to it would be an absolutely literal, character-by-character translation of

Tao Te Ching, since all our present translations are really paraphrases, and the original is much more exciting.

I have at last used Mr. Fred's drawing of St. Thomas's arms for a new letter-head drawing for Canterbury House, and will send my next letter on it for you to see.

Herewith are some stamps from China and Japan which just came on some of Ruth's mail. The Japanese occupation stamps may be of some value and interest.

This is, I think, all the news for the present. I can't say much of our English visit yet as it must depend to a great extent on what happens about my work, where we are to live, and when, etc. I am hoping, of course, that my book will create enough interest, both here and in England, for someone to invite me over to lecture and pay some of the expense! That's not beyond the bounds of possibility.

With lots of love from us all, Alan

JW: By now, Alan's indiscretions were becoming obvious to Eleanor. She became quite depressed. She made several trips to see her mother in New York and to counsel with a priest that she and Alan had known while living there. By then, Alan was having a full-blown affair with a graduate student, Dorothy DeWitt (known as Dottie), a mathematician that had been involved at the university with a naval project during the war. When our parents had to go out, she would babysit for us. She was, to us, very dour. A humorless woman, completely unloving and no fun at all.

In her loneliness, Eleanor started to take piano lessons from Carlton Gamer, a young music student at Northwestern who volunteered as a choirmaster for Alan. They fell in love. Eleanor confessed her indiscretion to Alan, thinking he would demand that she end her relationship, but instead he applauded it and decided that they both should have their lovers live in and be one happy family. He said he didn't want a divorce, however, and he expected her to carry on her duties as his wife and the wife of the chaplain. Alan's letters to his parents portray none of these things. He merely comments on Eleanor's health and says that she needs to get away to rest.

This living arrangement went on for some months. In a letter to his parents dated July 19, 1947, Alan mentions that he and Eleanor were making a monthlong trip out West, but he doesn't mention that Eleanor's lover went with them. Dottie conveniently babysat for us. No mention is made of the fact that Eleanor was pregnant until his letter of January 10, 1949, to his parents. She came to me (I was ten at this point) one evening and told me she was pregnant. I was too young to understand the situation, other than that Anne and I now shared a bedroom, the adult couples each had a bedroom, and the new child, Michael, born in January 1949 — the son that Eleanor had longed for — had the fourth bedroom. There was little mention of the event of Michael's birth, but his birth certificate lists Alan Watts was his father. Eleanor later claimed that Carlton was the real father.

CANTERBURY HOUSE | EVANSTON, ILLINOIS | JULY 5, 1947
John Grey Murray, Esq. | Publisher | London, England
My dear John,

In answer to your letter of June 13th, I am enclosing a biographical sketch and two alternative descriptions of the book [*Behold the Spirit*], designated A and B. A is more staid and solid, B has an eye to advertising value. I leave the choice up to you; edit them as you like if necessary.

I don't know whether I have any further suggestions as to the way in which the book should be publicized. You will of course be sure to send review copies to leading religious papers — especially the *Church Times*. Are you planning to print your own dust jacket? If so, I suggest something in Eric Gill's "Perpetua" in red and black on ivory, confining descriptive material to the back, or inside flaps.

Might it not be a good idea to try and get some prepublication comments for publicity use from various bigwigs? I suggest Dom Gregory Dix, Nashdom Abbey, Bucks; T. S. Eliot; Dorothy Sayers; E. I. Watkin; Christopher Dawson; Canon V. A. Demant; and the Bishop of St. Andrews (Lumsden Barkway). I am sure Pantheon would let you have some bound-up page proofs for this purpose.

Yours ever, Alan

CANTERBURY HOUSE | EVANSTON, ILLINOIS | JULY 19, 1947
Dear Mummy & Daddy,

Thank you both for your letters which arrived this week. I am anxious about your being unable to use fruit for lack of sugar, and therefore am sending you 5 lb. by air express on Monday. This is a special service considerably cheaper than airmail. This delay in putting the Marshall Plan into effect promises to make a difficult winter for you, and I'm afraid that most of the English news we get makes rather depressing reading.

Eleanor and I are going to be in New York for the first week in August to pick up Joan and make some final arrangements about my book. Its prospects look fairly good over here as Canon Bernard Iddings Bell has given it a big boost, saying that it will probably prove to be "one of the half-dozen most significant books on religion published in the 20th century."

After September 1st we are going to spend three to four weeks in the West, visiting California, Arizona, and Texas by car. We ought to get well thawed out in the Southern deserts; the weather here is still none too warm, though the water is just beginning to be tolerable for swimming. This is the only time we can get for the trip, and so I don't suppose we shall be able to get together with E.G.B. and Joy [Buchan] on their way out to Minneapolis.

This has been a very quiet and pleasant month. We have both been taking things very easily, keeping going at a leisurely pace with the Chinese work, and taking lots of walks. However, we have had good attendances at the Sunday evening seminars, but I am not giving any individual instruction this summer.

We have built ourselves an outdoor fireplace for a charcoal grill, and several evenings a week cook our meat there. It's a great improvement over gas broiling and a lot of fun to boot.

It *seems* that we shall have this house for another year as we've had no notice to quit as yet. Future plans will still depend to a large extent on what sort of an impression my book makes.

I'm sorry to hear about the Rutherford-Twentyman affair; I had forgotten all about Ralph, but now his face comes vaguely to mind. The Rutherford boy married Grace Halliday, didn't he?

It is good to know that there hasn't been the expected slump in HSF collections, and I hope that will be counted a feather in Daddy's cap. Are you going to get a summer holiday away this year, or did you spend too much money coming over here? You can, of course, count on the English royalties of my new book — though I have absolutely no idea what they will amount to!

This being the quiet season there just isn't any other news. Give our love to the folks at Bromley and to Sam Blyth; it must be grand for you to have him next door, amazingly waited on by two whole minions!

Lots of love from us all, Alan

PS. Sorry, but I find that even air express is too expensive for a package of this weight. Am sending the sugar at once by regular mail, so it will at least be in time for your apple jelly in the autumn. Takes about 6 weeks.

CANTERBURY HOUSE | EVANSTON, ILLINOIS | NOVEMBER 18, 1947
Dear Henry Miller,

I have been meaning to write to you for some time to express appreciation of your book *The Wisdom of the Heart*, and am moved to do so the more now that I have just read *Remember to Remember*. It's a long time since I had such a good belly laugh as I got out of the *Staff of Life* and you have things to say in your studies of Varda, DeLaney, and Rattner which are really profound. Also, the excellent piece on obscenity, and *Murder the Murderer*, a fine unsentimental job, which, on this subject, is unusual.

I wonder if I may make two comments, which may perhaps be suggestive to you. While I agree heartily with your general depiction of our "air-conditioned nightmare," it seems to me that you put yourself in a false position by wanting (if I understand you rightly) to be among the expatriates. You have realized that Europe offers no further escape from the nightmare, and I am afraid you will find the same true of Asia. This "civilization" of ours has left no corner of the earth untainted, unless it be some lamasery in Tibet, shortly to be rationalized by the USSR. Isn't it rather true, as in the Inferno, that the way out of hell is through its very center — revolution by involution? This mess is a manure to nurture fine plants — such as you already see in DeLaney et al.

It seems to me, as one born and bred in England, that the European culture is quite dead and the very soil in which it grew exhausted. But I have been enormously stimulated by the mere geography of America, though its present culture is a bad seed transplanted from Europe — dying along with it, but a little later. Yet the soil remains fertile.

American culture is a mulch, thrown across the ocean to land on new ground. It presents certain characteristics of the end period of European culture in a very exaggerated form just because the soil, the mere geography, is so stimulating. Here even manure thrives. Now it seems to me that you, for example, have done your best work in this country. I presume that earlier works (such as *Tropic of Cancer*) were done in France, and while in these I feel decay most vividly and bitterly portrayed, it does not seem to me to be fruitful decay. No spirit, no mysticism, comes out of it, as it does in your present work.

The second thing: you indicate, very rightly, that our state has to get much worse before it gets any better. Yet you seem to hope that at the very nadir of despair another messiah will emerge — "a radiant figure in whom the new time spirit is embodied." Perhaps. And yet the last of such figures made a remark which has not yet been realized, and which the present state of our culture (and especially of our religion) renders ripe for realization: "It is expedient for you that I go away, for if I go not away the Paraclete cannot come to you."

In other words, as long as we look for salvation to an external figure (or idea, or method) we cannot realize the interior Spirit. The present debacle is precisely a cosmic debunking of such figures — of faith in the past, of hope in the future, of trust in any external panacea — in order that we may be forced to look into the eternal Here and Now. As you know, this is what Krishnamurti is trying so hard to say — if only he could express himself better.

At this time hope in another avatar would surely perpetuate and give a new start to the old vicious circle. It seems that in the name of Christ the eidolon of the external Christ must be destroyed, as in Zen, "Wash out your mouth every time you say 'Buddha!'" Neither the Protestant Reformation nor the Secularist-Humanist revolution did this properly; they put new and worse idols in place of the old. The paradox, which few reformers ever see, is that the eidolon (in our case the Catholic mythos) has to be preserved in order to be destroyed, as Zen preserves the forms and rites and scriptures of Buddhism along with its own iconoclasm. Revere the symbol you smash, for it is the indispensable vehicle of the life which comes out of it.

Do you know that our mutual friend Graham Howe is planning to come over for some lectures in February? He wrote me about it some months ago, but as I have not heard from him recently I am wondering if difficulties in England have changed his plans. He is so little known in this country that he may also have had difficulty in getting enough engagements. Do you think some audiences for him could be found out West? I have one contact in Palo Alto, and one in San Francisco that would help him.

I was hoping to be able to stop by and talk to you about this when I was out West this summer, but had to move on down the coast quicker than I expected. One of these days I shall hope to have this opportunity, as I am making tentative plans to do some work in Carmel or thereabouts — if you have not by then taken off for the Orient.

With many thanks for much intellectual, and other kinds, of stimulation — and with every wish for more power to your work.

Sincerely yours, Alan W. Watts

CANTERBURY HOUSE | EVANSTON, ILLINOIS | DECEMBER 1, 1947
Mr. Kurt Wolff | Pantheon Books, Inc. | New York, New York
Dear Mr. Wolff,
Thank you very much for your letter of November 26th with enclosures which I return herewith.

So far I have seen no reviews of my book at all, except the accompanying excerpt from the *Living Church*. This is to be followed in due course by a full-length review by the dean of one of our theological schools. I am very glad to hear that *Time* will review it. If you have had any reviews sent in to date, would you be so kind as to send me the cuttings? I will return them promptly.

Two questions: (1) Have Murrays succeeded in getting an import license for their copies as yet? (2) I see Kegan Paul have published a new book of essays by Jung. Are you going to publish this soon, or should I order it from England?

Please will you have a copy of [my] book sent (charged to me) to the Rev. G. W. Robinson, Nuestra Ranchita, Hemet, California.

With very best wishes from us both to yourself and Mrs. Wolff,

Very sincerely yours, Alan Watts

CANTERBURY HOUSE | EVANSTON, ILLINOIS | FEBRUARY 9, 1948
Dear Mummy & Daddy,
When I returned from my trip to Madison I found the book you sent for my birthday, and was most delighted with it. It contains a wonderfully representative set of illustrations, with some types of writing that I had not met before. These books are most useful in that I am often asked by students to teach them lettering, and I like them to study really good examples.

I am so glad to hear that you liked the parcel from Denmark. I have already ordered another to be sent to you. Did our other parcel containing the canned chicken never arrive? I am afraid that many must have been lost through getting battered to bits in the Christmas rush.

Tom and Barbara's baby was safely baptized last Sunday; she seems to have come through with no ill effects at all, and the baby is good and healthy. I had just returned from Madison, where I had a very interesting time, staying at the very elaborate headquarters of the Church for the University of Wisconsin and talking every evening at one of the parish churches. A good crowd turned out. "Why has no one ever told us this before?" is becoming a rather oft-heard refrain!

Did I tell you that a little while ago I attended a most interesting conference with one of our bishops — Austin Pardue of Pittsburgh — and was amazed and delighted to find a whole live bishop in total agreement with most of my major ideas about everything, including the necessity of some synthesis between East and West in religion? Pardue is quite a power in the Church and may someday be presiding bishop. He is presenting a copy of my book to every priest in his diocese; nice for sales!

Winky is down at the moment with some kind of stomach flu. I was up much of Saturday night with her — cleaning up a two-ended explosion — but managed to catch up on my sleep yesterday afternoon. Joan was just as sweet as could be looking after her while we were at church, and in the evening put her down to sleep and got herself into bed without even being asked or reminded. Miss J. is becoming rather competent at some things.

Eleanor is working hard at the piano and coming along better and better all the time. Is at the moment in the midst of composing one of the most strangely haunting melodies for a song that you ever heard. It is intended for a flute accompaniment. Also — she is going in for the "new look" in clothes, with really very charming results.

We are all still very much up in the air what turn our work will take in the near future.

All I can do at the moment is to get myself known as far and wide as possible, to which end I am busy going hither and yon for lectures, retreats, etc. I could with relative ease get a job as rector of a parish, but would much rather get into teaching. A rector can sink into an organizational rut much too easily.

Daddy, would you please ring up either Toby or his secretary at the Buddhist Society, and find out whether they ever shipped a consignment of my *Zen* booklets to me. Orientalia (a bookshop) in New York has had them, but is now out of stock, Ruth has had one — everyone except the author! I wrote to Toby about this on Dec. 11th, but never had a reply.

Have had long letters from Ashton-Gwatkin, Babs Brinkley, and Christine Dunker in response to Christmas cards. A-G has a fascinating job working with the great Arnold Toynbee, and seems to be enjoying it. His mother is still alive, living at Bognor.

I had a grand time with Uncle Willie when he came through with Joy and Auntie. I think he understands now that I am not a terribly narrow-minded mediaevalist! He is quite the life of a party.

This afternoon, I am planning to go out with Joan and get her some modeling tools. We find she is less and less interested in "toys" and more and more in things she can make. She says she *wants* toys, but when she gets them hardly ever plays with them. Everything she plays with is something she has manufactured out of all conceivable odds and ends.

We are getting pretty crowded on Sunday evenings these days. Last night we had a perfectly fascinating discussion with Holt Graham, one of the seminary pandits, whom the students kept going until midnight. The week before, one of the fellows made a recording on wire of the whole proceedings, and it was rather instructive to be able to listen to oneself give a lecture. Each roll of wire runs for an hour, and so you can get an enormous amount recorded. Maybe I will buy one of those gadgets, record a few talks, and set them going on several loudspeakers, so that I can lecture in several places at once! That would be the duckiest way of getting time to write!

It's still very cold and snowy, and spring gets later and later. Fancy the green things turning up in February with you. It seems quite unimaginable. We won't see a bit of it until April, and then it will probably be wet and cold until July. However, Joan is getting lots of skating, and Eleanor has now begun it too — and has incidentally acquired a bruised butt!

Our love to you both, as always, Alan

CANTERBURY HOUSE | EVANSTON, ILLINOIS | APRIL 20, 1948

Dear Mummy and Daddy,

I have a sensation that it's altogether too long since you heard from me, but the aftermath of Easter has been just more of the same. Next week I am going to New York to stay with Ruth, take a rest, and loaf luxuriously. But I can only spare the inside of a week. Fortunately the time of year has come around when I can get some of the students to lecture for me on Sunday evenings, which will cut down some of the work.

I had a wonderful time last night giving a lecture on religious education at one of the big parish churches a little way north of Evanston. I was plied with all kinds of very intelligent questions, and spent until 1 AM with the rector and his family discussing the problem of evil! This looks as if it's going to have to be the problem of my next book, which I am clearing the decks for. But it will have to be discussed against the background of some pretty deep metaphysical problems, and I shall have to do quite a bit of preparatory reading just to be sure that I am not too tiresomely repeating things that have been said before. But the current of thought is taking me into some rather deep water, and I begin to wonder at times whether there are such things as true ideas which are too dangerous to publish! That is a trial for me, as I find it terribly hard not to say what I think.

Would it be too much to ask you to settle the enclosed bill for the Buddhist Society out of royalty funds? These will be building up during the year, as the *Spirit of Zen* is to appear again in June.

I was a little puzzled by your reference to the adverse effect of some announcement which Murray made about *Behold the Spirit*. I have asked to see their publicity material on it, but so far have had nothing. What a bright idea to subscribe to a press cutting service. For some reason the reviews here a very few and far between, but word-of-mouth advertising is working rather well. Officialdom greets it with a wall of silence!

We went the other night to a perfectly marvelous concert of French music from the 13th century to modern times. Two harpsichords, two violins, and a good contralto. I have never before attended such a thoroughly *superior* performance. Everything about it was right — the music, the setting — everything. And they played lots of lesser-known pieces by Couperin, Rameau, de Machault, Lully, etc., things just perfectly suited to such an orchestra. It was given in connection with an exhibition of French tapestry being held at the Art Institute in Chicago. Eleanor has seen it, but I have not yet had the chance. However, I am putting the illustrated catalogue in the mail for you. Eleanor was much impressed by some of the modern work, but says the catalogue gives little idea of it because of the absence of color. [...]

A rather large Japanese colony is settling in Chicago, and we have a perfectly delightful Japanese friend who works at Northwestern who has introduced us to some of its leading lights. The other evening we had a sake party for some of them, including one of the three local Buddhist priests! Eleanor is so pleased to be able to buy Japanese goods again — especially the little things like sandals, tea, rice bowls, etc. Our friend, Mr. Harada, came in on Sunday evening with a whole mass of reviews of my *Zen* booklet from the Japanese-American papers. But I can't read them! Many Japanese goods are now being produced in this country — surprising things like records of Japanese classical music, sheets of edible seaweed, sake, and so forth. I wonder — sometimes a military defeat is a cultural victory. It is going to be enormously interesting to watch the effect of the Far East on America in the coming years.

Spring is here on time for a great change! On Monday morning the trees were looking so lovely in their thin green mist that I took the car out to a large forest preserve and just wandered around in it for a time. Today even more were out. Unhappily the vacant land next to our house is no more an allotment, but is in process of becoming a parking lot, which will make the summer dustier than ever. I keep getting the itch — ever itchier — to go and live near mountains, and lead a more contemplative existence. One day I think I will have a school for clergy, and let them do the general circulating and public speaking for me!

Tonight is a sort of final breathing space before a very full three days of appointments. I think I'll go and get me a beer.

With lots of love from us all, as ever, Alan

Canterbury House | Evanston, Illinois | June 18, 1948
Dear Mummy & Daddy,
At last I am free from the trammels of all the things that go on at the end of the academic year. I have been worked off my head! Now everyone has gone away — even Eleanor has left for a week in New York with her mother, and I am alone with the children.

This should arrive in time to wish Daddy a very happy birthday. A gift is on the way, together with some more of that biscuit mix; the gift is Eleanor's handiwork. Also there is another Danish parcel in the mail.

I have had some letters from England about my book, but thus far no reviews, except a very silly one by Toby in *The Middle Way*. He gets "personal" and shows himself rather small, I am afraid. Had a most delightful letter from a Miss Maisie Spens of Colchester, who was put on to the book by E. I. Watkin, a very famous Catholic lay writer. Also from a sister at one of our own convents in Malvern, who seems to be a particularly charming person.

Bishop Conkling is on his way to London for the Lambeth Conference. You might ask him to lunch someday in the city. After June 30th he will be at King's College Hostel, Vincent Sq., S.W. 1. During the summer you will also be getting a call from a very charming young woman — Marily Krum — who has been one of my students this year; you might take her out to lunch too, if Mummy approves. She is very pretty and very intelligent. Paula Fowler will also be flying to London for a short visit later in the summer.

We have just finished a conference of clergy engaged in university work at which we had as leader a professor of philosophy at Yale, who is also master of one of the colleges in the university — Dr. Theodore Greene. He was a particularly fascinating person, unfortunately lame. I introduced him to Eleanor, as it turned out that they were both taking the same train for New York, they rode together and had a terrific philosophical powwow! Eleanor and I have been working for months on the problem of freedom and the origin of evil, and she has been looking around for a trained academic philosopher to try it out on. Well she got it, and I gather the results were very successful. I have to see if I can get it into a book this summer, which will go down to the most basic metaphysical problems.

Well I was suitably and ceremoniously given my degree last week, together with a splendid hood embellished with red velvet! I am wondering how soon it will be before I get asked to do some teaching in a seminary, as this is certainly something I would like to try my hand at. All this spring I have had a group of six seminary students coming for a weekly course in theological fundamentals, and they seem to have gotten a lot out of it.

We received the book of tapestries — really a much better production than the one we sent you, and Joan is delighted with the cross-stitch book although she takes rather slowly to this kind of work. I think she is principally interested in painting and drawing, and this term has done some really excellent work in school, including a lovely picture of a tree and falling leaves and an abstract design. We are sending her to art school this summer, and are looking for a good music teacher for Winky, whose sense of rhythm has become quite developed. Her strumming on the piano is at times pleasant to hear!

Eleanor has bought some beautiful new records lately, including the astonishing guitar playing of Andres Segovia. He plays such things as Mozart, Haydn, Scarlatti, etc., with an effect that sounds like a combination lute-harpsichord-piano. I never imagined that a guitar could produce effects of this kind.

Weather is still a bit on the chilly side, though we have had a few warm days. Oh this climate!

Lots of love from us all, Alan

The following letter is to the author of Meeting of East and West.

CANTERBURY HOUSE | EVANSTON, ILLINOIS | JULY 30, 1948
Dr. F. S. C. Northrop | Yale University Law School | New Haven, Connecticut
Dear Dr. Northrop,
Thank you very much indeed for your extremely interesting letter and article.
The latter is returned herewith. I have found both of great value and stimulating
power, as I am in the middle of doing some writing on the essential principles
of Oriental metaphysics. It seems to me that you have posed the problem of the
relation of the indeterminate continuum and the determinate theoretic logos in a
marvelous way. You have asked the right question with very great precision and
clarity; but I do not see that you have given the right answer. However, I think
the right answer is so extraordinarily difficult to express that it is to be doubted
whether language can cope with it at all!

First, let me say that I entirely agree with your point that, in general, Western religion and philosophy are concerned with the absolute as a determinate
logos. At the same time, St. Thomas (following St. Dionysius) most certainly
tries to identify, or at least relate, this determinate *logos* to a negatively described,
indeterminate, strictly infinite and eternal, metaphysical *ground* — a ground
which may be known mystically through the apophatic technique of the Areopagite, which has so much in common with the Vedanta.

I think we would agree that St. Thomas was not very successful. His failure
seems to me to spring from the same cause as the failure of the Cartesian dualism.
I think your own solution comes to grief through the same cause, namely, the
assumption that the indeterminate infinite continuum is in some way *opposed* to
the finite theoretic *logos*, making the two mutually exclusive in such a way that
they can only be related by a plus sign.

If the absolute is designated as indeterminate, the problem which the Western mind does not seem able to solve is this: How can an indeterminate absolute
be the sufficient ground and *cause* of structure, finitude, and determination? Or,
as you have put it, how can mystical knowledge of such an absolute bring any
creative and transforming power to bear on the order of the finite world? As a
passive continuum, how can it do anything but "accept" that world, enabling the
mystic to live in it with equanimity?

On the other hand, if the absolute is the determinate theoretic *logos*, it is
quite easy to conceive it as a sufficient cause of the finite order, and as a world-
transforming factor. *But*, is it still possible to conceive it as an absolute? If it is
determinate, what determines it? If it is principally finite, must it not have limits
in space and time, and, if so, where does it come from? Furthermore, although
Christian theology treats God as determinate from the practical standpoint, it is

equally bound to regard him as essentially indeterminate and infinite. Obviously, this has been a profoundly difficult problem for theology. We say that God is *self*-determining, but this must mean that in essence he is pure indeterminate freedom.

I notice that you do not give very much weight to the Vedanta and the Mahayanist concept of strict nonduality. To me, this is the essence of the Oriental doctrines. It means that the infinite and the finite, the indeterminate and the determinate, are in no sense opposites. The former includes the latter by definition, though not by necessity. By definition the infinite is free and has the power to manifest the finite. If it lacked this power, it would be neither infinite nor nondual, for it would by definition exclude and oppose the possibility of a finite order.

Perhaps we are misled by analogies. The idea of the infinite Brahman as a continuum suggests a passive mirror, field, or space in which the finite is produced. We feel, then, that the finite must originate from some seed (*spermatikos logos*) principally other than the continuum. But the Oriental doctrines assert that this seed (*bhutatathata*) is the infinite itself. The "continuum" has the power to produce a contraction (*sankocha*), a concentration of itself into particular points of view, particular expressions of infinite possibility, at an indefinite number of points or nodes within the continuum. Hence the paradox, "*Tao* is ever inactive, but there is nothing that it does not do."

In other words, just because the absolute is principally infinite it can for that very reason afford to "abandon" itself, to identify itself, with particular points of view, with definite forms and structures, the nature of which it thereby determines out of infinite possibility. This point comes out far more vividly in Zen than in the Vedanta, I think for the simple reason that people in a tropical climate are less interested in transforming the finite than inhabitants of the northern temperate zone! This concept of the infinite giving itself to the finite, of the absolute compatibility of the undifferentiated and indeterminate with the differentiated and determinate, is the central meaning of most of the Zen anecdotes — especially those which involve some sort of affirmation of a finite thing or action.

Bokuju was asked, "We have to dress and eat every day, and how can we escape from all that?"

"We dress; we eat."

"I don't understand."

"If you don't understand, put on your clothes and eat your food."

You are perfectly right in saying that whereas Brahman is known by immediate knowledge, the theoretic *logos* is inferred by logical intuition. (I prefer to give "intellectual" its scholastic meaning!) But I think that the reason why we cannot know the *logos* immediately is precisely that we have the viewpoint of Atman rather than Brahman. We are a self-limitation of Brahman, a kenosis, in which Brahman abandons omniscience and thus immediate knowledge of the *logos*. Just because in each one of us Brahman is identifying *himself* with a particular point of view, *how* he manifests the particular is not a datum of immediate consciousness.

Is not your identification of the Oriental viewpoint with the aesthetic and the occidental with the theoretic perhaps giving the term "aesthetic" too wide a meaning? It would seem to me that while theoretic knowledge is an analogical knowledge of the real in terms of concepts or ideas, aesthetic knowledge is analogical knowledge in terms of sensations and values. Surely immediate knowledge transcends both. It is intellectual knowledge in the ancient sense — i.e., the mode of knowledge proper to pure consciousness, whereby it is aware of its own existence. Aesthetic knowledge is surely a knowledge proper to certain objects within consciousness. It is knowledge of sense-impressions and values and moods as distinct from ideas. But immediate knowledge, pure consciousness, underlies both.

Maybe I don't properly understand your idea of epistemic correlation, but I feel that if you are going to set up the relation aesthetic plus theoretic you are going to get a dualism requiring some third term in which to ground the other two. The same goes for the formula W [West] plus E [East], if you identify E with the aesthetic. But it seems to me that immediate knowledge of Brahman transcends both aesthetic and theoretic knowledge, although Orientals have in practice paid more attention to the aesthetic content than to the theoretic. I would say that E includes W *potentially*, just as the nondual infinite includes the finite potentially.

The fact that the East has ignored the theoretic content of consciousness in preference for the aesthetic does indeed give the impression that Oriental mysticism is an aesthetic knowledge. But I don't think it is. Vedanta mysticism can include the aesthetic standpoint just as easily as the theoretic. That it has not so far included the latter is, I am quite sure, due to other causes than the nature of Oriental mysticism. The lush tropical climate of India — too hot to be very busy — is one explanation. In China and Japan, however, Zen has had a transforming effect. But it is a different kind of effect from the transformations carried out by Western technology because the Taoist mentality has the most profound respect for the "balance of nature." Chinese creativity is not to do violence to natural limitations, but to get behind nature and push — a sort of jujitsu.

But Western technology is always trying to make the finite infinite; its aim is the "bigger and better," expressing a hunger for more and more and more which hasn't the faintest idea where to stop. This is not purely modern. Modern man expresses physically the same itch for infinitude which mediaeval man expressed spiritually. It is the result of separating the infinite from the finite, making an opposition, a dualism between the two, between God and man. As a result man feels isolated, lonely, and infinitely hungry — so that he devours the world like a swarm of locusts. To give himself the craved sense of omnipotence, he wants to subject the entire natural order to his conscious control. I am sure that the East will eventually be sympathetic to a jujitsu use of technology which will not blow the balance of nature to hell.

I forget just what I said in my letter to Sister Rachel that gave the impression of disagreeing with your thesis of the unity of Oriental spirituality. What I meant to say was that you had underemphasized certain differences of nuance which are rather important. But the essential unity simply cannot be denied. And one of the great merits of your book was to call attention to this fact.

You see, then, that my object is to bring the Western, determinate *logos*, the transforming atonement doctrine, inside the realization of Brahman — not the other way round! I admit that *Behold the Spirit* gave the impression of discarding it because I was more concerned to describe the other point of view to Christians. It is precisely because of the nonduality of the Oriental viewpoint that I feel it to be *in principle* the more inclusive, even though it has not yet been so historically. The *logos* transforms the existential matter of the world, but surely no Vedantist would be such a gross pantheist as to identify Brahman with existential matter! René Guénon, a most perceptive exponent of the Vedanta, makes this particularly clear. I wonder if you know his *East & West, Crisis of the Modern World*, and *Introduction to the Study of the Hindu Doctrines*. They are very suggestive books, and Coomaraswamy thought most highly of him, though I must say his attitude is at times rather too patronizing.

With many thanks and all good wishes,

Very sincerely yours, Alan Watts

Canterbury House | Evanston, Illinois | August 8, 1948
Mr. Kurt Wolff | Pantheon Books, Inc. | New York, New York
Dear Mr. Wolff,

I am enclosing a copy of one of the Church of England newspapers including both a review and editorial about *Behold the Spirit*, as well as a review from *The Friend*. Please put them in the scrapbook.

I think you may be interested to know that I am making quite rapid progress on a new book [*The Supreme Identity*], which I hope to finish early in the fall. It deals with the principal metaphysical problems underlying the mysticism of *Behold the Spirit* — in particular the relation of the infinite to the finite, eternity to time, the nature of man and his consciousness, the problem of evil, etc. These various problems are woven together in a general discussion of the relation of religion and mythology to metaphysics, the latter being understood not as merely speculative philosophy, but as actual knowledge or realization of the ultimate reality.

The point of the book is to clarify the relations between religious knowledge and metaphysical knowledge as represented by Christianity on the one hand and, more specifically, by the Vedanta on the other. My idea is that these are not two competitive religions, and are thus wholly consistent as are, say, music and dancing. Though different in principle, the one is related analogically to the other. I am sure that if this idea can be established a tremendous amount of misunderstanding can be cleared up, both as regards the relation of Christianity to other "religions" and as regards the relation of theology to dogma.

In the latter connection I am trying to show that most of the real difficulties of theology — such as the problem of evil — are the result of mixing religious and metaphysical concepts in the same framework without recognizing that one is jumping from one language to another.

In general the book is an appeal for the necessity of metaphysical certainty to the sanity of the social order and the meaningfulness of religion. I am using the term "metaphysics" in preference to "mysticism," because it is much more exact and less liable to be confused with "religion."

In some quarters there was considerable criticism of *Behold the Spirit* because it seemed to be watering down the historical and sacramental aspect of Catholicism. By this clear distinction of metaphysics and religion I have found it possible to get the desired results without watering down anything. Religion remains in toto as a historical, space-time analogy of the eternal and infinite order of metaphysics. The religious point of view is necessarily conditioned by space and time; it must conceive infinity in terms of immensity, and eternity in terms of everlastingness. It expresses chronologically and concretely what metaphysics apprehends simultaneously and immediately.

The outline is approximately this:

Introduction: The necessity of metaphysical certainty in the social order. Confusion in every realm, the result of absence of the knowledge of man's true end. Definition of metaphysics, and its relation to religion briefly sketched.

I. The Infinite & the Finite: How infinity and eternity are conceived metaphysically as distinct from religiously. The infinite does not stand over against the finite as its opposite, but principally *includes* the possibility of the finite order. Contrast with pantheism, monism, and dualism. The unity of the infinite does not annihilate the multiplicity of the finite, or deprive it of meaning. Eternity does not abolish time, and union with the eternal does not involve absorption or loss of personality.

II. The Supreme Identity: The problem of man's nature and identity. The need of distinguishing the self (spirit) from the ego (soul-body), the former considered as the ground of consciousness, the latter as something *in* consciousness as a known or knowable object. Religion, absolutely and necessarily silent on the nature of the self as consciousness or spirit. The self, as a "point of view" taken by the infinity, and thus ultimately identical with it. That this is neither monism nor value-abolishing pantheism shown by a comparison with the doctrine of the Trinity.

III. The Problem of Evil: Does the absolute all-inclusiveness of the infinite annihilate moral value? Moral value cannot be made absolute without absolute dualism. But relative moral values may be maintained without annihilating them, because the absolute includes the relative and does not overwhelm it. In trying to make values absolute, theology precipitates a possibly dangerous and immoral dualism. From the eternal standpoint good and evil constitute a harmony (like light and shadow in painting) which, when known, is of such beauty that the suffering and evil experienced in time seem immeasurably worthwhile. Logical objections to this idea not born out in experience. Reasons given.

IV. Involution and Evolution: The self in man and its progress to realization through three stages, the unconscious, the ego-conscious, and the self-conscious. This progress is a finite image of the eternal distinction and union of the son and the Father in the Godhead. Because the finite image is in time, the distinction and union are known successively. Consciousness experiences distinction from God before union with God. How religious doctrine and symbolism corresponds with this. The function of the concrete and historical emphasis in Christianity. Relation of metaphysics to the uniqueness of the historic Christ. Religion and the gnosis — a historical tension.

V. Realization: The means whereby metaphysical realization of the union of the self and the infinite comes to pass. This is all-important because metaphysic is a realization rather than a theory, and as theory or doctrine has not the adequacy of religion. Realization is perhaps possible only for a minority, but the influence of such a minority out of all proportion to numbers. Discussion of spiritual techniques; various types of yoga. Because the infinite does not oppose the finite, material existence and experience [are] no obstruction whatsoever to realization.

Inevitably there will be a lot of material for controversy in this. I am doing my best to deal with some pretty difficult subjects without too much technical jargon, and I am certain that readers of *Behold the Spirit* will in general want to read it. Let me know, won't you, if it interests you. I am very happy with you as a publisher!

> With very best wishes to you and Mrs. Wolff,
> Very sincerely yours, Alan Watts

CANTERBURY HOUSE | EVANSTON, ILLINOIS | SEPTEMBER 22, 1948
Mr. Kurt Wolff | Pantheon Books | New York, New York
Dear Mr. Wolff,
Herewith is the manuscript of *The Supreme Identity*. About the same length, I think, as *Behold the Spirit*, though in some respects a rather different style of book for reasons explained in the preface. I have done my best to reduce technical jargon to the minimum, and I think I have succeeded in being considerably less polysyllabic than Northrop's *Meeting of East and West*!

I wonder if you and your reader would give me your opinion on two matters: (a) Should I append a glossary of all Oriental terms used? I have tried to define most of them as I go along, but some people have difficulty in memorizing them. (b) Would it serve any useful purpose, such as greater readability, to insert a number of subheadings within each chapter?

Writing this has been a little frustrating in some ways. It could have been expanded into a three-volume affair, and it was hard to know what to leave out.

> With very best wishes to yourself and to Mrs. Wolff,
> Very sincerely yours, Alan Watts

CANTERBURY HOUSE | EVANSTON, ILLINOIS | OCTOBER 29, 1948
Dear Mummy & Daddy,
I am so sorry to write so infrequently, but I have a terrible time keeping ahead of my work. It seems that the moment one sermon or lecture is given I have to prepare another, and in the interim see and talk to endless people. I have hardly had time to read since the fall term began, though I have managed to get through Toby's *Via Tokyo* in short snatches as it was quite "light."

I wonder how much Willie will be delayed because on November 9th I am due in New York! I think I had better write him at his hotel there and explain the situation. I have to lecture in Pittsburgh on the 8th. Maybe if I take a plane to New York I could catch him there, and then Eleanor could entertain them in Evanston so that they could see the children.

We shall be very delighted to have some more needlework from you. Your long stool with the devils always excites interest, but I am afraid it is getting rather too much use. I think we shall put the new piece somewhere else than in the living room; I will inquire about the Danish package and send you another in any case. Excuse the delay; I should really put this first on the list of my awful pile of unanswered letters. I need a secretary. Sometimes I get help from Northwestern girls, but those I have had type so untidily. What about duty on a biological kit? If it would not be a nuisance, I will gladly send you one. We are also sending over a black suit which Daddy may be able to use or, if not, give to someone else.

Monday night we got out to see the Russian Ballet: not so good as in the old days at Covent Garden, there being but one remaining ballerina of the old school. We had two shows for the price of one, as shortly before the affair started President Truman came by on his election campaign. How different from a Royal Procession! He travels in an open car, standing up, the running boards crowded with Secret Servicemen, and preceded by a fire engine with searchlights to floodlight the buildings on either side of the street. There was, however, a magnificent display of fireworks.

Daddy, your comments on the "problem of evil" are very much to the point. I have worked out something resembling this, but your own remarks give me an extra idea which I am most glad to have, though all its implications will need some thinking through. The idea of God setting up the condition of chaos as something to "play against" gives a rather startlingly simple basis for the continued validity of the conception of law and order as something absolute rather than merely relative. Possibly the idea contains some hidden snags, but I am going to work on it. I have been using the analogy of a photograph. Seen under a microscope (the viewpoint of time) it is a meaningless series of black, white, and grey patches. Seen as a totality (the viewpoint of eternity) it is a meaningful whole in which the dark areas have a definite value, and the light even more value than they had by themselves. Your idea, however, contains a certain dynamic quality that this lacks.

The whole problem is further complicated by the question of freewill, which in turn hangs on what we are to consider as the ultimate relationship between the individual and God — whether, for example, the essential consciousness or self in man is or is not a temporary self-limitation of the divine mind. That it *is* so seems to me to be the undeniable testimony of Oriental metaphysics and of much Western mysticism. This thesis, and its relation to Christian doctrine, is the main theme of the book I have been writing. It involves some problems of such great delicacy that I am never quite sure whether I have dealt with them satisfactorily, and thus am a little hesitant about letting the book out as yet.

I was much interested, and somewhat amazed, at Toby's *Via Tokyo*. Have you read it yet? It contains a lot of thought-provoking information about the postwar state of affairs in Asia, but I am simply floored at the man's mixture of wisdom and superficiality, his response to beauty and apparent insensitivity to others' feelings. A weird air of lighthearted conceit permeates the whole thing.

I'm very glad you liked *Zen*. It certainly has been printed beautifully, and I had a lot of fun copying the illustrations from the originals. They all had to be in deep black, rather than shaded, so that they would reproduce for zinc blocks. I don't know yet how it is selling; only 1,000 were printed.

A French woman in London has written to me about arranging a translation of *Behold the Spirit* into French. She has been very well recommended by Rom Landau, a writer and sculptor, whom I used to know in connection with the World Congress of Faiths. She works for the French section of the BBC.

Last week I gave a lecture to the Diocesan Altar Guild (some 50 women) on making vestments! I was chiefly concerned with problems of basic design and pattern rather than embroidery, and was trying to get them to depart from certain "fussy" violations of essential simplicity. They certainly seemed to take to heart what I said, though as one man talking to so many experienced needlewomen I felt as if I were really putting my head in the mouth of the lioness. But I don't have a mother for nothing!

Wasn't that chipmunk a dear! They are very tame, and I took his picture from about three feet away. Joan has made a model of one in clay, which has been painted, glazed, and baked. She is getting along quite well with her artwork, and does best in line drawing. I am, however, troubled about her other schoolwork. Here she is, ten years old and only just beginning long division — and lazy about it at that. The level of education around here is absurdly low, and yet Evanstonians are smugly satisfied at having the best schools in the land. Among other things they have the lamentable arrangement of one teacher for all subjects — which does not redound to the communication of an enthusiasm for knowledge.

I wonder if, when my subscription to the *Church Times* comes up for renewal, you could possibly switch it to the other Church paper, *The Guardian*. It contains much better material, and is not so appallingly bogged down with trivia and legalism and stuffiness. I am receiving the *Times Literary Supplement* from a clergyman in Cheshire, in return for a subscription to one of our magazines. It maintains a remarkably high level of writing and reviewing.

Lots of love from us all, as always, Alan

CANTERBURY HOUSE | EVANSTON, ILLINOIS | NOVEMBER 3, 1948
John Grey Murray, Esq. | Publisher | London, England
My dear John,
Pantheon Books are at present considering the publication of a new MS of mine entitled *The Supreme Identity: An Essay on Oriental Metaphysics and the Christian*

Religion, a synopsis of which is enclosed. In the next few days you will also be receiving, via Pantheon, a copy of the preface, which will give you a further idea of its nature. Kurt Wolff wants to know whether you would be prepared to consider an arrangement on this book similar to the one on *Behold the Spirit*. If such an idea is at all feasible, we shall send you either a copy of the MS or of proofs so that you may reach a final decision.

Stupidly enough, I did not make an extra good copy of the MS, though I have one which is just legible, because I had my doubts as to whether you would care to enter into another arrangement of the same kind in the present state of economics. However, I may be wrong, and this letter is to find out whether you would even contemplate such an arrangement again at this time.

Another matter: a Mlle. Monelle Desselle wishes to make a French translation of *Behold the Spirit* and arrange for its publication in France. I gather from our agreement that the author retains all rights of translation. Please let me know if this is in order, and I will take up negotiations with her.

I have seen a few very good reviews of *Behold the Spirit* from English papers, but I gather that there are others which I have not seen. Would it be possible for you to loan me your file of press cuttings, which I would of course return to you without delay?

Yours ever, Alan

CANTERBURY HOUSE | EVANSTON, ILLINOIS | DECEMBER 6, 1948
Mr. Henry Schuman | Publisher | New York, New York
Dear Mr. Schuman,
I am sorry not to have been able to answer your letters before, but I have been out of town and have only just returned. While away I made a start on writing the book [*Easter: Its Story and Meaning*], but your letters have raised points which will have to be settled before I can continue.

1. The outline. The actual titles of chapters, and the order in which the subject matter is presented is a very adaptable thing. My outline was to give you an idea of the content rather than the manner of presentation. However, a work professing to explain the feast of Easter which minimizes its Christian character and gives *primary* emphasis to the non-Christian cults which it has absorbed would be a manifest absurdity. If what you want is a book on "Pagan Equivalents of Easter" the title and overall presentation of the book should make it perfectly clear that this is what is being done.

I realize you want a book which is a contribution to the cultural history of Easter as a "folkway," but you can't treat Christian history as something sacrosanctly separate from cultural history. In this particular case Christian history is precisely the main element in the cultural history we are considering. To minimize it would be an offense against historical accuracy, quite apart from religious sentiment.

I am puzzled by your comment that the outline suggests the "essay" rather than "narrative" approach, for the outline is precisely designed to tell the story in its historical order — with occasional and subsidiary comments on its meaning. Surely it is clear in the outline that chapters 2, 3, 5, 6, 7, 8 & 9 are strictly narrative and descriptive, and I cannot see how you get the "essay" impression. The fact that in the outline I use such words as "preliminary grasp of what Christianity means by the Incarnation" is merely for your information; it is not the kind of phraseology I shall actually use.

Oddly enough, it is incorrect to suppose that "the purely religious and spiritual meanings of Easter have been dealt with a good deal in books." The vast bulk of modern Christian literature on the subject is concerned with a discussion of the historicity of Christ's Resurrection, and the inner meaning is characteristically ignored.

If I may say so, my *forte* as a writer is an ability to reveal a universal and "inner" meaning behind religious symbols — quite distinct from a merely moralistic or homiletical meaning. A book that did not offer this kind of insight into the subject of Easter would be utterly out of character for me, would seriously disappoint the considerable public I now enjoy, and would do my reputation no good. One can easily discuss profound meanings without being academic and pedantic, but a book which simply touched superficially on various "cultural curiosities" connected with Easter, which was designed to give information rather than understanding, a book which reached a conclusion as platitudinous as Mr. Count's final paragraph on the meaning of Christmas, would not be a book by me! If you want a book which treats Easter in *exactly* the same way as Mr. Count has treated Christmas, I think it would be better to get someone else to do it. I will write simply, but I will not "write down" to a hypothetically sentimental and superficial audience.

2. The time factor. I contracted to finish the book by the end of January, and there it will have to remain. If the work is to be any good, it cannot be rushed. If it is really essential for advance publicity purposes to have the complete MS by the middle of January, I think I shall write a bad book and you will have bad sales. It would be better from all points of view to wait until Easter 1950, or get the job done by a professional journalist.

3. The jacket design. Your artist has done a somewhat weird job of mixing a strictly symbolic and conventional theme with a strictly realistic and sentimental one. I favored the former because it is (a) arresting, and (b) in keeping with the symbols for use as chapter heads, and (c) will cost you ever so much less to reproduce. But those lilies have all the frightful sentimentality of the ordinary Easter greeting card, and to me that sort of approach to matters of religion is the very devil!

In short, then, the position is this: If you want something that will sell by an appeal to the large public for sentimental literature, which wants information without understanding, you will fall hopelessly between two stools by not asking an expert *journalist* to do the job. If, however, you want something of permanent value, that will go on selling over a period of years, and that will satisfy the ever-growing public of thoughtful but dissatisfied people who want something else from religious symbolism than platitudes, moralism, mush, and odds and ends of insignificant information, then I'm your man.

Please reconsider the matter and let me hear from you at the earliest opportunity.

Sincerely yours, Alan Watts

AW: In the second paragraph of the following letter, Alan mentions, for the first time in this collection, that Eleanor is pregnant and almost due. He had made no previous mention of her pregnancy.

Later, on January 25, 1949 (four days after Michael's birth), Eleanor writes to Henry Miller, saying that she has been "producing a son for the family." (We have included two of Eleanor's letters to Henry Miller for context.)

We have no further letters from Alan to his parents until March 6, 1950. He writes to them that Eleanor is getting a divorce in Reno. In fact, she was granted an annulment, something that would have been difficult for his parents to understand.

This was obviously a very stressful time for both our parents. While Eleanor had been seeking guidance from her mother, her therapist, and a priest in New York, Alan was challenged to explain things to his parents in as palatable a fashion as he could.

In the March 1950 letter, he says that Eleanor and he agreed that he would have the care of Joan and me and Eleanor would keep Michael, "whom she loves as she has never loved anyone." As adults, visiting our mother's cabin in Westcliffe, Colorado, Joan and I discovered a diary that Eleanor had written starting from Michael's birth. It bears out Alan's words: Joan and I in particular were barely mentioned.

CANTERBURY HOUSE | EVANSTON, ILLINOIS | JANUARY 10, 1949
Dear Mummy & Daddy,
Your letter came this morning saying that our Christmas package had arrived. We are so glad it has come through at last, and I hope the suit enclosed will turn

out to be useful. I have not written for so long because I got a commission when last in New York to write a book on Easter by the end of this month! Well, I am most of the way through with it by now, and so can afford some moments for much-neglected correspondence.

Eleanor is well, but the infant has not yet arrived. We had a false alarm the other day, and sent her to the hospital to be watched, but they let her go home the next day. Probably nothing will happen for another ten days or two weeks.

We got the things from Uncle Willie, as well as your Christmas packages. That stool is a perfect marvel! And I am as delighted with the needlework book as Eleanor, and of course turned to the page where the Turk's head knot is and tried my hand at it again. I have got the idea, only I need some better kind of cord for making it. I love my book of icons, and only wish I had some time to study them at the drawing table and so improve my own. One of these days I shall get at it again. The photograph of your needlework is most interesting, but I forget just where it is now. I wish they didn't have to use those dreadful round-backed chairs for the congregation: makes the place look like a cheap restaurant turned over! But I suppose you have to take what you can get.

We certainly had a splendid Christmas with Ruth here, although work didn't give me much of a holiday. I collected some good cigars, a lot of records, and Thomas Mann's new book *Dr. Faustus*. Gave Eleanor and her mother each a splendid new book on Chinese painting with lots of glorious full-page reproductions.

The *Guardian* has started to come; it really is much superior to the *Church Times*, the latter having such a tendency to stuffiness, and we are also most grateful for *Punch* again. We love Emett, and it is interesting that his jokes get reprinted quite frequently in our magazines.

We are trying to arrange joint publication with Murray again for my next book — not the Easter one — but for the one I did this summer, *The Supreme Identity*. *Behold the Spirit* is now to be translated into German. Notoriety gets me lots of work. The Bishop of Pittsburgh has been angling to get me into his diocese, and though he is a perfectly grand person who thinks much as I do, I don't fancy living amid the steel mills! Since last writing to you, I have been down to Tennessee for a week giving a "mission" at a very remarkable parish close by the Smoky Mountains, where the hill-folk are the purest Anglo-Saxon stock in the US, and still speak Elizabethan English. (Education is sadly changing all that.) I had to go by plane both ways, and the trip was beautiful — especially returning to Chicago at sundown. Sunset above the clouds is a sight for the gods.

Am off to Pittsburgh twice again this spring, once in February to speak at the university chapel, and once in May to give another mission. In April I have to go to Carleton College in Minnesota, and throughout Lent am conducting a School of Religion at a parish nearby. I suppose all this has to be done; it keeps the home fires burning and has, I hope, some beneficent influence. But sometimes I want to be able to stop and think for a year. At this rate one has to talk first and think later! Between trips one gabbles incessantly in endless conferences with individuals and groups.

Tenure on the house here is still a bit uncertain, but the bishop is taking steps to hold it, which will, I think, be effective. If I were a bishop I'd go nuts! Yes, Fr. Bruce is still around, and we see him often. Dorothy is working at a college in Iowa, but comes here frequently. The Dolezals were in for an evening over Xmas with their now very plump and splendid baby boy. Gloria Love is taking a graduate course in anthropology; Pris Clark is likewise doing graduate work in psychology at U of Minnesota; Muriel Pinder is just married and living in Hawaii; Rose Adamek is about to get married this spring, to a future philosophy professor. And so it goes!

Lots & lots of love from us all — As ever, Alan

CANTERBURY HOUSE | EVANSTON, ILLINOIS | JANUARY 17, 1949
Mr. Henry Schuman | Publisher | New York, New York
Dear Mr. Schuman,

I am very sorry to have made things so difficult for you, but I am afraid the difficulty is rather in the nature of the case. To a writer on religion, also a clergyman (!), the subject of Easter is primarily, and incurably, a religious subject, and only secondarily a matter of folklore and custom, and would have to be presented that way even in talking to high school students. The reverse mode of presentation is necessarily, from this point of view, a laying of emphasis on nonessentials.

My difficulty is this: If I present the subject au Frazer, the reaction will be, "What a charming and diverting account of old superstitions; how interesting to see that the Christian Easter is just the vegetation myth of Attis in other terms!" To anyone under the influence of modern education I cannot make it clear that the Easter story is something more than this without argument. This might have been possible two hundred years ago, when the Christian Easter story was almost universally accepted as a supreme spiritual truth and a historic fact. Today it is very largely *not* accepted in this way. What is more, various essentials of the story such as the idea of Christ as the Son of God, the notion of "redemption through his blood," the concept of eternal life, and the significance of "physical resurrection" mean nothing to the modern mind save pure superstition. How can I make it seem otherwise without explanation and argument?

I see your point of view. You know that a relatively smaller public wants to hear such an explanation. As a publisher you naturally want the book to reach as large a public as possible, and hence it must entertain rather than educate. Please — I don't blame you; it is perfectly legitimate to provide such entertainment, but a person in my position cannot, on this particular subject, assume the role of entertainer.

I have tried extremely hard to present the whole matter as simply as possible and to include as much narrative and mythology as space will allow. But at every point I find myself up against points of the narrative which, to the modern mind, look like one thing and mean another — points of symbolism which I know from long experience with young people are totally misleading when unexplained. In looking over what I have written I am myself aware of a "falling between two stools": the religious argument is not strong enough, and the descriptive narrative has not enough local color except, perhaps, in chapters 5 and 9. But how on earth is one to do both in so small a compass?

At the moment I am in course of preparing two final chapters, one on Easter observances in the modern world, and the other on eternal life. It would, I think, be possible to let you have these by the end of the week, but to rewrite the rest and prepare all the illustrations by the end of January is, with the vast load of other work I have to do, impossible.

Now what would you have me do? Let me make it plain: I cannot, in my position, write a primarily anthropological book, consisting of the mythology with a few hints as to meaning, because —

(a) If I were to narrate the Christian story as history and the pre-Christian as myth (and leave it at that), your readers will say, "Look at this old fuddy-duddy who believes in an obvious fairy tale!"

(b) If I tell both in such a way as to be very noncommittal about the historicity of the Christian story, and leave the impression that the deepest meaning of Easter is "joy in the eternal recurrence of life," my own public and my Church will say, "Good God, what has happened to Alan Watts? Doesn't he know any better than that?"

To do the job in such a way as to give a colorful story, to let the reader see that I am not being an obscurantist advocate of superstition, and to avoid the impression of having gone "woolly and vague" in religion is a terrific job. You see, I cannot write any book on an even remotely religious subject without keeping my ordinary readers in mind. They consist of Church people who I am trying to give a deeper and less superstitious idea of their religion, and of freethinkers who I am trying to give a deeper idea of the Church. The former watch me like hawks for heresy, and the latter for any signs of selling out to blind literalism. I am trying to persuade both to meet each other at the deepest level, the level of the mystical and interior meaning of religious forms. My position is thus critical, but I enjoy it and think it very necessary. I have an important work coming out in the fall on these matters which I cannot afford to prejudice.

Now if you think all this makes me quite impossible to deal with, please be frank and say so. I am terribly sorry if my previous letter of explanation did not make this clear enough, and so to cause you so much waste of time and expense, but if our positions and points of view are irreconcilable (and it is for you to judge), I think we had better cancel the contract and write it all off to experience.

I have received your telegram, and await the full critique with interest. Your courtesy and consideration in all this is, I assure you, very much appreciated. I dislike to see it end in nothing, but I wonder if your necessary objectives and my unavoidable position are not mutually exclusive.

With very many thanks and best wishes,

Sincerely yours, Alan Watts

CANTERBURY HOUSE | EVANSTON, ILLINOIS | JANUARY 19, 1949
Mr. Henry Schuman | Publisher | New York, New York
Dear Mr. Schuman,

Thank you very much for your letter of January 18th. I am, indeed, most embarrassed to have caused you to get so far "out on a limb" in the preparation of this book, and I have been trying hard to think of some solution to the problem. I don't think that it can be solved without getting us both into further difficulties.

It seems to me that the root of the misunderstanding is just what kind of "explanatory material" the readers you have in mind can take. I knew you wanted to avoid *technical* theology, and I sure avoided it! I think we differ very widely in our estimation of how much "theology" the proposed readers can both take and like. Since my main job is interpreting such matters to the young, and since I find many of them extraordinarily interested in even "mystical theology," I have reasons — warped maybe by professional optimism — for a very different estimation. I think we agreed that Dr. Count's book was not the *ideal* model. To you, I think, a "difficult theological essay" (from the readers' standpoint) means one thing, and to me another. And, to my mind, Dr. Count left out the real point of Christmas, which is inescapably theological.

I am returning the advance herewith for the cancellation of the contract. May I thank you again for your courtesy and consideration, and express my deep regret for not having been a more satisfactory author.

Sincerely yours, Alan Watts

EVANSTON, ILLINOIS | JANUARY 25, [1949]

Dear Mr. [Henry] Miller,

Sorry to have been so long in acknowledging your card concerning the print. I have been very much occupied since Christmas producing a son for the family.

The print arrived in fine condition. There are one or two tiny cracks but not enough to be noticed. I was so glad that the card announcing the print arrived while my husband was out of town — it allowed me to give him a surprising as well as welcome Christmas gift.

He and I have both followed your literary works with great interest for many years and we are now doubly impressed with your work as a painter. I should like to be able to see more of it.

Thanks for your interest. Eleanor Watts

CANTERBURY HOUSE | EVANSTON, ILLINOIS | MARCH 16, 1949

Mr. Kurt Wolff | Pantheon Books | New York, New York

Dear Mr. Wolff,

I am sorry to say that John Murray [Publishers] do not feel they can handle *The Supreme Identity* — expressing the opinion that the book is very interesting, but too difficult for their readers. Now I wonder if you would consider action under the following possible alternatives:

1. To publish yourselves an American edition more or less as the book stands at present, perhaps offsetting the cost by some arrangement for reduced royalties if this still be necessary. I don't imagine that production costs are any less since I last talked with you.

2. To seek another English publisher, perhaps Faber & Faber with whom I have good contacts. This will take time, of course, and might delay fall publication, which I am rather anxious to achieve.

3. To turn the book over to the Bollingen Foundation. Isn't Mr. [Joseph] Campbell associated with the foundation, and, having read the manuscript, he might be able to give advice on this point? I found most of his remarks very helpful, and am in any case making corrections in line with them.

If we were to follow course (3), would you consult Mr. Campbell, or whoever might be the right person, as to the advisability of (a) bringing some of the terminology more into line with Jungian concepts — e.g., stressing four "functions" of the soul rather than three; and (b) annotating the text in a fuller and more scholarly fashion, with particular attention to extra quotations from original sources to corroborate statements in the text.

I am well aware of the fact that the book is in some respects "difficult," but I should hesitate very much to simplify or popularize it because, in my position, I must keep the theologians in mind. In any case, this is a work in "creative theology"; it is exploring new ground, and must be intellectually respectable! Popularization would have to come later.

Perhaps you can think these points over and let me know what you consider the best course. I am sending the photostat of the manuscript to you while I retain the original for a while to make corrections. I am in any case going to introduce some clarifications into the rather too difficult second chapter, "The Infinite and the Finite." Substantially, however, the work will remain as it is, unless, should alternative (3) be followed, the Bollingen people would recommend the Jungian terminology and the additional annotation.

Please let me hear from you soon. With all good wishes,

Very sincerely yours, Alan Watts

EVANSTON, ILLINOIS | MAY 9, 1949

Dear Mr. [Henry] Miller —

I was so delighted to get your letter and hear firsthand of your interest in Zen. Yes. In a way Zen is "IT" for me too. My husband calls me a Taoistic Vendantist in Christian garb — a bit of a mix-up but I suppose he's right. Strangely enough, I never understood the Eastern doctrines until I became a Christian but without them I could never have become one as it is rather a "robbing Peter to pay Paul" affair at best. My mother, whom you probably know through her husband, Shigetsu Sasaki, remains a "scholastic Buddhist" but is producing some very valuable material through the First Zen Institute. She is working on another book which she hopes to publish in the fall. I do feel that Sokei-an's (his religious name) work is the most lucid we have had in English and it is wonderful that she is able to give it to the public.

Yes, I am familiar with *The Smile at the Foot of the Ladder* and consider it (so far) your finest, I am looking forward to *Draco and the Ecliptic*. I find your newer works far more satisfying than your early ones — somehow I sense in them a greatly deepened understanding — a real appreciation of phenomena rather than a merely sensitive observation. To me this is the great ideal — to realize, or would it be clearer to say, understand as real, the phenomenal universe just as it is. I know, intuitively, that perfection is at this moment but I find myself cut off from it by my refusal to accept the negative side of life as an integral part of that perfection — that, too, is part of it but happily one is not static and there is always change or what we choose to call growth.

The essay on the "Staff of Life" is also one that comes home to me — How far from reality can we try to get! I come from a rich and social family and as the years have rolled along have found my life growing simpler and more fundamental every day and I find myself not only able to adjust to a retired and penurious (in comparison) existence, but far happier in it. Gradually I desire to strip more and more. St. Francis in many ways was the supremely enlightened Christian. In many ways, I have been hampered by my background. When I married I had never cooked a meal or bought a piece of meat, but I am grateful because I know what I have left and can never *want* that sort of life again. Even *this* is far too complex.

Alan and I are planning to move West as soon as possible — next year this time, I hope. We find it far more conducive to the kind of life and state of mind we enjoy. We have seen quite a bit of the West the past two summers and have decided that somewhere in the Carmel–Big Sur area is where we should ultimately like to settle. If it is not too much to ask, I wonder if you could give us a helping hand — if you should hear of any living quarter of the sort that might suit our large family and meager purse, we would appreciate if you could let us know. It is so difficult to handle that sort of thing from a distance of 2,000 miles and estate agents just wouldn't have the sort of thing we are looking for. We shall probably be able to get a nice piece of property near Carmel in a few years. It belongs to a friend who has become a confirmed New Yorker. But our problem is to have a roof to land under until such time as jobs and permanent dwelling can be arranged.

Your watercolor is at last under glass — the more I see of it the more I enjoy it. My eldest daughter is in a fair way to becoming some sort of artist. Her feeling for line is amazing. I should love to find some really fine artist to whom she could be apprenticed for a while. Such an education seems much more valuable than the utter crap they grind out under that name these days. Northwestern is a case in point.

Perhaps I shouldn't trouble you with all this but Alan and I both feel closely allied to you, too.

Sincerely, Eleanor Watts

CANTERBURY HOUSE | EVANSTON, ILLINOIS | MAY 16, 1949
Dear Mrs. Gamer,
I want to thank you very much indeed for your letter of May 10th as well as for your tithe, which I am putting into a special fund, together with the $13.00 you gave me some time ago. This fund will be the nucleus for the School of Religion

which I plan to establish, and I am hoping to be able to make some material moves towards it during the next year.

I entirely agree with everything you say in your letter. To me, it is the soundest good sense, and I think it is beginning to be so for many others, who, even if they constitute a minority, can be a very influential one. I have just been spending a whole week in Pittsburgh, lecturing every evening on the general theme "Can We Know God?" — and, I found a group of some two hundred people very eager to listen and learn. They asked so many questions after the lectures that for three evenings running they had to be *told* to go home after sitting in church for nearly three hours. Are the sheep hungry! Furthermore, they bought a rather large quantity of books on this particular question which I had carefully selected for them.

Shouldn't we have enough faith in human nature to believe that very many will respond to this kind of teaching if it is really made available to them? Part of the trouble is that the present state of the theological schools in which our clergy are trained is really deplorable; they get a most uninspiring collection of not very relevant bits of information, and as a result come to the pulpit and classroom with no message but moral advice. As a result I am a little divided in my mind as to whether I should direct my energies towards the training of clergy or to the training of layfolk. Maybe both could somehow be combined in one!

With many thanks and very best wishes,

Most sincerely, Alan Watts

JW: The letter above is most interesting. I found myself wondering if Alan wrote it tongue in cheek, thanking her for a thirteen-dollar tithe. Mrs. Gamer was the mother of Alan's choirmaster and Eleanor's lover, Carlton Gamer. Having met her on several occasions (when I was an adult), I have to wonder what she knew and what she thought of Carlton's situation. Did she know that Michael was her presumed grandchild? Alan is totally cool in his thank-you — giving away nothing. But Carlton's father, Carl Wesley Gamer, was so upset with his son's circumstances that he threatened to sue the church for aiding and abetting the entire travesty.

While Alan continued his priestly duties, he was obviously beginning to question his choice of vocation. We begin to see less of Christian doctrine surfacing in his letters and more of Buddhist thought. He's also hinting that what he really needs is to live in the mountains and to lead a quieter life. He asks his peers in other states if they know of any teaching openings. In a letter to Henry Miller (with whom he and Eleanor had established a correspondence), Alan asked if he knew of any "small places" to live in California. Interestingly, Eleanor had asked the same question in a previous letter. Did she imagine the three or four of them continuing to live together? Eleanor left to live with her mother, Ruth, and took son, Michael, and my sister, Anne, with her. I was sent off to an Anglican convent school in Kentucky. Finally, in his March 6, 1950, letter to his parents, he admits that Eleanor is leaving him and they are divorcing.

This had to be incredibly difficult for him — to reconcile his own beliefs with that of the Church, and to acknowledge that he'd been so drawn in to the dogma of Christianity as to lose his own identity therein. He had created a trap for himself, trying to lead a Christian life, yet, within the Church, living a communal and unconventional lifestyle. His wife, so unhappy and displeased with the arrangement, had their marriage annulled. The impending scandal was terrifying. He also was panicked at the effect this would have on his parents, particularly his mother. Amazingly, despite the turmoil in his private life during this time, he managed to finish three books for publication.

CANTERBURY HOUSE | EVANSTON, ILLINOIS | MAY 26, 1949
Dr. F. S. C. Northrop | The Law School, Yale University | New Haven, Connecticut
Dear Dr. Northrop,

I have long had it in mind to answer your last letter (September 24!), but I must confess that the problems which our correspondence raised require anything but hurried thought. Before I try to reach any real conclusion on this highly suggestive differentiation between the aesthetic and theoretic components and their relation to Oriental and Occidental approaches to knowledge, I am trying the problem out on a few people whose competence in the Oriental doctrines is far beyond mine. Your letter certainly cleared up for me the precise sense of your use of the word *aesthetic*, and, with that definition in mind, there is no call for objection in using it for the Oriental mode of knowledge. But, so far as I am concerned, there is a good deal more thinking to be done about the nature of theoretic knowledge and its relation to Christian theology. It is a very fascinating line of thought.

However, my immediate reason for writing is a different matter. It has occurred to me that you might know of some college, preferably in the West, looking for someone to teach the philosophy and history of religions. I am on the lookout for work which will give me more time for writing and study than I can take here at Northwestern, and also for a climate that will be kinder to my wife's health. Here at Northwestern I do not teach on the faculty, and am simply the Episcopal chaplain.

As to qualifications, I have a master's degree in theology and am the author of half a dozen works in this field, the special point of concentration being, as you know, Chinese Buddhism and Zen in particular. Incidentally, I have two more works coming out next year, and, at the age of 34, ought to be good for plenty more! If you have any ideas, I would be most grateful.

Sincerely yours, Alan Watts

CANTERBURY HOUSE | EVANSTON, ILLINOIS | AUGUST 16, 1949
Mr. Henry Schuman | Lanesville, Massachusetts
Dear Mr. Schuman,
In answer to your letter of August 11th, the problem of the Catholic reception of the *Easter* book is rather difficult. From this point of view the whole subject of pagan antecedents of Easter is very ticklish, and the treatment would require the distinctly theological approach attempted in the first draft — with certain modifications. It would involve treating the Christian Easter story in the most literal way, and explaining the pagan antecedents by what is known as the "theory of types" — i.e., prophetic foreshadowings of Christ.

A book on such lines would be acceptable to most Christians of the traditional kind, but I believe they constitute a minority of the public you are aiming at. A treatment of the subject which would have the broadest possible acceptance would have to involve the highest degree of superficiality, and I am afraid that it would please no one. How did Catholics receive Count's book?

Sincerely yours, Alan Watts

The following letter is addressed to Adolph Teichert.

CANTERBURY HOUSE | EVANSTON, ILLINOIS | AUGUST 24, 1949
Dear Tolly:
The problem of Eleanor's health has now reached the point where I have had to tell Bishop Conkling that I must give up the work at Northwestern in the near future. I forget whether I told you in my last letter, but I have had to arrange to send her off for a prolonged vacation this fall and to put the two girls in private school. She must have a complete rest, both from the climate of the Middle West, and from some of the hectic duties of a clergy wife.

This means that I am on the lookout for new work, for which I expect to be available by Christmas at least. I don't know that I particularly want to get involved with the diocese of Dallas, but I noticed that you are going to General Convention in San Francisco. It is just possible, therefore, that you might hear of things and especially of any openings out West.

I am still set on this idea of a lay school of "spiritual studies," but the problem of setting up such a thing on the West Coast is that it is really impossible to do much about it unless I am first out there. Thus a job in college work in seminary, or even in a small parish, might be the entering wedge. So far as college work is concerned, I am more and more interested in the teaching side, and would like, if possible, to be somewhere where I could also be in the department of religion as faculty.

So will you please keep your eyes and ears open with yours truly in mind. I wish I could get out there for the convention myself, but, aside from the expense, it coincides with the opening of the fall quarter at Northwestern, for which I must be on hand.

Love from us all, Alan

CANTERBURY HOUSE | EVANSTON, ILLINOIS | NOVEMBER 8, 1949
Mr. & Mrs. Kurt Wolff | Pantheon Books, Inc. | New York, New York
Dear Mr. & Mrs. Wolff,
This letter is to both of you, to answer your two letters of October 31st and November 2nd.

Thank you very much for the contract, which I return duly signed. I presume you will send another copy for me to keep. I do hope we can get the book out in the spring, for it has been delayed so long already and is holding up my writing schedule! You see, I have another one in preparation, on quite popular lines. So many people have asked me to do something which does not require quite so much academic background.

I am writing to Faber [& Faber] to hurry on their end of the business.

Now as to Warner Allen's books. I feel strongly that *The Timeless Moment* is the better of the two. I found it a very interesting book, confirming many of my own ideas. It does not, as you say, fit in with any religious orthodoxy, but no more do many other books, such as those of Gerald Heard, which sell quite well. The problem is mainly that Mr. Allen has no following in this country, whereas Heard has. This means simply that the book would require quite a lot of promotion, and it would probably be necessary to get it read before publication by the kind of people whose comments you would use for promotion purposes. If they were favorable, you might risk it.

Do you have the impression that the style of the books is *peculiarly* British? There is a certain easygoing, rambling, poetic quality about them which I find very pleasing, but which does not, I think, appeal to the average American reader, who is in a hurry to get to the point.

Under the present conditions of publishing in this country, it must be risky indeed to launch a "discovery" of this kind on the public. Thus I am very hesitant in advising you in the affirmative, much as I like and enjoy the books myself.

With all good wishes,

Very sincerely yours, Alan Watts

EVANSTON, ILLINOIS | NOVEMBER 10, 1949

Miss Dorothea Oppenheimer | Henry Schuman, Inc. | New York, New York

Dear Miss Oppenheimer,

Thank you for your letter of November 8th. Let me answer your questions in the order presented:

1. Eleven chapters are okay!

2. Let us not capitalize except where absolutely necessary. Let it be "resurrection" and "crucifixion" throughout, and especially let the printer avoid the typographical piety of "He" for the divinity.

3. p. 10. *Association.* Italics please.

p. 26. Yes, insert "or Ishtar." The spelling Inanna is arbitrary, so let's keep it as written.

pp. 29–30. No way of simplifying without undue lengthening.

p. 42. Yes, it comes from *hilaros,* but we get it through the Latin. So it comes from *Hilaria,* too.

pp. 89, 93. Present tense is okay, even if some of these things are much less common than they were.

4. Corn. I don't know. People accustomed to the King James Bible are used to understanding it as a generic word for all kinds of grain. Thus the phrase "corn and wine" has a musical association which "grain and wine" doesn't have. Would you please discuss this with Mr. Schuman and perhaps one or two others, and I will accept your decision. Being English I can't judge very well!

Sincerely yours, [Alan Watts]

Following is promotional copy written by Alan for Easter: Its Story and Meaning, *published by Schuman in 1949.*

Easter: Its Story and Meaning
By Alan W. Watts

Why do we dress up in our newest finery when we join the Easter parade? What is the origin of the Easter egg? And why do toy stores display Easter bunnies in their windows at Easter time?

This book provides the answers to a host of such questions — some of them taking us back thousands of years, to the dawn of history. For the central theme of Easter — that of death and rebirth — is one that runs in various forms through all cultures and is as old as man himself.

In fresh, lucid prose the author initiates us into ancient and pagan spring rites, pointing out the many parallels to the Christ story. He elucidates the role the sun cycle played in these festivities and its relationship to Easter Week and explains the many symbols surrounding the Easter story, both in their deeper significance and in their practical application.

There is a chronological account of the Christian Easter story, to which has been added a number of legends not to be found in the gospels.

There is a chapter describing the dramatic rites of Holy Week as celebrated in medieval times which, in its precise reportage coupled with subtle poetic evocation, is unequaled.

The reader is introduced to a host of colorful folk practices and beliefs that have accumulated around Easter and are still to be found in many places.

The inclusion of an Easter calendar in which the significance of each day of the Easter week is made clear will give the reader added insight into the observance of the Easter festival.

Here is a book which takes us to the central meaning and message of Easter, which is that eternal life is not just a pious hope for the future but something which we have already in the present — not a dream but an actual reality. Here is a book to be valued alike for its account of an unfamiliar aspect of cultural history as well as for its interpretation of a spiritual truth.

CANTERBURY HOUSE | EVANSTON, ILLINOIS | NOVEMBER 14, 1949
Mr. Eugene Exman | Harper & Brothers | New York, New York
Dear Eugene,
Are there any copies of *The Meaning of Happiness* left? I particularly want one to be sent to Mr. Henry Schuman, East 70th St., NY, and charged to me.

I have just spent a most delightful two days with Elton Trueblood at Earlham College — a place with which I am most highly impressed.

I am still doing a lot of writing, and have two books coming out this spring, one a popular study of Easter, and the other an "opus" called *The Supreme Identity: An Essay on Oriental Metaphysic and the Christian Religion.*

The work here is terribly hard on the family, and I am seriously contemplating a change. The thing I want is to teach comparative religions and the philosophy of religion in some college. If you hear of anything in this line, please put in a word for me.

With all good wishes,
Very sincerely,
Alan W. Watts

CANTERBURY HOUSE | EVANSTON, ILLINOIS | [CIRCA 1949]
To the editor, *The Middle Way*
My dear Miss Cameron,
I wonder if you would be so kind as to give me space to write upon a personal matter which may be of interest to many readers of this journal, of which I was formerly editor.

Back in 1937 I published a book called *The Legacy of Asia* in which you may recall the following passage (p. 8):

> It is a common fallacy to imagine that the West can cut adrift from its Christian roots, to regard Christianity as an outworn creed in no way suited to the development of a rational civilization. But it is precisely to preserve us from a rational civilization (i.e., a purely humanistic, mechanized, secular culture) that a vital Christianity is necessary — a Christianity reinforced by all that Asia (i.e., Buddhism, Taoism, Hinduism, etc.) can give.

That passage was the first glimmer of a belief which has, since then, grown stronger and stronger, namely, that the true purpose of studying the wisdom of Asia was to reinvigorate Christianity. Such a thing has happened before, for Christian philosophy would hardly have reached its present development had not Origen been a student of Plato and St. Thomas Aquinas of Aristotle; in these non-Christian philosophers they found tutors to the wisdom of Christ and his Church, tutors who opened their minds to the profundity of the Christian faith. In a rather different way Buddhism, Taoism, and Hinduism have done the same thing for me; they have led me to appreciate as never before the wisdom of the Catholic religion, and they have led me so far that I am now a minister of the Church — in that branch of it known as the Episcopal Church in America and as the Church of England in the "old country."

I am afraid that some people will take this as a clear sign that I have gone somewhat crazier than usual, for what, it will be asked, can be more effete and decadent than the Church, and what more crude and unspiritual than the Catholic faith? While it is perfectly true that the visible Church is at present in a state of frightful mediocrity (not, however, without certain signs of awakening), the trouble with it is simply that, it has neglected its own treasures. Because of this neglect, the pagan public is not aware that it has any treasures save certain crude and crass dogmas which have long gone down the drain of washed-out superstitions. How, then, has a philosophy and a way of life so lofty as Mahayana Buddhism led one of its enthusiastic students to so dismal a conclusion?

Two things have always impressed and excited me in Mahayana (particularly as it is exemplified in Zen). First is the teaching that ultimate reality, variously termed sunyata, Tao, Tathata, etc., is so alive that it cannot be grasped in any rigid form of words, ideas, or feelings. Second is that sense that ordinary every-day actions and common material objects are in no way foreign to this reality, but, on the contrary, have a mysterious and intimate relation to it. This sense is particularly evident in the Zen mondo and in Chinese painting, where the turn of a bird's wing or the kiss of the wind on a blade of grass express the Tao more eloquently than volumes of abstract philosophy.

Two things have always puzzled and annoyed me both in Mahayana, and still more in Hinayana, Hindu philosophy and their modern derivative Theosophy. First is the idea that this ultimate reality, which is supposed to be alive, is a princi-ple or law, a mere mechanism, exceeding description only on account of its sheer infinite magnitude. To me, a living principle or law is a contradiction in terms. It seems like asking a weight to be lifted by the first proposition of Euclid, or like trying to explain the beauty of a Botticelli Madonna in terms of pure math-ematics — an over-logical, stodgy procedure wholly repugnant to the Chinese philosophy of art. Second is the notion that this everyday world and its material objects are incompatible with reality and that in nirvana they will have no further place. There we shall disembodiedly contemplate pure principle, and realize that all distinct phenomena are one formless and undifferentiated is-ness. So what? I would rather be reincarnated forever in this illusory but interesting world. Only the highest type of Mahayana is free (practically if not quite theoretically) from this uninteresting line of thought.

Nevertheless, Buddhists, Taoists, Hindus, and Theosophists are not nearly so oppressive and uninteresting as these two latter views might lead one to sup-pose. On the contrary, we have the astonishing moral beauty of the bodhisattva life and the aesthetic beauty of Chinese painting, together with a genuine human warmth which is something quite other than the operation of a mechanical prin-ciple. Furthermore, a large number of them would protest indignantly against the charge that they look upon reality as a mere mechanism. No, they would insist, the Tao cannot be defined as a mechanism because it is absolutely free and spontaneous; reality is not a dead, blind principle but a living principle of love, for "compassion is eternal harmony, the law of laws, Alaya's very self." But this is an evasion; it is either not saying what you mean, or not understanding what you mean. For if life, freedom, beauty, morality, and love come out of that void which they experience in samadhi, that void is a void only to human un-derstanding, a light so intense that it blinds human eyes. In itself it is not a void at all, but a richness and a fullness which the human mind can no more conceive than color can be described in terms of shape. Now since both St. Dionysius and

St. Thomas Aquinas, the Catholic theologians par excellence, have said just the same things of God, the authentic Christian view of God is not quite so crude and unspiritual as some might suppose. The assertion that God is a person is really what Buddhists who believe that reality is alive are feeling after. "Person" is of course an etymologically bad word, but it is used of God, not to indicate that he has a form or a body or a locality, but to show that he is preeminently alive, free, conscious, intelligent, and individual (i.e., undivided and integrated). Over and above this, Christian philosophy asserts that God has a character, to wit, goodness, beauty, holiness, and joyfulness. This certainly raises the problem of evil in his world, but it answers the far more difficult problem of the good in the world; and if reality is not in some profound sense good, it is neither lovable nor worth trying to discover. Only this can explain the lives of those who have found union with reality.

A living reality which has some intimate relation to everyday life and its material existences is undoubtedly experienced in Zen, but I cannot escape the conclusion that the Christian metaphysic offers a better ground for this experience than the Buddhist. For God is the creator of a material universe which is inherently good, with which he has intimately united himself in Christ (the Word made flesh) in order that it may be transfigured. Hence the sacramental note in Catholicism, the hallowing of such physical relationships as marriage, the mysterious doctrine of the resurrection of the body, and the vision of a God who so loves the world that it is not beneath his dignity to unite himself with mere bread and wine that even the most simple minds may receive the gift of his eternal life.

This I find most impressive of all — the fact that union with God is not an attainment but a gift. Buddhist experience also testifies to this in the idea that enlightenment is a present fact to be realized rather than a state to be created and attained, and Buddhists have told me of the sense of gratitude aroused in their hearts by satori, the sudden flash of illumination. I too, and many others of us, have had intuitions of our present union with reality or with God — a union which, for my part, I know I have done nothing to earn or deserve, and which is so disproportionate to my personal wisdom and merits that I cannot claim it as a right, and am compelled to thank and love a being other than my own. Dualism? No, for there is no more subtly misleading dualist than a mere oneness which excludes and opposes the freedom to create things different from itself, "When the many are reduced to the One, to what shall the One be reduced?"

Here I can say only enough to suggest how Mahayana philosophy could lead to the understanding and acceptance of these cardinal Catholic principles from which the rest follow. And because it has so led I am grateful for its tutorship, and wish to remain in the fellowship of its respectful students.

Sincerely yours,

Alan W. Watts

AW: Alan and Eleanor's marriage had been strained since before my birth. Alan was constantly working and traveling, and Eleanor suffered from depression and bouts of ill health, which had begun in her teens and continued until her death. Furthermore, they were sexually incompatible.

Having Carlton and Dorothy living with us was a highly unconventional arrangement, especially for a priest and in the 1940s. I have very vague memories of this time, having been so young. I do remember that I disliked Dorothy, finding her cool, distant, and humorless. Carlton, on the other hand, I adored; he would play with me, talk with me, and commiserate with my woes, and was the single most caring, consistent adult I knew.

In 1948, Eleanor became pregnant; on January 21, 1949, Michael was born. Eleanor finally had the son she had longed for, presumably with the man she was deeply in love with.

Soon after the annulment was obtained, Alan married Dorothy, and they moved to Thornecrest Farmhouse in Millbrook, New York. I was currently living with Eleanor and Michael in an apartment on the top floor of our grandmother's grand townhouse on East 65th Street in New York City. Joan remembers our father meeting with us in the grand library of the Sasaki, i.e., the First Zen Institute, asking us which parent we wanted to live with. I do not remember this event. However, I believed that Eleanor did not want me.

The next thing I knew, I was sent from my mother's to live with Alan and Dorothy. With Dorothy as my new stepmother, I felt somewhat as if I had gone from the frying pan into the fire. Once again, Alan, who had wanted his daughters to be with him, immersed himself in work and was rarely available. This meant Dorothy had the responsibility of being a parent to a child with whom she had no connection (Joan was away at boarding school in England). She did, over the years, make gestures of caring with the gift of her considerable sewing talents, in the form of clothing and, once, a completely new bedroom decor for me. Unfortunately, her parenting style toward me was mostly cold and harsh; that, combined with Alan's lack of parenting, led to my having a stomach ulcer at the age of ten.

CANTERBURY HOUSE | EVANSTON, ILLINOIS | MARCH 6, 1950

Dear Mummy & Daddy,

Today it seems as if spring were on the way — after some weeks of ice, snow and bitter cold. I have been fighting with a fluish cold, and generally feeling overworked and exhausted, which is one reason why I haven't written for so long. Last week I went to the doctor for a general examination. I find my blood count is low (for which he is giving me liver injections and vitamins), but I was glad to discover that my chest is quite free of TB. I'm always afraid of that.

This season of the year is very busy. I am lecturing three nights a week, and after Easter I am to take two lecturing trips, one to New York and one to San Francisco — right the way from coast to coast! I shall be in San Francisco for a little over a week, mostly giving a series of classes for clergy. It will be wonderful to get 2½ days' rest on the train each way.

I have finished correcting proofs for *The Supreme Identity*, and you will probably see this published in England sometime in May. All kinds of plans are under way for more writing, and there is a very real possibility that I may be able to devote my whole time to it, with some lecturing on the side. But there is a special chicken here which I am not going to count until it is hatched.

I know you have been disturbed because I have been rather reticent about Eleanor. But her state of mind has not improved at all, so far as I am concerned, and I have not wanted to say very much while some hope of things mending remained. But there isn't any hope. She doesn't want to come back to me, ever. I have been terribly concerned as to how you would feel about this, since you reacted rather strongly when Eleanor gave you the first hint that something was amiss. But at this point I am so tired and disgusted with the whole complex business that I cannot do much more than give you the immediate facts. The "explanation" would fill a small book — and it seems to me that when facts have to be faced regrets and postmortem analyses are beside the point.

As it stands Eleanor is about to get a divorce — at Reno, on grounds of incompatibility, where such things are managed without fuss, publicity, or fury. We have agreed that I shall have the care of Joan and Ann. To ask for Michael as well, whom she loves as she has never loved anyone, would be impossible and cruel.

For some time I fought for the obvious point that this would be very bad indeed for the children. But I have become completely certain that, were we to stay together, Eleanor's completely uncontrollable depression and bitterness would be even worse for them. So far as I am concerned, I have no desire to compel anyone to live with me who doesn't love me; I see nothing healthy in "Holy Deadlock." I don't understand Eleanor's psychology, and I haven't understood it for years. But I can only accept it as a fact — and may I ask you to do the same. The damage is done, and at this point protest, recrimination, "hashing it over," and such can — aside from relieving one's own feelings — do nothing but harm. The past is best buried. I cannot impress this upon you too strongly.

When certain emotions get the upper hand, human beings are simply not responsible for what they do — any more than if they had been hit by a hurricane. One accepts hurricanes, but we blame human beings because we are all so proud, and like to fancy that we are in complete control of our lives. But we aren't; and there are things which happen to the mind just as measles or the plague happen to the body.

The most important thing now is the future care of Joan and Ann. I must provide them with a home, and to do this it might someday be necessary to marry again, provided that the right sort of person could be found — from their point of view and mine. The difficulty here is that the Church does not like this kind of thing — at any rate not for clergy. This is why it may soon be necessary for me to earn my living by teaching or writing — a shift, however, which I would not make were there not many other considerations involved than marriage. Within the next two months I shall be able to have a much clearer idea of where I am going than I have at the moment, though even now I have grounds for feeling confident that I can handle the situation.

Thus far we have been able to handle this situation without any open unpleasantness, since Eleanor and I are in agreement as to what practical steps should be taken concerning the children, etc. For the time being, it has been necessary to have Ann stay with Eleanor in New York because she is too young to go away to school, and I cannot possibly look after her properly in this chaotic establishment. Furthermore, neither of us want to put any obstacle in the way of the children seeing both their parents, and we are going to try to arrange things so that we live near enough together so that the children can manage this without difficulty.

I do not want you to think that all this has happened without long and most careful consideration. The problem has been "brewing" for nearly three years. I have worked desperately to do the right thing, and have been willing to make any sort of sacrifice to save the situation. But always the insurmountable factor has been the irrational but nonetheless real fact that, living with me, Eleanor feels utterly depressed and frustrated. Admittedly, I am not the most ideal person for anyone to live with! But, in the last analysis, our circumstances and our difficulties are the outward symptoms of our own inner states.

During the past few months I have been living under the tremendous strain of uncertainty as to what I shall do, where I shall live, how I shall look after the children, what will be the reaction of those near and dear when the facts come out. I have been able to talk about the situation only to two or three very intimate friends; otherwise I have had to act and speak as if nothing were the matter, and keep a bright front to the world.

Though the future contains many uncertain elements, during the last few days a possibility has arisen which at the moment I daren't talk about because it is simply too good to be true. As to this, the next few weeks will tell.

I am sorry, dreadfully sorry, that at your time of life a problem like this should descend — that you should see your son a victim of the characteristic instability and uprootedness of modern life, and your grandchildren of the notorious "broken home" situation. But it is so, and there is simply nothing to be done about it save to accept it and "walk on." One may at least be thankful, that the children are not in a DP [displaced persons] camp in Europe, or homeless in a ruined city.

For the rest, I am irrepressible — mentally, if not always physically, full of hope and energy for living and working.

Quite recently I went and spent a weekend with Joan at her school [Margaret Hall, Versailles, Kentucky] — went riding with her, an art at which she is making progress and thoroughly enjoys, and had a wonderful time. What a lovable and companionable child she has become.

I am terribly sorry about Auntie Gertie. Will you please give her my love; I think I may manage to write her just as soon as the spring vacation comes, in another ten days.

I am sending you a copy of the book on Easter today. It has been very beautifully produced. The picture facing p. 97 is one of which you may recognize the painter, but I hadn't the nerve to put my own name beside El Greco and Dürer! The reproduction isn't too good, but the effect is fairly pleasing.

It is no good, I suppose, asking you not to worry, considering I do a lot of worrying myself. But it will be helpful if, with me, you will try to accept the facts as they are, and make the best of them.

With very much love, as always, Alan

JW: Alan married Dorothy DeWitt in the summer of 1950, in an attempt to keep Anne and me, leaving Michael to Eleanor and Carlton (who Eleanor admitted to be the biological father of her much-loved son). I was witness to Alan and Dorothy's marriage and as a wedding present gave them a hamster. We left (more like "fled") Canterbury House and drove east to New York City, where I was deposited with Ruth, Eleanor, Michael, and Anne while Alan and Dorothy went upstate to Millbrook.

I am uncertain about many details of the demise of the household at Canterbury House. Eleanor, at some point, had moved most of the furnishings which were from her family into storage in New York City. There was no "ceremonial" locking of the front door or handing over of the keys that I know of. There seemed to be little planning of the marriage between Alan and Dorothy. Alan had said to Eleanor that he really did not want to divorce.

In a letter to Bishop Conkling, Alan resigned, with a barrage of criticism of the Church. Conkling had no recourse but to write a response, thanking Alan for his service and wishing him well: "I'm grateful for all you tried to do for good in your ministry and I commend you to the justice and mercy of God."

In a letter to his friends after departing Evanston, Alan wrote, "After long and careful thought I have had to take a step which will perhaps be most disturbing to many of you, though to others it may come as no surprise. I have come to the conclusion that I cannot remain in either the ministry or the communion of the Episcopal Church." He wrote further: "During the past years I have continued my studies of the spiritual teachings of the Orient, alongside with Catholic theology, and, though I have sometimes doubted it, I am now fully persuaded that the Church's claim to be the best of all ways to God is not only a mistake, but also a symptom of anxiety."

So ended the chapter of his life as priest and chaplain of Northwestern University.

PART V

Interlude — Thornecrest Farm, Millbrook, New York

1950-51

Alan's drawing of Thornecrest Farmhouse, Millbrook, New York, 1950.

JW: Alan's departure from the Church and from his post as chaplain of Northwestern University, along with the scandal that ensued, reverberated for many years. In the summer of 1950, Carlton, aged twenty-one, graduated with a BA in music from Northwestern. He joined Eleanor in New York, where they were quietly married by a justice of the peace in the Bronx. He mentions that years later, upon his return to the campus for his fortieth reunion, all anyone wanted to talk about was "the scandal." Carlton and his father never spoke again until just before his father's death. Carlton went on the following fall to teach at Boston University and obtain his master's in music.

It is interesting to note Alan's inability to face the truth about his failed marriage. In his previous letters to his parents and to Tolly Teichert, he attempted to put the fault on Eleanor, claiming that her constant illness or her frigidity was to blame. But it was apparent that Alan wanted the freedom of an open marriage, not to be bound by the responsibilities of maintaining a sacrosanct union, and this was obviously not in sync with the mores either of the church or of the times. Regarding sexual mores, Alan's philosophy was, as stated in his autobiography, "I do not believe that I should be passionately in love with my partner — though it is the best of pleasures under such circumstances — and still less, married. For there is a special and humanizing delight in erotic friendship with no strings."

Alan received many letters in response to the mimeographed announcement of his decision. His friends and Church associates expressed everything from understanding to shock, dismay, and outrage. The Reverend Robert Platman (one of many attendees of the Canterbury soirees and one of several to whom Alan dedicated his book The Supreme Identity*) wrote: "I am doing what I can to stem the tide of malicious gossip which is beginning to flow around here. The most preposterous and vicious lies are being said and it would break your heart to hear them. I should rather have my tongue cut out than repeat them." An admirer from New York, who was on the board of the New York Public Library, wrote: "I am sorry the Episcopal Church is losing you, for I have regarded you as its most brilliant ornament....I still feel that what you have to* *say is as important as what the Church has to do, and I want to hear and read every-thing you say while I continue to take part in what the Church does." Amusingly, a fan from Texas wrote: "Your little namesake has grown like a weed and the fact that you have left the Church causes no regrets in regard to our having given him your name."*

A few years later, the Reverend Richard Adams (another frequenter of Canter-bury House) wrote in his book Reflections: *"Some time after my ordination to the priesthood, Alan Watts sent me the chalice and paten which had been given to him on the occasion of his own ordination to the Priesthood on Ascension Day 1944. They had been given to him in memory of his father-in-law, Edward Warren Everett [by Eleanor's mother, Ruth Sasaki]. In a letter to me, which preceded the actual gift, Alan wrote urging me to remember that the work of every priest is for the sake of* serving and celebrating the Divine life throughout the world.*"*

Alan's transition to New York in the summer of 1950 was ours as well. While at Granny Ruth's brownstone in New York City, Anne and I were summoned into the grand library on the second floor, which also housed the zendo *of the First Zen Insti-tute. The scent of incense lightly wafted through the large room. There were bookcases filled to the ceiling with many books in Chinese; ceramic Chinese horses and jade screens interspersed on the shelves; a beautiful Steinway grand piano; tall windows looking out on a small patio garden; large overstuffed couches with chintz coverings. Alan stood by the piano and explained that Anne and I were to decide with whom we wanted to live. I think both our hearts sank. As I later said, I felt as if I had to decide between the devil and the deep blue sea. There seemed to be no question about our mother. At that point, neither of us felt wanted by her. To this day, I don't remember her ever hugging or holding me. Anne felt there was nothing she could do right and that she was constantly perceived as naughty. Our father, on the other hand, for all our early years, had entertained us with stories, dandled us on his knees, encouraged us to dance freely to classical music, and took us with him on outings.*

But the problem for both of us was Dorothy. We constantly felt her ire. Anne loved Carlton, but at my rather sophisticated age of eleven, I found him, at ten years my se-nior, to be immature and couldn't imagine him as a father. Alan won custody, despite his marriage to Dorothy. Eleanor was apparently disappointed, thinking that Alan was being rewarded with our custody even though he was responsible for the demise of their marriage.

We spent the rest of the summer at Thornecrest in Millbrook, New York. It was a rambling old farmhouse built in three sections, each section smaller than the first. We had the two smaller sections, which included a large farm kitchen, and that is about all I remember of the house. The farm acreage included several outbuildings where Anne and I liked to explore. I wasn't there for long, as I was sent on my own, via Pan Am

Clipper, to England to live with my grandparents for a year and to attend Farringtons School in Chislehurst.

In the letters that follow, it is evident that this is a period where Alan had to reinvent his life. He had to adjust to being penniless (he'd given Eleanor back her inheritance of stocks from her father) and to living with Dorothy, and figure out how he was to make a living.

During the months that Alan and Dorothy (and Anne) lived in Millbrook, they became acquainted, with Joseph Campbell, his wife, Jean Erdman, John Cage, and others. Alan, with the help of Joe, was assisting Luisa Coomaraswamy (widow of Ananda Coomaraswamy) in obtaining a grant from the Bollingen Foundation to publish her late husband's works. Joe, who was working with the foundation, aided Alan in obtaining a grant. Alan also received a grant from the Matchette Foundation, which, ironically, funded his writing of The Wisdom of Insecurity *during those months in Millbrook.*

One senses in Alan's letters from this time a joie de vivre, with new friends, new projects, and a totally different lifestyle, as if a heavy cloak had been lifted from his shoulders. In his letter to his parents (January 3, 1951) and in his autobiography, he writes of developing a love of the culinary arts and describes a feast prepared for Joe, Jean, John, and Luisa. The guests all stayed and feasted at the farmhouse for several days. John Cage slept on the living room couch despite Alan's concern that the hamster running nowhere in its squeaky wheel would keep him awake — but John assured him it would be a lullaby.

In Alan's letter to Reinhold Niebuhr, I am amazed at his prophetic view of our economy as a manifestation of insatiable desire and at his references to imperialism, the limitless exploitation of natural resources, and the "electric field" of technology.

In the last letter from Millbrook to Jacquie Baxter, Alan, Dorothy, Anne, a cat named Boots and the hamster I gave them, are headed west to California and Alan's future in San Francisco at the American Academy of Asian Studies.

The letter below is probably addressed to a fan.

AUGUST 21, 1950

Dear Mrs. Walter:

I'm very glad that you wrote to me "in the heat of the moment." One gets a good, genuine reaction that way, and not something powdered over for public appearance. I remind myself of the remark attributed to a Chinese sage when one of his students left him for some months (or it may be years) and then returned: "Why this ceaseless coming and going?"

I am sorry to be so confusing. But of course there is no guarantee at all that what I say now has, for you, any more validity than what I said four years ago. If I may quote from the preface to *The Supreme Identity*: "I am not one of those who believes that it is any necessary virtue in the philosopher to spend his life defending a consistent position. It is surely a kind of spiritual pride to refrain from 'thinking out loud,' and to be unwilling to let a thesis appear in print until you are prepared to champion it to the death. Philosophy, like science, is a social function, for a man cannot think rightly alone, and the philosopher must publish his thought as much to learn from criticism as to contribute to the sum of wisdom."

But the real point is that your own confused reaction is a rather marvelous object lesson in the very problem you say you do not understand — namely, this business of clinging to oneself. We *think*, don't we, that we want to stop clinging and get rid of self in such "projected" and external forms as belief in God or in some spiritual teacher. Now God may exist, and the teacher may be right. But when we approach them in the self-clinging spirit we can't understand them properly, and the belief achieves nothing.

To the extent that you, or I, make someone or something an authority to be followed, we are really fooling ourselves. For, the authority of the teacher is something that you give him. And you give it to him because you want an authority, that is, some kind of spiritual security for the self.

All right then: if we find that "believing" has merely been an indirect form of clinging to self, we want to know how to stop clinging, and insist, as you do, that we would love to be rid of self. Why would we? I don't want to dictate the answer to this question. Look into your own mind honestly, and find out why you want to be rid of self. You could easily find out that you want to do so because you think you (i.e., your self) will be happier that way. And then you get that frustrating "haven't-we-been-here-before?" feeling, because the mind is just going round in a circle. The mind will always circle so long as it is under the illusion that it can make itself something other than what it is, so long as it imagines there is some trick whereby it can jump out of itself, or change its own nature.

But it is really easy to see the futility of all this if you are really aware of what you are doing. And when you see the real futility of this constant attempt to escape what you are, you have no alternative but to stop. When you stop, you can function properly. You can walk straight ahead, or flow along instead of whirling in small circles, instead of short-circuiting the spirit. At that point the state exists which the mystic calls "union with God" or "eternal life." For that is the state of reality. Circling (samsara) is the state of illusion.

Here I am turning you round in circles again! Well, beware of me. I really think you will. Take me with the biggest grains of salt you can find. I do not talk or write to be followed, but to get you to look into your own mind and find out for yourself what the score is. I have no message, for the rose is red and doesn't need painting.

I shall continue to write because it's my nature. *The Supreme Identity* will be out in Sept., and represents an intermediate stage between *Behold the Spirit* and what I think now. What shall I think tomorrow? I don't know. The whole fun of life is that it's full of new surprises and new things to learn, provided you are willing to keep on growing and not settle into a rut.

I wish you a good adventure.

Most sincerely, Alan Watts

This letter is to Jacqueline Baxter, former Northwestern student and a frequent guest at Canterbury House.

THORNECREST FARMHOUSE | MILLBROOK, NEW YORK |
AUGUST 21, 1950
Dear Jacquie,

That stuff about four legs and a two-headed torso will do beautifully. As a matter of fact you can throw in "four balls and a purple goatee." However, despite the cyclonic surging of winds (boy, you can sure turn a good phrase!) I have had some really fine letters from somewhat unexpected people back in the old stamping grounds. Will you please drop me a postcard giving me an address for Tassie.

We are having a swell time here, having gotten simply covered in paint and odds and ends of dirt from an amazingly filthy basement. (Wherever I go there seem to be dirty basements to get rid of. They must symbolize the repressions in people's unconsciousnesses.) Otherwise, instead of milking chickens and mooing cows, we are taking a few pleasant days of loafing in neighboring mountain- and lakelands. We do, however, pick berries. Behind us are many bushes of great, gorgeous, gross, and galluptious blackberries.

It will certainly be good to see Emmy [Emerson Harris], if he can get a chance to stop by here. We had a former seminarist, Jim Dennison, in for this weekend, and expect to have Dick Adams around September 8th. I seriously meant the invite to you and Jack, in my letter to him, but I suppose you're all much too deeply involved. Glad he returned the rabbit. I was worried he might try to send it on, but was fairly sure he had gotten the idea we would rather not have it.

Joan is enjoying herself immensely in England, and little Ann is taking to the country in truly sylvan manner. The other day we found her bathing stark-naked in a muddy pond!

We, too, have a cat — or did I mention this in Jack's letter? — Mrs. Boots, who is fairly wild and scratchy, and who bites our toes in the middle of the night.

Sorry you have no job jet, though another year in Spich Skull [Speech School] will keep you among friends.

With love from us all, as ever, Alan

This is addressed to Gertrude Moakley, who was connected with the New York Public Library.

MILLBROOK, NEW YORK | AUGUST 22, 1950
Dear Miss Moakley:
I am glad that you are trying honestly to think through the issues which my letter raised. May I say that I have no doubts in my mind as to the reality of the Incarnation, and as to the fact that something actually exists which might be called the Body of Christ.

I am, however, just as sure that there has been more than one Incarnation of God the Son, and that the Body of Christ is not coterminous with that complex of institutions called the Catholic Church. Thus I cannot feel that my separation from the Episcopal Church is a separation from that Body, or that I have left anything other than (I want to say this without offence) an artificial and unreal "Body of Christ." Under these circumstances, I don't feel much like a hermit, although living out in the country is physically quiet and uncrowded. On the contrary, I have long felt that I am somehow a member of an uninstitutionalized Body which cuts way across all confessional borders — whose very strength is that it bears no label.

To me, then, the basic principles which the Christian Form incarnates are unquestionably true. But, in practice, the actual Church does not intentionally stand for those principles. It isn't that it just fails to practice them; it doesn't even intend to do so.

Apart from any nostalgia, I could indeed see that the form of the Church expressed the deepest truth. I hoped that, somehow or other, this expression might be made more effective — supposing that the Christian language is the language natural to Western man. My experience has been that this language is not only no longer natural to the modern mind, but positively obscure and repugnant. Such repugnance might be no more than modern man's unwillingness to face facts. But if there is any such unwillingness, I find the enthusiastic churchman just as "guilty" of it as the modern pagan. Thus I have the greatest difficulty in saying what I feel must be said in what is, to most of my hearers, a baffling tongue — not only because of its obscurity, but also because they suppose it to mean things

(a) which I don't mean, and (b) which Christian doctrine, in the traditional sense, doesn't mean either!

I am sure you understand that, in writing this, I am in no way wishing to persuade you to do what I have done, and that I respect your sincerity in adhering to the Episcopal Church.

Another copy of the letter is enclosed, and I am putting Miss Hughes's name on my list. For your own, and anyone else's, information, I think it should be clear that *The Supreme Identity* represents a position halfway between *Behold the Spirit* and what I think today. The book was actually written about two years ago. But I think they all show a consistent development of thought, expanding and applying basic principles which were there from the first.

With very best wishes,

Most sincerely, Alan Watts

The following is addressed to Dr. E. Stanley Jones, a theologian and Methodist missionary in India.

MILLBROOK, NEW YORK | AUGUST 29, 1950
Dr. E. Stanley Jones | New York, New York
My dear Dr. Stanley Jones:
Thank you so much for your interesting letter of August 23rd. I don't think we need argue about the relationship between Christ and the Church, although if the latter word is used in any true sense at all it means the Body of Christ, for which reason the Church must, in the highest sense, mean the extension of Christ and Christ's action in the world.

It is, I think, clear to me why you say that Christ is a Gospel, and represents, or rather, *is* God's search for man. Yet it has become very clear to me indeed that Christ is not the only incarnation of this gospel. I don't know that he *needs* any interpretation from outside. I only know that the identical theme of "God's search for man" is the essence of the Hindu doctrine (and likewise fact) of the avatars, and the Buddhist bodhisattvas. For me they are all incarnations of the "only-begotten Son." If this is syncretism, I do not see how it can be helped, for I must acknowledge a truth where I see it.

Such an interpretation of the avatar and the bodhisattva may seem strange, when it is the common opinion in the West that Vedanta and Buddhism are religions of "self-help." But I am convinced that this interpretation is profoundly erroneous — a conviction which I was glad to find confirmed in Dr. Coomaraswamy's *Hinduism and Buddhism*, to cite but one other example of the same view. For there are many.

I agree with you that "Jesus is Life." And for that very reason I cannot set him up as an example, an authority, or anything to which one can cling for spiritual security. To me, this is an attempt to make life into death, to shut the wind of the Spirit in a box. Thus, to use your own analogy, it makes no difference whether the Church "possessing" Christ is a vessel of earth or of gold. The moment Christ is "possessed" he is lost; the moment the vessel holds him instead of pouring him out, it holds only stagnant water.

This is perhaps an unfamiliar point of view, because we think it right and natural to make an example and authority of what is highest and best, but it is less of a truism than it sounds to say that to the extent we make Christ our ideal, he becomes unreal — a future dream instead of a present actuality. To me, all idealism, all setting-apart-as-an-example, is simply postponement; it is pushing the reality which is Christ to the elsewhere and the tomorrow. If he *is* risen; if he *is* the Truth and the Life, he must be immediately here and now. To set him up in any special way is then to "gild the lily" and so destroy it.

In other words: if Christ is really God's search for man, God, to have effectively "come down to earth," must be discoverable here in this very place and moment, but the emulation of the "Jesus of history" obscures that truth. It concerns itself so much with what happened 2,000 years ago that it misses the point, confusing the pointing finger with the truth. "Why seek ye the living among the dead? He is not here, but is risen." The disciples sought him at the tomb; we seek him in the tradition of the Church or the record of the Bible — or in the future, which is merely the past projected ahead. They are all tombs, and "he is not here."

I wonder if the latter part of my printed letter makes it clear why idealism is simply postponement, and following an example of self-deception. We are so conditioned into thinking the other way that this involves something of a Copernican revolution of thought. Were it clear, I don't think there could be any question of following either the Christ or the Buddha or Krishna or Lao-tzu or all four together. The problem would disappear as a case of asking the wrong question.

With very best wishes,

Most sincerely yours, Alan Watts

The following letter was probably written to Sister Rachel, head of Margaret Hall, the Anglican convent school Joan attended in Versailles, Kentucky.

MILLBROOK, NEW YORK | SEPTEMBER 7, 1950

My dear Sister:

Before reading this letter, will you be so kind as to go carefully over the enclosed "communication." It will caution you doubly not to take me as an authority, but

Children's party at Chislehurst, Kent, England, in 1918.
Alan is the third child from the left.

Times of London clipping showing Alan (*right*) carrying the train of the new Archbishop of Canterbury (Dr. Cosmo Gordon Lang) at his enthronement, December 5, 1928.

Alan's drawing of a chess game, 1929.

Alan (*center front*) with classmates at King's School, Canterbury, circa 1932.

Alan, circa 1936.

Alan reading at Rowan Tree Cottage, Chislehurst, Kent, England, circa 1937.

Left to right: Ruth Everett, Warren Everett, and Eleanor Everett (age 15) in Kyoto, Japan, 1933.

Alan's parents, Emily Mary (Buchan) Watts and Laurence Wilson Watts, Rowan Tree Cottage, Chislehurst, Kent, England, circa 1937.

Alan, circa 1938.

Alan and Eleanor (Everett) Watts, on their wedding day, April 2, 1938.

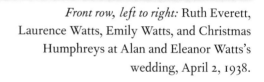

Front row, left to right: Ruth Everett, Laurence Watts, Emily Watts, and Christmas Humphreys at Alan and Eleanor Watts's wedding, April 2, 1938.

Alan, circa 1938.

Left to right: Shigetsu (Sokei-an) Sasaki, Ruth Everett, Eleanor Watts, and Alan at a Halloween party, circa 1940.

Eleanor Watts and Alan, April 1946.

Left to right: Alan, Eleanor, Anne, Laurence, Joan, and Emily Watts, with Jimey the dog, Christmas 1946, Canterbury House, Evanston, Illinois.

Eleanor (Everett Watts) Gamer, circa 1949.

Joan Watts in a dress
made by Emily Watts for a
children's party, Lord Mayor of
London's Mansion House,
January 13, 1951.

Left to right: Michael Gamer, Carlton Gamer, and Eleanor
Gamer, New York City, circa 1952.

Tia

Mark

Ricky

Lila

Diane

Tia Watts (age 10),
Mark Watts (age 7),
Ricky Watts (age 5),
Lila Watts (age 8),
and Diane Watts (age 6),
school photos, Mill Valley,
California.

Dorothy DeWitt, circa 1945.

Anne Watts, Trafalgar Square, London, 1956.

Alan's mother,
Emily Watts, 1953.

Dear Mummy & Daddy: I have been having a very busy time, all of it very interesting, though little opportunity for travelling about. Travel is pretty expensive here. I have had a most fascinating conversation with Jung and spent yesterday evening with Count von Dürkheim, who is the main German authority on Zen. A most charming man. Will be back Wednesday morning, & am

† VERLAG BERINGER & PAMPALUCHI, ZÜRICH 27

Z 6859 Zürich und die Alpen

flying in company with a most delightful old lady — the Hon. Mrs. Frost — from Devonshire. Dorothy & the children are all well, & have acquired 15 frogs for our stream! Mark sent me a wonderful drawing of the sun and planets, with their moons. Was in Basel Saturday night having dinner with the Prof. of Psychiatry at the University. What a beautiful old city! Lots of love, Alan.

Postcard from Alan to his
parents from Zurich,
Switzerland, 1958.

Dec 15th – p.m.

My darling Jano:

Your utterly lovely note of the 12th just came — with enclosures. I have returned the form to the New School, though this is strictly a case where they should pay a flat fee & not withhold tax. Am not their employee. I clinched the deal on the studio today, and D. is in a much better mood about things. Also I sent off the Realist interview with a few corrections and amplifications. . . . Had a recurrence of some LSD insights in the half-waking state early this morning — something I can't quite pin down at the moment about the micro-microscopic view of things. There is some puzzle in this whole business of magnification. . . . Jano, dearest one, it is simply glorious to get such a whopping expression of love from you. It glows all the way through me, like psychic wine. And, dear lady, it's as mutual as can be. I adore you, Jano, always and always.

Your Alan x x x
                    x

Do you think I should reply formally to Tom Phelps' letter?

Letter from Alan to Mary Jane ("Jano") Yates (King) Watts, December 15, 1959.

Jano Watts, circa 1963 (photo by Richard Borst).

Anne Watts and Chungliang Al Huang, aboard the ferryboat *Vallejo*, circa 1963.

The *Vallejo* in Sausalito, California, circa 1965 (photo by Joan Watts).

Alan in the galley of the *Vallejo*, circa 1965, with Joan Watts's son and Alan's
grandson David Sudlow (age 7; *far right*) (photo by Joan Watts).

Alan's fiftieth birthday party on the
Vallejo, January 6, 1965. *Left to right:*
Jean (Janko) Varda, Gert Davenport,
Anne Watts, Alan, Joan Watts, and Elsa
Gidlow (photo by John Sudlow).

Alan's father, Laurence Watts, circa
1965 (photo by Richard Borst).

Alan with sleeping Jano Watts, Kyoto, Japan, circa 1965.

Elsa Gidlow and Alan perform the Japanese tea ceremony on the *Vallejo*, circa 1970.

Jean (Janko) Varda, circa 1970.

Alan, Gary Snyder, and Snyder's son Kai at Snyder's home,
Kitkitdizze, in the Sierra Nevada foothills, June 1971.

Arthur C. Clarke and Alan, circa 1971.

Alan and a bevy of admirers. *Left to right:* Virginia Denison, Helen Janiger, Ruth Denison, and Alan, 1971 (photo by Jano Watts).

Alan at Esalen Institute, Big Sur, California, circa 1972 (photo by Joan Watts).

Exterior of Alan's library at Druid Heights,
Mill Valley, California, circa 1973.

Interior of Alan's library, built by Roger Somers from a redwood
water tank, at Druid Heights, Mill Valley, California, circa 1973.

Myra Andrews with her mother, Anne Watts, and Alan, April 1973.

Alan delivering an address at his granddaughter Elizabeth Sudlow's eighth-grade graduation in Bolinas, California, June 1973.

to take what I say on its own merits, and see for yourself whether it is true. For so long as you, or anyone else, simply take a thing on authority, you will not really be able to understand it. After all, even the initial acceptance of authority is an act of "private judgment."

What you say about Canon Fison's book sounds extraordinarily interesting, and I shall obtain a copy of it for study. There is, indeed, a real sense in which the Bible, the Ministry, and the Mass can be, and are, used as idols. Not only these, but Christ's own human nature can be made an idol, as well as the *ideas* of God, eternal life, etc., since they are all, as ideas, images of thought.

While I am personally of the opinion that the Church is irremediably committed to using all these things as idols, I do not believe that it is at all necessary to do so. I see no reason why God should not incarnate himself in Jesus, in the Mass, and in all the sacraments, and there is no doubt in my mind that he does so. But *for this very reason* it is quite fatal to confuse the forms with the One incarnate in them. This indeed is the heresy of confusing the two natures in Christ. The nature of Spirit is such that we "have" it to the precise extent that we do not cling to it. Thus to use its forms *to* cling to it is the most radical contradiction of their meaning. To me, this is the very reason why the Mass employs the perishable and to-be-consumed elements of bread and wine, and, indeed, the whole meaning of Eucharist is the attainment of life by giving life away — *not* by grasping it.

The eating and drinking of Christ's true Body and Blood in the Mass may, and I think without irreverence, be clarified by the popular proverb, "You can't have your cake and eat it." Holy Communion is through eating, not having. What we eat enters into the stream of life, but what we merely have remains isolated and ineffective. Thus the Mass and its elements are a sort of stream, and you cannot grasp water in your mental fingers. The flesh of Christ could not be grasped by the tomb (i.e., the past) and his Blood *flows*. You know the Hebraic symbolism: the blood is the life principle, the *nephesh*. All grasping (idolatry) is really a holding on to the past, an attempt to keep Christ in the tomb.

I repeat again: I find no contradiction of these principles in the external forms of the Church as such. The contradiction is entirely in the intents and the attitudes of churchmen. I should add that by *forms* of the Church I mean those which are strictly traditional — the mass, the office, the sacraments, etc. I do *not* include the hymns and books of devotion. They cling to the point of cloying. Do not forget that one says the office on the precise understanding that the psalms (symbolically interpreted) are the words, the songs, of the Holy Spirit being uttered through you.

Reservation and Benediction are, perhaps, slightly suspect, and the latter a relatively modern innovation. But again, they are of no harm and of much good so long as one does not think of Christ as the "Prisoner of the Tabernacle," but sees the Host as an agency through which he flows into the world — flows, not to be clutched and hugged, but to energize us into a like flowing, a like letting go of our own lives. For "whosoever would save his soul shall lose it."

Yours most sincerely, Alan Watts

THORNECREST FARMHOUSE | MILLBROOK, NEW YORK
SEPTEMBER 12, 1950
Dear Jacquie [Baxter]:
Thank you for your wonderful letter. Quite obviously, you now *understand* what I and others have been talking about these many years. You don't sound crazy. You have simply seen the thing directly for yourself, and your "incoherent" attempt to describe it is what always happens in these circumstances. Indeed, the very words and phrases are splendid "old stuff," yet ever new, straight from the original stream. I am always very happy when this happens to anyone.

Sometimes the immediate "glow" which such an understanding brings to the emotions passes away. This is usual enough, for the emotions cannot always be bright — any more than the weather. As and when this happens, you will also understand the futility of trying to wish yourself back into a past state of joy, for emotion cannot be caught and held without getting mummified. There is really nothing to do but, without expectation, to be what you are, what you think/feel, at each moment, for, as you say, in this acceptance you have everything. Then you see that each moment is alpha and omega, so self-sufficient that nothing else is needed. From this insight come all the theological definitions of God as the eternal *is*, the infinite, the complete.

You know how weak language is in expressing what you see. You know, too, that the very words can be twisted around to mean something quite opposite. Hence the problem of explaining it to anyone, such as Mrs. Colton. For this reason, we don't try to explain it directly, by way of positive description. It can't really be done, and, anyhow, it doesn't help because a God or a spiritual experience positively conceived is something that people try to cling to, imitate, and expect.

The best approach is therefore negative — removing obstructions to insight rather than trying to fabricate it. If you tell a person to accept this moment without expectation, she will do it *in order* to get away from it! And this is merely *not* doing it. Thus the thing is to try to make her see that escape from "what is" at this moment is quite futile. The attempt to get away from fear or depression simply *is* fear, and so can only engender fear. The same is true of selfishness or anything else. Suicide is not an escape from depression. It is depression, and the notion that death will bring release is due to an entirely unwarranted projecting of the experience of sleep into death. We don't know anything about death, and all our attempts to imagine what it may or may not bring are totally meaningless.

So the "technique" of revealing this understanding to another person is to question their desire to change, to get away from "what is" — so showing them that the very desire is part of "what is," and that they cannot escape it. Under these circumstances, acceptance is not a matter of choice. It is the only thing to be done. Indeed, there is really no question of "I" (on the one hand) accepting "my experience" (on the other). The apparent opposition of "I" and "experience" is a mental trick. In reality the two are one. Questioning can reveal this, too. What is *you?* Describe, discover, this "I" which seems to be separate from the stream of life and experience. It can't be done, because at any given moment, there is no "I." There is just the experience, or the experiencing. Part of this experience are certain memories. By a trick, these are abstracted from the present experience to which they belong, and woven into a supposed static "I" who was, is, and will be. If a person can see that the "I" is an illusion of memory, the original integrity of the mind will be rediscovered, i.e., that the mind *is* what it knows, and there is no split, no schizophrenia, of "I" and "me," "self" and "experience."

At this point, all that remains, all that really can be done, is to accept or be completely aware of "what is" — and this, which is for many so hard to believe, is a healing process, since most of our inner conflicts are created by the split.

It's hard to explain all this in a letter, for what you are asking for is the mastery of an art, which, like any other, takes time and practice. I can only say that you must go on what you know for yourself, and get it into her understanding, not by statement, but by questions which show the fallacy and futility of anything else. Keep me informed, if you like, of how things go.

Will you give my love to Pris and ask her to write sometime. Thank Johnny [Gouldin] for his remarks on the envelope of your letter, and give him our very best. Perhaps I shall be out in the Midwest around Oct. 5th, and, if so, may attempt to get into Evanston. I will keep you posted of developments.

Love from us all to y'all, as always, Alan

THORNECREST FARMHOUSE | MILLBROOK, NEW YORK | OCTOBER 23, 1950
Dear Mummy & Daddy:
I have been writing to Joan as regularly as possible, but I'm afraid you have been rather overlooked. There has been so much to do, and I am behind-hand two weeks with my letters, as I had to take a trip to Indiana and Chicago, for lectures,

and to Washington to see some of Dorothy's family. I drove all the way to Chicago, and stayed there at Ruth Goodkind's house. Spent a delightful three days lecturing at a Quaker college in Indiana. It is just the sort of place I should like Joan to go to when she is old enough.

Although this is in many ways a peaceful life, there is plenty of hard work both with the house and with writing. However, Jack Gouldin is spending a week with us, and yesterday and the day before we took some time off for "rural rambles." The autumn here this year is the most beautiful autumn I have ever seen anywhere. The colours of the leaves are indescribable, and with the blue hazy atmosphere, the smell of burning leaves, and the distant hills a dull blue against the vivid sky it is truly a paradise. Yesterday afternoon we began our compost heap, Jack being on hand to assist. Incidentally, he is the most energetic person, with a way of getting things done like buttered lightning. Not content with a day in the open air, with much walking and raking, he rearranged the entire attic after dinner (involving much furniture shifting) and made "spic-and-span" order out of the whole thing.

Last Friday we spent a most interesting evening in NY with my friend Joe Campbell, at his fascinating apartment. There was quite a gathering for dinner, including the wife of the great German Orientalist Heinrich Zimmer, a charming composer, Jack [John] Cage, and a couple connected with the Bollingen Foundation. Joe has been editing Zimmer's manuscripts and notes for the foundation, including a marvelous work on Indian philosophy which I have been "inspecting for small errors."

Joan's letters seem quite happy, and I only hope that she doesn't find the atmosphere of Farringtons *too* restricting, though I am sure it won't hurt her! I find it just a little strange that she takes such a violent reaction to Carl. Something of this kind is perhaps understandable under the circumstances, though in actual fact he is not the buffoon which she sees. Due to a certain youthful exuberance, he does "act silly" at times, but this is quite on the surface. Underneath he is a quiet and deep and even conscientious person, though certainly unconventional. I do think that in the interest of objectivity she might learn to see things a bit more clearly, and if you can help her in any way to see life a little less in terms of mere black and white, it would be good for her.

I *am* going to try to get you and Joan something better in the way of a picture of myself. Admittedly the old one was pretty poor, but it was something I had to get done in a hurry. Also, when I can get around to having it printed, I have an excellent coloured one of Dorothy. I did receive the negatives of the one you had taken of yourselves with Joan. My "photographic trouble" at the moment is that I haven't been able to find a good developing place out here. I tried one, but they ruined a whole film. In some respects this part of the world, only 80 miles from New York, is strangely primitive.

I am just getting over a bad cold I caught while on the road. It poured with rain all the way back from Chicago, and as I had to make the trip in two days it was a tiring and difficult drive. Then I had just a day's rest here before leaving for Washington, which involved the better part of a day's drive each way. However, the general effect of living here on my health seems to be wonderful. Everyone out in Chicago thought I looked ten years younger!

Ann is really coming along very well, and although she certainly has a "will of her own," she is certainly not the problem child that Eleanor made out that she was, during their year together in NY. I am afraid Joan may have received the impression from her mother that Ann is "a bit queer." It really isn't so: I know of so many children who are ten times the trouble that she [is]. But somehow or other, Eleanor got hold of some perfectly fantastic ideas, including the notion that she was on the way to becoming a nymphomaniac at the tender age of seven! The child merely likes affection.

Well, I must to work. I am so very glad that Joan is with you and under your eye. It does, at the moment, make things so much easier for us, and I am certain that even were things not difficult it would in any case be an irreplaceable experience for Joan.

With lots of love, Alan

MILLBROOK, NEW YORK | NOVEMBER 28, 1950
Dr. Reinhold Niebuhr | Union Theological Seminary | New York, New York
Dear Dr. Niebuhr,
When I learned that you might be reviewing my book *The Supreme Identity*, I was very much looking forward to the kind of penetrating criticism of positions with which you do not agree, such as I find in your books. Having published this work somewhat tentatively, I am rather anxious to know just what are its faults from the standpoint of theological positions such as you own.

Now that I have seen your review of my book in *The Nation*, I am at a loss what to think. I thank you for your comments on the book's intellectual caliber. But what you have criticized is a viewpoint as remote from that of the book itself as one could imagine. Indeed you have criticized it for holding ideas which it most plainly opposed.

The comparative quotations which I enclose are but a small part of what might be produced to show the total difference between what I said and what you have alleged that I said.

I cannot conceive that you "rushed into print" without reading the book, nor that my meaning can have been all that obscure — especially to one trained in philosophical and theological discourse.

What you have criticized is that odd travesty of Oriental metaphysic which is an idée fixe in the minds of some theologians — a version of the Oriental doctrines which it was an express purpose of the book to correct. I can understand your taking issue with these corrections, but you have passed them by unnoticed, and represented me as holding to the original travesty!

I am still eager to know what your criticism of the actual book would be, and I wish you would ask Marguerite Block if you might review it again for *The Review of Religions* (or some such periodical) after, if I may tactfully suggest it, another reading.

Sincerely yours, Alan Watts

The following is addressed to an authority on Asian performing arts.

MILLBROOK, NEW YORK | DECEMBER 22, 1950
Mr. Jacob Feuerring | The Asia Institute
Dear Mr. Feuerring:
I am very sorry that you should have been embarrassed by gossip about me, but, as everyone knows, there is always gossip about any minister who leaves the Church; it is the "old standby" in tactics for discrediting his motives. But I certainly would not want this to reflect unhappily either upon yourself or upon the Asia Institute. Hence this letter.

Enclosed is my public letter of resignation from the Church, the contents of which were previously communicated to my former superior, the Bishop of Chicago, who accepted it regretfully, although a year must elapse before he can accept it officially. Oddly enough, such "pressure" as came from the Church authorities was not to resign, but to remain in my position! The romantic tale about the "immorality" for which I am supposed to have been "unfrocked" is presumably the fact that, *after* I had left the ministry, I made a second marriage — many people not even then realizing that my former wife had left me some time before. Church law would not have permitted this, despite the fact that it was very necessary for the proper care of my two girls. All of this is so much a matter of public knowledge, that it is truly marvelous to find more exciting versions of the story still in circulation!

As to the other matter, I suppose that my somewhat "cheerful" style of lecturing might give a stranger the impression that I was intoxicated — as I hope I am, with the Tao! But those who hear me regularly know that I always speak in much the same way, and that it requires no help from the lesser kind of "spirit." Perhaps I was more "cheerful" than usual that evening, being somewhat struck · by the humor of my talking about Zen with Dr. Suzuki in the audience.

As to the smell of liquor on my breath — this is the natural consequence of having stopped by a friend's apartment on the way, where we indulged in the immense orgy of one cocktail. I must apologize for forgetting that even in New York City today there are those who do not like the aroma of a three-ounce glass on the breath. I should have eaten a peppermint, but some people like that even less, for I always think of Koko's "People who eat peppermint and puff it in your face, They surely won't be missed, They'll none of them be missed!"

Most sincerely yours, Alan Watts

THORNECREST FARMHOUSE | MILLBROOK, NEW YORK | JANUARY 3, 1951
Dear Mummy & Daddy:
At last, after the pleasant furor of the holidays there is time to write you! We were simply delighted to get your letters about Christmas with Joan, and we do both want to say a big thank-you for that lovely piece of Chinese embroidery — a piece I remember so well as one of my special favourites in your collection. Joan's bunny rabbit and horse were splendid, though I must say the rabbit looked mostly like her granny's work. I do hope you got our Christmas letter with the money for Joan's present. We are still behind-hand with some other things for her, but when I tell you what we were doing over the holidays you will understand why Dorothy has been as busy as ten bees.

We spent Christmas with Dorothy's brother in New Jersey, and had a big family gathering as her mother was there with us also. We had a lovely time as well as a lively one as there were four children running around in great excitement. Dorothy gave me a huge and amazing cookery book as a present, the like of which I have never seen, for it is a work of art both in its contents and its printing. To make it a somewhat culinary Christmas, I gave her an electric coffeepot and Ann gave her a cake icing outfit. For Ann, Dorothy had made a lovely ballet dress.

When we got home we set about preparing for a New Year's house party for four guests. These were Joe and Jean Campbell — he being the person who has helped me so much in getting to work with the Bollingen Foundation. His wife is a ballet (modern) dancer and teacher, and they are both delightful friends. I think Joe is one of the most inwardly happy, generous, and "integrated" people I have ever known. Then there was John Cage — a composer of extremely "advanced" music — who is a quiet, humorous person with infinite zest for life; I believe it would be impossible for him to be bored, for he has a way of being able to detect the beauty in the most ordinary and unlikely sights and sounds.

The fourth member of the party was Luisa Coomaraswamy, the Spanish wife of the late Ananda C., who, as you know, was one of the greatest scholars of Oriental art and philosophy. She is a very vivacious person, and a model house-guest who never tires of being helpful. They were all here from Sunday afternoon to Monday evening.

I have always longed to have the sort of meat pie one used to get in England — the cold kind, made of veal, ham, or pork. You don't often find them here, but my new book provided the recipe for a French version of the same thing, which I set about cooking for this party. Dottie made the pastry. You make it with a veal forcemeat, surrounding fillets of veal and ham which have been marinated in red wine with onions and various spices, and decorated with truffles.

You line the pastry shell with small French pancakes. It came out perfectly, and I am shamelessly proud of it! I also made chestnut stuffing for the turkey, and Dorothy prepared a trifle which was, as we say, "out of this world." Our huge kitchen here is a great temptation to taking cooking seriously. On top of all this, we made French onion soup, fruitcake with almond paste and icing, and a multitude of canapés for a midnight feast. There are enough leftovers to feed us for a week, which they will do very nicely.

You see, the kitchen has become quite a hobby for me. Most days, I get through work around four-thirty, and come down to chatter with Dottie in the kitchen. Usually I make the main course and she the dessert (sweet or pudding to you!). The most fun is seeing what you can do with nothing, with leftovers and butchers' odds and ends.

With all this the party had itself a great time, the only blemish being that Ann had to stay in bed with a wretched cough and cold. Mrs. Coomaraswamy brought a marvelous album of records with her, consisting mostly of the music for Japanese Nō drama.

This will be a busy month. There is a book still to finish, courses to prepare for San Francisco, income tax to calculate, three lectures to give, many people to be seen, and the usual mountain of correspondence. We hope to leave as early as possible in February, and to spend some time in Chicago, Dallas, and Los Angeles on the way. It will be quite a procession, what with Ann, Mrs. Boots the cat, and Furball the hamster in tow.

It is getting late, and before going to bed I must drop a line to Jack Gouldin in Evanston who has just had an operation for hernia, and is in hospital.

I am so glad you received our gift safely. Dottie joins me in sending very much love to you both. Do let us know about the Mansion House Ball [a fund-raising event for the Hospital Sunday Fund that Joan attended].

With love as always, Alan

MILLBROOK, NEW YORK | JANUARY 3, 1951
Dear Dr. Niebuhr,

Thank you very much for your kind letter of December 6th.

It seems to me that the difficulties between the Christian and mystical-metaphysical views of the nature of selfhood cannot be clarified so long as it is thought that the latter involves a denial of particularity. I insisted again and again in my book that this denial is not involved — except in the sense that "if any man would be my disciple, let him deny himself." The Christian and the mystic — as I understand the latter — both agree that this denial is the necessary prelude to the flowering of personality in all its uniqueness.

After many years' study of the Oriental traditions, I am absolutely convinced that, only with certain exceptions, do they envisage any obliteration of particularity. Mahayana Buddhism in particular, in the bodhisattva doctrine, culminates in a tremendous affirmation of the finite and the particular — so much so that no informed person can go on saying that Oriental mysticism omits the "nevertheless I live."

I don't think that we can begin to discuss this problem unless that much is clear. The reduction of all differentiated forms to the one or to the void is not the final word of either Buddhism, Taoism, or even the Vedanta. But what lies beyond this point cannot really be expressed in words. Negative language is used to negate, not the real world, but the adequacy of all verbal symbols for the understanding of reality. When it is said that the ultimate reality is non-finite, nonbeing, nonformal, the "non," the negation, applies to the words *finite*, *being*, *form*, etc., and not to the realities to which these words are attached. This is simple semantics. The word *tree* is a noise; the objective tree is not this noise, nor is it some static "idea" of tree in the human mind. In other words, the metaphysical traditions are saying that reality, whether divine or finite, is not comprehended in any static system of words or concepts; the negations apply to all these systems, not to the real things which they attempt to symbolize and comprehend.

This point of view seems to me to coincide exactly with the Hebraic second commandment — no graven image, whether of wood or of thought, can be anything but a misleading symbol of God. We must know God as we know the tree, not by defining it verbally or conceptually (save for conventional purposes not to be taken seriously), but by immediate perception. Thus the "mystery" of life is not seen as a problem to be solved but a reality to be experienced. The real dynamic world can never be made to correspond to any static system of symbols, measures, ideas, etc. These are useful conventions like imaginary lines of latitude and longitude.

As to the harmony of man and nature consisting in a "low-grade" agrarian economy, I think you are begging the question by calling it low-grade. I think there are finite limits within which man must live, and that our "high-grade" economy is something like the dinosaur — too big to be manageable. Do you know Wiener's book *Cybernetics?* He points out the danger that both the civilized brain and the civilized society have become like an overloaded telephone exchange, or a skyscraper too high for efficiency — because the higher you build it, the more floor space must be devoted to elevators.

In being redeemed from the agrarian economy, Oriental society (witness Japan and Communist China) is becoming an immense danger — because our economy, which they are adopting, is a manifestation of insatiable desire. It must expand or collapse, which means Imperialism and limitless exploitation of natural resources. This, rather than any metaphysical mysticism, seems to me to be the spirit which would abolish finite particularity. For to technology the world ceases to be solid, real, and substantial; it becomes a vast electric field in which anything is possible, and in which the splendid boundaries of time and space (i.e., the shapes of things) are obliterated.

With best wishes for the New Year,
Sincerely yours, Alan Watts

MILLBROOK, NEW YORK | FEBRUARY 1, 1951
Dear Jacquie:
We hope to be seeing you all the weekend of the 9th, but the roads are gosh-awful, and unless they clear off somewhat we shall have to go south. We shall leave here the 6th, and stay overnight with Dottie's family in New Jersey. On the 7th we shall have to decide which way to take, and when we make up our minds I shall let Ruth Goodkind know. So you can discover what is going to happen by calling her on Thursday or Friday.

I do very much want to make it, particularly in order to see Jack. How is he? If 'n when, under the circumstances, are you going to get married?

Things here have been a 3-ring circus. I have been rushing to finish a book before leaving, and it's all done but for the final corrections. Sunday night we went to Jean Erdman's (Campbell) dance recital, and the Sunday before to Merce Cunningham's. Both were vastly interesting, but I still think that Shearer is the genius.

If we don't succeed in reaching Chicago, our address on the coast will be [in] Palo Alto, CA, (after March 15) where we have rented a furnished house, complete with garden, fruit trees, etc. Until then, make it c/o American Institute of Asian Studies, [in] San Francisco, Cal.

Hoping to see you,

Love to Jack, love to you, love from ev'body,

Alan

THE DALLAS ATHLETIC CLUB | DALLAS, TEXAS | FEBRUARY 13, 1951

Dear Jack and Jacquie:

It was a hell of a thing to have to miss seeing you, but the roads were such as to require skates and reindeer instead of wheels and combustion. We skidded all the way from New Jersey to Harrisburg, dodging whole trains of trucks stuck on the hills. That was enough! In Harrisburg the AAA told us that the Turnpike was even worse, so we headed pronto for the sunny South. After Tennessee it was really sunny! It's sort of uncanny to step from 10 degrees below into this balmy spring weather.

We shall be here in Dallas until Sat. AM, and then we head out for El Paso and Los Angeles. Shall be lecturing for a week or so in cloud-cuckoo-land — i.e., S. California — and then we shall think about heading for SF. Our address will be [in] Palo Alto, Cal.

We have, you see, succeeded in finding a house.

I wonder how the weekend weather *did* turn out in Chicago. Snow and ice were promised, but I felt sure that if we decided not to come it would be perfectly beautiful! However, we shall have to make the return trip sometime this summer, and may be right back again if we decide to remain in Cal. Though God knows how another move will be managed! Yet the work in SF looks good, and as soon as I can get some extra copies I will send you some literature about the outfit. The quarter ends May 31st but we shall probably stay on until the middle of June.

Well this must be a short one as it's almost time for breakfast. Give my best to Bob Platman and say I will drop him a line as soon as possible.

With much love from us both, as ever, Alan

PART VI

California and the American Academy of Asian Studies

1951-57

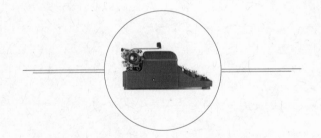

JW: *Alan, Dorothy, Anne, Boots, and hamster arrived in southern California in March 1951. They made their way up the coast, stopping in La Jolla, Los Angeles, Big Sur, and Carmel on their way to San Francisco, meeting and making contact with a number of interesting people — those whom Alan had wished to meet and those who wished to meet him. One gets the sense in his letters that the move was all he expected and more. They rented a small house in Palo Alto, near enough to San Francisco and the fledgling American Academy of Asian Studies.*

By the summer of 1951, they had relocated to a small but charming log cabin among giant redwood trees near Woodside. This was just in time for the birth of Dorothy's first child (the first of five), Marcia (Tia), born in August. I returned later that month from spending a year in England and came via New York, where I briefly visited my mother. Anne and I loved the redwoods and spent much time exploring the neighborhood and playing with the four-year-old twin boys from next door. Their family had horses and allowed me to ride whenever I wanted.

Things were not easy for Dorothy. Alan spent long hours at the academy, and the drive into San Francisco was tedious. Anne and I attended Portola School, seven miles from the cabin down a tortuous hairpin-turn road, which, when foggy, was enough to make one carsick. In January 1952, I was quite unexpectedly sent off to boarding school again. This time I went to Happy Valley School in Ojai, founded by Theoso-phist Annie Besant, Krishnamurti, Huxley, and others. (Today it is called the Besant Hill School.) Alan had become acquainted with the school's headmistress, Rosalind Rajagopal, through Huxley and Krishnamurti. The students, like me, were mostly the children of writers, artists, movie people, and generally offspring of the avant-garde. Happy Valley was then what today would be referred to as "new age." Alan, Huxley, Krishnamurti, Gerald Heard, and Guido Ferrando, among others, were frequent speakers during the years I attended. The artist Beatrice Woods was also involved with the school.

During the summer of 1952, Alan's parents came to visit from England. Because the cabin was quite small — only two bedrooms — a tent was pitched in the backyard for Anne and me. All of this activity put more stress on Dorothy, who just prior to their arrival had suffered a miscarriage. Our grandparents became particularly concerned about Anne's welfare.

Alan was beginning to spend more and more time away from home. Between his duties at the academy and his lecturing schedule through California and Oregon, he was also becoming popular as a lecturer on the radio with programs on KPFA and a growing number of similar stations around the country. Gradually over a period of six years, the school went from the directorship of Frederic Spiegelberg (who eventually left and returned to Stanford University) to having Alan at the helm. Alan was able to keep the school going through innovative programming, but overall funding was hard to come by. Part of the conundrum was that the board and the faculty could not agree about the status of the school — whether it was a specialty school, a graduate school, or an accredited program for university students attending other schools.

The faculty had included such notable scholars as Haridas Chaudhuri, from the Krishnagar Government College in Bengal; Sir C. P. Ramaswamy Aiyar, chancellor of the Benaras Hindu University; Judith Tyberg, teaching Sanskrit and yoga studies; Tokwan Tada, a Japanese lama trained in Tibet; Rom Landau, a Polish expatriate who taught Islamic studies (Alan had met him in London); Princess Poon Pismai Diskul, curator of the National Library of Thailand; and Sabro Hasegawa, a Japanese artist known for sumi-e (black ink painting) and the study of Japanese culture.

The academy also had guest lecturers including S. I. Hayakawa, D. T. Suzuki and our grandmother, Ruth Sasaki, who, Alan said, "entranced the whole student body with her formal and definitive lecture on the use of the koan in Zen meditation."

In 1954, the school was absorbed by the College of the Pacific. Even though classes were well attended, Alan left the academy by 1957 over disagreements with the college's board. After several transformations over the years with Chaudhuri at the helm, the academy became the California Institute of Integral Studies.

Alan wrote in his autobiography, "In retrospect one can see that the Academy of Asian Studies was a transitional institution emerging from the failure of universities and churches to satisfy important spiritual needs. It was a bridge between the idea of a graduate school and the idea of a 'growth center,' such as Esalen Institute...but in those days we were still troubled with the elaborate nonsense of accreditation, degrees and academic status."

Interestingly, among the participants at the academy were Michael Murphy and Richard Price, who eventually founded Esalen Institute in Big Sur. Others noteworthy at the academy were Crist Lovdjieff, whom Eldridge Cleaver later dubbed the "Saint of San Quentin"; Ananda Claude Dalenberg, once part of the Canterbury

House group in Evanston, who ventured west to study with Alan and who was eventually ordained a priest at the San Francisco Zen Center; and Gary Snyder, a beat poet and Chinese and Japanese scholar (fictionalized as Japhy Ryder in Jack Kerouac's The Dharma Bums). *Of Gary, Alan wrote, "When I am dead I would like to be able to say that he is carrying on everything I hold most dearly, though with a different style…my only regret is that I cannot formally claim him as my spiritual successor… he is just exactly what I have been trying to say."*

During this time, Alan established an office in San Francisco for "personal counseling," which added to his time away from home. But the academy afforded him a never-ending list of interesting people, and he developed friendships with some who lived on the north side of the Golden Gate Bridge, in Marin County: a charming poet, Elsa Gidlow, whose partner, Isabel Grenfell, turned out to have been a student of Alan's mother in England; surrealist painter Gordon Onslow-Ford and his lovely, delicate wife Jacqueline; poet James Broughton; and builder Roger Somers. In early 1953, through friends Alan found a house in Mill Valley (in Marin County). This meant a much shorter commute, but nothing was easy. Dorothy and Alan's first son, Mark, was born in July 1953.

Alan lamented that his work kept him from home fourteen hours a day and felt that he was a terrible father who couldn't spend enough time with his children. I never thought of him as terrible, I quite adored him, but absent he was. He would often fail to show up or make arrangements for me to stay with someone on home weekends from my school in Ojai. And he never defended Anne against Dorothy's unrelenting strictness or ire. One Easter vacation I became so upset with Dorothy's bullying of Anne that I yelled at her to stop. She barely spoke to me again and obviously started to fear me. I, on the other hand, away at school, feared for Anne's well-being. Fortunately, Alan's parents, Granny Ruth, and our mother came to Anne's rescue, and she was sent to England to live and attended school at Farringtons in Chislehurst. She spent five years there. Anne says, "I knew at the time that they had saved my life."

We often spent vacation time in Big Sur, visiting with ethnologist Maud Oakes, Louisa Jenkins, Henry Miller (for whose children I occasionally babysat), architect Nat Owings and his wife, and Margaret Lial, who had a wonderful music store in Carmel. We frequently dined on the very edge of the Big Sur coast at the Fassetts' Nepenthe restaurant — a favorite haunt in later years for the Hollywood set.

By 1955, Alan had developed quite a following. His lecturing was beginning to extend beyond the West Coast and his books continued to do well. He also maintained a lively discourse with theologians regarding his books, The Supreme Identity (Pantheon, 1949) and Myth and Ritual in Christianity (Vanguard, 1953), *both having been published abroad as well as in the United States.*

PALO ALTO, CALIFORNIA | MARCH 8, 1951
Dear Henry Miller:

We were so sorry to miss you the other day when we stopped by at Partington Ridge, but were delighted to meet your wife [Janina Lepska] who entertained us nobly in your absence.

As you are but 2 hours or so from here by road, we should love to run down and see you one of these days, perhaps a Saturday, or a weekday if it can be managed before the school ("academy") opens here on the 20th. Do let us know what might be a good day — the 13th, 16th, and 19th are "out" for us. I have been looking forward to a talk with you for a long time.

I was much interested to meet Hugh Chisholm and hope he will still be there when we come as we had to rush off after a very brief chat.

Your wife was kind enough to let me have a copy of Suares's *Mythe Judeo-Chretien*, and though I have only had time for a brief look at it, it seems to be saying what I have felt about this problem for quite some time, and I am very glad to have it.

With all good wishes,
Very sincerely, Alan Watts

PALO ALTO, CALIFORNIA | MARCH 22, 1951
Dear Jacquie-on-Lake Michigan:

Hon. Rice Cake of 1951 sends you greetings from the Pacific, and thanks for two very delightful letters. I can hardly begin to tell you of the delightful adventures and encounters we have had. It has been a glorious trip.

We spent some time in southern California before coming up here, and there did much lecturing and discussionating. We stayed in a fabulous Mauresque house in the Hollywood hills, and met all such celebrities as Huxley, Gerald Heard, Christopher Isherwood, and Fritz Kunkel. We also stayed for a couple of days at a small piece of paradise in La Jolla — a house on top of a mountain overhanging the ocean, with a view of 100 miles of coast, and mountain-land to the north. We then returned to LA, and came up here via Ojai and Big Sur, at the former place meeting the remarkable Mr. Rajagopal, who is Krishnamurti's right-hand man — and he was certainly far and away the most impressive of all the characters encountered. A man, apparently, of utter inward peace and naturalness; no axe to grind, no "holy" atmosphere, no self-pushing.

Palo Alto is a sort of sunshiny Evanston with palm trees. The house is comfortable and convenient, but nothing romantic. The decor of this house is a bit gloomy, so I promptly added color by printing a violent picture of Shiva dancing.

If we stay on here I think we shall try to find something with a view, and I have heard of a place in Sausalito, across the Golden Gate from SF, which might do very well.

But I do not know what is going to happen. The power behind this academy is a charming but unpredictable millionaire who doesn't know what he is going to do until he has almost done it. It is all marvelously interesting and insecure. It is, however, most probable that we shall come east for part of the summer. If we can find a good billet out here, here we shall stay. One has to live somewhere, and a place where the heating bills are not exorbitant is the best.

I will get in touch with your friends Colton and Janice. The music teacher (for Tassie) is Dr. Oswald Jonas, whose address I can never remember. He is in the Chicago phone book, somewhere on N. Park Ave. I recommend unreservedly. A great character. If he embraces Tassie and calls her "my darling" don't let her take it seriously. That's just "Ossie." His step-daughter Irene Schreier just gave a concert here in SF, and it was quite superb. Ossie is a close friend of Ruth Goodkind, through whom I met him.

The fact that you have been enjoying [Reginald H.] Blyth's books puts you into a very special and select group of initiates. There simply isn't anything better on Zen to be had. I recommended them to Aldous Huxley, and he is likewise vastly impressed with them, not only as Zen but as literary criticism.

We saw Bob Morse [from Canterbury House days], who came for dinner the day after we got in, bringing gifts of bread, salt, and wine. He is very impressive in clericals, and I only hope they don't get the better of him. He finds me somewhat incomprehensible, which is natural enough, because we all are. Boots produced kittens the same day — four of them, respectively Boots Jr., Tiger, Monkey-face, and Clown. It was immensely considerate of her to wait until we hit home base.

I must tell you about the fabulous tea party in Hollywood at the Vedanta temple, which is a sort of miniature version of the Taj Mahal in stucco. *Everyone* with the exception of Gerald Heard was there, including the swami and some half-dozen sisters — i.e., Vedanta nuns, only they were wearing afternoon-tea dresses. Well, we had much conversation, but the swami got me into an argument as to whether the atman can feel a pinch or not. I said it could, and he said it couldn't, and so in the end I was pretty much dubbed as a heretic. I hear he preached against me the following Sunday. However, I think they still want me around as they are publishing an article of mine in a forthcoming symposium to be entitled *Vedanta, East and West*, which is coming from Harper in June.

In Ojai we stayed with a remarkable French artist, Guy Ignon, whom I used to know in NY. He is busy on a *moderne* version of the Temptation of

St. Anthony, and has done a weird picture of Don Quixote armored in newspaper. Has a charming Russian wife. Going through Big Sur we stopped off and saw Mrs. Henry Miller, in H. Miller's marvelous "retreat" about 1,000 ft. above the ocean on the side of an incredible mountain. Mist turned everything into a sort of Chinese landscape.

Here in [Palo Alto] I have been busy talking at Stanford, and with various groups in town, making them simultaneously happy and furious. The enclosed will give you some idea of what is going on at the academy.

I was very much interested in all the news of Jack, and would love to see the renovations in his apartment. Glad also to have news of Dick and La Breslauer (anything cooking there?). Please tell Platman I will write him very soon.

Dorothy is just fine and no end of a help with my work, and I have been delighted to see how well she has been received wherever we go. So, here's the end of the last piece of paper I have at the moment, and I must sign off with lots of love to you and to all the clan.

As ever, Alan

PALO ALTO, CALIFORNIA | MARCH 27, 1951
Dear Mummy & Daddy:
The work here is turning out to be most interesting. We have an excellent group of students, and in addition to the teaching at the academy I have already two groups of private students here in Palo Alto. We are getting to know a great many people, and find life considerably easier than in Millbrook where, particularly during the winter, we were very much cut off.

For very many reasons I am quite sure that it will be best for us to live here for a while. There is the prospect of more or less permanent teaching work here at the academy. I have a far larger "public" here in the West than anywhere else (I find bookstores carrying respectable stocks of my work). The climate is very reasonable, and in the icy winters of the East and Middle West you get the feeling of simply burning up your income to keep warm. From the beginning of November we were using up more than 2 tons of coal a month, and getting very erratic heating from it, with coal at $21.00 a ton. We had to use electric heat as well.

So the position is that it would be crazy to spend another year in the farmhouse. We must move, both because of the winters, and because it is really too far from the city, upon which my work depends. Furthermore, the school was poor. It was an area without any "middle class" — just very wealthy landowners who send their children to private schools, and then tradesmen and artisans of a rather rundown kind sending their children to the public schools. As a result, Ann was getting in with the wrong set, and learning to talk like a shop girl. Here all that is changed, and in the past month she has improved enormously in every way.

Moving means either going closer to New York or coming out here. So far as I am concerned this part of the world is hard to beat. It has "everything" — mountains, ocean, flowers, beautiful trees, friendly and rather easygoing people. Everything grows here, and the stores are full of fruit and vegetables of all kinds, which makes for much healthier eating.

Under these circumstances, I plan to drive back to Millbrook starting June 1st, and close up the house. We have much too much property — heavy furniture, much of which is getting old and decrepit. More and more I am finding that many possessions are a liability and a burden, and I intend to get rid of ballast, and sell everything which is not quite essential. Then I shall ship the remainder out here and return about the end of June.

Another factor is that Dorothy expects a *baby* about the end of July. This is another reason for avoiding Thornecrest in the winter, and also why I wouldn't want her to do any travelling this summer.

Now — moving and having a baby is a fairly expensive business, even though I have been doing well this year and prospects look good. Likewise we have some debts — I had to borrow on my life insurance last year — but in another year out here we should be able to clear that off. But in these circumstances I do not feel able to guarantee that I could underwrite Joan's school expenses for another year in England, and at the end of that time carry her extra fare back to New York plus her fare out to California. I might be able to do it, but I am not in a position to promise it.

On the whole, I think it would be best for her to return this June. Then I can meet her in New York, and she can come out to California with me in the car, which will, incidentally, be a very lovely and thrilling trip. Then, if all goes well in the year following, we might be able to consider doing something about you. I very much wish that both of you could come and live with us in this very benevolent climate, and I think it is becoming time to think carefully as to whether this would be a practical proposition from your point of view. If, by summer 1952, I am in a position to afford it, do you think you would be equal to the adventure?

The difficulty of making promises about anything is that in my circumstances and in this particular work, I never really know what is going to happen. The man who runs this academy, [Louis] Gainsborough [the principal financer], does not know what he is going to do almost until he has done it! Not very convenient, perhaps, but it seems to me that all life is pretty much like that, and you just have to get used to the idea of living perpetually on the edge of the unknown. He is a sincere man, however, and I think he is to be trusted. But I have long given up the idea of expecting to be secure. In this world today, anything can happen. You can be run over on the street or hit with an A-bomb; so why worry? I don't know of anything else I can do to be more secure. Yes, I could earn less money by taking some kind of work that would be very dull and very regular — like investing in gilt-edge stocks. But that seems to me to be mortgaging your life, and planning to live tomorrow instead of today. Tomorrow never comes, and today you are a drone. And the drones only imagine that they are safe, being just as liable to the misfortunes of life as anyone else. So — one must gamble all the time, and get used to doing it with a light heart. In the end, we are all losers, which is tragedy if you don't accept it; and if you do accept it — "he that loses his soul shall find it."

For days now it has been sunshine and springtime. Last week I took Dorothy and Ann to see the country just north of San Francisco across the harbor entrance. We went for a walk in a redwood forest [Muir Woods] — great trees hundreds of feet high — and drove to the top of a mountain [Mount Tamalpais] 2,500 ft. straight above the ocean with a view of the whole SF area. I am considering the idea of living in that neighborhood. We have this house until the end of June, but it would be wonderful to move into an area where you are only 15 minutes from the heart of SF and yet in the most romantic surroundings. There is a little town called Sausalito, which clings to the side of a mountain overlooking the harbor. Below it is a fishing village. Above it is a pleasant "residential area" not too crowded, where almost every house has a view of the water, the mountains all round the harbor, and the distant cities of San Francisco, Berkeley, Oakland, etc. At night it is a fairyland of lights.

On Easter Day we had Jim Delkin and his wife for dinner. He was the man who published my *Zen* here; he runs a small publishing business as a hobby, and specializes in fine printing. Earlier in the day we had a breakfast party at the home of a Mrs. Besse Bolton whom I have known for some years, and who has been such a help in getting us settled here. She found this house for us, and has introduced me to all kinds of people.

Dorothy made Ann a lovely new dress for Easter — a pale yellow "dotted Swiss" material, with frills. We found a couple of orchids for Dorothy in a little Chinese flower shop, and so everyone was very happy and "decorative." Dorothy makes "quite a hit" these days, and seems to be very much liked wherever we go having a marvellous gift for being unostentatiously pleasant.

Last Friday night we had the first meeting of what we call the Colloquium here at the academy. This is a panel discussion between three members of the faculty — Spiegelberg, Chaudhuri, and myself. Chaudhuri had not arrived from India then, so we had a guest, a professor from Mills College in Oakland. There was a splendid audience, and the three of us got rapidly into an animated conversation about the contributions of Asia to Western life.

At present I am teaching two courses, one on the comparative mentality of East and West, and the other in conjunction with Chaudhuri on "The Application of Asian Psychology to Modern Psychiatry." The latter was given to me as a surprise, and I still feel very unprepared for it!

I gave the first lecture yesterday, as Chaudhuri still wasn't here, and Spiegelberg said it was the best lecture he had ever heard from me. The first course has about 17 students and the second about 12. Spiegelberg wants me to do a course on Buddhism in the fall.

Now will you, as soon as possible, let me know your reaction, and suggestions, if any, about all these plans. I hate to have to suggest bringing Joan back this year because I know what a pleasure she is to you, and I am quite sure that she is deriving many advantages from Farringtons. But I feel very responsible for her being so far off, and, in the uncertainties of things, cannot guarantee that I can manage

    i. School expenses in England;

    ii. Extra fare to New York in 1952;

    iii. Fare to California.

I *might* be able to do it very comfortably if everything works out all right, but it would be a mess if I couldn't. And that seems to me too big a chance to take.

I am sending you another food package, with best wishes for April 15th, and the hope that there may yet be many more birthdays for both of you.

With lots of love from us all, as always, Alan

WOODSIDE, CALIFORNIA | AUGUST 11, 1951

Dear Jacquie:

It's about time I kept you up with the news, though you may have heard something of our doings through Ruth [Goodkind]. To wit, that on August 3rd Dorothy produced 5 lb. 5 oz. Marcia Ruth Watts — a cute little bundle with a fine round head and deep blue eyes. Then, yesterday, Joan arrived from London and New York, making our vast family up to five humans and five cats, symmetrically grouped since each "class" contains one male and four females.

Our place in the mountains is perfectly lovely — peaceful, beautiful, and very comfortable. There is even a bamboo bush at our front door, so I feel justified in this Chinese stationery, which says "A-lan Wa-tsz" and means "Ah, billows-in-puddle-sir," which is a good name for someone who writes much about what can't be described.

We are very much charmed by the effect upon Joan of a year in England.

She has acquired a very natural English accent, and seems to have matured quite a bit. Not quite a "woman" yet, but getting there, and nearly as tall as Dorothy.

Happily there has been little work to do in the way of school affairs, so I have been able to concentrate on the house, taking a leaf out of Jack's book and manufacturing some furniture, including a desk some seven feet long in a kind of Japanese-modern style. The weather has been heavenly, and we have been spending some absolutely idyllic days which give one the feeling of living a floating rather than an earthbound existence. We do get some fog up here, but on such cold days we resort to our enormous stone fireplace and popcorn.

Distant rumblings reach me about the outbreak of a marriage between you and Jack sometime this month. Do tell. Should this miracle occur, I am going to send you a telegram and — all the way from California — a gas balloon carrying a wad of flaming Kotex soaked in gasoline. Golly, I love you both and, whatever happens, wish the very best for you.

Sometime will you please give me the address of the seminary for young gentlewomen where you are going to work this fall. It must be the notorious Convent of St. Ench, with the motto *Gyrovagulam Facit Sorore*, which, idiomatically translated is "Makes a bum out of a nun."

I hear from Joan that Platman has been in New York. I wonder if he will return to Highland Park before leaving for Dallas. I heard from his future rector today, who has been having much trouble with his new baby girl, Nancy — born with one lung not functioning, resulting in an enlarged heart.

Other than all this, there is really no news. It's just that the stars are bright at night, the mist lies on the valley, the redwoods grow higher, and the mountain streams flow on to the ocean. Oh yes, I did climb a redwood this afternoon in an attempt to rescue a cat — a very *dumb* cat called Monkey-face — who fell off before I could get her down, but was none the worse.

With love to you all from us all,

As ever, Alan

THE AMERICAN ACADEMY OF ASIAN STUDIES | SAN FRANCISCO, CALIFORNIA | AUGUST 30, 1951
Mr. Henry Miller | Big Sur, California
Dear Henry Miller:
I thought you might like to see the enclosed program of the work we are going to do this year. I am sending a copy of it to almost everyone I know who is interested in things Oriental, because I really don't know where else anyone could find such a unique and complete group of courses.

I would hate to think of any potential student missing the opportunity of studying here just because he had never heard of our work. I wonder, therefore, whether you would be kind enough to circulate information about what we are doing among any of your friends and acquaintances who might be interested.

With all good wishes,

Sincerely yours, Alan Watts

WOODSIDE, CALIFORNIA | JANUARY 22, 1952

Dear Henry Miller:

As far as I know *The Spirit of Zen* is still available from E. P. Dutton in New York, who are the US agents for John Murray in London. I have also heard of someone in Florida who seems to be handling the Wisdom of the East series direct from London, more or less in competition with Dutton.

On the West Coast, my book is generally available at Perkins' in Pasadena, Abbey and Pickwick in LA, and the Metaphysical Town Hall Bookshop in SF. In New York it is always in stock at Orientalia and Gateway.

I am looking forward to your latest from New Directions, but it doesn't seem to be out yet.

One of these days I shall probably be stopping by in hope of taking you out to lunch. My eldest daughter Joan is now at the Happy Valley School in Ojai, and my trips southwards are rather more frequent.

All good wishes, Alan Watts

SAN FRANCISCO, CALIFORNIA | OCTOBER 11, 1952

Dear Henry Miller:

Thanks for your postcard, and apologies for the delay in replying. My former wife's address is:

Mrs. Carlton Gamer

East 65th Street

New York, NY

Will you please let me know the price of the book as I want to buy one, and would rather get it through you than from a bookstore — since you make the profit.... God, what one has to do for a living! I wonder when writing will ever pay. Just look at what I am now doing to help make ends meet.

I hope to be down your way soon, and would like you and spouse to come out for a meal with us. Do you expect to be home and visible during the coming month? Let me know, because we are planning a visit to friends in Pacific Grove and haven't set a definite date yet.

All good wishes,

Sincerely, Alan Watts

The following is undated. It contains a side note from Henry Miller: "replied to: 11-5-52."

REDWOOD CITY, CALIFORNIA
Henry Miller:

Supposing we came down Saturday (Nov. 8th), would you be at home, and what time would you prefer that we came? Will bring the wine. (Sunday would do also.)

I have a copy of your *Tropic of Cancer* in good condition save that it has no cover. Perhaps this is something of a collector's item which you could dispose of to your advantage, and if so I would be glad to give it to you. [The original Obelisk edition of *Tropic of Cancer* was banned in the United States until 1961.] It would probably need to be rebound.

I don't know how fast your mails are, but if you judge a reply to this letter won't reach the above address by Thursday, please reply c/o Mrs. Dorothy Tainton, Pacific Grove, where we shall be staying on Friday.

All the best, Alan Watts

WOODSIDE, CALIFORNIA | NOVEMBER 4, 1952
Dear Mummy & Daddy:

Oh dear! This is so long overdue, but ever since you left I have been incessantly on the go.

First it was a trip to Los Angeles for lectures. Then school opened, in a new building. Then I had to get my office fitted up in San Francisco, and I am not through with this yet. I found a perfectly charming little place in a friend's house, but it has required a lot of painting and other work, and all this has taken up an immense amount of time.

I had quite a successful time in Los Angeles. The lectures were very well attended, but I think the most delightful part of it was an afternoon spent with Aldous Huxley and his wife at their home. I had met him several times before, but this time felt I really got to know him, and to achieve a real meeting of minds.

The academy is now in a new building, all its own. It is a large house on Pacific Heights in San Francisco with a fine view of the harbor. I have some very well-attended courses, including an extension course on Buddhism every Wednesday to which about 60 people have been coming. I am assisted by Dr. Malalasekera from Ceylon; a very famous Buddhist scholar, though he is in some ways so Westernized that I feel that he is the Westerner and I the Oriental!

As I told you, I am doing some work in psychological counselling, for which purpose I have taken an office in the city, quite close to the academy. It is on Steiner Street, the home of Margaret Tilly, who has been one of my students at the academy. She is a charming, rather intellectual middle-aged woman who teaches music. I have three rooms at the back of the house, approached through a delightful little garden with a fish pool and tubs for maple trees, fuchsia plants, etc. One of my students has been helping me with the painting, though we have covered most of the wall space with burlap, which gives a very pleasant texture.

Tia managed to walk the day after you left, and by now is careening around at great speed and getting mixed up with everything. Dorothy's father sent her a small peasant costume from Sweden, in which she appeared at a dress-up party given by Mrs. Repetto on Halloween for the whole neighborhood. We made Ann a sort of Elizabethan costume out of crinkled paper, and with the aid of some batik I fixed up Dorothy as a South Sea Island girl.

About ten days ago we had both the Delkins and the Greenes up for dinner. Jim Delkin's printer is doing a wonderful job on a new edition of my *Meaning of Happiness.* Yesterday I took a look at Felix's new shipment of antiques. One rather interesting item is a fine chest of drawers lined with newspapers dated 1815, and describing the surrender of Napoleon. I happened to make this discovery and called it to Felix's attention. Hope it will increase the value for him!

Last Saturday we had dinner at the Davenports' — a very nice party given for a woman who is an architect just setting up business in San Francisco. She showed us a set of perfectly beautiful slides of New York City in all its varying lights, as well as some marvelous pictures of Switzerland. Gert and Dave seem to be in fine form, and ask after you frequently.

We are planning another trip to Carmel this weekend, and shall stay with Dorothy Tainton, and then visit friends in Big Sur. Blanche Matthias has been away in New Mexico, but called this morning to say that she had a considerable amount of fine glass from her mother's home for which she had no use and wondered whether we would like it.

The Listener has started to arrive — for which very many thanks. The first issue had an article by John Ward-Perkins about the discovery of the tomb of St. Peter in Rome. It really is a most informative and interesting magazine, and we are very glad indeed to have it. The book reviews are particularly good.

I have heard a rumor to the effect that Toby [Christmas Humphreys] has been made a judge. Do you know whether this is true, for if so I should really write and congratulate him. And, I completely forget, but what is the correct form of envelope address for a judge? — the Rt. Hon. Mr. Justice X or what?

Joan seems to be happy as usual at Ojai. Felix and Elena saw her down there just a little while ago, and said she was looking both happy and healthy. She doesn't write much, which I suppose is good on the principle that no news is good news!

The weather here is gorgeous. Dorothy and I had a lovely walk on Sunday — up past the Christensens' — and spent about an hour lying in the sun at the spot where you discovered that fine view behind the enclosed orchard.

Everyone joins me in sending lots of love to you both, with the hope that you are not completely exhausted after gathering in your harvest. What a job!

With love as always, Alan

The following is a circular from around January 1953.

SAN FRANCISCO, CALIFORNIA

Alan W. Watts wishes to announce that he is now setting aside a number of hours each week for conferences on personal problems. This is by way of regularizing a practice which has been carried on intermittently for the past ten years, in response to requests as they arose, but so frequently that it has become advisable to put it on a professional basis.

Appointments may be made at any of the numbers listed above, or by letter. For the convenience of those living further down the peninsula, Mr. Watts will also keep appointments at 1527 Byron Street, Palo Alto, at least one day a week.

SAN FRANCISCO, CALIFORNIA | MARCH 30, 1953

Dear Mummy & Daddy,

We are still working on settling down in the new house [in Mill Valley, California]. The main job is getting furniture together: but, with the help of an electric sander, we are busy renovating and remodeling all sorts of odds and ends into pretty decent-looking shape. We have had a present of two very fine modern chairs, from Blanche Matthias and another friend, and I think that within another ten days the place will look quite interesting and habitable.

I was down in Los Angeles all last week, and had a very interesting time, including a whole morning's discussion with one of the top men in the Ford Foundation — mostly on the subject of their plans for assisting education, which are almost unbelievably intelligent!

On my way home I picked up Joan at Ojai, and brought her back for the Easter vacation. The school there is getting larger and larger, and they plan to divide it before long into two smaller schools so as to maintain the "individual" character of the teaching. Ann has gone off on a week's trip with a party of children from the Portola School. I think this will be a real thrill for her, as they are going to Death Valley — a part of the California desert lying to the east of the Sierra Nevada. It is below sea level, and within sight of the highest peaks of the Sierra, and is particularly celebrated for the intensely vivid colours of mountain and desert landscape.

Ruth will be over here from Japan about the 12th, on her way to New York for a short visit before returning to Kyoto. Joan will stay over to see her, and go back to school later.

Jim and Barbara Delkin will be leaving for England this month to see the coronation [of Queen Elizabeth II], and I will of course be sure that they have your address because I know they will want to see you. Felix [Greene] has recently returned, and is mainly concerned now with finding an American market for a special type of furnace construction which his brother has invented — one of those very simple little ideas which completely revolutionize former procedures. It is already in use in England, and the interesting thing about it is that no theoretical engineer will believe that it can work. But it does! It is essentially a device for insulating furnaces working at tremendous temperatures.

Dorothy has reupholstered the long stool [a beautiful needlepoint fireplace stool of devils made by Alan's mother], and done a very good job with it. I have just about finished my book for Thames & Hudson, and I think it will appear under the title *Myth and Ritual in Christianity*. The other volumes in the series for which it has been written are very beautifully produced. I have still to do a lot of drawings for it.

We are to have a dinner party this week, with Grace Clements, together with the Onslow-Fords. Now that we are in Mill Valley we see quite a bit of the latter, and they have been enormously helpful. Gordon helped me move a refrigerator into the house, and Jacqueline gave me one of those amazing old stand-up desks which used to be used for bookkeeping. I have always wanted to have one. Combined with a lower table for the typewriter, they are wonderful for spreading out books and making notes while you are writing.

Did I tell you that my radio programme is now going all over the country? It can now be heard over forty-one stations, and as a result my "fan mail" is assuming rather formidable proportions. The radio station has given us an FM receiver, so that I can check up on myself — but it is wonderful to have it for their other programmes, which are very fascinating.

Thanks so much for that cutting from *The Times* about the plans for the study of comparative religions. If any more information about it appears, please will you let me have it.

Little Tia is doing splendidly. Her vocabulary is growing fast, and she shows considerable intelligence in fetching and carrying, finding things which she has misplaced, and generally "making sense" out of what goes on around the house.

Everyone joins me in sending their love, and we hope that your spring will be as beautiful as ours. It has been simply heavenly.

With love as always, Alan

MILL VALLEY, CALIFORNIA | JULY 1, 1953

Dear Mummy & Daddy:

Thank you very much indeed for *The Times* coronation supplement. We have enjoyed the pictures very much indeed. To judge from all the reports, the whole thing was a marvelous success, and seems to have given the country a tremendous sense of renewed life.

We have just returned from a trip south. The whole family went camping in Ojai for ten days, during part of which I was on a very gratifying lecture visit in Los Angeles. Joan's school asked me to be the principal speaker on their equivalent of Speech Day, and the children put on a really wonderful performance of the Midsummer Night's Dream, as well as a puppet show and some excellent folk dancing. We camped on some property owned by a friend, and Dorothy particularly enjoyed the open air. She is in wonderful health — expecting, as I think I told you, towards the end of this month or the beginning of next.

This year in school has been wonderful for Joan. She is becoming so grown up and companionable, and in every way the place seems to be an excellent influence on her. Her work in ceramics is coming along splendidly, and she has brought home a large fruit bowl which is really quite beautiful. We need it, for our trees are pouring plums down upon us!

My work is in a very curious state. As I said, the last lecture visit to Los Angeles was most successful. I tried a new kind of programme — a four-evening conference on Zen, which was most well attended. I also had lectures in Ojai and Santa Barbara, and on all sides the work seems to be "in demand." But the academy is just about falling apart from lack of funds. My problem is whether to try and save it or simply to go ahead and work as a "lone wolf." To save it, I shall more or less have to take initiative in such a way as to make it my own "baby" and run it according to my own ideas. This seems to be the necessary course, and so I am organizing a summer school there for July and August and in the meantime trying to get Gainsborough to collect a working group of trustees who are really interested people instead of the present bunch of stuffed shirts with big names.

I have two books coming out in England this autumn — the *Myth & Ritual in Christianity* from Thames & Hudson, and *The Wisdom of Insecurity* from Rider. I am sending you a copy of the new edition of the *Meaning of Happiness*. Sorry I forgot to let you have this, but, seeing that it was just a reprint, I didn't think about it. In the meantime, I am doing another small book in collaboration with Gordon Onslow-Ford. This is to be a "weird and wonderful" affair called *Nothingk* [*sic*] — an essay on the philosophy of inspired nonsense!

I'm afraid I have to bring this to a rapid conclusion as I must be off to town — to broadcast and to organize things at the academy. I have quite a programme of radio talks to do, as the National Assn. of Educational Broadcasters wants another series from me to send all over the country — and I am doing a series on the great philosophical classics of Asia.

Lots of love from us all, as always, Alan

MILL VALLEY, CALIFORNIA | JULY 6, 1953
Dear Mummy,

I must write to you about a rather interesting coincidence. During the past month I have come across two of your old pupils at Walthamstow Hall. One of them I have known for years without ever realizing that she had been there, and the other I have just met recently.

When I was in Los Angeles I had a long talk with a Mrs. Jennings, whom I first met in Oxford at the World Congress of Faiths in 1937. She has lived out here, mostly in Santa Barbara, ever since, and is a very ardent Buddhist — having now adopted Ananda as her first name. In the course of conversation I discovered that she had been the daughter of a missionary in China, and was educated in Sevenoaks, so at once I asked the obvious question. She was delighted to find that I was the son of her "favourite mistress — Emily Buchan!" Her name was then Mabel Hunt. Do you remember her?

You should have less difficulty in remembering the other, who was Isabel Grenfell, daughter of John Grenfell, the Baptist missionary to the Congo. She was half Negro, and one of three sisters. She remembers Miss Glover, Miss Fletcher, and the Rhys (or was it Rees?) sisters very well, and showed me photographs of both Miss Glover and Miss Hare. From her own accounts she was a very naughty little girl, who used to escape from her room by climbing down the ivy. She remembers how pleased you were when the school built a new gymnasium.

At the present time she is a woman about 55 years old, or perhaps a little less, of extraordinary charm and beauty. She lives with one of my students, Elsa Gidlow, not very far from Mill Valley, with whom we all had dinner last Saturday.

It seemed such a surprise discovering these two instances of "how small the world is" in such quick succession that I just had to write to you about it.

Today I begin a fortnight's teaching assignment at Mills College in Oakland — another girls' school! So I must get busy and be off.

Lots of love to you both, as always, Alan

MILL VALLEY, CALIFORNIA | AUGUST 8, 1953

Dear Mummy and Daddy:

What an eventful summer! I'm glad that you got the cablegram all right, and Mark bubblingly thanks his Granddaddy for the letter. He was born at 2:43 AM on July 31st, and the doctor was so pleased with him and his mama that he let them come home from the hospital the following day. The hospital had never had such a short maternity case before, and it was the more surprising because it was a rather conservative doctor. Dorothy is just glowing with pleasure, and everyone in the family is delighted. As Mark "jells" into full human shape, he is said to resemble his father — particularly in profile. The full name is Mark DeWitt Watts, joining Old Dutch with Old English.

Ann and Tia received the Coronation Crown pieces [of Queen Elizabeth II] with great delight, and thank you muchly. I hope Ann will write to you soon, but she doesn't ever write a letter unless made to do so, and Dorothy has stopped forcing her. And thank you for the *Country Life*, with the lovely article about the Chinese gardener, and, also, did I thank you for *The Times* coronation supplement with its splendid photographs?

The Delkins have returned with good news of you both, and seem to have been most pleased with their visit at Holbrook Lane. Felix is not going over again this summer, but I have seen quite a bit of him here — partly because both of us are interested in getting him on the staff of KPFA, my pet radio station. This summer I have come into much closer association with this work, having helped them through a big internal crisis arising from a conflict of personalities. Also my talks have been instrumental in getting them a fairly large financial grant from the Ford Foundation.

Plans are well ahead for the publication of my Christian mythology book [*Myth and Ritual in Christianity*] in England this autumn, as well as *The Wisdom of Insecurity*, which has been taken by Rider & Co. The former book will have some perfectly splendid plates in it, and many drawings. I had to delegate the task of choosing some of the plates to the publisher, and they have done it with exquisite taste.

The summer school at the academy has been going quite well, but the general picture of things there is very dubious. I simply don't know whether to devote myself entirely to trying to save it, or whether to look elsewhere. There is a lot of goodwill for the work, but so much of it seems to be attached to me personally from people whose interest in the project is more "spiritual" than "academic." This presents a conflict, for the more one would emphasize the "spiritual," the less one would acquire academic status and respectability. This is a ticklish problem. Lest the thing should collapse, I am busy lining up outside lectures for the autumn, having worked out a new system of lecturing which is much more remunerative.

Tia is beginning to talk fluently and is at times alarmingly intelligent. Our only troubles with her are that she does everything with such gusto that she needs some watching, and that she is very restless at night — kicking, screaming, and whatnot. She shows good signs of development in drawing, and can be trusted to help with quite a number of household affairs, which she attacks in odd ways that turn out to be intelligently thought out even when unconventional.

Joan is a real dear despite many symptoms of typical American adolescence. She has become almost arrestingly beautiful, and I can only hope that her brains will somehow approximate to her beauty. She is very slow in all literary subjects — but oddly does have some capacity for writing! I wish to goodness I could spend more time with these children, but earning a bare living takes up so much time, especially in the evenings when they are home.

This is also rather a fertile summer. Our baby comes just after loads and loads of plums, and now all the cats have kittens! Gordon Onslow-Ford gave the family a beautiful Japanese dwarf tree in honour of the arrival, and both he and Jacqueline have been so very kind to us in many ways.

Incidentally, Mills College thanks you for the picture of the girl who married the Oxford "stroke." They put it up on the main notice board.

Well, I think this is almost all the immediate news, though I must have forgotten some things seeing that there are so many. One may at least be thankful for a full life!

With lots of love from us all, as always, Alan

AMERICAN ACADEMY OF ASIAN STUDIES | SAN FRANCISCO,
CALIFORNIA | FEBRUARY 23, 1954
Mr. Walter Neurath | Thames & Hudson, Ltd. | London, England
Dear Mr. Neurath:
Thank you very much for your interesting letter of February 18th. Before going further, I do want to say how very pleased I am with the way in which you produced my book [*Myth and Ritual in Christianity*], especially with the selection of the photographs for illustrations.

I was most interested in Mr. [R. F. C.] Hull's reactions, and I wonder if we shall get any from Dr. Jung. As to his suggestion about an edition of the works of Dr. Coomaraswamy, steps have already been taken to do this under the auspices of the Bollingen Foundation. They have given Mrs. Coomaraswamy a grant to do the necessary editorial work.

I wonder if you would get in touch with the editors of *Nimbus* [the editor was Hull's son] and ask if they will let me have some copies of the edition in which my piece appears. I already mentioned this as one of the conditions of allowing them to print it.

With many thanks and all good wishes,

Yours very sincerely, Alan W. Watts, Dean

JW: R. F. C. Hull was an Englishman best known for his translation of The Collected Works of Carl G. Jung. *In a letter to Walter Neurath, Alan's editor at Thames & Hudson, he commented, "I agree with you that both* Divine Horsemen *[Maya Deren] and* Myth and Ritual in Christianity *are exceptionally good. I read the Alan Watts [book] in a couple of evenings and found it a remarkable achievement. To my mind it is streets ahead of a book like Fritz Schuon's* Transcendent Unity of Religions, *recently published with much aplomb by Pantheon Books, New York."*

AMERICAN ACADEMY OF ASIAN STUDIES | SAN FRANCISCO, CALIFORNIA | MARCH 17, 1954

Dear Henry Miller:

Thanks so much for your card. If the English publisher, John Murray, won't supply you with *The Spirit of Zen*, the US agent is an outfit by the name of Transatlantic Arts, Hollywood-by-the-Sea, Florida. It's no longer Duttons. If you have difficulty in getting them from him, and I gather the fellow who runs it is rather lackadaisical, the best plan is to order from an English bookseller.

I have been meaning to write to you for a long time to thank you for Gutkind's *Choose Life*. The delay is due to the fact that I haven't really had time to get into it, though what I have read is marvelous and powerful.

I shall be staying in Carmel between May 4th and 9th — giving a powwow on Zen — and I hope at that time to be able to run down to Big Sur and see various friends, including you.

Buddhadeva Bose is going to give a lecture here on April 16th. I haven't met him, but he was very highly recommended by Kenneth Rexroth.

Please make a note of our changed address, as above. We've been here for more than a year now, and I seem to be managing to hold the place together despite lack of funds.

All the best to you and family,

Very sincerely, Alan Watts

AMERICAN ACADEMY OF ASIAN STUDIES | SAN FRANCISCO,
CALIFORNIA | MARCH 22, 1954
Eric Peters, Esq. | Thames & Hudson, Ltd. | London, England
Dear Mr. Peters:

Thank you very much for your letter of March 18th with all the enclosures. Will you also thank Mr. Neurath for his letter, but as yours is the one which seems to need the answer I would be glad if you would just acknowledge his.

At the present time I am rather burdened with some writing commitments that will not make it possible for me to start work on another book until the autumn. My plan is to do something on Buddhism, probably on Zen Buddhism.

I do not think I could in any near future do another book for the Myth & Man series, because my study of symbology has been somewhat restricted to Christianity and my interest in Oriental philosophy has taken other lines. However, I would very much like you to be the publishers of the British edition of my next book, provided that it would be possible for Pantheon Books to handle the American end of things, since I have promised them my next book here.

I will keep you informed of any developments in my plans and will let you know as soon as the subject of my next book is clearly formulated.

Thank you so much for all the reviews of *Myth & Ritual*. It seems to have stirred up quite a little furor and I hope it will sell a lot of copies.

With many thanks and best wishes,

Yours sincerely, Alan W. Watts, Dean

AMERICAN ACADEMY OF ASIAN STUDIES | SAN FRANCISCO,
CALIFORNIA | APRIL 14, 1954
Dear Mummy:

I'm afraid this will arrive a day or two late to wish you a very happy birthday. But I wanted to wait until I had seen Mary Blashko and her husband. They stopped by our home in Mill Valley on Monday and took some pictures of the family, but I was out at the time, and so did not see them until yesterday, when we had lunch together in San Francisco.

We realized that our last meeting must have been when I was about seven years old: consequently I had only the haziest recollection of Mary. She is certainly a most charming woman, and her husband I found very congenial indeed. We found that through her association with the Quakers there were several rather interesting people in this country with whom we were both familiar — and I was most interested to hear of Ian's work, teaching in one of the Rudolf Steiner schools.

The weekend before this last one I spent in the old town of Columbia at the foot of the Sierra, at the country home of Robert Burns, who is the president of the College of the Pacific.

It was quite a party, for the guests included Louis Gainsborough, two deans of the college, their public-relations expert, and their chief fund-raiser. We spent two days laying all the plans for the affiliation of the academy with the college — which is the oldest in California. It was founded in 1851, and the academy in 1951! Now all the formalities have been completed, so that we are now a graduate school of the college, retaining our own spiritual and intellectual independence. The arrangement has the immense advantage of giving us much greater academic prestige, and it will make the thorny problem of raising money considerably easier. To me all this is not only gratifying — but a bit of a chuckle goes with it, since I never expected to become the head of a respectable university graduate school in quite this way! There's nothing like the back stairs.

Joan is coming home for the Easter holiday tomorrow, and one of the other girls [Olivia Westberg] at the school, who happens to be Aldous Huxley's niece, is coming with her. Ann was out until late last night on a roller-skating party which she enjoyed enormously — organized by the "Camp Fire Girls," a sort of scouting affair, to which she belongs. Mark has just started crawling. Tia has been bothered with a boil on the top of her head, and Dorothy has been having a terrible time with some sort of impetigo on her hands and legs. I had a brief spell of it, but my Chinese doctors got rid of it in short order. The family doctor is not doing so well for Dorothy, so I think I shall have to take her over to the Fung brothers. This is a little embarrassing since they never send a bill, but they are good doctors.

We have been doing a lot of work in the garden this spring — clearing out the jungle of undergrowth and giving the good plants room to breathe. At the front entrance of the house there is a sort of courtyard overhung by a weeping willow. I am turning it into a Chinese-style garden with interesting rocks and potted trees. You can get the most wonderful pickle tubs from the Japanese groceries, wooden barrels bound with strips of bamboo. I picked up four of them the other day, and have thus far transplanted a small plum tree. Hope it will flourish! In a few days I shall go to a nursery and get an orange tree, an azalea, and perhaps a camellia. We also have a dwarf Japanese cypress.

The weather has simply pulled us out of doors. Day after day it has been simply gorgeous, although there has been enough rain to keep things from drying out. But at this time of year, with all the blossoms out, every direction in which you look is beautiful. So much of it is almost overwhelming!

Thanks for sending those letters from the *Sunday Times*. The book has set some controversy going in other places besides — and the Catholic papers, in particular, are in what we call "quite a tizzy" about it. It is a sort of hot potato which you can't drop and can't swallow. I had a very nice little note from

Jacquetta Hawkes, and was interested to discover that she is Mrs. J. B. Priestley, and lives at Brook on the Isle of Wight.

We all hope that there will still be many more happy birthdays for you. Breathe gently and live to a hundred! So this letter comes with all our love to you, and to Daddy —

As always, Alan

AMERICAN ACADEMY OF ASIAN STUDIES | SAN FRANCISCO, CALIFORNIA | MAY 13, 1954
The Very Rev. Dom Aelred Graham, OSB | The Priory | Portsmouth, Rhode Island
Dear Father Graham:

I am sorry indeed that I never received your letter of October 28th, 1952. But "better late than never!" It was a very pleasant surprise to hear from you because I think you are almost the only theologian who, to my knowledge, has not reacted suspiciously to *The Supreme Identity*. It was really an essay in a type of "theological semantics," which is both fascinating and tricky because of the great difficulty of getting one's readers used to the idea of different languages in the same tongue.

I do not know whether you will like *Myth and Ritual* quite as much, although it takes the liturgy as its basis, and deals with the very difficult problem of confusing the language of myth and dogma with that of science. I had to write the book in circumstances where I was without access to some important reference materials, and so there are some inaccuracies. It is published by Vanguard, NY. I would value your frank opinion of this book, since one of my purposes in writing is to clarify my own thought by discussion with others.

Another of my books that might interest you is *Behold the Spirit* (Pantheon, NY). As to other materials along the same lines as *The Supreme Identity*, I would especially recommend the very scholarly work of Dr. Ananda Coomaraswamy, *Time and Eternity* (Artibus Asiae, Ascona, Switzerland), Gai Eaton's *The Richest Vein* (Faber, London), and Frithjof Schuon's *Transcendent Unity of Religions* (Pantheon). All these are works representing a rather new point of view in comparative religion.

Some of the important books along more specific lines are R. L. Slater's *Paradox and Nirvana* (Chicago UP), a most interesting study of negative theology in Buddhism; and René Guénon's *Introduction to the Study of the Hindu Doctrines* (Luzac, London), a work in which the gold of positive content has to be sifted from the dross of a rather unfortunate hauteur. If you were specially interested by the references to Zen in *The Supreme Identity*, I would recommend D. T. Suzuki's *Living by Zen* (Rider, London) read alongside his *Introduction to Zen Buddhism* (Philosophical Library, NY).

My clues to the schema of theology/metaphysic, analogy/negation, kataphatic/apophatic, etc., come from a vast complex of sources. This makes it rather difficult to recommend books, because some of them were of value to me for a single page, or even sentence! But you are naturally familiar with St. Dionysius, Nicholas of Cusa, and others who formulated the *via negationis* for Christianity.

Currently I am much interested in the theological implications of the "meta-linguistics" of B. L. Whorf, concerning which there was a rather sketchy article by Stuart Chase in the April *Harper's*. The most interesting article on these lines is Whorf's own *Language, Mind, and Reality*, published in *ETC* spring 1952.

With very many thanks for your kind words,

Very sincerely yours, Alan Watts, Dean

AMERICAN ACADEMY OF ASIAN STUDIES | SAN FRANCISCO, CALIFORNIA | MAY 20, 1954
The Very Rev. Dom Aelred Graham, OSB | Portsmouth Priory | Portsmouth, Rhode Island
Dear Father Graham:

Thank you very much for your letter of May 10th. Your comments on *Myth and Ritual* were interestingly the reverse of the greater part of the criticism which it has received thus far. Occasionally I do come to the East, but I am never quite sure when these trips are going to occur. But I will certainly let you know when another opportunity arises, since I would surely enjoy a discussion with you.

I agree with you that Aldous Huxley has done some extremely useful work. My only objection to the general trend of his thought is that he has a certain element of Manichaeism, in that there are so many passages in which he seems to feel that the finite world order is definitively evil — a sort of very regrettable mistake on the part of the creator. Some of his most recent writing seems to have modified this position, and I think he has begun to realize that, when one understands it more deeply, Oriental metaphysic does not insist upon the incompatibility of Maya and Brahman, the finite and the infinite.

With all good wishes,

Very sincerely, Alan W. Watts, Dean

AMERICAN ACADEMY OF ASIAN STUDIES | SAN FRANCISCO, CALIFORNIA | JUNE 8, 1954
The Rev. John Dunne | Ss. Peter & Paul's Church | Wilmington, California
My dear Father Dunne:

Having never before been sent joyously to Hell, I feel that this is a rather unique situation, for which, I thank you!

I am sorry that, so far as I know, I cannot claim Celtic origin. My mother was Scotch, but from the east coast, and my father English, so I can only assume that I must have had a nurse who put raven's blood in my milk. But when I lived in England I certainly fell under the charm of the west country, of the lonely dolmens on bare hills, and the ancient tree circles where the old magic seemed to linger.

I think it was the Chinese painter Wu Tao-tzu who vanished into the cave, which he had painted on the wall. These gentlemen felt very much at home in the realm beyond the noun, where the Word has not yet created the world — not, perhaps, without the initial terror of falling into outer darkness. For there is a Zen poem which runs:

> To be able to trample in the Great Void,
> The iron bull must sweat.

But, since you were talking of the Bird, perhaps I should also quote another:

> In the sky-realm there is neither back nor front,
> The path of the bird annihilates East and West.

"*Non est servus neque liber; non est masculus neque femina; omnes enim vos unum estis in Christo*" ["There is neither bond nor free, there is neither male nor female: for ye are all one in Christ." Galatians 3:28].

Your reference to Coventry Patmore interested me very much. I know of him only through odds and ends from *The Rod, the Root, and the Flower*, though I have never had the book itself in my hands. I remember, in particular, a wonderful passage which begins, "Love raises the spirit above the sphere of reverence and worship to one of laughter and dalliance..." But where did you get your information about the writings which he destroyed?

It is usually most disappointing to meet authors after you have read their books, but I shall be lecturing again in Los Angeles next week and take the liberty of enclosing an announcement.

With many thanks and all good wishes,

Sincerely yours, Alan Watts

THE AMERICAN ACADEMY OF ASIAN STUDIES | SAN FRANCISCO, CALIFORNIA | JULY 22, 1954

Dear Jacquie:

Your letter came while I was on vacation, and since returning I have been getting a summer school under way. There is always something, and most of the time I feel as if I were Shiva with ten arms all doing different things at the same time... All of which is the real reason why you have not heard from me in such a long time. This is not the silence of condemnation! It is just that it takes forever to get around to the sort of letters you don't dictate to a secretary.

What an amazing coincidence that you sent me the "Mud-Pill Court!" For years I have had a large rubbing of the identical chart. About two years ago I began to translate it, but a lot of other things interfered. So I am absolutely delighted to have this key to its mysteries, because I discuss this kind of thing in a course which I give on "the Tao in Far-Eastern Culture."

The study of Chinese has become a sort of delightful necessity for me, because the students here want to study Lao-tzu in the original, and the regular Chinese language teachers know nothing about it. So, as usual, I find myself rushing in where angels fear to tread. Worse than that, we now have a seminar working on the translation of the Rinzai-roku, a very important Zen text which is supposed to be too difficult to translate. I have the assistance of two almost spherical Chinese MDs, the brothers Paul and George Fung, who are learned Buddhists and present me with excellent cigars. Both have taken their MA here, and are now working towards the PhD. After hours we go to Chinatown and eat fabulous meals, at which they try to get me under the table with offerings of vodka by the tumbler.

Besides all those goings-on at the academy I give periodical lectures and seminars in Carmel, Santa Barbara, and Los Angeles, and conduct a weekly radio program over KPFA in Berkeley. This is an ultra-highbrow, noncommercial station supported by listener subscription. One gets an audience that really listens.

Since March '53 we have been living on top of a hill in Mill Valley, in a rambling house amid a jungle of fruit trees which are now bombarding us with plums. Joan is nearly 16, is unbelievably beautiful, and even [...the rest of the letter is missing].

MILL VALLEY, CALIFORNIA | OCTOBER 13, 1954
Dear Mummy & Daddy:
Thank you both so much for your last two letters. You will have received quite a long letter from Dorothy by now, and at last I have the chance to write one of my own. The past month has been very full indeed, mostly with getting the academy started again for the new academic year.

When a chicken lays an egg, nature permits it to cackle a bit. So, I want you to know that as of this year I have made the academy a self-supporting institution. We have a little more than 50 students, and the fees which they pay for tuition, plus the fees which a rather smaller number pay for their living quarters, enable us to run the whole school and to pay something that begins to be decent salaries. In a very uncertain world, no one can tell how long this will last. But actually there is no reason why we should not get even more students, since we are only just beginning to be known throughout the country and the rest of the world. The gratifying thing is that for a graduate school to be self-supporting is felt to be something of a miracle, for such institutions do not usually exist without large endowment. In all this I have had the help of two former students who have been working their heads off to make a go of it, Lois Thille the secretary and registrar, and Bill Swartley the house manager. For the past year, Louis Gainsborough has been able to put in very little money, since the expenses of the first two years almost broke him. But he has taken the risks in some of the gambles we had to make, and now that things are running themselves he is finding time to go back into his business and improve his fortunes. It has meant an enormous amount of work, but it is mostly so interesting and worthwhile that I don't regret it at all. I really think we have succeeded in bringing to birth a school of Oriental studies which has nothing quite like it anywhere else in the world.

Some weeks ago I was in touch again with Mr. Richardson who asked you for a photograph, so now he has one. As to the royalties from John Murray, I had imagined that you had used them for your trip out here. This was always my intention, and though books would certainly be welcome, I am sure that you could use the money yourselves and would love to have you do so. Over all these years I have been able to contribute so little to you, and I would feel very happy if you would accept it all as a gift for this Christmas. Thanks so much for renewing *The Listener*. I still read it regularly and carefully, for it is one of my main sources of "outside news." Thank you also for the announcement of Francis Crowdy's engagement. If this is his first marriage, he has certainly been a long time in making up his mind! I am glad that this very wet English summer has at least been of benefit to your garden. I have heard such bitter complaints about it from Rom Landau, who writes me often from Devonshire. He is coming over here permanently in January, and I have been helping him with his immigration papers... I think you know we are expecting another baby sometime in January. Big families seem to be becoming "the thing" again, especially out here. And now that the academy is so well on its way, I don't feel so anxious about it.

Very much love to you both from us all,

As always, Alan

The address of the following shows that by this point Jacquie Baxter had married Harry Doolittle. She never married John (Jock) Gouldin.

THE AMERICAN ACADEMY OF ASIAN STUDIES | SAN FRANCISCO, CALIFORNIA | NOVEMBER 3, 1954
Mrs. Harry Doolittle | New York, New York
Dear Jacquie:

I wish I had time at the moment to answer your delightful letter with suitable illuminations. But since you need the enclosed, I'm getting this nearly perfunctory reply off at once.

Thanks very much for the news of Em [Emerson Harris]. I'm about to see one of his teachers on Sunday, to wit, Stella Kramrisch, but be sure to give him my congratulations and very best wishes. Bob Platman is in Syosset, Long Island. I think the Episcopal Church of St. Bede is a sufficient address.

I note that your letter came in an envelope bearing the address of Ted Bates. What is your connection with this outfit? One of Eleanor's cousins, Walker Everett, used to be a big shot in the firm and handled the account for some inflated fluff called "Wonder Bread."

Thanks very much indeed for all you are doing to spread the news of our work. We certainly need to be better known on the East Coast and these kinds of contacts are very valuable.

Things occasionally go "whoomph" in the night when Pins, our chief tomcat, makes a false step while trying to raid the kitchen.

With love from us all, Alan W. Watts, Dean

THE AMERICAN ACADEMY OF ASIAN STUDIES | NOVEMBER 15, 1954
Mrs. Harry Doolittle | New York, New York
Dear Jacquie:

Thanks for your letter about Ch'ao-Li. I have no immediate contact with anyone in Washington who might help him, but since there are already fifty people trying to influence the immigration authorities it would be as well not to add any more. Government circles sometimes get ornery when too much pressure is applied. However, I presume he is in touch with the China Institute in New York City. They have Chinese Nationalist funds and are very influential indeed.

In any case, you might keep me notified of the progress of his case, and if there is time let me know a little bit more about him personally, as I have a kind of collector's interest in Chinese scholars.

With love and best wishes, as ever,

Alan W. Watts, Dean

AMERICAN ACADEMY OF ASIAN STUDIES | SAN FRANCISCO,
CALIFORNIA | JANUARY 12, 1955
E. C. Peters, Esq. | Thames & Hudson, Ltd. | London, England
Dear Mr. Peters:

Thank you very much indeed for your letter of December 30th, enclosing the interesting article by Arnold Toynbee. I feel that his position is sufficiently close to my own that I could only take issue with it on rather minor points, but I was certainly glad to read it.

I am not at this moment at work on any new book, but I am making many preparatory studies for what will probably be a two-volume work on Zen Buddhism, with the assistance of a number of collaborators. The first volume will be an interpretative study, and the second an anthology of translations from original sources. It will be a fairly scholarly work and I do not know whether you would be interested in this kind of thing. Routledge have already expressed their interest in it, but if you think there is any chance of it being suitable for their list I would give you the first opportunity for the English market, and have informed Routledge accordingly.

Would you be so kind as to let me know when I might expect any royalties from *Myth & Ritual*? I have already received those for the American edition, but I do not know at what times of the year you are accustomed to make payments.

With all good wishes, sincerely yours,

Alan W. Watts, Dean

AMERICAN ACADEMY OF ASIAN STUDIES | SAN FRANCISCO,
CALIFORNIA | JANUARY 24, 1955
E. C. Peters, Esq. | Thames & Hudson, Ltd. | London, England
Dear Mr. Peters:

Thank you very much for your kind letter of January 19th. In view of your interest in the work on Zen, I will certainly let you see it first before other English publishers and will also keep you informed about other writing projects which may actually mature before this one.

As to the royalties on *Myth & Ritual*, I am wondering whether you would be so kind as to ask the accounts department if they could expedite payment as it would be a great help at a time of the year when one is suffering from the after-effects of Christmas and the imminence of a new baby!

With all good wishes, very sincerely yours,

Alan W. Watts, Dean

The following is an invitation addressed to "Henry Miller, Big Sur, Calif."

The American Academy of Asian Studies
A School of the College of the Pacific
San Francisco, California

ALAN W. WATTS
Dean of the Academy
will give a public lecture at
THE CARMEL WOMEN'S CLUB
Friday, April 29th, 8:00 PM
"DEPTH PHILOSOPHY"
In the cultures of Asia there are various forms of "psychotherapy,"
such as Zen Buddhism, which suggest that conflicts and disorders
of the mind arise from confused premises of thinking
rather than repressed emotional experiences.

Tickets ($1.50 each) may be obtained at Lial's Music Store on Ocean Avenue in
Carmel, or at the time of the lecture.

AMERICAN ACADEMY OF ASIAN STUDIES | SAN FRANCISCO,
CALIFORNIA | JUNE 9, 1955
Mrs. Kurt Wolff | Pantheon Books, Inc. | New York, New York
Dear Helen:
I am afraid you haven't heard from me for a long time, since my circus has developed a fourth ring and writing seems to be the last thing I can get to. However, I am enclosing herewith two unedited transcripts of radio talks in the Great Books of Asia series, for your meditations and comments.

Would you ask your shipping department to let me have five copies of Anne Lindbergh's *Gift from the Sea* and charge it to my account? This is a very charming book and one of these days I would love to meet its author.

With all good wishes to you both, very sincerely,
Alan W. Watts, Dean

AMERICAN ACADEMY OF ASIAN STUDIES | SAN FRANCISCO,
CALIFORNIA | JULY 26, 1955
Mr. Kurt Wolff | Pantheon Books, Inc. | New York, New York
Dear Kurt,
I have been approached by a New York publishing firm, unknown to me, as to whether I would be willing to let them republish an old book of mine entitled *The Legacy of Asia and Western Man* — a book for which some relatively small demand has existed since it went out of print during the war. Apparently there

are a number of firms specializing in reprints of this kind and I have assumed that this type of publishing is somewhat outside of your sphere of interest. The firm in question is called University Books, Inc., in New York City, and the man who writes to me is a Mr. Jay Dreyer. I would be very grateful indeed if you could let me know anything about the reputation of this concern.

I'm giving some serious thought to the possibility of writing a book along the lines which you suggested, as I do want to keep up my association with you and am very eager to find time to write down some of the many things on my mind. But I seem to be in a phase when life has presented me with material, rather than verbal, problems.

I think you are right in feeling that the talks on the Great Books of Asia should be accompanied by the texts which they discuss, but it is obvious that this would involve a very expensive kind of book. The radio talks on the Great Books of Asia have produced an enormous correspondence and innumerable requests for having them in published form, but probably it would be just as well to turn them off on the mimeograph.

With all good wishes to you both, very sincerely,

Alan W. Watts, Dean

AMERICAN ACADEMY OF ASIAN STUDIES | SAN FRANCISCO, CALIFORNIA | AUGUST 1, 1955

Dear Henry [Miller],

I'm sorry we couldn't get together Sunday because there were several things I wanted to talk to you about.

First of all, I'm sending under separate cover six copies of *The Way of Liberation in Zen Buddhism*. These retail at $1.00 each, less 20 percent to the profession, but maybe we can make a swap for some of your things I don't have.

Eve told me of your projected trip to the Orient and suggested the idea of our renting your place [in Big Sur] while you were away, if this would be satisfactory to you. Certainly we would like to consider the idea if we can't find a place of our own any sooner.

With all good wishes, sincerely yours,

Alan W. Watts

JW: In the summer of 1955 I visited my mother and Carlton in Colorado Springs. Carlton, by now, was dean of the music department at Colorado College. My half-brother, Michael, was six years old, and behaved just as one would expect of a six-year-old boy. I enjoyed the more settled lifestyle and, to Alan's dismay (although, I think also, with some relief), I chose to live my senior year in high school with my mother. Anne was still living in England with his parents.

Alan and Dorothy moved again, this time to a small house in a wooded area on the flats of Mill Valley. Alan's personal stationery letterhead called the place "Four Pines." Dorothy presented Alan with yet another child, Richard (Rickey), born in February 1955. Alan's schedule kept him on the go and out of town much of the time. I visited there briefly, for after my graduation from high school, I was sent off to Japan to live in my grandmother's subtemple, Ryosen-an, in Daitoku-ji Temple, Kyoto. I was to study sumi-e (Japanese brush painting), pottery making, and the Japanese language. The irony was that I would visit Japan before Alan.

Alan was, during his heavy travel schedule, writing what was to become possibly his best-known book, The Way of Zen. *He asked me to take photographs of the famous rock garden at Ryoan-ji Temple to include in his book. His writing and lecturing was garnering national attention along with that of several other proponents of Buddhism, and Zen was beginning to be somewhat of a fad.* Time *magazine published an article in their February 4, 1957, issue about the burgeoning interest in Zen Buddhism, crediting Alan Watts, the First Zen Institute in Manhattan, Ruth Sasaki at the Kyoto branch of the institute, and D. T. Suzuki at Columbia University as interpreters of Zen to avid students and followers through lectures and meditation.*

It was then that a US naval officer, moonlighting as a correspondent for Time, *interviewed my grandmother for the above-mentioned article and introduced me to a fellow officer, LTJG John Sudlow. I was married in Grandmother Ruth's grand style in the only Catholic cathedral in Kyoto, Japan, in late summer of 1957. Alan wrote me a cautionary letter about marrying someone of the Catholic faith.*

Time *published a subsequent article, "Zen: Beat and Square" in their July 21, 1958, issue, which quotes Alan as saying, "For Anglo-Saxons the main obstacle to the achievement of Zen's peace is an inability to purge themselves of the need for self-justification. This urge to prove oneself right has always jiggled the Chinese sense of the ludicrous. The Chinese [who] rated human-heartedness ahead of righteousness, felt that one could not be right without also being wrong. At the roots of Chinese life there is a trust in the good and evil of one's own nature, which is peculiarly foreign to those brought up with the chronic uneasy conscience of the Hebrew-Christian cultures."*

During this period, when Alan was working on The Way of Zen, *there are a number of letters from Ruth, answering Alan's queries about aspects of Zen as related by ancient Chinese scholars, about which she was becoming quite the authority. Unfortunately, he didn't make copies of the letters he sent her. During this written exchange, Ruth apparently hinted that she would be ordained. It is remarkable that the two of them maintained a professional, though somewhat guarded, relationship throughout their lives.*

Alan's dear friend Sabro Hasegawa died in March 1957. He was a man Alan greatly admired, who taught him calligraphy and from whom he learned much about Japanese culture. Around this time Alan began to wear a kimono (in honor of Hasegawa), finding this form of clothing far more comfortable than the traditional Western-style trousers, ties, and suit jackets which were quite constricting.

It was on the heels of publishing The Way of Zen *that Alan had begun a new book for Pantheon:* Nature, Man and Woman. *With so many demands on his time, he was finding it difficult to finish the manuscript. It seems, though, that he was getting quite a bit of help with the book from a woman who was considered an inspiration for the work.*

During the mid-1950s, Alan became interested in Aldous Huxley's experimentation with psychedelic drugs, specifically mescaline, about which Huxley wrote in his book The Doors of Perception *(1954). This led to Alan's own experimentation, especially as it related to religious experience and psychosis. Huxley and Gerald Heard were suggesting that the use of psychedelics in treatment of psychotic patients might be productive. In the late fall of 1957, Alan was asked to fill in as a speaker for Huxley at a symposium of psychiatrists in Los Angeles regarding the use of consciousness-changing drugs and religious experience.*

THE AMERICAN ACADEMY OF ASIAN STUDIES | SAN FRANCISCO, CALIFORNIA | JULY 28, 1956
Mr. and Mrs. Kurt Wolff | Pantheon Books, Inc. | New York, New York
Dear Kurt and Helen:
You should be receiving the typescript of *The Way of Zen* on Monday morning, about the same time as this letter. I think it is rather longer than it looks, for it contains a lot of quotations which have been typed in single spacing.

I am quite pleased with it, and as it represents the outcome of more than twenty years' study on my favorite subject, I shall naturally assist you to the utmost in "blowing its trumpet"! I plan to come to NY for lectures at the time of publication, and then get back here as soon as copies reach the coast. I will arrange with Lengfeld of Books Inc., and with Harry Hill in Los Angeles to give special displays, and I am sure both will get time for it on their radio and TV outlets. The initial sales should be quite high in this area, and we will use our three to four thousand mailing list at the academy for an advance notice.

Although it is not as popular in style as *The Wisdom of Insecurity* or Herrigel's book, it is [at] about the same level as my *Myth and Ritual*, which has done rather well. It can be represented as the only comprehensive introduction to the subject, and the only standard work readily available. (Suzuki's books are only published in England, and are always going out of print.) Libraries should be advised of its "standard" character, as well as of its complete bibliography.

Now as to various matters of detail:

Illustrations: The last chapter really needs some illustrations to go with it — from four to six at the least. If you feel that the extra cost is justified, I can supply the photographs by the end of August at the latest.

Chinese characters: I hope the inclusion of a few Chinese characters will not make it look too formidable. But the book is supposed to be useful for the more scholarly reader as well as the layman, and romanized Chinese terms are terribly ambiguous. At the end of the MS you will find a list of all the characters needed, which can be sent to the firm supplying the type. If there is any difficulty about this, I can obtain the type here, or have the characters written for photographic reproduction. The MS includes them in the text, but, if you think it better, they can go to the foot of the page, or be put in a special appendix at the end.

Format: I would like to make some suggestions about the format — especially the dust jacket — which should have an "authentic" character, especially in view of the interest in Zen in the art world. One could make a very attractive calligraphic jacket with the two words "Zen Tao" (i.e., "The Way of Zen"), and am sure Sabro Hasegawa would do this for me. (Ask John Cage about him.) Otherwise, we could use a black-and-white *ʒenga*-style drawing by one of the old masters.

Index: I will prepare this as soon as page proofs are available.

Supplementary material: In due course I will send you a suggestion for the "blurb" and a list of acknowledgements. There will not be many of the latter, as very few modern authors are quoted, and I have done almost all the translations for the original texts myself. Are books published in English in Japan copyrighted in the US? I have quoted a number of Blyth's translations of haiku, but should probably ask his permission as a matter of courtesy.

I have just had a very pleasant letter from Anya Seton Chase, who mentions having seen you recently.

With very best wishes from us all, most cordially, Alan

MILL VALLEY, CALIFORNIA | AUGUST 30, 1956
Mr. Donald Ludgin | Field Enterprises, Inc. | Chicago, Illinois
Dear Mr. Ludgin:
Herewith is the article on Easter which you requested for *The World Book Encyclopedia*, together with a list of sources.

As I did not have a list of related subjects with your specifications, I was not quite sure how much I should explain such terms as Mass, Good Friday, equinox, etc. However, if I have said too much about some of these things, you can cut them down and refer to the other articles in question.

Your request for a section on Easter in the Arts has me puzzled. Almost every important painter has treated the Resurrection, if he painted religious subjects at all, and if he lived before 1500! So I am not quite sure what you want in this respect. It seems more of a subject for an art historian than for one whose field is primarily the history of religions.

I have tried to avoid anything that would arouse controversy in dealing with the religious aspects of the subject. A good deal of information about these is unavoidable in such an article, since the feast of Easter has much more of a religious character than Christmas, and many more special religious observances connected with it. Furthermore, it seems to me essential to say something about the activities of Holy Week preceding Easter, as the theme of death-and-resurrection is very much of a piece.

Sincerely yours, Alan Watts

THE AMERICAN ACADEMY OF ASIAN STUDIES | SAN FRANCISCO, CALIFORNIA | NOVEMBER 7, 1956
Dear Mummy & Daddy:
I'm sorry to be late again, but our affairs are still unsettled — like everything else in the world! Mr. Gainsborough has halfway resigned, but in such a fashion that we are at the moment without any responsible head of the organization — making it impossible for me to raise funds and get lots of the important work done. Furthermore, it seems that he may renege on his resignation as chairman of the board. Tonight we are having a meeting of the Directors of the Friends of the Academy, to see if we can work out any solution. I am afraid I am dealing with an utterly unreasonable man, who would rather see the work collapse than run by anyone but himself.

To add to the problems, Mr. Hasegawa, our beloved Japanese art professor, has a very serious cancer condition, and although he has just undergone a major operation, the doctors feel that it has spread too far to be of much use. Fortunately he has made so many friends since he has been here that many people are doing their utmost to help him and his family.

We continue to get excellent news of Joan in Japan, where she seems to be maturing rapidly. Ruth is so pleased with her that she may prolong her stay. Little Tia is making very interesting progress with her painting and writing, and has drawn some really marvelous cats.

I am very busy getting out another small booklet, to be ready in time for people to buy it for Christmas — this time on "Eastern Philosophy & Western Psychology." My new Zen book [*The Way of Zen*] is to come out in March, and as soon as proofs are ready — by the end of this month — we shall begin making arrangements for an English edition. Sales on *Myth and Ritual* have rather trailed off, but this one should at least have a large initial sale in England, and I will turn it all over to you.

I heard first about Uncle Harry from Ann, and I'm afraid he must be terribly missed. What is Joy doing? Where is she living now? Is she staying on at Garden Road? I must, I'm afraid, stop, as a student is just coming in to see me, and the day's work gets under way.

Lots of love from us all, Alan

THE AMERICAN ACADEMY OF ASIAN STUDIES | SAN FRANCISCO, CALIFORNIA | DECEMBER 16, 1956

Dear Mummy & Daddy:

Sorry to have had to have been holding off for so long, but we have been in a stupendous mess with the academy. However, today seems to have brought some clarification, and I think we have a new president, a new treasurer (praise be!), though still the same old chairman — considerably curtailed in power. His last acts as treasurer have been to keep my pay back; hence the delay. Will you please call Toby when you can and tell him that our new president is none other than Ernest Wood. He's a very fine old gentleman: honest as a rock, and an excellent head for business. His wife is a perfectly charming Britisher (so's he for that matter), so that with myself and Rom Landau this is really becoming the Anglo-American Academy of Asian Studies!

But with all these problems we are even more behind-hand than usual with preparations for Christmas. I am sending things off to you this week, and in the meantime am adding $10.00 to the check for Ann so that she can get something for herself in England, with no duties. I will write her this week.

I haven't seen the Tillys yet, but have talked with Dorothy on the phone. I think she is going away again, but I know I shall see Margaret very soon.

Despite all the problems, my Dorothy and the family are in really wonderful shape. Day by day Tia is practically teaching herself to read and write, without the slightest effort or push from us. Mark is all muscle, and it looks as though we may have an extremely husky young man on our hands. Rickey is beginning to say sentences now, but his greatest delight is to push around a model lorry which thunders through the house with almost as much noise as a real one. (Incidentally, he learned to walk on a sloping path, and I think it would be almost true to say that he learned to run before he could walk.) Several mothers in the neighborhood have formed a "playgroup" and we all take turns in having a bunch of pre-school children together for the morning twice a week.

Like you, Margaret and Dorothy Tilly were very alarmed about the international situation, but, strange to say, the American press has had no "war scare" at all. The situation is very strange, for there has been some well-informed talk about the US and Russia making a deal together to finance the building of the new Aswan Dam. What of our president's attitude? Well, I didn't vote for him! We think quite highly of Mr. Stevenson, but are afraid that after two tries he will not get another chance.

I have to get ready to go to the meeting at which we shall be hearing about the final arrangements for the academy's new regime. So — this will be to wish you all a most happy Christmas. Whatever happens, don't worry about me, for if the academy runs into difficulty I have other things lined up. Do give our love to Ann. Tia has just made her the most priceless Christmas card — with Ann and her granny standing beside Christmas trees. Only she drew both of them without any clothes on. "Tia, I don't think your granny will like that. I think you had better get both of them dressed." So on went the dresses, with a wiggly design.

Much love and a very happy Christmas from us all,

As always, Alan

THE AMERICAN ACADEMY OF ASIAN STUDIES | SAN FRANCISCO, CALIFORNIA | JANUARY 8, 1957

Dear Mummy & Daddy:

On my birthday we had Felix and Elena to dinner, and Felix told us that he is leaving for London on Thursday, and plans to see you all very soon. I have given him a little gift to convey to Ann.

For the time being, at any rate, the academy problems seem to be settled. Ernest Wood got the conditions he demanded to accept the presidency, and he and his perfectly charming wife are working together here. Richard Gump, the owner of a very sophisticated art, antique, china, and glass shop in San Fran, has become treasurer, with the result that almost all effective power is out of Gainsborough's hands — and I don't think he likes it very much. Especially as Wood listens to me and not to him. The problem now is to get ahead with raising money, and fortunately the Bollingen Foundation have come through with their promised $5,000 and another friend in New York has just given $3,000. So this is a good start for the year.

I have arranged a whole series of lectures for January and February (leaflet enclosed) and this does not include some special lectures for closed groups in Los Angeles and San Diego early in February. So I think things are shaping up pretty well.

I was very pleased to get Ann's last letter. There is a marked change in her handwriting, which has suddenly begun to mature, and the way she expresses herself has become much more grown-up, without losing a certain very delightful enthusiasm.

I do hope everything went off all right for your trip to see the *Yeomen of the Guard*. Your Christmas sounded a really fine old-style affair. By now you should have received the album of pictures I took of the children on Christmas morning. They were done in rather poor light with an extraordinary new type of film, which enabled me to take them as fast as 1/60 of a second, so that I could catch some "action."

I don't know how much rest I got over the holidays, as there were ever so many things to be done. I managed to prune five of the fruit trees (a new experience for me) but I have had a stiff neck and shoulder ever since. The rains are beginning to start now, and the view from my window here at the academy is quite lovely. A light rain has splashed the glass, the wind is rising, and I can see all colours of clouds over the mountains across the harbour. The sun comes through the clouds and has just picked out the village of Sausalito, which clings to the opposite slopes of the harbour right across from me.

Lots of love from us all, as always, Alan

THE AMERICAN ACADEMY OF ASIAN STUDIES | SAN FRANCISCO, CALIFORNIA | FEBRUARY 1, 1957
Dear Mummy & Daddy:
I have so many things to thank you for — first the delightful Fougasse book which has given us many a laugh. My favourite is the chipmunk (or maybe hamster) having a drink. Also I was delighted with Ann's *Hoffnung Orchestra*, and now with Mummy's very newsy letter of January 28th.

The enclosed page from *Time* will show you one reason why I am agog with activity. This coming Monday I go to Los Angeles for a series of private classes, three public lectures, a lecture at San Diego State College, and back to LA for still another lecture! Then at the end of April I plan to go to New York, since my book is due to come out on April 26th, and we are expecting that it will have a very considerable sale. I think Ruth's cryptic reference to surprising everyone means either (or both) that she is going to come out with a series of important translations or that she is going to be recognized as the first woman Zen master. The latter is just guessing, but she is *very* ambitious, and the top is none too high!

The academy's material situation is improving. Richard Gump is redecorating the interior of the building and new students and some money are coming in. However the atmosphere is not what it might be — getting a bit stodgy. With Hasegawa sick and Gi-ming Shien slow on his English there is no one on the faculty who has any real imagination — save some of the young instructors. I find them quite a drag. Wood, while having distinct advantages, is too old and too set in his ways to do anything very creative, and students and faculty find him difficult to get along with. So don't be surprised if one of these days I pull out and start something else. I am no believer in continuing institutions for their own sake, but I don't intend to make the jump until I have firm ground to land on.

Congratulations to Capt. Walpole, if and when he turns up in Chislehurst again. I like to see that sort of spirit in an old gentleman! And do please give my very best wishes to Mrs. Macfarlane. See if you can get the full name of Mr. Hills; it would be very easy to call them.

Lots of love from us all, Alan

THE AMERICAN ACADEMY OF ASIAN STUDIES | SAN FRANCISCO, CALIFORNIA | MARCH 14, 1957
Dear Mummy & Daddy:
Late again, I'm afraid! But there has been more complicated business about the academy, and Sabro Hasegawa died early this week and I am in charge of all the funeral arrangements. The poor man had the most terrible cancer of the sinus and neck. He leaves a wife and three children — twenty-two, sixteen, and fourteen — with no obvious means of support. The service is to be held tonight at the Japanese Zen temple.

I am going to New York about April 26th, and return May 5th. I think I shall be quite busy there as several lectures have been arranged, including two for the general public. Then I come back by way of southern California for still other lectures at Pomona College! Such a chatterbox, but people seem to enjoy it.

The academy really has me puzzled. Although with Ernest Wood as president, things are in some ways more stable, and this year — due, however, to my efforts — there is rather more money available, the atmosphere of the place is deteriorating and becoming very formal and prissy. Wood is such an honorable old fellow that it is intensely difficult to criticize him, and his years make it hard for him to change. I have suggested that he take charge of the overall business administration while I handle the academic side, but the president of the College of the Pacific has declared that he will not stand for me in any administrative position at all. Otherwise the college will dissolve its connection with us. The root of the matter is that COP is a very mediocre, small-town college, quite terrified of anything imaginative. Many of us think we should be much better off without them.

I think I am now in a position where I could afford to pull out of the whole thing, which would just about wreck the institution, but I really hesitate to be so violent since the work means a lot to many people, and we have some splendid students. It is quite astounding to be in a position where you supply both the money and the brains of an organization, yet cannot formulate its policy!

We have had a long spell of rain, and the grass gets higher and higher, but too wet to mow. Trees are in blossom again, and fortunately the neighbors' three white ducks are busily eating up a plague of snails — just when I was beginning to wonder how on earth to get rid of them!

Last week Mark started in a new play school where he goes five mornings a week. There are no children his age in the immediate area, and so this is a means of finding friends for him. He has become very particular about his clothes, and simply loves to dress "nattily." It's really quite funny, since he carries it off with some style. And it isn't as if he were foppish. I never saw such a husky little boy. Tia goes to a painting class every Saturday and does amazing abstractions, but, fortunately, can also handle other styles as well, though I think this work gives her a fine sense of space and design.

No word from Joan for some time. Hope all goes along well with her. It's nearly time to leave for the city, so I must close with lots of love from us all,

As always, Alan

The following letter was sent to Joan in Kyoto, Japan.

THE AMERICAN ACADEMY OF ASIAN STUDIES | SAN FRANCISCO, CALIFORNIA | APRIL 22, 1957

Dearest Joan:

Thank you for your most interesting and very beautifully written letter about John [Sudlow]. If he's as nice as his picture you're doing fine. In any case, you know my attitude: it's your life and it's now up to you to choose whoever you want, and I will naturally welcome him as a son-in-law. If there is a question of formal permission, just let me know when the date is fixed.

I think you know, too, that I hold the Roman Catholic Church in high respect, though not the version of it which flourishes for the most part in the United States — which is really Jansenist and more or less heretical. It lacks the humane sunlight of the Mediterranean, and has absorbed much too much of the native Puritanism of the cold North. Catholicism is excellent when taken, as in the South, rather lightheartedly, with a touch of gentle cynicism about the clergy, and with full reservation of one's right to interpret its doctrines in the light of one's own intelligence. This attitude is not insincere so much as it is mature. It is the simple recognition of the fact that no person of culture and intelligence can go along 100 percent with a Church which is both a spiritual society and a vast political machine. At the same time, one is not so naive as to renounce and reject it just because it involves a lot of all-too-human folly.

This is why born Catholics are usually so much nicer people than converts. They are not using the Church so much to bolster their own sense of inner in-security. They therefore tend to lack what is, for me, the most unfortunate and, indeed, childish aspect of Christianity — the insistence on being the rightest religion in the world. This kind of overweening zeal always betrays an inner lack of faith. An extremely strong sales pitch is needed only for an inferior product!

As to your own situation there are some things I might say only because you have asked my advice. And these are merely warnings about certain pitfalls which lie in the course you are taking. Other courses would have other pitfalls.

Becoming a Roman Catholic, especially in the United States, is a step for which one should have pretty good reasons — as distinct from rationalizations. You are obviously in danger of taking this step (a) because you are in love with a Catholic, and (b) because you may need to show your independence of a family of Buddhists, infidels, agnostics, and whatnots.

Taken for these reasons, the step will certainly lead to conflict later on. (That may, of course, be okay — for there is always conflict about something.) But the trouble is that they make your choice of the Church automatic rather than free, and this, by the Church's own standards, is unfortunately sinful. Of course, its own marriage laws lay the Church wide-open to this abuse, which only goes to show that they have the propagandist purpose of increasing numbers, rather than the sincere intent of winning souls.

Reason (b), which I detect in what you say about Happy Valley [School], is just cutting off your nose to spite your face. Of course, everyone needs to show some independence of their family and upbringing. But it is pretty costly, to yourself, to do this by assuming what will later be the suffocating role of the stuffed shirt — (i.e., to offset HV's phoney Bohemianism). I am not saying that Catholicism, even Jansenist, and stuffiness necessarily go together; only that you yourself have a slight tendency in this direction. Forgive me this criticism, for it is perhaps my own fault!

However, these dangers are serious only to the degree that you and John might take your Catholicism without humor, with excessive zeal, and with overmuch respect for what comes from the pulpit. But if you can take the birth-control nonsense with a grain of salt, you should be able to do so in other matters as well.

I could wish, of course, that you would not have to identify yourself with any "-ism," nor have your mind stamped with any ready-made pattern of ideas

— which goes for Zen as much as for Catholicism. But, as you know from HV days, this too can be an affectation!

If the tone of what I have said about the Church sounds a bit on the flip and cynical side, it is only because it would take me a great deal of time to dwell on the more positive aspects. And then I would only be saying again what I said in *Myth & Ritual*. I wish you read books! At this distance it's the only way of communicating with you.

I have sent you *The Way of Zen* with many thanks for your help in getting me those pictures of Ryoan-ji. I'm also sending you a few things to be mounted kakemono style [traditional Japanese style, in a paper scroll rather than framed]. The two longish pieces of calligraphy, from Dogen, belong to the Davenports. Have them done with the same color. For the rest, I trust your judgement. Does it add very much to the cost to have them boxed [in a slim cedar or sandalwood box designed to fit the scroll]? If so, just send them plain. And send me the bill.

I'm off to NY for a week on Thursday — will be stopping with Ruth [Goodkind] in Winnetka, and returning the following weekend via Los Angeles, where I am to talk to the Canterbury Club (!) at Pomona College.

Give my very best wishes to John. Also to Granny [Ruth Sasaki], hoping she feels better, and looking forward to hearing from her. Send me one of your tea bowls if you can.

Lots and lots of love from all, as always, Daddy

JW: I was married to LTJG John Sudlow in August of 1957. Alan did not come to Japan for the wedding to give me away. In order to be married in the Catholic Church (even in Japan), I had to convert to Catholicism. Somehow, my grandmother came up with an Irish priest from the Maryknoll Mission in Kyoto who provided the appropriate catechism to enable me to be formally baptized as a Catholic. The lessons were private — over breakfast — at his offices. I remember he smothered his scrambled eggs with catsup, something I had never seen done. I was horrified! He was equally horrified when, during his teaching, he had to discuss sex with me, explaining that the act of coitus was strictly for creating a child. I, in my innocence, asked how one would handle the sexual needs of a husband if sexual activity was so limited. He turned beet-red and told me I shouldn't concern myself with such things.

We were married in the very beautiful (seventeenth-century, I believe) St. Francis Xavier Cathedral in Kyoto, with an odd assortment of guests, dressed to the teeth. Included were John's naval friends and associates stationed in Kobe, and many of Granny Ruth's Japanese and foreign friends involved with the First Zen Institute in Japan. My sister Anne and my mother Eleanor came over from the States for the wedding. None of John's family (Catholics all) attended.

Needless to say, some things never last. The cathedral was torn down some years later, and my marriage to John lasted twelve years. As my father predicted, the dichot-omy between my straight side and my bohemian side caught up with me, and I found the corporate lifestyle suffocating. Out of the frying pan and into the fire, I married a Catholic Marianist monk who had left the Church, and we fled the Midwest for California in a Volkswagen camper with three children, a dog, two cats, and a gerbil. Sound familiar?

MILL VALLEY, CALIFORNIA | MAY 13, 1957

Dear Mummy & Daddy:

Here is the check for Ann: $30.00 for May, plus $72.80, which is the equivalent of £26. I think for some of these things, especially extras, we should draw on Ann's savings account here, which we opened for the purpose of giving her funds for things she really needed, instead of running downtown and frittering it away on gum-balls. I think everything will go all right, but the future is somewhat uncertain because, unless a miracle happens, I am going to leave the academy. The situation is absolutely out of hand, and the new regime is forcing through a program which is merely silly. While I was in NY I got an offer for the academy of $20,000 — to be given if I would give the work my personal approval. But I cannot do so, and even $20,000 won't make them change their minds about the new program.

However, the trip was otherwise very successful. My lectures were crowded, Pantheon gave me a contract for a new book, *The Way of Zen* had sold 1,500 copies on the day of publication (without even any reviews yet), and two of my other books are to appear in paper-cover cheap editions. It is quite apparent that lecturing is my best source of income, and I can do a great deal more of this without the academy on my shoulders. Cornell University has invited me for a week in November, so I shall make another round of lectures in New York City at that time.

As you may have heard, Joan is making serious plans to get married. Ruth seems to approve very much of the young man — at present an officer in the US Navy. He is, however, a Catholic and Joan is inclined to become a Catholic — at least for the purposes of this marriage. Fortunately, he does not appear to be a particularly rabid Catholic. Thus I have raised no objections on this score; and, in any case, raising objections is one of the fastest ways of getting nowhere! Ruth has written me an immensely long letter about his background, and she has even gone so far as to have her lawyers check up on his family. The name is John Sudlow — originally of Polish descent — and from all accounts he sounds, and looks, a very nice fellow. They plan to live in Japan until his time with the navy is over, and then to return to Chicago, where he expects to go into business.

I really had a delightful time on this trip. I saw Ruth (Goodkind) Roberg and her husband in Chicago, spending the weekend with them, and met all kinds of fascinating people in New York. Kurt and Helen Wolff, of Pantheon, arranged a cocktail party for me, to which most of the Bollingen Foundation people came — and I had a long, long talk with the very charming man who directs it, Jack Barrett. They have long-range plans for a marvelous research institute, in which I may perhaps become involved. We shall see, but it will take some time. The flight back was really thrilling — 8 hours from NY to Los Angeles, with the whole varied panorama of the country rolling below. This always gives me the funny feeling that I am living in the future.

This June we are all going up to Lake Tahoe in the Sierra for two weeks, where I am to take part in a philosophy institute, and then the family will go to Santa Barbara while I do a week of lecturing in Los Angeles, followed by another week in Santa Barbara itself. A friend is lending us a beach cottage there. After that I must come home and start writing the next book!

Mummy, are you recovering all right from that horrible contretemps with the gate? Good old Pond's Extract is quite a charm, and I still keep it handy here.

Lots and lots of love to you all, as ever, Alan

JW: There were several interesting reviews of The Way of Zen. *One in* The New York Times *(August 5, 1957) was very complimentary. It was by Joseph Campbell, who wrote, "*The Way of Zen *[is] the most readable systematic introduction to Far Eastern thought now available." But in* The Middle Way *(the journal of the Buddhist Society of London), Sohaku Ogata (a Zen priest at Chotoku-in, Shokoku-ji Temple, Kyoto) wrote, "Although this is certainly the best book that had been written by any Westerner who has not gone through the [Zen] training, it was like an artist drawing a big cat instead of a tiger." In his autobiography, Alan countered, "But indeed, one of Zen Master Sengai's paintings shows a tiger being scared by a cat!" He notes another in the* London Observer *as "a marvelous review of* The Way of Zen *by Philip Toynbee."*

OCTOBER 29, 1957 | THE AMERICAN ACADEMY OF ASIAN STUDIES | SAN FRANCISCO, CALIFORNIA
Mrs. Helen Wolff | Pantheon Books | New York, New York
Dear Helen:
I'm afraid that the time for my visit to New York is approaching extremely rapidly, that during the past week I have been slowed down with a horrible cold, and

that during my recent trip to Los Angeles there were too many distractions to do as much writing as I had intended. All this means, I fear, that I am not going to be able to come to New York with the completed manuscript, and naturally I am terribly sorry to disappoint you, as well as to destroy my reputation for being the man who always makes the deadline. I am disturbed as to whether this will put you to any serious inconvenience, since I know you plan things so far ahead.

However, I do feel that the book would be greatly improved if I could give it a little more time, even if this were to mean postponement of publication until the fall of 1958.

In the meantime, I want to thank you very much indeed for the help which you have given in connection with my forthcoming New York lectures, and I am looking forward very much to seeing you both again in a couple of weeks' time. I shall be staying, as before, at Charlotte Selver's place.

With very best wishes,

As ever, Alan W. Watts

PS. Will you check with your mailing department as to whether copies of *The Supreme Identity* and *The Way of Zen* were mailed to a Mr. Alexander Baillie, Honolulu. I had thought I had asked you to send them sometime during the summer.

MILL VALLEY, CALIFORNIA | DECEMBER 2, 1957

Dear Mummy & Daddy:

Since I returned from New York we have been battling with flu in the family, though not the Asian kind, and I have been trying to catch up with all the chores that have piled up in my absence. However, I had a very fruitful trip, visiting Cincinnati, New York, Ithaca (Cornell University), and Los Angeles, where I spoke to a meeting of the American Psychiatric Association. The lectures were almost all crowded, and the last one in NY had them standing! Pantheon asked me to join them as an associate editor, working on my own time to find books for them and to watch their interests here in California, and this will give me some stable income — since lecturing is always unpredictable.

I had a very fascinating time at Cornell, as one of a panel of three speakers for their Campus Conference on Religion. We had about 3,000 at the first meeting, and the visit concluded with a delightful dinner with six members of the faculty which was a real meeting of minds. In Los Angeles I was taking Aldous Huxley's place, talking to the psychiatrists about "consciousness-changing drugs and religious experience," since they have found that certain new drugs produce states that are extremely close to the mystical kind. Aldous was in NY and couldn't come.

I am planning a set of lectures in Hawaii at the end of March. After that, New York again at the end of April... and then, I have been corresponding with Dr. Eric Graham Howe (whom you may remember) about the possibility of a lecture series in London. There is as yet no fully workable plan for this, for the scheme which he has suggested would not pay for the trip, and it has to to justify it. Naturally, however, I would love to be able to do this, and I am wondering if you would know anyone or have any ideas as to how I might get some paid lecturing in England. Toby is no help since he is firmly opposed to charging admission for lectures of this kind. Meanwhile, I shall see if Thames & Hudson have any ideas, and will consult others here who give similar lectures in England. As I said, this is still only a notion; it may not be possible to carry it through, but it is certainly worth exploring.

All this fall I have been hard at work on a new book which is to come out in June with the title *Nature, Man and Woman*, a study of the Taoist philosophy of nature and its relation to love. I have had this book "up my sleeve" for years, and I think the time is now ripe for it. But it is not easy to write, and the going has been a little slow.

We have had some nice chatty letters from Ann, and at last we have heard from Joan, who seems to be extremely happy. They think they will return here at the end of January. The other children have been, aside from flu, doing very well. Mark is making extraordinary progress.

He can draw almost as well as Tia, and already makes some letters. Some time ago he constructed a "machine" in the garden to stop the rotation of the earth so that the sun wouldn't set! Some imagination! Lila Jean is now giggly and conversational, gruntishly, and continues to be very pretty. Rickey enters the mischievous state, and has learned how to climb shelves, very silently, and explore where he shouldn't.

Seems I am also going to get into television, as there are plans for a special series on Asian thought and culture, which will be filmed and distributed to stations all around the country. There's lots to do, but it's a great relief not to be tied anymore to the academy. Philip Wheelwright, a professor of philosophy at the University of California, says I'm the only philosopher he knows who — outside of university teaching — makes something of a living by philosophy!

All our love to you, my dears, and I hope the winter is not being too hard on you. I will do my best to make it to England next year, but I can't promise, so don't be too disappointed if it doesn't work out. (I tried once before, in the fall of 1956, but all the academy trouble came to a head, and it was impossible.)

As always, Alan

PS. I have just had an invitation to lecture at the C. G. Jung Institute in Zurich between April and July (my choice of times), and this may make things a lot easier. If you want to get in touch with Dr. Graham Howe, you can reach him in London.

MILL VALLEY, CALIFORNIA | DECEMBER 6, 1957
Dr. Jolande Jacobi | C. G. Jung Institut | Zurich, Switzerland
Dear Dr. Jacobi,
I am very much honored by your kind invitation of November 28th. I would indeed like to come to Zurich this next spring, and am wondering if it would be possible, in view of my rather crowded schedule, to give the lectures twice a week between May 5th and 24th? The terms which you offer seem perfectly reasonable.

The lectures would fit in very well with my tentative plans to lecture in London between April 21st and May 3rd.

I presume that what you would like would be a short course on Zen Buddhism, perhaps stressing its relations with some problems of psychotherapy. But if a more general theme would be welcome, I would suggest a series on the "Ways of Liberation in Eastern Philosophy."

Incidentally, your letter mentioned an enclosure, which was somehow left out.

Please let me know just as soon as you can whether these dates will be acceptable, since I also have to make arrangements for the London lectures.

With many thanks and all good wishes,

Yours sincerely, Alan Watts

AW: We were interested to note that, even though Alan had many lovers over the years, few love letters exist in this collection besides those to Jano, his third wife. We are left to surmise that if there were copies of any, Jano destroyed them. Alan did mention in a letter to his lover Jean Burden that sadly he had to burn all her letters to him. We later learned of his letters to Jean in the Jean Burden Collection at Syracuse University and we were able to include the following letter to her.

This letter to Jean Burden was written about a year or so into their relationship. The "knot" in her stomach was apparently due to the admission by Alan that on October 13, 1957, he had had a one-night stand with a "Miss D." In another letter from that time, Alan had written that early on he had learned to lie about such liaisons so as not to incur wrath for stating the truth. But he had decided to tell Jean the truth, and the truth made her physically ill. It seems that she had had another significant blow of some sort as a young woman that also occurred on October 13. She was shaken by the significance of the date. Despite his statement of love for Jean, he again compromised their relationship in 1959, when he confessed his love for Jano as the person he had waited for all his life, but beseeched her to not leave him, as he still loved her as well. Jean finally terminated their relationship in mid-1960.

Their correspondence during their four-year relationship fills a two-inch binder. He wrote Nature, Man and Woman *during his relationship with Jean and shared several chapters of the book for her comments prior to its publication. As has been mentioned here before, he dedicated the book to her in a cryptic poem. She in turn wrote a magnificent poem about him entitled "For a Sleeping Man," which was published in* Poetry *magazine in 1958. About it Alan commented, "What a voice you are!"*

MILL VALLEY, CALIFORNIA | TUESDAY [LATE 1957?]

Beloved Jeanie,

I simply can't find the heart to deal with the heap of stuff waiting on my desk while you have that knot in your stomach. I am "catching" it too, and since I talked with you last night you have, if possible, been more in my mind than ever, with those sad, loving eyes floating behind the film of the visible world. But I don't know what to do. You want to understand me. Does that mean to make one part of me consistent with another? Does it mean to explain me in such a way that my actions seem predestined by my past? Does it mean that I must defend myself to you and offer excuses? Somehow I don't think you want any of these, especially the last...I think, dearest, that we have moved into a new world in which I am as a little boy, and you a little girl. I don't say this, as it were, to offer the excuse of ignorance for irresponsibility, but rather that we are both perplexed before mysteries which almost no one can explain. But there is one thing I must say, however much it may sound like self-defense. I have told you that for 25 years or so I have been almost constantly fascinated and tormented by the psycho-physical beauty of women. I have never resorted to mere sex, with a partner whose personality was indifferent to me. But I have lived morning, noon, and night, with an utterly insatiable fascination, and until just a few years ago the opportunities to satisfy it were few — mostly because I was too inhibited. Now that I am older and less self-conscious (and also perhaps more attractive) I find myself surrounded by all-too-willing recipients of my desire, and the whole of my past rises up with glee and says, "*This* is what you have been waiting for!" And somehow it always seemed to me, in the past, that I had to be content with the somewhat less attractive women. As an adolescent it was impressed upon me that I was not the kind of man who was physically appealing to girls — that the beauties went to the handsome — and though I have long known that this isn't so, the feeling still lurks around. When I told my mother that I wanted to marry a really lovely woman, she pooh-poohed it and emphasized *character*. I said, "But I don't *want* an ugly wife!" "Well," she said, "of course I don't mean someone you have [to] seat with her back to the light at meals!" Another queer (i.e., inconsistent) thing is that I have always "lived every day as if thy last," in the sense that I have never felt that I was going to live much longer. Thus I have lived with love and with death, in a kind of Omar Khayyam atmosphere of rather awful and awesome intensity — when I must make haste because the caravan starts for the dawn of Nothing. All this will obviously explain the compelling attraction of a girl like "D.," but just as obviously, it is inconsistent with most of my philosophic position. Yet I understand and can explain the ins and outs of the vicious circle of samsara so well because I myself am such an example of it.

And now I have discovered you — the one and only woman for whom my *love* far exceeds my (not at all negligible) lust. This has never happened before, and it has caught me smack in the full momentum of my more characteristic pattern of cherchez la femme. For my inner life this is a head-on collision. For you it is a bewildering tangle with a runaway bandwagon with a harem on board. It will run some yards while the other girls tumble one after another to the road. In other words, I can only ask you to recognize the momentum in the man — met just at the time he was accelerating in the roaring forties.

But this will not at once make you feel any better, simply because you have been hit. Wounds don't just vanish immediately. I have hurt you and I cannot soothe the hurt except by a long work of love to which I shall devote the rest of my life, not out of pity, but with the utmost exuberant joy. For though we have begun with an awful wrench, there is not a shadow of doubt in my mind that you and I are to grow into each other endlessly.

Now I realize this begins to sound like a guilt-ridden confession with contrition and sincere promise of better things to come. I know you have told me that the knot in you isn't me but you, something you have to understand for yourself. For you, too, have your momentum — a pattern, which like mine, is unreasonable even by your own lights. By conditioning we are both to some extent "just male" and "just female" and,

Higgamus, hoggamus, girls are monogamous,

Hoggamus, higgamus, boys are polygamous.

But we mustn't get into the idiotic impasse wherein the more we try to explain things to each other, the more hurt and confused we become. This happens when people imagine that they *can* explain themselves, instead of saying, "Such knowledge is too wonderful for me; it is high, I cannot attain unto it...for I am fearfully and wonderfully made." Thus when I reread what I have written, I am half inclined to tear it up and begin again, and forbear only because I want, by writing, to be with you, and want you to feel my presence with you between the clumsy lines. I am, at the moment, a cloud of confusion in which the only clear thing is that I love you in a way that reduces even me to silence. I have spent my life trying to express inexpressible things, but this is too much for me. I give you everything — my confusion, my silence, my heartache, my foolishness, my perplexity to myself and to you — a collection like the contents of Hotei's bag. [Drawing of Hotei with bag below.] And in this wild assortment is the string that ties it all — the clear, strong, joyous certainty that you are the only person I love in the way I never believed it possible that *I* could love. Yes, I knew this last Sunday; but not with the clear, firm certainty that I know it now. I want to lay my hands and my lips upon that tight knot below your heart, and soothe you with all the tenderness and warmth that is in me. Jeanie, Jeanie, you are the dearest creature to me on earth. [...]

With all my heart I love you, I love you, Alan

PART VII

Further Writing
and Lecturing

1958–59

JW: In the spring of 1958, Alan went on an extended lecture tour to New York, London, and Zurich, ending at the University of Vermont, where he was awarded an honorary doctorate in divinity and delivered the baccalaureate speech at the school's 154th commencement.

At Cambridge, he had been invited by the faculties on theology, anthropology, and oriental studies to lecture, and said he had never met such an unresponsive audience in his life. He found during his time in England that everything was pretty much the same as he had left it back in the 1930s, that authors and journalists were still yearning for the imperial past, and that those academics in his particular field were sitting in a "tower of decaying ivory." Fortunately, it was quite the opposite in Zurich.

He found Zurich much more stimulating and to his liking. The C. G. Jung Institute was located in the old section of the city, which he found very charming. There he lectured to young students from all over Europe and America who were studying to become psychotherapists. This was the first opportunity he had to meet Carl Jung. He had attended one of his lectures in England back in the 1930s but had never actually met him. They spent several hours together at Jung's summer home on the edge of a lake in Küsnacht.

The following postcard was sent to his parents while in Zurich.

ZURICH, SWITZERLAND | APRIL 1958

Dear Mummy and Daddy,

I have been having a very busy time, all of it very interesting, though little opportunity for traveling about. Travel is expensive here. I have had a most fascinating conversation with Jung and spent yesterday with Count von Dürckheim, who is the main German authority on Zen. A most charming man.

Will be back Wednesday morning, and am flying in company with a most delightful old lady — the Hon. Mrs. Frost — from Devonshire.

Dorothy and the children are all well, and have acquired fifteen frogs for our stream! Mark sent me a wonderful drawing of the sun and planets, with their moons.

Was in Basel Saturday night having dinner with the prof. of psychiatry at the university. What a beautiful old city!

Lots of love, Alan

AW: In the late 1950s, Alan was introduced by his good friend Hilde Elsburg to Charlotte Selver. Alan described Charlotte as "exuding a bewitching tranquility, a profoundly interesting stillness." Hilde and Charlotte had studied a unique form of body awareness with Elsa Gindler in Germany. Alan had enormous respect for them both.

Hilde went to India to study with Sri Ramana Maharshi of Arunachala. Soon after, Alan and Charlotte began leading workshops together. They formed a deep friendship and lasting partnership, leading workshops primarily at Charlotte's studio in New York and at Esalen Institute in Big Sur, California.

Alan coyly remarks in his autobiography that he was falling in love "with a lady of unobtrusively aristocratic appearance, blond, Roman-nosed, thoughtful, and attentive, with open eyes rather than a frown, who kept turning up at our seminars." This was his first mention of Mary Jane Yates King, known as "Jano," who was to become his third wife.

By May 1958 Alan had clearly begun a deeply intimately relationship with Jano. He wrote the following poem on an American Airlines postcard, apparently while in flight. There will follow many other love letters.

One of these days I shall ride again
On this hot, sighing arrow
To take your whole living body in my arms,
And tell you, where breath mixes and eyes
    dare to touch
That then within my grasp there lies encircled
The last deep center,
The inmost star
To which my comet swings.

MILL VALLEY, CALIFORNIA | AUGUST 22, 1958
Mrs. Helen Wolff | Pantheon Books, Inc. | New York, New York
Dear Helen:
I have had a note from Kyrill, referring to a letter from Neurath and a reference to "The History of Hell." This is a book that Neurath suggested I write, and I

turned over the idea for a while in my mind while I was in England, but it doesn't particularly interest me and I'm not going to do it. On the other hand, I am cooking up quite a big idea for my next book, and I will talk to you about it when I am in New York.

I also received yours of the 19th. Never mind about the proofs [for *Nature, Man and Woman*]. I just wanted to be sure that some lines of verse from the Zenrin Kushu had been taken out and the dedicatory verse [a cryptic poem for Jean Burden] put in.

All the best, yours ever, Alan W. Watts

MILL VALLEY, CALIFORNIA | AUGUST 22, 1958
Lawrence Ferlinghetti | City Lights Books | San Francisco, California
Dear Mr. Ferlinghetti:
Thank you very much indeed for your letter of August 8. I am delighted to find someone who wants to publish little books in paper covers, for I am a confirmed pamphleteer. It is always possible to say almost everything in fifty pages, and I have often chided my New York publishers with encouraging authors to pad because of their practice of selling books by the pound.

I like your idea of making a booklet from an expanded version of the *Chicago Review* article. But I have also an enormous amount of material in typed script that has been used for talks over KPFA.

Will you therefore let me know when you return from Big Sur, so that we can look the material over together and decide which idea would be the better.

Another idea which occurs to me is that I have still a considerable number of copies of *The Way of Liberation in Zen Buddhism*, and we might be able to work out an arrangement whereby you could take over the distribution of this.

With all good wishes,
Very sincerely, Alan W. Watts

JW: The recommendations in Alan's long letter below, to his longtime friend Frederic Spiegelberg regarding Frederic's book The Religion of No-Religion, *nearly amounts to a rewrite. (The book was first published by James Delkin in 1948. It should not be confused with* Buddhism: The Religion of No-Religion, *a compilation of some of Alan's lectures that was edited by Mark Watts and published posthumously in 1995.) We see no response regarding this critique, but we do have a charming letter from Spiegelberg over a year later, with ecstatic compliments to Alan for his book* Nature, Man and Woman.

MILL VALLEY, CALIFORNIA | OCTOBER 7, 1958

Dear Frederic:

Mr. Hartog came yesterday with the new material for *The Religion of No-Religion*, and I have been immersed for some hours in the whole thing, both old and new. It is possible that, with some minor adjustments, Pantheon would take it as it stands. But, on the basis of past experience, I'm inclined to feel that they would want a greater degree of formal unity. (For incomprehensible reasons, most publishers retreat from books of collected articles and papers, so that one can only get away with such delightful grab bags if you are already "made" like Aldous Huxley.)

However, the problem of giving this material a greater formal unity is not too radical. Chapters 1–4 hang together pretty well anyhow, but the section on alchemy though splendid in itself breaks the continuity and has the effect of preventing the whole work from coming to an effective and dramatic conclusion.

Now I feel very strongly indeed that it is worth taking a little trouble to perfect this book. To begin with, it contains some really magnificent thinking, especially in the first three chapters which, on rereading, seem to me as profound as ever. Furthermore, this is preeminently *your* book. It is not a textbook, an exposition of someone else's ideas. I conceive this as Frederic Spiegelberg's unique contribution, not a professorial commentary but an original work of philosophic art. You absolutely owe it to your students and friends, to the world, and to yourself to put this jewel into final brilliance and finished setting. It will never get the recognition it deserves unless you do so, and you just mustn't hide your light under the bushel of literary laziness.

My suggestions are as follows:

1. It needs a preface or foreword by yourself, saying that though this book has been formed from materials written at sundry times and in diverse manners, it has a dominant theme which is as follows... You should then outline the intention of the book, projecting the development of the theme through the various chapters, or showing how they round out, rather than develop, the main idea from various points of view. Envelop, perhaps, rather than develop.

2. Chapters 1–3 should remain pretty much as they stand. If I go over them more carefully I might think of a few details needing improvement.

3. Chapter 4 seems to me to need a few introductory connecting paragraphs. Surely this would be the point to bring in some such idea as this: the vital movement of the spirit never arises where it is expected. Every man and every age has to discover it for itself by going its own unique way, which is often a way that from the standpoint of traditional authority seems to be evil. (Hesse's *Demian*.) But the discovery which everyone must make for himself always turns out to be

the same perennial insight. Perhaps then, for us, the vital movement passes from its traditional guardians, the churches and clergy, to the secular, unrespectable, and amoral sphere of the artist. When we seek God in the sacred, he vanishes, at the same time revealing himself openly in the secular — where no one is looking!

4. But it doesn't do to conclude Ch. 4 with so weak a reference to the fact that the ritual of the mandala may become an obstacle. Surely the mandala is the sacred symbol par excellence, and the religion of no-religion precisely the bursting asunder of the mandala sanctuary, which you will be showing in those marvelous rocks and waters. (Have you seen Joe Campbell's *Symbol without Meaning*? If you take the *Eranos-Jahrbuch* regularly you will have it, but if not I will lend you my copy. It is totally germane to your whole theme.) I think our Jungian friends are so prissy and dull just because they are captivated by the mandala archetype. A stronger ending here makes a beautiful preparation for a final section presenting your rocks and waters instead of the piece on alchemy.

5. But now comes a bit of a problem. "The Being of Being in the Most Common Things" doesn't quite come off. Were you in a hurry, or just overwhelmed by the pictures? About these one should say either nothing, or much more than you have said, and I would be tempted to interweave my text with many quotations from Zen poetry. This isn't to say that some of your comments aren't very good indeed — but I feel a miasma, a lack of crispness, which I fear you have contracted from the metaphysical flatulence of Aurobindo. Surely it is just at this very point that "the Being of Being *in* common things" is the most unhappy phrase — as if, in looking at a rock — just *that* — the mind is supposed to be led off to such an extreme abstraction as Being, and worse, the Being of Being! "Big Beings have little Beings upon their back to bite 'em." I know what you mean — the existential *zang* of the rock — but somehow you must convey this without falling back into the language of transcendentalism. Otherwise you are once again making the rock a symbol pointing to a beyond, and the situation is dualistic even when you say that the B. of B. and the rock are one. As a Zen master said, "It's true. But it's a pity to say so."

Specifically, this is the place to say something about controlled accidents, the asymmetry of the forms of Tao (as distinct from the symmetry of the mandala, where the balancing of the yang and yin has hit *dead* center), the technique of sumi-e painting, and the Taoist-Zen appreciation of nonsense. Also stick in some mondo.

The whole chapter needs a conclusion after the last picture, or else the book will fizzle out. Personally, I feel Plate XV is rather bad. There are many calligraphic drawings of Bodhidharma which would be much better. Incidentally, isn't there any material in your *Die Profanisierung* which you can incorporate here, apropos of the Hokusai drawings?

6. After inserting these wonderful pictures, the rest of the artwork suffers terribly by comparison. I think the diagrams at the end could well be left out. Hui-neng tearing up the sutra should be replaced by the original. I don't see the relevance of the Izanagi picture, but may have missed the reference to it. The fan at the end of Ch. 3 is really horrible, and I would like to see a mediaeval original of the geocentric universe.

Now! I hope I have been persuasive, for you should not undervalue the enormous importance of this book — which is just what makes its perfect presentation so necessary.

Am sending you an inscribed *Nature, Man and Woman*.

As ever, Alan

AW: The following letter is a startling anomaly. We have no other love letters to Dorothy, even though he was frequently far from home. Further, it seems that he was already falling in love with Jano. This letter seems to be a desperate attempt to mollify Dorothy and repair their damaged marriage.

I can only imagine that this letter must have been very confusing to Dorothy, while at the same time giving her a crumb of hope.

JW: The original of this letter was handwritten, and the file copy was typed from Alan's original and sent to Jano with the notation in Dorothy's handwriting: "This is a copy of a letter that Alan sent me at the above date. It so happens that I read it to him sometime around the end of Jan. and asked him if he still meant it and he said 'yes.' This letter is to show the terrible state of our marriage before all this nonsense."

NEW YORK, NEW YORK | NOVEMBER 12, 1958

Darling Dorothy,

For some reason or other I am suffering from insomnia and haven't had what you'd call a real thorough night's rest since I left San Francisco. It's just crazy, for it isn't as if I were lying awake, worrying about something. Just perfectly humdrum thoughts and impressions wandering along, and neither reading nor the liberal offerings of alcohol at after-lecture parties make the slightest difference. The only constant motif in all these wakeful reveries is you. I must be helplessly in love with you, even though when I am at home I must so often seem to take you for granted. The only thing that relieves the boredom of feeling wide-awake with nothing to do in the wee small hours (it's now about 3 AM) is to think about you, and to delight in the thought that you are my wife! The best thing that comes out of so much time to think about you is that I have no desire at all for you to be different from what you are. It used to worry me that you were *so* reasonable and *so* emotionally reserved, but now (now being a period of several months long) it strikes me it is just this outward reserve that gives you such enormous inward sweetness. You don't dissipate yourself in mere expression; you keep fire in reserve for moments of wordless communication in which you are the most exciting woman imaginable — and I have a pretty good imagination! (Reading this in the harsh medium of writing may embarrass you, but it's the only effective way of making love to you at a distance.) You seem to me to be an entirely complete character, in which the elements I thought I didn't like are found to be the energizing sources of those which I love, and this has taught me a great deal not only about you, but about human nature in general. (One has always known the theory, but it is the actualization of it which is so persuasive.)…Also, I want to say something which I don't think I've ever really been able to get across to you. What excites me and stays with me from the moments in which you give yourself so completely is not only (and this is no "mere" only) your physical attraction, but the revelation of a certain attitude in you which probably underlies everything you do. I think I could define this attitude if I tried very hard, but it might make you too self-conscious if I did, and this is why I am afraid of saying just exactly why I love you — often though you have asked why. The devil of being a good writer is that one can kill things by expressing them too well.

So — I wish I could sleep a bit. But there is no you to cuddle, which would make it such fun to stay awake. Darling, I love you so much that if I were to try to write it down you would think I had gone nuts. At least I have two pictures of you.

Don't try to write if you haven't time or energy. I know how it is!

All my love, Alan

AW: Shortly after Alan's love letter to Dorothy, he wrote to Jano. It is just the beginning of many letters to follow as their passion builds. With regard to space, we have chosen to edit out those that feel merely repetitive.

MILL VALLEY, CALIFORNIA | DECEMBER 3, 1958

My dear Mary Jane:

It was so good to talk to you today — having had you much in my mind since leaving NY. Also it was a pleasant relief having been scratching my brains all day to get started on the article "Religion" for the *Funk & Wagnalls Encyclopedia*!

Such an impossible subject, since none of its standard classifications are valid — so that there is no easy way of breaking it down into orderly sections.

Here is the article I promised you — being more or less what I talked about at the session you missed. This is one of my "between books" efforts [*Beat Zen, Square Zen, and Zen*], designed as a "thinking out loud" affair for the simplification of my ideas. It could still be much, much simpler. I'm always working towards a clarification of these things which will be so plain that the very idea will strike us with a wallop, so that everyone will say, "Why in hell didn't I see that before!"

Satori is fundamentally a new kind of common sense — seeing an obvious relationship which has not before been noticed, and the "intellectual" seeing is so convincing that you *feel* it as well. Like realizing that the earth, or perhaps the moon, is round and not flat.

This is why all the writing and thinking is such an adventure, for the clarification is always just on the tip of my tongue. Perhaps a mad dream, since all the sages say that it *can't* be put into words. Yet the artist in me says it jolly-well can! Now you know how crazy I am.

Dear lady — will you drop me a line occasionally, however merely "chatty" it must be? I am ever so happy to have discovered you, and have no hesitation in sending love and kisses galore to a most delightful girl.

As ever, Alan

MILL VALLEY, CALIFORNIA | MAY 5, 1959

Beloved Mary Jane:

From the feel of things you are going to be hearing from me very often! Although the last letter was penned when very slightly tipsy-ish, I don't withdraw a word. I mean all of it and more so. I only hope it doesn't sort of scare you that you have come to mean so much to such an involved man. Talk of R. H. Blyth's "becoming as deeply attached as possible to as many people as possible" — you alone are enough to do duty for as many people as I can imagine! Quite aside from its intrinsic beauty, I feel that this experience is going to do something for me of very special importance — being a kind of radical "test" of my philosophy, of being able to hold an immense feeling without either repressing it or being blown to bits by it. Perhaps life is asking me to "put up or shut up." It's about time it did, so I have no intention of backing out of the storm. If I can be a ball in *this* mountain stream there will never be any doubt that the Tao works!

But I'm sure all this can be worked out if I can feel that you are with me. I need nothing but your love, but I am never, *never* going to demand it.

Spent all yesterday morning being photographed for *Look*! They are doing a feature around Sumire Jacobs, the girl in the records, daughter of Sabro Hasegawa and wife of my crazy "real cool" friend Henry Jacobs. Incidentally, I have told him to send you the haiku record. I have also mailed you a copy of *The Meaning of Happiness*, and herewith comes another work — just to keep your library complete with Watts!

I have to rush out to a dentist's appointment. Am sending $25 to help out with phone calls.

I dreamt of you last night. I absolutely adore you.

Later. Dentist has just cleaned up the lowers! Now in the peace of the post office instead of in a big rush I can go on. The sunshine here continues to be absolutely gorgeous. Yesterday, walking little Lila in the garden, I watched the big jet planes making their white tracks in the brilliant blue sky, and of course was just wishing I was on one on the way to you! Wouldn't it be great if there were some way of arranging your vacation out West, with me borrowing a house or apartment in Hollywood or somewhere. I suppose an idle dream. But I guess I'm allowed to dream.

Tomorrow morning is the press conference for my TV show. Don't specially relish these affairs as some of these pressmen are so bloody hard-boiled. But they are going to show one of the films first, and I guess that will make an easy introduction for interviews. Great Books Foundation have just asked me to do a late-June lecture for them at their Asilomar summer conference. Asilomar is a big conference center near Carmel...Hope you had a good evening with Sam and the tapes. One of these days I'll get you your own recorder and send you *personal* tapes. Sooner or later I'll have to outfit myself with all this sound-scribing machinery, instead of having to drive over to KPFA in Berkeley whenever I have to make a tape. Sweetheart, let me have news of yourself and your goings-on, everything and anything. As I said, best to typewrite the envelope and perhaps leave off a return address. 'Specially if you write often. But don't try to keep up a one-to-one correspondence with me. I'm crazy, and will doubtless be deluging you.

Once again, dear Mary Jane, I love you with all my heart. Let me know (just approximately) what early evenings you're likely to be home from the office. This is often the easiest time to call.

I love you again, and again, and again, and again, and again, and again!

Devotedly, Alan

MILL VALLEY, CALIFORNIA | MAY 14, 1959
Most beloved Mary Jane:
Hot from the press, here is the first copy in New York! I hope that letter in the 8½" by 11" manila envelope got through all right (there were photos in it), and I

guess today you should have received the Reps book [Paul Reps, *Zen Flesh, Zen Bones*] — plus the Watts addition! It's such fun to be able to have so many things to send you. My astral body is almost living in your little apartment, wondering ever so often whether you're lonely and what you are doing...Have you noticed anything new about your wooden effigy of Winston Churchill?

In getting steamed up for my new book I have been reading something quite astonishing — Norman Brown's *Life against Death* — a study of Freud and psychoanalysis which in many ways is startlingly close to *Nature, Man & Woman*, only in some ways almost more daring. Not having finished it yet, I'm not quite certain what he's driving at, but the general trend is becoming clear. He's trying to transcend the Freudian duality of pleasure-principle vs. reality-principle. Eros vs. Thanatos, as a theory of the instincts. But what seems to be coming out is the most interesting, full-blooded, and philosophically competent affirmation of "faith in nature." The book isn't easy reading. It's a close argument, full of all sorts of references. But as you have been in analysis and know my work as well, I think you might find a lot in it. Naturally, I have been thinking about you while reading, and your relationship to me provides a kind of material embodiment for what he is writing about. My thoughts sing.

My only worry — from our last phone conversation — is that all this is too much for you, especially the long separations. I really mean what I said in my last letter: if you can be willing to feel whatever love is, its aspect of anguish starts to transform itself. Our "inner," as Charlotte calls it, is amazingly intelligent. One can, I am quite sure, only grow through this kind of suffering, especially if it is suffering without resentment. It might be different if I had jilted you. My own feeling begins to move in this way — though I have bad moments when I see a girl in the distance on the street whose coloring or build reminds me of you — and at the same time I love you more than ever. The impression of your whole personality just *grows* on me, and I don't think I've ever before been able to relate to anyone on so many levels.

Darling, I will call you next Monday evening or night (latish) so either way you won't have to wait in for the whole evening (i.e., it will be around 6 PM or 12:30–1 AM). I think it's better for me to originate calls, as it would be such a pity for you to reach me at a moment when I could only speak rather stiffly. Don't worry about writing at length — but an occasional postcard in envelope saying "I love you" would warm me like anything.

Golly! I wonder how it would be if you came to work in SF. I'm sure I could figure out a modus vivendi of some kind, and your nearness would be consoling, to say the least. Also we might be able to do a lot of work together. Wish I could afford you as *my* secretary.

City Lights have printed 5,000 of these booklets [*Beat Zen, Square Zen, and Zen*], and the NY distributor has already ordered 2,100 — so you should be seeing it all over the village.

Mary Jane, I wish I could project myself along with this ink and tell you face-to-face how completely I love you. (Incidentally, being in this state of feeling seems to have cured me of all sorts of minor bodily ailments; I seem so alive.) You wonderful, lovely creature — innumerable kisses to you. My imaginative arms are around you all the time!

Most devotedly, your Alan

PS. The bow and the *matching* cuff links — complete with rose petals — have just arrived! Thank you ever so much, darling. Such taste you have. They are very beautiful and will remind me worthily of the beautiful giver. By the same mail Vanguard Press say they have sent you a copy of *Myth and Ritual*. Will you ever get through all this reading? Never mind, I just want to be on your shelves. Thank you again, dearest one. You make me so happy!

MILL VALLEY, CALIFORNIA | MAY 15 [1959]
(Nuts! The prints weren't ready when I went to pick them up. But so this letter isn't utterly zany, I enclose a slide. Not quite the best, which I need more than you!)

Well here you are, dearest! Can you blame me for loving such a face? Or is it always a case of "would that some god the gift he'd gie us, to see ourselves as others see us"? If you could see yourself as I see you everyone would pay $100 to touch you: the world's happiest woman. Or maybe you'd just blow up... Mary Jane, I hope I'm not "bugging" you by being such a crazy lover. But I did promise I would shower you with little communications so as to keep my presence with you as much as possible, and it's such a good promise to keep. This is just the literary equivalent of the conversation I would carry on with you if we were living together, and if a day went by without my speaking to you, you would certainly think something was amiss. I'm just reveling in having found someone with whom I can share everything I enjoy, for it's often rather lonely being an oracle. And one of the things I enjoy most of all is you, but I don't want to bore you with you. You must tell me if I'm too overwhelming with my enthusiasm for you. But in a world so full of strife, it's wonderful to be able to turn on the full force of delight in another human being.

In my last I sent you a photo of our house, and I wish you could see it now. One of my students here is a landscape gardener, and has been working all day around the place getting the flower beds in order. The day has been perfectly lovely — blue sky slightly dusted with thin clouds to keep the heat off. This afternoon

I drove into SF for a long conversation in my favorite bar at the St. Francis with my old friend Frederic Spiegelberg — a prof. at Stanford — whom I have known since 1936 when he was a refugee from the Nazis, in London. I am helping him to prepare a book in which Pantheon is interested — a marvelous collection of Chinese and Japanese paintings of cloud-like rocks with Zennish comments, entitled *Vanishing into Reality.* So we have been discussing it over vodka and amazingly black (tho' mild) Brazilian cigars which he supplied. Spiegelberg has a very strange child, about the age of my own daughter Joan (21), a girl who lives completely in the present, gets an immense bang out of everything and anything, and is therefore 100 percent unadapted to American culture. And it's the culture, not the girl, that's disturbed! Spiegelberg is the most honestly selfish man I know, an absolutely brilliant teacher, and one of the most stimulating conversationalists. He's preparing a study of the psychological and mythological symbolism of scarecrows. He collects Tibetan ghost traps (amazing erections of sticks and colored wool, like TV antennae) and makes sculptures of his friends based on the ghost-trap technique. This is a pretty "gone" world I live in!

The seminar on Zen, Ethics and Esthetics is going very well. The group is most congenial, and the hostess, Sally Parks — who makes picture frames! — has been successfully knocking herself out to create a good atmosphere. More later — I must sign off now.

I love you most tremendously, Alan

PS. Just got your lovely letter — Joy, oh joy! More later. — A.

JW: Alan was working on a compilation of his essays to be published in a book, This Is It, *which was published in final format by Pantheon in 1960. Lawrence Ferlinghetti, a San Francisco poet who still operates the wonderful bookstore City Lights, was involved with some esoteric publishing, mostly of small works, and was interested in forming a relationship with Alan.* Beat Zen, Square Zen, and Zen, *originally published in the* Chicago Review *in 1958, was City Lights' first Watts pamphlet. This was one of the essays included in* This Is It.

This is also the beginning of Alan's serious study and experimentation with psychedelic drugs. The following three letters are significant for the glimpse they offer with his fascination of the psychedelic experience.

MILL VALLEY, CALIFORNIA | MAY 20, 1959
Darling Mary Jane:
This is one of the "gonest" documents you'll ever get — consisting of immediate reactions to last night's LSD experiment. The handwritten part was done while

still under the influence. Feel free, if you want to, to show it to Charlotte, though I would rather you clip off the last paragraph of the handwritten piece. This is only for *your* eyes.

A note of warning: please don't feel afraid of this kind of thing. As a student of semantics you know how "loaded" is the word *drug*. So far as we know, chemically, LSD does nothing more than *suspend* certain inhibitory mechanisms in the nervous system.

Well, you'll gather a bit from things you have aroused in me. On another simultaneous level I'm still aware that you are Mary Jane in her own right, with her own life, in this sane, humdrum world. Don't let me overload you with ecstasy if you don't want to take it — but I think you are strong enough. I don't want you to get the too-much-cream-and-strawberries feeling — but that belly laugh of yours reassures me.

Also — don't feel you have to make some sort of "adequate response" to this communication. Nobody could. It's simply for your enjoyment, and no strings attached. For I just have to share this with the person I love most in the world.

Your Alan

MILL VALLEY, CALIFORNIA | WEDNESDAY [LATE MAY 1959]
Dearest one:
So glad everything worked out okay with the New School. Thanks *very* much. Dinner last night with the *Time* man again, at Henry Jacobs's place. Sumire made a fantastic curry, but it hasn't settled too well on the internal economy. This morning to a lecture at Langley Porter by the two doctors who worked the LSD with me: a most fascinating presentation, about which I'll tell you in LA this afternoon. I'm sitting here waiting for a couple of Japanese Zen priests to visit. Allen Ginsberg just phoned — also with a long story about *his* LSD sessions! What a bunch of dopeheads we must be!

I love and adore you, darling — Alan
Hereafter: c/o Books in Review, LA. Mark *Personal*

MILL VALLEY, CALIFORNIA | THURSDAY [LATE MAY 1959]
Beloved Mary Jane:
That haiku was fine. You ought to enter it in the TV haiku competition which Don Sherwood is about to start here. First prize, a free trip to Japan! If I get a chance, I'll put it in for you. Tonight we go to see Eric Hawkins in his new kind of dancing, the philosophy of which he says he owes to me. I wonder very much what it will be like. At Langley Porter yesterday the two doctors gave a splendid presentation on LSD and mescaline, and this morning I got a big supply of the

latter from a psychiatrist in Santa Barbara. Want to try it? My contact number there [is at] Books in Review.

My fondest to you, beautiful person. Alan

MILL VALLEY, CALIFORNIA | MONDAY [MAY 1959]
Darling:
I have just spent the whole afternoon with *Time*'s SF editor. He got word from NY this morning that they wanted a story on me for next week's issue. We'll see. They're none too reliable. Saw a fantastic show last night, James Broughton's "The Rites of Women." One gag, "I've been to Albert Schweitzer, Suzuki, Alan Watts, and even Krishnamurti, and I *still* can't find myself!" Thanks for the Mod. Museum p.c.'s [postcards] — I simply couldn't make out where you got my doodle until I read the small print!

I love you most dearly, sweet Mary Jane. Alan

MILL VALLEY, CALIFORNIA | TUESDAY JUNE 30 [1959]
Most beloved Mary Jane:
So much warmth exudes from little things you left with me — those two beautiful ties, and the case for sunglasses. Sort of centers for positive radioactivity. Thank you again ever so much, but most of all, thank you for you...I'm seriously wondering whether I should try to go to England in late July, as my mother is failing fast. If so, this unhappy business will have compensations that will make me look forward to it. Trouble is, I can't afford to go unless my uncle in Minneapolis takes a broad hint...And other miracles besides. The better to keep in touch with you, I'll send you copies of my manuscript [*This Is It*] as I write it, so as to be able to do it actually as talking to you. More than ever, I am completely convinced that in you I have found the person I have been looking for all these years, and what particularly convinced me was the way you responded when I tried to show you and share with you so many things and places that I love... Time to get going to catch the mail...so here's kisses on your lips, fingers in your golden hair, and the staff of my love plunged deep into your body.

Mary, I adore you — Alan
[PS.] I've put your home address on the outside, just in case.

MILL VALLEY, CALIFORNIA | JUNE 30, 1959
Dear Mummy & Daddy:
I have just come back from two-and-a-half weeks in the Los Angeles area, busy as a bee, and interminably behind in correspondence. Just before I left a friend

took a whole lot of photos of the whole family that are absolutely splendid, and as soon as I can get some enlargements I will send them on.

I have been trying to think how on earth I can get over to see you within the next months. This is a period of financial slump (the summer almost always is) as I am drawing into my own hole to write a book which should be ready by November. But it could be delayed. All I can say at the moment is that I am trying to find a way, despite finances and the problem of travelling at this time of year. If it was my affair alone, I would borrow the money and gamble on having a prosperous autumn. But we can never predict our income accurately, and this is sometimes problematic when you are responsible for so many people! Wait a little, and see what develops. Dorothy and I went out for dinner last night to celebrate our wedding anniversary, and had a long discussion of ways and means of getting over this summer — but it's still inconclusive. If there should be urgent need of getting in touch with me, use the telephone and reverse the charges. I shall be in southern California again between July 13th and 16th.

Dorothy's mother is coming to stay with us for a few days in July. I have seen her fairly often on my trips to the East Coast; but Dorothy hasn't seen her for 8 or 9 years, and of course she has never seen the children.

These last months have been very active for me in the "inner" aspect of my work, since many new ideas and experiences have been coming to me through the many fascinating people I have been meeting, through books, and through my continued consultations with psychiatrists in various parts of the country.

Did I tell you that I have been invited to be one of four contributors to a symposium on mythology to be held at Harvard this November? My friend Joe Campbell will be one of the others, and the whole thing is being paid for by the American Council of Learned Societies. Quite a big affair, and I'm very thrilled about it. Also Lance [L. L.] Whyte has written me the most glowing letter about *Nature, Man and Woman*, which pleased me tremendously as I feel him to be one of the most brilliant minds in the world.

While in LA I had dinner with Aldous Huxley and also with Nancy Wilson Ross and her husband — she being a very well-known novelist, and a most charming and cultured woman for whom I have considerable respect. I once visited their lovely home in Long Island, where she has an extremely fine collection of contemporary paintings.

How rapidly the children are growing up! I will get Tia to write you a letter soon just so that you can see her beautiful handwriting. Now that they have no school until September they are busily playing with friends all over the neighborhood and learning to find their way around by themselves. Lila wants to be right in there with the rest of them, and with all this competition she is being brought, or dragged, up a good deal faster than the rest. We are about to get another enormous crop of fruit, and I'm glad to see that the apricots are doing well this year. The children have planted their own garden, the main hope of which is a crop of corn — you know, the kind with the big ears or cobs which you eat in your hands with butter. Greasy but good!

This is, I think, everything for the moment, but I'll let you know the instant I see any way of coming. I've just had a letter from Uncle Willie to which I must reply. He has strained a ligament in his leg, and has had to rest up a bit.

Very much love from us all,

As always, Alan

CHISLEHURST, KENT, ENGLAND | WEDNESDAY [JULY 15, 1959]
Mary Sweetheart:

I had a wonderful time in London yesterday, taking Ann around and seeing old friends. We had dinner with Christmas Humphreys, the president of the Buddhist Society, and cocktails with my first publisher, John Murray, an extraordinarily witty and genial fellow about my own age. I think they will do my next book. Their "office" is a venerable private house, where the firm has been located since its beginnings, some 200 years ago! The whole place is a museum of venerable literary traditions — Byron's manuscripts and all that. London is very attractive at this time of year and seems much more prosperous than a year ago. Makes me feel I could *almost* live here again, though I know I should loathe the winters.

Darling Mary Jane, your face is always before my eyes, and I love you as intensely as ever. Many kisses on your lips, most beautiful one.

Your Alan

AW: In the letter above, Alan describes the joy of connecting with old friends and places. It is interesting to me that I have no memory of that day. What I do remember is his visiting me at Farringtons, the girls' boarding school that I attended for five years. I was delighted to have him come. Interestingly, the teachers and older girls were all agog at how handsome he was. This was very strange, as I had never considered my father in that light; it was somewhat unsettling to me.

In the following letters, Alan is really struggling between his desire to have more time with Jano, with whom he feels so totally compatible and deeply in love, and his marriage to Dorothy, for whom he describes feeling fondness. He is torn between not wanting to hurt Dorothy and the freedom and joy he feels when he is with Jano.

It is my theory that during this time, he became very aware of how his need for varied female companionship (Jean Burden was quoted as saying, "Women were like catnip to him") was leaving great pain in his wake. He began drinking more and more, vodka being his libation of choice. He once told Joan that he drank so much because it was the only time he liked himself. This was painful to hear, and led to my belief that he drank to cover his immense feelings of guilt.

MILL VALLEY, CALIFORNIA | JULY 31, 1959

Most beloved Mary:

Your letter of Wednesday contained some of the loveliest things that have ever been said to me. As I've said before, you are marvelously communicative in writing, though still more so in sheer personal presence. I was also very glad that you sent me that very pretty photograph, but specially so for the delightful reason that — if the picture doesn't lie too much — you are many times more attractive today: almost startlingly so. The picture shows a bright, conventionally good-looking girl, but now you have a gentleness and a kind of glowing, elegant femininity which doesn't seem to be back there in 1945. Of course, so much of you is in motion, and pictures don't always catch it.

Jano, dear, I am always a little cautious of discussing a relationship because it can so easily develop into a kind of obstructive self-consciousness. But, naturally, I have been thinking a great deal about what might be the best possible arrangement between us. It is true, as you say, that we have been together under rather ideal circumstances. The prosaic and humdrum aspects of marriage might make things much more difficult, though I would gamble on going through hell and high water with you.

Marriage would make our relationship "kosher" in the eyes of certain sections of society which don't mean much to either of us. It would assure you of support and companionship in later life — quite a factor. It would provide the necessary background for your having a child or children, but aren't the 40s a little late in life for starting a family? I have rather a lot of experience in this and, even were things ideal, would now have considerable qualms about starting another child with Dorothy...At the same time, I hunger more than I can say for your continuous companionship, for the opportunity of being able to settle down to do certain things with you in a very leisurely way, just as we go strolling together around the village.

In the wilder moments of fantasy I have imagined all kinds of things that might make it possible for us to be together in this way — even the outrageous expedient of simply deserting to New York and sending home a monthly check until the dust settled and a reasonable arrangement could be made. But this would be an awful blow to the children, even though they are now accustomed to my being away for lengthy periods.

Well now, since getting back things have entered a new and problematic phase. Dorothy's mother has been here for some days, and the effect has been strange. On one hand, she has said an awful lot to D. about how lucky she is in having me for a husband. On the other hand, she has been such a suburban fussbudget that D. has seen her own bourgeois aspects caricatured, so much so that she has said to me, "I really think now that I want to be a Watts instead of a DeWitt or a Jones." (father and mother's names.)

Also, D. has apologized, almost abjectly, for her last spat with me (just before I left), partly because I didn't react as usual, which scared her, and partly because she really loves me. She has said something, which I'm not too clear about, as to not doing anything drastic for at least two years. All this came out after a somewhat drunken party the other night, and under the influence she is either very amorous or very quarrelsome.

Now the plain fact is that I do not love her as I love you, but at the same time I feel tender and affectionate towards her. *At the present moment* it would be insufferably mean of me to jolt her with any talk of separation, or with the suggestion that I have found someone else who is "it." (I should say, however, that I have seriously considered asking her whether she can accept me as I actually am, whether she can still accept me in the realization that I have a real need for the special relationship that lies between us. But on such a revelation I have to feel my way. I might have serious trouble if she knew that every trip to NY was to you, and I don't want to do anything to endanger our all-too-brief times together.)

It is my general feeling that, try as either of us may to please the other, Dorothy and I are emotionally so different that we will not ultimately be able to conceal the cleavage, and that therefore it is only a matter of time before the old difficulties will arise again. (Her own "two year" idea suggests that this is also in her mind.) I predict a new shift around December or January.

So, then, adding all things up there is the possibility that the ideal relationship between us two is the extracurricular one, with you not the wife but the "Shakti" — a word which I use very seriously. It means, among other things, that we should not, perhaps, think about ourselves in the stereotyped terms which our society provides for a man and woman in love. At the same time it is urgent both to me and to you that we see a great deal more of each other, and this requires yet further thought. Is it possible for you to be happy with the following rather suspenseful situation?

That we stop thinking of ourselves as oriented towards the social institution of marriage as the permanent relationship, since marriage is primarily a bond between people intent on founding a family. That we are not just content with, but find it actually best to be, in the relationship of institutionally untrammelled lovers — without undue secrecy, and with every possible effort to be frequently together. Would it not actually be a serious loss to be in any situation where you and I might take each other for granted? Would we not discover that the actual tension of our relationship is, like the taut string of the violin, the secret of its music? Or part of it?

At the same time, I cannot help thinking of the possibility, nor conceal these thoughts from you, that something might happen to enable us to be very constantly together, married or unmarried as suited our convenience. I confess that "might happen" sounds very irresponsible on my part, but I have told you and I think you understand that it has always been essential to me to work on the principle that

> There is a tide in the affairs of men
> Which, taken at its flood, leads on to fortune.

I have always found myself foolish in any forced issue, and I believe you respect my Taoism enough not to force me.

So much for my wisdom, and now, since I am really showing my guts to you, for my foolishness. For my sake, will you please endure the pain of this suspense? I am very, very conscious of what all this asks of you because I have to endure it too, perhaps in a different way. (In your absence I have my family — but it reminds me of you.) I am saying this even though you have given no hint of backing out, and though I trust your love for me as I have never trusted anyone — and perhaps I'm just trying to say how utterly grateful I am for your existence. But I must say that this, still imperfect time-wise, love between you and I has become the center about which I swing. As I said, it has brought color into my sumi picture of the universe. Watch the results! Though my new book starts quietly enough, it will make even *NM&W* seem chilly. Dear one, it is getting late and I've been up since 6:30 AM, but you have come to mean life to me and this attachment does not just possess me; I will it with everything!

As to my thoughts on our seeing each other more often, it is striking me as a most practical possibility that trips to NY may most profitably (despite air-travel costs) be substituted for those to LA — since NY is also Boston, Philadelphia, and Washington! With a little patience, I think the family can get used to that idea, and now travel time between the two spots diminishes astonishingly.

Charlie Brooks and his equally delightful brother, Kenyon, stopped by for a while today, and we plan a picnic with them Sunday. Also I did a lot of writing. Sunday morning I have a harangue at the Fellowship Church (interracial) and Monday night we tape a TV show on haiku.

Golly I must to bed. Dearest, don't feel you have to react to all this in detail, and please remember that, aside from my love for you, it expresses things as of the moment. You seemed to have considered all these things in your last letter, but I had to tell you all this so that you would know I don't just presume on your patience and your beautiful self-giving.

All, all my love, dear Mary Jane — Alan

MILL VALLEY, CALIFORNIA | AUGUST 6, THURSDAY [1959]
Most beloved Mary Jane:
Here, at last, is the introductory chapter [of *This Is It*]. It shows the usual problem of getting under way, sticky at first and then getting into stride. Usually I find that I have to rewrite some of it, and make some of the language less ponderous.

Thinking over yesterday's talk, I am very eager indeed to get your general impressions of the David-Neel book [Alexandra David-Neel, *The Secret Oral Teachings in Tibetan Buddhist Sects*] as well as a detailed description of the vision. It seemed to arise so spontaneously that you may have a natural gift for this kind of thing, brought to the surface by intense emotion. If so, there is, as I said, a need for caution — the simplest form of which is a limitation of the number of times you let it happen. It is very naturally a most attractive substitute for physical contact, and well, oh how well, do I know what the yearning for this can be. But just because there is an alliance here between sexuality and psychic experience, the combination of forces is peculiarly strong and potentially dangerous. I am sometimes prone to look at things in the most apprehensive light, and, therefore, taking this peculiarity of mine into account, let me say that nothing would horrify me more than my being the cause of your getting into any serious psychological trouble. It is well known that ordinary masturbation fantasies can sometimes become more attractive than normal intercourse. Visions of the kind you described are much stronger, and there is, as a matter of fact, a whole mediaeval lore about them — incubi for females and succubi for males! However, in an instance such as this, I couldn't close my own mind to the chance of some sort of ESP between us. I know two separated ones who do it regularly, but on a "high spiritual level!"

Sometimes I wonder whether in encouraging your enthusiasm for matters Zennish I am assuming too much background. It's so easy for me to forget all that I have read and thought and wrestled with for thirty years. But, as I said, I have so much faith in a kind of belly laugh that you have, though I don't know whether this is a recent acquisition.

These long enforced abstinences are asking an awful lot of you, and I'm afraid my own relations here are, increasingly, no substitute. So I'm really in this with you. But even with the burden of your absence, time is just flying past so that I can't keep up with my work and October and November are racing towards me. I get incredibly absorbed in my writing, and I wish you had some fascination of the same kind, other than Socony.

I wish I could really make out D's state of mind. An invitation came today to speak at Bryn Mawr in October or November, and she twitted me with going off to find a 20-year-old wife. The subject of Picasso, Henry Miller, Edward Weston, and others with very young wives had been the subject of conversation at cocktails last night, and I had said that in general this was no solution for me. The companionship of the maturer woman was too important. And, as you know, the main problem between D. and I has been this matter of companionship. Both feel its absence acutely... with you I should probably find so much that it would interfere with my work! In the long run I think (as of this moment) that I have two alternatives. One (improbably as it may sound) is to get D. to accept the Shakti principle, and then make arrangements for you to live out here. The other is the more conventional divorce. Both will need "playing it by ear" and very gentle handling, but I am absolutely intent on getting a far better arrangement between us than we have now. After all, Frank Lloyd Wright had three wives. Coomaraswamy had four. Sages, as well as movie stars, can get away with this kind of thing!

In the meantime I have fairly successfully broached the subject of substituting the East for Los Angeles, and I have no doubt that invitations from Eastern colleges will be trickling in fast. Either way, it's in practice a day's journey SF to LA, or SF to NY. It's a function of money, not time.

Sweetheart, I have a mountain of work to do, and this must be enough for today. Funny, I was thinking of giving you that Persian art book for *your* birthday!...Dear, dear Jano — I could write on and on and still not say how much I love you.

Most devotedly, your Alan

[PS.] There may be some errors in this copy, as I haven't had time to go through it.

Have just checked my Memphis dates — Oct. 19–20–21. Will try to be as much as possible near you between Oct. 22 and my Cleveland date, Nov. 3.

I love you all over again, Alan

JW: During most of 1959, there are very few letters to anyone but Jano. Alan wrote to her almost every day, as she did to him. His energy and thinking must have been completely absorbed with his relationship with her. For daughters of Alan, parts of these letters are difficult to read (as today's vernacular puts it, TMI: too much information). One of the files included a line drawing he had made of them together, reminiscent of the Indian Konarak sculptures. In many ways, he was like a besotted teenager with occasional twinges of anxiety about where this relationship was headed and with mixed feelings about Dorothy and his young children with her.

Mary Jane Yates King ("Jano" was her self-given nickname as a child) was originally from Casper, Wyoming. She became a journalist and was noted as being the first woman reporter for The Kansas City Star. *Born in 1918 (the same year as our mother), she was briefly married to a Mr. King (no children), and held several other journalistic jobs before joining Socony Mobil Oil's corporate offices in New York City in April 1951. She worked in the public-relations department there for at least ten years. Her involvement with Alan perhaps diminished her enthusiasm and capabilities as a senior public-relations officer. There was also some rumor that she had participated in a few too many two-hour three-martini lunches. Nevertheless, in December 1959 one of her former superiors wrote her a glowing employment recommendation addressed to Alan at his Mill Valley home, which was probably read by Dorothy. There's no doubt that Jano was very much capable of handling Alan's public-relations needs and assisted him in lining up lecture engagements and the publicity required.*

In addition to her administrative capabilities, Alan found her fun to be around. She had an optimistic, rather playful personality and an overwhelming curiosity about all of Alan's activities. She had an eye for beauty in the simplest to the most extraordinary objects — from found pebbles on the beach, a leaf from a tree, and beautiful weavings from Oaxaca to exotic jewelry from India. Alan found her love of such things fascinating, and she constantly sought to draw Alan's attention to her through them.

In the first years of their relationship they were quite in love with each other. Their affair went on for five years before Alan divorced and they would be able to marry. Companionship with Jano was more compelling than it had ever been with either Eleanor or Dorothy — a relationship on an entirely different plane.

Alan noted during this time that he wished to direct more of his travels towards New York instead of Los Angeles. This may, in part, have been because he did not want another relationship to be compromised — with Jean Burden, who was living in Los Angeles at the time.

MILL VALLEY, CALIFORNIA | AUGUST 18, 1959

Dear Henry [Miller]:

We're coming to Big Sur for 10 days or so this Friday. I'm giving a seminar at Margaret Owings's, Monday through Thursday…I've a lot of things I'd like to talk to you about, including this amazing book of Norman Brown's [*Life against Death*], which you must have seen, and some recent experiments I've made with LSD. What an adventure in alchemy!

We shall be staying with Jack and Helen.

All the best, as ever, Alan

BIG SUR, CALIFORNIA | AUGUST 24, 1959, MONDAY

My darling, beloved Mary:

I have been sitting this morning over on the grass with an extraordinary little Englishman, the poet Eric Barker. He has a shack here underneath someone's garage — I guess rent free, as he has practically no money. Bald, with a fringe of longish white hair around ears and neck, reddish bronzed complexion, and eyes like a very intelligent deer. The hill where his shack stands is just north of Nepenthe, and looks south along the coast for miles, and back inland to those golden mountains with their patches of green forest — today topped with just a very few white clouds. We were listening to a flute and guitar record by Laurindo Almeida, with Salli Terri singing — mostly Spanish songs — some just the voice without words — songs of such incredible longing and far-off-ness that I almost wept, hit in the solar plexus with the unbearable combination of the scene, and thinking of you. Eric has nothing and everything. He was spending his morning with a pipe, a book, and an orange, sitting at a rough wooden table below his shack. The people we are staying with are rather like this, too. The *true* beatniks, living in a $7.00-a-month house, surrounded with a very lush vegetable garden, high over the ocean and on the edge of a deep canyon. They also have four children, same ages as mine, running naked most of the time. Jack [Morgenrath] is a Polish Jew, great nature mystic, handyman, painter and sculptor in wire. Helen is a dancer, with a flair for kathakali and Indian things. Homemade bread, mostly vegetarian food, but everything tasting unspoiled. Yesterday we went further south to the Bay of Lucia, where Camaldolese Benedictines have just set up a hermitage. It's the most idyllically Mediterranean place on the coast. We were visiting a most gifted potter, Jay Kipp, who lives on a promontory where there was once a noble mansion, long since wrecked by an earthquake. He lives with wife and baby in the old servants' cottage, surrounded with the overgrown gardens — jacaranda trees, oleander, eucalyptus, potato vines, pampas grass — all hanging above the bay. There was a light rain which had cleared the atmosphere, giving us the rarity of a visible horizon. Jay's pottery is very much in the finest Zen tradition, and somehow, if I can possibly manage it, I will try to get you a piece. Jay is gone on Subud, has done a jail sentence for growing marijuana, and was really pumping me about LSD. Oh, it's a strange world — this great quest for ecstasy.

This morning Jack and I also stopped by the Owingses' house, where the seminar starts tonight, and spent some time with Margaret and Nathaniel [Owings, an architect with the international firm Skidmore, Owings, & Merrill]. He is like a younger, and probably nicer, Charles Laughton — pudgy and sensuous, with a slight atmosphere of power that goes with great success and wealth.

Margaret told me the seminar is now fully subscribed — and people are coming from as far as Berkeley and Ojai. I'm sort of hoping Burt Kaiser may turn up, too. I suspect some may come just to be in that house. Jano, it's totally fabulous, and decked with objects of contemporary art that you would adore. They've just brought in a bronze statue of a girl, from Italy, that's like an extended, lankily pregnant Tanagra figurine. The loveliest thing.

I wish I could acquire one of those shacks here. They can be made very cozy, and I have been having visions of you in blue jeans and a soft sweater, sitting by a fire with me on a stormy night. I can see your hair against a background of stone and grey, weathered wood, and I am pouring you wine from a brown ceramic bottle.

There are hummingbirds here that are quite tame, and hover from flower to flower right under your nose, and last night I caught sight of a sphinx moth doing the rounds of the garden. The house is covered with a passionflower vine, mingled with a canarybird vine, so called because its leaflike blossoms look like canaries. In the front Jack has collected an astonishing assortment of rocks and driftwood as a basis for a cactus garden, where there's every kind of spotted, spiny, and extravagant plant.

I have to collect my thoughts for tonight's session, and perhaps also do some work on my book. I'll write again in a day or two and will tell you how the seminar is going.

Jano, sweetheart, as always I am just bubbling over with the love and warmth for you — and feeling more and more the almost uncanny naturalness and fitness of our relationship. I know, I *know* you are just peculiarly the lock which fits my key — my rather complicated key — and that somehow life will allow us to fulfill each other and belong completely without claims. My dear, dear Mary — for the present I can give you at least my most unreserved and uninhibited love.

Your Alan

BIG SUR, CALIFORNIA | AUGUST 29, 1959, SATURDAY
Beloved Jano:
Sort of flattened out with this cold, and 30 miles or more away from any means of getting my usual "remedy" — vodka! But, thus incapacitated, I have been reading all Wilson's pamphlets. Funny — but so much of what is said, even by the great AK, seems thin. Chisholm has one very interesting remark: that the psychiatrist must concern himself less with psychotherapy and more with social prophylaxis — and this is at least a step towards my own view that the trouble lies in the communication matrix, in a pathology of thought, and during the last days I have been trying to sharpen my ideas about this. Chisholm's urgent plea

for immediate action, necessitated by the brief interval at our disposal before the co-annihilation of World War III, seems to me only to highlight the utter futility of all ordinary kinds of "doing something about it." (Apologies for this scrawl, but I'm writing on my lap, lying down.) Dangerously close as it may seem to come to pure apathy, I think human beings have to see that this is a problem being created by attempted solutions — or at least partly so, for there are plenty of troublemakers who are not idealists. But note Chisholm's own cocksureness as to the immeasurable superiority of scientific rationality, and his desire to impose it by authority — if necessary, by violent authority. Perhaps what I am trying to say is that (politically) we have to continue in our present defensive course — *knowing at the same time* that it is not solving anything. In other words there has to be a profound disillusion with the competence of the dualistically think-ing will — a realization that its activity can bring nothing but vicious circles of trouble. My only grounds for hope that co-annihilation will be averted is that the political scene will be sufficiently controlled by canny gangsters who value their own skins. The really dangerous men in politics are those moved by symbolic inducements, whether "goodness" at one extreme or "empire" at the other. Poli-tics is the art of keeping people turning from side to side on a hard bed. In other words, it is a perpetual problem to which the whole idea of solution is absolutely irrelevant — and this very insight makes it a less crushing problem. The trouble with the American mentality is its readiness to believe that big solutions are pos-sible. But solution is a static concept — allied to the Christian heaven. Note, too, that when we try to absorb Buddhist and Taoist ideas we project this same static quality and think, for example, that satori is a definitive state at which one arrives, whereas — on the contrary — satori is the realization of the "state" of no fixed state, or, as it is sometimes called, of "nonattainment." The secret is that there is nothing to get, nowhere to arrive, and, indeed, no secret! But this no-*thing* and no-*where* must of course be understood to mean the *things* and *wheres* of dualistic thought, the spurious concretions of happiness, goodness, success, wisdom, etc. Thus in place of "enlightenment" or the "inner meaning" of Buddhism, there is just "it is windy again this morning." Perhaps the artist can show this much better than the philosopher.

As soon as I get home, dear, I will get busy on arrangements about the Oc-tober seminar, answer a letter I have had from Mrs. Ziegler, and phone you about the whole situation. Still no word from Charlotte. I wonder if she got my letter.

Mary, this brings my fondest love to you, loads of it. I adore you immoder-ately and in spirit cover you with kisses.

Your Alan

AW: The letter above to Jano seems incredibly relevant to today's political environment. I'm not sure who "Wilson" or "AK" are. Chisholm is, perhaps, the philosopher Roderick Chisholm (Perceiving, 1957). In any case, I find Alan's philosophical thoughts on politics useful in today's climate.

So much of what Alan wrote throughout his life in regards to politics vis-à-vis the human condition is relevant today.

MILL VALLEY, CALIFORNIA | SEPTEMBER 3, 1959

Most beloved Jano:

I hope all my various letters are getting through to you, for when we talked on the phone today you didn't seem to have had a postcard bearing an illuminated B (mailed Tuesday) nor a long letter on yellow legal paper (mailed Wednesday). Today yours of last Friday was forwarded from Big Sur, and I forgot to say that I was very much interested in the [Allen] Ginsberg article. We don't take any newspaper here, so I hadn't seen it in the *SF Chronicle*.

Here is the rough draft of the announcement. Your suggestions will be most welcome, and, also, would you please be so kind as to call the New School and get details of time and price of admission. A copy has also gone to Charlotte. Here, too, is a copy of the current announcement for this part of the world, which I had to get done in a big hurry because of the Big Sur trip. I think I'll have the NY one set up in type. It takes me hours to type the thing on an Olivetti with the right-hand margin adjusted.

As I told you, Tynan and crew came out today and made movies — mostly in the garden, though they did one shot in the entryway to the house where I had hung a fine piece of calligraphy saying, in effect, "Heaven on-high, sentient beings okay" — the Buddhist equivalent of "God's in his heaven, all's right with the world!"

This weekend we are going to be invaded by the entire Morgenrath family. Helen came up with us to do some work with Shivaram, a marvelous Hindu dancer now working here, and Jack is bringing all the rest tomorrow.

I still haven't said anything like all I wanted to say about your Sunday letter, for there remains the possibility of total upheaval. Ever since my return Dorothy has at least been repressing her usual critique, but it's hard to say whether or not she's feeling it. I think so. I have been more than usually involved in work because of time lost out through the trip, but in other ways the summer has not been quite so troublesome with the children. They are of course used to long absences on my part, and often when I get through work I'm much too tired to play with them very actively. I'm afraid I'm becoming the abstracted American husband. But I'm also afraid of playing with them in some ways that come naturally to me, because they are much too riotous and nonsensical for Dorothy's taste. I know she was piqued last night because Helen started singing and I joined in with her — always agog for a songfest — and this "excludes" D. because she can't sing. Oh dear, it's all so unhappy because D. doesn't mean to be colorless and tries so desperately hard to be a good mother, housekeeper, and so forth. But she can't understand why I become a totally different person when anyone, male or female, who has anything in common with me comes around — and this always leads to bad feelings. Mary, this is sometimes an awful sad world, but I don't think I'm sorry for myself.

Dearest one, I have to get all my stuff to the mail and then get over to a neighborhood cocktail party. I am excited that you are steaming up for a big change in your life and work. Be sure I will do my utmost to help you, not only for my sake, so that we can be closer to each other, but also to see you using your own lovely mind in some more appropriate way. Mary, beloved, I adore you, hold your image tight, and fill its hair with kisses.

I am always yours, and will be more so — Alan

MILL VALLEY, CALIFORNIA | [CIRCA 1959]
Gary [Snyder]!
Have been reading all about you in *Dharma Bums*. Terrific!!! Am going to LA until Sep. 29, but want to see you after that. Will you buzz me? I hope Kerouac has done a good true job of characterization. If so, I know you a lot better.
    Alan Watts

MILL VALLEY, CALIFORNIA | OCTOBER 5, 1959
Dear Henry [Miller]:
Thanks so much for yours of the 2nd. No, I don't have *Crisis and Resurrection* and would be most grateful if you could let me have that extra copy.

I was instrumental in getting Pantheon to publish the American edition of *Segaki*. I think it's magnificent, and was, like you, very struck with its resemblance to *Ugetsu*, not only for the incident with the woman but also for the curious uncertainty as to whether the action is taking place in the natural or the supernatural world. Stacton lives in Berkeley, and though I have talked with him on the phone I've never met him. Otherwise I really know nothing about him.

I'm off to New York and the East on the 18th, and will be back at Thanksgiving. I don't suppose I'll be down in Big Sur again before you take off for Asia, so bon voyage to you.

Love to Eve, and to Maud [Oakes]. As ever, Alan

MILL VALLEY, CALIFORNIA | OCTOBER 7, 1959, WEDNESDAY

My beloved Jano:

Oh dear — what a morning! Having composed a delicately diplomatic letter to Margaret Rioch about my visit to Washington, I receive an awful blast from my former girlfriend [Jean Burden] in LA (more sorrow than anger) pointing out the dreadful defects in my character and intimating that I will exploit you just as I exploited her. Oh Jano, aren't you simply scared to death of getting so involved with me? I feel like someone in a novel, blundering through life leaving a whole swath of broken and bloody hearts, headed by poetic justice for a garret on Skid Row. Perhaps I can console myself with the fact that only for you have I dropped the desire for all other relations, and have cut off all other affairs, and there is the sort of objective fact that no one else has ever inspired me to write every day, and keep on wanting to for months at a stretch. Of course, of course I have my blind spots, being human, but you never seem to judge me. Mary dearest of all creatures, *please* don't ever fail to tell me if you feel exploited or in any way misused by me. Your love is incredibly precious. It's not that asking this is a way of trying to make you responsible for what I do to you; it's only that it is so difficult to be always completely conscious, and to make one's communications to others mean what they mean to oneself. And then explaining them always seems to make everything more confusing! As is, I'm not aware of being in any sort of false position with you. It seems quite inconceivable to doubt that this is as love as love can get. I even feel sure enough of it to see whether it can be doubted!

Had a very good session with the psychos yesterday. I had never been so far north in Calif. before, and the country was most beautiful. It was 100-mile drive from here, part of it along the Russian River. Had dinner with one of the doctors afterwards — a man also very enthusiastic about LSD.

Henry Murray, of Harvard, has written that he will be in NY the 23rd and wants me to lunch with him, Joe Campbell, and Jack Barrett of the Bollingen Foundation. Sounds important. About Margaret Rioch. She and David [of Walter Reed Hospital] have invited me to stay with them in Washington. I have replied very tactfully explaining my relationship with you, saying you'll be with me, and suggesting that under the circumstances it might be better for me to stay at a hotel — but leaving the door open for them to invite us both. If they don't, what hotel would you suggest? Or have you any understanding friends there? This will be a kind of test as to what we can get away with, and I'll be damned if I'll let you down. I feel I know them well enough to expose myself.

All for now, darling — most beautiful, lovely, adorable girl. Time gets closer to the touch of your real lips — and the light in your eyes and hair.

I love you — Your Alan

MILL VALLEY, CALIFORNIA | OCTOBER 15 [1959]

Dearest, most beautiful Jano:

That was such a perfectly delightful note I got from you yesterday, written with the echo of my voice in your ears. I couldn't reply right away as yesterday was an outing — to lay in a store of wine for the winter. I had a lecture date in Livermore for the evening, and as the Livermore Valley is just about the most superb wine country in the US, I had a friend there show us the way to two of the wineries I had wanted to see for a long time, Wente and Ruby Hill, the former very modern and the latter marvelously decrepit and run by an old Italian boozer. Golly, it was good tasting and buying wine on a hot afternoon that came to an end with a great pale moon in a pearly and then red-golden twilight!

The lecture afterwards, sponsored by the Unitarian Fellowship and the AAUW in the Episcopal church, was very crowded and a great success. Livermore is full of scientists, working at the U of Cal Radiation Lab — all very top-secret and *Scientific American*-ish. My host was an electronics man, and the friend who showed us the wineries — young woman, student of mine for some years — an astronomer. She has had the most highly passionate and utterly frustrating love affair with a rocket expert, dawdling on dreadfully for years. What that fellow really wants to screw is the moon! While there she showed us a fantastic book which I have just ordered for you — Feininger's *Anatomy of Nature*, the most gorgeous photographs of all the things we love from galaxies to insects' wings. When I get my studio in SF I am going to make it a place of such things: not so Oriental, but with great pictures of stars and cells, and wonderful objects from the sea. We just have to go to the Natural History Museum together and look at their plastic models of animalcules that live in water — immense, surrealistic jewels. If I could only get one of those to hang from the ceiling!

The lecture in Washington is also to be at an Episcopal church! (Christ Church Georgetown.) I come home to roost in the funniest ways!

A thought struck me yesterday while people were questioning me about Western Zen. Chinese Zen is Buddhism in terms of Taoism; Western Zen will be Zen in terms of the philosophy of science. I have oodles of young scientists in my audiences out here. You see, they are coming to the end of their thinking.

I really have to make a list of all the numerous odds and ends I must bring with me to show you, articles, tapes, and whatnot. Could you get Sam to lend his Wollensak [projector] to us for the day with Charlotte? Dear one, I am so full of ideas these days that I am having trouble sorting them out. And there is so, so much to read that bears on my work. I really think that Suzuki, and I, and a few others have stirred up something. I need a huge foundation grant for one year's meditation, with you as Shakti. Wouldn't it be fun to think up a formal application, specifying just exactly that!

Oh dear — no word from you today, and yesterday's was written Sunday. But I suppose it is I that am keeping your nose to the grindstone! Still, I hope you're all right.

I wonder if you have further news on the big shake-up at Socony. It miffs me somewhat, that NET [National Educational Television] is only talking about a 6-month project, though I may be able to change their minds in NY. But still it doesn't make any difference to my overall scheme. The way things are going I simply must have help, and nobody else will do!

Jano, it is only a week now. I will, of course, call you from Memphis, if not before. I love you, darling, I love you with seashells and stars, pebbles and ferns, leafy branches and immense clear skies, and above all with this body to hold you and give myself to you.

Your Alan

WHEATON, ILLINOIS | SUNDAY NIGHT [APPROXIMATELY NOVEMBER 1, 1959]
My darling, beloved Jano:
Late Sunday night, and all the guests from a party which Joan gave have gone. Tomorrow evening I return to Minneapolis, with a rather heavy heart, although it is a "good deal." I was so eager to be with you tomorrow, and, though it's only a few days' delay, being in love makes one such a fool! But I'll call you tomorrow night — before you get this. "Stay me with flagons and comfort me with apples, for I am sick with love." And the business at Minneapolis is all so involved with very special things that we have shared together — for there are the rocks and shells, the whole "uncalculated world," in a collection which they are amassing to be a library of forms and images rather than words or ideas. A similar project exists at the Museum of Modern Art, and Bryan plans to come to NY in April to consult with me and Karpel — the MMA man who runs it. I let out the idea that such a collection might be of far vaster application than a reference library for artists — i.e., a kind of dictionary of ideographs, capable of expressing and relating patterns that could never be expressed in words. I suggested that we pass the idea on to L. L. Whyte, Don Hayakawa, Bateson, David Rioch, and others to get reactions, and then perhaps have a brainstorm session with these people in the summer. Bryan jumped on this bat from my belfry, swearing this was the vision he'd been looking for all his life. You know, he's a magnificent-looking man of 61. Has made a great success of this school, but avows he is depending very heavily on me for his inspiration — and he seems to want my moral support in a way that is almost desperate. At the same time, I see the most colossal

technical difficulties in the way of such a project, and when I discuss it with the school's faculty, I realize how difficult it will be to get the idea across. The real point is that the collection could be a sort of apparatus for Hermann Hesse's idea of the Bead Game. Well, it's certainly worth 2½ days' discussion and experimentation...

Much love, your Alan

MILL VALLEY, CALIFORNIA | NOVEMBER 30 [1959], MONDAY
[Jano,]
Today I'm really getting to work. Have made up the LA program, have circulated all kinds of inquiries for studio, etc. Please get my schedule to me as soon as you can. The weather is gorgeous and it only needs you to make it utterly wonderful. Am all agog for your arrival — already! But, darling, please do reconsider driving out *alone*. There is so much thuggery going on, and though it would be wonderful to come that way I really question its advisability. Would Nathan Horowitz want to share with you? Otherwise, I'd be most willing to help out on plane or train fare. You are absolutely precious to me, and I'm missing you terribly. I have a lecture for the SFGS group on your birthday; they're taking the Unitarian church for it. Are you going out that evening? If not, I'll call you.

Dearest Jano — Thank you for clearing up so many odds and ends I left behind! For the rest, our long time together in NY has convinced me more than ever that my love for you is no whimsy, and that I want you more than anything. I can never have enough of you.

Adoro te. Your Alan

MILL VALLEY, CALIFORNIA | DECEMBER 8, 1959
Mr. Gerald Gross | Pantheon Books, Inc. | New York, New York
Dear Gerry:
Well here we are, even if a day or two late! This is not the finished product, but I think quite adequate to show you what I have in mind [the *This Is It* manuscript]. The theme is quite consistent — the mystical (satori) experience, and the problem of finding it, describing it, and expressing it in action. I have tried to avoid articles that reduplicate material in my books, since so many of the short pieces I have written are just preliminary sketches for something that gets said much better in a book.

Now if this seems satisfactory to you at this stage, please send all the material back to me as quickly as you can, and I will try to let you have the final version by January 15th. Also would you let me have a contract. I could do with an advance on or about January 1st. Would $500 be reasonable for this one? Also — serial rights for items 1, 2, 5, 6 would be in the clear. I ought to try and sell these myself, but at present I haven't the time, so if you want to take a shot at it we'll split by the usual arrangement.

It is okay with Lawrence Ferlinghetti (of City Lights) to use *Beat Zen, Square Zen, and Zen*. I imagine you have a copy in the office, but if not it's certainly at the 8th Street Bookstore.

Please register the return. I have no copies of one or two items!

Very best wishes, cordially, Alan

MILL VALLEY, CALIFORNIA | DECEMBER 12 [1959], SATURDAY
Most beloved Jano:
Just got some new letterheads, and naturally the first to be used goes to you! Today it has rained here for the first time in weeks, and everything is smelling wonderful — except that I *still* have [a] cold and can't join so well in the smelling…I'm fairly sure I'll take the studio at 1807 Broadway. It's in a very dignified old mansion, two blocks from my former stamping grounds, The Academy of Asian Studies. On the 1st floor (above street level), facing the street, which is as wide and airy as the city has. Mostly residential. Hope there are no zoning snags, but I'll find out on Monday. Tonight we're off to a party in Palo Alto — driving down with Maud Oakes (Jerome Hill's cousin) and the astonishing David Hunter — a kind of Zen drama teacher, and also rather a fine painter… Pantheon say they can't publish the essays [*This Is It*] until late summer, but Gross wrote before he had seen the material. City Lights have just paid me a royalty of $313.00 on *Beat Zen*! They've sold almost 8,000 and are printing another 5,000!…Gee, we must get going, so must stop.

Dear, sweet, lovely Jano — I adore you as always.

Your most devoted Alan

MILL VALLEY, CALIFORNIA | DECEMBER 19 [1959]
My darling Jano:
This morning I was in San Quentin, giving a talk to about 50 inmates. What an incredibly fascinating audience — including Neal Cassady, who is the "Dean Moriarty" of Kerouac's *On the Road*. In there for passing out marijuana for free. An amazingly depressing place — but the very progressive Protestant chaplain organizes courses in comparative religion conducted by many of my former students. So my works are widely read there! Many are as far from "criminal types" as could be imagined — just victims of our appallingly vicious sex and drug

laws...I rather hesitate to call, beloved, now that your parents are with you, since I might find you compelled to be frustratingly taciturn...Last night a cocktail party at KPFA. Hal Winkler again tried to persuade me to take over WBAI! If you were stuck in NY, I might well be tempted.

This afternoon I was looking over furnishings for our studio — floor covering and all that. I hope to get decoration started immediately after Christmas. Don't see how I can get at it earlier. But as soon as I begin working I'll have a phone installed so that we can talk to each other. Oh Jane, sweetheart, how I love you and miss you.

All my love to you, beautiful lady, watching the horizon for you —
Your devoted Alan

MILL VALLEY, CALIFORNIA | DECEMBER 25 [1959]
Most beloved Jano:
What a magnificent Christmas Eve! By the late post came both your little package and that absolutely beautiful letter of Monday the 21st. You know, just as everyone is about to shut themselves in for the holiday: stores close, no mail, you spin in under the gate and make everything wonderful. Jano, I *love* you! Now the amulet you sent me — and this is just what it is — is a late classical example of the head of the Gorgon Medusa, used as a charm against the evil eye. You probably know the story — she was an incredible monster who had an affair with Poseidon (Neptune), and her head was cut off by Perseus. It had the power of turning all who looked upon it to stone. But from the head sprang Pegasus, the winged horse (!), sired by Poseidon. Subsequently the head was borne upon the shields of Zeus and/or Athene. The Gorgon Medusa is sometimes considered as a sort of dark counterpart to Persephone, Queen of Hades, and seems to me to correspond somewhat to Kali in Hindu mythology. Earlier forms of the head show the same fangs and protruding tongue. Don't be alarmed that you sent me such a terrible personage, for now she is mine she will do as I tell her!

Something I put in Mark's stocking has given me an idea for a tabletop for the studio. This is a set of "playing-card" colored photographs by Eames — just gorgeous things: assorted marbles, reels of thread, skeins of wool, butterflies, an old abacus, scattered clock hands on a white ground, medical capsules of all colors, heads of wax crayons, a marvelous snail shell, a crab, a walnut, old jewels, a Buddha face, and heaven knows what else. All slotted for building card houses.

Yes, the cheese from Gail and Lynne was just the one. Joe Campbell sent a huge mince pie. Back to the amulet. It must be quite old, for no one carves stones like that nowadays. Isn't it fascinating how the green is flecked with red? Wow, I love it. Trust you for picking out marvels. It might also be used as a seal. Nothing like taking off one's tie clip and sealing a letter with the Gorgon's head! I wonder if anyone still sells sealing wax. I often bought it in England.

I'm glad you've decided to airmail Saki and Cho-cho (Cio-cio?) — "cho-cho" is "butterfly" in Japanese. Probably you won't be settled here until the 26th, but a day or two won't make much difference. (I can hardly concentrate. The children are rushing all over the house exploding balloons!) So — continuing the following morning: The dust has settled, and now all is quiet. Brilliant sun this morning with a slight frost on the ground. But we have also had a good downpour during the week and thus an end to the drought and fire danger. I did all my Christmas shopping amid the deluge.

I was enquiring about Sausalito waterfront places for you last night. Apparently they come as low as $65, but are apt to be small and are getting very rare. The land there is becoming extremely valuable, and one of these days they will sweep away all the barges and put up swanky apartments. Same old story as the village.

Darling, how soon will you be going over to Charlotte's? I'm not so sure of being able to get to LA the 17th, but of course I'll let you know. The morning of the 18th is much more likely. Meanwhile, I'm getting still more eager with longing to see you, and have you with me from now on as number-one collaborator in all my multi-nefarious doings. What *could* be better?

Dear Jano — I love you, I love you, and will kiss myself into every pore of your body.

Your Alan

MILL VALLEY, CALIFORNIA | DECEMBER 29 [1959]

My beloved Jano:

What a treat to get those pictures! Will you thank Dick very much indeed — for there is one of them which has caught exactly the peculiar smile which invariably drives me out of my mind — smile which started the whole trouble! I went to bed very early last night, and so am up this morning at 4. Everything is so peaceful and un-interfered with, and I have taken out all my pictures of you for a good long look. I *love* you!

Jano, what an adventure we are starting out on together. I am going into SF with Roger Somers today to start work on the studio, and the joy of getting it ready is very much like preparing for the setting for a jewel, for I want to provide surroundings that you will love to work in. Maybe I can get a phone installed by tomorrow (Wed.), and as soon as that is done I can start seriously on hunting for your apartment. I'm sure I can get something satisfactory for $75 or less...

In calling me on your trip, the best times will usually be from about noon to 3:30 on weekdays. I will see if I can get a credit card for the new number, and then you can simply use the card number in making your calls. Would you like me to have the office number listed under your name as well? Much as I hope to have enough work to keep you fully occupied, I also want to encourage your own line as a writer, and have you feel that this studio is your own place as well as mine.

That was a lucky accident with La D [new auto]! Of course it must be freezing in NY now, though hard to imagine here. And I suppose you have been driving around on snow and icy roads. But I hope you've been able to stick the seller with the responsibility. The advantage of the Volkswagen in this respect is that it's air-cooled.

The records and the Persian miniatures have arrived, my dear — the latter as a perennial and fabulous delight which we'll keep around the studio. Yesterday I bought another set of those Eames cards to make a tabletop.

If you're in touch with Virginia Glenn again — I don't see how I can fit a Chicago affair into the February trip, but it might be managed in the first week of April. The Minneapolis School of Art wants me to spend some extra time with them helping to plan a course on the cultures of Asia, and I don't want to be too long away from SF at this time. Another session at Pendle Hill would be splendid — but I think it must wait until the fall. I don't want the April trip to run more than a month. A question about the trip is where we can stay together: will you sound out Charlotte? Of course if Dick gets that fabulous place from Madeleine that also might be a possibility, though it would be best to have a spot in town. Also, since there are only 2 seminars this time I think it would be best to have both at Charlotte's if that is okay with her. Another business matter: I am puzzled by the deduction of NY state income tax from my New School lectures. Does this mean that all income earned in the state is subject to tax? If so, my joint account with Charlotte may occasion some trouble, and it might be well to shift it to California! Or pay the tax! I don't want to get in trouble so that I have to stay clear of NY state!

Lovely girl, I adore you, love you, lust over you, and respect you — I hope I can always make you as happy as you can be!

I love you, sweet Jano, I love you — Your Alan

PART VIII

Psychedelics, Love, and Divorce

1960–62

JW: During the sixties Alan became well known as a lecturer, writer, and radio and TV personality, both in philosophical and psychological venues and among the youth of the nation, who were disenchanted with the Vietnam War. In addition to being a gifted writer, Alan was a gifted speaker. He could stand up to a podium without notes and deliver a lecture with such lucidity as to leave his audience spellbound. His speaking voice, like his subject matter, was commanding. He spoke at universities and colleges all over the country and participated in think tanks and psychiatric forums.

His books continued to do well in the United States and abroad. He was contributing to various prestigious journals and magazines, including Playboy, *where some of his more provocative essays were published. His most popular books were published during this era:* This Is It: And Other Essays on Zen and Spiritual Experience; Psychotherapy East & West; The Joyous Cosmology: Adventures in the Chemistry of Consciousness; *and* The Book: On the Taboo against Knowing Who You Are. *Additionally, he took part in the development of a mythology project, published by George Braziller as* The Two Hands of God: The Myths of Polarity.

With his interest and self-experimentation with psychedelics, he became increasingly interested in how the brain works and sought out pioneers in the field of brain science, including Karl Pribram of Stanford University and David Rioch of Walter Reed Hospital. He was involved with Timothy Leary and Richard Alpert during their studies of psilocybin and LSD at Harvard. Alan was involved with their experimentation with prisoners at the Concord Prison Project in northern California.

For Alan, the use of psychedelics was a religious experience. He felt that the abuse or constant use of such drugs was to nullify the spiritual effect one could garner from the experience. It was like finding a shortcut to satori or samadhi, but on an entirely different wavelength. To Alan, drug-induced altered states could be compared to certain states experienced in some Buddhist (and other religious) practices.

Alan began to break out of his mold. The sixties were carrying him, along with many others (the Vietnam War objectors, the hippie movement), to look at life differently, through a different lens, so to speak — to abandon societal norms and to disencumber one's psyche of needless constrictions. He was becoming an idol of the counterculture. Alan decided to move Jano to the West Coast. She left Socony Mobil Oil during a corporate shake-up, bought a car, and headed west. Meanwhile, Alan had secured a small office in San Francisco and hoped to find a living space for her in Marin County. The excitement and anticipation of this decision is very evident in his letters to her.

It was amazing that Alan could carry on his long-distance relationship with Jano for as long as he did — with love letters, gifts, and photos being sent and received. Dorothy, who now had four children to look after, was finally fed up with the indignity of it all.

AW: For his part, Alan had reached the point where he could no longer live under the constraints of his life with Dorothy. In his attempt to protect Joan and me from our own mother, he had chosen to marry Dorothy. In his autobiography he wrote: "I imagined — erroneously, as it turned out — that her extraordinary good sense about practical matters would rub off on me."

I think he and Dorothy each struggled to fit the other's picture, with dismal results. While Alan's popularity grew, he sought solace in work, the fascinating people he was meeting, women, and vodka. Dorothy, meanwhile, stayed home with the children, feeling abandoned, uncomfortable with many of Alan's friends, and suspecting he was having affairs. All of this, understandably, incited fury in her.

I am struck by the fact that, while Alan describes much of his discomfort with Dorothy, at the same time he consistently avoids blaming. For example: "As an old friend of mine once said, 'She [Dorothy] knows the words, but doesn't know the music.' And I am really past blaming her for this, because it's quite something to know the words so well." He goes on to say, "Perfectly good water doesn't mix well with perfectly good fire." He puts no one in the wrong. He also hoped that their children would be cared for.

It seemed to us that he always had tender feelings for all of his children; he just had no idea how to be a fully responsible father. He did know how to work, and his work was extraordinary.

Furthermore, as we have seen, Alan was now head over heels in love with Jano, with whom he was experiencing the kind of intellectual and sexual rapport he had always longed for.

GRAND RAPIDS, MICHIGAN | FEBRUARY 15, 1960
My darling Jano:
Just to say that I have arrived here and send you my love. We got off just after I phoned you and the trip was very comfortable. Spent the night with old friends

in Evanston, John and Lynne Gouldin, wonderful relaxed characters — he with an amazing flair for all kinds of creative nonsense — weird sculpture, drama, singing, mad exploits. Has a mobile in the bedroom, made up of separate though connected parts so as to be flexible in the breezes, of a complete male apparatus confronting a female — fallopian tubes and all! Installed in a glass cage in the living room are two doves, which cooed at me most restfully through the night.

Jano, your image is with me all the time. I love you as madly as ever. My host, Duncan Littlefair, met me in a Dauphine just like yours, and my heart jumped. Dear, lovely creature — I am always yours — Alan

San Francisco, California | April 4, 1960
Dear Daddy:
I have just had a letter from Ruth in Japan saying that she has deposited Ann's return fare with BOAC. By now you will have heard from Ann that as I would like to spend a little time with her in New York (before she goes to stay with Joan), I would like to get her there on or just after April 26th. My address in New York will, as usual, be with Charlotte Selver, in New York City. I shall be in New York from April 7th to May 1st, with the exception of a trip to Harvard from the 22nd to the 25th. This is for the big lecture event for the American Academy of Arts and Sciences, where I am to give a paper on "Mythological Motifs in Modern Science," as part of a symposium on "Myth Today" along with my friends Joseph Campbell and Mircea Eliade — the latter a Romanian-born scholar who is now at the University of Chicago.

The last two months have been unbelievably busy. I have been again to Minneapolis and seen Uncle Willie. Also to Wheaton for a weekend with Joan and John, who are now about to move to Quincy, Illinois, as John has had a promotion. Your little great-granddaughter, Elizabeth Ann, was then still very much "baby" and so it was difficult to make out any family resemblances. Well, Joan and John seem to be very happy, and little David is a magnificent boy. The new studio in San Francisco has been going along well, and the last seminar here was very well attended.

I haven't written you for rather a long time because there have also been troubles and uncertainties, and no way of seeing how they might turn out. As you probably gathered on my last visit to England, things have not been going well between me and Dorothy. I have tried very hard to love her, but for nine years I have been quietly nagged with much the same attitude that you saw being accorded to Ann, and, with a person of my temperament, the cumulative effect of this kind of life is a search for companionship outside the home. My travels have been a blessed relief, even though I am very fond of the four children — who exist because in the act of the creation of children there was almost the one and only point where I could get into communication with Dorothy, and where her immense emotional reserve could be penetrated. And when this reserve is off, she is either exceedingly amorous or the opposite — a fury, with nothing but a pent-up torrent of resentment expressed in "billingsgate." It has been very hard indeed to support a home life for so long in which I feel free only to be about one-third of myself, the other two-thirds being basically unacceptable to someone who I have discovered to be profoundly lacking in imagination.

I am writing this letter to you alone, because I must leave it to your discretion how much of this should, at this time, be told to Mummy. I do not want her, in particular, to be saddened and depressed because of a son who has had such a difficult time in finding the right partner for marriage, or with the fear that this will be an irremediable blow to four little grandchildren.

The problem is that if I have to continue in a home life in which most of me has to be suppressed, they will never really get to know me at all. Under other circumstances they may at least have a chance to spend time with me as I am, without my having to give constant heed to Dorothy's sort of schoolmistress attitude to life, which throws a wet blanket over all that goes on. As an old friend of mine once said, "She knows the words, but doesn't know the music." And I am really past blaming her for this, because it's quite something to know the words so well. But the problem is that perfectly good water doesn't mix well with perfectly good fire, and I think it wiser to admit that certain human relationships just don't work than to go on and on trying to achieve the impossible just for the sake of maintaining the proprieties.

As things now stand, I am still not sure how they will turn out. But it is most likely that Dorothy and I will come to a parting of the ways, and, if so, I don't want it to be a total surprise to you. The discussion of the whole thing between us is at present in the hands of a very wise and warmhearted lawyer who has the respect of both of us, and who can be trusted to work out an arrangement most reasonable for the children.

If the change comes, it will not directly affect Ann, since she will be spending most of the summer with Joan and with her mother, and then be going on to college. In any case, I was not particularly happy at the prospect of Ann and Dorothy being together again. I think too, it would be better if you do not mention the problem to Ann before she leaves; I will explain matters to her when she gets to New York. Furthermore, whenever she may need a home with me there are very adequate facilities here in the building where my studio is, which is a very large house in the nicest part of San Francisco.

So, I will of course let you know how things go, and please don't fret over it too much. For my part, this is obviously a change over which I am not too unhappy. The greatest worry is the children, though as they are Dorothy's own she has an affection for them which was not the case with Ann. From my side they will not lack for ample support. I wish I could come to England this spring and discuss the whole thing with you. It is all very complex, and one letter can't begin to tell the whole story.

Among the circles in which I move, separations of this kind are quite common, and occasion more gossip than censure, for times have changed very much indeed. You may feel that they have changed for the worse, but that was, of course, always the feeling of older generations. What happens, I think, is that each generation shifts its standards of the good life, concentrating now on one ideal, now on another, so that in effect plus ça change, plus c'est la même chose.

I have discussed this problem at great length with Felix Greene, who is in a rather similar situation, as is our mutual friend, also English, Gregory Bateson. In some ways we are three of a kind, still very much British in temperament, so that at least a part of our problem is the curious difference between English and American conceptions of what a husband should be, a difference which becomes quite crucial for men who have artistic or intellectual vocations. In my case, this factor is perhaps somewhat secondary: I mean the British-American conflict. But the "professorial absentmindedness" of a man absorbed in work, which his wife hasn't the temperament to understand, has been one of the chief targets of Dorothy's resentment.

This is not, therefore, a situation by which I feel crushed or set back, but rather relieved to get on with my work. I may have sounded quite sour about Dorothy, but do not blame her because she has acted according to her lights, which are not, however, mine. Will you write to me in New York, and thereafter to my studio. I don't think it would be wise at this time to try to bring any influence to bear on Dorothy.

Very, very much love to you both,

As always, Alan

AW: I arrived in New York fresh from girls' boarding school in England in April 1960. On the way from the airport, Alan explained to me the situation with Dorothy. He told me that he was in love with Jano, whom I was about to meet. I think, because I was feeling close to him, I found it all surprisingly easy to digest. When I met Jano, I liked her twinkling eyes, her obvious intelligence, and her love for Alan.

I also met Charlotte Selver, in whose studio we all stayed. I found her to be a wise, fun, and magical woman. While we were there, LIFE magazine was doing an article on Alan which included Charlotte — my father and I were in a photograph participating in one of her sensory awareness seminars.

Sadly, the road to freedom was not so free. Alan was plagued by financial burdens. Dorothy, in her fury, did everything in her power to make his life as miserable as possible. She took to bombarding him with daily hate mail and requests for more money, and writing to universities, publishers, and foundations, trying to get them to stop funding him. This, of course, was like the proverbial cutting off your nose to spite your face! If she had been successful, he would have had no income to support her and the children. His visits with their children were so traumatic that he felt his presence was more hurtful to them than supportive; he eventually stopped going.

His writings, his public contact, and his close friendships with Elsa Gidlow, whom he frequently called his "adopted sister," and Roger Somers, in addition to his relationship with Jano, were of great solace; these friends being a source of delightful play and exuberance through the madness in his deteriorating marriage.

SAN FRANCISCO, CALIFORNIA | MAY 26, 1960

Dear Mummy & Daddy:

Oh how the time flies! Ever since returning from New York I have been up to my ears in business, both family and otherwise. But the best thing lately has been to see Ann. She had a really wonderful time with us in New York, and at a very jovial party one evening I was surprised to find that she is a really accomplished dancer. She "follows" very complex moves like one's own shadow. I saw her off to Joan's in Chicago, and then she will be with her mother until about the middle of August, and then out here to me. The college question still isn't settled, but I'm expecting to hear daily.

The Harvard affair went off splendidly, and I had the nicest letter from Henry Murray, the prof. of psychology, about my contribution. Quite a group of my students came up from New York, and the university entertained us in the grand style. A party of us spent the Easter weekend far out on Long Island, including a day at Montauk Point, away out in the Atlantic, beaches loaded with the most glorious shells.

Other adventures in New York included three hours with Clare Boothe Luce, former ambassador to Italy, and wife of the owner of *LIFE* and *Time*. We had a most absorbing discussion, and I found her a most intelligent and charming woman — however, with a considerable contempt for the public intelligence! Other excitements included a private lecture which I gave at a friend's flat in the midst of a beautiful collection of Chinese art, and sitting right in front of me was Charlie Chaplin's former wife, Paulette Goddard — a very bright person, who has apparently been "reading me" for some time.

And then final arrangements were made for my next book, which is to come out in October — a collection of essays called *This is It: And Other Essays on Zen and Spiritual Experience*. I have lately received an exquisitely produced Italian translation of *The Way of Zen*, and the French version is on the way. The paper-covered edition has now sold over 100,000 copies!

Back here, I had to get the essay book ready for the press, and begin a new series of TV programs which will run until about the end of July. Future plans involve lectures in Los Angeles from June 10th to 17th, and more lectures at the New School in New York in October and November.

During the past two weeks I have spent some time with the Davenports and the Onslow-Fords; both asked after you and asked to be remembered. Likewise the Delkins, though I saw them early in April.

Things at home are no better, and pro tem I am living here in the city and Dorothy is doing some work with a psychiatrist which I hope will help her, though my hopes aren't very high. Gert Davenport has always been very close to Dorothy, and isn't a bit surprised that this has happened. Neither, of course, was Ann — and I think she's very relieved that she doesn't have to go back into that situation. I got some stories about things which happened between her and Dorothy while I was away from time to time which were very unpleasant. Nevertheless, the whole thing is harrowing because at the same time I am very sorry for Dorothy and most concerned about the children — though at present they seem to be swimming along pretty well. But it all brings out her least attractive aspects, at any rate in relations with me. Yet there is the compensation of some real peace!

Now I hope things are going along fairly well with you now that Ann has left. I wish I could get over again, but I'm so loaded with responsibilities. However, with jets and so on it's so quick from New York, and even a few days would be something if I could get hold of the money. It only means a bit more work!

Much, much love to you both — As always, Alan

San Francisco, California | June 2, 1960
Mr. Kyrill Schabert | Pantheon Books, Inc. | New York, New York
Dear Kyrill:
I have just sent Gerry a very full outline of the next book I want to do, *The Joyous Cosmology*. In New York, I described it to you rather vaguely because it was in my mind more as a feeling than as a form. But in writing this outline I have most of it structured so clearly that I think I can write it very quickly, and perhaps bring it with me when I come again in mid-October. What's more, I have become so full of the subject that I'm all agog to get to work on it.

I wonder if you have had a chance to talk further with Weybright about NAL's [New American Library's] interest in my future work, for if there *is* any interest there it would certainly help in financing this next work. However, I'm still puzzled about paper editions — whether the increased volume of sales really pays the author so well as, say, five years of a steadily demanded hardcover. After all, the royalty per copy, in paper, is way down, and even then is split 50:50 with the original publisher. Incidentally, is this a fair division? I honestly don't know, since publishers must live too, but even a literary agent takes less. Anyhow, do what you can, and I'll give you a real opus!

I'll be starting another run of TV shows here on June 9th, and by the fall they will be circulating again nationally. From the 10th to the 17th I'll be lecturing in Los Angeles, and from July 6th through August 24th I'll be giving weekly public lectures in Berkeley on "The Joyous Cosmology." Then, as I said, to NY again in the middle of October, when I do want to get a chance to come out to be with you and Mickey.

Nothing official has as yet happened about my private affairs, but we are living in de facto separation. This gives me a great deal of peace for work, and Mary Jane is being a wonderful help. Almost all my friends seem to be very understanding about it, for which I am very thankful.

All good things to you, as ever, Alan

SAN FRANCISCO, CALIFORNIA | JUNE 2, 1960
Mr. Gerald Gross | Pantheon Books, Inc. | New York, New York
Dear Gerry:
Herewith is (a) the very full outline of *The Joyous Cosmology*, and (b) a selection of photographs. Please return the latter to me after use.

You will see that the book as outlined takes up themes that were discussed in *The Supreme Identity* and *The Wisdom of Insecurity*, and, to a lesser extent, in *The Way of Zen* and *Nature, Man, & Woman*. But I think the outline makes it clear that I have found a much sharper formulation. The outline is really something like an artist's preliminary sketch for a painting. In wanting to get it to you in plenty of time, I have skimped somewhat on the final section. I apologize for giving you so much to read, but this was the only way of working it out clearly in my own mind.

With luck, I think I could have the manuscript ready when I come to New York in mid-October, especially if Pantheon and NAL can finance me! I am very enthusiastic about this book and really want to get at it. The material is "hot" and I think this will be much more "It" than *This Is It!*

Very best wishes, Alan

Los Angeles, California | June 17, 1960
Mr. Kyrill Schabert | Pantheon Books, Inc. | New York, New York
Dear Kyrill:

Thanks very much indeed for yours of the 13th, from Chicago, forwarded to me in the midst of some very busy and productive lecturing in Los Angeles!

Please don't be concerned about my enquiry as to the 50:50 division on subsidiary income, I have to find out about these things somehow, and the most direct way is to ask you. I raised the question on the basis of a memorandum from the Society of Authors, pressing me to join them, though I don't feel particularly inclined. Also, I raise such questions because I dislike very much to deal with a publisher through such intermediaries as agents. So set your mind at rest; you have given a fair answer to the question.

As to whether we should become so beholden in advance to NAL, assuming they like the books, I think only the figures can tell. Being away from my records, I can only speak from memory, but it seems that thus far I have received from NAL only my portion of the advance payment on both *The Way of Zen* and *Nature, Man, and Woman.* As to the former, if they have sold approximately 100,000 copies, the total royalty at 7 percent (which I think was the figure) should be about $3,500. Has anything come in from NAL since your last royalty statement to me? And is there any way of guessing, say by comparison with *The Wisdom of Insecurity*, what sales of *The Way of Zen* might have been had it not gone into paperback? It is difficult for me to judge this question without all the figures in front of me. And one would also have to take into consideration, in making a comparison with the *W of I*, the popularity of Zen as such. All I can ask is that you take a look at the figures as they now stand, and make as good a long-run guess as you can. I'll accept your judgment.

Now as to the new book, *The Joyous Cosmology*. Gerry tells me he is taking the outline to Helen, and of course NAL have yet to see it. So I have yet to receive a full reaction to the idea from both publishers. However, I want to start work on it as soon as I can, and most of the work will be concentrated into August, September, and the first half of October. To work on it full speed ahead I should, ideally, need $2,500, and I say this just to give you the exact amount of income I have to make during that period. Whether that's practical economy for you is another question!

The jacket design for *This Is It* is stunning. But my bookseller friend's reaction is, "Must it be white?" I love white jackets myself.

Back to *The Joyous Cosmology*: ideas for it are pouring into my mind all the

time, making the outline very much a skeleton. I don't think I have ever felt quite
so worked up about a book in advance of writing.

Mary Jane sends very best wishes. We shall much look forward to seeing you
and Mickey in October, and, in the meantime, I seem to be saying a lot only to
leave the decisions in your good hands. And many thanks indeed.

Yours ever, Alan

SAN FRANCISCO, CALIFORNIA | JULY 28, 1960
Prof. Raynor C. Johnson | Queen's College, University of Melbourne |
Melbourne, Australia
Dear Professor Johnson:
I have just read with great delight your wonderful anthology with commentary,
Watcher on the Hills. I find these records of the mystical experiences of "ordinary
people" in modern prose immensely convincing and moving. I wish I had known
you were collecting them, for I could have added a number to your files from my
own correspondence.

I have just finished a book of essays on the same topic, and will see that a
copy is sent to you. It bears the title *This is It* — "this" being the present mun-
dane moment, and "It" the — well, there are no words. It also contains an account of my own experiments with LSD, and I find your own remarks on this
matter very much to the point. Have you ever taken it yourself? I feel that like
the elixir in Lytton's *Zanoni* it is both illuminating and dangerous, and has to be
handled with some wisdom. With its aid I have seen the "void of terror" as well
as "*L'amor che muove*," but the former is the threshold to the latter.

One thing in your book I find vaguely dubious, and that is the conception
of hierarchies of souls and spirits in the afterworld beyond death. I realize that
the grounds for your belief in this are largely communications from sensitives,
and that similar communications keep coming up with similar ideas. I have a
strong intuitive feeling that we must not jump to conclusions here. First of all, I
feel that we need to revise our language in such a way as to eliminate the whole
spirit-matter duality. Secondly, I have discovered that very profound Buddhists
do not take the reincarnation hypothesis at all literally, and simply do not believe in the survival of any sort of individual soul. (Have you seen Alexandra
David-Neel's book, *The Secret Oral Teachings in the Tibetan Buddhist Sects?* Published by the Maha-Bodhi Society, Calcutta. Sounds Blavatskyish, but, having
studied Buddhism for years, I have no hesitation in saying that this is a *very* profound little book.)

My feeling, though vague, is that there is something wrong in the multiplication of entities — i.e., souls, spirits, etc. — and that the clue to "psychic"

communications of this type lies somehow in a strange sort of reticular intercon-
nection between all parts of the total pattern of the world, past, present, and future. The clue is on p. 153 of your book, middle paragraph. This strikes me in an
indefinable way as deeper, more profound, more interesting than detached souls
which drift about independently of bodies like chauffeurs without cars. My own
feeling is that what we call the body, though finite in time, has many more dimensions than four, and that somehow it will be easier to think about the universe in
terms of pure pattern, instead of such "substances" as spirit, mind, matter, etc.

I also enjoyed your *Imprisoned Splendour*. So — I just wanted to get in touch
with you, and to wish you all power in your fascinating researches and writings,
and to thank you for the encouragement they have been to me.

With all good wishes,

Sincerely yours, Alan Watts

SAN FRANCISCO, CALIFORNIA | AUGUST 8, 1960
Mr. Kyrill Schabert | Pantheon Books, Inc. | New York, New York
Dear Kyrill:

Many thanks for your kind letter of the 5th. Although the way in which the lectures on *The Joyous Cosmology* are coming out is not exactly repetitious, I do see
a basis for your concern as the outline actually stands. For it does not show what
volume of the work the various topics mentioned will occupy, nor can it indicate
the strange and often radical transformations and new ideas which arise in the
actual writing! So let it wait. As I told Gerry on the phone, I am ready to go ahead
with *Psychotherapy East & West*, and I deeply appreciate your "unbusinesslike"
efforts to make it possible for me to do so. Let me say, then, that in principle your
kind offer is acceptable, and that I understand it as follows:

1. That you will at this time advance a further $1,000, applying this sum
against one or all of my books currently in print.

2. That you will endeavor, in addition, to obtain an advance for NAL, the
first (half) installment of which will be payable to me entirely, and the second
installment kept by you.

Two questions arise: (1) A royalty payment generally comes sometime in
August, and I don't have any idea what it will amount to. Will you deduct the
$1,000 from this? If by any chance it amounts to as much as $1,000, and if you
intend to deduct the advance from it, what we have is not so much a second advance on *Psychotherapy E & W* as an early payment of royalties due. But with
both *The Way of Zen* and *Nature M & W* in paperback, the royalties due may be

less than usual. (2) Will you need an outline of *Psychotherapy E & W* for Victor Weybright in order to get his advance?

Please let me know about these details just as soon as you can, since the time is ripe for me to start work.

Best wishes and very many thanks, as ever, Alan

SAN FRANCISCO, CALIFORNIA | SEPTEMBER 17, 1960

Dear Mummy & Daddy:

I have been silent for so long that you must have wondered what on earth goes on. I am sorry, because I know how much letters mean to you. For the past several weeks I have been completely immersed in writing a book that must be finished by the middle of October, when I go to New York again. My writing plans were changed, and the publisher wants the book on *Psychotherapy East & West* before anything else. So I set to it; the writing has been enormously fascinating, but hard work, since by now the subject is colossal, and I have to keep reading as I go along. Pantheon gave me a very generous advance on this book, but it just keeps up with responsibilities!

Ann is of course here, and I'm delighted to have her. She has started school at the College of Marin, and hopes to transfer next year to the University of California. Through our friend Elsa Gidlow (you remember Isabel Grenfell, Mummy's old student who lived with her?) I have found a wonderful little house in Fairfax. This is on the other (north) side of Mount Tamalpais from Mill Valley, on the side of a hill overlooking a valley that's almost always sunny. Has a rocky garden full of fuchsias and moss. The place is divided into self-contained (small) flats — so here is Ann and also my secretary-assistant, Mary Jane King, to help us. So this is the place to send on Ann's things — though it's best to keep mail going to the Broadway address in San Francisco.

Tuesday afternoon every week I do two television programs, and the talking part of it takes care of my radio programs which are now running not only here and Los Angeles, but also New York, Philadelphia, and Boston. Otherwise I have not been going into the city very much recently; I have all the books I need out in Fairfax, a huge desk, and a wonderful view of hills and sky.

Ann has had something of a struggle deciding whether to live with me or her mother, and I have let her make up her mind completely on her own. But she just didn't feel she was really wanted in Colorado. Same old story. Here at any rate she is most generously received by all my friends, and we've had a great deal of fun together.

Otherwise, I'm much too busy to worry about much else. But as we're close to mountains and ocean we all get lots of fresh air and look pretty brown. Sunday before last we found a lot of agates on the beach.

Nothing yet settled with Dorothy. It will take time.

Thanks very much for sending on the *Sunday Times*. I always read it with considerable interest, as it sort of keeps me in touch with another world. How on earth am I going to get over again? I'll have to make a real "cleanup" financially one of these days, and we'll pile into a jet plane! Lots and lots of love — from Ann too.

As always, Alan

NEW YORK, NEW YORK | NOVEMBER 3, 1960
Dear Mummy & Daddy:
Here I am in New York, and will be staying here until at least November 25th. In a separate package I'm sending you the new book, *This Is It*. I've now finished the other one, which, at least in this country, will have the title *Psychotherapy East & West*.

This visit to New York promises to be pretty exciting as I seem to be spending much of my time meeting terribly famous people. I was up until 3 AM one morning after a dinner party discussing the troubles of life and the world with Clare Boothe Luce (former ambassador to Italy; her husband owns *Time* and *LIFE* magazines). Then at various parties I have run into John D. Rockefeller, Senator Jackson (who is chairman of the Democratic party), the Dalai Lama's brother, Ludwig Bemelmans, and so on and so on! Had a delightful weekend in Washington with David and Margaret Rioch, giving another seminar at the Washington School of Psychiatry, and soon I'll be going up to Cambridge for a session at the Massachusetts Inst. of Technology.

This coming weekend I go out to Long Island to stay by the beach with friends who run an art gallery here, and later on I expect to spend some more time in the country with my publisher, Kyrill Schabert.

I've just had a long chatty letter from Ann, who seems to be having a splendid time. She had just been to the opening of an exhibition of painting by Gordon Onslow-Ford. Ann has a really astonishing capacity to make friends. On my way back to the West I hope to be able to see Joan, as I have a lecture assignment at a college not far from Quincy.

Your life is so very quiet, and mine, just the opposite! But I do get days now and then when I can let down the pace and really relax, though it's easier to do that in California than in New York. I do wish I could get to England, but there are so many responsibilities and so many mouths to feed.

Lots of love to you both, as always, Alan

San Francisco, California | December 12, 1960
Dr. Timothy Leary | Department of Social Relations | Cambridge, Massachusetts
Dear Tim:

I am most indebted to you! I don't know what CY 39* does for other people, but for both Mary Jane and myself it has been profoundly healing and illuminating. She will write you independently as soon as she can find time. She has a very interesting story of using it to carry her through a nasty situation with her mother, and is now saying, "For the first time I feel really weaned!"

I took it yesterday at 10:30 AM. The external circumstances were ideal as we were spending the day in a kind of earthly paradise owned by some very dear friends, all of whom have experienced LSD. This made it very easy for me to talk with others during the experience. Otherwise, things were rather gloomy. I was very tired after my trip east, suffering from a virus throat, financially harassed, needing a rest, and quite disinclined to work!

During the hour after taking the first five pills I felt terrible — very weak, rather sick at the stomach, no appetite for breakfast, throat feeling as if I were swallowing a billiard ball. I had the feeling that this medicine was no escape, no rest, but an intensification of reality, so I just lay down and waited. About 11:25 everything changed, and I decided to take the second dose, at this point we were listening to some Hindu music — a set of London records prepared for UNESCO, edited by Alain Daniélou. As I listened I was quite startled to realize that the music was pure nonsense, and yet it said on the label, "Classical Music of India" and Daniélou is a very stuffy scholar. Nevertheless the singers were not singing words: they were lulling, playing with syllables (dit-da stuff), and blowing their oboes just to make weird spontaneous noises. There was nothing "classical" about it; it was the most abandoned, delightful blathering. Now at the time I thought that this was the usual LSD effect in which everything ceases to be serious. I thought my friend had just put on a record of some sort of jam session. But he said, "No, this is serious Hindu music." I asked to see the record envelope and that's what it said it was. Now the joke is that I listened to it again six hours later, and nonsense is what it still is! These happen to be very unique records in which the human voice is used as an instrument: no Sanskrit or Hindi, just bwa-wa-bwa.

I think you can see how this set a pattern for the rest of the experience. What is serious, classical, and terribly important is at root nothing but play; it doesn't have to happen; it needn't go on; life is not indebted to anyone. But, though

---

* A synthetic psilocybin manufactured by the Swiss pharmaceutical company Sandoz for therapeutic research.

under the influence of a drug, I realize that this is what the record really is; my "sober" companions see the same meaning in it and confirm all my impressions. (You listen to those records too.)

Next, I was looking at a nonobjective painting and projecting images into it — an airplane view of Manhattan, my own face, a camshaft made of transparent cubes, all seen in vivid, photographic reality. Again, I point these out to Mary Jane and my host, and they confirm it: yes the painting could very well be seen that way. My host even makes a more elaborate description of the face in the picture.

I guess it must have been about 12:30 by now. I was lying on my back on a divan, looking at the ceiling, which is made of rather thin slats of wood, beautifully grained. Again, I was projecting figures into the grain patterns and asking Mary Jane if she could see them too. Yes, she could follow me so long as the projected figures were contained within a single slat, so long as the natural grain pattern was continuous. But then I pointed out images running across several slats — vague limb- and body-like forms. These had the curious effect of making the ceiling appear to be transparent. One could look right through the socially real grain to a higher order of pattern. The higher pattern "captured" the lower, including it without destroying it.

Thereupon I was somehow plunged immediately into the most vivid cosmic-consciousness experience I have ever had. It was so marvelous that I called everyone to come into the room, "I've got to explain this to you," I said, "but there's no reason why you have to understand. You're all divine, you're all buddhas just as you are without having to know what I'm talking about, but the point is that life is a gesture — a gesture of motion, of color, of sound — and there isn't anyone making the gesture or to whom or for whom it is happening. There is simply no problem of life; it is absolutely purposeless play; it doesn't *have* to continue; there is no reason whatever to explain it, for explanations are just another form of complexity, a new manifestation of life on top of life, gestures gesturing. If there is any problem at all it is to find out how people come to think there is a problem, whatever made them imagine that life is serious. Basically there is the gesture. Time, space, multiplicity are all complications of it. Pain and suffering are very far-out forms of play, and there just isn't anything at all to be afraid of. There isn't any ego. The ego is a kind of flip, knowing that you know — like being afraid of being afraid. It's a curlicue, an extra jazz to things, a sort of double take or reverberation, a dithering of consciousness which is the same as anxiety."

I don't know if I can say anything more about this experience. I realized at the time that I had made it perfectly clear in my books, and was only amazed that

I didn't always understand what I was saying. But I saw that I didn't need any answer to the mystery of life because there is no question. I saw that the state of consciousness in which I was could, like the projected pattern in the ceiling, capture and include all other states. I felt almost identical with Mary Jane, and remember saying that what people call the difference between us is about 65 steps down in the order of complexity!

I spent the rest of the day just living in the glow of this experience. The surrounding world looked much more "natural" than with LSD or even mescaline; there was no distortion of any kind. But the world and people were just incomparably beautiful. We sat in the garden, drinking wine and eating homemade bread. It tasted vaguely mushroomy, and my friends thought I smelled a little of mushroom. I found it easier to relate to people than with LSD, and to be very open and honest. As the sun went down the garden began to be chilly, and it was suggested that we go indoors. I felt a bit regretful. It was so lovely out on the terrace that I thought I might feel depressed inside. But no; we went in and everything was just as delightful there. By this time, direct effects were wearing off. But even now, some 24 hours later, the fundamental tranquility remains. I still understand the basic principle of my "vision." It is quite lucidly explained in the last sections of Wittgenstein's *Tractatus*! But I wonder if *he* knew what he was saying.

Under separate cover I'm sending you my LSD tapes. I didn't have a recorder for this session, but if you would be so kind as to send me a further supply of this beneficent magic I'll very gladly make a tape for you.

Very many thanks indeed, and best wishes from us both — yours, Alan

SAN FRANCISCO, CALIFORNIA | DECEMBER 15, 1960
Mr. Edwin Seaver | George Braziller, Inc. | New York, New York
Dear Ed:
We've just had a meeting of the San Francisco end of the mythology project. I'm glad to say that Maud Oakes has teamed up with Dr. Henderson to do some research for him. I had hoped that she would do one of the volumes, but this is better than nothing. She wrote *Beyond the Windy Place*.

But we have some problems. You will see from the enclosed letter that Dr. von Franz can't make our deadline. Dr. Eliade's student, C. H. Long at the U of Chicago, told me that he would love to participate but couldn't even begin writing until June. All the other authors here would like more time, and what about Dorothy Norman? She should have been in touch with you.

As things stand, then, we are still in need of an author for Myths of Creation. We can:

1. Extend the time, and take on Dr. von Franz.

2. Invite instead Dr. Carl Kerenyi (c/o the Jung Institute in Zurich), author of *The Gods of the Greeks*, etc. The director of the institute was in on our meeting and thought Kerenyi might accept the assignment.

3. Let me divert my work to the Myths of Creation and cut the series back to six vols.

4. Get a happy inspiration for another author!

Solution #1 would seem to please everyone except, perhaps, the poor publisher.

I would have written earlier, but I only reached home a week ago and have been very tired.

All the best, Alan Watts

SAN FRANCISCO, CALIFORNIA | JANUARY 9, 1961
Simon Young, Esq. | John Murray, Publisher | London, England
Dear Simon:

Many thanks for yours of December 27th.

This Is It has the same connotation of finality and doom in this country, and this was part of my intention in choosing the title. For "this" includes not only this immediate living moment, but also the moment of death. Doesn't the phrase also carry the superlative connotation in England?

If, in your opinion, the present title simply won't do, what about the following:

"This, this is IT." Like a line from a poem, stressing "this" as if to say, "This, indeed is it."

"THIS is It," capitalizing it the other way. Rather an easier typographical problem for jacket design.

"It is Here."

"Now is the Time." ("Now is the time of our salvation.")

"See it Now!"

"Here and Now."

"This is the Day" ("...which the Lord hath made.")

The problem of changing the title is what to do about the title of the first essay. It enters so much into the actual text. Furthermore, it has a force which the others lack, and is doing very well indeed for the book over here. "Zen and Spiritual Experience" would solve the problem to some extent, but it sounds feeble.

We're also going to have a problem with the title of *Psychotherapy East & West* if you decide to take it on. I remember you didn't like that title, but the publisher here loved it.

Sincerely, Alan Watts

SAN FRANCISCO, CALIFORNIA | JANUARY 9, 1961
Dr. Timothy Leary | Center for Research in Personality | Cambridge,
Massachusetts
Dear Tim:
Many thanks for yours of the 28th. By now you should have my tapes, and I only
regret that I never taped some of the later and more rewarding sessions. I don't
always have a machine available. The trouble with these things is that it seems to
take several sessions to learn how to use them.

Your observations about our latent monotheism are very important. I, too,
have felt that certain types of psychotic break are instances of satori without the
cultural context or personal preparation to support them. And so many psychiatrists seem to have either a vested interest or neurotic compulsion to uphold the
social definition of reality.

I can think of all kinds of creative and opinion-making people who might
benefit from the experience, but how do you handle them at a distance? So much
depends upon the context of the experience both physically and socially. I have
an ideal setup for my own use, but can one trust even supposedly intelligent people to find a suitable environment and at least a minimum of cool supervision?
People one could trust to handle it on their own would be anthropologists Gregory Bateson and Maud Oakes, Wilson Van Dusen at Mendocino State Hospital,
Dr. Keith Ditman at UCLA, and a number of others who have already had experience with LSD. But they are already turned on!

The other night I talked with a group of Jungian psychiatrists, trying to
give them the line that, as doctors, they ought to make LSD respectable just by
claiming the right to prescribe it whenever it seemed indicated. After all few, if
any, drugs are really specifics, and in a field of medicine where diagnosis is always
vague there should be great latitude in suiting the prescription to the individual
rather than the disease. I pointed out that if they didn't claim this right they
would lose an occasionally useful medication to the crooks. But no bite. Not even
to an offer to turn them on personally!

We'll be east at the end of March, for over a month, and will certainly come
up to Harvard.

As ever, Alan

JW: Alan's involvement with Timothy Leary, Richard Alpert, and the Harvard Psychedelic Club continued during this era. There were many others interested in the Harvard project, including Huston Smith, Allen Ginsberg, Aldous Huxley, and Gerald
Heard, as were a number of medical doctors, psychologists, and law-enforcement

groups. Psychedelics were becoming a national interest. At a big meeting of the American Psychological Association (APA), held in September 1961, Alan was one of the main speakers. Alan wrote in his autobiography: "In retrospect, it must be said that the Psychedelic Decade of the sixties [had] really begun to awaken psychotherapists from their studiedly pedestrian and reductionist attitudes to life." He said further that: "In the early days when LSD, psilocybin, and mescaline were used more or less legitimately among reasonably mature people, there was little trouble with 'bum trips,' and episodes of anxiety were usually turned into occasions for insight. But when federal and state authorities began their systematic persecution, the fears invoked to justify it became self-fulfilling prophecies, and there was now real reason for a paranoid atmosphere in all experiments conducted outside the sterile and clinical surroundings of psychiatric hospitals."

His written communications with Leary are fascinating, both sharing their experiences with various mind-altering drugs. Alan finished his manuscript for The Joyous Cosmology *during this time, quite lucidly describing his experiences, although he notes that the book was a compilation of several experimental sessions, condensed into one "trip." His clarity was exceptional. When Leary read the final draft, he wrote Alan saying, "You have such a rare combination of talents — insight plus that astonishing felicity of expression. I'll be delighted to add a couple of pages — in spite of my unwillingness to let my prose stand [in] close comparison to yours." (In fact he and Alpert wrote the foreword.) Alan credits Sterling Bunnell at the Langley Porter Clinic in San Francisco for setting him off on a series of experiments that were the basis for* The Joyous Cosmology, *in which he was compelled to admit that LSD had brought him into an undeniably mystical state of consciousness. Fortunately for Alan, he was quite circumspect about his use of these materials and his involvement in the Psychedelic Era. Timothy Leary was not so fortunate, and Alan always said he felt that Leary "went too far."*

During this time, Alan and Jano moved to the ferryboat Vallejo *at Gate 5 in Sausalito, owned by artist Gordon Onslow-Ford. Alan always referred to it as his "oyster" — rough on the outside and beautifully smooth on the inside. It was, indeed, a wonderful place. At low tide, the vessel rested in the mud of Richardson Bay (an arm of San Francisco Bay) and at high tide it floated. It gently swayed in the currents except during storms when it rocked and sometimes took on water in the bilge. The main room had teak floors that had seen a century of traffic, and shone beautifully with the wear. Through a long wall of windows where the paddle wheel had been, one had a magnificent view of the bay and Mount Tamalpais. Richardson Bay was an artists' colony of sorts — people living in small boats and other structures in alternative lifestyles. The halyards from nearby sailboats would make a wonderful musical sound as they slapped against the masts in the breeze and as fog came off the hills or up the bay from the Golden Gate. A well-known Greek collage artist and wonderfully companionable neighbor, Janko Varda, lived on part of the vessel, and there was a secret door between the sections. It was a magical living space. Interestingly, Alan mentioned to his father only that he had moved to Sausalito. But in fact Jano was living there too, as they had given up the San Francisco studio and Elsa's cottage in Fairfax. His only mention of Dorothy was that he had to put pressure on her to be allowed to visit with his children.*

Alan's father asks an interesting question about Anne's relationship with a divorced older man. Alan attempted to clarify the situation. This had some rather involved family history to it. The man in question was the gifted concert harpist Joel Andrews. Joel's brother Oliver was a well-known sculptor. Both were originally from Santa Barbara. Their uncle, Gavin Arthur, an astrologer and the great-grandson of President Chester Arthur, was also a friend of Alan's and lived on Octavia Street in San Francisco — a rather colorful character whom I met once with my father. I remember that our grandmother Ruth was shocked when she learned of Anne's proposed marriage to Joel, as many years before, Gavin had been the lover of her brother, our great-uncle David Fuller.

Alan's mother, Emily, was taken ill again and died in October 1961. Alan's sense of guilt for not going immediately to be at his father's side is palpable in his letters. His father suffered a brief period of illness, and again Alan wrote that he was unable to visit, but he promised that he was trying to get a grant to take a couple years off from writing and lecturing, in order to do what philosophers are supposed to do — contemplate! — and that he hoped to make a trip to England and Europe.

Again, Alan was on the lecture circuit, and his writing continued, as did his appearances on educational TV shows and radio lectures. There's reference to a book on yoga which, despite a signed contract, seems never to have materialized. His first trip to Japan was in the planning stage, scheduled for May and June of 1962.

AW: I met Joel Andrews, fourteen years my senior, through my father. I felt a deep connection with him the moment I first saw him. I have no idea of what my mother told my grandparents. Joel was indeed divorced when we met, and his ex-wife was greatly encouraging of our marrying. We were married for ten years, had two amazing, gifted children, and lived a rich, colorful bohemian life that overlapped frequently with Alan's.

SAN FRANCISCO, CALIFORNIA | JANUARY 11, 1961
Mr. Kyrill Schabert | Pantheon Books, Inc. | New York, New York
My dear Kyrill:
I am enclosing herewith an outline of the proposed book on Yoga. It may take me a year to finish, and therefore I would like to begin work on it as soon as possible.

There don't seem to be any great difficulties in the way of it except that I do not see how I can write anything about Yoga and Indian philosophy without saying *some* things that I've said before. The only solution seems to be to say them in a different way. Indian spirituality seems to lend itself more to the exuberant style of *Nature, Man & Woman* (chaps. 4 and 5) than to the more philosophical style of either *Psychotherapy E & W* or *The Way of Zen*. This strikes me as a good approach, for not only has it been very well done in the Zimmer-Campbell books, but almost all the usual Yoga literature is horribly dry and cook-bookish. It should be about the same length as *The Way of Zen*.

Of course, what I have to say about Indian cosmology in both *The Way of Zen* and *Psychotherapy E & W* is pretty concise. Here I shall spread myself more, and of course the material on the history and techniques of Yoga will be something new. This goes, too, for the chapter on Yoga and psychiatry, which will cover the ground from another angle than used in *Psy E & W*. It will, I think, be the first popularization of Campbell's and Eliade's theories about the shamanistic connections of Yoga.

Our understanding was, wasn't it, that this is in the first place to be a Pantheon book unfinanced by NAL, they having the option to take it up after a stated period in hardcover.

From January 23rd to 31st I shall be lecturing in Los Angeles, c/o Books in Review, LA.

Back to NY at the end of March.

Very best wishes — also from Mary Jane, who's been struggling with virus pneumonia, not serious but a nuisance.

As ever, Alan

Los Angeles, California | January 26, 1961
Dear Daddy:
What delightful letters you have been writing recently!... Of course, the experiment with clouds and trees is difficult when sky area predominates, for a small concentration of the darker against the lighter always captures attention. It is easier to make the sky the figure and the trees the ground if you look through branches, standing so close to them that they frame the sky. The Gestalt school of psychologists have worked out the rules as to what forms and motions take precedence over others in capturing attention, but it doesn't follow that what has the advantage in capturing attention is more real or more important. Seeing figure and ground in reverse is easier on the mottled surface of a pebble or a moth's wing or in the designs on seashells.

Since writing the essay on "The New Alchemy" I have been collaborating with a professor at Harvard in studying a substance called psilocybin, derived from a mushroom found in Mexico. This seems to bring about a very deep and absolutely pure mystical experience with no bizarre effects at all. Used for centuries by the Indians of Oaxaca in their religious ceremonials. I met him through Aldous Huxley.

Lance Whyte, the British biophysicist, is again in this country. I have been very greatly indebted to him for a number of important ideas. He is now at a university in Connecticut where there is an institute for advanced studies for independent research and contemplation. I hope to be invited there for a while so as to be with him, though in any event I shall see him in April. Today (I am writing from Los Angeles) I'm going to spend the afternoon with Gerald Heard, who's always crackling with bright ideas.

I am now working on the idea of getting one of the big foundations (Ford or Rockefeller) to give me grants for two or three years' study and thinking. I have been talking and writing so much that I think I ought to "refuel," particularly by having time to discuss various problems with other philosophers and psychologists both here and in England and Europe. This would take some of the pressure off me.

It has been a very dry, foggy, and cold winter here, but at last the much-needed rain is coming. Driest winter in 84 years!

Ann is blooming. She decided, I think very rightly, to postpone college for a while. I didn't want to press her, but I suggested long ago that she should spend a year here just getting accustomed to the new environment before plunging into studies. So this is what she has decided to do, and now has a part-time job at our favorite bookshop, facing the delightful waterfront of Sausalito. It's one of those easygoing places where they invite browsing, serve coffee and cakes, and have tables for playing chess.

Very much love to you both from us all. When I can get to it, I'll send you some pictures of the ménage at Fairfax. Greetings, too, from Mary Jane.

As always, Alan

SAN FRANCISCO, CALIFORNIA | FEBRUARY 12, 1961
Mr. Kyrill Schabert | Pantheon Books, Inc. | New York, New York
Dear Kyrill:
Many thanks for yours of the 8th. I'm very glad you liked the outline, and by all means pass it on to Arabelle and see if they want to take up their option right away. Am again the penurious author, facing the ravages of the tax season! I gather you'll send the contract in the next few days. As I remember the one on

Psy E & W, it carried a $1,500 advance of which $1,000 was payable on signing. I suppose some royalties are due about the 15th of this month, but much of these will have been eaten up by the second advance on *Psy E & W*. However, *This Is It* should be fuelling things up again. I'm a bit pressed because this is always the off-season for lectures in San Francisco.

I'm now pulling all available wires in New York to get a hefty foundation grant for the next two or three years. I am very concerned not to have to write and talk so much that I start repeating myself or losing quality. I've written Jack Barrett for advice although what I need is beyond the scope of Bollingen, but if you have any bright ideas or "right people" to whom you can drop a hint I shall be very grateful. What about Gordon Wasson? I think I told you that I've been working on his mushroom with Timothy Leary at Harvard, and he has invited me to Harvard at the end of March for conferences and an open lecture under his department. Also, to a special meeting of the American Psychological Assn. in NY in September.

Sorry that you, too, have been struggling with sickness, with storms and strikes thrown in. Mary Jane is now over the virus, but still a bit weak. She was down for a month with it, and thus all my routine work went to pot.

Your salesman in LA showed me the jacket for *Psy E & W*; it's really most effective.

All the best from us both, yours ever, Alan

SAN FRANCISCO, CALIFORNIA | FEBRUARY 27, 1961
Mr. Kyrill Schabert | Pantheon Books, Inc. | New York, New York
Dear Kyrill:
Many thanks for yours of the 24th. Herewith the contract [for the book on yoga], and if you can accommodate my request by wire of this date, grateful thanks!

Of course you have the option on my next book-length work, so I want to feel you out on something. I have a 10,000-word manuscript, just completed, on my experiences with LSD, mushrooms, etc., going into them in pretty vivid detail, and using almost entirely different material from "The New Alchemy" essay in *This Is It*. It will make a small book, like Huxley's *Doors of Perception*, but much more lively. I am transferring to this the title of *The Joyous Cosmology*, "a view of the world through the instrumentality of mescaline, lysergic acid, and psilocybin." It has a carefully reasoned introduction, followed by a free-flowing, poetic sort of description of the kind of world these things reveal. People who've read it here are out of their minds about it.

If you published it late fall, it would be just right for Christmas. On the other hand, in former times Pantheon has resisted the idea of little books, but then, again, I am quite sure this will sell abundantly. Wherever I go, people want to discuss this subject.

On the other hand, it might be better to put it out as a paperback pamphlet, like *Beat Zen*, and use it later in a book of essays. The point is, I'm pretty pleased with it, and feel it's worth a good offer, and don't want you to be excluded. Let me know, then, if you want to see the manuscript.

Best wishes, as ever, Alan

SAN FRANCISCO, CALIFORNIA | FEBRUARY 27, 1961
Dear Tim [Leary]:
Thanks very much for yours of the 14th and 23rd. I've been terribly busy with some writing, of which more in a moment, so overlooked acknowledging the mushrooms. Many thanks indeed! More reports and, soon, a tape are in store for you.

We'll probably drive east this time, leaving here about March 16th. Expect to be with you the 31st and for the weekend. I have to lecture at the New School on the evening of April 4th, but if anyone at Boston U or Brandeis or MIT wants a lecture, I'd be available Monday the 3rd or even Thursday the 30th... Just exactly what do you want the Harvard lecture to be about?

Yes, ask Jo Bartlett to call me. I'll see what I can do for him. Many a time have I handled these initiations, but a guy in my position has his hands full. Just everybody wants to be turned on, and I have to act a little esoteric!

I have just completed a 10,000-word manuscript entitled *The Joyous Cosmology* — a view of the world through the instrumentality of mescaline, lysergic acid, and psilocybin. Purpose: after a rather square introduction, to launch into a free-flowing, poetic account of this particular universe. Will make something like Huxley's *Doors of Perception*, but more vivid. Am taking it round the publishers, looking for the highest bidder! But you shall see it when I come.

One of my main objectives on this trip east is to get myself a foundation grant to contemplate for a year or two. I've been writing and talking too much, and want to go down into the depths to see if I can find some new fish.

What a blessing to the poor jailbirds you are going to be! I often lecture at San Quentin, where a very bright Protestant chaplain conducts courses in comparative religion. All the tea masters turn out for me.

Mary Jane and I are very much looking forward to being with you. I'll probably call you as soon as we hit NYC (about the 27th) and make last-minute arrangements.

All the best, Alan

SAN FRANCISCO, CALIFORNIA │ FEBRUARY 27, 1961
Mr. R. B. Silvers │ *Harper's* magazine │ New York, New York
Dear Mr. Silvers:
I'm afraid your letter of February 9th about my article "Eros & the American Way of Life" poses a very ticklish problem.

If I get as specific as you want me to be, I'm not going to be particularly welcome as a lecturer at many of the colleges and universities which I customarily visit. (Vide: the references to Koch and Russell, and a weird experience I had recently at Bryn Mawr.) Sure, I could illustrate the whole thing autobiographically, which would be fine if I were Henry Miller — though I'd do it in quite a different way. However, my tactics and, I think, my strong point in these matters, is to approach them (broach them?) with a certain indirection. The reader reads, and somewhat later does a double take.

I would be fascinated if, in place of my article, you could find someone who could do exactly what you want. But I think you may have difficulty! Otherwise, I agree almost entirely with all the criticisms of my article which you make. But if I follow your suggestions, I'm going to have difficulties in making a living, and supporting dependents, for which I'm sure the fee for the article won't compensate!

So, do you want to reconsider the article as is, or let me ungracefully "chicken out" and see if you can get something better?

Best wishes,
Sincerely, Alan Watts

c/o CHARLOTTE SELVER │ NEW YORK, NEW YORK (UNTIL APRIL 31ST [*sic*]) │
MARCH 24, 1961
Christmas Humpheys, Esq. │ London, England
Dear Toby:
At last, a chance to answer yours of February 17th. Of course I didn't get around to reading *Zen Comes West* until some time after publication, but it seems to me that the issues raised in my letter are perennial and not relative simply to any dated book. Surely by "contentious" you meant "controversial" — and I think that some answering remarks from you would be very much to the point. I don't see any real need to publish the first two pages alone, as I wrote only incidentally to comment on what you said about me. The main point was to discuss the absolutely radical problems which face the Westerner trying to practice Zen.

Presumably you saw the unbelievably ignorant article on this and other books in the *Times* Lit. Sup. of February 14th, by someone who couldn't even get the titles and authors' names straight. I hope someone wrote a letter to the editor; I get these things too late to make timely comments.

Edwin Halsey was going to the West Indies first and then on to London, so I gather you should expect him any time now.

Am now en route to New York and Harvard for sundry lectures; also to see if I can raise some funds to do a bit more travelling and maybe get over to England again.

Love to Puck, as ever, Alan

SAN FRANCISCO, CALIFORNIA | APRIL 15, 1961
Dear Mummy & Daddy:
Happy birthday, Mummy, though this will be a little late for it. I am in New York now, until May 2nd, at Charlotte Selver's. I had intended to write last week, but suddenly found myself in a lot of work helping the editors of *LIFE* magazine prepare an article about me which is supposed to come out this week. Will send it to you as soon as I get a copy. Lots of pictures.

This time I drove across the country instead of taking the plane, and it was a very interesting trip until reaching the dreary Middle West. This season in New York is going very well indeed, and I am working hard on getting foundation grants so that I will have some time to travel during the next year or two — I mean travel abroad, to England, Europe, and Mexico.

On the way across I spent a night with Joan and John, who are now in Indianapolis, and had a most delightful time with them. Her two babies are absolutely charming. Every ten days or so I talk with Ann on the phone, and all seems to be going well with her. She still has her part-time job at the bookshop in Sausalito, and is making innumerable friends.

Had a most fascinating weekend at Harvard, staying at my friend Timothy Leary's home. It was like the United Nations, for guests included both a Chinese and a Negro family — the latter with twins aged 2. The father was a psychiatrist, I think one of the best I have yet met, and with a sense of humor that almost had us rolling on the floor. Next week I am going to the University of Chicago for two days, and after that we shall be spending the weekend in the country, at the home of Dan and Marian Johnson in Long Island — a perfectly gorgeous place full of some of the finest modern paintings. Marian runs one of the main art galleries in New York.

So much goes on that I hardly know how to remember it. New York surrounds one with friends, and I must say, really wonderful ones, so that from now until May 2nd every evening is booked! In spite of all this I am managing to get a lot of work done, and am just finishing another (short) book to be called *The Joyous Cosmology*, to come out in the autumn. *Psychotherapy East & West* will be out in August, and Murray will be publishing *This Is It* in May. I am so glad to be back with them...I'm hoping to get together soon with Lancelot Whyte, who is now staying in Connecticut. Increasingly I find him the most intelligent and stimulating person that I know.

After leaving New York, I have a string of engagements in the West — Montana, Washington state, and Denver, Colorado, and will get back to San Francisco about May 20th, but then very shortly go on to Big Sur and Los Angeles, and again back here to New York at the beginning of September for a meeting of the American Psychological Association.

In all this whirl of travel and activity there are, happily, islands of rest — in Big Sur, at Elsa Gidlow's retreat in Mill Valley, and sometimes with Bob Balzer, in his exquisite place in the mountains about 70 miles east of Los Angeles.

Now I have to go to work. I have classes in conjunction with Charlotte Selver this weekend, and one of them is just about to start.

Best wishes from the Davenports and the Onslow-Fords, as well as love from Joan and Ann. The faster and the better all this work goes, the sooner I shall get to England again!

Very much love to you both, as always, Alan

SAN FRANCISCO, CALIFORNIA | MAY 23, 1961
Dear Mummy & Daddy:
Now we're back in California for the summer, but will go to the East Coast again about September 1st. The weather is lovely, the cottage is covered with roses, and the garden is star-spangled with daisies of all sizes. The fuchsias are in bud and will open in a few days. The day of our return we all had dinner with Elsa Gidlow — Ann and her boyfriend, Joel, and Mary Jane — and though there was some fog in the valley, Elsa's garden was just ablaze with flowers. (Mummy will remember that Elsa was living with Isabel Quallo of Walthamstow Hall — the Negro girl.)

This last New York trip was really very delightful. Since I last wrote there have been visits on Long Island with Nancy and Stanley Young, and Bob Platman who is the vicar of Syosset, an old friend and student of mine from Northwestern University days. Nancy Young writes novels under the name Nancy Wilson Ross and has just edited a marvelous anthology of modern writings about Zen. Her husband is a playwright — one of the most humorous people I've ever met, a sort of lovable, teddy-bear man. Their home is on one of the old estates of the island, and they have a wonderful art collection of both modern painters and Chinese and Japanese masters.

On the way back I gave lectures at two universities in the gorgeous mountain country of the Northwest, in Montana and Washington, and stayed (in Montana) with [a] professor of philosophy [Robert M. Pirsig? Alan reviewed his book *Zen and the Art of Motorcycle Maintenance* prior to publication] whose wife is an architect and designed their own home. Lovely place with a roaring mountain stream at the edge of the property. Then drove through Yellowstone Park and saw the geysers spouting, herds of buffalo, wild bears, and ospreys catching fish from the river. Got marooned for a day in mid-May in a blizzard (!) in Wyoming, and then drove to Denver for a weekend series of lectures at the home of an old friend who lives in the foothills of the Rockies. It was like sitting on a terrace overlooking the whole US.

On the way home, drove through Lake Tahoe on the border of California and Nevada, which was more beautiful than I had ever seen it. Vividly blue among mountains still covered with snow, and no crowds of tourists around. The Sierra was in full spring bloom with all the deciduous trees just bursting into leaf and the streams bubbling with melted snow.

That was quite a masterful comment on Uncle Willie's book. I helped him to edit it, and did what I could to smooth some of the rough edges. To judge from a letter he sent me at Christmas, he and Auntie Jean have not been too well. Daddy, you should perhaps have been a writer after all! I'll never forget your rewriting a play that I made up (aged about 11). We sat on the garden seat just behind the house and did line by line, and I was simply astonished at the way you polished up my crude efforts!

At the beginning of June we'll be off for two weeks to Big Sur and Los Angeles. In Big Sur we have a dinner coming up with one of the very great architects out here, Nathaniel Owings, who is inviting me to meet Laurance Rockefeller — the one who has done so much for the conservation of the wild country here in the West. Clare Luce told me he has been reading my books for some time but was diffident about approaching in person! Incidentally, the Owings house is amazing. A concrete prism perched on a rocky promontory 600 feet above the ocean and a nursery of sea lions. Margaret Owings is a superb artist and has just been working on a new medium — a sort of appliqué embroidery on burlap: vivid and joyous stuff.

I really have to get to work this summer: two books to write...but I'm glad I have a peaceful place to do it. Poor Aldous Huxley just had his home burned down as the result of a brush fire in the Hollywood Hills. No one hurt, but an awful loss of fine books and paintings. Expect to see him next month. He has a perfectly enchanting daughter-in-law, Ellen, whom we regularly see in New York and hope to see this summer as she is driving out to California in a Volkswagen bus to make geological films. She works for the NY Museum of Natural History.

Nothing yet settled with Dorothy. Sorry to say that more and more she becomes what Elsa Lanchester describes in one of her songs as "a righteous woman with a military stride."

I am still working on the project of getting grants from foundations for a two-year research and reflection period. If anything comes through I'll take the first jet plane to London and spend some time with you. Are you still making that excellent beer? It's impossible to find decent beer here, except in the spring when there is a so-called "bock" beer that comes from the bottom of the barrels.

Charlotte Selver will be coming to stay with us after the trip to Los Angeles and to do some work with me in San Francisco. She's just received $14,000 in reparations from the German government (was hounded out by Hitler), and may build a house out here. She was in the *LIFE* picture that also showed Ann.

It's now just about midnight and I think I must get to bed. Much, much love to you both.

As always, Alan

SAN FRANCISCO, CALIFORNIA | JULY 19, 1961
Dear Mummy & Daddy:
How very good to hear from you! But too bad this is a poor year in the garden. Here the weather is exceedingly hot and dry, making the whole country like a tinderbox, but the fruit seems to be plentiful — judging by the tree outside the window.

Main news is that after August 1st I am moving to Sausalito, the charming little fishing town just across the Golden Gate Bridge from San Francisco. You remember Gordon Onslow-Ford? Perhaps you never saw the old ferryboat which he has tied up in the harbor there, and which is converted into two enormous apartments. Well, I am taking one of these — comprising an immense studio, a very large living room, with sleeping quarters, and two additional bedrooms. The whole is in very solid condition, needs hardly any decorating, and has the most superb view of the bay and surrounding hills.

We'll give up the cottage in Fairfax, the studio in SF, and concentrate everything there. Our neighbor is a famous Greek artist, Janko Varda, a very exuberant old boy, who plies a large dhow-style sailing boat of many colors. So after August 1st, my address will be: The Gate Five Gallery, Sausalito, Calif.

I'm working hard at my book on "The Myths of Polarity" (i.e., of the pairs of opposites) [*The Two Hands of God*], and last week took a short lecture trip to two universities in Michigan, which was extremely well received. Met a Russian doctor and his wife who have a fabulous collection of Italian masters, including a Leonardo and a Raphael, as well as a collection of musical instruments from all over the world.

Let's see — since I last wrote I have also been again to Los Angeles and Big Sur, and on a visit to the latter had a dinner party at Nathaniel Owings's with Laurance Rockefeller, who seems to have been interested in my work for some time. Lectures in LA were more than usually successful. Ann is now spending a couple of weeks with friends in Santa Barbara. I have recently forced Dorothy into giving me proper access to the other children, and so have been seeing quite a lot of them lately.

It's so hot today that I'm sitting around in swimming trunks and just sweltering, so it's rather hard to think of things. Also I have to go into the city quite soon, and only hope it's cooler there. I'll send you pictures of the new place.

Lots of love to you both. I'll try to make it over next year.

As always, Alan

SAUSALITO, CALIFORNIA | AUGUST 24, 1961
Dr. Timothy Leary | Cambridge, Massachusetts
Dear Timothy:
Yesterday I picked up a letter at the post office from your address. Quite mysteriously, it vanished between picking it up and getting it home. Apologies, but what was it?

As you see, we have moved — into an absolutely magnificent old ferryboat, converted into a studio with enormous rooms and a marvelous view of the bay and the mountains. Gulls, herons, pelicans, ducks, and ever-changing moods of light.

Two other questions, with regard to the APA meeting:

1. Am I supposed to present a written paper in advance? I shall talk as if impromptu. It holds the audience better, but if somebody needs it, I will work up a preliminary outline, or whatever is required.

2. Do you suppose APA might pay my plane fare in advance? It's just possible that I might not have quite enough in the bank at the time to cover it.

I'm sure you had a fascinating session in Copenhagen. My plans require that I fly to NY for the APA meeting and then return here until about September 23rd, at which time I shall be coming east for about two months or more.

Mary Jane sends very best wishes. So all good things to you and yours.

As ever, Alan

SAUSALITO, CALIFORNIA | SEPTEMBER 5, 1961

Dear Daddy:

I'm sure you will have received my telegram. Under the circumstances I feel rather helpless, tied as I am here with so many responsibilities and an exceedingly busy season. But in any contingency, do please use any funds from my royalties that you have set aside. Of course, we knew that Mummy's strength could not hold out indefinitely, for you this must be a terribly difficult moment. My very warmest affection goes to you, and please, if you can get it to her, presuming she is still aware enough, tell Mummy that I love her for the wonderful courage that she has shown all through her life, and for giving me, above all else, a sense of the beautiful. And can you also convey something like this: I have had the privilege, especially in recent years, of seeing what I believe to be very deeply into the heart of this universe and its life — and there isn't anything to be afraid of. The end and bottom of it all is not emptiness, but a love beyond anyone's imagination.

Now as to Ann. I understand your concern, but I don't think you have been correctly informed. Joel is divorced, and his marriage broke up long ago. Under California law, remarriage cannot take place until a year after divorce, but that won't be so long now. In any case, what seems to me important in these things is not so much the legal and formal definitions as the genuine feelings and relationships between people. As you well know, my own standpoint in these matters is rather liberal, and so is that of the great majority of those in this country with whom I associate. Ann's marriage to a divorced man would hardly so much as raise an eyebrow in the milieu in which we live, which, I must say, comprises people of very high culture and character. Of course, standards change, and as we get older we're always inclined to feel that the children are "going to the dogs." The same feeling is expressed on an Egyptian tablet 6,000 years old! But I'm afraid Eleanor likes to make trouble. Ann feels totally rejected by her and, since she is now of legal age to make her own decisions (and mistakes), Eleanor is putting a finger into matters that are no longer her business. Incidentally, Ann's feeling in this regard existed long before she even met Joel. For myself, I'm inclined to feel happier that Ann loves a man with some experience of life and its difficulties than a callow youth still "wet behind the ears."

Ann has been working this summer in Santa Barbara, as companion to a wealthy family, where she has had room and board as well as salary. We're expecting her back today.

Yes, I have moved a lot. This place happens to be quite the most beautiful spot I have ever lived in. It is permanently moored, and reached by a short gangway. It is also amazingly capacious, and those who come aboard for the first time usually draw in their breath a bit. There is a vast studio room the whole width of the boat. At one end of this room there is a second, very large, room which I use as office, library, and living quarters. Beyond this a stairway leads to a small deck cabin. At the opposite end of the main room there are two other good-sized rooms, a kitchen and an enclosed sundeck. Above them another small deck cabin. The main room has a great window, where the paddle wheel used to be, looking out over nothing but water and birds to Mount Tamalpais in the distance. A similar apartment, on the other end of the boat, is occupied by a Greek artist Janko Varda, now 70 years old — a most robust and colorful figure. He has made himself a capacious sailing boat with a lateen (dhow-type) rig, all painted in brilliant hues, in which he takes out sailing parties of 12 or 14 people every Sunday. To see it go by makes you think you are in the Mediterranean. And the whole place is very shipshape and cleanly and restfully decorated.

Now let me give you some details of my future whereabouts. I'll be here until about Sept. 20th. Then I go east for the usual autumn lecture trip, making my headquarters with Charlotte Selver (Brooks), now married. I'll be in and out of New York, but she will always know where I am. Plan to be back here about the end of the first week in November. Perhaps, for a few days between Sept. 20 and Oct. 1st, I'll be at Harvard, but in any case you can always reach me through Charlotte.

Well, again, my fondest love to both of you and great sympathy at this very difficult time. Please have courage.

As always, Alan

SAUSALITO, CALIFORNIA | OCTOBER 22, 1961

Dear Daddy:

Joy's telegram came while I was "on the road," at Beloit College, Wisconsin. I returned here, to New York, this weekend to find your letter, as well as one from Joy written before the telegram and seemingly hopeful that Mummy's condition was improving.

I feel very sorry indeed that I cannot come over right away, but I am going all out and full time. Although this was all very much to be expected and puts the end to constant worry and suffering for both of you, the event itself leaves a void. It would be rather hollow to say that I hope you won't be lonely, after nearly fifty years' companionship. But would I be wrong in the impression that over the past years you seem to have gained a very marked degree of inner peace and resourcefulness? I often say, when complimented for philosophy, "Well you should meet my father. He doesn't write, but he really has it."

Naturally, I have been very fully prepared for this since the emergency in 1959 when I last came over, but now I am really concerned as to how you will fare. I can understand your distaste for a housekeeper, and wonder if you can manage just with Mrs. Chance to help and by confining yourself to the ground level of the house. I am sure that in your position I would want to be left alone and not fussed over by some stranger.

I have to catch a plane for Boston in a few minutes, but could not let another day go by without at least sending you my love and affection at this difficult moment. You are very constantly in my thoughts. I will write again later in the week. I know you will be strong.

As always with love, Alan

SAUSALITO, CALIFORNIA | NOVEMBER 17, 1961
Dear Daddy:
I have been spending a couple of days in Indianapolis with Joan and John, and their two bouncing children. It has been a very delightful interlude after a long period of lecturing, though today I'm off to Chicago for one more lecture before returning to the West. Your great-grandchildren are, I am quite sure, all that you could want them to be: robust, to say the least, as good-looking as their parents, and most talkative. Last night Joan cooked a wonderful Japanese sukiyaki dinner, and we all ate so heartily that this morning we're feeling rather wobbly below!

Thank you for the details of Mummy's funeral. I would always agree to the principle of cremation. We have complex laws about it in California, but I wonder whether it would be permissible to scatter the ashes in the garden. There is something very fitting about returning to the very ground one has loved to cultivate.

I have answered a letter from Francis Everington, saying that I would be glad to serve as an executor, and he will send me the necessary papers for signature. I do want to get to England as soon as I can, and I may have told you in a previous letter that I am trying to get two years' income from foundations for a special research project that will involve some travel to both England and Europe. But such funds would not be available until July 1st, 1962, at the earliest — unless there is some unusually lucky break. In the meantime, it seems most likely that I shall go to Japan for May and two weeks of June, taking a party of students to visit Kyoto and a few other places.

I hope you have received *Psychotherapy East & West* by now. The next book, *The Joyous Cosmology*, is already in production and will be an extraordinarily beautiful volume. Pantheon's designer is most enthusiastic about doing a good job with it, and we have selected about 24 full-page photographs to go with the text: highly magnified views of the intricate patterns of nature — crystals, water, butterfly wings, leaf structure, and so on. Just before I left NY we made a final selection of the pictures and settled on the typographical style. I always enjoy these problems.

Spent a lovely weekend with Dan and Marian Johnson at their beautiful home on Long Island. They run one of the great art galleries in NY, and have a personal collection of their own which is one of the best selections of modern painting that I have seen.

Their home is the former dairy of her grandmother's estate — a house with walls about 3½ ft. thick, supporting an upstairs which overhangs the downstairs — each room having its own balcony overlooking a large pond where two wild geese make their home for part of the year. They gave a dinner party, inviting some of my best friends, including Nancy and Stanley Young (she a novelist and he a playwright), and Alan Dunn and his wife Mary Petty, both cartoonists for *The New Yorker*. She did the cover drawing I sent Mummy several years ago; the one of the elegant old lady warming her legs in front of the fireplace [in *The New Yorker*, March 14, 1942]. The party also included Michael Collins, junior partner of Collins, the London publishing house, a most likable and intelligent young man.

Please give my love to Joy and Sybil. I do so appreciate what they are doing for you, and I hope there can be some satisfactory solution to the housekeeper problem. Joan, John, and family ask me to send you their love. You should have heard from Ann by now. They will meet my plane on Saturday. I'll write again just as soon as possible after returning.

Much, much love, as always, Alan

SAUSALITO, CALIFORNIA | [LATE NOVEMBER 1961]
Dear Daddy:
I have just heard from Joy that things have not been going so well with you. I saw your delightful letter to Ann, and have, of course, received the one you wrote me from the hospital. I am keeping in fairly constant touch with Joy, and wish I could do more than telling her how very deeply I appreciate all that she is doing.

I thought you might like to have these pictures of the ferryboat. In the colored one, I am standing at the top of the gangway with two friends, and it gives you an idea of its size. The black-and-white ones show the main fireplace under the central funnel, and the large window looking out onto the bay. The arrowhead beams beyond the window used to support the paddle wheel. Other people in the pictures are students at one of my seminars.

Things here in New York are most active, and, among other things, we are making final arrangements for my TV series to appear on one of the two main stations (National Broadcasting Corp.) starting November 5th. It has not hitherto been seen in New York City. I don't know whether you have any appetite for reading, but a copy of the new book has been sent to you at Holbrook Lane. The package carries Pantheon's label.

I do hope you are comfortable in the Farnborough Hospital. Joy seems to have a very good impression of the sister in charge. Please don't try to write if it's too much strain. I'll simply let you know how things are going from week to week, and rely on Joy for news from you. We love you very, very much and hope that all the rest you can get will tap the source of life and give you a long time with us yet.

Most affectionately, Alan

SAUSALITO, CALIFORNIA | NOVEMBER 21, 1961
Mr. Laurance Rockefeller | New York, New York
Dear Mr. Rockefeller:
Further to our talk on the telephone, I am writing as you suggested to give you a concise outline of the project I have in mind, and upon which I have already been working in a preliminary way.

The problem is essentially one of communication: to find the clearest possible language for expressing the fact that man is an organism/environment, or, in other terms, that the individual and the world constitute a unified field of behavior.

Although I first came across this idea in my studies of Chinese philosophy, I later realized that it was also emerging in such sciences as ecology, biology, and social psychology (e.g., in the "transactionalism" of John Dewey and A. F. Bentley).

But it seems to me that scientists and philosophers alike run into the most peculiar difficulties in expressing this idea clearly even to the intelligent layman. Our common sense and the very structure of the languages in which we think are so committed to the notion of the individual as a *thing* acting all on its own *in* an environment, that a transactional relationship between the two is hard to grasp — especially in terms of specific problems in ethics, law, and technology.

I do not believe that the rather urgent recommendations of conservationists, ecologists, and others concerned with the proper "control" of our environment can make much headway until we can get around these difficulties.

My specific task, then, is (a) to study the built-in resistances which our languages and patterns of thought offer to this "field" concept of human behavior, and (b) to consider what forms of speech and conceptual models will make the idea much more readily intelligible.

I am therefore looking for a two-year grant for study, including the opportunity to travel and discuss particular aspects of the problem with authorities in the various fields involved, leading up to the publication of my findings in book form. I am not satisfied with my own presentation of these ideas in *Nature, Man, and Woman* and *Psychotherapy East & West*, and feel certain that I can do very much better.

I would like, if I can, to get a grant of $10,000 per annum for the two years of study, and in any situation where grants are not payable directly to the individual concerned, I am sure I could arrange to do the work under the auspices of the New School for Social Research or perhaps the Department of Social Relations at Harvard.

Any help you can offer will be most deeply appreciated. With many thanks and best wishes,

Sincerely yours, Alan Watts

PS. (An explanatory footnote.) Just as an example: what social psychologists and ecologists have to say about the influence of the social and natural environments upon individual behavior always *sounds* like determinism, and is thus repugnant to the individual's sense of freedom.

This is partly because the individual has adopted a sense of identity which excludes the environment and restricts "himself" within the boundaries of his skin. But this sense of identity is arbitrary and even demonstrably false. Yet it cannot be changed without the clearest and most cogent description of an alternative. — AW

SAN FRANCISCO, CALIFORNIA | NOVEMBER 26, 1961
Mr. Kyrill Schabert | Pantheon Books | New York, New York
Dear Kyrill:

May I answer in one letter yours of November 13th, Paula's of the 14th, and Gerta's of the 17th?

1. Many thanks indeed for the extra $500 against royalties due. I'm so sorry I had to leave before you returned from Europe, but I certainly hope we can see each other when I get back to NY in March — somewhat after the middle of the month, and staying on until about April 10th.

2. Thanks for the credit to *Books In Review* in Los Angeles. Harry Hill has been of immense help to me, and I want to keep relations between this store and Pantheon as cordial as possible. I am sure he will appreciate your consideration in

this particular problem, and I feel you have been most courteous. *Beyond this, will you be sure to let him have proofs of* The Joyous Cosmology *as soon as available?*

3. The subtitle for *The Joyous Cosmology*. The problem of those suggested by Gerta is that mescaline is not the main chemical involved, but LSD-25. Now I think "Ventures into the World of LSD" might not be too comprehensible. So let's try instead: "Adventures in the Chemistry of Consciousness," or "Experiments with Drugs and the Mind," or "Experiments in the Chemistry of Mysticism," or "An Exploration with Consciousness-Changing Drugs." I think the last is the best, even though "consciousness-changing" is a bit awkward. However, it's terribly difficult to find the proper vocabulary in this realm, and the term was at least invented by Aldous Huxley!

Very best wishes, as ever, Alan

SAN FRANCISCO, CALIFORNIA | NOVEMBER 29, 1961
Mr. Klaus Gemming | Pantheon Books | New York, New York
Dear Klaus Gemming:
It seemed best to deal with the problem by making up a dummy. There are just a few author's corrections (it has been wonderfully printed) and these could be transferred to another galley set.

So, I've done my best to get things as you wanted them. The space seems to allow for 21 pictures instead of 20, though I have calculated on 6 pp. of front matter and 6 pp. for the foreword. I doubt if it will be that long. I have also assigned the last page (100) for the description of the plates. But I haven't succeeded in getting p. 28 blank as you wanted it. None of the pictures seemed appropriate to the prologue.

I'm not quite sure whether I like the idea of grey background for part titles and grey for initial caps. It makes the text itself look photographic (which of course it is, being offset), but I prefer the impression of clean letterpress. But I leave it to your judgment. Again, for the main title page I would prefer just type. I am not quite clear as to the idea you have in mind, but wouldn't the letters *J C* appearing as a sort of decorative background suggest "Jesus Christ"?

I enclose copy for (1) the "by the same author" page, (2) the dedication, and (3) the description of plates. But on (3) note that I have no information as to subject and photographer on 55, nor of photographer on 50 and 64. None of these were included in *Forms and Patterns in Nature*.

I am sorry that you are going to leave Pantheon, but I am sure you must have found a better opportunity. I don't know where Pantheon will get someone to do such marvelous designing, and I deeply appreciate the skill and enthusiasm you have shown with this particular volume.

Sincerely yours, Alan Watts

SAUSALITO, CALIFORNIA | DECEMBER 11, 1961
Mr. Edwin Seaver | George Braziller, Inc. | New York, New York
Dear Ed:

This is in answer to yours of the 6th.

I have received the Ackermann MS, and am working on it. Simply from a stenographic and copy editor's point of view it's in poor shape, and she will really have to do something more to provide or indicate sources of proper illustrations.

Talked with Perry a few days ago, and I regret to say that he, too, is lagging and does not expect to be finished until about mid-January. I am dismayed that Dorothy Norman has now put it off until March, but she is an extremely busy person. On all sides, however, I am getting the reaction, "Please don't rush us if you want a really good job. Surely the publishers want something of quality, and not just a hack job." This is, of course, the perennial problem — that scholars and philosophers, as distinct from journalists, have the most terrible time writing to order and making deadlines.

I still am confident that you will have my complete written MS by January 1st. It will take me a little longer to collate the pictures.

Best wishes, Alan

SAUSALITO, CALIFORNIA | DECEMBER 20, 1961
Dear Daddy:

I'm afraid you have had such a long wait for a letter, but since I last wrote I have been travelling and working almost incessantly. But perhaps a little relaxation is in sight: two weeks ago I talked with Laurance Rockefeller, and he seems really interested in picking down into the pockets of his vast foundations so that I can get a grant for the philosopher's duty — contemplation!

This may not arrive quite in time for Christmas — but what I hope will arrive in time is a copy of Fosco Maraini's book *Karakoram*, one of those marvelously photographed epics of mountaineering which I know you enjoy. I have had it sent to you c/o Joy, as I'm not quite sure whether you've yet returned to Holbrook Lane.

I got back here from New York on November 20th, and then took another trip to the East, or, rather the South, to Atlanta in Georgia for a week's lecturing at a group of Negro colleges. Then back here again, to be immediately involved in toting up the accounts for the year, getting announcements ready for the next round of lectures and seminars, and dozens of little odd jobs around the boat such as stopping leaks from the rain, and getting the place adequately heated. But in all this incredible whirl of activity there are compensations. For the last several days the water has been quite literally thick with birds — ducks of all kinds, grebes, herons, gulls — I have never seen such a multitude before. The herons glide past the windows; the grebes dive for fish; the ducks bob up and down on the misty water. There are literally hundreds of them within a hundred yards of the boat, and occasionally flights of geese pass over on their way to Mexico and the Gulf of California for the winter.

I am planning a big Christmas dinner here with Ann and Joel, Gert and Dave Davenport, Elsa Gidlow and her sister (you may remember her as a friend of Mummy's student, Isabel, at Walthamstow Hall), and one or two others. Mary Jane, my indefatigable secretary, has set up a tiny potted Christmas tree decorated with bees, dragonflies, grasshoppers, bluebirds, and minute angels — all perfect little creatures made, presumably, in Japan!

Speaking of Japan — it seems that at long, long last I shall be going there for the month of May and the first two weeks of June, but in the line of work, taking a group of students to visit some of the great shrines and gardens around Kyoto. The whole thing is being arranged by a travel agency connected with my television station here in San Francisco.

I have recently completed all the work for my next book, *The Joyous Cosmology*, and Pantheon's production manager has done a really exquisite job of typography with it. It includes some 20 photographs of the near-in view of pattern in nature — crystals, seashells, leaf skeletons, ripples on water, wings of butterflies — all designed to give some idea of the incredible rhythm and detail of the dance of life which drugs like LSD reveal. It's going to have a foreword by Timothy Leary, who, as I may have told you, is doing the main research in this domain of psychology at Harvard. I spent some more time with him this autumn, and on this visit went with him to the prison at Concord, where he is doing some really remarkable rehabilitation work with a test group of some 30 inmates.

On the way back from New York I spent a couple of days with Joan and John in Indianapolis. Joan is expecting another baby, and I found both David and Elizabeth perfectly delightful. They are very beautiful children, and both of them highly talkative and intelligent. Joan and John seem marvelously happy together and, as one might have expected, Joan has become a young lady of such amazingly good looks that I can hardly believe she's my daughter. They have a modestly "elegant" house in one of the most charming parts of the city (though

Indianapolis isn't any San Francisco), and I must say that Joan seems to have "fallen on her feet" very well indeed...Ann is another story, but no less interesting. Ann has become a red-blooded, vibrant, and exuberant personality, with a capacity for dancing which is really extraordinary. At present she is studying with the best Hindu dancer we have in the West — Shivaram — and a few nights ago she joined with him in a public performance here on the boat, demonstrating the primary movements and disciplines. About 75 people came, and we had a most delightful evening, with Shivaram and his wife, Janaki, performing in their gorgeous costumes a series of dances in which everything moves — eyes, face muscles, individual fingers — so that human beings seem to be transformed into the gods and goddesses of Indian mythology.

Well, it seems to be getting very late at night, and I think I must stop. Do please let me know what are your immediate plans. I'll be here in Sausalito until mid-January, then to Los Angeles for two weeks, and then back here until mid-March.

Lots of love, and best of wishes for Christmas and the New Year,

As always, Alan

SAUSALITO, CALIFORNIA | JANUARY 4, 1962

Dear Joe [Campbell]:

Many, many thanks to you for two feasts: that fabulous mince pie, and now the proofs of volume 2. I have spent three hours giving the latter a fairly thorough skim, and returning three galleys to you, which may perhaps belong to the set which you were correcting.

I am really flabbergasted by the scope and detail of your knowledge, combined with a flair for writing that makes such a learned work positively poetic. I have specially enjoyed the wealth of historical and archaeological background, which makes tremendous sense out of things that are otherwise confused and puzzling.

I have two comments that may be useful. I may not have skimmed thoroughly enough, but have you given adequate treatment to the dramatic aspect of Hindu mythology — the theme of Brahman-Atman as the player of all the parts in the world? There are, indeed, lots of references to the theme, but I think the book would be enriched by more substantial quotation from the appropriate sources.

Galley 40. Haven't you put the precession of the equinoxes backwards? The sun is now rising at the vernal equinox in Pisces, and is on the verge of moving into Aquarius. Or rather, I should ask whether your version is up-to-date, not backwards. You are putting it *now* in Aries, but this is where it was when astrology was invented. Anyhow, I think you might check on this. Astrologers today make a lot of the fact that the vernal equinox was moving into Pisces at the time of the birth of Christ, and that we are now entering the Aquarian Age.

I think you did a great job with the Egyptian materials, usually so out-of-this-worldly confusing. I've also been working on the Horus-Set polarity. I've turned up in Mercer's *Religion of Ancient Egypt* (p. 55) a marvelous figure of the two heads on one body.

So — all good things and a most happy New Year to you both. When I've been through the galleys more carefully I'll write you again.

Love from us both — Alan

The following is addressed to a Jungian psychologist at Harvard.

FEBRUARY 2, 1962
Dr. Henry Murray | Cambridge, Massachusetts
Dear Harry:
Laurance Rockefeller is offering me a two-year grant for research and study on a project that has long been dear to my heart, and I am, at the same time, in rather urgent need of letting up on this incessant lecturing and doing some deep thinking!

The grant would be approximately $10,000 per annum, but it has to be handled through an academic institution. Mr. Rockefeller is particularly interested in Princeton and wanted me to apply there first. However, the project was submitted to Charles Page, of their Council on Human Relations, who felt that my approach was too philosophical for their scheme of things even though "its long-range results may have important implications for the social sciences."

Well, I'm not so unhappy about this as I have no special connections with Princeton and do not know what I would find there by way of inspiration. What I would much rather prefer is the opportunity of working through your own Department of Social Relations, because my visits with you and others at Divinity Avenue have been uniquely stimulating. Would you, therefore, consider the possibility of sponsoring this grant and project?

As you can see from the enclosed outline, the project calls for quite a bit of travel (for discussion with persons in the same area of interest) and for this and other reasons should not require residence at the sponsoring institute — only frequent visits, and perhaps residence for short periods.

As you know, my work does not lie within the formal boundaries of any one academic discipline, and my *forte* is for provocative conceptualization rather than piecemeal research. My outline does not, therefore, pretend to any specific predictions of the project's results because I cannot really say where it may lead until I am deeply involved with it.

I expect to be in Cambridge in the latter part of March, but an early indication of your interest in this idea would be very welcome. I shall be most grateful for your consideration, and positively elated if we can work together.

Very sincerely, Alan Watts

SAUSALITO, CALIFORNIA | (UNTIL APRIL 20: C/O CHARLOTTE SELVER, NEW YORK, NEW YORK) | MARCH 15, 1962
Dr. James Hillman | C. G. Jung Institute | Zurich, Switzerland
Dear Jim:
Apologies for the delay in answering yours of January 15th, but I've had mountains of work on my hands and a lot of travel.

I wish I could get over to Europe again soon. I have had thoughts of trying it this coming autumn, and am going to discuss the prospects with Jack Barrett.

As to "hara-kiri" (lit., belly cutting), get in touch with Karlfried von Dürckheim, who will, I think, have a good deal of information. Otherwise, see:

E. J. Harrison, *The Fighting Spirit of Japan*. O.p., but published in England about 1913. (Unwin.)

B. H. Chamberlain, *Things Japanese*.

These are rather old sources, for much of my reading on Japanese folkways was done years ago and I haven't kept up with it. However, I have just this minute called Donald Keene, quite the authority on these matters, and he suggests:

Nitobe, *Bushido: The Soul of Japan* (o.p.).

Mamoru Iga, "Cultural Factors in Suicide of Japanese Youth" in *Sociology & Social Research*, vol. 46, 1, Oct. 1961.

Tatai, "A Further Study of Suicide in Japan" in *Report of the Dept. of Physiological Hygiene*, Inst. of Public Health, Tokyo, vol. 7, 1.

Haring, "Japanese National Character" in *Personal Character & Cultural Milieu*, Syracuse, NY, 1956.

Robert Bellah, *Tokugawa Religion*, Free Press, Glencoe, Ill., 1957.

Maybe this will help.

Very best wishes, Alan Watts

NEW YORK, NEW YORK (UNTIL APRIL 20TH) | APRIL 9, 1962
Dear Daddy:
My rather long silence has been due to constant travel and work, but now I'm settled here for a few days and there's a little peace for writing. Slowly, but I

think surely, plans are moving ahead for those foundation grants as I need to get some rest, and to make it possible to think of coming to England again. The Jung Institute in Zurich is also asking for more lectures, and I have a very good relationship with the young American doctor who is its new director. Happily divorce proceedings are at last under way, and we are beginning to get all those troubles settled. But it involves an enormous amount of legal and accounting work, in which I have been blessed by the help of one of my students who is a public accountant and a very expert financial advisor.

Charlotte Selver and I have swapped homes for some weeks, as she is with her husband working in California. I have been in and out of New York since March 15th, giving lectures in St. Louis, Washington, and Boston. I'll be back in California from April 20th to May 1st, when I set out for six weeks in Japan, and then back for Ann's wedding in the middle of June.

Just as soon as a copy is off the press I'm going to send you this astoundingly beautiful new book, *The Joyous Cosmology*. I have seen unbound sheets, and the publishers have really gone to extremes to make an exquisite book with the most extraordinary photographs of detail in nature. They have promised me copies by April 18th.

A day or two ago Aldous Huxley was here and I had a chat with him on the phone. He has just been appointed a visiting professor "of nothing in particular" (as he says) at the University of California in Berkeley, and so we shall be getting together on my return. He has just published a very fascinating new book called *Island* — essaying the very difficult task of writing a convincing utopia. I think you might enjoy it, so long as you do not expect it to read like the novel it claims to be. It's more of a philosophical and social essay in dialogue, and what interests me so much is that over the years we've both come to adopt pretty much the same views about most major problems. Aldous is close to 70 now and is beginning to look rather frail. We see a lot of his delightful daughter-in-law, Ellen, who lives in a charming old house in Brooklyn. Had dinner there last week with a very intriguing company of guests. Ellen is a zoologist, and makes up for not being particularly pretty with a sprightly personality, interested in everything under the sun.

Although I haven't seen her yet, Ruth Sasaki is here in New York. Apparently she came to my lecture last Tuesday, but there was such a crowd I didn't see her. I am rather astonished, as I know she considers me a sort of black sheep of the Zen movement, but I suppose curiosity got the better of her!

I have replied as promptly as possible to Francis Everington's letters, and I hope all the formalities are now satisfactorily completed...And how are things with you? Is the new housekeeper working out all right? And are you regaining your strength? I manage to keep pretty well, despite all the work, though I had a brief bout with some sort of chest cold the week before last. But I just have to "refuel" and let down the pace. I have just heard, via the grapevine, that the Bollingen Foundation has awarded me a grant for two years at $5,000 p.a., but the one I'm really waiting for is from Laurance Rockefeller, who has promised $10,000 if I can get a university to handle it. So I'm working on my old friend Henry Murray at Harvard to put it through their Department of Social Relations. If all this goes through, I shall aim at coming to England sometime between September and October. The project for which I have applied for these grants requires some travel — for brain-picking, as I want to consult a lot of people both here and in Europe who are working on related lines, such as Lance Whyte in London.

Very much love — and please hang on to this existence for a while so that we can get together again!

As always, Alan

NARA HOTEL | NARA, JAPAN | MAY 23, 1962
Gary Snyder and Joanne Kyger
Dear Gary and Joanne,
It seems now that there will be an opportunity to see you again before leaving, and we would enjoy it enormously. We shall be in Osaka two extra days, Saturday, June 2, and Sunday, June 3 — so we could get together Saturday about 6 PM, as before? We'll come out to your place unless you drop me a line to the contrary c/o Japan Travel Bureau, in Kyoto. Looking like my research grant is definitely going through, so I want to talk further about staying in Kyoto for a time.

Love to you both — Alan

PS. Can you pick me up a Zenrin Kushu — Chinese-style binding as it's *lighter*?

PPS. Why don't we arrange to bring dinner (sushi, etc.) that evening so that we can have undistracted conversation.

NARA, JAPAN | MAY 23, 1962
Dear Daddy:
There is increasing probability of being able to come to England in September. I have just heard from the Dept. of Social Relations at Harvard that they are willing to appoint me as a research associate, and this should clinch the grant which Laurance Rockefeller has offered for a two-year period. (The grant had

to go through a university.) The idea of the grant is to give me some rest from intensive writing and lecturing so that I can "refuel." I don't have to stay in any one place, since part of the idea is that I should be able to travel and have talks with people in various countries who are working on similar lines.

Now if all this works out, I shall also be lecturing at the Jung Institute in Zurich sometime in October, and in this case it would be great fun if you could come, too. You could meet my old friends Kurt and Helen Wolff, who used to be my publishers at Pantheon Books, but have now retired to Switzerland. Well, we can plan all that nearer the time.

We are continuing to have a most fascinating journey, and are now in Nara, which was the first capital of Japan, back in the 8th century. Yesterday we saw what I feel to be one of the most beautiful works of art ever created, the enclosed image of Maitreya (the future Buddha), which is in a convent at the Horyu-ji Temple.

We had all kinds of wonderful experiences in Kyoto: tea ceremony with Soshu Sen, the number-one master of the art, a fabulous dinner with the abbot of Myoshinji (Zen) who is 92 years old, and amazingly alert as well as bubbling with humor. The rock-and-sand gardens are far more lovely than I had imagined, even with the aid of excellent photographs. Photographs can never convey the subtle qualities of light, nor include the whole context in which these gardens are set: the surrounding temple buildings, whose rooms are entirely walled with "fusuma" screens painted by the very great masters. (Fusuma is a sliding door, or wall panel.) Nor do they catch the forested mountains and the neighboring roofs of building which enclose these gardens. It is so strange, in looking at this landscape, to realize what realists the great screen painters were — that Chinese and Japanese painting is neither fantastic nor stylized, but really just the way things look.

We return to California June 15th, after a brief stop in Hawaii. Saturday June 16th will be a great celebration for the announcement of Ann's wedding, and then I'll have to be off to Los Angeles until July 1st — to settle down for the summer!

Lots of love,

As always, Alan

JW: Alan's first trip to Japan was in May and June of 1962. He and Jano, with a group of more than twenty fellow tourists, billed as "The Alan Watts Tour of Japan," traveled to a number of historical areas, notably the city of Kyoto, where much of the tour's time was spent. They visited many of the famous Buddhist temples and gardens, including Nishi Hongan-ji, Ryoan-ji, and Daitoku-ji, where our grandmother, Ruth Sasaki, lived and maintained the subtemple, Ryosen-an. Alan makes no reference to having had the tour visit her subtemple or meeting with her. Alan and Jano did spend time with Gary Snyder and Joanne Kyger in Kyoto. Alan gave lectures to the group during mealtimes about the various sects of Buddhism, Japanese arts, theater, temple architecture, and gardens.

Alan was, understandably, struck with the beauty of the old Japan and its contrast with the modern Japan, which developed after World War II. The architecture (something I was keenly aware of when I lived there in the 1950s) became an abomination of cement and glass buildings, as square as the blocks with which they were built. Interestingly, the ancient temple buildings (some of which date back to the ninth century) are often rebuilt every few hundreds of years by craftsmen trained by older generations of carpenters in the intricate techniques used in the construction, with cedar grown specifically for the purpose. Japan is one of the few countries having a classification for such artisans as "national treasures." Alan relished the old streets and neighborhoods, which still catered to silk weaving and sold scented sumi inks and calligraphy brushes, tea bowls and exotic teas, and handmade papers, along with, of course, the wonderful food vendors.

Alan took four tour groups to Japan between 1962 and 1967. He was forty-six years old on his first trip, whereas I was eighteen when I first went to Japan. I lived there for two years, first in Daitoku-ji with our grandmother, and later, after I was married, in the seaport of Kobe. (Anne was fourteen when she came from England to Japan to attend my wedding.) Daitoku-ji, considered the main temple for the Rinzai sect of Zen Buddhism, is an absolutely beautiful temple compound with a huge main gate, a main temple, and many subtemples within the compound, with famous walled gardens, carefully maintained by monks.

My fondest memory of Japan was the rain. Alan's last chapter in his autobiography is "The Sound of Rain" (also published in Playboy*) and, to my childish delight, I found it before he did. Our grandmother's house in Ryosen-an was old-style Japanese — wood, glass, and paper. At night, a futon would come out from a closet and be laid out on the tatami, and I would lie under a quilt of silk. I'd awake at four in the morning to the deep, resonating sound of the main temple gong, calling monks to meditation. In my waking dreams, I would often hear this echoing sound, muffled by softly falling rain — almost a mist — dawn light barely breaking. To me, it was the most beautiful way to start the day. Alan, too, mentioned this as his favorite impression of Japan.*

Alan's wish to take a sabbatical from his heavy schedule of lecturing and other public appearances was granted. Harvard agreed to take him on as a research fellow to accommodate the rules for grants from both the Bollingen and Rockefeller

Foundations. This arrangement gave him more freedom to travel, rest, study, and write. It also promised light at the end of the tunnel of his marriage. Jano quietly disappeared from the scene to New York City, supposedly to make it seem for purposes of the divorce that she had left Alan. Dorothy apparently believed this and wrote him that she'd heard that Jano had left, but too bad — she wasn't taking him back. Mutual friends spent time trying to counsel Dorothy not to be so bitter and hateful. Curiously, Alan even had Gavin Arthur read her horoscope in an attempt to nudge her into a different frame of mind.

After many months of legal discovery and depositions, haranguing with the IRS about his actual income, Alan, with the aid of his friend and accountant Donald Gates, was able to finally reach a settlement with Dorothy, and the divorce was granted in August 1962. According to California law, however, Jano and Alan would not be able to marry for a year. Jano was quite unhappy about this and begged to find a way to get around the law. She wanted to be legally married.

In July 1962, our stepfather, Carlton Gamer, visited Alan on the Vallejo. *He had become highly respected, both as the dean of the music department at Colorado College and as a composer. His music has been featured at Carnegie Hall and many other venues. He, too, had toured Japan and was about to visit again as an Asia Society fellow. Their conversation was mostly about Japan.*

Anne and Joel were married in several ceremonies, including one in which Alan officiated. Alan speaks of Anne's wonderful bohemian lifestyle, treating mine as something just short of conventional. I was married to an up-and-coming business executive in Ohio, and Anne, to a concert harpist in San Francisco. Quite a difference. I could get Alan to come visit if I arranged lectures for him, which I did. He was written up in the local newspaper, which attracted the attention of talk-show host Phil Donahue (then in Dayton), and Alan and I appeared on his show. A few weeks later, Phil had comedian Tom Smothers on his show; he invited me to be in the audience and introduced me to Tom. This eventually led to a meeting between Tom and Alan in the hopes that they could collaborate on a show. Alan wrote up a rather humorous British-style script, which never aired. He felt that "Tom just didn't get it!"

There is a brief mention of one of the Northwestern University students who frequented Canterbury House, Jacqueline Baxter Doolittle, a pretty, vivacious young woman who had been close to Alan and his friend Jack Gouldin. She had been in a terrible auto accident on a New York freeway. She had severely damaged her face and was suffering from aphasia. Her husband, Harry Doolittle, worked at the Ted Bates advertising agency, and Alan was hoping that while Jano was in New York she could garner some information about how Jacquie was doing.

Alan continued to be politically involved with the ongoing debate on whether psychotropic drugs should be criminalized. The reader will see a few letters addressing this issue, which also involved the Native American tribes and their use of such drugs as sacraments in the Native American Church. He participated in conferences with the Oglala and Shoshone tribes and pleaded that their religious rites and lifestyle honoring the earth should be respected.

Alan's two-year sabbatical was jammed full of travel: Chicago, New York, London, Zurich, and Los Angeles. Reading his letters, one wonders how he kept up the pace. He turned fifty on January 6, 1965. A formal dinner party was held aboard the Vallejo, with a colorful array of guests in formal dress, all close friends. James Broughton was the master of ceremonies and delivered a wonderful poem; there were many toasts and much ribald gaiety.

Alan's frequent mention of Jano's illness was a cover for her alcoholism. I noticed that she kept a pint of vodka hidden behind the watercooler in the galley, and I often caught sight of her taking a swig while I was visiting. Vodka had the ability to put her almost immediately into a stupor from which she couldn't recover for hours. I often thought she was allergic to it because it seemed to take so little to have that effect. This was quite frustrating to Alan. Whereas he could consume a quantity of the beverage and still appear to function, Jano disappeared and went to sleep. Over time, this became an embarrassment to him.

Alan met and became friends with Bishop James Pike of Grace Cathedral in San Francisco. Pike, an outspoken theological liberal, had been charged with heresy but was vindicated by the Episcopal House of Bishops in 1965. In September of that year he and Alan held a conference at Esalen Institute in Big Sur, on "Christianity in Revolution." Pike also made news in a nationally televised séance in which he attempted to communicate with his son, who had recently committed suicide. Alan was grieved when in 1969 Bishop Pike died from a fall in the Judean Desert while doing research with his wife.

In a letter to his friend Laura (Archera) Huxley, Alan had reviewed an article Laura was writing about Aldous, to whom she'd been married, all too briefly, from 1956 to 1963. Her book, Timeless Moment: A Personal View of Aldous Huxley *(Celestial Arts, 1968), was written after his death. Alan also makes mention of Jano's "illness," wondering if a Dr. Niehaus would be of help.*

SAUSALITO, CALIFORNIA | JULY 7, 1962

Miss Kim N. Cohen | George Braziller, Inc. | New York, New York

Dear Miss Cohen:

I returned from Japan only to have to go on the road again for some lectures; hence the delay in answering yours of June 28th.

Now all is set to go ahead full blast on the [mythology] series for the next two months. I will get in touch with Perry at once so that we can work out the cuts to be made.

I will come east as close as possible to September 1st, and then will be off for Europe until the end of October, whereafter I shall be back and forth between NY and Harvard until mid-December.

I'm afraid I'll be off the air for quite some time. At present I have to give full time to finishing this book and getting the series in order, and thereafter I need time for a lot of thinking and discussionating with people in various parts of the world. Am brewing some new ideas.

All good wishes,

Sincerely, Alan Watts

SAUSALITO, CALIFORNIA | JULY 9, 1962

Mr. Kyrill Schabert | Pantheon Books | New York, New York

Dear Kyrill:

Here is a list of a few more pundits who should receive complimentary copies of *The Joyous Cosmology*. I thought that some of them were on the original lists, but they have not received copies.

I had an absolutely marvelous time in Japan and look forward to telling you about it when I come east in September.

My present plans are as follows: Seems I have coming up a 2-year fellowship for study and travel from Harvard plus a Bollingen grant for the same period. So, I intend to come to NY and Cambridge as early as possible in September, than leave for London and Zurich (Jung Institute) from about mid-September to the first of November. Back to NY and Cambridge for November and the first half of December.

Jim Russell is coming to see me tomorrow with ideas for a party for booksellers on the boat here. How is the *JC* [*The Joyous Cosmology*] doing, and what did you work out with NAL about the Yoga book contract? ... Oh, and RH [Random House] should inform their agent in Milwaukee that I'll be lecturing there, Art Department of the U of Wisconsin, from July 17th through 19th.

Very best wishes to you, Kyrill, and looking forward to getting together again soon.

As ever, Alan

Complimentary Copies of *The Joyous Cosmology*

Dr. Joseph Henderson, San Francisco, Cal.

Dr. Oscar Janiger, Los Angeles, Cal.

Dr. Benjamin Weininger, Santa Barbara, Cal.

Dr. Eric Graham Howe, London, England

(Checking back through the files I see that none of these were on the original lists.)

SAUSALITO, CALIFORNIA | JULY 10, 1962

Dear Ed [Halsey],

So glad to get your letter. Our present plans are to go east early in September, then on to London, Zurich, Rome, etc., and back to the Cambridge–New York axis from November 1st to December 15th. Then out here until March, unless there is the opportunity to go directly from NY to Mexico on the way west.

Japan was a most marvelous experience — so full that I can't begin to write about it without going on and on. Some excellent things are going on there, and the Zen life is not at all a bad scene. Gary Snyder has been at it for four years, and I must say he seems to bloom with it.

I wanted to let you know that Timothy Leary is in Mexico this summer, and I think you would like to meet him. I have told him you might get in touch with him. He is Mr. Mushroom at Harvard, and I gather is setting up some sort of untrammelled research center in Mexico. Address: Dr. Timothy Leary, Hotel Catalina, Zihuatanejo, Guerrero.

I'm hard at finishing a book that doesn't really interest me, which is a lousy chore. I don't know quite what sort of fuel I'm going to bum for the job, because smoking gave me up last April. With the help of LSD; just vanished.

Our love to you both, and we'll keep you in touch with our orbits and try to meet as soon as we can.

p.m.p. yours, Alan

Ed Halsey died in an auto accident in the autumn of 1962.

SAUSALITO, CALIFORNIA | JULY 20, 1962

Beloved darling Jano:

It was so good to get your long, long letter today — as well as that juicily sexy one late last night when I got home from dinner with Joel and Ann, and Carlton. Of course, of course, baby there is no problem. We'll certainly get married by whatever means are best and as immediately as possible. I trust you completely, so don't worry about it. I haven't been able to talk to Phil yet; he is down in Salinas today, and won't be home until late. But we'll do it even if we have to stop off in Iceland on the way!

I've been answering letters all day, save for a brief interlude with Janko [Varda] and the usual joyous repartee. Enclosed are various items. Have written Henry. You should call Kim Cohen at Braziller — a very pleasant girl — and she will help you when it comes to assembling the photos for my book. They haven't yet sent the extra $500 promised, but I plan to start work on Monday. I've had two letters from Kyrill, and it transpires, very conveniently at the moment, that I owe Pantheon $2,375. I've told him you are in town and will get in touch. *JC* has sold 3,000 thus far, which is way, way ahead of what *The Way of Zen* had attained in a comparable period . . . Elsa called this morning and sent you her love, and for the first half of the day the phone was busy with seminar and lecture reservations. I've arranged for an answering service beginning Monday, so you'd better call me person-to-person if you have to, or hang up quickly if I don't answer after the first 2 rings. (Then you could try another 2.) Remember Joe Campbell's code: ring twice, hang up, and ring again.

I will send you the letters and all that as soon as I can get to it. Now I must run out to catch the mail before the PO closes up. This is short, but much more will come over the weekend. Endless kisses dear one — Alan

SAUSALITO, CALIFORNIA | JULY 26, 1962
Miss Kim Cohen | George Braziller, Inc. | New York, New York
Dear Miss Cohen:
About ten days ago Dr. [John] Perry and I went over his manuscript, but things have piled up too fast for me to write until now.

Unfortunately the only simple cuts seem to be the sections of the Shilluks, the Hittites, and the Philosophy of Nature, a total of 40 pp., or about 10,000 words.

Cuts can be made in the repetitious material of Part IV, but for the rest it is up to Dr. Perry to prune his chapters bit by bit, and I have suggested that he work on the principle of cutting out whatever is not strictly relevant to his psychological commentary — i.e., source materials unessential to the unity of the book.

Dr. [Joseph] Henderson and Miss [Maud] Oakes have assumed that you will take care of permissions on pictures in the same way as on quoted sources for the text. This was my original understanding with Ed Seaver, especially since the decision to include as many as 32 pp. of plates.

My assistant, Miss Mary Jane King, is now in New York and will be on hand to consult with you. She will call you.

Best wishes,
Sincerely, Alan Watts

SAUSALITO, CALIFORNIA [UNKNOWN DATE, PROBABLY SUMMER 1962]

Darling beloved Jano:

Your beautiful, long letter about the Lassaws and Lonkisland in general came today. I love it. Don [Gates] and I have been hard at it all day, as it has suddenly transpired that the filing of accounts for the first half of the year involves another court hearing on Monday, which seems to all of us an absurd waste of time, though Dorothy's lawyer wants to insist on it. Well, we'll see...I just talked to Van Heuven, who called LD from San Diego, and have told him that I will go along with him on the 1963 Japan tour. There hasn't been a word of follow-up from Mimi. We had a very good time last night at Sally Crane's place in Berkeley. Lee Sannella was there, and I was happy to hear that the Fuzz have not pressed further charges against him. But Van's situation is still uncertain. He will be attending some existential convention here in August — so apparently is not locked up. So I asked Lee to convey, if he could, Tim Leary's interest in having him at Harvard. The evening also involved a long and very friendly chat with Carlton Gamer, mostly about things to do in Japan. Which reminds me — a letter came today from Gary Snyder — asking about another of Morimoto Roshi's students who wants to come here and set himself up in the Bay Area. The idea is to have him learn English well enough to act as interpreter for Americans who might study with Morimoto. Darling poppet — I am having a very, very rough time getting to work on this idiotic book I'm supposed to do. Perhaps it will work itself out spontaneously, but the art of writing seems to require, for me, surrounding circumstances which are fairly well at peace. Alas, I am not a machine!...Dear Jano, I love you ever, ever so much. Early this morning you appeared to me in incredibly concrete fantasy.

I love you Mary Jane — I love you, love you. Alan

SAUSALITO, CALIFORNIA | JULY 29, 1962, SUNDAY NIGHT

Beloved Jano:

I shall probably call you before this arrives. There is no doubt that "I know who's going with me." Your absence at once recreates all those feelings of the summer of 1959, and packing your clothes to send them off to you (REA tomorrow morning) is just plain sad. Moreover, I'm frustrated at the idea of coming more than two-thirds of the way in your direction, only to turn round and go back. I went sailing with Janko today. Gorgeous weather and a boatload of beautiful girls, but all somehow lacking a heart. Same way with the cuckoldry party the night before. Best thing about it was Jim and Joel and their harpoems [sic]. I had Joel, Ann, and Gavin here to dinner before the party, following John and Anne Perry for lunch.

This evening I took Janko and some friends of his, the Murphys who run Holiday House at Malibu, to the Greenes' garden party. This was a very fine occasion, beautifully arranged, and there were quite a number of old friends present, including Norman Woodberry. No Davenports. We left early and came back to discover that a very high tide had poured gallons into the hold because Warren had borrowed the pump. He is to return it first thing tomorrow, but Janko's end of the boat was very nearly awash.

This vivid, sudden absence of you is quite a shock, bringing into consciousness how much I must have taken you for granted. But that old fire is burning inside as bright as ever, dear Jano, my poopipoppet, I adore you... Have shifted date of Random House party to the 15th so as to get to you sooner.

Love you, love you, Alan

Sausalito, California | July 30, 1962, Monday
Beloved, beautiful Jano:
Today has been fairly constructive. Don [Gates] has done a beautiful job on the accounts, which will be turned over to the opposition tomorrow afternoon. It was erroneously scheduled for a court hearing today, but Phil had that coshed as a waste of time. At the same time I have steamed up somewhat on the book, mostly by way of digging out further source materials and getting a clearer idea of how I want to shape the general presentation. Tomorrow AM we are both going into SF for a powwow with Phil on the way to work things out. And tonight we have a date with Louisa at Sanpei.

Lord, what a full house I have! Not only Don, but also Debbie Pollock's ex, a very beautiful but amazingly mixed-up young man (Clem), his not-exactly girlfriend, Ruth Costello, and Jack Selzer — all from St. Louis, all quite sophisticated fun. I wish I were in less of a hurry so that I could pause to describe this scene. Last night Jack barbecued a really excellent breast of lamb dinner, and one of the results of not smoking is that today I can smell breast of lamb as everyone's basic essence!

As yet no word from Gordon. So I still can't make definitive bids for fall rental, to Bass's or anyone else. One possible is Pat Traubel (singer's sister) who is chief purchasing agent for Cost Plus. Friend of this St. Louis trio and a very delightful woman. Another is Sophie Harpe from Carmel.

I have just talked with Gavin, who had yesterday a session with Dorothy, and is going to see her again Thursday about her horoscope. He is apparently trying, to use his own words, to stop her cutting off her nose to spite her face, and is at the same time dutifully spreading the rumor about us which, at least until yesterday, certainly hadn't reached her. I await results.

Talked with Mimi this afternoon, and gathered from her that Dick Moore is attempting to put some sanity into Ruth and, via her, Dorothy. But this is real ticklish. Van is obviously the best person to handle the 1963 tour, and so I have put off Mimi until September, but will write her to clean things up just as soon as the divorce action is over. Damn these mixtures of business and friendship.

What I missed most yesterday was you on the voyage with Varda. It was the most beautiful and thrilling trip I have had with him, all with naked girls swimming in the water beside us! The light, the birds, the sky, the spray, the bread and wine. Oh Jano, my heart ached for you. But soon we'll have it too. I long for you and can't sleep for thinking of you.

I love you, darling — Alan

SAUSALITO, CALIFORNIA | JULY 31, 1962, TUESDAY
Most beloved Jano:
Don [Gates] and I have just had a long, long session with Phil including lunch. His opinion on the remarriage situation is this: that all states known to him, including Mexico, would require a divorce in the first instance (conducted in said state) and that these are not granted unless the party sued signs a waiver of contest. One could just get married, but there would always be a risk that evidence of it could get into Dorothy's hands, and then I would be liable in California for bigamy. DAs don't like to prosecute for bigamy, but if the offended party screams enough they have to. His advice is bluntly, just play you are married, and then legalize it when the year is up. Nothing in the law prevents you from just changing your name. The only point in going before a court to do so is to make it a matter of record. However, I suggest you make further inquiry as to legal change of name in NY, Conn., NJ, and Penn., and then put it on your passport. It makes things so much easier when travelling, for in some European countries they demand passports when registering at a hotel.

We still do not know whether Dorothy is aware of the SCP [Society for Comparative Philosophy]. I'm fairly sure Gavin advised her of your departure, but there's no mention of it in her almost daily diatribes to me, which have lately been harping on how envious I am of her psychiatrist, and how I myself will be completely responsible for any bad publicity she has to make. Motivation: either self-punishment or to have an excuse for the eventual and certain failure of my enterprises!

So, darling poppet, things must remain dangling for a few days yet. I wish there were some more secure course available for hitching ourselves together within the next month — not, perhaps, for security as such: it would be more like giving you a very deep kiss. There are times when one cannot get close enough even when fucking.

I must get this to the PO and do sundry marketings. I love you most fantastically, you dear beautiful, galluptiously glorious babykins. Alan

SAUSALITO, CALIFORNIA | AUGUST 2, 1962

Darling, beloved Jano:

After your phone call this morning I picked up your note of the 31st. Yes, have Pantheon send a *JC* to the Baillies. Am just off to get supplies for the dinner I'm giving for Ann's birthday, which will include Gavin, Varda, Vagadu [Varda], and perhaps Rita Hamilton. Roger and Barbara [Somers] will stop by later in the evening.

Don left this morning, and will be back the weekend of the 11th so as to be on hand for the trial. He has brought all accounts and tax matters so up-to-date that I am financially clarified for the first time in my life.

Come to think of it, the connection

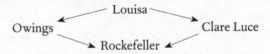

makes a good deal of sense, doesn't it? I hope all this comes through all right, and that neither Harvard nor Rockefeller will be put off by the divorce publicity. Since *l'affaire* Nelson they shouldn't be too stuffy. We depend on it absolutely for the trip to Europe. You will see from the enclosed London *Sunday Times* cutting that we may be in Rome for the most crucial Ecumenical Council in centuries [the Second Vatican Council], and as soon as things get a little bit more certain I will write Nat Owings to jog his memory about the Amer Academy. Van will arrange our tickets and reservations. Do you remember that couple from Rome who came to a seminar in NY? She took pictures of me, and they said, "O do join us in Rome one of these days and meet all the people interested in your work." Check with Kyrill or Gerta on the address of Feltrinelli who's my Italian publisher. We must also write him.

Jano, I love you. Alan

SAUSALITO, CALIFORNIA | AUGUST 3, 1962

Beautiful, beloved Jano:

I'm absurdly lost without you. Every day brings a mass of odds and ends so that I can't really get to work. Today Kyrill sends a letter from Dorothy trying to upset my figures about royalties, but he's replying expertly. But it took 2 phone calls, one to Phil. Last night Gavin had much to say, but we need to talk further. Apparently he has had some success in mollifying the unreasoning rage, talking with her for three hours. But we couldn't really discuss it in full with all the others around.

We had Varda and Vagadu, Roger, Gavin, and (later) Jerry Walters. I don't think I have had such an astoundingly convivial scene for a long time. After about 3 glasses of wine, believe it or not, Vagadu opened up and ceased to be an adolescent. She recited French poems with terrific style and verve. I did the poached salmon, hot, with a rice pilaf, plus Chenin Blanc and Chateau Wente, with salad. Varda was absolutely magnificent, and neither Gavin nor I got sleepy. Ann, in her condition, probably had a little too much; when I phoned her today she had a bit of a hangover. She was delighted with your gift, which Joel had intercepted so as to spring it on her at the dinner.

I enclose some odd letters, some routine, some very interesting — like the one from Alan Dunn. You might call him. Also Kyrill would like to hear from you when you get back into town.

In fishing around for a birthday gift for Tia (marvelous jingly sparkly blue necklace) I came across some fascinating jewelry from Nepal in one of those shops in the Village Fair. All little Buddhas made of coral, turquoise, and something like jade; then strung out into necklaces, etc.

Shortly I'll be taking off for Olema to spend the evening with Steve [Charter]. Then the seminar tomorrow... Got into an LSD state this morning by looking very carefully at a little wiggle in something I had written. It's funny: if you concentrate in a certain way, you get down to the basic *it*. And then there just isn't any problem. None. But at the same time I don't want to give up the problem that there is a psychophysically luscious girl called Jano with whom I want to be most indecorously entangled. I love that picture of you they took at Idemitsu. I keep looking at it, and just don't know how to describe your atmosphere.

I love you! Alan

Sausalito, California | August 4, 1962

Adored and beloved Jano:

Your little note of Thursday arrived this morning. I will forward letterheads, etc. Meanwhile here is a lengthy letter from Phil which should answer all the technical questions, quoting also the Code sections so that Moskowitz can look it all up in any law library.

Harvard tells me that the Rockefeller grant is strictly limited to $10,000 p.a. I expected that. But some wangling has to be done to diminish the amount taken out by Harvard's retirement fund.

I have no wife's name on my passport, and it is not in the least unusual for husband and wife to have separate passports especially when they travel independently. So there won't be any trouble there. Much more difficult to pretend to be brother and sister, because of different birthplaces, etc.

I am waiting to begin the seminar, not yet knowing how many to expect... Had the most delightful evening with Steve, Mary, and Pier. Steve wants particularly to send his love to you; he thinks you are perfectly magnificent. He baked excellent bread, but, alas, the stew was a flop. Another strong LSD sensation came over me driving out to Olema — again having to do with the basic *this* which is so unproblematically *thus*.

This is, I think, all for now — except that I'm all lusty for you! I adore you, love you, my absolutely darling Jano.

Your Alan

SAUSALITO, CALIFORNIA | AUGUST 7, 1962
My beloved Jano:
So much is going on! I have a 5-page letter from Dorothy on her reactions to your having left me, much of it so incoherent that I can't make any sense of it at all. But she admits toward the end that she has at last a boyfriend, or at least some man interested in her, and that is very good news. In general it has the tone of "You poor sick creature, please come to me for help, but don't be afraid that I want you back as a husband... But I would still hold out for $1,000 a month." Kee-razy. Kyrill has sent a perfect letter in response to her inquiry about my financial situation with Pantheon: viz., that in 1961 they advanced $3,500, all of which remains unearned; that, in addition, I am indebted to them for $2,375 on *The Way of Yoga*.

Sunday night with Joel and Ann to a rip-roaring performance of *Kismet* by the SF Light Opera Co. Corny and pseudo-Persian as hell but expertly done. Last night with Clem Pollock and Ruth to Sanpei, and then on with Clem to a party on a neighboring barge: Rudd and Dixie Garrett, who came to the last seminar, and are the warmest and most delightful beatniks. He makes a home brew that is better than my father's, and will supply us vastly in exchange for seminars. They are coming this afternoon for tea ceremony. (Which reminds me that I've mailed you the essentials to 315.) Just before the party I served Janko and a couple of others, and he was ecstaticized.

As a way of giving thanks for accommodation here, Ruth [Costello] is typing all the extra selections I need for *Myths of Polarity* [*Two Hands of God*]. But there is still a problem of pictures, and on this I am going, if I may, to put you to work very shortly. I think most of the things needed can be obtained between the Met and Bollingen. Braziller's have at last paid up, so I feel justified in going to work on it.

For the rest of the week, we have the Pantheon party tomorrow night, Joel and Bob Garfias supplying the music. Then Gavin to dinner on Friday, followed by an LSD session with Roger on Saturday to include both Gavin and Don Gates. Funny, Don has asked me in all sincerity how not to be a square.

An unidentified couple (beautiful brunette) has taken over the stranded boat to our north. They go back and forth on a small green dinghy.

And what else? Don plans to be here again Friday or Saturday, and we sail with Varda Sunday (the last voyage of the season before he goes for an extended stay with Louisa's Benedictines). I expect to conclude arrangements with Gordon [Onslow-Ford] before the end of this week, and if the Basses aren't interested in renting there is a very strong possibility that Helen Traubel's sister Patricia may want it.

That, I think, is all the news. For the rest, I look at your picture and long for the very special light in your eyes when you laugh, beholding in me the irreducible rascal. At night, or when I wake very early while it is still dark, I can visualize you with almost total clarity, and look far down into your magical eyes... Jano, darling,

Love you again, with kisses in all places. Alan

SAUSALITO, CALIFORNIA | AUGUST 7, 1962
My dear Daddy:
A long delay in writing, not just because of the multitude of things to be done, but also because I wanted to be able to give you quite definite word on coming to England in September. I can say only that prospects still look good. It all depends upon official confirmation of my appointment from Harvard as well as from one of the Rockefeller Foundations which is putting up the money. Final action will be taken early in September, and as things look now it is just a formality. But "as there's many a slip twixt the cup and the lip," I don't want to be absolutely definite.

If all goes as planned, I shall leave NY for London about September 15th. The dates for Zurich are mid-October, about the 11th to the 17th, and after that I thought we might go on to Rome. I have to be back in New York for lectures by November 6th.

I will bring all my color slides of Japan with me so that we can take up a couple of evenings going through them. I didn't realize how good a photographer I was, but I think the landscape did it for me! Also I will reserve all my impressions of this astonishing trip until we can just talk about it. It is all much too much to write.

I hope it won't grieve you to hear that I have given up smoking — not by grim effort but by simple falling away of something that, at this particular time, just isn't for me. It just "happened." But I haven't given up drinking, and I hope you can arrange for a barrel of that magnificent cider to be on hand. I don't suppose you brew anymore. Last night I visited one of my neighbors who also lives on a houseboat here, and he served the most splendid home brew. But he doesn't have the hops [that are] available to you. His are dried in some way and have lost their perfume. Anyhow, there just isn't anything like Kentish hops.

A comment on literary style and the changing fortunes of words. Do you remember when it was pretty awful to say, "Damn it" (Pinafore) or "Bloody," and now how some of these terms have become either comic or adjectives of endearment. As we say to some man we respect and admire, "Well you old rascal!" Forty years later it's the same with "son of a bitch" and "shit." For our generation they have completely lost their outrageousness, and have become simply and almost innocently funny. The really dirty words of today would curl your hair: which is just the point of them — to curse by uttering what, at all costs, must not be said. But when it has been done long enough no one is impressed anymore. The taboo word is admitted into the dictionary, though for a while it retains the same sort of interest as the lady of loose virtue who has gone straight and made a respectable marriage.

I will write you more definitely after August 15th or thereabouts as to the exact plans for travel. Will you let me know a little bit as to how you have things arranged at Rowan Tree Cottage. I ask because it is most highly probable, as things go, that I shall be accompanied by the final and definitive Mrs. Alan Watts — a humorous and affectionate and deliciously intelligent lady who is second from the right in the enclosed snapshot, taken at an art exhibit in Tokyo. Third from the left is Catherine Peck, who called you recently while she was in London, and second from left and third from right are Elizabeth and Jan Pokorny, New York architects who are very special and longtime friends of ours. So, on Jan's left is Mary Jane King, for four years my assistant, manager, lecture agent, and secretary, much loved by my closest friends. At the present moment, she's in New York, doing various jobs with my publishers.

Much thought has been given to helping Ann and Joel to come to England, but it's beyond our financial reach. Ann would love to see you again, and I know you would be thoroughly delighted with Joel. You know, travel in jet aircraft is astonishingly comfortable and easy. It's just like gliding, only at a vast speed. If anything goes wrong with our plans we might still get you over here for a while if you think you could stand it. Many's the time when I simply walk out of the house with nothing more than a briefcase and go off for a job 2,000 miles away. I have shirts and even a suit that you can wash yourself, hang up over the bathtub, and it dries and irons itself overnight. The hardest part of your trip would be the drive to the airport.

Joan and John have moved to Dayton, Ohio, because he has a much better job, and I suppose you know that you have another great-grandchild, Christopher. Joan keeps a very beautiful home, just off the conventional, but only just. Ann, on the other hand, has a place on California Street in San Francisco that is quite startlingly interesting, and I wish I could give you some sort of glimpse of the fascinating personality she has become. Incidentally, much of Ann's happiness today is due to Mary Jane, who became a sort of older sister to her when she came back from England.

Well, I must get this off to the post office and get on with my work. Tonight we have a party on the ferryboat, given by my publisher, for San Francisco booksellers! Joel will bring his harp.

Much love to you,

As always, Alan

SAUSALITO, CALIFORNIA | AUGUST 8, 1962

Most beloved and longed-for Jano:

This is a quickie before getting ready for the Pantheon party. Apparently things are afoot to cool this divorce jazz. Phil has arranged a conference with Don and Anne Diamond the day before the trial so that the financial facts can be looked in the jolly old face. Now that they have Kyrill's letter things are pretty clear, and I do believe that Anne D. is a sensible woman. ·

I have just written a long letter to my father announcing you and enclosing pictures. Van Dusen is going to be in the area shortly, and has written to see if we can get together.

Very probably I shall call you tonight, but I thought I might just as well write if only to send on the enclosed photo taken at Milwaukee with Prof. Suppan.

Last night I discovered a really marvelous Japanese restaurant for all the usual things like tempura and sashimi. Very reasonable, but I think it's also a whorehouse. Many more waitresses than necessary, and the one we had was the swingingest lass, who claimed to be from Yokohama. Japanese face; Western figure.

Please call Kyrill (greetings), Harry Doolittle, and Kim Cohen. You ought also to call John Abbatte, but he's a killer. I love him but I love you a lot more!

Darling poppet, kisses on your lips and each side of your neck. I am confirmed in the opinion that you are the loveliest woman I know. That isn't sensible but it's true.

Your Alan

SAUSALITO, CALIFORNIA | AUGUST 10, 1962
Darling and most beloved:
The craziest party last night! I had to do something about the leftovers from the booksellers' binge. So I invited Ann and Joel, Mary and Herb Beckman, and Calvin Kentfield, who has latched on to Ruth Costello (from St. Louis). Then I screamed out to the couple who have occupied the abandoned boat (rowing by), and they turned out to be very charming. Even so, we didn't finish it all! Sushi galore, plus a rock bass which I acquired for 95 cents (3½ lb.) from a fish place on the waterfront, and served up as sashimi. Jim Russell's son, about 19, was around helping out on chores for the party, and he introduced me to this fish place. It's about halfway between here and the center of town, and is the real wholesale place where the boats bring it in... Because of the tide the other-boat-couple had to leave early, but everyone else spent the night aboard. So we went on with sushi for breakfast, and Ann took home the half of the rock bass which I didn't use!

Tonight I am having dinner with Gavin (in town) and will treat him to yaki-tori, or something like that. I am really on a Japanese diet thing. (This was where we talked on the phone.) It's very strange, but I simply have no appetite at all for standard food and therefore don't eat properly unless it's oriental. After dinner we will meet Don Gates and all drive out here for the night. Then on to Druid Heights tomorrow. Did I tell you I've had a letter from Van Dusen? He will be here next Saturday after the seminar, for dinner.

I am so sorry that tea bowl smashed; I thought I had it very securely packed. Do please buy another one. There must be lots of places where they are available. Today I have sent you a magnificent illustrated annual called *This Is Japan*, which I'm sure you'll love.

Jano baby, I have to go out. I love you, love you, just simply like that and completely. You have taught me the wisdom of not making promises: however, when I get to NY you shall have the full snow treatment. Massage and hot tub included. I absolutely love you, and trust you to be completely yourself — you dear, beautiful, utterly screwtable [*sic*] creature. My lips upon yours. Goodnight.

Your Alan

SAUSALITO, CALIFORNIA | AUGUST 16, 1962

Beloved, adorable sweetheart and poppet:

We will doubtless call you this evening. Don has been through everything with the IRS accountant and reduced it to nothing but technicalities, and the guy has more or less indicated that he will delay his reports so as to give us maximum time to pay. No trouble. We are now trying to figure out our income and expenditures for the rest of the year so that we know exactly what we can afford to do.

You can practically get married courtesy of the State Dept. I called them today, and all you have to do to get your passport name changed is ask for a form which will be signed and notarized by any friend who knows you both as Mary Jane King and Mary Jane King Watts. No lawyers. No $100 fee. No nothing. It's up to you to choose whether you want to be MJK Watts or just MJ Watts. (I love you, either way.) There must be something equally simple for a driver's license.

Last night I went on a zany radio program to publicize the *This Is It* [LP] record. Done over KGO from the "Hungry I" by a cat named Les Crane, at 1 AM. We got into the floor show for free before it started (Don and I), and heard Prof. Corey, who satirizes the Eng. lit. teacher, and three just ger-luvly Negro girls constituting a sort of female Kingston Trio. Apparently the Les Crane show has a very vast audience, and people phone in with questions and comments. I stayed long enough to hear a very obviously Negro (male) voice saying how my philosophy was "the most." We conducted this thing along rather uninhibited lines.

I enclose multitudes of self-explanatory bits. Ruth Costello and Pat Traubel will take over the ferry from Sept. 15th to Dec. 15th, but in between I may let it out to Nancy Mehl, Virginia Glenn's friend. I haven't met her yet, but she's coming for the seminar this weekend and has nowhere special to live. I just want the place occupied. I am now arranging and classifying papers and other oddments for packing, and therefore still expect to be with you Monday night. I am out of my mind, insatiable, demented, crazy, and beside myself to be with you... Yesterday I had an absolutely delightful conversation with Varda on the subject of light and color, arising out of remarks I made at the Pantheon party apropos of a substantial display of Varda paintings which we hung in the studio that evening.

Tonight Don and I go to the Berkeley Buddhist Church, first for Japanese dinner and then for a lecture I am to give on Buddhism and Christianity. Then again for a second installment tomorrow.

This should be quite a seminar this weekend. Some gal is coming all the way from Ft. Lauderdale, Fla., and I also expect Dr. Shelton (Sandy's friend) with an extra supply of LSD. Have I told you that I have met an absolutely charming couple of boat neighbors, Rudd and Dixie Garrett, plus two babies? They live just north of us on the other side of the big San Rafael ferry, and want to exchange seminars for work. She's going to wash all the windows Friday morning!

Darling, absolutely adorable Jano, this must do for the moment. Much work accumulates. Meanwhile I can't wait to get my hands on you, you light-engendered, floating beauty, fair daughter of the sun.

I love you, Alan

SAUSALITO, CALIFORNIA | AUGUST 17, 1962
Mr. George Brantl | George Braziller, Inc. | New York, New York
Dear Mr. Brantl:
I plan to arrive in New York this coming Monday, and perhaps it will then be best for us to discuss the Perry manuscript directly. I have had another long talk with him about it, and we have arrived at a number of proposals.

My reason for coming immediately is that I need the facilities of the NY Library and Metropolitan Museum for finishing off my own manuscript.

I'll look forward, then, to seeing you next week.

Sincerely, Alan Watts

SAUSALITO, CALIFORNIA | AUGUST 17, 1962
Dear Daddy:
Yours of the 13th has just arrived. Slow. I leave for New York on Monday the 20th. I plan then to go to Harvard and make final settlements on my fellowship, making absolutely sure that funds are available for our trip. I am aiming for September 15th, which probably means arrival on the 16th. Will you arrange for Barrett to meet us? When things are quite certainly settled I will send you a telegram.

Probably what we should do is to fly as far as Paris — much more comfortable than a Channel crossing. Jano wants to visit her sister and brother-in-law there, and then there is an excellent direct train to Zurich. Then Geneva, then Rome. I will have to work it out with my travel agent, for the only difficulty might be that we can't get a return trip by air from New York to Rome that simply includes London, Paris, and Zurich as stopping-off points at no extra cost. We would want to return with you to England before leaving for New York.

You do not need to worry about cooking while we are with you. Both of us love to cook, and are delighted that you are once again brewing.

This has been a hectic week. Divorce proceedings went through, and, so far as we know, without any publicity. But then the income-tax people decided to investigate me (at Dorothy's instigation), but fortunately my accountant is staying with me and he got rid of them in short order.

We'll leave the problem of skill in using vulgar words until we can talk!...I don't remember having met the Usdanes from Mill Valley.

So — somehow or other I think we'll get as far as London. According to the way in which finances work out, we'll see what else we can do. The main thing is that I want to see you and want you to meet Jano.

Lots of love, as always, Alan

NEW YORK, NEW YORK | AUGUST 22, 1962
Dear Daddy:
This is just a brief note to say that everything seems to be going ahead in order. I have talked both with Harvard and with Laurance Rockefeller's office, and there shouldn't be any hitch.

Now how would you feel about flying to Paris about October 1st and then renting a car for the rest of the trip? Would it be too much of a strain? We would get something reasonably comfortable and capacious so that you could stretch out, and then we could make a sort of tour gourmet, with the aid of the Guide Michelin, Paris-Geneva-Zurich-Locarno-Venice-Milan-Florence-Rome, and then back along the Mediterranean coast.

Meanwhile would you please be so kind as to call Toby. He has asked me to give a powwow at the Buddhist Society on September 26th. This is fine. But I shan't be available after that date, so that anything else he might want to arrange, such as a dinner, should be between the 17th and the 26th. I have told him that I particularly want to meet D. E. Harding. Tell him also about Mary Jane.

Will you need a passport for Europe? I hope they are obsolete.

Lots of love,
As always, Alan

NEW YORK, NEW YORK | AUGUST 23, 1962
Mr. George Brantl | George Braziller, Inc. | New York, New York
Dear George:
Here is the letter I propose to send Dr. Perry, but I thought I would let you see it before putting it in the mail.

Then it occurred to me that you might send it off together with a letter of your own explaining the plan of publishing the series in two stages. This would ease his mind with regard to the time required for the changes we are suggesting.

Kim said that she made quite a lot of notes on the manuscript, and the substance of these might be given to him if he agrees in principle with the suggestions in my letter.

Please call me if you want to suggest any changes.

Sincerely, Alan

NEW YORK, NEW YORK | AUGUST 23, 1962
Dr. John W. Perry | San Francisco, California
Dear John,
I have had a long discussion of your manuscript with George Brantl and his assistant, Kim Cohen, to see what ways there might be of shortening it without destroying its integrity. As a writer, I am rather vividly aware of the fact that when, having just finished a piece of work, I am very "close" to it, it is difficult for me to see it objectively — especially as regards the order and balance of its total structure.

Our feeling is that the book would not only be shortened but positively improved by the following steps:

1. Concentrate all theoretical discussion into the introduction. This would include material both from the sections dealing with various cultures and from the psychological observations. If this is done, I think you will see that there is a good deal of unnecessary repetition in the discussion as it now stands.

2. Cut out almost all material on the historical backgrounds of the various cultures. After all, this may be necessary knowledge, but the book cannot take on everything, and the reader can always refer to an encyclopedia for details of this kind.

3. Let the chapters after the introduction consist, then, almost exclusively of the texts themselves, or summaries thereof in your own words (but not both in any one case). To this should be added explanatory comments on terms or names whose meaning is not clear from the text, plus comments of your own when, say, the form of a given myth is significantly different.

I am asking Mr. Brantl to send some additional information by the same mail which will, I know, make the task easier. Now, if these suggestions seem to you sound in principle, perhaps we can go ahead and make some quite specific recommendations.

All the best, as ever, Alan Watts

NEW YORK, NEW YORK | SEPTEMBER 10, 1962
Dr. Norman W. Storer | Department of Social Relations | Emerson Hall,
Harvard University | Cambridge, Massachusetts
Dear Dr. Storer:
I have heard from Mr. Rockefeller's secretary that he has just deposited $25,000 with the university for my project. So, at last things can get going.

If it is convenient with you, I will come up to Cambridge this week, either Wednesday or Thursday. But I will call you first. I am planning to leave for

London on Saturday, and therefore would appreciate it very much if you would ask the university to make funds available as follows:

First month's salary out of the annual: $4,000.

Half of the annual travel allowance of $6,000, i.e., $3,000.

Best wishes and many thanks,

Sincerely, Alan Watts

NEW YORK, NEW YORK | NOVEMBER 28, 1962

Dear Gary [Snyder],

Apologies for taking so long to answer your letter, but we have been travelling all over the place, including Europe, and everything gets behind-hand.

I will give you the final word on sponsoring Asai sometime around Christmas. I'll be back in Sausalito then, and can work out with the accountant how to handle the bank accounts and all that. I don't see why there should be any problem.

Mescaline. Standard dosage is 350 milligrams, and you can take up to 500 without difficulty. Any liver trouble is a contraindication. Procedure the same as for peyote: i.e., lie down and rest for an hour after taking to avoid nausea. As to brain deterioration, tell your friend to get hip with the literature.

What I am working on in this brain-picking spree is: in what ways are we all hypnotized by language, metaphors, social rituals, etc., etc., so that we ignore what should be our startlingly obvious *ji-ji-mu-ge* identity with the whole cosmos? In other words, I am just going on with my usual interests, but with some time for contemplation.

Still look forward to seeing you in the fall of '63.

HO [Gary describes the meaning of this as an exclamation, as in "Ho!"]

PS. After December 1st, use the Sausalito PO box.

PART IX

Becoming a Guru

1963-73

JW: The Society for Comparative Philosophy was incorporated in 1962 to establish an educational organization that would generate income to promote the work of Alan and others in the philosophical/religious field. The ferryboat Vallejo *became a seminar center. The original board members were Alan, Henry Denison, and Don Gates. Grants were given over the years to individuals and groups involved in projects that fit the society guidelines, including Lama Anagarika Govinda, Charlotte Selver, Krishnamurti, Douglas Harding, and Lama Chögyam Trungpa. In 1970, Elsa Gidlow deeded her property at Druid Heights to the society. A library was built on the property to house Alan's extensive library away from the dampness of the* Vallejo *docking. The library was available as a retreat to students doing research associated with similar interests. The US government added the Druid Heights properties, on the southwest flank of Mount Tamalpais, to the Golden Gate National Recreation Area and Muir Woods National Monument, giving the residents ninety-nine-year leases. The society continued with Robert Shapiro, Elsa Gidlow, and Anne Watts on the board for a few years after Alan's death but eventually disbanded.*

Alan always admonished those that said he was a guru, stating he was in fact a philosophical entertainer, or perhaps a trickster guru.

MILL VALLEY, CALIFORNIA | JANUARY 30, 1963
Mr. Henry Volkening | New York, New York
Dear Mr. Volkening:
On the assumption that you are still willing to be my agent, I am enclosing a copy of a letter to Paula Van Doren of Pantheon which is largely self-explanatory.

But I am wondering what sort of information *you* will now need to help you in your negotiations. My last book, *The Joyous Cosmology*, has been doing pretty well for the sort of thing that it is. At $5 retail it had sold over 3,000 within two months of publication. My TV programs are still running in various parts of the country, and there are more to come. Braziller will be publishing (Book-Find

445

involved) a book provisionally entitled *Yang & Yin*, or the *Myths of Polarity* in a series on The Archetypes of Myth this fall. *Psychotherapy East & West* has just appeared in *Mentor*.

The stage therefore seems to be set for a book that is at once by me and about me.

We need to get a substantial advance to give Mr. Ashby the opportunity to get the work done. Seeing, however, that the bulk of the material is mine, how should contracts be set up? Should the publisher contract with me, and I subcontract with Mr. Ashby, or what?

With all good wishes,

Sincerely yours, Alan

NEW YORK, NEW YORK | MARCH 14, 1963

Dear Daddy,

I'm so sorry; it seems I haven't written since Christmas. One reason is that I have been trying to come to some definite arrangement as to our next visit, and as things now stand it seems that Christmas 1963 will be the most likely. I think we shall just fly west from Tokyo on November 8th, with stops in Hong Kong, New Delhi, Rome, Paris, and London. Jano wants to see her sister again, so I think this will be the best way to manage things. We had thought of coming in September on our way to Japan, but we have been travelling so much that we want to have a real long summer's rest at home in Sausalito.

This January and February on the ferryboat have been most exciting. We have had several storms with very high tides, so that there has been some motion aboard, but the most fascinating thing has been the swarms of birds and the seals — all apparently encouraged by huge shoals of herrings.

We are in New York, just on the way to Harvard, and planning to stay there until April 18th. Then back to New York until the end of the month. On our way back to Sausalito in May we shall spend a few days with Joan and John. They were here in the city a few days ago, and we had a most delightful time with them including a dinner party at a Japanese restaurant. John was here on business.

We have been making some changes on the ferryboat — mostly in the form of painting and cleaning things up. In our absence, one of my students is staying there and using the car in return for various jobs around the place, and I think the results are going to be very beautiful. Especially the new dining room with its pale-yellow walls and brick-red floor and huge windows of very small panes of glass. It's a veritable sun trap.

Arrangements seem to have been made at last for publishing *The Joyous Cosmology* in England — by Sidgwick & Jackson. I don't quite know when it will be out, but they are publishing in the expectation that I will come over from time to time for lectures, and since our last visit I feel very much inclined to do so. I'm sure you realized how much we enjoyed it, and for me it was a sort of rediscovery.

Will you give our very best wishes to the Usdanes and the Salomons, and to Mrs. Forsdyke. I hope you are by now "digged out" of all the snow and freezing weather. I haven't seen any snow this year, but we may run into it on the way home, for we shall be stopping in Denver, Colorado, to do some work. And the last time I was there (in a May) it really came down.

This morning I have a lecture, starting at 11, and I want to get this off to the post in the hope that you will get it Monday morning.

Very much love from us both,

As always, Alan

PENNSYLVANIA | MAY 3, 1963

Dear Daddy:

I have been working on a lot of plans since your last letter. We shall be in Japan, as I may have told you, from Sept. 23rd until Nov. 8th. If we then flew on round the world to London, it would cost us $600 extra at the very least. Wouldn't it make a lot more sense for us to save this and buy you a ticket direct from London to San Francisco (return) so that you could leave in time to be with us here for Christmas? We would then travel eastwards with you late February (when I have work in NY) and you could stop off to see Eleanor and Uncle Willie on the way.

The idea of sailing via Panama is of course thrilling, but at that time of year it could be abominably rough, and I would feel much more at ease about you if you would come here by the magic carpet, and then do the earthly travelling after arrival. This would include Big Sur and other delightful places in California, and perhaps the Grand Canyon... We are now resting in a beautiful log cabin in the woods (Pennsylvania) and will be staying with Joan and John next week. This trip to the East has been most exciting and productive, but we are longing to get back home to our boat and the quiet waters... A delightful dinner in NY with Mummy's old student Isabel Grenfell (Walthamstow Hall), and her 2 daughters. More soon.

Lots of love from us both —

As always, Alan

SAUSALITO, CALIFORNIA | JUNE 5, 1963
Dear Tim [Leary]:
The *Psychedelic Review* is really very good, if I do say so myself, as contributor.
Please congratulate Ralph [Metzner], if he is with you.

I just hit on a rather remarkable discovery, when I hit upon the follow passage in the Benn article:

> 1300 years before this socle, in the southern part of our continent, the
> concept of reality began to be formed. The Hellenistic-European *ago-*
> *nistic* principle of victory through effort, cunning, malice, talent, force,
> and the later European Darwinism and "superman" was instrumental
> in its formation.

What I had just discovered [was] that the Greek word for "games" we had
been looking for was *agony*! To be exact: so the term for the transcendental life
is *megagonic*, a state of metagony or perhaps paragony, and thus comes through
the evolution of words to have the same sense as nirvana — the state beyond
suffering!

Also think about the possible meanings of catagony, epagony, peragony
(peri-agony), apagony, anagony, prosagony, etc.

Yes, I would contribute to the *Consciousness Expanders*, and along the lines
you suggest. But someone from their office must get in touch with me officially,
or with my agent Henry Volkening, 551 Fifth Avenue, New York.

Do let me know about the history and prospects of the liquid solution as
soon as you can. You must be swamped with correspondence, and I know what
that is!

Love to you all —
As ever, Alan

SOUTHERN CALIFORNIA | JUNE 20, 1963
Dear Gary [Snyder]:
I am disturbed that so much time has gone by without further action on Gisensan. The trouble is that I am so much on the move, and will be settling down in
Sausalito for the summer only after July 4th.

But the suggestion that he come in under the missionary classification
seems admirable. Asia kicks back. I would very gladly cooperate with this, but
it is up to your end to figure out the sort of statement or form that the Society
would have to sign. The only thing holding this up is secretarial work and red
tape.

Does Gisen-san have any other friends or contacts in Calif.? How will arrangements be made for his residence, etc., when he arrives? What about Claude's East-West House?

We still plan to hit Kyoto about September 24th or 25th. Could still bring a little LSD if you have any interested *roshi* lined up, though, if you've heard the gossip, the situation on LSD here is in the dept. of utter confusion. Timothy Leary (Harvard) and his project for experimental LSD groups was kicked out of Mexico, which is about as low as you can get.

This time I'll reply right away when I hear from you!

All the best, Alan

SAUSALITO, CALIFORNIA | JULY 4, 1963

Dear Daddy:

Yours of June 29th was here when we returned from a three-week's trip to southern California, and I hasten to reply because it's been such a long time since you heard from me. We have been almost constantly on the road since early March, and now at last will be able to settle down at home until September 23rd, when we leave for Japan. The boat is quite beautiful now. We have had the kitchen, dining room, and the spare bedroom (which will be yours) painted in gay colors appropriate to the sunny end. It's all rather like an oyster: shabby without and pearly within.

Yes, we had heard about Sonja, and I had been afraid for some time that it would end that way. I never was fully able to understand what was bothering her, even though we had had some pretty deep discussions back in 1958 when I first met her. The immediate problem was that she felt completely unable to go on with her painting, and at the same time felt terribly guilty for being so dependent on her parents. And there was still more to it than that, but let it go until we can talk. We know from mutual friends that her mother was quite a problem!

How would it be for you to come here about December 15th or 20th? I think there is a BOAC flight which comes from London to San Francisco nonstop, across the pole. We could then spend the whole Christmas season in Sausalito, and thereafter go to Big Sur and to my friend Bob Balzer's wonderful place in the mountains (6,000 ft.), where he has established one of the most beautiful restaurants in the world, where the view — of snowy peaks — is as good as the cooking. We have just been there, since the place has facilities for conferences, and I had a class of 54 for the weekend...After that we could take a look at

Hollywood, and then move slowly eastwards. You might go first to Colorado Springs and Minneapolis, and then meet us at Joan's place in Dayton. I will set up all the plane reservations well in advance. I have to start some lectures in New York at the beginning of March, and so this would be the time for you to head back for London. Will the garden stand your absence that long? If I can somehow manage it, I would like you to see Harvard; it's one of the very great places of this country, and the buildings, the atmosphere, and the people have a wonderfully unobtrusive elegance.

Minette Kuhn wrote me a postcard about their visit with you, and you will very probably see them again when we reach New York in March. I will look forward very much to seeing the Usdanes when they get back to Mill Valley, and perhaps we will still meet thereafter as I make very frequent visits to Washington.

This summer I'm going to stay at home and write a book that's been in the back of my mind for a long time — a book in a new style about very ancient ideas. More or less in the "poetic" language of *The Joyous Cosmology*, but treating the very basic theological problems from the standpoint of the Hindu view of the universe as the maya of the Godhead — a sort of drama in which it loses itself in a game of hide-and-seek. Against this background comes a discussion of Christianity from a point of view that I have never quite taken before: seeing its extreme emphasis on the difference between creator and creature, and on the momentous and terrifying choice between heaven and hell as an extremely "far out" situation of the Godhead getting temporarily lost in its own game of hide-and-seek. The immense energy and individualism of Western culture is thereby generated, and the phenomenon is seen, not as something to be condemned, but as a work of art, a fantasy of preposterous dimensions like a dinosaur.

I'm trying to learn some Japanese cooking, since the shops here are increasingly supplying some of the essential ingredients. It is now quite early in the morning, and I think I'll shortly be livening us up with a bowl of miso soup. Always served with breakfast in Japan, and it warms and encourages one all the way through.

Sorry to hear about poor Mrs. Forsdyke. I wonder how old she is. It always struck me that she must have been tremendously attractive as a young woman. Who is in her house now?

So then, very much love to you — in which Mary Jane joins me, and as soon as I get more details of SF–London flights from our travel agent I'll be letting you know about the plans.

As always, Alan

SAUSALITO, CALIFORNIA | AUGUST 10, 1963

Dear Father [Aelred] Graham:

I wonder if you have seen the enclosed, in which we are both taken to task by Ruth Sasaki, who is more or less Mrs. Zen.

For my own part, I marvel at this way of dismissing someone's work with an airy shrug instead of real criticism, as did also that reviewer in the *Times Lit. Supplement* whom you quoted. Incidentally, that article "The Appeal of Zen" was not only distinguished for factual errors, but [the writer] couldn't even spell.

My position on Zen and morals, of which you make quite a point, has been considerably developed in *Nature, Man & Woman*, and *Psychotherapy East & West*. I simply do not understand your criticism on p. 111 of your book, firstly because you seem to assume that putting Zen beyond the ethical standpoint makes ethics unimportant. There is no opposition between "reality" (i.e., the absolute) and "mutual agreement"; it is entirely a question of different levels in a hierarchy, as when the clear difference between up and down in this room is contained in interstellar space, where there is no such distinction.

Buddhism as a whole concurs here. Perhaps the best way of putting it is to say just what you say in the last sentence of par. 1 on p. 111. But, surely, in Christianity the individual conscience responds primarily to the moral authority of God — and this is precisely the ethical standpoint universalized and absolutized. My feeling is that to invoke divine sanctions for ethical misconduct is to go against ethics. It's like putting a million volts through the toaster. As the Chinese say, "Don't swat a fly on a friend's head with a hatchet."

I was glad to see that you didn't perpetuate the Maritain-Zaehner distinction between natural and supernatural mysticism. Obviously, if the Holy Spirit works extraordinarily, i.e., outside the regular channels of the Church and the sacraments, its grace is always supernatural. The Catholic position would be stronger by distinguishing between natural (speculative) and supernatural (revealed) systems of doctrine, in terms of which the existential fact of mystical experience is interpreted.

I don't expect to be in the East again until late in February, when I shall be spending some time in Cambridge, and I shall try at that time to get in touch with you again.

Oh yes!...I did want to say that I am most grateful to you for sending me your book for the obvious reason that it gave me a great deal to think about, especially because I am just starting a new theological work.

With all good wishes,

Pax tecum, Alan Watts

SAUSALITO, CALIFORNIA | AUGUST 12, 1963
Dr. Edward W. Maupin | Neuropsychiatric Institute |
University of California Medical Center | Los Angeles, California
Dear Dr. Maupin:

Many thanks for your kind letter of the 8th. Really, no apology is needed. I was only teasing.

Zen people speak of many degrees of satori, of little satoris and big satoris, and are also strangely unconcerned with its relation to behavior change. I have discussed this quite a bit with people in Japan, and am going to take it up again when I return this fall for another visit.

Have you seen Sanford Ungar's article on behavior change and LSD? There is no question in my mind that LSD by itself does very little, and that its usefulness depends almost entirely upon who is therapist and who is patient. It is like a scientific instrument, such as a microscope, which, though fun for a layman, is extremely useful to a person with chemical or biological training.

Have you run into my friend John Whittlesey yet? I think he is still working with [Keith] Ditman.

With all good wishes and many thanks,

Sincerely yours, Alan Watts

SAUSALITO, CALIFORNIA | SEPTEMBER 20, 1963
Dear Daddy:

We are just about to take off again for Japan, leaving Monday afternoon with a party of about 20 people, including many old friends. Joel's older brother, Oliver, will be with us, and also Ruth Goodkind Roberg, whom I have known since Northwestern days, from about 1947. Didn't she call you once when she was in England? Also a very dear friend from New York, Milly Johnstone, the most skittish matron in the sixties you ever saw — wonderful at cross-stitch embroidery, and wife of one of the directors of Bethlehem Steel. I've been in touch with her since 1940!

All this summer I've been writing another book, this time a theological work, though its title will probably be *Beyond Theology: The Art of Godmanship* [Pantheon, 1964]. I have been so absorbed in it that I have simply forgotten the passage of days, and only as the departure for Japan has approached have I stopped to consider the calendar and the days of the week! But in the meantime I have still another book coming out, which I am sending you now. It is an anthology, with commentary, of the myths of polarity (light/dark, life/death, good/evil, etc.) entitled *The Two Hands of God.*

The weather here has been so lovely that we almost regret to leave this place for Japan. Though I am absorbed in writing all week, we often go sailing on Sundays with our neighbor, Varda, and this keeps us well tanned with the sunshine.

We return from Japan about November 10th. Shortly thereafter I will send you your ticket to leave by BOAC about December 15th, plus or minus a day or two. Maybe we can get better connections through Qantas. The travel agent who handles my Japan tour is very expert in all these matters, and he will get you here by the best way. We are planning a great and glorious Christmas dinner for the whole family and some of our very close friends. We so much enjoyed your last letter, and were particularly pleased to know how well surrounded you were with friends, and that with Mrs. Chance's help you could entertain so often. We had a visit, late one evening, from Saloman's son and two of his friends — one a British boy from the Isle of Wight, and the other an American from Los Angeles. They arrived rather late and we invited them to spend the night with us, since, as you will see, there's lots of room here. We had a really fascinating talk with them over late supper and (also late) breakfast, before they took off for Canada. It seemed that they are living pretty close to the bone, but enjoying it thoroughly. It's a hand-to-mouth way of life, but I feel encouraged that there is still such a spirit of adventure. Right near us here there are also a couple of English girls, about the same age as Saloman's son, and making their way completely on their own. All very refreshing!

We look forward so very much to having you here. This boat has been so beautiful this summer with all the changing lights on the water, but by the time you get here the birds will be arriving. If I didn't have to travel around giving lectures, this would be the perfect and ideal place just to sit and contemplate!

Our address in Japan will be Yachiyo Inn, Higashiyama-ku, Kyoto, and we shall be there until November 1st. This is a Japanese-style inn on the outskirts of the great Nanzen-ji Zen monastery, close to the mountains on the eastern side of the city. I'll write next from there.

Lots of love from us both, and also from Ann and Joel. I saw them this afternoon and the baby [Myra] was utterly delightful. You will lose your heart to her!

As always, Alan

The following letter is to Louisa Jenkins, a resident of Big Sur and a neighbor of Maud Oakes and Henry Miller.

BETHLEHEM, PENNSYLVANIA | MARCH 23, 1964

Dear Louisa:

I have been having a round of talks with Jack Barrett, Nancy, Marian, and others here interested in Ogata, including one member of my tour who spent some time at Chotoku-in.

What has developed is an almost unanimous feeling that he is doing a much better job in Kyoto than he could do here, considering, especially, the state of his health and vitality.

Part of the purpose of arranging a visit to the USA was that his lectures and classes would not only cover expenses, but also raise funds for Chotoku-in. We are all, then, inclined to think that the best we could do for him is to raise a fund for Chotoku-in and his work in Kyoto. We could base it on a fairly substantial contribution from SCP, and have SCP collect the funds so that they would be tax-deductible. Jack indicated that Bollingen would certainly give sympathetic consideration to helping. I plan, therefore, to write Ogata to this effect (in about a week's time) and ask for the names of all Americans who have used the facilities of his temple. I, perhaps in conjunction with one or two others, would then circulate personal letters asking for support.

Please let me know what you think. Until April 5th we can be reached c/o Mr. and Mrs. Wm. H. Johnstone, Bethlehem, PA.

We have been having a most interesting and busy time here in New York, and in odd moments I have been fascinating myself with Bucky Fuller's *Ideas and Integrities*. I hear he is in Hong Kong en route to Japan at this moment. Am most interested in his mystique of the sailor and his idea of the sailor-priests of ancient times. Have you seen his:

OM

DOME

DOMINUS

WOMB

TOMB

HOMO

BOMB?

Fantastical, but suggestive.

We both send very much love to you, and please give some of it to Maudie.

As ever, Alan

SAUSALITO, CALIFORNIA | MAY 24, 1964
Miss Nancy Foster | KCBS | San Francisco, California
Dear Miss Foster:
The characteristic features of English haiku would be approximately as follows:

1. Each poem should consist of *approximately* seventeen syllables. This rule is not rigid; it is merely suggestive of the desired length.

2. It should be set out in three lines, of which the last is often the "punch line" as in:

> A fallen leaf
> Returning to the branch?
> Butterfly!

> It walked with me
> as I walked:
> The scarecrow in the distance.

3. English haiku should in no circumstances be rhymed.

4. The mood of haiku is always objective, and the poet does not speak of himself and his feelings directly. Haiku expresses a vivid instant of experience in which the duality of external event and inner response is transcended. At such an instant we say, "You could have knocked me down with a feather!"

5. Each haiku should have a seasonal reference. The two above are respectively fall and spring.

6. A serious fault in haiku is "cuteness," and the first one quoted above just steers clear of it.

With all good wishes,
Sincerely yours, Alan Watts

SAUSALITO, CALIFORNIA | JUNE 22, 1964
My dear Judge Harris:
In re: *US vs. Roseman and Copley*
I believe that this is the first time that illegal use of the drug LSD-25 has come before the courts in a criminal context. The case is therefore of very great concern to the many scientists, physicians, psychologists, and philosophers who feel that proper research with chemicals of this type may contribute enormously to our understanding of the human mind.

Specifically, our concern is that this drug should not be associated, either legally or in the public mind, with such narcotics as heroin and opium. It would be a real disaster if a criminal traffic in these chemicals were to arise, and nothing seems to foster such traffic more surely than legal and police methods designed to suppress it. (Shades of the Volstead Act!) You probably know as well as anyone of the increasing agreement among penologists that harsh measures against drug addicts have been a total failure, and that strong legal prohibition of their unauthorized use is an open invitation to organized crime to take control of them.

The FDA is quite properly exercising its authority to control the use and distribution of research drugs. But LSD-25, and similar substances, are highly anomalous as *drugs*. For drugs are normally authorized by the FDA when proved to be therapeutic as well as reasonably safe for consumption. But it is doubtful whether LSD-25 will ever be widely used for therapy. Its function is instrumental and exploratory, augmenting the power of the senses internally much as telescopes and microscopes do so externally. Most experienced experimenters with LSD-25 agree that it can be dangerous when used in any situation that disturbs or seems to threaten the patient or subject. But as a menace to life, limb, and sanity it is mild indeed compared with a hurriedly swallowed pint of bourbon.

I know the defendants in this case only slightly, but it is my definite impression that they should be treated as misguided enthusiasts rather than persons of criminal intent. Please deal with them kindly.

Very truly yours, Alan Watts

June 25, 1964
Mr. Gordon Ragle | Kansas City, Missouri
Dear Mr. Ragle:
Thank you for your most interesting letter of June 6th. These questions about the reality of the ego involve many semantic difficulties. My purpose in *Psychotherapy East & West* was not to deny that there is a certain kind of psychic functioning which achieves the feedback or doubling (*operación redoblada*) associated with the ego: it was to show that this operation is not the authentic self in its fullness, and is not an actual entity separate from and confronting the panorama of experience.

There was a young man who said,
"Though it seems that I know that I know,
What I *would* like to see
Is the I that knows Me
When I know that I know that I know."
Knowing about knowing about knowing is a series of comments, each succeeding one upon a higher level of abstraction than the one before. But this does not require a new and separate ego for each level. It requires only memory and

(in the widest sense of the word) language, that is, a system of symbols, which can stand for, and apart from, events as money stands for real wealth.

I regard the actual self as the entire cosmos (or whatever *it* is), operating in that particular way, time, and place that we call the individual organism. The organism's sense of ego is an additional operation of this totality — a kind of resonance or echoing (like singing in the bathtub), which enhances experience. I also connect the ego with the organism's capacity for conscious attention, i.e., for a type of awareness similar to a spotlight, that can focus upon those areas of experience that we call things and events, simultaneously ignoring everything outside those areas.

All these ego functions seem to be real and effective. But they are functions of the larger self, and I cannot feel the ego as something apart from that self, and certainly not as the real and final ground of my being.

Sincerely yours, Alan Watts

OAXACA, MEXICO | AUGUST 26, 1964
Dear Daddy:
We are now in the southern mountainous region of Mexico, and this city is in a wide valley at about 5,000 ft. A marvelous, restful place — part Spanish, part Zapotec Indian. Our hotel room overlooks the central square with bandstand, large trees, cafés, and endless activity, and the hotel is right next to the 17th-century cathedral. There is also a Dominican church like a jewel box inside with all the gold and polychrome work on the roof and walls. The Indians make extremely beautiful blankets and the town is famous for a kind of Toledo steel. We have been in Mexico since August 1st. Spent some of the time in Mexico City, which is an immense international metropolis, and then hired a car and drove to Guadalajara and back, visiting some fascinating old towns and villages. We are now in Oaxaca with Madeleine Low and Dick Borst, and I enclose two of his photographs. There are also many other Americans — some most congenial, and we plan a party tonight at one of their homes — at which we are to cook the dinner. Many foreigners — American, British, French, etc. [—] live here because houses and servants are very cheap and the climate is gorgeous. Cool and clear, with rain in the afternoons. We have visited the vast ruins of Mitla and Monte Alban, going back to about 500 BC, but no one really seems to know much about the culture that built them. We also went up into the remote mountain village where Juarez was born, but Jano got terrible flea bites on the ankles and we have had to have the doctor for her. We shall be flying back to Los Angeles on September 3rd, and staying in southern California for lectures until the middle

of the month. Then home to Sausalito. In LA we'll be staying with Henry and Ruth [Denison]. We were delighted to hear of your convivial doings and hope the summer is being sunny and genial for you.

Very much love from us both —

As always, Alan

PS. Forgot to tell you that I was present at the birth of Ann's lovely baby boy [Michael]. He came with a beautiful dawn, and was helped in (or out?) by a most interesting and happy-tempered doctor.

SAUSALITO, CALIFORNIA | SEPTEMBER 16, 1964

Dear Dick [Richard Alpert], Tim [Leary], Ralph [Metzner], and all:

Many thanks for your letters, received on return from Mexico.

Here is my schedule for the fall, though it looks as if we are going to cross one another. I shall be back here about December 4th. I've just had a wonderful seminar at Big Sur, and it seems that the Esalen project is really hitting its stride. I am sure your session there will be a whopping success.

As to slides, I still have lots, but thanks all the same. I can't look at them very often, and when I do, they stimulate me so much that I have almost six months' worth of material for lectures.

The New Republic has asked me to do a review of Sid Cohen's new book *The Beyond Within*, and I have consented — suggesting that I work it up into an article-length review on the chance that they would make it the main feature of one issue. Ralph asked me to review *The Psychedelic Experience* for *PR* [*Psychedelic Review*]. How soon would it be needed? I would like to if I can work it in. But as yet I don't even have a bound copy!... I think (and this is what I have partly in mind for *The New Republic*) that it is very necessary to disarm the prevalent idea that those who have taken psychedelics are "permanently altered" so as to be not quite human. This is of course a revival of superstitions about witches and sorcerers who made pacts with the devil, but it could be a very dangerous notion unless quickly and clearly identified for what it is.

Before leaving for Mexico I saw rather a lot of Roseman and Copley. The latter is utterly uncool and is doing no one any good. He is really determined to be a martyr.

Our love to you all, and please let's get together as soon as our various schedules permit. We have much to discuss.

As ever, Alan

JW: Three interesting letters below from the mid-1960s include a letter to Margaret Rioch, a clinical psychologist with Zen training from Washington, DC. Alan's letter is in answer to hers regarding his topic for an upcoming lecture at the Washington School of Psychiatry that October. He had given the title of the lecture as "Controlling Consciousness," and Margaret was hoping that Alan wasn't going to "lecture on the use of LSD and related substances."

In fact, in his letter he presents a rather alarming description of his proposed topic, in which he mentions that the future of psychotherapy could be involved with the neurological manipulation of the brain and controlling genes. He wonders who would have the authority and wisdom to make such decisions of "neuropolitics."

In a letter to a woman who is terrified of flying in small planes, Alan kindly takes the time to counsel her on how she may overcome her fear of flying. He compares her fear to a fear of spiders and how one can overcome such a fear by thoroughly studying the subject. An unusual request, but his response shows Alan's humanity.

In the third letter, which is to Peggy Morrison of the Episcopal Diocese and Church Center of New York, he was asked to review a study regarding the future of the family. He somewhat chides her about the Church's view of the family, noting that the present-day family is far from what it had been — either at the time of Christ or for some hundreds of years. He goes on to say that the Church's view of the family may well be obsolete. His thoughts on this subject were expressed fifty years ago and are certainly true today in 2017.

SAUSALITO, CALIFORNIA | SEPTEMBER 21, 1964
Dear Margaret [Rioch]:
I had been meaning to write to you, but the pile of business that has accumulated during our absence (presence) in Mexico during August is phenomenal, and I think this is also how we missed you.

As to the subject of my lecture "Controlling Consciousness." The topic is simply this: As we perfect our skills in psychotherapy, neurological manipulation by electrical stimulation of the brain and by drugs, by new methods of propagandizing the unconscious, and even by the control of genes, we come within sight of being able to produce the kind of human beings we consider desirable. The problem is then: what sort of people should we desire, and who has the authority and/or wisdom to decide? One of the biggest issues of the future is therefore what might be called neuropolitics: the debate and the contest of how the nervous system should be controlled, assuming that we gain the power to control it. The subject of psychedelic drugs is incidental to this lecture, but you can bet your life that the audience will stress it to the limit in the question period.

Off the record. Isn't it simply contemptible that at a time when there is immense public curiosity about LSD, etc., that the psychiatric profession puts its head in the sand, and doesn't want to have anything to do with it? Given a chance to look into the inmost workings of the psyche, they slam the lid on!

Of course, we'd love to join you for dinner on the Saturday night, and I'm wondering if you know Robert Evett, the editor of *The New Republic*. I have been corresponding with him and would much like to meet him if it can be wangled.

I have recommended you as a possible participant in a panel on the psychology of personality at the University of Florida in late January. Do you speak well in public? I was sure you did, but have only heard you in private.

The trip to Mexico was most fascinating, and the thing that I found most interesting was the cult of pain in Mexican Catholicism. Someday I shall understand this and work it up into a writing, related to the general theme of my *Beyond Theology* book.

Incidentally, we are having a dinner meeting tonight for the leading psychiatrists and psychologists in this area interested in psychedelics. Cold poached salmon Vallejo, *riz aux noix et petits pois*.

Much love to you from us both, Alan

SAUSALITO, CALIFORNIA | SEPTEMBER 28, 1964
Miss Marianne Winder | Editor, *The Middle Way* | London, England
Dear Miss Winder:

Delay in answering your letter of August 18th is due to the fact that we have been on our travels again, this time in Mexico.

I'm sure you want to get your query settled right away, but alas I don't have a copy of the article and am not exactly sure of the content of the paragraph you want omitted. From the context of your letter, it seems to be a section casting doubt on the usual interpretation of the psychic powers supposed to be possessed by high gurus, *roshis*, etc.

I cannot, of course, speak from any direct knowledge of Tibetan Buddhism or of the more esoteric forms of Hinduism, but so far as Japanese Zen is concerned, it may interest you to read the (slightly fuzzy) copies of letters from Ruth Sasaki when I questioned her on these points several years ago. My much more intimate discussions with both Western and Japanese people in Kyoto confirm her opinion, though one *roshi* demurred on her flat rejection of the literal interpretation of reincarnation.

One should not, of course, go out of one's way to give offense. But it seems to me that an editorial policy which goes out of its way *not* to give offense might make *The Middle Way* read like a Buddhist version of the *Church Times*...I would much rather you left the article unchanged.

Toby should soon be getting a copy of *Beyond Theology*. In the meantime, very best wishes for the anniversary!

Yours sincerely, Alan Watts

Sausalito, California | October 13, 1964

Dear Tim [Leary]:

I have been unconscionably long answering your letter of September 19th. Sorry, but what a whirl!

I don't think I should attempt a workshop at Castalia on this trip. There is just too much already. But we would both love to come up for a few days midweek, around either Nov. 12–13 or 17–18, depending on when I have to go up to Harvard.

As yet I haven't received Cohen's book, so haven't worked out how to review it. I appreciate your point of view on alterations to the brain. It really doesn't make any difference, does it, as to *what* gets changed! The whole thing is process and pattern anyhow, whether brain, or memory, or behavior. What I feel concerned to "disarm" is the charge that those so changed have become subhuman, as if lobotomized.

Had a very pleasant dinner two nights ago with Jack Downing and John Whittlesey. Most constructive.

Jim Watt has come out here, and wants to stay. I hope you will see him. Confidentially, I am very concerned about him, and I think he is tormented with guilt about breaking up with his family.

Love to you and all from us both. As ever, Alan

Winnetka, Illinois | October 21, 1964

Dear Milly [Johnstone]:

I'm at present on the road across the country, now staying a couple of days with Ruth Roberg before going to Washington, DC, to meet Jano (flying direct from SF) and give a seminar at the Washington School of Psychiatry this weekend.

Jano may have replied already to your long and most fascinating letter about cha-no-yu [the Japanese tea ceremony] at the Fair. She has been staying home to catch up on all the correspondence, while I have been gadding about in Milwaukee and Chicago. (Fancy, I was taken to one of those dreadful Playboy Clubs last night, with their bunnies. *Ne touchez pas les lapins!*)

I didn't open up the question of a seminar for this fall in Bethlehem because it seemed that by the time we could get east, the weather would be too cold. I think we should look forward to the latter part of April, if that will be a convenient time for you.

We plan to reach NYC on the 26th, and will be staying for a few days at the Shoreham Hotel before moving into Charlotte's new studio when she and Charles go west. Then we shall be in town more or less continuously until November 25th.

Hope you got our postcard from Mexico, where we spent a fascinating August, and came back with blankets and other textile objects to make your mouth water. Well, there'll be much to tell you about that.

I thought you would particularly appreciate the following koan: Is a zebra a yellow horse with black stripes, or a black horse with yellow stripes? Answer: Neither. It is an invisible horse, striped black and yellow so that people won't bump into it.

Ruth sends much love to you. And please give our very best to Bill — hoping, too, that all goes well with him.

Fondly, Alan

NEW YORK, NEW YORK | NOVEMBER 4, 1964
Dear Daddy:

We are here in New York until November 25th. I am wondering if you received the (very controversial) book, which I sent you by airmail almost three weeks ago.

The last letter from you said that you had made a privet bow and had taken up archery. The odd thing was that just at the same time I, too, had acquired a bow, together with some very highly colored arrows that can easily be seen in the grass — with the idea of playing a sort of archery golf. You take a walk in the wilds, simply following the arrows from point to point, using what they call "field arrows" as distinct from target and hunting arrows. We can get them here for about 40 cents each. My bow is made of fiberglass, and has a 45 lb. pull.

We are all immensely relieved that Mr. Goldwater has been utterly squelched in the election, but wonder how you feel about the narrow Labor victory. The situation looks very unstable, and I just can't understand the Labor opposition to the common market. They used to be so internationally minded.

We are going full speed ahead with plans to take another tour to Japan in the autumn of 1965, and this will definitely involve passing by London and Paris on the way there, or on the way back. Which end is not yet decided, but the Japan period will be approximately six weeks, ending October 31st, and this should get us to London (if we follow this plan) in the latter part of November.

As to more immediate things, we shall leave here for Sheridan, Wyoming, to spend Thanksgiving holiday with Jano's mother, and then I have to make a quick trip to the University of Saskatchewan, and then on home to Sausalito until Christmas.

Friends in London, in particular a fellow by the name of R. L. Pulton, are trying to set up arrangements for my giving the same kind of "seminars" as here. This will be marvelous if it goes through, because in this jet age it might justify a London visit as an extension of any New York visit.

Very much love from us both —

As always, Alan

NEW YORK, NEW YORK | NOVEMBER 10, 1964
Mrs. M. D. | Santa Barbara, California
Dear Mrs. D.:
Thank you for your letter of October 26th, and also for being about the only person thoughtful enough to realize that an author's reply to a correspondent takes a fair amount of time. So you get a prompt answer!

I have a friend who, some years ago, moved into a country house afflicted with black widow spiders. She was terrified of all spiders, and black widows gave her the most especial creeps. But there they were, lurking in her shoes, behind jars on the shelves, and in the piles of logs in the garage. I am sure they were quite as horrible to her as private planes are to you.

My friend thereupon bought a book on spiders, and read up on everything known about black widows. She got colored slides of them from the Natural History Museum, and some specimens of the creatures encased in plastic from a biological supply firm. These last she studied carefully with a magnifying glass. Then she managed to capture a live specimen with a tumbler, and watched it closely too. As a result, she lost her fear of them entirely. She understood their habits. Knew how not to anger them. Knew what precautions to take before putting feet or fingers into places there they might lurk. In the end, she felt quite friendly to them and to spiders in general.

You, therefore, should purchase a book on small aircraft and learn to identify all the different types. Take a few afternoons at the Santa Barbara airport, and, if at all possible, make friends with someone who owns one and take a ride. Get an aircraft map of the whole area (they are really terribly interesting), and know where all the ports are and all the standard routes. You should get the magazines on small aircraft that are on sale at almost any large magazine stand, and, incidentally, I believe the best identification book is *The Observer's World Aircraft Directory*, published by Warne at $3.50. The only way to overcome nuisances of this kind is on the principle of "If you can't lick 'em, join 'em." Also the only way to subdue dragons is to look them straight in the eye. If you run, you are immediately devoured.

Sincerely yours, Alan Watts

SAUSALITO, CALIFORNIA | JANUARY 20, 1965
Mrs. M. Gershbein | Brooklyn, New York
Dear Mrs. Gershbein:

Mr. Eisley of Japan Airlines has passed on to me your letter of January 2nd.

As I originally formulated them, the rules for the JAL haiku contest did not call for a rigid adherence to the 5–7–5 or 17 syllable form. I indicated that this was simply suggestive — that an English haiku should be approximately of this length. Even in Japanese, haiku do not adhere strictly to this rule. For example, this one by Issa: *Toyama ga / tsuki ni utsuru / tonbo kana*. R. H. Blyth translates it: Reflected / in the eye of the dragonfly / the distant hills.

In my opinion, Blyth is far and away the best translator, and to get the spirit of this poetry you should consult his four-volume work *Haiku* published by the Hokuseido Press in Tokyo. In New York this would be available from Orientalia, Inc. I think he has also published a one-volume *History of Haiku*. He does not follow the 17-syllable rule, nor does he make Henderson's mistake of rhyming English haiku, which invariably gives the effect of doggerel.

The old pond. / A frog jumps in / Plop!

Sincerely yours, Alan Watts

cc. Mr. Richard S. Eisley, JAL

SAUSALITO, CALIFORNIA | FEBRUARY 2, 1965
Mr. Peter John | *The Psychedelic Review* | Cambridge, Massachusetts
Dear Peter:

When you write one surely does get news!

Jim Watt is working with Stolaroff at Menlo Park, but their operations are confined to mescaline. No LSD. Rumor hath it that they are reporting all bootleg LSD to the FDA, and thus the scene is not very cool.

As to those who are still working with LSD in the North American continent: there is a fellow at the University of Saskatchewan, but I forget his name. However, you can get it from Dr. Duncan Blewett, Dept. of Psychology, Univ. of Sask., Regina, Sask. I was there early in December, and it's a very swinging crowd.

Let me know, some months from now, how things work out with University

Books. They've made me a proposition, too, but I am wondering just a little about Morrow's reliability.

I saw Sid Cohen in LA a couple of weeks ago, and had a very constructive talk with him. Have you heard about the conference on LSD that is to be held at Amityville, NY, in May? Harold Abramson is in charge, but I shan't be able to attend because I am due for a session at that time with the Oglala Indians in Nebraska who belong to the Native American Church.

I too get dozens of letters asking How To (?), but there's nothing to be done except using *ipomaea purpurea*, and I don't readily recommend it because of the insecticides used on many seeds. I imagine that the best-informed person on who is doing what (if anything) would be Sandy Ungar, since he's with NIMH.

Very best wishes to you and good luck with the *Review*.

As ever, Alan

SAUSALITO, CALIFORNIA | FEBRUARY 18, 1965

Dear Daddy:

The encyclopedias are coming in now, and I'm simply delighted. Not only are they a mine of cooking information, but also a veritable document of high-style manners and tastes of the 1890s. They have also been very well rebound, by someone who understands the hard use that such volumes may get, and was imaginative enough to put in pockets for the loose plates and for sundry recipes clipped from magazines. Thank you very much indeed.

I am so sorry not to have written for so long, but things have been in a fantastic whirl. Since Christmas I have been on rapid trips to Los Angeles, La Jolla, Florida, and New York. We have so much mail that filing baskets of various classifications are spread over about 30 feet of table area! Yesterday, at a relatively small local college, I gave four lectures — the last of which was attended by well over 1,500 people, standing room only and lots turned away. The professor who was introducing me felt that they might even be reproducing while in queue outside!

We had two birthday parties: one here on the boat and one at the Denisons' in Hollywood, and people took us at our word to come dressed "formal and colorful." It was like being in the middle of an exquisite Italian Renaissance painting. We had thirty all told here, and I enclose a copy of the invitation for your amusement. John Sudlow took photographs, which you may get soon (but see below). I made two *poupetons* or stuffed rolls of boned turkeys. Ruth [Denison] served individual squab pigeons in a wonderful sauce, and for her party I finally persuaded Jano to wear her Indian sari, which is light, bright-blue silk woven with an intricate gold pattern. She had expert help in putting it on. Joan had made a bow tie and a cummerbund for John out of the most marvelous white Japanese brocade, which he wore with a white dinner jacket, and, in general, the men came in similar colored-up versions of evening dress. At the party on the boat James Broughton acted as toastmaster, and all the old-time formalities were observed. (I must somehow send you a copy of the illuminated poem he composed for the occasion.)

Not so happy — John had a bad motor accident about a week ago. He was driving from Cincinnati to Dayton a bit too fast and hit the back of a slow-moving lorry. Fortunately was wearing a seat belt, but had injuries to his face and nearly bit off his tongue. But with luck he went to the new Kettering Hospital where it's their policy to have a top-rank surgeon in constant attendance, and he did the necessary work to eliminate scars and heal the tongue. (I have tried to call for the most recent news, but Joan is at present out.) But all-in-all they seem to be optimistic about his being able to get back to normal fairly soon.

Something that is simultaneously good and bad is that Jano has discovered that she has a mild case of diabetes, a condition which is hereditary and must have existed for quite some time. It was responsible for her lack of energy and necessity for sleep. Only quite recently new methods of correcting it have been discovered — not insulin injections but a pill called tolbutamide. So — her chemical balance is being readjusted and she is full of new life. In fact, it has changed her body chemistry in ways that are almost startlingly positive.

We are going ahead with our plans for the autumn tour of Japan, with Jano and I continuing via Hong Kong, Bangkok, India, Paris, and London so as to reach you early December. I don't see quite how we can stay for Christmas, unless on the chance that Robert Pulton (the man with a beard who made a mint in toothpaste) can arrange seminars in London. Otherwise we will have to go to work in New York on the way home.

Recently we have made very good friends with the Episcopal Bishop of California, James Pike, and his wife Esther. He and I gave a joint television program on Christmas Eve, whereafter he invited us to the midnight mass at Grace Cathedral. We went with his party and had seats in the choir. It is a huge (vaguely Perpendicular Gothic) building with central altar. They use the Coventry-Sarum Rite, facing the congregation, and did it with considerable dignity and beauty, with the help of a very fine boys' choir. After that, we went back to his home for drinks and a discussion that went on until almost 3 AM. Since then they have been here to dinner, and we plan a joint seminar in Big Sur for September. He is noted as a sort of American equivalent of the Bishop of Woolwich, and has all ears open with great readiness to learn of things that might put life into the dear old Church. His wife is a distinct asset to him.

We also had a very pleasant visit from the number-one Protestant theologian Paul Tillich, who is a close friend of Frederic Spiegelberg. This was extremely interesting. We are living in very exciting days so far as things religious are concerned. Everything is in flux, and there is even a real possibility of Roman-Anglican reunion in a not-too-distant future.

I'm afraid this must be it for the time being. Much, much love from Jano, and Ann and Joel, and from

Yours as ever, Alan

PS. Not to mention — thanks for your cablegram [of birthday wishes]! And for the most pleasant little book in Italy. We have thoroughly enjoyed it as a reminder of that splendid trip.

SAUSALITO, CALIFORNIA | FEBRUARY 23, 1965
Miss J. H. | Portland, Oregon
Dear Miss H.:
Thank you for your letter of February 11th, which has just been passed on to me by the travel agency.

Though it is always impolite to ask a lady her age, I think this has something to do with your eligibility for the Japan tour and whether your mother has some say in the matter.

I do not "use" drugs as a habit — like smoking. I have made a few very carefully controlled experiments with some of the new chemicals that change consciousness in an attempt to give investigators a very accurate account of their effects. One of my main interests is the psychology of religious experiences and the description of states of mind that are very difficult to put into words.

If your mother doesn't have time to read *The Joyous Cosmology* or other books on the subject, such as Dr. Sidney Cohen's *The Beyond Within* (which is a highly authoritative study) she is really not in a position to form an opinion.

Obviously such experiments are dangerous, but so is flying to the moon, climbing Mount Everest, and exploring the jungles. Nothing worthwhile is ever achieved without danger.

With all good wishes,
Sincerely yours, Alan Watts

SAUSALITO, CALIFORNIA | MARCH 1, 1965
Dear Henry [Miller]:
I was very glad to get your letter, though most sorry to hear that you have all this surgery to cope with. As you know, everyone is always giving advice to their friends about favorite doctors. I happen to know the most un-knife-happy

blinking genius of an orthopedist here in Marin County, who healed a real bad broken back of a friend of mine in one instead of the usual six months. No cast, no nothing. He is Dr. Adolph Segal of Kentfield. Louisa Jenkins went to him and was delighted. Ask her. Of course he knows of you and digs your work. It might be very well worth your while to risk a simple consultation. "Second opinion" sort of thing. I hate to think of you stuck away for two or three months, and there is just the bare chance that a quick plane ride up here might change things radically. Why not phone him and explore the chances?

As to *The World of Sex* the man who approached me is Robert Carr, at The Wax Museum in San Francisco. I will try to get in touch with him, but in the meantime you might get your agent to make appropriate noises in his direction.

Warmest greetings and all good things to you, Alan

New York, New York | April 12, 1965
Dear Daddy:
We were so glad to get your last letter and to know that all goes so well with you. (Yes, I *did* get the watch compass. I am so sorry to have overlooked saying thank you. It looks as if we may well need it if we take a projected camping trip with friends — including Ruth and Henry — to Baja California this summer.)

We're now, as you can see, on the spring tour. I left March 19th for Dallas, and Jano joined me here on the 22nd. We've seen a lot of Madeleine Low and Dick Borst [a photographer], who made the accompanying print specially for you. Sam and Minette Kuhn send their very best wishes; they took us to the theatre last week to see a play from London (light and witty) called *The Knack*.

We went to the symphony in the new Lincoln Center auditorium with Amyas and Eve Ames, and since he is president of the NY Philharmonic Society we really had the "red carpet" treatment. They are utterly delightful people. It's quite an accomplishment to be amazingly rich and lovably human!

I've been doing a lot of writing (articles and reviews), though in New York it's difficult to settle down to anything. Time goes faster than in California. But I'm on a round of meetings with publishers, editors, and TV people (also the dentist!). We have had two seminars here with excellent audiences, and there's another to come at the Johnstones' place in Bethlehem, Pennsylvania. Then we go on for a couple of lectures and two seminars in Michigan, and May 3rd we head out for home via a place in western Nebraska where we have been invited by an Indian tribe to take part in their peyote ceremony. Peyote is the cactus from which mescaline is derived, and it is used as a sacrament in an Indian religion which is now called the Native American Church. This should be quite an experience, and I shall probably write something about it. Then we return to Sausalito, and during May I'm going to have a couple of meetings with Bishop Pike prior to a joint seminar that we're going to give at Big Sur in September on the current "revolution" in Christianity.

Did I tell you that Jano has discovered that she has a mild case of diabetes? She has been getting a new kind of treatment (not insulin, but a drug taken orally) from our doctor at home, but a specialist here in New York thinks that the case is so light that she hardly needs it. Just stay off excessive sugar and starches, which is no trouble because she doesn't go for sweet things anyhow.

Have Joan and John sent you any of the colored photos which they took at the big birthday party? If not, I'll pass some of them on. John seems to have made an excellent recovery from his accident.

We have recently seen Mummy's old pupil Isabel Grenfell Quallo. We went to her place on her birthday and met most of the family. She has a daughter, Phyllis, who looks exactly like a very beautiful Hindu woman. If she wore a sari, no one would know the difference, and since she is quite deeply interested in Eastern philosophy we invited her to the seminar this weekend.

I have to go out to lunch now to discuss plans for a new TV show, so I'll have to finish up. We're still working on plans to see you in December after the trip to Japan, but we won't know for certain until about July 15th, when registrations for the tour should be complete. The only thing that might seriously interfere would be a Far-Eastern blaze-up from this sorry business in Vietnam. Incidentally, this war is not at all popular here, and there is considerable protest against its continuance.

Jano joins me in sending very much love.

As always, Alan

NEW YORK, NEW YORK | APRIL 16, 1965

Dear Gary [Snyder],

I don't know whether you have had any official notification as yet, but Bollingen is going to give you the grant. I've no information as to the actual figures.

You should be hearing from Fr. Buckley, asst. prof. of theology at the Univ. of San Francisco. He will be hosting a Japanese Jesuit fascinated with the Zen-Catholicism bit, on or about April 24. I told him to get in touch with you.

Love from us both, Alan

PS. Until Apr. 24 in New York City. Back in Sausalito about May 8.

SAUSALITO, CALIFORNIA | MAY 6, 1965
Dear Laura [Huxley]:

I think the article is a very good idea, and fine as far as it goes. But it needs a little more local color — the environment of Aldous's home on Kings Road, which I remember as a most attractive place, and other such details. Try to revive the atmosphere around the man, as well as the man! I have made a few slight corrections of spelling and typographical errors.

It appears that Jano has a mild case of diabetes, coupled with "nervous intestines," whatever that may be. The diabetes is controllable with tolbutamide. There is apparently no other glandular trouble, but she still sleeps excessively. I have heard much of Dr. Niehaus, for surely he is the man who enabled Maugham, Hewlett Johnson, Churchill, Russell, and so many others to live to such great antiquity. I wonder if Jano's problems are in his line.

We come to Los Angeles on May 28th and will be staying until June 4th — presumably with the Denisons. By all means let's get together. Thus far all evenings seem to be free, but it would be as well to consult with Henry and Ruth.

Love from us both,

As ever, Alan

SAUSALITO, CALIFORNIA | JULY 6, 1965
Dear Daddy:

We are back again from extensive travels up and down the West Coast. Last weekend we were in Seattle, Washington, guests of a very charming couple who are heirs of one of the great lumber concerns. The occasion was a seminar held on their 50-foot motor cruiser, a wonderful and very shipshape craft made in 1929 — all beautiful wood and brass, and none of that plastic streamlined stuff! Their home is on the shores of Lake Washington, about a mile wide and eight long. Lovely place. The trip also included a visit to one of the innumerable islands in the Puget Sound area to visit the sculptor Phil McCracken and his family, who has a wizardly technique for carving birds and animals in wood. He also makes excellent home brew! When it is not raining (which is seldom) this part of the world is an unbelievable paradise of blue waters, green hills, islands, and white mountains in the distance.

Also we went to dinner with the curator of the Seattle Museum, who lives in a sumptuous villa reminiscent of the place where we stayed in Rome. The dinner was preceded by croquet on the lawn, for which Jano has unexpected talent. He has a lovely collection of Chinese things, including some very fine embroidery.

Then — let's see — we went down to La Jolla to stay with Eric and Betty

Bass and conduct a seminar at a local bookshop, all of which was a most delightful experience, in the course of which I picked up (on tape) some absolutely astonishing Indian music from Madras. The night before last we had a party just to listen to it.

In Los Angeles we stayed again with Ruth and Henry [Denison] (who send their love to you). On one of those wretched freeways I had a freak car accident, escaping without a scratch. As a result of some construction work ahead there was one of those frequent and terrifying slow-ups of traffic going at 60. I had the choice of slamming into the car in front of me or dodging. So I switched into the empty lane to the left, hit the curb, and turned the car right over. But as I was wearing a seatbelt I didn't fall on my head, but was just hanging upside down, and quickly escaped through an open window. Seven husky young men appeared from nowhere, put warning flares on the road, and flipped the car back onto its wheels. Well, we decided the thing was a total loss. The insurance paid the bill, and Don found me another — this time a big, heavy Pontiac with power brakes. Fortunately I was alone, and there were no bad nervous reactions. It all seemed perfectly natural!

Jano is still having some troubles with tiredness, dizziness, and headaches, but actual symptoms of diabetes are very slight. The trouble is that she can't work consistently, so I have a former student, Crist Lovdjieff (from Yugoslavia) as part-time secretary. He is marvelously reliable and willing. But in her bright intervals, Jano is very bright!

Ruth Denison has been making the most exquisite mosaic coffee tables, of which I enclose a transparency. Here, too, are pictures of the birthday celebrations. The crown is the creation of Suzanna Broughton, since Epiphany is the feast of the Three Kings.

Maud Oakes and Nancy Young (the novelist whom I am sure you met in New York) stopped by for lunch a day or two ago — both in great form and on their way to the Northwest. We also had Joe and Helena Henderson to dinner. They are on their way to London and will be calling you. (He, you will remember, was in Zurich with us, and is the number-one Jungian analyst in San Francisco.)... You'll be glad to know that the magnificent encyclopedia of cooking comes in very useful, even though many of the recipes are designed for banquets and busts for fifty guests!

Plans for Japan are well ahead, and the party now has 20 members. We need just a few more to justify circling the world, but I think we shall get them. I think we shall know for sure by mid-August, if not before. We shall be here in Sausalito for the rest of the summer, except for a brief weekend in New Mexico at the beginning of August. (Another seminar.) Varda leaves for Europe at the end of this month, and I am sure he will get in touch with you when in London, though his plans are vague. He will be away for a whole year, and we shall all miss him very much.

I am very concerned about your eye trouble. Is the doctor you are seeing a really tip-top specialist? If it would help, I would be very willing to fork out some extra funds for you to see one of the big shots. Otherwise, I think I am going to have to get you a tape recorder so that we can send tapes instead of letters. Please let me know about all this.

Very much love to you from us both, and much looking forward to being with you again.

As always, Alan

SAUSALITO, CALIFORNIA | SEPTEMBER 15, 1965
Dear Daddy:

We have just returned home from a most exciting and stimulating weekend conference at Big Sur with Bishop Pike. He and I held a dialogue on "Christianity in Revolution" before a very lively audience of about 50 people, and came to substantial agreement on all the main issues. He had just returned from a meeting of the House of Bishops, at which charges of heresy against him had been completely turned down (by unanimous vote) and he was naturally in high spirits. He is now about to leave for a few months' vacation for study at Cambridge, so don't be surprised if you get a call from him... Varda wrote that he had a very pleasant time with you and thoroughly enjoyed the garden.

Now as to our plans: the war in India and some temporary financial problems make it unwise to attempt to go on round the world from Japan. Instead, we plan to come to London about April 25th (from New York) and return about May 20th. This will include a visit to Vince and Pegy in Paris, on which we hope you will be able to join us. The season is better in any case, but I'm sorry for the delay, because we had hoped to see you sooner. How good to hear that your eye problems are improving so well. We have been very touched by everything that Phyl Salomon has been doing for you. Please give her our love and most cordial best wishes.

I so often wish that we would be more frequently on hand to help out, but as yet the problem of paying my way in England is sticky, and I haven't found the solution. There isn't yet a publisher for *Beyond Theology*, although Gollancz made an offer for it which was unacceptable. (By the way, call Murray about those royalties. I know of no reason why you shouldn't have received them.)

Jano's health problems are still puzzling, though she has had some very good days lately. More and more it seems that the diabetes diagnosis may have been faulty. She has had medical tests galore, and there seems to be nothing seriously wrong to account for the lack of energy and need for so much sleep. She gets furious at herself for being so inert, but when she brightens up, she really comes alive in a big way... We saw Henry and Ruth this weekend, and they send much love. Joel played the harp (and Roger Somers the drums) by way of an interlude at the conference, adding much to the gay atmosphere of the whole affair... We shall be leaving for Japan on the 26th, and returning about Nov. 10th, after a few days in Hawaii. Did I tell you that Elsa Gidlow will be travelling with us?

I am coming close to finishing the manuscript of my next book, and may have it done before we leave — though there have been constant interruptions all summer. For example — I was working all this afternoon on a TV program for the Japan Broadcasting Corporation, which they filmed here on the boat, and which will be shown all over Japan on Oct. 26th, while we are there. It all seemed good "public relations" — so I set aside the time.

Our address in Japan will be the Miyako Hotel, Higashiyama, Kyoto, and we will be there until October 31st. Of course, any letters sent here will be forwarded.

Ann and Joel send their love to you, as do Gert and Dave, with whom we spent a very delightful evening 2 weeks ago to celebrate his birthday.

Very much love from us both, dear Daddy —

As always, Alan

SAUSALITO, CALIFORNIA | NOVEMBER 11, 1965
Michael Thomas, Esq. | London, England
Dear Mr. Thomas:
I'm very glad to hear, through Henry Volkening, that Hodder & Stoughton seem to be going ahead with my *Beyond Theology*.

Is Paul Hodder-Williams, who should be just over 50, connected with the firm? We went to the same prep school. Please tell them that I am planning to be in London late April and early May, and that if I can be of any help in promotion I'll be happy to do what I can.

It's just possible that a "quotable quote" for dust jacket or whatever could be had from the Rt. Rev. James A. Pike, Bishop of California, now resident at Cambridge. They should also try the Bishop of Woolwich; I'm pretty sure he has read it.

Best wishes and many thanks,
Yours sincerely, Alan Watts

Sausalito, California | November 11, 1965

Dear Henry [Volkening]:

Many thanks for yours of October 29th and for the good news from England. I've taken the liberty of writing directly to Michael Thomas, as you will see from the enclosed copy.

We are just back from Japan after 3 days in Hawaii. By all means let Spectorsky in on *The Book*. I enclose copy of a letter from Paula which gives me a little more time, but I want to finish it as soon as possible in any case. "The Circle of Sex" was to have been published in the December issue [of *Playboy*], but the forecast of contents doesn't include it.

The tour was great since we had a most congenial and relaxed group with us, and must have consumed hundreds of gallons of sake, which I recommend as an eminently civilized drink. Delighted to hear that you were once Chinese! I, too, have real Chinese blood in my veins — courtesy of a transfusion — but still, I'm rather proud of it.

Do you have any contacts with *Holiday*? I want to do an article on "The Paradox of Tourism" — Americans wanting escape to romantic foreign atmospheres, and all the natives going American as fast as possible — to the ruination of the tourist business! You should see what is happening in Japan. I can walk down the street in the most vividly colored Mexican clothes and no one bats an eye, but the moment I put on a restrained and very correct kimono I get my picture in the paper and endless giggles. But the old ladies approve. They feel the cloth and murmur, "Naisu," which is Nihonglish for "Nice."

All the best, AWW

AW and JW: Elda Voelkel, the addressee of the next letter, was a Broadway and Hollywood starlet when she met and married filmmaker Irving Hartley. Together they made newsreels and travel films from the 1930s through the 1960s.

Elda went on a vacation tour of Japan with Alan and Jano in 1965. This was the beginning of both a friendship and a partnership. The Hartleys formed the Hartley Film Foundation, and Elda began producing documentary films of a spiritual nature, realizing a long-held dream. Together she and Alan collaborated on half a dozen films, including The Art of Meditation; Buddhism, Man, and Nature; *and* Zen and Now.

Alan enjoyed working with TV more than film. He was much more at ease with the spontaneity of television production. The movie-making process seemed cumbersome to him — the constant "cut" and "action" were interruptions to his train of thought. He never worked from a script, hence, the changing of settings and inevitable fussing irritated him. He and Elda did not always agree as to how a scene should be filmed.

Despite their apparent close friendship between the two couples, Alan still sternly criticized the final product. (See his letters of April 19 and May 14, 1971.) Elda fiercely defended the production, citing people who liked the films as they were. At one point, she also sent Alan a long and impassioned letter begging him to stop drinking. This was an obvious deeply caring plea, regardless of their working differences.

SAUSALITO, CALIFORNIA | DECEMBER 20, 1965
Dear Elda:
How good to hear from you! We had just sent off a card with a slide of you enclosed when your letter arrived.

Yes, I should indeed like to see John Clayton when he comes through, but I shall be away in southern California from about January 5th to February 1st.

I will try to have a Zen tape by the time we come to NYC, which will be the end of March. We plan to leave April 25th for Europe for just less than a month.

Glad your slides and films turned out so well. I shall be interested to see what Alfred got when we pass through Chicago in May. Hope your packages have been coming through, as ours have been very slow and they're not all here yet — even some mailed quite early in the trip.

Interesting about Ann Patai. I wouldn't want to live in Japan either, but I think a year in Kyoto could be very well spent — before the place vanishes under an immense modernistic pagoda made of wire, plastic, and neon lights!

Very much love from us both to you both —
As ever, Alan

This letter to Christmas "Toby" Humphreys mentions a new home and conference center for Alan and Jano — a reference that remains mysterious.

SAUSALITO, CALIFORNIA | MARCH 19, 1966
Dear Toby:
It seems that we are going to have to move house early in May, which will therefore postpone our visit to England. We shall be acquiring a new home and conference centre for the society just a little north of here, and I am trying to persuade my father to come and live with us as he seems to be getting a bit too feeble to take care of himself. The senses of sight and sound are closing down as he withdraws back to the center.

Now as to radionics. The literature you have sent me whets the appetite but remains exasperatingly vague. Just what is inside all that electronic equipment? The climate of scientific opinion here is very rigid and stuffy, and commendatory speeches by various aristocrats without minute statistics and details will go over like a lead balloon! I say that it "whets the appetite" because it sounds as if it were a confirmation of the whole *ji-ji-mu-ge* philosophy of the Avatamsaka. But we really do need to know what is inside those little black boxes.

Incidentally, have you seen John Blofeld's account of his mescaline experience? Graciously, if reluctantly, he acknowledges that Aldous Huxley and others, such as your humble servant, may be right in thinking that certain chemicals may be powerful aids to the practice of meditation. In any case, it is one of the most astonishing descriptions of samadhi that I have ever read. If you want, I'll send you a copy.

Much love to you both, as ever, Alan

SAUSALITO, CALIFORNIA | MARCH 22, 1966
Dear Don [Hayakawa]:
Although this is written in the form of a personal letter, I am submitting it as a "Letter to the Editor" of *ETC*.

In your foreword to the Psychedelic Issue you have, I feel, committed the cardinal semantic sin of using loaded language, as well as the journalistic device of employing derogatory and derisive quotation marks. Of course, the advertisement in the *Gater* for the Psychedelic Chapel was a sitting duck for derision, but you should have been above shooting at it with words so reminiscent of *Time* magazine as:

> I shudder as I see in my mind's eye, sitting in the "chapel," the Jet
> Set and the Sin Crowd, "turned on" and "tripping through the Astral
> Plane," with the music of Recording Artist Ivan Ulz (whatever he sings
> or plays) crashing and reverberating through their skulls, each member
> with a dog-eared copy of this issue of *ETC*. in his pocket.

You are simply using the easy device of begging the question by exploiting the obvious bourgeois prejudices against beatniks, and I don't think this is worthy of General Semantics. Beware lest "the stone which the builders rejected becomes the head of the corner." Beatniks may have something.

All that you say about having vivid awareness of the world without psychedelics is true enough, but I would love to know what you would say if you had actually experienced the changes of consciousness which they involve. Kipling's saying that "he does not know England who only England knows" is also true of our normal sensations of the world.

Best wishes, Alan Watts

AW: In some of the following letters in this collection, Alan takes a bold and impassioned political stand to keep psychotropic drugs such as LSD, mescaline, and marijuana free from the rigid and punitive hand of the law. He argued, quite rightly, that such laws would only drive these drugs underground and thereby make any quality control impossible. His own experiments with these drugs were careful, occasional (unlike his daily consumption of alcohol), and treated with respect and wonder. He shared his experiences with those doing research into the effects of these drugs spiritually, psychologically, and medicinally.

In his letter of September 1967, Alan wrote to US Senator Henry Jackson, making an eloquent and knowledgeable plea on behalf of Native Americans and their sacred ceremonies. He had on occasion been invited to share in these events with different tribes.

This letter refers to The Varieties of Psychedelic Experience *by Robert Masters and Jean Houston, which later became a standard work in the field.*

SAUSALITO, CALIFORNIA | MARCH 23, 1966
Mr. H. R. Cohen | Holt, Rinehart & Winston, Inc. | New York, New York
Dear Mr. Cohen:
Many thanks for sending me the proofs of *The Varieties of Psychedelic Experience*. I have mixed feelings about this book. On the one hand, it really is a serious effort to achieve an objective study of the various changes in consciousness brought about by psychedelic chemicals. I feel that the authors did their lab work very well.

On the other hand, I have reservations about their way of presenting it. If you are really going to be scientific, there is no room for vague generalizations about any alleged basic differences between Western and Eastern thought. There are too many varieties of both, and, for example, there is no way of deciding whether Islamic culture is Western or Eastern.

Furthermore, I find too much use of loaded language and deprecatory quotation marks. To entitle a section "Instant Love and Galloping Agape" is to invoke and exploit the most obvious bourgeois derision of the so-called beatnik subculture, and, together with other matters, gives the impression of striking a scientific posture rather than being scientific. I find repeatedly that people who make strong claims for representing an attitude which is, e.g., "Western-oriented, nonmystical," etc., are insufficiently aware and critical of their own metaphysical assumptions.

It is not correct to say that Huxley and I have imposed essentially Eastern ideas upon the psychedelic experience. Both European and Asian literatures abound with accounts of mystical experiences, which obviously have the same general character, and in much of my own work I have stressed, not so much the mystical, as an awareness of ecological and transactional relationships as a common feature of the experience. (See especially my contribution to the Solomon Symposium.)

In general, it strikes me that the authors would be in a better position if they had a wider knowledge of the psychology of religion. However, I hope you and they will realize that I wouldn't have taken the time to comment at this length if I did not consider the book very important and worthwhile. It is all in the right direction; it is an excellent counterbalance to current hysterias; it gives very sound directive for controlling the use of psychedelics instead of merely repressing them.

Sincerely, Alan Watts

SAUSALITO, CALIFORNIA | APRIL 29, 1966
Mr. George P. Hunt | *LIFE* magazine | New York, New York
Dear Mr. Hunt:
You were welcome to my "grandmotherly panic" phrase for your editorial of April 29th on LSD. Your attitude is entirely correct and will help very much to bring sobriety into this silly hysteria.

For future reference, may I urge you to consider the following outline of a policy which should be adopted for the control of drugs of this type, for which I commend the neutral and unbiased term "psychotropic" or "mind altering."

1. The wide public interest and irregular use occasioned by these drugs puts them in a special category beyond the normal and proper procedures of the FDA for testing new therapeutic chemicals. They are likewise outside the province of the Federal Narcotics Bureau, which is supposed to confine its attentions to habit-forming and torpor-inducing opiates and barbiturates — i.e., true narcotics.

2. Panic legislation against the simple possession of such drugs (including even marijuana) is socially demoralizing and productive of disrespect for the law and its officers. Consider the horrifying possibilities of "planting" something so concealable as LSD upon innocent persons for purposes of blackmail and

entrapment, political smearing, and generally getting rid of one's commercial, political, or domestic enemies.

3. Responsibility for the control of these drugs should be adopted by a national committee of physicians and other scientists experienced in their use: (a) To inform the public and the professions as to their properties and dangers, and to advise on the treatment of those who have suffered from bad side effects; (b) To recommend measures of control to federal and state agencies; (c) To sponsor further research (now more needed than ever); and (d) To establish centers where carefully selected individuals can use such drugs under optimal conditions and proper controls.

Sincerely yours, Alan Watts

Society for Comparative Philosophy | Sausalito, California |
April 29, 1966
Mr. Pearce Young | Chairman, Assembly Criminal Procedures Committee |
Sacramento, California
Dear Mr. Young:
Your committee is very much to be commended for resisting the pressures for "panic legislation" in regard to the problem of LSD-25 and similar psychotropic chemicals. This is much more a matter for physicians than for the police, and I think you should know that a group of prominent New York doctors are in the process of forming a national committee of scientists for public information and advice as to the control of these chemicals, as well as to sponsor future research. You will be kept informed.

The principal mistake that "panic legislation" on LSD, DMT [dimethyltryptamine], and even marijuana, can make is to define simple possession as illegal. The great majority of both Jewish and Christian moral theologians have agreed that no material substance is in itself evil. Evil can arise only in the misuse of a substance, and the law should therefore require proof of misuse in any criminal action relative to these chemicals.

Otherwise, the illegality of mere possession can create highly demoralizing situations that can bring both the law and its enforcement officers into disrespect. Powerful quantities of such a minute and undetectable substance as LSD-25 can be "planted" upon innocent persons and used for blackmail or entrapment, and one shudders to think of the potential exploitation of such possession laws for political "smearing" and generally getting rid of one's commercial or domestic enemies.

Sincerely yours, Alan Watts, President

SAUSALITO, CALIFORNIA | JUNE 4, 1966
Mrs. Peggy Morrison | Episcopal Church Center | New York, New York
Dear Peggy Morrison:

Well — this is a most impressive document, a very skillfully constructed anthology of persuasive authorities, and I feel fairly sure that the Church is ready to act on at least some of it.

I think a little more might be made of the point that the ethical teachings of Jesus must be seen in historical and cultural context. He couldn't have been laying down principles that are valid for all times and places whatsoever. Thus a divorced Palestinian woman of his day was simply returned home "used," and no man would look at her again.

This leads to a larger and more disquieting problem. He was also teaching in the context of an agrarian society in which the family is a very real entity. Father, mother, and children all live and work together in a meaningful vocation. Today's urban and industrial family does not have the same reality. Father goes off somewhere to a job which, so far as the rest of the family is concerned, simply produces money. The children go to school, where they are in effect, brought up by other children, and as soon as mama can get them out of her hair she takes a job herself or goes to the women's club. Home is merely a dormitory.

Now, the Episcopal Church is very largely a bourgeois, suburban, or small-town institution, acting as a conservative force to keep the family intact. "The family that prays together stays together." Naturally, then, that part of your study which deals with heterosexuality, marriage, etc., is based on the assumption that family preservation is the great desideratum, allowing that divorce may be a very necessary evil when the association just won't work.

But you don't consider the possibility that the family as such may already be obsolete — that it has widely ceased to exist as a fully functioning organism, and that therefore we are trying vainly to put new wine in old bottles. It seems to me, then, that the Church should stop considering the family as a sacred cow, and try to come up with some humane and rational alternative. Otherwise, we are all drifting into a ridiculous muddle in which children are the chief victims.

I think the family really began to break up when children were sent to school instead of learning to work along with their parents, on the farm or in the shop. Later, the family went into mitosis — i.e., every grown child wants to get the hell out of home and set up his own private *ménage à deux*, away from the generally disapproving atmosphere of parents and grandparents. This is because rapid means of communication increase the speed of social change, creating ever more acute disharmony between the generations.

Thus the modern 30-to-40-year-old parents aren't so much afraid that their adolescent kids will jump into bed with each other, but that they will go to the University of California and become beatniks, hipsters, and acidheads, attend happenings designed to "blow your mind," and grow up totally uninterested in business! You should take a look at the *East Village Other* (circulation 11,000 within a few weeks of existence).

The Church sure has its work cut out! Thank you so much for letting me see the study, and very best wishes to you.

Sincerely yours, Alan Watts

SOCIETY FOR COMPARATIVE PHILOSOPHY | SAUSALITO, CALIFORNIA |
JULY 21, 1966
Mr. Pearce Young | Chairman, Assembly Committee on Criminal Procedure |
Sacramento, California
Dear Mr. Young:
Many thanks for your letter of July 14th, and for your consideration and courtesy in taking time to reply to my letter. It really is rather reassuring to know that some of our legislators will take the trouble to discuss such matters with concerned citizens.

I still feel that the unamended SB 6 was unnecessary in view of existing laws, both state and federal, and you may have seen the editorial in *Look* magazine (July 26th) which criticizes both California and Nevada for "panic legislation" which hinders rather than helps the proper control of LSD-25.

Such laws are paralyzing legitimate research into one of the most crucial and exciting problems facing mankind, and, once made, they are incredibly difficult to repeal. Can't you do something to get the whole question reconsidered?

With all good wishes and repeated thanks,
Sincerely yours, Alan Watts, President

SAUSALITO, CALIFORNIA | JULY 26, 1966
Mr. Henry Volkening | New York, New York
Dear Henry:
Since we are on the brink of making another contract with Pantheon, I really think we should take a hard look at my situation with them. For I don't really need to write the *Philosopher in the Kitchen* book from a financial point of view; I can spend the time far more profitably by lecturing, and thus the only real reason for doing it is that the project fascinates me. Which is as it should be — from my standpoint, but not in the economics of publishing.

Pantheon has goofed completely on *Beyond Theology*. If I do say so myself, it's a good book as well as being highly relevant to the whole "Death of God" uproar, and they really should have made capital out of this.

They are also about to goof on *The Book*, to judge from the promotion you sent me in the *Publishers Weekly*. No publisher should accept a book with that title and not play it up. It just doesn't make sense to announce *The Book* among one's "also-ran" titles.

So may I ask you to do some rather tough diplomacy for me with Paula, or whoever actually runs Pantheon in the Random House organization. Is the amount of the advance a critical factor in deciding the advertising budget? If so, let's ask for at least $5,000. (Authors less well-known are getting even more than that.) You could say that otherwise I shall just stop writing for a while, or go into publishing myself, or take up with that crass and vulgar promoter who sells Laura Huxley's *You Are Not the Target*. He happens to be interested! Anyhow, I leave the tactics up to you.

Pantheon has also made a deal with Felix Morrow to sell some of my books through the Mystic Arts Book Club, though I don't think that these were books that you handled. I would rather not do business with that outfit. The terms are terrible and they don't pay their bills. We'll be lucky to get the $200 he owes us for my introduction to *The Circle of Sex* [by Gavin Arthur].

All this is terribly depressing stuff for me to write to you upon your return from what was, I trust, a most pleasant vacation. But I'm sure you're used to it!

Best wishes, Alan

SOCIETY FOR COMPARATIVE PHILOSOPHY | SAUSALITO, CALIFORNIA |
JULY 30, 1966
The Chairman | Local Draft Board #51 | Oakland, California
Dear Sir:
Re: Mr. J. D. M., Conscientious Objector
I have known Mr. M. and his mother, Mrs. V. M. M., since about 1952. Mr. M. attended a course on comparative religions which I conducted in the Fall and Winter of 1961–62, under the auspices of this Society, and has been an earnest student of this subject since that time — during which I have been in contact both with him and his family.

Though I do not expressly advocate conscientious objection in my courses, it is highly possible that a person exposed to and sympathetic to the teaching of Hinduism, Buddhism, and Taoism might find it against his conscience to serve in the armed forces. Both Hinduism and Buddhism exalt the principle of ahimsa, or nonviolence towards all living beings.

I am fully satisfied that Mr. M. has held such convictions from at least the age of 17, and that his whole family background would have predisposed him to this viewpoint from an early age. I have no reason whatsoever to question either his moral character or his sincerity.

Although Mr. M. has signified, on the appropriate form, that he is uncertain on the "Supreme Being" question, I have advised him that this phrase is intentionally vague and does not absolutely specify belief in a *personal* God. He does, however, subscribe to the belief of the above-mentioned religions that there is a universal intelligence and order superior to the human will, compelling all those who recognize it to respect other lives as one's own and to refrain absolutely from slaughter as an instrument for bringing about social order and peace.

Very truly yours, Alan Watts, President

SAUSALITO, CALIFORNIA | AUGUST 14, 1966
Dear Gary [Snyder]:
So glad to know that we shall see you again soon. I shall be here until mid-October, and then we take off for New York and Mexico until Christmas. I didn't see nearly as much of Gisen as I would have liked. In the last months of his stay he was very difficult to reach, and I tried several times. I saw Sally several months ago, at a party for Bob Dylan. But it strikes me that what *you* should do is pick up Mihoko Okamura on your way back! I've just finished an article on Suzuki for a memorial edition of *The Eastern Buddhist*. [...]

Jano sends much love.

As ever, [Chinese character signature] Alan

SAUSALITO, CALIFORNIA | AUGUST 15, 1966
Mr. Henry Volkening | New York, New York
Dear Henry:
Many thanks for yours of the 5th. Chaos reigns here too. We are having the interior painted, and next week I have to take time off for a visit to Albuquerque to consult with the USAF Weapons Research Lab! They want to talk with philosophers. Must be pretty worried.

But by the end of next week I shall be at work on the first chapter of *Philosopher in the Kitchen*. The *Playboy* people are pressing for it. For their purposes I'm going to call it "Murder in the Kitchen." Which reminds me that I am trying to work out a better title for the book as a whole, so let me know if a bright idea should come to you while shaving.

As to terms with Pantheon, let's see if we can get away with the $5,000 request. It's high time they did some worrying about one of my books, and you might also look into their plans for *Beyond Theology*. I don't want them to remainder it without warning. (Harper might buy it as a Cloister Torchbook.)

By all means wait for bound copies of *The Book* before trying England. I guess Hodder & Stoughton should have first choice.

Oh yes, I talked at length with Spec [A. C. Spectorsky, of *Playboy*] when I was in Chicago in May, but we didn't discuss finances because I thought he would be taking that up with you.

Present plans: to stay here until mid-October. Then to Chicago and Virginia, arriving in NYC about November 1st and staying until Thanksgiving. Back to Chicago for the weekend, and then a vacation in Mexico until Christmas!

All the best, AWW

MEXICO CITY, MEXICO | NOVEMBER 29, 1966
Dear Daddy:
Since October 18th I have been "on the road," and we are now, at last, at our ease in Mexico. This energetic, though profitable, trip was from home to Los Angeles, to Chicago, to eight different colleges in Virginia, to Washington, to New York, to various universities in the Northeast, to Dayton for Thanksgiving with Joan and John, then back to Chicago for the weekend. So now we are in Mexico City, and tomorrow we shall be taking off for three weeks' rest with friends who have a house in Puerto Vallarta — on the Pacific coast of Mexico.

Jano stayed home until November 7th and, with the help of her doctor, concentrated on getting well, and thus met me in New York in wonderful shape. She really has made the most remarkable improvement, and everyone is delighted. Among other things, Bill Paul has become permanent caretaker of the boat, secretary, and general handyman. He is not only competent but very easy to get along with, and is also a man of many gifts. In another age he would have been a Jeeves for a duke!

So — we have seen many friends on this trip — although briefly, because there was so much ground to cover. Thus you have greetings from Madeleine Low, Dick Borst, Joseph Campbell, Charlotte and Charles, Ruth Roberg, Henry and Ruth Denison, and Joan and John. Henry and Ruth were very sorry not to see you, but they returned home only just before I left. I spent the night with them in Hollywood on my way out.

So much has happened in the past month that it's hard to remember it all. Among other things I have been offered a resident fellowship at the Center for Advanced Studies at Wesleyan University in Connecticut. This would be for a four-month period, probably early in 1968. I am thinking it over. It is quite an honor since they get very eminent and remarkable people there, though it means just more time away from home.

Joan has just had her kitchen remodeled and is about to finish off improvements to the living room that will make it very beautiful indeed. She has such a wonderful sense of color. She is rather disturbed about both her mother and grandmother. Eleanor, she says, has become very coarse in manner and overly addicted to the bottle. Ruth is aging rapidly, has been very sick, and although warned by her doctors not to return to Japan for the winter, has nevertheless gone back. Rather characteristically, she has made an extremely complicated will!

Well, at least Joan and John are healthy, and their children are doing excellently. All three are very bright and seem well on their way to be part of this really astonishing influx of highly intelligent and unusual young people which impresses me, and many others, so forcefully in travelling around the universities. I am really amazed how quickly and easily they catch on to what I am saying — almost as if they were as born to it as ducks to water!

Well, on the lighter side of things Jano and Barbara Somers (Roger's ex-wife) saw a delightful performance of *The Pirates of Penzance* by the D'Oyly Carte Company in New York, and in Chicago we were taken to the opera to see *La Traviata* done in the grandest style with a most extraordinary soprano in the leading role. Today we are going to see the new anthropological museum here, which is supposed to have the world's best collection of pre-Columbian antiquities. Puerto Vallarta is reputed as an idyllic harbor with a lovely beach — accessible only by plane and ship because of the surrounding mountains. Our friends there are Roger and Louise Randolph. He is a lawyer from Tulsa, Oklahoma (of all places!). They are really charming people who have rather recently become deeply interested in my work, and it seems that they have a house overlooking the ocean from the top of a cliff and that we shall be installed on the lower floor, complete with a Japanese bathroom!

I'm afraid the winter in England must be most trying for you, and naturally we're concerned but feel rather helpless at this distance. We shall definitely come over at the end of April, just as soon as I get through with a stint at the University of Minnesota. Then we can discuss things with the Caves and make plans for setting up a Chislehurst-Sausalito "axis" for our multifarious operations! I haven't seen any reviews of the London edition of *Beyond Theology*, though I gather that the *Times Lit. Supp.* gave it their usual pish-tush treatment. It's too early to judge reactions to *The Book* here, though Jim Broughton gave it a fine review in the *SF Chronicle* and word-of-mouth recommendations are doing very well.

Jano joins me in sending lots of love and we hope to be able to get some photographs to you from Puerto Vallarta.

As ever, Alan

PUERTO VALLARTA, JALISCO | DECEMBER 14, 1966
Dear Daddy:

Yours of December 3rd must have crossed mine of November 29th, written from Mexico City. I am very sad that you will have to spend Christmas in the hospital, but with the cold weather and feeling run down it's doubtless the most sensible and comfortable arrangement. I have asked Sybil to take care of a Christmas gift from us, and, naturally, you simply must not be concerned about cards, presents, and such things under the circumstances. We, also, are cutting down on Christmas this year as a good rest seems more important than anything, and we plan to stay here until December 26th. Though successful, this last round of lectures was rather exhausting.

Here is a postcard of the place where we are staying — the home of our friends Roger and Louise Randolph. Puerto Vallarta is subtropical and lies on the edge of a large, sheltered bay surrounded by mountains and forests — the latter abounding with coconut palms and bananas. Excellent fish are plentiful, and last Sunday Jano and I caught a big mackerel and a yellowtail. The Randolphs have many friends here, and we made up a big party for a hike to a lake and waterfall in the hills — going first by boat to a fascinating Indian village. The Mexican Indians here are amazing — physically beautiful and healthy, living very simply in palm huts called *palapas* with beautifully woven conical roofs. Three small boys were our "bearers" on this expedition, and the children seem to have the same kind of gaiety and physical competence as the Japanese kids.

The town itself is agog with religious festivities at this time of year, and almost every night there are fireworks and processions. Mexicans and fireworks don't mix too well: their idea of fun is half a stick of dynamite inside a bamboo tube, light the fuse, and throw it as far as possible!

Streets are cobbles and roads pitted, so we drive around in a jeep. But the marvel of a Mexican town is that nothing shows on the outside. Streets are enclosed by long, ancient walls with high and massive doors, but inside are endless surprises in the way of courtyards with overlooking galleries and external stairways, gardens fountains, trees, and potted plants — all set about with Spanish tiles. There is a peculiar coziness to this way of living, though by our standards it seems exactly inside out, or rather, outside in. Mexican builders are masters in handling bricks and tiles, making the most attractive "filigree" screens out of short sections of tile piping which can be mortared together in all kinds of designs. They are also expert in wood carving and bent ironwork, and this is still a culture where small boys work along with their fathers so as to learn trades and arts which will, alas, disappear as soon as the government compels them all to go to school.

Puerto Vallarta has a small but increasing population of American and British expatriates bent on "getting away from it all." We found some old friends of ours and the Davenports' who used to live in Palo Alto; also the former head of the London String Quartet, Warwick Evans — a feisty old gent devoted to bridge and bawdiness. He still does some composing, but most foreigners (or "gringos") here come to loaf. The social center is therefore a small cluster of beach cafés, and you go there to make appointments and arrange affairs since there are no telephones — and their absence has a curiously socializing influence, because people visit one another spontaneously instead of ringing up.

The main industry seems to be making highly colorful clothes — for export — since the native women have largely been beguiled by wretched machine-printed frocks. I wonder when Japanese, Mexicans, and others will wake up to the fact that the sophisticated modern world, which they think they are imitating, is now imitating *them* as they used to be!

I hope Christmas in the hospital won't be too utterly boring, though I'm sure your marvelous capacity for making friends will hop things up. I will write again very soon, and in the meantime much, much love from both of us —

As always, Alan

PS. Thanks for Daisy Cave's address. I'll get in touch with her.

SAUSALITO, CALIFORNIA | JANUARY 3, 1967
Mrs. Elda Hartley | New York, New York
Dear Elda:
Herewith the first rental order [for films], and they seem to be in a hurry! We've advertised the sale price as $125 and rental for $25; see enclosed, which also gives our spring dates for New York.

One of my most effective TV programs was a recitation of Chinese and Japanese poems with the camera panning (if that's the right word) across sumi paintings. Sudden changes between paintings and actual landscapes might be very effective, with the additional point of showing how true to nature Chinese painting can be. For TV we used only good reproductions, not originals.

Puerto Vallarta was most interesting: an idyllic paradise with human beings not knowing quite what to do with it. We returned the day after Christmas, and shall be here until the 6th — returning the end of January. Meanwhile, off to Big Sur and southern California.

Much love from us both, and a prosperous New Year to you.

As ever, Alan

SAUSALITO, CALIFORNIA | FEBRUARY 9, 1967
Dr. R. D. Laing | Institute of Phenomenological Studies | London, England
Dear Dr. Laing:

Thank you very much indeed for your kind letter of January 31st. I was most happy to hear from you because I have just finished reading the proofs of *The Politics of Experience*, sent to me by Paula McGuire of Pantheon Books, my own publisher. This is really a marvelous book, and I am already talking about it to friends and colleagues. Reading between the lines, I assume you have ventured into the world of psychedelic experience?

I have plans to come to England during May, and rumor hath it that you will be in California in March. If so, please call me and let's get together. You can always be our guest overnight.

As to "The Dialectics of Liberation" conference, I would certainly like to be there — at least for part of the time — but it will depend upon your being able to supply my plane fare, round-trip, between London and San Francisco. I had thought of advancing my May visit to July so that no expense would be involved, but rather urgent family business compels me to come earlier.

Didn't we meet at Graham Howe's place in 1958?

So, congratulations on a splendid book, and let me hear from you as soon as you can manage.

Yours sincerely, Alan Watts

SAUSALITO, CALIFORNIA | JUNE 20, 1967
Mr. Paul Mellon | New York, New York
Dear Mr. Mellon:

During the past years I have twice been privileged to receive a grant from the Bollingen Foundation, and have followed almost all aspects of its work with intense interest.

Now Joseph Campbell tells me that the foundation is more or less winding up its operations. Doubtless you have good reasons for this, and what must be must be. But I would like to add my voice to, I hope, many others in telling you what a unique and magnificent venture this has been. There was nothing else like it in imagination and scope, and, as you doubtless know, foundation money is not too readily available for these rather profound and adventurous intellectual interests. You, and the other trustees, are to be thanked and congratulated for a very great achievement.

I think you should know, too, that those of us who knew the work of the foundation were constantly amazed at the courtesy and the excellent taste of Jack Barrett and the staff.

With many thanks and all good wishes,

Sincerely yours, Alan Watts

[JAPAN, CIRCA 1967]

Dear Gary and Masa [Snyder]:

We'll be back June 25th, and trust that all is going well in building your mountain retreat. Pantheon has given me a good contract for an autobiography, and with luck I'll be able to stay put for the rest of the year and write it. Please get in touch sometime after our return.

Love to you both — Alan and Jano

SAUSALITO, CALIFORNIA | JULY 7, 1967

Miss Marilyn Kelso | *Look* magazine | San Francisco, California

Dear Miss Kelso:

Thank you very much indeed for your letter of July 5th, enclosing the article by George Leonard and Marshall McLuhan.

I am at once astonished and delighted that such an article can appear in a great national periodical. This country is in serious trouble, both at home and abroad, because of the dominance of what McLuhan and Leonard call "the narrow-gauge, specialized male." A total, 100 percent male has, of course, nothing in common with women, and therefore cannot relate to them except as dames to be "made," and then chalked up as evidence of masculine prowess, as an ace pilot notches his plane for every enemy shot down.

These unhappy brutes are so terrified of the tender, voluptuous, and yielding aspects of their own biology that they identify them with homosexuality and sissiness, and build up the hard-shell, crustacean character-armor that is so commonly affected by our police, military men, business tycoons, and politicians. Their substitute for erotic ecstasy is to grind a hobnailed boot in someone's face. One can only hope that McLuhan and Leonard are right in feeling that this kind of masculine role-playing can be dissolved in laughter — instead of blood.

Sincerely yours, Alan Watts

SAUSALITO, CALIFORNIA | JULY 9, 1967
Mr. Henry Volkening | New York, New York
Dear Henry:

I want to try an experiment with one of the young, small, and very up-and-coming publishers here. He has asked me for a book of nonsense ditties, to be illustrated by Rick Griffin — one of the best hippie artists contributing to the *San Francisco Oracle*.

Herewith is the copy, minus one poem yet to be added. The drawings on the epic limerick were done by me at the age of 19, and will not be used.

The publisher is Jeff Berner, Stolen Paper Editions, Mill Valley, CA. (He did the notorious *Love Book* by Lenore Kandel.) He is proposing a royalty of 12 percent of the retail price, and I'm not asking for an advance because the job is already done, and anyhow he doesn't have that kind of capital.

What do you suggest? Do you have some kind of ready-made contract form which could be used?

Aren't some royalties from Random House due about this time of year? We should be doing well on *The Book*, though the contract with Eugene Schwartz of Information, Inc., has only just gone through.

Best wishes, Alan Watts

SAUSALITO, CALIFORNIA | AUGUST 9, 1967
Dear Gary [Snyder]:

You will surely remember Donald Gates, who was with us on one of our trips to Japan, and who helped out in making arrangements for Gisen to come here. He has a very attractive and intelligent son, Randy, aged about 15 — as I judge a real sweet (but not sugary!) guy. Randy is enthused with the idea of going to Japan to study aikido and other *bushi* arts, and his father is prepared to support him in this venture — as a splendid alternative to getting brainwashed in the ordinary high-school routine in the US.

I have advised him to enroll immediately at a Berlitz school and study Japanese. What he needs is simply an introduction to an aikido dojo and directions for finding some suitable YMCA-type place to live. I think he would really apply himself wholeheartedly to the discipline, with the idea of returning eventually to the US as an aikido teacher.

I don't know at the moment when he plans to leave, but he is looking up the local LA *roshi*, Joshu Sasaki, to consult with him. The question is, then, would you be able to put him on to an aikido school (when the time comes)? If not, where else should we apply? Any advice is most welcome!

Our plans are well in hand for arriving in Kyoto September 29th. Sometime soon you will be getting a visit from a most remarkable Benedictine monk, Dom Aelred Graham, who wrote *Zen Catholicism*, and who is now on his way to Japan with his very intelligent young disciple Harold Talbott. I am sure you will enjoy them, as Dom Aelred is a most witty and scholarly man in the very best Benedictine tradition. Very far-out theologically.

That was great news about the head monk of Daitoku-ji!

Our love to you, and many thanks.

As ever, [Chinese character signature] Alan

SAUSALITO, CALIFORNIA | SEPTEMBER 4, 1967

Dear Father Gillet:

When you review a book unfavorably you should at least do the author the courtesy of reading it. However, I realize that when there is an immense quantity of publications crossing your desk, it is really difficult to do more than skim. I am, of course, referring to your remarks on my book *Beyond Theology*, which appear in your 26th Book List for the USGR [United States Global Resources].

For example, I simply did not say that Christianity is "the most impossible amalgamation of odd ideas." If you will turn to p. 85, you will see the proper context of this phrase, I said only that many people have this feeling about Christianity, and the whole intent of the book is to change this very impression.

I wrote this book in a spirit of tremendous respect for the Christian tradition, and if, for example, you will read through pp. 120 to 128, you cannot possibly accuse me of lacking in a sincere and reverent intent. I also wrote the book to help many of my friends in the priesthood, who feel troubled and dishonest in holding to the old catechism party line, to stay on the job. Dom Aelred Graham recently told me that it was a real eye-opener for him.

If my humor seems vulgar to you, that is really a matter of personal taste. I feel, with G. K. Chesterton, that God is not incapable of some transcendental equivalent of the belly laugh. "He that sitteth in the heavens, he shall laugh, the prophet said," But I am afraid that you probably turned to Ch. 7, "The Sacred Taboo" (about sex) and read it out of context. I jest in this way only because the sanctimonious spirit which plagues the ecclesiastical world needs some un-stuffing.

Furthermore, please note that my reputation for being the "bonze [monk or priest] of California Zen" is quite unjustified. I do not even label myself as a Zen Buddhist. I have made it clear in innumerable writings and lectures that I do not adopt any religious label. The "bonze of California Zen" is a very able Soto-shu master named Shunryu Suzuki, who has a large, devoted, and sincere following. And they really work at it.

Otherwise, your Book List is a very useful compilation for helping students of comparative religion keep abreast of the burgeoning literature.

Yours sincerely, Alan Watts

SAUSALITO, CALIFORNIA | SEPTEMBER 16, 1967
The Hon. Henry M. Jackson | United States Senate | Washington, DC
Dear Senator Jackson:
Many thanks for your kind letter of August 15th, with information about S. 1816.

I wrote for information because the enclosed statement was given to me by a Shoshone chief, who came to see me while in San Francisco. I have also talked with some of the Sioux people, who have rather the same attitude.

The point is a very difficult one to get across to the general American public, because a sizable proportion of Indians simply do not share our values. They just do not want to "enhance and expand their participation in American society," because they regard our ways as insane, and our aggressive "conquest-of-nature" use of technology as a violation of the earth, which, as they have not forgotten, we stole from them.

Considering their attitudes to us, and ours to them, and also their lack of our style of education, it is hard indeed for most Indians to compete successfully in our economy. I am afraid, therefore, that the net effect of this very well-intentioned bill will be the progressive loss of their land, and an increasing migration of Indians to city slums...For many of them will mortgage their land, blow the money in some unworkable enterprise, and then lose their land to the loaner.

I am reminded of the saying, "Kindly let me help you or you'll drown — said the monkey putting the fish safely up a tree." Seriously, wouldn't it be better to respect the independence of the Indian nations, let them follow their own culture, and protect them from all further exploitation from whites? We need to preserve a great variety of lifestyles in this world, since our own begins to look more and more suicidal.

With all good wishes,
Sincerely yours, Alan Watts

SAUSALITO, CALIFORNIA | SEPTEMBER 21, 1967
The Rt. Rev. John A. T. Robinson [Bishop of Woolwich] | London, England
Dear John:
Stanford has just sent me *Exploration into God*, and, believe me, this is really getting somewhere. Of all that I have read in the field of "New Theology" or

"Death of God" theology, this is the most profound discussion since the work of such very great ones as Berdyaev and Tillich. I particularly like the way you work up, step by step, to the panentheistic conclusion, and your treatment of such metaphors for God as "rock," "Father," etc., is beautifully lucid. This book more than makes up for anything that was lacking in *Honest to God* [also by Robinson]. Indeed, it is full of passages, both your own and in quotation, that are going to keep me busy for quite a while.

I am off for seven or eight weeks to Japan and Ceylon next Tuesday (the 26th), and thus I don't quite know how I am going to find time to do an immediate review of the book. But since it won't be published until October 30th, there may be a chance.

So — thank you very much for a most fascinating and illuminating experience. And please give our love and greetings to Ruth and your delightful daughters.

Yours very sincerely, Alan Watts

The following is a response to a request for a foreword to Richard Wincor's novel Sherlock Holmes in Tibet, *published in 1968.*

SAUSALITO, CALIFORNIA | SEPTEMBER 21, 1967
Mr. Victor Weybright | Weybright & Talley, Inc. | New York, New York
Dear Victor:
How good to hear from you again, and how thoughtful of you to bear me in mind in connection with Wincor's book.

I am just off to the Orient until November 19th, but I have seriously considered whether or not I should write an introductory essay. My real problem is that this book is so oddly balanced. The material presented as the lama's discourse is quite sound so far as it goes, and the notion of Holmes as a *tulpa* is very clever. However, the appendices from Berkeley and the "Bardo Thodol" are sort of bottom-heavy. I think readers will be disappointed in getting a book this padded.

The author should have worked out a full-length story of Holmes's adventures in Tibet, perhaps on the lines of some of Talbot Mundy's romances, and in this case the initial vignettes of London could somehow have been given relevance to the story. Nor does the work really live up to the title *Conan Doyle and the Creative Process*, which lends one to expect a psychological study of Doyle as an artist...Or is the actual title to be *Sherlock Holmes in Tibet*?

If the author could be persuaded to fill out the present material into a novel of adventure, I would feel much more enthusiastic. As is, I think it's a bit of a literary mess.

    With all good wishes and many thanks, sincerely yours,

    Alan Watts

SAUSALITO, CALIFORNIA | NOVEMBER 22, 1967

Dear Elda [Hartley]:

We arrived back on the 19th, to find your long and very interesting letter. I expect you have seen the Klines by now and have heard something of our doings and adventures. We certainly did enjoy that couple; they have a kind of "style" which I find most pleasing.

    Now as to the happening with Judy [Hollister]: I shall be out of town on April 25th, and as things stand my free evenings will be April 3rd through 5th, 8th, 9th, and 16th through 19th, and then perhaps April 29th through May 3rd. It's a terribly hectic schedule, including trips out to Houston and the Finger Lakes area.

    The comment on the film from the University of California is exactly what I would expect from them. Their Oriental Department is celebrated for stuffiness, and I am scarcely ever invited to lecture there — under any department! I guess it's the "prophet in his own country" syndrome.

    Ceylon and Thailand were extremely fascinating, and I am thinking seriously of taking a tour, by invitation only, through South Asia (but not India) in two years' time, hoping that the whole area will not by then be total mayhem.

    I have some ideas for a third film: one on tea ceremony [cha-no-yu], in collaboration with Milly Johnstone and her friends, in which I would be commentator, sitting in as a guest. Sound in this would be "live," since I would contrive to talk during the actual filming. Or, if this presents technical difficulties, I could again superimpose it. Another could be on methods of meditation, showing yogas of various kinds, zazen, postures, breathing methods, mantra chanting, and all that.

    Best regards to Huston, and much love to you both. As ever, Alan

    PS. If the small black and white [photo] is too small, you can get another from Dick Borst in New York City.

SAUSALITO, CALIFORNIA | JANUARY 30, 1968

Dear Elda:

I'm afraid the omission of the films from our last bulletin was a stupid oversight. I had to get the thing together in a huge rush between visits to Sioux City and Vancouver, in the midst of all the details that had accumulated during our absence in

Ceylon and Japan...I am between two stools: well-known enough to have lots of busy-ness going, but not enough to afford an efficient organization! But we shall rectify this matter in the next issue.

Now as to Judy Hollister's suggestion. I don't want to offend her, but this invocation piece just isn't my style. I find it corny and full of clichés, in fact quite a hot-air job, despite the obvious beneficence of its motivation. I feel that no one should, on film or radio, lend his voice to any utterance which does not have his full approval in both content and style. (This principle would get rid of most advertising!) On the other hand, if some poem could be found with the same essential message, and which was also the work of a first-rate artist, I would be very happy to record it as track for a film. As of today, our best poets have long abandoned such phrases as "children of the earth," "guardians of the flame," "frontiers of darkness," "blasts of wintry selfishness," and "darkened window of the world." This may have been fine in the age of Tennyson, but not in the age of Frost, Cummings, Rexroth, Spender, or Dickinson — which is already old hat in comparison with Ginsberg and LeRoi Jones. True, there is the ageless poetry of Virgil and Shakespeare, but this piece just isn't up to that.

As you know, we arrive in New York about April 1st, for three weeks, and much look forward to seeing you.

Much love to you both, Alan

The following letter is addressed to Gary Snyder, who was in Japan at the time.

SAUSALITO, CALIFORNIA | JANUARY 30, 1968

Dear Gary:

I'm enclosing some funny reactions to your piece on "Buddhist Anarchism" — especially the one from Joe Campbell.

There was one fellow who said that Mr. Snyder should clobber the redneck of his own ego and dunk the scab in his own heart. I returned the letter, asking the writer to hold it up to a mirror and clobber the redneck of his own self-righteousness and the scab of his pomposity...Such games we play!

Under separate cover come the materials you asked for.

Rumor hath it that you plan to return here permanently this summer, plus Masa and baby. Should I confirm these tales?

We had a really marvellous time in Ceylon. I don't remember whether you have been there, but it's still an essentially agrarian culture of high and exquisite fertility, though lacking international exchange for industrial products — and therefore formally "poor." This excites resentment among the younger, and thus the politics swing leftwards and anti-USA. Universities train the kids for industrial and technological jobs which are simply not to be had.

Our love to you both.

As ever, Alan

SAUSALITO, CALIFORNIA | FEBRUARY 15, 1968
[Name withheld] | Middletown, Connecticut
Dear Madam:

Thank you for your letter of February 6th, I understand your concern. When several of us began experimentation with LSD back in the 1950s, we did not expect that its use would be driven underground — with the inevitable results of which I and many others tried to warn government and law-enforcement agencies. (See my book, *The Joyous Cosmology*, Vintage paperback.)

It simply is not a good idea for anyone to use black-market LSD, much less methedrine, DMT, STP, or other irregularly manufactured psychedelics. There is no control of the quality or quantity of these preparations, and sometimes "LSD" is mixed with other chemicals that may be extremely harmful.

Undoubtedly, the press has exaggerated the dangers of genuine LSD-25 (as produced by the Sandoz company), but, even so, it should be employed with the utmost care as to the mental stability of those ingesting it and to the circumstances under which it is given. As yet, there is no clear evidence that LSD causes any serious chromosomal damage; much more is caused by substances taken quite commonly and legally. There is also no evidence of brain damage, but there may well be changes of personality — sometimes beneficial, sometimes otherwise.

As to marijuana, its principal danger lies in the enormous legal penalties attending its use and possession. Three major scientific studies of the subject (including the so-called "LaGuardia Report" made by the New York Academy of Medicine) have found it relatively harmless, and there is no proof that its use leads to addiction or to the use of such dangerous drugs as heroin. However, I have reason to believe that immoderate use of marijuana may bring about states of apathy and disorientation. But then the immoderate use of anything can be harmful. I knew a very teetotalitarian Methodist minister who contracted a disease from drinking too much milk!

On the positive aspects of LSD, I would refer you, not only to my own book *The Joyous Cosmology*, but also to *LSD: The Problem-Solving Psychedelic* by Stafford & Golightly (also in paperback) and *The Varieties of Psychedelic Experience* by Houston & Masters.

I would suggest to your daughter that relatively few "trips" on LSD are enough. If after, say, ten times you haven't "got the message," you never will. Many experienced users of LSD have now stopped taking it entirely and are, instead, practicing various methods of religious meditation. Quite definitely, LSD at its best is a medicine and not a diet. With luck and intelligence it will get you into a higher state of consciousness, but thereafter you must proceed on your own.

Naturally, I will keep your letter in absolute confidence.

Sincerely yours, Alan Watts

SAUSALITO, CALIFORNIA | FEBRUARY 15, 1968
Mr. Henry Volkening | New York, New York
Dear Henry:

Many thanks indeed for your letter. I don't know if I can get acquainted with your friends in Sausalito right away: I am slowly suffocating under mountains of paper. I presume that this condition is becoming more or less universal, and have occasional qualms of guilt about contributing to "the multiplication of books." There was once a New York "underground" paper called *EVO* which was, at first, quite interesting. I contributed an interview and an article to it (see enclosed). But this paper has now become what even I would describe as a filthy rag, with personal ads presumably inserted by members of the city vice squad.

However, the former editor, Walter Bowart (who had some sense) is compiling a volume of contributions to be entitled *EVOLOVE* (published by Harris Wolfe & Co., Jacksonville, IL). I am telling them that before they include anything of mine they must clear with you, and if they are not in a position to make any deals they will refer the matter to Bowart.

I am suggesting then, that you be a little on the tough side as to terms, although I am not sure what the copyright status of these pieces may be, since out of general enthusiasm and liking for Bowart I originally contributed them for free.

Otherwise, you will soon be getting a copy of my next piece for *Playboy*, and I am trying to wangle out of them a commission for two articles instead of one. They will be "USA 2000" (in conjunction with article by Herman Kahn and Carl Rogers) and "The Future of Ecstasy."

For the rest, I am much looking forward to drunching with you early in April.

All the best, Alan

Sausalito, California | March 15, 1968
Dr. James L. Goddard | US Food and Drug Administration |
Washington, DC
Dear Dr. Goddard:

As one increasingly impressed by your attempts to bring some rationality into the control of psychedelic drugs, I am much looking forward to meeting you at the Illinois Medical Society conference on April 11th, in which we are both involved.

I am concerned, however, by your apparently reluctant acquiescence to new federal legislation which would make mere possession of LSD-25 a criminal offense.

The point at issue here is not primarily one of drug control but of the very nature of law and its enforcement in any country where police cannot always be relied upon to stay out of politics or involvement with criminal activities.

It would be the simplest thing in the world to "plant" a substantial quantity of LSD-25 upon one's political enemy or business competitor, and then inform the police indirectly of its whereabouts.

Isn't it fundamental to legal ethics that no substance is, in itself, evil — but that evil can arise only from its misuse? Any sound law should require proof that anyone possessing LSD-25 (or any other dangerous drug) has in fact used it in some unauthorized way. I am inclined to the opinion that guns and automobiles are considerably more dangerous to life and limb than LSD, but the law penalizes their misuse rather than their possession.

I really think you should reconsider your stand on this particular point, and advise the Congress very strongly against passing a law with such sinister side effects.

With all good wishes,
Sincerely yours, Alan Watts

Sausalito, California | March 26, 1968
Ian I. Mitroff | Assistant Professor, Graduate School of Business |
University of Pittsburgh
Dear Professor Mitroff:

I am sorry to be so long in answering your letter of January 15th, but I have been traveling away from home.

I found your paper on the "Mythology of Methodology" extremely fascinating. I read many of your examples of games that science could be playing to a group of people interested in systems theory, out of which we got many laughs. I was particularly interested in the last two sentences of your letter: "Once you realize it's all a game, 'things' are never the same. You only want to play mean-ingful games or not play at all." The question that occurs to me is how could we state the notion of a meaningful game and also ask whether there is such a thing as not playing at all, because it seems to me that existence itself is, in some sense, a game. In Hindu philosophy, the production of the Universe is sometimes called "Lila," which essentially means sport or play, because of the idea that the world is itself a game of hide-and-seek — now you see it, now you don't — now it's on, now it's off. It is thus the game of hide-and-seek in which the Self forgets itself and remembers itself, loses itself and discovers itself and that this on-and-off vibration is simply what we call Being or Energy.

Please keep in touch with me because I think you are working on extremely interesting lines.

Sincerely yours, Alan Watts

SAUSALITO, CALIFORNIA | JUNE 20, 1968
The Editor | *San Francisco Chronicle* | San Francisco, California
Sir:
The reports of the American Medical Association and the National Research Council on the effects of marijuana have disquieting implications that go far be-yond the immediate problem of marijuana itself.

As reported in the *Chronicle*, there is no clear indication as to what these re-ports mean by "psychotic symptoms." In my own considerable experience I have found that most psychiatrists will dub almost any unusual state of conscious-ness "psychotic," especially if the subject (or patient) connects it with religion. In psychoanalytic circles at least, religion is by definition a delusional system, and religious or mystical experience [is a] downright hallucination. In fairness I should say that a strong minority of psychiatrists dissent from this view, but they are seldom represented on "official" research teams.

When psychiatrists become involved with government and law enforcement, they are dangerously tempted to set up arbitrary and even tyrannical standards of what are "sane" or "acceptable" experiences or states of consciousness. This can go beyond infringement of one's freedom of thought: it invades the inmost privacy of one's freedom to *feel*.

Must we all, then, be condemned by these guardians of sanity to an official way of feeling the "real world" — e.g., as reproduced in an ordinary color snap-shot or as seen on a bleak Monday morning?

It may be of significance that when many psychiatrists are shown, without prior explanation, the alpha brain rhythms of a person in deep meditation, be he Buddhist or Christian, they will at once suspect some form of psychopathology.

Any responsible psychiatrist will admit that his science, if science it is, is as yet far from being exact. He will therefore refrain from using the damning term *psychotic* for states of consciousness which he does not understand and which do not issue in destructive behavior.

Yours, etc., Alan Watts

JW: In the summer of 1968 I went (solo) from Ohio to visit my father and spend time in Big Sur. It was on this trip that Alan introduced me to LSD. Under his guidance, I experienced the drug on the ferryboat listening to, first, Gregorian chants, then the Beatles. I was overwhelmed by the experience — the absolute wonderment of the rich and harmonic sound of the Beatles against the beautiful longing sound of the celibate monks, drifting off in a lonely gray existence. It was an "aha" moment where I clearly saw that the Beatles were the new classical music. I wonder if the following letter to Tom Donahue was influenced by my sharing those thoughts with Alan that day.

SAUSALITO, CALIFORNIA | JUNE 28, 1968
Mr. Tom Donahue | KSAN | San Francisco, California
Dear Tom:
I have been away from home since the end of March, and it is good to come back and find you nicely settled in at KSAN — which I leave on most of the time, as I did KMPX when you were there.

I often wonder why I do this, since there are excellent classical programs on other FM stations, such as KPFA, and good jazz from KJAZ. There is definitely a "new sound," strong, joyous, and lilting, coming from within the general class of "rock" music, often combined with astonishing technique and musical competence far beyond what has hitherto been heard in popular music.

This is so much so that I begin to believe that, within a few years, we shall all be saying that derivatives of "rock," which will include Baroque-rock ("barock"), raga rock, and electronic rock ("electrock"), constitute the main stream of serious Western music.

Bob Dylan has persuaded millions to listen to real poetry, and with Donovan, Cohen, and others, seems to be creating a contemporary form of lieder. Malachi is quite intentionally offering a new form of sacred music, and there are many times when in listening to such groups as the Beatles and Wyatt Day's Ars Nova (not to mention Harum) I know very well that I am listening to music in direct line with the best classical traditions.

Modern music written specifically for the concert hall and symphony orchestra scene is, to my ears, pretty insipid. By and large, it ended with and in John Cage. It complicated itself into chaos. In a not-too-distant future we shall regard many forms of "rock" as classical music — a continuation of the tradition of Vivaldi, Bach, Haydn, and Mozart.

Good luck to you, and call me next week so that we can start work on the university project.

Sincerely, Alan Watts

The following is addressed to D. G. Garan in regard to his book Relativity for Psychology: A Causal Law for the Modern Alchemy, *published in 1968 by Philosophical Library.*

SAUSALITO, CALIFORNIA | JULY 11, 1968
Dear Dr. Garan:
I am sorry to say that I have mislaid the letter which came with your book, and so am writing c/o your publisher to thank you for it. I am also asking my publisher to send you copies of *Psychotherapy East & West* and *The Book*, both of which bear very directly on your interests. *The Meaning of Happiness* is a very old book, written when I was 24, and that was in 1939!

It may not strike you as odd, but I found the most stimulating part of your book the section on physics, gravitation, the field, etc., for when people get on the subject of cosmology they demonstrate their truly basic ideas. On this, your thinking is very close to mine, except that I had not thought of space, the field, as something more dense than matter.

In many ways, however, I think you are an oppositionist rather than a full relativist. From my standpoint, the explicit polar differentiation of opposites conceals an implicit unity, and thus I do not think of their relationship as causal. I prefer to call it transactional (e.g., buying and selling). Causality implies a time lag between + and –, whereas I can conceive them only as arising mutually, just as heads and tails are different faces of a single coin.

You might ponder on the difference this viewpoint might make in your critique of psychotherapy. I agree with you on so many points, for long experience in psychiatric circles has made me increasingly dubious of the whole enterprise. But, e.g., in the education of children, I don't think we are going to have much success by going back to an (albeit) scientific updating of the Bible and birch-rod method. It got us where we are now!

If you don't already know it, I think you might be most interested in the work of A. F. Bentley (behavioral scientist), especially his book *Inquiry into Inquiries* (Beacon, 1954), in particular the essay "The Human Skin: Philosophy's Last Line of Defense."

On second thought, would you please drop me a card with your home address so that I can have the books sent to you directly.

With best wishes and many thanks,

Sincerely yours, Alan Watts

The following letter refers to an otherwise unknown project of Alan's called The Pillow Book.

SAUSALITO, CALIFORNIA | AUGUST 6, 1968
Edward Victor, Esq. | Jonathan Cape Ltd. | London, England
Dear Ed:

Thank you so much for yours of August 1st. It will still take me a little while to get around to giving you plans for *The Pillow Book*. Currently there are other attempts being done over here to do something rather similar, though from the ads they don't seem very attractive. (See enclosed.) I want to study this material, and then let you know. Already I have a couple of artists in mind.

When you print the book [*The Book: On the Taboo against Knowing Who You Are*], please note that the emblem on the title page is out of alignment, and should be rotated clockwise until the (long) right edge is at 90 degrees to the horizontal. However, you may prefer to reset the whole page to conform to your usual format, which would be perfectly acceptable to me (i.e., with the flower-bowl emblem).

While you are considering *The Joyous Cosmology* I might remind you that there has never, to my knowledge, been a UK edition of *Psychotherapy East & West* (Pantheon and Mentor). It's odd that Houghton Mifflin takes so long to reply.

Very best wishes to you and to Tom — Alan

The addressee of this letter, A. C. Spectorsky, was senior vice president of Playboy.

SAUSALITO, CALIFORNIA | AUGUST 16, 1968
Mr. A. C. Spectorsky | Chicago, Illinois
Dear Spec:

Many thanks for yours of August 6th. I will get the MS of *The Future of Ecstasy* to you in about a month's time.

Otherwise, I will send you chapters of *Ethics in a Floating World* as they come off the typewriter. Catholic books on moral theology have always given about 75 percent of their content to sex, and a miserable 25 percent to murder, lying, stealing, swindling, and other more serious problems. Since *Playboy* has done such a good job on sexual ethics, I think I am going to put my emphasis in another direction and concentrate on the ethical aspects of war, violence, gluttony, drugs, usury, the family, money, patriotism, civil rights, police power, and other such matters. It might be quite a jolt for some people to realize that "the unspeakable crime against nature" could be dumping chemicals into a river.

This letter doesn't need a reply. You'll be hearing from me in due course.

Very best wishes, Alan

AW: The following letter is a fascinating look into the various aspects of the Playboy *organization. The man Alan is writing to, Jacques Mousseau, is a French journalist who was director of broadcasting at TF1 (a private national French TV channel), president of the Multimedia Institute, general secretary of the Television History Committee, editor in chief of the magazines* Planète *and* Plexus, *and director of the journals* Psychology *and* Communication and Languages.

SAUSALITO, CALIFORNIA | SEPTEMBER 30, 1968
H. Jacques Mousseau | Paris, France
Dear Jacques:
I owe you for two letters now; but hasten to reply primarily because you want information and reactions about *Playboy*.

This magazine is one of two major operations run by Hugh Hefner — a rather troubled and unstable man with a genius for making money. I have not met him personally, but his staff finds him an impetuous prima donna, who may, for instance, want a whole issue of the magazine changed at the last moment, keeping his staff working around the clock. He maintains a luxurious mansion on the near north side of Chicago, housing his staff and some 20 young ladies. The whole place looks as if set up for an orgy, but this *never* happens because his scene is strictly titillation. He may take on one of the girls for a year, give her everything she wants, and then give her a good job in his organization.

The other operation is the Playboy Clubs, spread throughout the US. These are flamboyant restaurant/bar clubs, served by shapely girls dressed as bunny rabbits with long ears and cottontails. Behind the scenes, these girls are disciplined as if in a convent school, and are absolutely forbidden to date or even touch the customers. They are very well mannered and well spoken, but many of us feel that the costume is insulting to women. Average membership of the club consists of wealthy businessmen, in their forties, and over-superannuated fraternity boys. (*Don't* quote me on this by name!)

The magazine is quite a different affair, run by an extraordinarily intelligent editorial staff headed by A. C. Spectorsky — a man of high culture and imagination, who is undoubtedly the most helpful editor I have ever worked with. The various (young) men working under him are all on their way to higher objectives in their careers, and are one and all bright, mildly cynical, but creative.

Playboy is superficially a voyeuristic "nudie" magazine, with sophisticated articles on fashion, cars, gadgetry, sports, etc., but in the minds of Spectorsky and most of the editors, this is simply a "come-on," an attractive front for serious discussion of civil and sexual liberty, political, economic, social, and even religious issues. I have no qualms at all in being one of their authors. Through the Playboy Foundation, the operation pays legal expenses for people being persecuted under archaic sexual laws. They have been able to discourage the post office from prying into private mail in quest of "obscene" literature and communications. Hefner was manhandled by the Chicago police in the recent riots, and I am quite sure that this is going to result in a tough campaign for police reform in this country. With a circulation of 4,000,000 (largely sold on newsstands), it exercises quite a powerful influence.

My general impression is that Spectorsky, with Hefner's compliance, is playing a sort of jujitsu on American culture — going along with all its phony materialism in order to blow the readers' minds into radical change.

Thank you very much for sending me Michel Lancelot's book. It is an excellent piece of reporting — in fact, quite the best thing I have yet read about the whole "hippie" phenomenon. But, as of today, the entire movement seems to be in a state of confusion. Haight-Ashbury has deteriorated terribly, and the original hippies have dispersed, mostly to the country, although there is quite a concentration here in Sausalito. Politically, they are rather sharply divided into activists and contemplatives!

Do you have enough photographic material for your interview with me? If not, please let me know at once and I will send you more.

I plan to be in Paris again next May, and shall look forward to seeing you again.

With very best wishes,

Sincerely, Alan Watts

The mention of Eliot Elisofon below has to do with a project that he and Alan were working on: Alan's book Erotic Spirituality: The Vision of Konarak *would later be published with Elisofon's photographs. It is discussed further in Alan's letter of August 2, 1969. The "developments with Eugene Schwartz" mentioned at the end have to do with the project that would become the* Alan Watts Journal.

Dear Henry [Volkening]:

By all means keep a tough line going on the Elisofon project. At this rate I, too, might be losing interest!

Why don't we propose to Paula another book of related essays, like *This Is It?* It would consist of the following:

"Wealth vs. Money," (*Playboy*, December 1968).

"Murder in the Kitchen," plus most of the second chapter written for *Philosopher in the Kitchen*. She has this material.

"The Spirit of Violence and the Matter of Peace," (*Alternatives to Violence*, Time-Life Books).

"Psychedelics and Religious Experience," (*California Law Review*, January 1968).

A longish essay, as yet unwritten, called "When Clothes Make the Man (or Woman)," which will be to the matter of dress as "Murder in the Kitchen" is to food.

This will give us a perfectly consistent set of essays on man's relation to material. We might entitle it *Does It Matter?* I would write a brief introduction which ties the whole thing together. Paula could have all this in the very near future, in substitution for *Philosopher in the Kitchen*, and then we could go ahead and draw up a new contract for *The Rules of the Game*, which is my proposed title for a book on ethics in the late 20th century.

In Chicago Sunday night I spent the whole evening with Spec, and he encouraged me very strongly to write as much for him as I can, even suggesting advances (which I do really need). The situation is that I am being released from overmuch lecturing by some heavy contributions to my Society for Comparative Philosophy, which we are about to expand into a new version of the Bollingen Foundation, giving grants to individuals working in my general areas of interest.

Will you please make an inquiry for me when talking to anyone at Random House. Months ago I wrote an introduction, at the request of Jay Thompson, for *The Book of the Love Generation*, a picture-article anthology on the hippies. What became of this project? I was supposed to be paid for it, but I really forget the details.

I am trying to "move in" on Paris! The current (November) issue of *Planète* has a long interview with me by Jacques Mousseau, and since *Planète* is also a publisher of books we ought to take up with them the possibility of French translations of *The Book* and other such works as *The Joyous Cosmology* and *Beyond Theology*. Thus far, only *The Way of Zen* and *Nature, Man & Woman* have appeared in French.

So — I think that's everything for the moment. I will keep you informed on developments with Eugene Schwartz.

Very best wishes, Alan

Alan received an award from Playboy *for best nonfiction in 1968 for his article "Wealth versus Money."*

SAUSALITO, CALIFORNIA | NOVEMBER 22, 1968
Mr. Jack Kessie | *Playboy* magazine | Chicago, Illinois
Dear Jack:

Thank you all very much indeed. In some ways I prefer this award to getting, say, an honorary degree from Harvard. I am most touched, and trust that my future writings will come up to your expectations.

The check can come at any time convenient to you, I guess I could use it for Christmas.

What is the procedure on getting some reprints of the article? I think I could use about 500, though it might be more convenient to get City Lights to issue it as a pamphlet.

With gratitude and all good wishes,

Sincerely, Alan Watts

SAUSALITO, CALIFORNIA
For either Dear *Playboy* or the *Forum*.

Under the cover of lusty and curvaceous chicks (of whom I approve), and of silly bunnies (of whom I disapprove), you have turned *Playboy* into the most important philosophical periodical in this country. I am a little nervous about admitting this, but, by comparison, *The Journal of the American Philosophical Society* is pedantic, boring, and irrelevant. Your recent interviews with Marshall McLuhan and Allen Ginsberg, your articles by Romain Gary, Arthur Clarke, Justice William O. Douglas, Alan Harrington, and many others — all these are intellectual stimulation of the highest order. How on earth do you get away with it?

However, in an entirely friendly spirit, I would like to take issue with Alan Harrington's fascinating article "The Immortalist" (May 1969), on the desirability of abolishing death, and the possibility of doing so through medical techniques.

The immortalization of any biological individual runs into the same logistic problems as building indefinitely high skyscrapers: the lower floors are increasingly taken up with channels for elevators. It's called "the law of diminishing returns." A brain that continues intact for 100, 500, or 1,000 years is increasingly clogged with memories, and becomes like a sheet of paper so covered with writing that no space is left for any visible or intelligible form. Thus a human being 500 years old would be as inert as a turtle of the same age.

Consider the following points: (a) Death is not a sickness or disease; it is an event as natural and as healthy as childbirth or as the falling of leaves in the autumn. (b) As the "natural childbirth" obstetricians are training women to experience the pains of labor as erotic tensions, there is no reason why the "pangs of death" should not be reinterpreted as the ecstasies of liberation from anxiety and overloads of memory and responsibility. (c) Suppose that medical science achieves a method of getting rid of the overload of memories and anxieties: Isn't this what death accomplishes already? (d) The funk about death is the illusion that you are going to experience everlasting darkness and nothingness as if being buried alive. (e) The "nothingness" after death is the same as the "nothingness" before you were born, and because anything that has happened once can happen again you will happen again as you did before, mercifully freed from the boredom of an overloaded memory.

Along with most of us, Alan Harrington doesn't see that this "nothingness" before birth and after death is simply the temporal equivalent of, say, the space between stars. Where would stars be without spatial intervals between them? The problem is simply that civilized and brainwashed human beings lack the perception that we are all one Self, marvellously varied and indefinitely extended through time and space with restful intervals. As St. Thomas Aquinas said, "It is the silent pause which gives sweetness to the chant."

Instead of trying to turn us into living mummies, the medical profession would be better advised to reform the present morbid rituals of dying in hospitals and turn them into celebrations in which the patient is encouraged to let go of himself by cooperating with death. You only die once, and why not make the best of it?

Alan Watts

SAUSALITO, CALIFORNIA | JANUARY 11, 1969
[Name withheld] | San Jose, California
Dear S. C.:
In answer to your enquiry on the "Racism & Violence" manifesto of the SDS [Students for a Democratic Society]:

1. I was invited and hired as "visiting scholar" to San Jose State by the College Union, a student organization, and not by the administration or any academic department of the college.

2. I was allowed total freedom of speech, and therefore expressed nothing other than my personal opinions.

3. I made it very clear (I thought), that both the so-called capitalistic and Marxist-socialist forms of economy are obsolete, being equally based on the economic situation of pretechnological societies. I refuse, absolutely, to take sides in an archaic and irrelevant argument. For documentation, see my article "Wealth vs. Money" in the December 1968 issue of *Playboy*.

4. I am opposed to violence, especially on the college or university campus, because (in the long run), brains are always superior to brawn, and it is therefore the business of students to outsmart and not to outmuscle an establishment of which neither they nor I approve.

5. The establishment is managed by very puzzled and unhappy people, since every miser is of necessity miserable. Let's be aware of the ghetto of the rich, be compassionate to them, and try to seduce them into the art of enjoying life instead of figures on inedible paper.

Thank you for giving me an opportunity to make this clear.

Sincerely, Alan Watts

SAUSALITO, CALIFORNIA | FEBRUARY 28, 1969
The Hon. John F. McCarthy | Sacramento, California
Dear Senator McCarthy:
Thank you for your thoughtful letter of December 11th, and apologies for my delay in answering. To identify me, see Marquis *Who's Who in the West*. I am tremendously concerned about two problems, which arise out of my work with university students:

1. *The bad image of the police.* We are running into very serious trouble by reason of lack of respect for and mistrust of our police. Obviously, we cannot revamp and retrain the entire force. But we are embarrassing and confusing our policemen by asking them to act as armed clergymen, enforcing sumptuary laws against crimes without victims, laws in fundamental violation of the constitutional separation of church and state. Confine their duties to traffic control, protection against violence and robbery, and giving due assistance to lost children and little old ladies. Let them have no authority over private morals.

Question needing no answer: "What sort of character would volunteer for service on a vice squad?"

2. *Reform of the marijuana laws.* We have hundreds of young men and women in jail for violation of purely ritual crime, at the great expense of taxpayers. I am a research consultant to the Maryland State Hospital project for investigation of mind-changing drugs, and can say with some authority that all scientific and rigorously conducted research as to the use and effects of this herb has, as of this date, been showing that it is far less deleterious than the use of alcohol. Furthermore, prosecution of possessors of marijuana is seriously hindering, time-wise, the normal business of our courts.

Please take note of the enclosed proposals from Dr. Stanley Krippner of the Maimonides Hospital in Brooklyn, NY, in a letter to the US Attorney General.

With very best wishes for your work in the State Senate,

Sincerely yours, Alan Watts

SAUSALITO, CALIFORNIA | JUNE 7, 1969
Mrs. Paula McGuire | Pantheon Books | New York, New York
Dear Paula:

I, too, am disappointed at the delay in *Does It Matter?* But if *Playboy* was to have the "clothes" piece and you didn't want any kind of substitute — say an essay actually entitled "Does It Matter?" and announced as original for the book — then it can't be helped.

I talked with Cape's editors, Tom Maschler and Ed Victor, at length, and we have come up with the idea of publishing a much larger volume, containing all Hearn's major writings on Japan and the Orient, including of course those originally proposed. They think it high time for a general Hearn revival. How about that?

You will be hearing from Jacques Mousseau, of *Plexus*, about one or two forthcoming books which I think might well be of interest to you. Paris was, as usual, delightful, with all the chestnuts in flower and its vaguely aristocratic-looking population. The London climate was the usual rather damp cold, but food continues to improve. The population looks like a human zoo: I have never seen such an assemblage of grotesque, eccentric, and hippie-looking characters.

All the best, Alan Watts

THE SOCIETY FOR COMPARATIVE PHILOSOPHY, INC. | SAUSALITO,
CALIFORNIA | JUNE 19, 1969
Mr. Michael Maitland | Warner Brothers Seven Arts | Burbank, California
Dear Mr. Maitland:

Our friend George Greif tells me that he has spoken to you about the possibility of reacquiring the rights to my record *OM: The Sound of Hinduism*. We would like to obtain the present stock of unsold records, plus the original master tapes, because we feel that at points the music outbalances the voice, and would like to produce at least tapes of a corrected version.

Would the enclosed check for $1,000.00 be satisfactory to conclude this arrangement?

May I point out that we are a federally recognized nonprofit corporation, and that any loss you take on this specific arrangement would be tax-deductible if represented as a contribution to SCP.

With all good wishes,

Sincerely yours, Alan Watts, President

THE SOCIETY FOR COMPARATIVE PHILOSOPHY, INC. | SAUSALITO,
CALIFORNIA | JUNE 23, 1969
Dean Gerhard Friedrich | Office of the Chancellor | California State
Colleges | Los Angeles, California
Dear Dean Friedrich:

Your interesting letter of June 12th regarding a degree program for Asian studies enclosed a questionnaire which does not quite apply to my situation as I do not conduct regular courses on any campus. I am associated with a nonprofit educational corporation, which has, as its principal interest the furthering of the philosophical dialogue between Asia and the West, and other forms of cultural intercommunication. However, I'm constantly in and out of the colleges and universities as an independent lecturer and consultant.

I think I can answer the last two questions at once:

(a) Our "shrinking globe" urgently requires that more and more Americans become familiar with Asian customs and languages so that we do not behave like barbarians among people whose cultures are highly sophisticated, but along different lines than our own.

(b) The study of Chinese, Japanese, and Indian ways of thinking and speaking shows that the basic assumptions and common sense of their cultures are subtly, and sometimes profoundly, different from our own. Familiarity with these points of view gives us a sort of "triangulation" upon the real world, comparable to establishing the position of a distant object by observing it from widely different positions. Furthermore, to alter Kipling's words, "He does not know America who only America knows," and Asia offers far more interesting contrasts than Europe or Russia.

(c) As automated production increases our leisure, the high cultures of Asia offer immense enrichment for our own intellectual and aesthetic lives — as witness the current popularity of Hindu music. Thus far, Western scholarship has only scratched the surface of Far-Eastern literature, and most English-speaking Japanese and Japanese-speaking Americans (a mere handful), can converse only at the level of small children.

(d) Of necessity, America is going to have to play a major role in easing the tremendous economic crisis and famine predicted for Asia and Africa in 1975 unless drastic steps are taken now. But we must not make the usual mistake of, "Kindly let me help you, or you'll drown," said the monkey, putting the fish safely up a tree. We must help Asians to the kind of affluence they want for themselves, not to such as we think is good for them. In offering help, we must not be patronizing; we must treat them as equal human beings, and this can hardly be done without intimate and appreciative knowledge of their ways of life.

I think these are four very good reasons for going full speed ahead for extended programs for Asian studies — *if* you can find the faculties. I sure wish you every success, and please feel free to call upon me as, and when, you feel the need for consultative assistance.

With all good wishes,

Sincerely yours, Alan Watts, President

SAUSALITO, CALIFORNIA | AUGUST 2, 1969
Mr. Peter V. Ritner | The Macmillan Company | New York, New York
Dear Peter:
Herewith is the manuscript as promised. A second copy goes to Henry Volkening, and would it be asking too much to have you Xerox this one for Eliot Elisofon?

Including the quotations, it is something in excess of 14,500 words, and you will see that I have suggested a new title: instead of "The Black Pagoda," it seems to me that we might call it *Erotic Spirituality: The Vision of Konarak*.

I have a set of Elisofon's pictures. Should these be returned immediately, or are there sufficient copies on hand for both you and Elisofon?

I assume that, as per our original discussion, Elisofon will supply some identificatory notes about each plate. The aim and function of my commentary is fully explained on p. 3, and I have made various production suggestions on a separate page following the title page.

As to the matter of a dedication, I would prefer Elisofon to decide on this. There might be someone whom we know in common, and it occurs to me that we first discussed the idea at the home of Louis and Bebe Barron in Hollywood, if my memory is not playing tricks.

I have had the manuscript "vetted" by Gary Snyder, who has much first-hand knowledge of all these matters, and has made some very useful suggestions. In some way his help should be acknowledged. But I don't want to bury this in a mere footnote. Perhaps Elisofon and I should write a joint preface.

With all good wishes — Sincerely, Alan Watts

SAUSALITO, CALIFORNIA | AUGUST 21, 1969
Dr. Stanley Krippner | Dept. of Psychiatry | Maimonides Medical Center | Brooklyn, New York
Dear Stan:

In answer to yours of the 15th: As I am sure you realize, I am most eager to support your work in any way possible because I have great confidence in your ability, and if you really want to go ahead with this ESP survey I shall naturally give the green light.

However, I am puzzled by your interest in it. Does it really matter what members of the APA think about ESP? Will their increased belief in it be of any more real significance than, say, their having almost unanimous consent to some idea that was later shown to be folly? What would have been the value of a survey of pediatricians in 1930 as to their opinions about the regular feeding of babies?

What I am trying to say is that I have difficulty in seeing how a survey of scientific opinion can have any scientific value. How will it promote our understanding of ESP? At best it could be a gambit in getting increased funds for this line of research, but I feel that your abilities would be much better employed in a more basic form of research. [...]

Also, I am always suspicious of the corporate attitudes of professional associations. The more everyone agrees about something, the more I am inclined to question it. So, just for my own enlightenment, I would like to know something of your real reasons for this project.

My two sons were also at Woodstock and from all I hear it must have been quite a scene. At one point the younger climbed a 100 ft. mast for lighting and said he could see no limit to the crowd. As Burt said, "When I was that age what on earth could have persuaded 500,000 of us to gather together?"

All good wishes,
As ever, Alan

Sausalito, California | August 24, 1969
Dear David Gordon:

Sorry to have been so long in answering yours of July 3rd, but I have been writing books — and at such times I pay as little attention as possible to my mail!

I am so glad that Macmillan is going to handle your book. I have just finished one for them, in collaboration with Eliot Elisofon, using his pictures of the sculptures of Konarak for a discussion of "erotic spirituality." I feel that Macmillan, as represented by Peter Ritner, is one of our most imaginative publishers.

Alas, there's no chance of my being in Washington at the end of this month, but I shall be in NYC during the week of which September 24th is the Wednesday, for a public lecture at the Unitarian Church on Central Park West. I'm not sure where I shall be staying, but Paula McGuire of Pantheon Books will know.

I have been trying my hand today on a "This Is How I Live" article for you. The trouble is that, if it is to be in any way honest, it becomes much too intimate and I do not want to yield to the temptation confronting so many well-known people of sacrificing privacy for notoriety. I don't think I want the rest of the world to know how I live, not because I am ashamed of it, but simply because I want to retain some measure of private life. A world in which there are no mysteries is a familiarity breeding contempt.

With all good wishes,
Sincerely, Alan

Sausalito, California | September 4, 1969
Confidential: To Those Particularly Concerned
Subject: Refugee Tibetan Lamas & Others

We are troubled by the present situation of Tibetan lamas, scholars, and artists who have most cruelly been ousted from their country by the government of Mao Tse-tung and are, or have been, living in India under most unsatisfactory circumstances. Although the Swiss government has admitted some thousand of these refugees to a congenial village in the Alps, the United States, for all its avowed opposition to the Communist regime in China, has done virtually nothing to help exiles from Tibet.

We believe that these people can offer a unique spiritual and cultural contribution to the USA, and that we should look forward to the eventual establishment of a center for their relocation in the Sierra Nevada — including even the Dalai Lama himself, if he were willing to come.

As things now stand, this society has undertaken, in conjunction with Mr. Douglas Campbell (investment banker of Los Angeles and New York) to contribute $10,000 (i.e., $5,000 from each of us) to Sonam Kazi, the Dalai Lama's chief interpreter, for a year's visit to this country with his wife and 14-year-old child. He is a citizen of Sikkim, but his wife is Tibetan. He wishes to translate into English various texts of the Nimarpa branch of Tibetan Buddhism, and to instruct a few selected students in its disciplines. In our opinion, he is most highly qualified to do so, since his comprehension of Buddhism and his command of English are excellent.

We also wish to assist Tarthang Tulku, a lama of very high rank now in Berkeley, California, to establish there a center for Nimarpa Buddhist studies, and are seeking for that immediate purpose a sum of $25,000 to get his work under way for the next two years. His command of English is fair. He is about 35 years old, is married, and has an infant child. In our opinion his knowledge of Buddhism is both scholarly and profound.

Contributions to the society for this purpose are, of course, tax-deductible.

Alan Watts, President

Sausalito, California | September 8, 1969
Mr. Peter V. Ritner | The Macmillan Company | New York, New York
Dear Peter:

Herewith the official copyedited typescript of *Erotic Spirituality*, courtesy of Mary Jane Watts, who worked on it for two-and-a-half days, 9 to 5, so you will at least owe her an invitation to lunch when we come to NYC for the inside of a week on or about the 22nd of this month! Not every author is married to a trained copy editor.

The trouble with the copyedited script you sent me was that it was done by someone (probably a graduate of Radcliffe) who is too intelligent for that kind of work but not intelligent enough to rewrite me. She thinks too hard to get the point. (And would want to substitute "hardly" in the foregoing sentence.) However, Mary Jane thinks she is probably a very interesting person and would like to have her for lunch too.

A friend of mine who teaches yoga professionally has just read the script and is ecstatic — hoping that the book will not remain so high-priced as to exclude the young student readership.

With all good wishes,

Sincerely, Alan Watts

AW: The following letter is an invitation to Sonam Topgyal Kazi to the United States. Sonam (mentioned in the letter of September 4 above) was, among other things, the main interpreter for the Dalai Lama from 1959 to 1972.

THE SOCIETY FOR COMPARATIVE PHILOSOPHY | SAUSALITO, CALIFORNIA
October 23, 1969 | Sonam T. Kazi | New Delhi, India
Dear Sonam:
This is a formal invitation to you, to your wife, Psede Lhamo, and your daughter, Jetsun Pema, to visit us in the United States for a maximum period of one year, during which we will provide for your expenses and housing at an amount not exceeding $10,000.00. We will also provide you with economy-class round-trip plane fare from New Delhi, for which tickets will be sent as soon as we know your date of departure.

For much of the time you will be able to reside at the Esalen Institute in Big Sur, California, which is a peaceful resort on the mountainous coast, and there carry on your translation work and instruct a few selected students in the Nying-mapa discipline. You will be free to use your time as you wish.

Otherwise, we would like you to visit our own center here in Sausalito, and some of the other growth centers (like Esalen) in this country for the purpose of giving practical instruction in Buddhist sadhana.

I think we can discuss your daughter's schooling when you arrive. Travel is often a more educative experience than sitting in classrooms.

I see no reason why you should not make brief stops on your way out, provided that you can cover your own hotel expenses at such times.

The US Consul in New Delhi may be assured that this society will be your sponsor, in conjunction with Douglas Campbell. We are inviting you as a visiting scholar, having special competence in the field of Tibetan Buddhism which is not available from any US citizen.

Our very best wishes to you and your family —
Sincerely yours, Alan Watts, President

SAUSALITO, CALIFORNIA | DECEMBER 6, 1969
Mrs. Paula McGuire | Pantheon Books | New York, New York
Dear Paula:
This is to put on the record an idea which I may or may not have mentioned in one of our recent phone conversations. This is the publication of a uniform Zen bookshelf, perhaps boxed, which would consist of the following Pantheon publications:

Zen and Japanese Culture (Suzuki), *The Way of Zen* (Watts), *The History of Zen* (Dumoulin), *The Supreme Doctrine* (Benoit), *Zen in the Art of Archery*, *The Method of Zen*, and *Zen in the Art of Flower Arrangement* (Herrigel) in one volume, plus *Zen Rocks and Waters* (Spiegelberg), *The Original Teachings of Ch'an Buddhism* (Chang), and another work which I am sending you under separate cover — this is *Zen Is Eternal Life* by Jiyu Kennett, a British woman *roshi* of the Soto school, with at least ten years' experience of study in Japan. It is a translation of the more interesting parts of the *Shobogenzo* by Dogen Zenji, founder of the Soto line in Japan, plus the *Denkoroku* of Keizan Zenji, which is a truly fascinating document. She is now here in SF, and agrees with me that the MS needs certain revisions and minor additions. I am not, for example, in agreement with the idea of publishing Book II, Ch. 1, the *Tai-Taikoho*, without some further preliminary explanation, and it also seems to me that certain terms have been unhappily translated. But she needs some money to go ahead with this, and so I am sending you the MS *as is* to see if you think it's worth it.

You might also attempt to capture the translation of the *Rinzai Roku*, which is now being completed at the Kyoto center of the First Zen Institute, at Ryosen-an, Kyoto. This is one of the most magnificent Zen books ever, coming from one of the greatest masters of the Tang dynasty.

Furthermore, the most important works of Suzuki seem to be pretty much out of circulation, i.e., the three volumes of *Essays in Zen Buddhism*, *Introduction to Zen* (a beauty once issued by Philosophical Library), *Living by Zen*, and *The Zen Doctrine of No-Mind*. You can get information on the copyright situation from his secretary, Mihoko Okamura, and find out her whereabouts from her mother, Mrs. Okamura, who runs the Aki restaurant in the environs of Columbia University. Perhaps she is still in Kamakura, but I'm not sure.

To alarm you, or whet your appetite further, there have never been either US or British editions of most of the works of Reginald H. Blyth. Dutton did his *Zen in English Literature*, but there are only Japanese (Hokuseido) editions of *Haiku* (4 vols.), *Zen & Zen Classics* (3 vols.), *Oriental Humor*, *Senryu*, and *The History of Haiku*. He died several years ago, about the same time as Suzuki. Hokuseido Press, Kanda, Tokyo.

So, dear Paula, a most happy Christmas to you and Bill,

With best wishes from us both, Alan and Jano

Robert S. de Ropp, the addressee of the following, was a student of the Gurdjieff-Ouspensky teachings. His books include The Master Game.

SAUSALITO, CALIFORNIA | FEBRUARY 6, 1970
Mr. Robert de Ropp | Santa Rosa, California
Dear Robert:
Many thanks for your stimulating letter. I think you are engaged in a very worthwhile project, but don't call what I am doing "trailing clouds of verbiage." "Verbiage" is a word that one uses with the same strategy as when one calls being

in love "infatuation." There is a way of using words like a dance. Furthermore, a great deal of what I am now doing is instruction in meditation practice rather than lectures, and this sort of thing happens to be the easiest way for me to make enough to support seven dependents.

Now, I never called you a mere Gurdjieffian, because I, too, learned a thing or two from old Mr. Gurdjieff. Unlike Ouspensky, he had such a marvelous sense of fun, and for me this is an essential ingredient of true humanity.

I will call you and come up and see you one of these days. Very best wishes.

Sincerely, Alan Watts

JW: In the summer of 1970, I moved back to California with my husband, Tim Tabernik, and three children. I had lived in the Midwest for twelve years and couldn't wait to be back on the coast. We lived temporarily on the Vallejo. *Alan and Jano were living in Druid Heights, but Alan still maintained an office on the* Vallejo, *with a delightful secretary, Hisayo Saijo. Then we moved, and for the better part of a year we lived on two different communes in northern California. Alan's son Rick had left his mother in Pittsburgh, to live with Alan, and Alan thought it would be good for Rick to live with us. (After her divorce from Alan, Dorothy had taken the children back to Pittsburgh, where they lived with her ailing father. This was at least partially to keep the children as far from Alan as possible.) We were a good one hundred miles from the Bay Area, and the isolation was not to Rick's liking. He had a very different "scene" in mind. By the winter of 1971, we had moved back to the ferryboat, disillusioned with communal life, but also, we hoped, to turn Rick back over to his father's care. We eventually bought a house in the coastal town of Bolinas.*

I started working for the Society for Comparative Philosophy, handling the publication of the Alan Watts Journal, *the bulletin for the society and its members. I also began to arrange seminars on the ferryboat with guest speakers, often as events combined with presentations by Alan. He was frustrated with the mountains of paperwork that would accumulate while he was away or writing at Druid Heights. Many days, when he and Jano would come down from the mountain together, there was much tension. She was often quarrelsome. This frustrated Alan further. Neither of them was functioning well. Alcohol was obviously taking its toll.*

Additionally, sons Mark and Rick had left their mother, and Alan now felt responsible for their well-being. Mark busied himself with his mentor-to-be — Alan's good friend Henry Jacobs, a recording specialist and a lover of Alan's recordings — while Rick was assigned maintenance jobs around the ferryboat and at Druid Heights. When Alan wanted to entertain, I was usually called upon to prepare meals. One evening he hosted a shared party on Varda's end of the boat and had me prepare a large pot of chili to take with us. Ali Akbar Khan was the guest of honor. Alan got seriously drunk, and Jano was unable to attend.

In another episode, Alan was due to speak at a local university. He rarely drove and relied frequently on my husband or Rick to drive him. With Rick and our friend Michael Symmes, we picked Alan up in our VW bus. He demanded to stop at a supermarket, where he purchased a case of six 1.75-liter bottles of vodka. Alan, sitting in the front of the vehicle, had to have a drink right away and reached back, rear in the air, and took a long swig from one of the bottles. When we got him to his lecture destination, we basically propped him up on the stage and watched from the wings. Somehow he managed to give a lecture; the audience appeared to be rapt with his words. The question-and-answer period was much more difficult. It was obvious to us that he was losing his train of thought. When he returned home, he found that Rick had put green food coloring in the vodka, hoping he wouldn't drink it. He was furious and yelled at us, saying that he would commit suicide any way he wanted and we were not to interfere.

Twice he tried to give up drinking and ended up in the hospital with delirium tremens. On one of those occasions I went to see him, and he thought I was my mother. He called me Eleanor and seemed to be in a different era altogether.

From the beginning, Alan and Jano's relationship seemed to revolve around their use of vodka. Looking forward to drinking together was a recurring theme in their love letters. Amazingly, he managed to somehow keep going. Jano didn't. When he was in town, she was comatose. When he went on tour, she would stop drinking and spend money. To justify her spending she'd say: "But I saved you so much money by not going!" During his lectures she attended, she became an embarrassment. She would often interrupt him and say, "Alan, tell them about the time when..." or, "Alan, that's not true!" in order to draw attention to herself.

It was a sad state of affairs. His friends and family begged him to stop drinking and to dissolve his relationship with Jano. But he couldn't face another divorce. Even when writing his autobiography, In My Own Way, *he had to be circumspect about his relationship with her. His editor at Pantheon, Paula McGuire, was disappointed with the book. She felt that it was too shallow, that he could have gone much deeper into his psyche.*

Despite his alcoholism, he continued his writing and lecturing. In the late 1960s and early 1970s, Alan began to address more political issues, writing some of his most remarkable letters.

Macmillan published Erotic Spirituality: The Vision of Konarak *in 1971, for which Alan wrote the text to accompany photographs of the Konarak Sun Temple in India by the renowned photographer Eliot Elisofon. Elisofon died the same year as Alan — 1973.*

There are some amusing letters to Gourmet *and to Sabella's Restaurant.* Playboy *continued to publish timely interviews and articles by Alan, including "Wealth versus Money," published in December 1968. The "Future of Ecstasy" was published in January 1971. These essays, along with "Murder in the Kitchen" and "The Art of Contemplation," were included in* Does It Matter? *and* Cloud Hidden, Whereabouts Unknown. *In a letter dated December 23, 1969, A. C. Spectorsky of* Playboy *wrote, "Please bear in mind, Alan, that you have a way of making virtually any subject fascinating for our readers, no matter how unlikely the idea may seem for* Playboy.*"*

There is a touching letter to Alan's friend Dez Peck, in which he lovingly counsels her about her pending death and possible reincarnation. Another, to his father, Laurie, expressed dismay about his "uptight" reaction to Alan's autobiography. He was in the midst of writing In My Own Way, *feeling overwhelmed with the magnitude of recording his life, and was concerned about the volume of manuscript he had written.*

*During this time, Alan took up an interest in quantum physics as related to Buddhism. He communicated with physicists Fritjof Capra (*The Tao of Physics*), L. L. Whyte (*The Next Development in Man*), whom Alan describes as a freelance theoretical biophysicist, and G. Spencer-Brown (*Laws of Form*), inviting the latter to come from England to California to participate in a conference regarding the subject. The AUM (Alan's tongue-in-cheek acronym for American University of Masters) Conference was held over several days at Esalen Institute in Big Sur in the spring of 1973. Alan made me coordinator of this event, which had an impressive list of participants, New Age thinkers all, including Capra, Spencer-Brown, Gregory Bateson, Claudio Naranjo, Karl Pribram, Ram Dass (Richard Alpert), and John Lilly.*

In June 1973 my daughter, Elizabeth, graduated from the eighth grade at Bolinas School. Her grandfather gave the graduation address for the occasion, dressed in a kimono and wearing a bandana. He announced his presence with a conch shell (much to the delight of the students). Elizabeth graduated with her pet rat, Quetzel, on her shoulder, happy to have had an unconventional ceremony for a traditionally conventional event.

Alan's seminar schedule for the summer of 1973 was, as usual, heavy with lectures at home and away. He and tai chi master Chungliang Al Huang gave several workshops together. Alan participated as the keynote speaker for a symposium on "Psychotherapy and Religion" at the New Jersey Association for Mental Health. He was a participant with Isan Sacco and Shuyu Singer in a public dialogue held on the campus at UC Berkeley and later gave a lecture and seminar for Cold Mountain Institute in British Columbia. He did all of this while writing Tao: The Watercourse Way. *His final trip, to England and Europe, began in late September 1973.*

His following letters show diverse thought on a variety of subjects — many of which are still very pertinent now (2017). It is no wonder that younger generations are so attracted to his philosophical teachings. Perhaps the time is ripe for a shift in the world paradigm.

SAUSALITO, CALIFORNIA | FEBRUARY 19, 1970

Dear Spec [A. C. Spectorsky]:

Herewith comments on the Romain Gary letter. Hope to be seeing you next week.

One does not wish to offend such a person as Romain Gary, a writer of great distinction, who served his country most admirably as the French Consul here in San Francisco for many years.

However, although the French are respected for their logical minds, his letter is an emotional outburst almost entirely unrelieved by any factual information or evidence of personal or clinical experience. May I make the following points:

1. The drugs, which M. Gary has in mind, are opium, heroin, cocaine, and hashish when used in excess. Their effects are entirely different from those of LSD-25, mescaline, psilocybin, and moderately used marijuana. The former induce torpor and passivity, as also, alas, does the immoderate drinking of Châteauneuf-du-Pape. The latter induce a sensation of intense though relaxed awakeness in which all details become vividly clear and astonishingly interesting. One sees, in the words of Shakespeare, that "there are more things in heaven and earth than are dreamed of in your philosophy." It should be noted that visual images of these experiences presented in the popular press and in such films as *Easy Rider* are completely misleading, for they're not vague and bizarre but as clear and articulate as, say, Persian miniatures or the stained glass of Chartres or the photographs of Eliot Porter.

2. There is no analogy whatsoever between the use of psychedelic chemicals for clarifying and expanding consciousness and the use of cultivated syphilis for the cure of bubonic plague. The choice of such an analogy indicates only a highly emotional prejudice. There is no evidence that small amounts of psychedelic chemicals damage the body, but a little syphilis goes a long way.

3. It is true that the British used opium in China for the same reasons that the French permitted hashish in Algeria — to keep the underdogs passive and amused. Oddly enough, it is only *since* my experiments with LSD-25 that I have become politically active, especially in the problems of man's relation to his environment.

4. To the best of my knowledge, no one on the panel, except perhaps Mr. Anslinger, has or has had any financial interest in the drug traffic. Mr. Anslinger

used it to maintain the Bureau of Narcotics in reasonable affluence, by arousing public indignation against marijuana after the failure of his efforts to enforce the Volstead Act's prohibition of beer, wine, and spirits. ("Alcohol" is an Islamic cussword.)

5. All the evils of these drugs, chemicals, or plants come from their excessive use. But I once knew a Methodist minister — a rabid prohibitionist and teetotalitarian who contracted a serious sickness from drinking too much milk.

Will governments therefore desist from turning their countries into nurseries? Freedom involves the right to go to hell in your own way, so long as you do no violence to others. And the whole problem of respect for the police, who are essential public servants, could be greatly eased by ceasing to ask them to be armed clergymen, and removing from their jurisdiction all sumptuary laws dealing with private morals and "crimes" without victims, such as gambling, prostitution, drug abuse, and sexual vagaries between consenting adults. Why isn't it understood that all such laws are immensely profitable for organized crime? The Mafia people lobby for their continuance.

Alan Watts

Spec, I think you might send a Xerox of this to M. Gary before publishing anything. I simply don't want such a fine man to make a fool of himself in public.

Sausalito, California | February 24, 1970
Sabella's of Marin | Mill Valley, California
Gentlemen:
My wife and I have been fairly regular patrons of your restaurant since 1961. Last night we wished to go out to dinner and found that the Trident was closed, the Blue Fin poorly supplied, the Buckeye closed, and the adjoining Mexican restaurant hopelessly crowded. We then bethought us of Sabella's.

But from your establishment we were rudely excluded by an arrogant young man for the peccadillo of wearing sandals over bare feet. Otherwise we were elegantly, if informally, dressed. Now your food has been consistently excellent, but you are not the St. Francis Hotel. If you have any eye for the future, bear it in mind that you are operating in an area where an increasing number of young people (your customers-to-be) are unwilling to dress like morticians.

By chance you might have seen my article "Murder in the Kitchen" in the December issue of *Playboy* magazine, which is, among other things, a discussion of the barbarous fare served in most American restaurants. Your own chef, or chefs, are very competent — and my standards may be considered fussy. But why must we be obliged to come to your restaurant with our feet sweatily enclosed in wool and tight leather, observing a mere ritual which, however appropriate in the snows of Chicago, is unnecessary in California?

I really believe that a change in your policy is in order, as well as an apology to a longtime customer.

Very truly yours, Alan Watts

JW: The following letter was written to the mother of a remarkable woman who had become a devotee of Alan's. From a blog, "The Psychedelic Adventures of Alan Watts," by psychologist Stanley Krippner, we learned that Virginia Glenn suffered from advanced diabetes and had decided to commit suicide. She changed her mind after hearing one of Alan's taped lectures and thereafter took to playing his lectures in the 1950s to whoever would listen. She met Alan in 1957 while working as a waitress and began to schedule talks for him with the help of Krippner, who wrote, "Alan looked upon her as a Bodhisattva." She died July 3, 1970, in a diabetic coma. Krippner further wrote, "The lasting fruits of my relationship with Alan Watts are a testament of Virginia's divine gift. Her talent of introducing [people] would prove to be a lifelong benefit and the reason I can now write about Alan Watts with such a personal perspective."

Alan's letter to Virginia's mother shows how deeply touched he was by her daughter and how much she meant to him. The photo of the tablet he mentions has unfortunately not been found in his files.

Sausalito, California | July 6, 1970
Mrs. Walter Glenn | Ottumwa, Iowa
Dear Mrs. Glenn:
Perhaps you have not seen one of these before. It is a Far-Eastern-style memorial tablet, bearing the posthumous, or religious name of a departed person. Such tablets are displayed at the funeral and are afterwards kept in some place of honor in the home.

The name I have chosen for Virginia is not too easy to translate, but it's something like this: the first (top) character (and the top is the rounded end) means both music and happiness, and is pronounced *raku*. The second means flower, and especially the lotus flower, and is pronounced *ge*. The third and fourth, pronounced *bosatsu*, mean Bodhisattva; which refers to a person of especially great wisdom and compassion, and is reserved for those rare people we call "spiritual giants." Virginia, in her humble way, richly deserves such a title.

In all, it means something like "Harmonious Flower Bodhisattva" (*Raku-ge Bosatsu*), and I send it to you as some sort of symbolic representation of my admiration for this marvellous woman, who was uncomplaining under intense suffering, and who worked with immense enthusiasm to promote intelligent friendships between people concerned with man's enlightenment and liberation.

On the back of the tablet I have permitted myself a joke which Virginia would most certainly appreciate, I have changed the word "posthumous" to "posthumorous." No one will forget her laugh.

With all good wishes, and thanks for mothering such a wonderful child.

Sincerely yours, Alan Watts

The following is a form letter from around 1970 sent around to various police departments.

SAUSALITO, CALIFORNIA

Sir:

Recent and current "race" riots have many causes, but one of them is most certainly hatred of the police. In this country, the big-city police forces have, at present, an extremely bad public image, which must be changed *now* — because nothing is more basic to the morale of the community than respect for the law and its officers. May I therefore submit the following simple and practical proposals. They will not solve the entire problem, but will make a substantial contribution to that end.

1. Clothes all too easily make the man, and those who dress like Nazi SS troopers tend to behave like them. Police uniforms should therefore be changed from black or blue to khaki-green, and, instead of helmets or vizored caps, we should restore the old campaign hat, as worn by forest rangers and Mounties — officials generally liked by the public as helpful "scouts." If there must be helmets, let them be those of the British "bobbies."

2. The police must cease to carry armaments other than truncheons or nightsticks. Concurrently, the civilian public should forbid themselves to own firearms other than shotguns or rifles for use in sport and hunting. Handguns and automatic weapons should be outlawed, and I say this even as a former member of the National Rifle Association.

3. In accordance with the constitutional principle of the separation of Church and State, the police must have no further jurisdiction in matters of personal and private morals. Nothing brings them into greater disrespect than being required to act as armed preachers, enforcing sumptuary laws against gambling, wenching, boozing, and drug-taking. Such jurisdiction is also a major cause of police corruption, inviting blackmail, harassment, entrapment, and acceptance of bribes. The drunken driver, for example, should be charged with bad driving — not with intoxication. All efforts to get rid of the *causes* of crime, by force, end as

attempts to get rid of human nature, and all truly moral behavior is, by definition, voluntary.

4. Police duties should be confined to the essential functions of (a) directing traffic, (b) protecting the citizenry from murder, robbery, and violence, and (c) giving due assistance to lost children and little old ladies.

If these four basic principles are worked out in detail, we in the United States will have loved and honored police forces, as distinct from officially sponsored corps of racketeers, hoodlums, and booted bullies — all the more dangerous for being allowed to vent their spleen with a clear conscience.

There will be respect for authority when, and only when, authority is itself respectable.

Very truly yours, Alan Watts

SAUSALITO, CALIFORNIA | AUGUST 23, 1970
Dear and beloved Dez [Mrs. Sherman Peck]:
If this letter does not reach you while you are still on this level of existence, I would like your sister to read it to you at your funeral.

I have studied much, lately, with those Buddhist lamas of Tibet, and I believe they know a thing or two about the basics of existence. They have sat for hours and days in those quiet mountains, feeling out and testing the root and ground of consciousness.

They say that when you die, you have an immediate experience of a clear, transparent, and electric-blue vivid light — which is the same as "the love that makes the world go round." They suggest that, at that moment, you give in completely to absorption in this light, because it is the final ground and base of your own mind, and of the energy of the universe.

If, however, you can't make it, you will next experience visions of everything which you have ever considered sublimely blissful, but must understand that it is secondary to the Clear Light, and simply a product of your own mind.

If you get caught up in this blissful vision, it will automatically turn, by what Jung called enantiodromia (or the flip-flop ability of opposites), into a vision of everything you have always hated and feared — though it is to be understood that this, too, is the work of your own imagination.

If you run away from this horrifying vision, you will seek shelter in a womb, and thus be reborn according to your karma.

Dez, I don't know whether all this should be taken factually or symbolically, but just watch out in case it happens. I know only that the real "I" is the eternal energy of this universe, and that it is the nature of energy to vibrate, to come, and to go. Thus the word *tathagata*, which is the name for a Buddha, means equally one who comes thus, and one who goes thus.

It would be stupid and irrelevant for me to wish you well, for what else is there? All nature follows gravity, for doesn't one fall both into love and into the grave? So just keep on falling, and at the end of the down you will swing up.

These days Jano and I are living in retreat — in a cottage on Mount Tamalpais above Mill Valley, close to Muir Woods, and I am immersed in writing a book to be called *Coincidence of Opposites,* which is actually the story of my life.

My old friend Elsa Gidlow, who owns the land here, has just deeded it to our Society for Comparative Philosophy so that it will be kept quiet and preserved from "development," and we shall simply keep it as a place for retreat and meditation, possibly putting up an unobtrusive kiva-type building to house my library. We overlook a huge forested valley, which is a state park, and in which no single human habitation is to be seen — and we are only 40 minutes from San Francisco.

Well my dear, much love from us both, and let the ideas, the words, "life" and "death" drop away from your mind.

As ever, Alan

SAUSALITO, CALIFORNIA | DECEMBER 20, 1970
Mr. Henry Volkening | New York, New York
Dear Henry:
I'm in a bit of a quandary with this autobiography. Although it is not strictly chronological record, I find myself over 180 pages in and still only 29 years old. The going is slow because I am not used to the narrative manner of writing, which is why I have never been a novelist.

But obviously I am not, as I hoped, going to get it done by the end of the year. There is free time set aside in January, and some in February, but with March and April the round of lectures gets going again — since I shall have to pay my income tax and fill the coffers of the Society for Comparative Philosophy since we lost a benefactor in the 1969 stock-market fracas.

As soon as it is all copyread, I will send a Xerox of the whole thing for you and Paula up to the end of Chapter VII. Much additional material has gone into the chapters you have already seen, and there have been a few cuts.

What do we do? Break it up into two volumes? Even so, to round it off at 1950 will take quite a bit more work, and what I have thus far received by way of advances, though generous, is spent. The two-volume idea does not altogether appeal to me, but this sort of thing has been done often enough before. I think of Robert Graves and Anaïs Nin. But if I am to get the whole thing in one volume, I doubt if it will be ready until the end of June, and then publication won't be until late spring or summer 1972.

The remainder to be written breaks down somewhat as follows:

1. My adventures as a priest and college chaplain. (To 1950.)

2. Going to California and working with the American Academy of Asian Studies.

3. The Zen boom. My freelance career. Work with Charlotte Selver, and the beginning of Esalen. Kerouac & Dharma bums.

4. The psychedelic adventure. Huxley, Ginsberg, Leary, Alpert.

5. Travels in the Orient, Mexico, and Europe. Jung, von Dürckheim, Ronald Laing, Suzuki, R. H. Blyth, Gary Snyder.

6. The hippie uprising and Spengler's "second religiousness." Growth centers, communes. The concern for ecology.

7. Going with the Tao.

This means yet another seven chapters, so would you please consult with Paula and let me have your suggestions.

All best wishes, and happy Christmas!

As ever, Alan Watts

SAUSALITO, CALIFORNIA | DECEMBER 20, 1970

Dear Gary [Snyder]:

This is a most belated reply to your two letters, with the incantation, but I have been as much of a hermit as possible for the last months, working up at the Mandala on the autobiography — which is slow going because I'm not used to a narrative style of writing. We made two trips to Canada — one to Cold Mountain, which I found very impressive and to which I plan to return in the summer. The Weavers have their feet on the ground, and it's the only such place where the food is good.

At the beginning of October I decided I was drinking too much and simply stopped. I was surprised to get rather startling withdrawal symptoms and, had it not been for my experiences with LSD, might have been scared. My metabolism is not fully adjusted to sobriety, but my insides are sorting themselves out and I feel more and more drawn to a sort of Taoistic existence in the mountains.

I understand you are planning some teaching at UC Riverside. I shall be at Claremont and Palm Springs in February, and perhaps we could get together...

Have you seen a little book called *EST* by Clark Stevens? It quotes "Four Changes" and is a marvelously concise survey of the current scene.

David was so enthused about La Barre's *Ghost Dance* that I bought a copy. As yet I've only skimmed it, and must have missed the cause for enthusiasm, for I find only a broken-down 19th-century Freudian scientism in which the cleavage between man and environment is a matter of high dogma. His own phrase: "The objectionable objective world." Tell me if I'm missing something.

How are you going to publish the Fudo Incantation? Maybe I could put it forth somehow.

Much love to you all from us both,

As ever, Alan

Sausalito, California | January 18, 1971

Dear Daddy:

It is really rather difficult to answer your letter about the autobiography, because the problem at issue is emotional rather than intellectual, or even moral. Jano and Elsa have both seen your letter (as they have also read the manuscript) and they are astonished, just as I am. It just doesn't seem like your usual self, but more as if you had put on a ritual mask that would better fit the features of Prince Albert or Mr. Gladstone.

First, I should have told you that this was simply a first draft of the manuscript, to which hundreds of corrections are being made. I sent it to you to be sure that there were no glaring errors of fact.

The main point at issue is obviously my inclusion of some passages having to do with sex and matters of human evacuation which you find "obscene." You are however, judging my work by the standards of a very short period of English literature, running from about 1830 to 1930, and I simply refuse to submit to the tastes of the genteel bourgeoisie of that time when such masters as Chaucer, Shakespeare, Marlowe, Swift, Smollett, Swinburne, Burton, Maugham, and Huxley have certainly outdone me in bawdy and ribald writing. You must remember that in school we read these classics as mutilated by such censors as Mr. Bowdler, who gave us the verb "to bowdlerize."

Further, I see no analogy between a book which is concerned with life as a whole and the genteel seclusion of a drawing room. A life story limited to things suitable to drawing-room conversation is obviously dishonest, and has the same grotesque and unnatural appearance as a statue sprouting a fig leaf between the legs, and thus blatantly drawing attention to parts conspicuous by their absence.

Moreover, if we are going to confuse matters of taste with matters of principle, I will readily take the position that accounts of battle, mayhem, and murder are far more obscene than those of the tender ecstasies and harmless humours of sex, and by this standard find Dickens, Conan Doyle, and Kipling obscene. Wouldn't you agree that a murder is far more immoral in a drawing room than a pleasant seduction?

Yet detective stories deemed fit reading for all abound with detailed accounts of the precise methods whereby people were poisoned at dinner or shot while playing bridge. I would rather open a finely printed book to find a smudge than a dollop of blood.

Surely, too, it just isn't true that my writing is cynical. My cynicism, if it exists at all, is always touched with affection and nowhere do I blame or condemn those adults who, appearing so formidable and serious to a child, are seen in retrospect as, after all, amusingly human. I was at some pains not to represent childhood experiences as hardships, and even said explicitly that I would not have had things otherwise. But this need not prevent me from a certain bemused amazement at some of the traditions of British schools and at the constipation rituals of our nannies.

My dearest Daddy, please light up your pipe, pour yourself a judicious glass of brandy, and reconsider the whole matter. My publishers are agog to see the rest of the work, and everyone in the office has been reading what I have sent them. They have also agreed to keep me comfortably financed for as long as it takes me to finish the job, and the people of Pantheon Books are anything but money-grubbing pornographers. You will see the finished manuscript as it comes along. So please don't be a skeleton at the banquet.

There have been all sorts of problems around here this month. Dear old Varda dropped dead of a heart attack in Mexico City, and I have to take care of all the rearrangements concerning his part of the boat and who is to live there instead — which requires much soothing of easily ruffled emotions. Furthermore, my son Richard has fled here from his mother, which, taking into account his precocious temperament and his mother's rage, is going to take some handling. Mark also hopes to join us this summer. I am thinking of taking the whole multitude, including Joan, Tim, and Joel's brother Oliver on a camping trip to the islands of British Columbia — which are as lovely as the Inland Sea of Japan. Did I tell you that we went there this past autumn, for a seminar on Cortes Island, and that I have been invited back for a much longer session?

Many thanks indeed for the guide to London and for the lacy kerchiefs for Jano. They have just arrived — and the latter are lovely if too delicate for the wretched colds we have had this winter, despite the vitamin C.

Very much love from us both — As ever, Alan

JW: The above letter was written in rebuttal to the foreword Alan had asked his father to write for his autobiography, In My Own Way. *His father, Laurence, took umbrage to some of the more blatantly sexual and, in his thinking, "amoral" passages of the book, hence Alan's tongue-in-cheek chiding. His father lived a full year after Alan's death and died, perhaps of a broken heart, having lost his only child.*

Some years after his death Alan's image as a learned philosopher was being questioned by those who thought he didn't live true to his teachings. One common criticism was his reputation of being a "womanizer." This became evident in public comments in various venues. One particular female commentator on a local radio station, who for years had praised his writings and lectures, began to denigrate him for what she began to perceive had been his attitude towards women. During his era of popularity, he wrote articles for Playboy *magazine and did, once, as shown in a letter above, experience a Playboy Club, which he called "dreadful" and "silly." He certainly always admired women and had formed relationships with a few that were equal to his intellectual caliber. As his fame broadened, and as he traveled more, "opportunity" presented itself everywhere he went.*

In his defense, I have to say that I saw firsthand that there were women, young and old, that pretty much laid themselves at his feet. Like a bowl of chocolate truffles, it is hard to say no to "just one." And of course, there was his aversion to Judeo-Christian mores regarding sex outside marriage or regarding sex in general. Especially in America. I quote Alan's thought from In My Own Way: *"My life would be much, much poorer were it not for certain particular women with whom I have most happily and congenially committed adultery...women to whom I am permanently grateful for but one or two embraces, and I have every reason to believe that they feel the same way towards me, for our sexual communion was the natural culmination of our admiration for one another as people." To Alan, there was a significant difference between being in love and the act of sexual intercourse as an act of mutual admiration.*

I rarely saw him as the instigator in any of these associations, although once I was particularly amused by his attempt to seduce a well-known woman. I happened to meet her briefly as my seat companion on a flight from San Francisco to Monterey. Later that week, she showed up at Esalen, where my father was conducting a seminar. One particular evening, everyone was dancing and Alan was obviously intent on seducing her, which I found amusing but embarrassing. (I am, after all, his daughter!) Later he confided to me that he just couldn't understand why the woman wasn't attracted to him! As a woman, I understood on several levels, but wouldn't explain it to him. The dent to his ego was justified. He could, however, on very rare occasion be known to brag, "I once had the privilege of sharing a mistress with one of the holiest men in the land."

Two women in particular have come up in biographies of Alan and on the internet

— *Jean Burden, mentioned earlier, and June Singer, a noted Jungian psychologist. June and Alan met in Chicago in 1964, shortly after her husband died. Alan had offered comfort and support in her grieving. They became on-again-off-again lovers and remained so, it seems, until Alan's death. He has been noted as having helped her decide on the title of her book* Boundaries of the Soul *(1972). We have found no evidence that either Dorothy or Jano knew of Alan's relationships with these women.*

In a letter to Jean Burden, Alan justified his behavior as follows: "If I appear, then, to be spiritually or physically frayed, this is the natural consequence of being highly strung, temperamentally and unsystematically energetic enough to get away with supporting a considerable number of dependents at the unlikely business of philosophy. Of course I am frayed, but I don't expect to make omelets without breaking eggs. Nor do I pity myself for the costs which my peculiar way of life entails. So if people expect me to embody their own conceptions of a sage, or of its rather watered-down modern equivalent, the mature man, they are going to be disappointed — but I hope, in the long run, enlightened, for at least they may get what I mean without having to reverence me as the source of the insight. For one of the things I am trying to do is to shatter the whole idea of the exemplary person, and of treating philosophy and life itself, as something that is supposed to 'work,' to be good for us."

In retrospect, Anne and I always felt that Alan had deep-seated self-destructive tendencies. His excessive use of tobacco and alcohol and his overwhelming need for sexual gratification (having been described even as sadomasochistic) is hard to understand in someone who was a brilliant scholar — a savant put here on this planet to impart the "wisdom of the universe" and yet a very vulnerable human being at the same time.

Together, Anne and I characterized Alan as suffering from a Pygmalion complex in his choice of wives. All three were basically very unhappy women from the time he had met them. His sense was that if he married them, he could heal their chronic unhappiness. Instead, in each case, he made their suffering worse. He had some wonderful mistresses whom we both knew and loved, but whom he didn't marry. He seemed hell-bent on complicating his life. How he had the energy as a highly demanded public persona to juggle women, write books, lecture, and travel around the world is unfathomable. Somehow, he did it, but toward the end, his orbit began to wobble. He burnt himself out. A tragic waste of a brilliant mind.

Sausalito, California | April 19, 1971
Mrs. Elda Hartley | Hartley Productions, Inc. | Cos Cob, Connecticut
Dear Elda:
Further reflection of *The Art of Meditation* film, discounting the technical snags of the last screening, convinces me that my part in it is simply not up to scratch.

You will remember that I expressed strong doubts about it after the actual filming. Even though it might pass muster with people unfamiliar with my work, the poor quality would be obvious to people who are used to me in good form, and, especially in a film on this subject, I would be seriously violating my standards not to do a very much better job. For one thing, even when the speed is right, my speaking is too fast and strained. You might ask Bea, for I think she is of the same opinion, though her initial reaction to the film was warm because of your photography — which is certainly exquisite.

I would be most willing to redo my part of it entirely when you come out to the West Coast, where we would not only have a lovely setting, but also the great gong bell and other interesting props. I realize that, at this point, you are understandably weary of work on this one project, but I feel that if we let it lie a little while our enthusiasms will revive. But I really don't want it to go out as it is.

We shall expect to see you at the Kleins' on the 22nd.

Love and best wishes, Alan

SAUSALITO, CALIFORNIA | MAY 14, 1971

Dear Elda:

Many thanks for yours of May 10th. The more I think about it, the more this film troubles me. You will remember that I expressed doubts about it immediately after we had done the filming. As it stands it might perhaps "get by," but I could not promote it with any enthusiasm for this is simply not the film on meditation I wanted to do, and I would not want it to prejudice any later film on the same subject. Although Jano is worried about my appearance, I am worried about the voice, for the tone and mood do not fit the visual scene, as they would if I had done it the other way round. As it stands, the voice simply distracts.

It is possible that I am being heavily subjective. So, if you must press the matter, I would like you to bring the film out here and show it, along with the others, to a group of friends and associates including James Broughton and Sandy Jacobs (who works with me on TV projects) and perhaps Gary Usher (who made the original record).

The trouble is that a film is a permanent record. If this were simply a demonstration I had put on for a single run, that would be all very well. But I am disturbed at the idea of having work that is by no means my best (and on a very basic and crucial subject) shown again and again and again.

For some reason the best night's sleep I ever had was in a trailer. It was by no means a fancy one. It was in a miserable small town in Illinois, and belongs to a Methodist minister! I think you will enjoy travelling this way.

Love and best wishes from us both, Alan

JULY 2, 1971
Mr. Fritjof Capra | Department of Physics | Imperial College of
Science & Technology | London, England
Dear Mr. Capra:
Many thanks for your letter of June 20th, the interesting article, and the beautiful photomontage.

This is, of course, a most important field of investigation, and your article prompts me to make two observations. The first is that we must somehow find a language to clarify, for laymen, the concepts of quantum theory and especially the nature of a physical field. I have been working very carefully on this from a somewhat different point of departure — not quantum theory, but the "field" character or reciprocal interdependence of such polarities as organism/environment, voluntary/involuntary, self/other, solid/space. Heisenberg, in *Physics and Beyond* (p. 206), says, "Those who are not shocked when they first come across quantum theory cannot possibly have understood it."

The second is that you must be much more specific as to what *kinds* of Oriental philosophy go along with quantum physics — and here you will find the most exciting parallels in Mahayana Buddhism, especially the schools known respectively as Madhyamika and Avatamsaka (Gandhavyuha). On the first, see T. R. V. Murti, *The Central Philosophy of Buddhism*. On the second, D. T. Suzuki in *Essays in Zen Buddhism*, vol. 3, and Fung Yu-lan's *History of Chinese Philosophy*, vol. 2. The latter has a theory of the "mutual interpenetration of all things and events" (*shih shih wu ai*), which is curiously like the restoration, by holography, of a whole photographic negative from a single fragment of the same — showing how the "part" implies the whole field.

I certainly wish you well in this project, and shall be interested in how it goes along.

Sincerely yours, Alan Watts

SAUSALITO, CALIFORNIA | JULY 16, 1971
Dear Lance [L. L. Whyte]:
I have read your essay "Towards a Science of Form" with real delight. For me, you are one of the six most stimulating people in the world and here, as in *The Next Development in Man* (which absolutely must be reprinted), you have done it again.

(In passing, have you read *The Laws of Form* by G. Spencer-Brown, published by Allen & Unwin in London? John Lilly brought it to my attention, and I think you would find it important and interesting.)

I want to think out loud with you. Our problem in understanding the morphic process is that we are trying to translate it into the terms of the English language or mathematics. If we can do this, we shall feel secure in our understanding. But what leads us to suppose that we need this kind of security? We may be creating a false problem, like that of trisecting angles with ruler and compass.

Hereafter the word *language* will mean both spoken, written, and mathematical symbols of process, strung out in lines, whether on paper or magnetic tape. Simply, is it really possible to translate morphic process into this form? Morphic process involves more simultaneous and rapidly moving variables than can be set out in lines occupying the same time spans as the processes themselves. What happens in a field cannot be scanned, linearly, in the same time as what happens.

If we cannot find language for morphic process this is to say what mystics have always said, that the vision of reality is ineffable. (Thus Korzybski called the physical world "unspeakable.") This seems to be saying that our efforts to understand morphic process must come to dead end, blind alley, failure.

But must understanding be restricted to understanding in terms of language? I understand how to open and close my hand, but I cannot tell you how it is done.

You are looking forward to the expression of a surprisingly simple and elegant formula for the explanation, in language, of morphic process. Could it be just that such a formula is neither possible, necessary, nor desirable? That just *that* is your formula? The trick is to see that this negatively phrased statement is a positive affirmation that unconscious and nonlinear morphic process is itself the answer to the problem.

The intellectual task is to demonstrate in intellectual terms (i.e., language), why this is so — as if to make it plain that an important event can really come to pass without its being reported in the newspapers or seen on television. Perhaps morphic process can take care of itself, and has no need of being monitored by suspicious inspectors who cannot in any case monitor their own monitoring, etc.

You are saying in a new way that "the Tao which can be explained is not the eternal Tao," for Tao is exactly what you mean by morphic process, which is *tzu-jan*, "of itself so" or spontaneous, and functions by a principle of order called *li*, which first meant the markings in jade and the grain in wood, which are, of course, the permanent traces of patterns in the flow of liquid. Needham translates it "organic pattern." (On which see also Theodor Schwenk's *Sensitive Chaos: The Creation of Flowing Forms in Water and Air*. Rudolf Steiner Press, London, 1965.)

But language and science are themselves events in morphic process, and their function is to go on putting themselves peacefully and reasonably to rest. Science is optimal when it is done in the same way as art — in the realization that it is not necessary. Thus anyone engaged in pure research cannot and must not be pressed for results or made to work by the clock. A fine intellect must be trusted in the same way as morphic process must be trusted.

Another related thought: What do we mean by clarity? We think, first, of transparency, a fine lens or crystal, or unobstructed space — that is, of something void. But at the same moment we think of form in perfect focus or clear definition. (The notion of substance is, of course, "stuff" — or the fuzziness which appears when the focus is off.) There is thus a polar, interdependent, or transactional relationship between void and form, space and solid. Western man has the fixed idea that *ex nihilo nihil fit*. Thus another aspect of the simple and elegant idea for which you are looking is that you can't have something without nothing, or articulate differentiation without undifferentiated space.

It is as difficult, but no more difficult, to see this point as to realize that Earth is not flat but globular. It is also important to see that neural efficiency is not to be attained through muscular effort...But the startling point here is that, if we look at it chronologically, form is the result of space, which is just another way of saying that it is inseparable from it, or that the universe is a closed system which, as St. Thomas Aquinas would have put it, is what all men call God. It includes its outside.

With very best wishes, and hoping to see you before long,

As ever, Alan Watts

SAUSALITO, CALIFORNIA | AUGUST 4, 1971
Mrs. Paula McGuire | Pantheon Books | New York, New York
Dear Paula:

Things are going ahead, and very soon I will have more chapters to send you. You probably know that *Playboy* has accepted the last chapter (in its brief form).

In the meantime — I understand Random House has bought Grove. They publish my *Spirit of Zen* and, as you will see from the enclosed, the original publisher has had difficulty in obtaining from them the illustrations for a new edition, which they would like to bring out as soon as possible. I sent the material to Grove many months ago.

Is there anyone you know in RH who could somehow get things moving?

Hope your summer is not unbearably sweltering. I'll be back in NY in October.

Love to you both, Alan

JW: Alan considered John Lilly, to whom the following letter is addressed, as his astrological twin. They were born the same day, in the same year, and about the same (real) time, John in Minnesota and Alan in England. They shared other coincidences

— both married the same number of times and had the same number of children, each with a daughter named Joan. John was a scientist known for his dolphin studies — primarily in communication. He was also noted for his research in computer sciences and was another of Alan's friends involved with psychedelic experimentation. He was the author of a number of books including Center of the Cyclone: An Autobiography of Inner Space, *which Alan is critiquing in the letter. John and Toni Oshman (a beautiful woman who was John's "grounding" partner) often participated in seminars at Esalen and on the* Vallejo *and were great friends of ours.*

SAUSALITO, CALIFORNIA | AUGUST 23, 1971
Dear John:
My comment for publication on your book would be: "This is the astonishing story of an eminent scientist who, having explored the limits of the intellect, of logic and technics, saw it as a dead end unless surpassed and then redirected by a mystical discipline. It may horrify his former colleagues, but they should read it, and then ask themselves the most basic questions they can imagine."

Now I go on to wonder: Is the work finished and already in proof? As things stand I am concerned lest those colleagues shrug it off saying, "Look what LSD did to a great mind!" I feel you have a responsibility for making it much more clear intellectually, why you passed from the scientific enterprise to the mystical. This requires a hard-nosed critique of scientific objectives and method, and at the point in the book where one expects it there are only those aphoristic passages which, for some reason, I found much less interesting than the more narrative parts of the story, which, including the dialogue with Oscar, are perfectly fascinating.

There are many minor errors which careful copyreading should correct. But it is *mantram* not *mantrum*, and *prakriti* not *prakreti* and I am unfamiliar with the yoga terminology you have used other than the term samadhi. I would like to look at the source book you have used and check out on it. A scientist who gets into these domains must continue to be intellectually respectable!

Thus: your use of the word *satori* is really improper. It should refer only to state +3, and to the state beyond it (numberless) in which it is clear that +3 and all other states are the same, and that there is really nothing to *do* at all. Other levels should simply be classified as spectrum bands of consciousness — C6, C12, C24, C48, etc. And you should explain more methodically why you use this number system, why you use astrological categories, and why you suddenly drag in prayer and a theistic image of God. You should also relate the isolation box and the hood to the sensory deprivation tank. You know, don't you, that the word *sufi* comes from an Arabic word for wool because of the practice of wrapping oneself completely with a blanket.

I would omit the appendices. These tables and diagrams don't give much information and, above all, they "look" phony — like something out of a bad book on occultism dated 1910. I have a real nose for these things, and know exactly what typography and layout will make an academician suspect (unconsciously) that a book is phony.

What I'm saying is, I think, that in your function as a bodhisattva you must have compassion on the scientific community you have left behind. Anyone can do what you have done, but only a John Lilly can convey the sense of it to scientists — and this delineates your position and role in the mandala of bodhisattvas. Mine is, perhaps, to convey it to theologians and psychoanalysts! It seems to me that a person who goes beyond science should not suddenly and indiscriminately accept the whole bag of nonscience or metascience: astrology, astral projection, telepathy, angelology, cartomancy, divination, and metaphysics — not to mention kataphysics, anaphysics, paraphysics, hypophysics, hyperphysics, and apophysics.

There is a position from which the stickliness of academicians, and having to deal with it, seems an utterly unnecessary waste of time. But so, also, does any attempt to communicate the mysteries by words. But once having decided to try it, we must speak to those whom we would reach in the best form of their own language. This means, then, some caution and/or expanded explanation in those parts of your story which deal with occult, rather than strictly mystical, phenomena. If this distinction isn't clear, Toni will have heard me explain it.

But I do wish you well with this whole undertaking, both the book and the work itself. Let me know your plans.

Much love to you both, Alan

SAUSALITO, CALIFORNIA | SEPTEMBER 18, 1971

Dear Spencer-Brown:

I was really delighted to receive your letter of the 13th. Immediately I telephoned my publisher and they will cable Allen & Unwin tomorrow (Monday) about rights. This is Pantheon Books, a subdivision of Random House, who distribute the *Whole Earth Catalog*, on p. 12 of which is a fine review and summary [by Heinz von Foerster] of [your book] *Laws of Form*. I'm reasonably sure they will take it; if not, I'll find someone else.

You may, of course, quote my letter in any way you wish.

As to lectures in USA I will get in touch with the Esalen Institute where they are already sponsoring a seminar on your work by von Foerster. Through my own foundation, The Society for Comparative Philosophy, I will sponsor a seminar for you here with a minimum guarantee of $500. Meanwhile I will alert my mathematical friends in various universities; they can't possibly afford to ignore you! It will probably take until the summer of 1972 to arrange this. Do you know Lance Whyte? He is very experienced in these matters and would gladly advise you, and his address is on Redington Road, London.

I assume you also know Joseph Needham at Gonville and Caius. Some years ago I had dinner with him and we discussed, among other things, the development of binary arithmetic from the *I Ching* and the possibilities of using ideographs with analog computers. How well do you know Chinese? I regard myself as not much more than a dabbler, but am always fascinated with it and have been through the whole of Lao-tzu.

Alas, I am the product of an English classical education in which we learned to despise mathematics. However, I have to some extent overcome this prejudice, though there are some tight places in your reasoning where I feel I need parallel analogies to follow you. Nevertheless I am amazed at the elegant simplicity of your language.

The relations between mathematics and language are fascinating; and mathematicians seem to use English in a peculiar way. Your notes help out a great deal, but I think you should consider, for the American edition, an expansion of the notes on Chapter 1. The two axioms could do with some extra commentary.

If you will bear with me, please turn over.

To a merely literate reader Axiom 1 seems to say, "The value of a (first) call made again is (only) the value of the (first) call," so as to say that my attempts to reach you many times by telephone would show no greater degree of urgent motivation than a single call... But the axiom seems to be correct if we assume that only *now* is real, and that therefore what *did* happen is no longer the case.

In Axiom 2 it is not perfectly clear (to me) as to what you mean by recrossing. If it is something like this [several lines of blank space] we are of course back where we started and "to recross is not to cross." But then what are we to make of the parable of the Prodigal Son?

In the First Canon (p. 3), "What is not allowed is forbidden" is, in political terms, the principle of a totalitarian state. For this reason the Ninth Amendment to the US Constitution affirms, in effect, that the people retain certain rights not specified in the Constitution — and leaves it at that. Has this any relevance?

Perhaps it raises the touchy question of what are the basic sanctions for any mathematical or logical directions, i.e., as to whose version of sanity is the right one.

I can see that some of these questions are resolved as one proceeds, but I do think fuller notes on the axioms would be helpful.

Incidentally, what is Cat Books?

Very best wishes,

Yours sincerely, Alan Watts

Sausalito, California | November 12, 1971
Mr. Henry Volkening | Russell & Volkening | New York, New York
Dear Henry:

I am just back from my trip to England, both rested and stimulated — the latter through long conversations with a philosophico-mathematical genius at Cambridge.

Meanwhile, thanks for your many communications, all necessary items of which I return herewith. In addition there are three problems:

1. The *LA Free Press* pirated this article from *EARTH* (enclosed), and they now have enough advertising and circulation to give some benefit to their authors. They used this article for their main front-page headline.

2. *EARTH* has paid no more than that $600, and I have refused to write further for them until I am paid in full. I think a very strong letter from you would be in order. They have had short articles by me in every issue from January–November 1971 inclusive, which amounts to 11 pieces at $350 each — i.e., $3,850 less $600 — so that they owe us $3,250, on which I have had two rubber checks, one for $1,000 and one for $2,000.

3. *Playboy* taped a dialog between me and Arthur C. Clarke, which they edited very skillfully and are going to publish in the January holiday issue as the longest single piece they have ever run. They are giving us $3,000 each, check for which is on the way to you, though I realize I should have notified you earlier, for they have thoughts of making a book out of it. Spec also wants an article from me on reincarnation. They are postponing publication of "The Sound of Rain" so as to coincide with the publication of the autobiography, for which I must still write three more chapters by the end of the year.

Otherwise, dear Henry, I am remaining analcoholic, having even passed up the port and brandy in the dons' common room at Caius College, which is the highest possible temptation. But I am feeling very well and frisky.

Sincerely, Alan

Sausalito, California | December 7, 1971

Dear Peter [Leith or Lord Burgh]:

Thanks so much for your very interesting letter of November 29th. What a pity I did not know of you a couple of months earlier, for I was in Cambridge during October, staying at Trinity, and visiting the philosopher/mathematician G. Spencer-Brown. You should make yourself known to him because he is a genius and his interests lie right along our lines. His address is Cat Books (Publishers). I think the phone is listed so you'd be able to find it. One of the most interesting people I have met.

There is also a young Sikkimese Lama at Trinity, Sogyal Lakar (full title: Tulku Sogyal Rinpoche Lakar, which is a very high rank). Speaks excellent English and has gone very deeply into Nyimapa esoteric stuff. My other friends there are Bishop Robinson (of *Honest to God* fame), who is now dean of the chapel at Trinity, and Joseph Needham, the sinologist, at Caius.

I am most interested in your thoughts of political activity. I concern myself with such immediate matters as prisons, police, and civil liberties, and thus, with confining policemen to their proper duties of protecting life and property so that they no longer serve as armed clergymen.

Varda, alas, died of a sudden heart attack in Mexico City last January. He was my close friend and neighbor for ten years, and we loved him very much.

I am so glad you have found my books to your liking. The reaction in England (my home country) has been extremely slow and sluggish but over here I am satisfactorily notorious, especially with the younger generations.

Do please let me know if you should be coming this way. Otherwise, I shall probably be in England again within a year.

With all good wishes,

Very sincerely, Alan Watts

Sausalito, California | March 14, 1972

Ronni Fiedler | *Harper's* magazine | New York, New York

Dear Ronni Fiedler:

Thank you very much indeed for sending me your April '72 issue with the extraordinary article by Thomas Szasz on "The Ethics of Addiction."

This is an exaggeration, but I have long regarded Thomas Szasz as the only sane psychiatrist writing for the general public. This man is, furthermore, one of the most interesting champions of civil liberty because he has so keenly detected the new disguises assumed by the ancient institution of the Holy Inquisition.

There are two reasons why his article on "The Ethics of Addiction" should have the widest possible circulation. The first is that our police forces are being corrupted and diverted from their proper tasks of protecting life and property by being required to serve as armed clergymen enforcing sumptuary laws against "crimes" without complaining victims. It is no business of the government to interfere in matters of gambling, sexual morals, and the use of natural substances arbitrarily defined as "drugs" or "narcotics." The work of our courts is clogged and our prisons overcrowded because of this ridiculous inquisition of private morals and tastes.

The second is that medical knowledge and expertise should be as freely available to the general public as the art of cooking. There are not enough qualified physicians and surgeons to serve our needs, with the result that doctors' offices and hospitals are as overburdened as the courts of justice.

There are serious risks in adopting such a policy, but without risk there is no freedom, and the United States of America is supposed, above all things, to represent the principle of liberty — the dangerous and splendid task of taking responsibility for your own life.

If you don't see fit to publish this letter, please pass it on to Thomas Szasz with my love and respect.

Sincerely, Alan Watts

SAUSALITO, CALIFORNIA | APRIL 12, 1972
Hugh T. Kerr | Princeton, New Jersey
Dear Hugh Kerr:
A good letter deserves an answer, although I am puzzled as to how there can be a "department" of theology in a theological seminary.

·I am not uptight about the Jesus freaks. I am simply and honestly angry. To be uptight about something is to pish-tush in a standoffish way. But my emotions seem to go naturally angry when people take on wallowing in guilt and anti-sexuality as a way of life and, furthermore, obscure the Gospel by insisting that Jesus alone was the son of God. Biblical fundamentalism is, to me, the nastiest religion on earth (whether in its Protestant form or as Catholic Jansenism) because it underlies white racism and colonialism, prohibition, prudery, and, equally, leering pornography.

I am not afraid of tangling with fundamentalists. I am very used to it, since all my mother's brothers were of this persuasion, though she herself was more liberal and had the good sense to belong to the Anglican Communion.

At the same time, I can see Billy Graham or a Southern Baptist deaconess as very far-out manifestations of God playing not God, as performing the function of making sex fascinating by forbidding it, but — for my taste — this is an ugly trip. It ends up with requiring the police to be armed clergymen, and filling the jails with people who have committed "crimes" without victims, and my anger is one and the same process as their suffering.

As to what's next beyond where I've been for a long time, G. K. Chesterton once said that progress is finding a good place to stop... Your course sounds fascinating, and, if you can persuade the seminary to invite me, I could visit with you for a day between the 9th and 12th of May. I am much concerned with the problem of what to do with churches on Sunday mornings, and have worked out a contemplative, as distinct from didactic, liturgy and am interested in showing the ministry how to do it.

Very best wishes to you — Sincerely, Alan Watts

SAUSALITO, CALIFORNIA | JUNE 6, 1972
Jim Spurlock | *Gallery* magazine | Chicago, Illinois
Dear Jim Spurlock:
Further to our telephone conversation, I have the following suggestions for an article:

1. "Must We Be Men?" On the utter tiresomeness of machismo, of going vrrooomm to know that you exist, and its results in the serious waste of the earth's physical energy. A man who has to prove that he is a man by competition with other men is probably a crypto (concealed)-homosexual, whereas the actual proof of maleness is more nearly the art of conferring pleasure upon women. But this can't be done as a "duty."

2. "Guilt in Pleasure." When a child is hurt it is cuddled, but when it is happy it is suspect. "Find out what Johnny's doing and tell him to stop it!" This would go into our curious devotion to self-frustration, especially as reflected in popular mythologies about alcohol, drugs, and sex, and into the tyranny of always having to be in the right state of mind to drive that death-dealing missile called an automobile.

3. "What to Do on Sunday?" Why don't we have the consideration to realize that God must be utterly bored with most of our church services, with being flattered, wheedled and told how to run the universe? If you were God, what would you like people to do in your honor — for you, with you, or about you? Revolutionary suggestions on what to do with all that real estate called Church.

4. "Armed Clergymen." In a republic where the separation of church and state is basic, the police are corrupted when asked to be armed clergymen disciplining private morals. The business of the courts is hampered and the jails are overloaded in dealing with crimes without complaining victims. Police are

essential and respected public servants in protecting life and property, in directing traffic, and giving aid to people in distress. No more. The economic and
logistic reasons for taking sumptuary laws against private morals off the books.

In making any financial arrangement, please contact my agent, Henry
Volkening, on Fifth Avenue, New York.

Best wishes and thanks for your interest,

Sincerely, Alan Watts

SAUSALITO, CALIFORNIA | JUNE 13, 1972
M. Dominique de Wespin | Society Pierre Teilhard de Chardin |
Brussels, Belgium
Dear M. de Wespin:
Please forgive me, first, that I am so long in answering your letter of last August
and, second, that I reply in English, for though I can read French easily I cannot
write it with good style.

I am not as yet sure when I shall next be coming to Europe. There is the possibility that I may come in November of this year. I will let you know, because I
would like to meet with you.

I feel that, as it were under the blessing of de Chardin, there is forming
a truly global ecumenicity which, in a few years, will be de facto rather than
de jure, and this will obviate the need for approval by official councils of the
Church. Such a meeting is, for example, being sponsored by the Benedictine
monastery of St. Saviour in Connecticut this August.

With very best wishes,

Sincerely yours, Alan Watts

SAUSALITO, CALIFORNIA | JULY 12, 1972
Dear Henry [Volkening]:
Many thanks for your long letter of July 8th. First of all, let me say that, although
I have not yet met him, I trust your choice of Timothy Seldes and see no reason
why I should not get along with him. Please have him call me before he comes
out here so that we can arrange a meeting when I am not out of town.

Apparently Random House has decided to distribute a cheap edition of *The
Art of Contemplation*. It would have to be somewhat smaller than the original
format, and not in a white cover — since these get dirty in bookstores. But we
have all the original offset plates here at Graphic Arts of Marin in case it would
be cheaper for them to buy these instead of making new ones. See if you can get
a good advance, for I am being persecuted by the IRS, lawyers, and children
screaming for pearls and caviar.

But on the matter of children: Please tell Bayless that I and my son Mark have made ten half-hour one-inch Sony colored TV tapes with the prospect of marketing them as videotape cassettes. They would also be available to educational TV for broadcast. We made most of them on the ferryboat in different locations, and most of them, if I do say so myself, are of fine dramatic quality. They consist of a series of talks on the nitty-gritty problems of life, and are currently available at $75 each through my old friend Henry Jacobs who runs Musical Engineering Associates in Sausalito and distributes all my tapes. He is also our technical director.

Also — tell Bayless to get friskier on my behalf. He let a Mr. Sam Parkins of the Westinghouse Learning Corporation get away with a two-hour interview with me for only $100, and charged no commission for himself. That's not business. The videotape cassette market is going to become very important within the next two years, and although I live mainly in the present, I keep my eye on "the life of the world to come."

Gene Schwartz assured me that copyright on all the *Journal* publications had been obtained, but his business has been in such a total mess since he was ruined by letting a finance corporation come in and take it over, that his records and his memory may be at fault. He is basically a very pleasant fellow, with a lovely wife and a great art collection. So call him back. My daughter Joan is securing copyright on all *Journal* publications since Sep. 1971, as she is now in charge of it and all my PR affairs.

I'm most grateful for your amicus curiae intervention with Bobbs-Merrill. This was very kind of you, and I'll await the results before making up my mind.

EARTH magazine has dissolved completely and is in receivership, and its hapless editor, James Goode, has gone to work for *Penthouse*. I suppose we had better write this off, but I can't see how they can possibly object to our use of the articles which I contributed since they are so heavily indebted to me.

It's really tough to sell parts of *In My Own Way* as separate articles, since the whole thing hangs together in an organic way. Don't trouble yourself about this, for the book will have to go over on its own. But don't you still have the piece on reincarnation, which I think I returned to you? A possibility is *Psychology Today* and another the *Intellectual Digest*, which last, incidentally, since it is a digest, might take over "The Sound of Rain" or any other articles which I have recently published.

I'm delighted to see that I am becoming famous in Spain. I'm reading the Spanish translation of *The Book* to learn the language!

The novel about the trickster guru is now a serious possibility. I am going to write the first chapter within a few weeks. As I told you, I have talked to Paula about it. She is interested and there is the obvious advantage that this would be a first novel by an author already well known, and writing the autobiography has given me practice in narrative. I'll figure out a tentative title within a few days and then go to work. I have discussed this project with Henry Gellis of Columbia Pictures, LA, with regard to possible movie rights, and also with James Coburn, actor, as I think he would play the lead particularly well.

I am full of energy and ideas, and wish that you were in fettle to go along with me for many years to come. But it can't be helped, and we all eventually vanish as the tip of a flame goes off into the air, though the flame itself keeps going. Yet I feel you have been very responsible to me in working out future plans for the agency, and am most grateful. Jano, who first insisted that I retain you, sends greetings.

All the best, as ever, Alan

JW: In the above letter to his agent, Alan makes reference to a series of videos that he and his son Mark have made. Alan's good friend Henry Jacobs, who for many years taped most of Alan's lectures, had with Alan's blessings married Sabro Hasegawa's daughter, Sumire (Alan having promised Sabro before he died to look after his daughter). Sandy (as he was called) took Alan's son Mark under his wing and taught him the science of tape and video recording. Sumire was an artist in her own right, and participated in several of Alan's recordings playing the koto and reciting poetry in Japanese. She also prepared amazing Asian meals and had a Japanese restaurant in Sausalito. Sandy made Alan's lectures available through Musical Engineering Associates, which after Alan's death became Electronic University. Mark is currently the curator of Alan's many taped lectures, videos, and films and is married to Tia, daughter of Sandy and Sumire.

Sausalito, California | August 4, 1972
John-David E. Robinson | Center for Spiritual Studies | Fairfield, Connecticut
Dear John-David:
I had been considering how best I might participate in the symposium when your letter of July 22nd came to my attention. I was away from home when it arrived. I had two things in mind: (a) to learn a spiritual discipline other than my own, and (b) to practice with Christians, and anyone else who cared, a contemplative form of liturgy.

As to the first, I am rather torn between the Sufis and the Hesychasts. As to the second, I am wondering if the sunset service could be a special form of the Eucharist preceded by silent meditation — a form which I call the *Missa Glossolalia*, and which I celebrated recently at the Oblate Seminary in Boston. It follows the traditional form of the Mass, but is contemplative and mantric rather than didactic, since none of it is in English, and its objective is to contemplate God through the manifestation of *shabda* or pure sound. Would this be acceptable? It would require the usual vestments, plus a deacon and subdeacon, and is celebrated *versus populi*. Otherwise I could do something much more simple, sitting in a big circle on the grass. In either case I would need a thurible with incense. (Only problem is that chanting is easier indoors!)

The idea of a talk on "Unity in Contemplation" is fine.

My wife may not be coming with me, so if we have to share rooms I would very much like to be with Baba Ram Dass...If Louisa Jenkins has applied to come, she would be a most worthwhile adjunct: a great Catholic artist of the de Chardin school.

All good wishes and many thanks. Pax — Alan Watts

Sausalito, California | August 5, 1972
Paula McGuire | Princeton, New Jersey
Dear Paula:
I have been away from home for over a week, conducting seminars and such things. So I am late in answering yours of July 20. Also I hope your office got a satisfactory version of my father's foreword, which we phoned in.

I am returning the first page of your letter. This is a good selection, put out in the right order.

The logos at the head of each entry should be the doodles in *The Art of Contemplation*, but made uniform in size. I can let you have black copies of these. And remember that Graphic Arts of Marin (Bernie Moss) can let you have the plates, negatives, or whatnot, from which a slight reduction can be made, as this may save you money.

I'm still in favor of calling the whole collection *Cloud-Hidden, Whereabouts Unknown: A Mountain Journal*. This is a line from a Chinese poem called "Seeking the Master in Vain," and we are working on a splendid photograph of the area for the jacket. If this doesn't work, I'll get some Chinese artist to paint it!

Trust all goes well with Bill and baby Mary.

All the best, Alan

Sausalito, California | August 5, 1972
Dear Henry [Volkening]:
Yours of July 22 and 24 came while I was away from home, doing seminars in Big Sur and Santa Barbara...I'm glad about [Jonathan] Cape, though they should be

urged to retain the American title, as much confusion arises from US and British books having different names. I guess £350 = $830. This, minus commissions, should be sent, as usual, to my father. Thomas knows the address.

Copyrights: James Goode is now at your end, with *Penthouse*, which I gather is run out of NYC. Gene Schwartz really *ought* to know what copyright is, since he produced many books as well as newsletters. But his office was a somewhat confused place, and they could either have forgotten to take it out or lost the records. Goode is something of an adept at not being reachable by phone. He might remember your name as my representative, so why not have Timothy call him?

I have started the novel, but the concentration needed for this kind of work is rendered difficult by the mountains of mail, some of it interesting, which follow from fame. I suppose people were offended by the inaccessibility of Salinger and Traven, and I am, alas, gregarious.

The small print on the title page of *EARTH* reads:

©1970 by *EARTH* publishing corporation. *EARTH* ® Registered trademark. Nothing may be reprinted without written permission from the publisher.

The enclosed copy of a letter to Paula should be self-explanatory.

British consular officials in New York and Washington get tropical pay. But here in the hills it's relatively cool.

All the best, Alan

SAUSALITO, CALIFORNIA | SEPTEMBER 26, 1972
Mr. Tom Maschler | Jonathan Cape, Ltd. | London, England
Dear Tom:
It concerns me a little bit that the remarks about St. Hugh's School in my autobiography might be considered libelous or in bad taste since the institution still exists, although it has long moved from Bickley, Kent, to Berkshire. It might therefore be advisable to change the name to St. Paul's School in all references as well as in the quotation of the school song which begins with the line, "Cold's the wind and wet's the rain." Perhaps your legal department will advise you about this, for, of course, in times past, writers like Hugh Walpole and Somerset Maugham have said terrible things about schools which are still established institutions.

All good wishes.

Yours sincerely, Alan Watts

This letter to William Mailliard, a member of Congress from 1953 to 1974, was also sent to the president of the United States, Sen. Alan Cranston, and The San Francisco Chronicle.

JANUARY 31, 1973
The Hon. William S. Mailliard | San Francisco, California
Dear Mr. Mailliard:

As a good Republican and believer in free enterprise, I trust you are as offended as I am with the conversion of our Republic into a nursery, where such agencies as the FDA regulate by law what we may, or may not, eat, drink, or even smell. As an educated adult, I am willing to take such responsibilities upon myself, and would like to be able to rely upon the FDA for advice, but not for legislation with criminal penalties.

On January 19th of this year the FDA published, in the Federal Register, an order stringently regulating the manufacture and sale of vitamins and mineral supplements to diet. Medical opinion on such matters is notoriously subject to whim and fashion and therefore should never be hardened into law, since laws are extremely difficult to repeal in the light of later knowledge.

I therefore earnestly urge you to support HR 643, which will restrain the motherly anxiety of the FDA and the consequent interference by policemen with our private lives in the role of armed doctors and clergymen.

Sincerely yours, Alan Watts

SAUSALITO, CALIFORNIA | MARCH 12, 1973
To the Editor | *Gourmet* magazine
Sir:

If I were to have been told three or four years ago that I was to become a vegetarian, a fruitarian, and a nuts-and-cheese freak, I would have been horrified. For in those days I prided myself in preparing *boeuf tartare*, *pate de veau en croute*, *poupetons de dindon*, and a steak-and-kidney pie better than anything to be found in London.

But something has happened to our meat and poultry. The meat has become mere chewing stuff, and the poultry (in particular the breasts) has come to taste like papier-mâché. Some of my friends who are health-food aficionados say that this is because I have ruined my palate by smoking too many cigars and imbibing too much spiritous liquor. This is not true. Several years ago I imagined that this was the cause of my finding American potatoes (even the little new ones) entirely tasteless. But when, after twenty years absence, I returned to my father's garden in England, the potatoes were as delicious as when I had been a child.

So I have not destroyed my palate. The truth of the matter is that our edible animals are being raised in vast cellblocks under the superstition that almost anything fed, say, to a chicken will turn into chicken. Why, they are even scheming to breed featherless chickens to eliminate the plucking process!

The reason is simply that the food industries are owned by syndicates composed of barbarians who are interested in nothing more than making money. Being barbarians, they do not understand that huge sums of money become increasingly worthless when there is no food on the market except the fraudulent plasticities produced by themselves and their equally uncivilized competitors.

You may not, perhaps, realize that your magazine (which I have been reading for years) is no mere slick and frivolous publication for affluent gluttons. You have been performing the almost religious and spiritual task of teaching people how to reverence food and drink, and thereby to arouse the rather scarce virtue of conviviality. I am thinking of the true *holy communion* of sitting around a scrubbed wooden table in a big kitchen with Louis Martini's incredible 39-year-old tawny port, the hard Monterey Jack cheese of California, and San Francisco's extra-sour French bread — with strings of onions and garlic and bottles of Chianti hanging from the beams.

I therefore urge upon you most strongly to give your readers more information about the actual raising and growing of foodstuffs: how to test out what is offered in the markets, where to go for high-quality materials and even how to raise your own. You give wonderful advice about cooking but the whole process depends ultimately on the farming.

Sincerely, Alan Watts

Charles McCabe, the recipient of the following letter, was a longtime columnist for The San Francisco Chronicle.

MARCH 15, 1973
Mr. Charles McCabe | *San Francisco Chronicle*
Dear Charles:

I wonder if you could somehow air some views for me. Much as I love this country and many of its people, I no longer feel free. The land is being turned into a nursery, and I am more oppressed than helped by government.

Item: As a reasonably well-educated adult, I resent sheer dictation as to what I may eat, drink, smoke, or even smell. I am willing to assume responsibility for that, and also to consider advice from such federal agencies as the FDA and HEW. But it is insufferable that, through such agencies, the police should be empowered to be armed nurses, doctors, and clergymen.

Item: In driving on the freeways (which in California is almost necessary to life) I am more threatened by the police than by drunken drivers, since it is necessary for them to prove their efficiency by making arrests. In many areas they have arrest quotas, and issue tickets on absurd minor technicalities. Furthermore, legislators don't realize that people driving under the influence of rage, anxiety, and depression may be far more dangerous than those comfortably relaxed with whatever measure of alcohol they can tolerate without becoming weaving drunks.

Item: Government has become a self-serving vested interest, taxing us exorbitantly for the maintenance of a vast, inefficient, and lazy bureaucracy, and of a huge military machine so incompetent that it could not subdue the "natives" of North Vietnam, and which, if it should come to nuclear war, can defend nothing but itself. Jolly to be in a plane at 35,000 ft. when the bombs hit the cities! Join the Air Force and be safe.

Item: Has anyone figured out what it costs to pay taxes, aside from the taxes themselves? Of maintaining the IRS, of employing accountants and lawyers, and of wasting hours and hours in calculating, recording, and filing papers? We are past the point where the recording of what happens has become more important than what happens. One exists only on paper.

Item: I am concerned about the omnipotence of credit agencies. At any moment I could arbitrarily be denied the use of a credit card, or be blacklisted for some idiotic reason (such as computer error) by a credit bureau, with no other recourse than an expensive lawsuit which, aside from its cost, would take months to resolve.

Item: The increasing multitude of young rip-offers (i.e., thieves) do not realize that their "liberated" attitude to property is precisely what will multiply police and security measures, and thus push the country into fascism. A community simply cannot exist without mutual trust, and when we all have to bar our doors and employ guards, we move into a vicious circle of mutual mistrust which ends up in wondering who guards the guards. Ethics are not religious superstitions; they are purely practical principles for getting along together — like agreeing to use the English language for communication.

Item: How can anyone imagine that if only the military and the police are allowed to possess guns that they will have our best interests at heart? If we should surrender them, they must surrender them too. Furthermore, do plain-clothes officers realize that if they invade a home on the no-knock principle, they may well be mistaken for burglars and be shot? Anyone can get a phony badge or ID card and represent himself as an officer of the law…and the FBI and the Narcs might think this over. And, incidentally, why is it that many plain-clothes men *look* like burglars?

Item: The "rule of law" has become government by books instead of human beings. Often an official will admit that what you were doing or want to do was perfectly reasonable, but nevertheless against the regulations. Because circumstances alter cases, reasonable behavior can never, never be meticulously defined in words.

Charles, you are a great defender of our freedoms. Use these observations in any way you see fit.

All good wishes, Alan Watts

MARCH 17, 1973
Richard Weaver | Cold Mountain Institute | Cortes Island, British Columbia
Dear Richard:
This is a horribly belated answer to yours of December 7th, but my involvements are such that I have to live entirely in the present and am therefore somewhat forgetful. Of course I will act as an advisor to the Yogacara Buddhist Sangha, and therefore let me proceed to advise.

Goddard's *Buddhist Bible* isn't really well translated. He reworked much of it without knowing what he was doing. A much better selection is Conze's *Buddhist Texts through the Ages*, and there are others. Get advice from Leon Hurwitz at UBC; he knows more about these things than almost anyone. Suzuki sort of renounced his (very early) *Outlines of Mahayana Buddhism*, though his translation of the *Lankavatara* remains the only, and Goddard's reworking of it isn't satisfactory. There just isn't a good comprehensive text on Mahayana. T. R. V. Murti's *Central Philosophy of Buddhism* is excellent, but is confined to *Madhyamika*. J. Takakusu's *Essentials of Buddhist Philosophy* is reliable but dull. I think the subject is simply too big for any one individual to take on. I might try one day, but for now I am about to do a book on Taoism, similar in style to *The Way of Zen*.

We have now moved my library to its new home (a small pagoda) near Muir Woods, and I am sorting out books for you.

I look forward to seeing Leslie Kawamura's translation of *Seikuro*. My own publisher (Pantheon) might be highly interested in this kind of thing.

Our love to you both — as ever, Alan

SAUSALITO, CALIFORNIA | APRIL 5, 1973
Pantheon | New York, New York
Dear Paula [McGuire]:
Some reflections about the next book:

1. *Title*: The one that appeals to me most is *Tao: The Watercourse Way of Life*.

2. After my return from Japan at the end of May, everything will be set to go. I have been reviewing many of the existing books on Taoism, and translations of the texts, so as not to be merely repetitious. I have all the important original Chinese texts in my library, and will get a Chinese assistant to help me out when necessary.

3. It is really essential that all Chinese terms in the book be accompanied by the proper ideographs. I can, of course, write them for reproduction, as in *The Way of Zen*, but I would rather have them set off in the margin like this, *hsin*. Can you find a printer with Chinese type at his disposal? The book will probably begin with an essay on the Chinese language and its peculiar advantages as a written system of communication, seeing that its visual form is immediately intelligible to people pronouncing it in at least seven quite different ways.

We do not need to know how to pronounce in order to understand the sign.

4. I would like a book of dimensions about 6¼ x 9¼, the better to display black-and-white reproductions of Chinese painting and calligraphy, as well as some photographs of certain natural forms. But this raises the question as to whether the Vintage series ever goes beyond 5 x 8, though this "giant" size might be satisfactory for paperback reproduction.

5. This is perhaps insane — but if we were really to splurge we would have appendices consisting of Chinese texts of Lao-tzu, Chuang-tzu, and Lieh-tzu accompanied by the translations, respectively, of Lin Yutang (Random House), Burton Watson (Columbia), or H. A. Giles (where there are, I think, no copyright restrictions), and Lionel Giles (John Murray's Wisdom of the East series). Chinese texts could be offset from materials at my disposal.

I shall be in New York from April 10th to 27th, and hope to see you during that time. Donna will know my arrangements.

Our love to you both — As ever, Alan

AW: During Easter vacation in April 1973, Myra (my daughter, then ten and a half) and I drove from our home in Raleigh, North Carolina, to Haverford, Pennsylvania, a distance of about four hundred miles, to see Alan. Little did we know that this would be the last time we would see him. This was a rare mother-daughter excursion, during which we sang a great deal of "Ninety-Nine Bottles of Beer on the Wall" just to help me stay awake! Michael, my son, was not with us; as best we can all figure, for that holiday he went to visit his father in Virginia Beach.

Alan had been invited by the lovely Grace Swanson to give a workshop at Haverford College, where she taught yoga and meditation. Grace had a beautiful, elegant home where we stayed with Alan and other guests. There was good food, great conversation, and hearty partying. Grace says that she and Alan loved singing together. One of the things Myra remembered was her grandfather handing her several eggs that he had exquisitely hand-painted for her for Easter. They were such a treasure that she could not bear to part with them until they became rotten!

Another of Myra's memories of this trip is written in her own words: "One of the most powerful memories I have of my grandfather, Alan, happened in Grace's kitchen early one morning. I found him seated at the kitchen table. It was a rare occurrence for me to find him alone. I remember he greeted me so warmly and with so much affection in his eyes. As I went to the stove to prepare tea, I could feel his eyes on me. He got up from the table and came over and said, 'I want you to hold out your arm with as much strength as you can, and I'm going to try to bend it, but don't let me.' I felt his hands around my small arm. He bent my arm with little effort. Then he said, 'Do you see that piece of tinfoil on the stove? I want you to stare at it, don't take your eyes off of it. Imagine that your arm is like a fire hose and the most intense amount of water is rushing through it. Now I'm going to try to bend your arm again, but don't let me.' I could feel his fingers around my arm, I could feel his arms begin to shake with the effort, but he was unable to bend my arm.

"This was one of the most transformative moments of my life. It was a revelation, a profound experience that altered my experience of myself and the universe completely. It was one of the many informative moments we shared in the few years we had and, as a dancer, one of my most cherished."

Myra's story is common to what many people experienced with Alan. In any case, that visit was a delightful connecting time with him, one that each of us treasures.

Seven months later, on November 16, 1973, I got the devastating call that Alan had died in his sleep, just a month and a half before his fifty-ninth birthday. I only remember snippets of what happened after that. In my experience, the thing we call "memory" is highly suspect. Joan says I came out to California for the intimate Buddhist ceremony for family only on November 18, two days after Alan's death; I have no memory of that event. I do remember being on the ferryboat Vallejo, *with Joan and the priest Ajari, who led us through a Goma (fire ceremony) in which we sat on the floor and made offerings to Alan of rice, beans, tea, and a bottle of rum (the only alcohol we could find!). I remember Ajari regaling us with interesting stories of his connections with Alan, and of his life as a priest who was a fire protector (lookout) on Mount Tamalpais.*

I also remember attending the traditional One Hundred Day Ceremony, held at the Zen Center, Green Gulch Farm, in Marin County. I remember the warm, sunny day, the large gathering of family and friends who quietly flowed from one small group to another, connecting and remembering. I remember Al Huang playing his wood flute. I remember sitting in the front row, sitting close to the altar with other family members, which included Elsa Gidlow (whom Alan had "adopted" as his sister). I remember

*Richard Baker-Roshi in his ornate robes, Ananda Claude Dalenberg (a longtime fam-
ily friend), and Philip Whalen presiding over the ceremony. The large, resonant hall
was filled to overflowing. I remember people filing up to the altar, where Alan's photo
rested, saying their farewells.*

*I felt his loss deeply, not only for myself and all who were close to him, but espe-
cially for his grandchildren. At the same time, I felt relief that he was free of his crip-
pling burdens. As I have read his letters and shared memories with my sister Joan, I am
profoundly struck by the rich complexity of our father: his brilliance, insight, wisdom,
kindness, and playfulness, along with his addictions to women and alcohol. I am clear
that he was a man who lived his life in his own way.*

*JW: There are many accounts of Alan's death in books and on the internet — mostly in-
accurate. Oddly, I don't remember my mother's death or the deaths of my various grandparents. I know the causes of their deaths, but not the dates or who notified me of their
passing. But Alan's death, over forty years ago as of this writing, is still vividly clear.*

*The morning of Friday, November 16, 1973, started like any other day — get-
ting kids up, fed, and off to school with their lunches. My routine was interrupted by a
phone call at about 7 AM. It was Elsa Gidlow. She asked if I was sitting down. I said,
"No, should I be?" She exclaimed, "Oh, Joan, Alan has died!" Distressed beyond
belief, I dressed quickly and drove to Druid Heights. I went over and over in my mind
my conversations with him the past ten days since his return from abroad.*

*Alan had undertaken an extensive and strenuous tour in England and Europe.
Gone a month, he had lectured in London, appeared on television, and visited with his
mentor Christmas Humphreys. He'd set out to visit with Bishop John Robinson, Joseph
Needham, and Dom Aelred Graham. He'd spent time with his father at Merevale, a
retirement home in Bickley, Kent, and with his cousin Joy and other relatives. His lecture tour continued through Switzerland, Germany, and Holland. Jano was supposed
to have gone with him on the trip, but at the last minute canceled because she was ill
(from her alcoholic condition). When he returned, he was exhausted and had called
me several times expressing concern about his health. (Alan was drinking again, adding to his debilitation.) He asked if there were any vitamins I could recommend that
might boost his energy. He was anxious to finish his book* Tao: The Watercourse
Way. *I had suggested he see Dolph Segal, his friend and personal doctor.*

*When I arrived at the Mandala in Druid Heights I was greeted by Elsa, dis-
traught over Alan's sudden and unexpected death. Jano was sitting, quietly sorting
through some things on his desk. She had been in one of her manic high moods while
Alan was gone, calling me every day with endless chatter. However, on Alan's return,
she succumbed to the bottle and became catatonic and slept all day. This distressed
him no end, and on top of Jano's dysfunction, he was dealing with new demands for*

additional child support from Dorothy for his two youngest daughters. He'd returned home to a hornet's nest of problems. I have often felt that he simply decided he'd had enough and just "checked out." As Jano said, "He left his body but couldn't get back."

As I sat on the floor in the Mandala, I leaned with my arm over the seat of his chair and was startled to feel him sitting under my arm. I'll never forget the sensation. The chair was Chinese style, made of teak, and there was no cushion. I sorted through the items in his briefcase, which had not been touched since his return, looking for I wasn't sure what, listening to Elsa explain the events of the previous evening and early morning.

Jano's niece Kathleen and her friend Jason had visited. They had brought two balloons — one had popped. Alan had been sounding his gongs, then laid on the couch bouncing a balloon in the air, idly chatting with them about the stormy night. When they all left, he'd gone to sleep. Jano awoke in the early morning to find him strangely still. His doctor was called. Dr. Segal surmised that he'd died of a heart attack and complications due to his enlarged liver. Several Buddhist monks appeared at the Mandala, friends of Alan's who watched over Mount Tamalpais (considered by some to be a sacred mountain). Their leader, Ajari, said they had been "visited" by Alan where they were camping during predawn hours, and knew he was dead. They kindly offered to take his body for cremation to the local funeral home at the base of Mount Tamalpais in Mill Valley. I went with Jano a few days later to pick up his ashes and wrapped the urn in a furoshiki, a traditional Japanese wrapping cloth. As Jano drove us back to the Mandala, I opened the urn to peek in. I'd never seen human ashes. Some were small chunks, the rest a fine granular powder. Jano and I each kept some of the smaller pieces, she in a necklace with a Tibetan amulet, and I in a small secret container.

In a condolence letter to Jano, Laurie Watts expressed his sympathy to her, writing that her loss was probably greater than his as Alan's death meant a great part of her life gone. He further wrote, "It was a kind thought of Joan's to get into touch with Joy [his niece] on the telephone and to ask her to break the news to [me]. It actually saved me from a worse shock as there was a small paragraph among the foreign news in The Times *announcing Alan's passing which I had not read before Joy came." Laurie was ninety-two when Alan died.*

A traditional Buddhist ceremony was held for members of the family, November 18, 1973, at the Zen Center, Green Gulch Farm, in Marin and was officiated by Richard Baker-Roshi, Ananda Claude Dalenberg and Philip Whalen. Some of Alan's ashes were scattered in a private extended-family ceremony at Druid Heights. Included were Alan's sons, Mark and Richard, and Jano's niece, Kathleen, the residents of Druid Heights, and a few close friends. One hundred days after Alan's passing, a public memorial service, with the interment of the rest of his ashes, was held at Zen Center's Green Gulch Farm. Monks erected a large stone stupa on the hillside overlooking the valley and off to the ocean in the west. Gary Snyder read his poem honoring Alan's death:

He blazed out the new path for all of us
and came back and made it clear.
Explored the side canyons and deer trails,
and investigated cliffs and thickets.
Many guides would have us travel single file,
like mules in a pack train and never leave the trail.
Alan taught us to move forward like the breeze, tasting the berries,
greeting the blue jays, learning and loving the whole terrain.

I wrote Alan's obituary for the December 1973 Society Bulletin, *an excerpt from which I share here:*

I had known him for thirty-five years and two days. Though it is hard to remember anything but fleeting glimpses into the past, back to our beginning, he'd told me many times with an affectionate pat on my rear end and a twinkle in his eye, that I was conceived on the common green in Chislehurst.

He was always playful, joyful, a rascal. We'd dance in the living room, bounce on his knees to nursery rhymes, be tickled by his whiskers, and giggle at the fantastic monsters, buddhas, and animals he would draw for us. He taught me how to "get inside" my favorite carved teak box.

Once, I lived in Chislehurst with his parents. I have fond memories of high tea, apple pasties and "doorsteps" of bread smothered with Lyle's Golden Syrup, the beautiful garden with "Queen Elizabeth" and "Queen Mary" (pruned hedges), the rose trees, and Henny Penny, my favorite hen. I rode the common greens of Chislehurst on horseback with my schoolmates.

There were hard times, family trauma, divorce. Somehow, he always maintained a sense of humor. When I grew older, he told me what it was like to make love.

I moved out of his life for many years. He became a stranger. I would see him once every one or two years and have to share him with followers, admirers, and disciples.

Then, several years ago, I moved back into his daily life, shared his friends, many, my childhood acquaintances. A gathering was always an opportunity for a party, gaiety, laughter, wine, and food. I felt uneasy with his way of life; our differences became intense to me. I was one of the "New Puritans." He made it very clear that he enjoyed what he was doing and would die doing so, and would have no one interfere with his enjoyment of life. I never said another word about his forms of enjoyment.

It was difficult to watch him age so quickly. He became tired and weighted with responsibility. Life was interfering with his work. Nine days after returning from a hectic lecture tour in Europe, he died peacefully in his sleep.

Alan is quoted as having said, "Death means going to sleep and never waking up, as if we had never been born."

ACKNOWLEDGMENTS

First of all, we wish to thank our editor, Jason Gardner, and publisher, New World Library, for having faith in us that we could, in fact, pull off this monumental project. There were hundreds of letters to sort through and to decide which might be most interesting and afford a window into the heart and soul of our father, Alan Wilson Watts.

There were others who helped along the way, either with encouragement, help in the organization of files, the scanning and transcription of often barely readable copies of letters into Word format, and putting up with us while we spent long hours on the project, which took almost two years to complete.

Included first and foremost are our spouses, Johnny Hale (Joan's) and Mark Kupke (Anne's). Laura Watts Georgiades (Joan's daughter) and Scarlett Daley for transcription and editing of letters, and Talitha Stills, who in 1992 helped organize the very disorderly and damaged literary files of Alan's papers we inherited when Alan's widow, Mary Jane Watts, died.

We also thank Gary Snyder for his permission to gain access to Alan's letters in Gary's collection at UC Davis Library, and we thank Syracuse University Library for allowing us access to the Jean Burden Collection and UCLA Library for letters in the Henry Miller Collection. We wish also to thank the Rev. Richard Adams, Carlton Gamer, and Paula McGuire for helping us remember things of the past. We are grateful to the California Institute of Integral Studies, which accepted the more than eight hundred volumes comprising Alan's library, making these books available to future generations of students and researchers.

INDEX

In subentries, Alan Watts is abbreviated as AW. Page references given in *italics* indicate illustrations.

Harris, Judge, 455–56
Harrisburg (PA), 283
Harrison, E. J., 418
Harry, Uncle, 74
Hartford (CT), 22–23
Hartley, Elda Voelkel, 474–75, 487–88,
    494–95, 530–31
Hartley, Irving, 474
Harvard Divinity School, 113
Harvard Psychedelic Club, 394–95
Harvard University, 366, 440; AW as
    research associate at, 420–21, 422–23,
    425, 432–33, 441–42, 446; AW attendance
    plan, 70–71, 73; AW divorce publicity
    and, 431; AW lecture tours at, 402, 408;
    Leary psychedelics research at, 377, 415,
    428; mythology symposium at, 353, 379,
    382; retirement fund at, 432; Social Rela-
    tions Department, 390, 412, 417–18, 420
Hasegawa, Sabro, 288, 318–19, 320, 321, 324,
    325, 347
hashish, 520
hatha yoga, 63
Haverford College (Haverford, PA), 551
Hawaii, 421, 473, 474
Hawkes, Jacquetta, 308–9
Hayakawa, S. I. ("Don"), 288, 368, 476–77
Haydn, Franz Josef, 228, 501
Heard, Gerald, 94, 120, 251, 287, 290, 291,
    319, 394, 398
Hearn, Lafcadio, xiii, 8, 83, 509
Hebrews, 197, 216
Hefner, Hugh, 503, 504
Heiler, Friedrich, 215–16
helicopters, 122
Henderson, Helena, 471
Henderson, Joseph, 392, 425, 427, 471
Hermetics, 126
Herne Bay (England), 6
heroin, 520
Herrigel, Eugen, 319, 515
Hesse, Hermann, 342, 369
Hesychasts, 544
Heuven, Van, 428, 430, 431
Hill, Harry, 319, 412–13

Hill, Jerome, 370
hillbillies, 51, 101
Hillman, James, 418
Hinayana Buddhism, 183, 185, 187
Hindu dance, 416
Hinduism: *ahimsa* in, 183, 185; Atman in,
    201; in AW's children's book, 66; consci-
    entious objection and, 482–83; enlighten-
    ment in, 43, 44; impersonal pantheist in,
    200; production of universe in, 499; as
    "self-help" religion, 271; theism and, 185
Hinduism and Buddhism (Coomaraswamy),
    271
Hindu music, 390
Hindu mythology, 416
Hinkle, Beatrice, 154
Hinsdale (IL), 20, 47, 104, 113, 114
hippie movement, 377, 490, 504, 526
History of Chinese Philosophy (Fung), 532
History of Haiku (Blyth), 464, 516
"History of Hell, The" (unwritten book),
    340–41
History of Zen, The (Dumoulin), 515
Hitler, Adolf, 51, 405
Hodder & Stoughton (publisher), 49, 473,
    484
Hodder-Williams, Paul, 473
Hokusai drawings, 344
Holiday magazine, 474
Holland family, 25
Hollister, Judy, 494, 495
Hollywood (CA), 290, 404, 450, 465–66,
    484
Holmes, Edmond, 9
Holt, Rinehart & Winston (publisher),
    477–78
Holy Cross (magazine), 99, 144, 158, 180,
    183, 205, 207
Holy Cross Press (New York, NY), 141,
    144, 182, 191, 202
"holy-rollers," 51
Holy Spirit, 206, 217
Honest to God (Robinson), 493, 539
Hong Kong, 446, 454, 466
Horner, Jack, 101

Myth and Ritual in Christianity (Watts):
British publication of, 301, 302, 304,
305–6, 315; reviews, 306, 307; royalties
from, 315; sales of, 322; sent to Jano, 349;
theological discourse over, 289, 310; US
publication of, 289, 309, 315; *The Way of
Zen* and, 319; writing of, 301
Mythe Judeo-Chretien (Suarès), 290
"Mythological Motifs in Modern Science"
(Watts), 379
"Mythology of Methodology" (Mitroff),
498–99
Mythos und Schicksal, 36
"Myth Today" symposium (New York, NY;
1960), 379

Nanshinken Roshi, 20
Nanzen-ji Temple (Kyoto, Japan), 20, 453
Napoleon, 51
Nara (Japan), 420–21
Naranjo, Claudio, 519
Nashdom Abbey (Bucks, England), 220
Nation, The, 277
National Association of Educational Broad-
casters, 303
National Broadcasting Company (NBC),
198, 411
National Educational Television (NET),
368
National Library of Thailand, 288
National Research Council, 499
Native American Church, 424, 465, 468–69
Native Americans, 129, 389, 492
Natural History Museum (Washington,
DC), 367
nature, 41–42
Nature, Man and Woman (Watts), 357; ad-
vance payments on, 385, 387–88; Brown
work compared to, 348; correspondence
praising, 341, 353; criticism of, 451;
dedication of, 341; Indian spirituality
and, 397; *The Joyous Cosmology* and, 384;
proofs of, 341; shortcomings of, 412;
translations of, 506; writing of, 319, 332,
334

Nazi Germany, 100
Nebraska, 468–69
Needham, Joseph, 533, 537, 553
neo-Thomism, 212–13
Nepenthe restaurant (Big Sur, CA), 289
Netherlands, 553
Nettie (domestic servant), 40, 51, 67, 78,
85, 107
Neurath, Walter, 305–6, 307, 340
Neuropsychiatric Institute (Los Angeles,
CA), 452
"New Alchemy, The" (Watts), 397–98, 399
New American Library (NAL), 384, 387,
397, 425
New Delhi (India), 446, 515
New fire, 198
New Jersey, 39, 279, 282, 283
New Jersey Association for Mental Health,
519
New Mexico, 471
New Republic, 458
New School for Social Research (New
York, NY), 351, 364, 373, 383, 400, 412
New Testament, 124, 147, 152
New Theology, 492–93
New York (NY), 8, 366, 465, 483, 484; as
artificial, 41; AW arrival in, 20, 87; AW
business correspondence from, 51–53,
81–85, 401–2, 440–42; AW church membership in, 71–72; AW correspondence
with fans from, 463–64; AW correspondence with parents from, 21–40, 45–51,
53–81, 85–87, 389, 418–20, 446–47,
468–69; AW friendships in, 276, 402–3;
AW–Jano liaison in, 369; AW lecture
tours in, 258, 319, 325, 329, 330–31, 339,
360, 379, 383, 402, 434, 450; AW life in,
29–30, 31, 32, 34–35, 39–40, 382, 389,
468; AW love letter to Dorothy from,
344–45; AW newsletters from, 39, 40–44;
AW radio programs in, 388; AW residence in, 24, 33–34, 56–57; AW seminars
in, 468; AW workshop partnership in,
340; boys' choirs in, 105–6; Eleanor's
visits to, 167; Englishmen in, 48;

ABOUT THE EDITORS

JOAN WATTS grew up in the United States and England, attending private schools, and then studied art at various institutions in the United States. She also studied sumi-e (Japanese ink painting) for two years in Japan. Her art has won awards in juried shows and hangs in many private collections.

In addition to her art career, she spent twenty-five years as a successful fundraiser in the nonprofit world. She retired in her fifties and moved to Montana, where for twenty years she was an occasional fishing guide and operated a bed-and-breakfast that catered to fly fishers from around the world. After retiring (again), she began, along with her sister Anne, editing her father's letters for publication and resumed her painting.

She is the mother of five successful, happy children and nine grandchildren. She lives in Livingston, Montana, with her husband, Johnny (Montana) Hale, a musician, songwriter, and retired motion picture–industry technician.

Most of her life decisions have been influenced in one way or another by her father, Alan Watts.

ANNE WATTS's philosophies were also strongly shaped by her experience as the daughter of Alan Watts. Anne is a certified hypnotherapist and an educator and counselor in the areas of human sexuality, sexual abuse, family stress, self-esteem, healing the inner child, and financial and aging issues. Since 1985, she has facilitated hundreds of workshops in the United States, Canada, Australia, Japan, England, and Germany with the Human Awareness Institute, work she is deeply passionate about. Since 2008, she has also been a regular faculty member at Esalen Institute.

Anne is the proud mother of two children, Myra Krien and Michael Andrews, and three grandsons, Max Krien, Oliver Andrews, and Eli Andrews. She lives in Santa Rosa, California, in a deeply loving relationship with her husband, Mark Kupke, who has been her partner since 1984.

NEW WORLD LIBRARY is dedicated to publishing books and other media that inspire and challenge us to improve the quality of our lives and the world.

We are a socially and environmentally aware company. We recognize that we have an ethical responsibility to our customers, our staff members, and our planet.

We serve our customers by creating the finest publications possible on personal growth, creativity, spirituality, wellness, and other areas of emerging importance. We serve New World Library employees with generous benefits, significant profit sharing, and constant encouragement to pursue their most expansive dreams.

As a member of the Green Press Initiative, we print an increasing number of books with soy-based ink on 100 percent postconsumer-waste recycled paper. Also, we power our offices with solar energy and contribute to non-profit organizations working to make the world a better place for us all.

Our products are available in bookstores everywhere.

www.newworldlibrary.com

At NewWorldLibrary.com you can download our catalog,
subscribe to our e-newsletter, read our blog,
and link to authors' websites, videos, and podcasts.

Find us on Facebook, follow us on Twitter, and watch us on YouTube.

Send your questions and comments our way!
You make it possible for us to do what we love to do.

Phone: 415-884-2100 or 800-972-6657
Catalog requests: Ext. 10 | Orders: Ext. 10 | Fax: 415-884-2199
escort@newworldlibrary.com

🌲 NEW WORLD LIBRARY
publishing books that change lives   14 Pamaron Way, Novato, CA 94949